CONTROVERSIES

CONTROVERSIES

Contemporary Arguments for College Writers

Alfred Rosa
University of Vermont

Paul Eschholz
University of Vermont

Macmillan Publishing Company
NEW YORK

Editor: Eben Ludlow
Production Supervisor: Publication Services
Production Manager: Aliza Greenblatt
Text Designer: Publication Services
Cover Designer: Robert Freese

This book was set in Palatino by Publication Services, Inc.,
and printed and bound by Arcata Graphics.
The cover was printed by Lehigh Press.

Macmillan Publishing Company
866 Third Avenue, New York, New York 10022

Library of Congress Cataloging-in-Publication Data

Controversies: contemporary arguments for college writers / [selected
   by] Alfred F. Rosa, Paul A. Eschholz.
      p.   cm.
   Includes index.
   ISBN 0-02-403611-0
   1. College readers.   2. English language—Rhetoric.   I. Rosa,
Alfred F.   II. Eschholz, Paul A.
PE1417.C654   1990
808'.0427–dc20   90-6532
                                                                CIP

Main Text: ISBN 0-02-403611-0
Instructor's Edition: ISBN 0-02-439118-2

Printing: 1 2 3 4 5 6 7   Year: 1 2 3 4 5 6 7

Acknowledgments copy begins on page 629 and constitutes a
continuation of the copyright.

Preface

Controversies is a collection of contemporary essays organized into fourteen topical units—the dominant concerns and issues of our day. Who hasn't thought about the problems of drugs, crime, divorce, AIDS, censorship, gun control, euthanasia, and the environment? You can hardly pick up a newspaper or magazine, turn on your television or radio, and not be confronted by these issues. Who hasn't seen a television special or news clip or read an article on the transformation of the American family; mandatory testing for AIDS; the clashes over abortion; the push for tougher drunk driving legislation; the plight of our nation's homeless; the shocking betrayal of date rape; the growing call for the legalization of drugs; the obscenity of rock lyrics and the attempts to censor them; and the problems caused by our seemingly never-ending stream of solid waste? And on a more personal level, who hasn't grappled with such questions as what to believe and why, how to find the proper balance between the spiritual and material in one's life, what to do after college, and what the choices are going to be as one grows old and can no longer care for oneself? These are issues and questions that we're sure you have opinions about, opinions that you'll bring to class with you. The controversies are real, and we are all struggling to find ways to resolve them.

Overall, our goal has been to seek understanding in controversy. We have tried not so much to push for resolutions to the issues or to advocate a particular point of view by the essays we have selected as we have sought to be stimulating and to get at the essence of each controversy. To this end, each topical unit in *Controversies* contains selections written by people representing a rich diversity of backgrounds and voices. In addition, we have supplemented the essays with an occasional cartoon or advertisement which gives both different perspectives to the topic and displays interesting techniques of persuasion. If you engage each of the issues in *Controversies* in a well-intentioned fashion, that is, without an ax to grind, you can reap the benefits of argument by coming to a better understanding of your own values, beliefs, and feelings as well as to a healthy respect for those of others.

Argumentation is being increasingly taught in our colleges and universities, and for good reason. Simply put, good argumentation is the product of an important set of critical thinking skills that include differentiating facts from opinion, analyzing sources, developing an arguable thesis, generating and ordering evidence, assessing the needs of a specific audience, and reaching a reasoned and logical conclusion. One tried and true method for mastering the art of argumentation is to read and analyze a number of arguments, looking for both their strengths and shortcomings. You'll see that the more arguments you read, the more you will begin to appreciate the different ways people think and argue, and the better you will see how to adopt some of these methods and strategies in your own writing.

Assuming that you have little experience in analyzing and writing arguments, we have provided you with a brief overview of the fundamentals of both reading and writing arguments to help you get started. Our introduction, "Reading and Writing Arguments," is divided into three basic units. First, we define the function and purpose of argumentation, how it works and what it is supposed to do. Next, we provide some advice for getting the most out of your reading of the essays in this text. We include here a list of helpful questions that focus on important aspects of content and writing strategies. To illustrate our approach, we have annotated Lynne Cheney's essay, "Students of Success." Finally, we offer suggestions on writing your own arguments. Within the context of the writing process, we break an argument into its components so that you can better understand what you need to do at each step along the way as you write. Our checklist format encourages you to think about the decisions and choices available to you while developing your argument. We conclude this general introduction with a student essay by Lisa Denis arguing against the use of disposable diapers because of their negative impact on the environment. This student essay is intended to set a realistic benchmark for the type of writing that you will be doing in your course.

In order to give you a foothold for each of the topics in *Controversies*, we have written short section introductions that define the crucial issues and set a context for the selections that make up the unit. Specifically, each introduction provides some historical perspective on the issue, identifies the dominant parties in the debate, clearly defines areas of agreement or common ground, and delineates those points of contention that are the focus of the current controversy.

Each essay has its own brief introduction that provides you with the essential information about the writer, the issue, the publication where the essay first appeared, and several rhetorical features of the essay. These biographical sketches are intended to help you assess the authority or bias that a writer brings to his or her point of view.

Following each essay are questions, "Analyzing the Writer's Argument," that focus your attention on both the elements of the argument and the particular strategies used to make the writer's case. Also included are several questions that we have called "Exploring the Issues in This Essay." These are intended to promote classroom discussion and to act as a springboard to either a broader investigation of the topic or a yet more focused analysis of the issue or some aspect of it. These study aids have a common purpose: to encourage you to think critically about what you have read.

Finally, each thematic unit concludes with 8–12 suggested writing topics based on the articles in that section. These suggestions offer you a broad choice of both topics and approaches. In some of them you will be asked to assume a particular role and argue a case to a designated audience. In others you will be asked to compare and contrast the arguments of two or more writers and to report on or summarize the arguments on one side of an issue. Finally, there are suggested topics that call for you to spend some time in the library doing additional research.

We are indebted to many people who read the preliminary drafts of *Controversies* and gave us the constructive criticism so necessary to the evolution and refinement of our thinking about this book. We are especially grateful to Nancy K. Barry at the University of Iowa, Donna Carter at George Washington University, Paul J. McVeigh at Northern Virginia Community College, Gail Stygall at Miami University, and Richard J. Zbaracki at Iowa State University.

We would like to thank a number of people who have been helpful and supportive of our work. Our colleagues in the Department of English at the University of Vermont—especially Molly Moore, Brian Kent, and Phoebe Bryan—willingly shared with us their expertise in teaching argument, as well as their experiences with their favorite essays and topics. We are grateful to all our writing students at the University of Vermont—particularly Lisa Denis whose essay appears in the introduction—for their enthusiasm for writing and their argumentative zeal in the classroom. Carol Ericson wrote all the authors and secured permissions to reprint the essays, cartoons, and advertisements; and Patricia Paquin developed the *Instructor's Manual* to accompany *Controversies*. Kristina Williamson of Publication Services expedited the production with dedication and unstinting eye for detail. At Macmillan Publishing Company, Nancy Cooperman and Wendy Conn were always available and responsive to our needs. It has been our pleasure to work with Eben Ludlow, our editor. His confidence in us has been inspiring, and his professionalism and cordiality have been exemplary. He has brought to *Controversies* a firm hand, one tempered by a wealth of experience.

ALFRED ROSA
PAUL ESCHHOLZ

Contents

CONTROVERSIES

Reading and Writing Arguments

What Is Argument?

We all know what arguments are. We get into them all the time. We've argued with our friends about music or sports; we've argued with our parents about money, using the car, and grades. And we've argued with the people we date, our teachers, our bosses, our brothers and sisters, and with anyone else whose views differ from ours. Arguing would seem to be natural. It's a by-product of our beliefs and values, of holding opinions and taking stands on issues that affect our daily lives.

If we stop to take a look at the situations in which we have found ourselves arguing, we would see that certain characteristics are common to all arguments. In each case there are at least two people who have a reasonable difference of opinion about an issue. And each is trying to show the other the truth in his or her own way of looking at the issue, ultimately with the hope of persuading the other person to this position or to a particular course of action. Because such arguments arise spontaneously, they are not always well thought out and there's always the possibility that tempers will flare when these encounters turn out to be inconclusive or, worse yet, emotional and hurtful.

The written arguments that you will be reading and writing in this course have much in common with the oral arguments that you are already familiar with, but they have a distinct advantage. Written arguments tend to be the product of reasoned and logical thinking. Ideally, in a written argument you are able to think about your subject and decide what claim you want to make about it. After determining your reasons for making this claim, you can plan a strategy, identify the type and amount of evidence you will need to marshal to satisfy your readers. Finally, you can check your facts and chart a course that will persuade or convince your

1

readers of your assertion. To argue logically is to think systematically, to move from assertion to evidence to conclusion with an almost mathematical precision. Your goal in each essay is not so much to win, to beat your opponent no matter what the costs, but rather to learn and to clarify and share your understanding. To this end you should learn to respect the intelligence and ideas of your audience and the fact that reasonable people may, and often do, disagree. By the end of the course, you will come to understand that to shed light and bring order where there was conflict and controversy is one of the most satisfying and rewarding of all intellectual pursuits.

As with all writing, the process of composing argumentative essays helps us come to a better understanding of how we think and what we believe. Seeing our ideas develop on paper gives each of us the opportunity to realize that all issues are fairly complicated if we look at them closely enough—and we must look at them closely if we are to ascertain the truth and to come up with something more than knee-jerk responses, either/or options, or black-and-white solutions. Writing helps us get beyond our biases, opinions, and prejudices—traits that don't really lead to greater understanding or social betterment. You can talk about the subjects and issues in *Controversies*, and you will probably argue about them in class, but only in writing about them will you clarify and refine your own thinking about them.

Reading and Analyzing an Argument

Each essay in *Controversies* offers its own challenges and rewards to you as a reader and writer. First you will want to know what the essay is about—what the author is arguing for or against and why. Next you will want to evaluate the evidence the author uses to persuade you to his or her position. Is it convincing? At the same time that you are reading for content, you should be paying attention to the writer's craftsmanship, the techniques and strategies the writer uses to construct the argument. An understanding of these strategies will be important to you when the time comes to write your own arguments. So that you can get the most out of your reading of the essays in *Controversies*, we offer the following set of questions to help you identify and analyze the key components of an argumentative essay.

What Is the Writer's Thesis or Claim?

It is important to come to an understanding of the author's main point or claim. In most cases the writer will present the central idea in a fairly concise statement, often called the *thesis statement*. Sometimes, however, the thesis is implicit and you will need to construct it for yourself by extrapolating the author's ideas. The thesis is not only the message of the essay, but also its magnetic center. All parts of the essay are held together by it.

The position of the thesis statement is the result of a strategic decision. In some essays you will find the thesis stated fairly early; in others it may be delayed or even put off until the closing paragraphs. A writer who anticipates a hostile or skeptical audience may want to present the thesis later in the essay after thoroughly preparing the readers for it. Even a shocking thesis statement might be presented right off if the writer believes the intended audience will be sympathetic to it. Once you have located the thesis statement, you should underline it for easy identification.

What Are the Writer's Assumptions?

One of the main reasons that people disagree is that they do not share a common ground. Their values, beliefs, and assumptions about the world are at odds. We need, therefore, to understand those differences before we can fully understand why people are taking a particular position. For example, doctors who write about animal experimentation might have one attitude toward the use of animals based on their professional goals and beliefs, whereas animal rights activists might operate on a completely different belief system. Those in the lumber industry do not view the world in the same way that environmentalists do. To loggers, trees are a livelihood; to environmentalists, they are a wildlife habitat and a necessary part of the ecosystem. Because these assumptions are seldom mentioned directly, you as a reader need to take special care in identifying them. Knowing something about the writer is always helpful, and that is one of the reasons we have provided a short biographical sketch of the writer before each essay.

What Persuasive Appeals Does the Writer Make?

When writers use persuasive appeals, they employ emotionally charged language and images designed to move you beyond the logic of the argument to decision or action. To call members of the National Rifle Association "gun-toting little boys," may rally antigun forces but does not make the argument valid or convincing. Similarly, when prodevelopment forces refer to environmentalists as "narrow-minded fanatics who want to bring us back to the Stone Age," they are not so much addressing the real issue of how to use the environment as they are appealing to people who believe as they do. Because emotions are so much a part of who we are, we use them almost unconsciously in all our interpersonal relationships and they become an integral part of our oral and written communications. While it is difficult to separate an emotional strand of an argument from its logical structure, it is nonetheless necessary that we become sensitive to the appeals that are playing on our own prejudices. Failure to recognize the persuasive power of emotional appeals can put readers in the unfortunate position of being manipulated by the writer's argument into making a decision or carrying out an action that they would later regret.

What Reasons Does the Writer Provide for the Thesis or Claim?

The basic structure of any argument consists of a thesis or claim (which you identified previously) and one or more reasons that are logically linked to and support that claim. For example, consider the following argument:

Claim:	Animals should not be used to test cosmetics.
Reason 1:	Many animals suffer great pain and even death during the testing process.
Reason 2:	Animal testing is not a reliable method of determining the potential harmful effects of the ingredients in cosmetics.
Reason 3:	Other means are available to test whether or not cosmetics are potentially harmful.

The logical link between the claim and the reasons can best be seen if we insert the word *because* between the claim and each of the reasons. For example,

Animals should not be used to test cosmetics *because* many animals suffer great pain and even death during the testing process.

It is not really possible to understand the thrust of an argument without identifying the writer's key reasons for making a claim. As you read an argument, be sure to label and number the writer's reasons so that you will be able to see the overall plan of the argument when you are through with your analysis.

What Evidence Does the Writer Use to Document Reasons?

For an author to convince a reader, he or she must provide evidence to support or document each of the reasons for the claim. Evidence usually takes the form of facts, statistics, examples, case studies, testimony from authorities, and, in certain cases, a closely linked chain of additional reasons. It is important to be able to identify the evidence that a writer uses and to assess its accuracy and relevance.

Does the Writer Consider Opposing Arguments and Points of View?

In any argument or debate the writer should always anticipate the key arguments of the opposition and be prepared to offer rebuttal or concede the reasonableness of those points. One of the common arguments for capital punishment is an economic one: execution is cheaper than mandatory life imprisonment. It has been shown, however, that because of protracted litigation the cost of execution far exceeds the cost of feeding and housing a prisoner for life.

How Has the Writer Developed the Argument?

As you highlight the main structural elements of the essay (the claim, the reasons, and the evidence), you should begin to see whether the writer has developed the argument by using *induction* or *deduction*, the two main methods of reasoning. Inductive reasoning moves from a set of specific examples to a general statement or principle. For instance, after presenting a series of examples of how language can be used to intimidate, frighten, harass, belittle, and totally demoralize children, the writer concludes that verbal abuse, although sometimes less obvious, can be as damaging to children as physical abuse. As long as the writer's evidence is accurate, relevant, and representative, the conclusion of an inductive argument can be regarded as valid. If, however, you detect inaccuracies in the evidence or know of contradictory examples, you have good reason to question the writer's claim as it stands. Inductive reasoning is the most common argumentative structure.

Deductive reasoning, on the other hand, is more formal and complex than the inductive approach. It moves from an overall generalization to a specific conclusion. A good way to both visualize and test a writer's deductive logic is to put the argument in the form of a *syllogism*, a simple three-part arrangement consisting of a *major premise*, a *minor premise*, and a *conclusion*. Consider the following syllogism:

Major Premise: Any condition that impairs a person's ability to drive should be avoided.

Minor Premise: Drunkenness impairs a person's ability to drive.

Conclusion: Drunkenness should be avoided.

The conclusion here is true because both premises are true and the logic of the syllogism is valid. There is a difference, however, between truth and validity. If either of the premises is untrue, although the syllogism may be valid, the conclusion will be false. For example,

Major Premise: All living creatures are mammals.

Minor Premise: A spider is a living creature.

Conclusion: A spider is a mammal.

The problem is clear. The major premise is obviously false, and therefore the conclusion is untrue. Yet, the syllogism remains valid.

A conclusion can also be invalid even though both premises are objectively true. Such failures occur when the writer jumps to a conclusion without accounting for obvious exceptions to one or both of the premises. Consider the following example:

Major Premise: If a person has a headache, he or she feels pain.

Minor Premise: Sally feels pain.

Conclusion: Sally has a headache.

This syllogism is invalid because the two premises, although true, fail to account for the fact that there are other sources of pain. Notice, however, what happens if the minor premise is put in the negative: "Sally does not feel pain." In this case, you can deduce the valid and true conclusion: "Sally does not have a headache."

What Does the Writer Want from You?

Once you have finished reading the complete essay, it may be useful for you to write a *summary*, or précis, of the argument. Such a summary should help you see the writer's point and purpose more clearly. You will find that writers very often wish to clarify their thinking about issues and at the very least wish to share their thoughts with us. Frequently, however, they go beyond the clarification of ideas. They wish to change our way of thinking, our attitudes toward a particular issue. And in other cases they may call upon us to do something, to carry out actions that reflect our beliefs and attitudes. If the final analysis you will want to determine if the writer has been successful in bringing you to his or her way of thinking and/or persuading you to pursue a specific course of action.

While these questions may seem a bit mechanical to you now, they will provide a process to help you systematically understand any essay that you encounter. The more you make use of these questions, the more they will become a natural part of any reading that you do.

Annotated Essay

As an exercise in reading and analyzing an argumentative essay, consider the following article by Lynne V. Cheney entitled "Students of Success." Cheney, a native of Casper, Wyoming, holds a doctorate in English from the University of Wisconsin and has taught at George Washington University and the University of Wyoming. She was the director of the National Endowment for the Humanities in 1986 when she wrote this article for *Newsweek*. Using a startling finding from a Carnegie Foundation study as her springboard, Cheney argues that today's college students should follow their hearts in choosing majors—and careers—and not follow the lure of big dollars.

As you read Cheney's essay, pay special attention to our marginal notations. Notice how these notations correspond to the questions discussed previously.

Lynne V. Cheney

Students of Success

Not long ago, my college-age daughter read about a software genius who became a multimillionaire before he was 30. "That does it," she said, "I'm going into computers."

This daughter, who has never met a political science course she didn't like, was only joking. But a study conducted by the Carnegie Foundation shows that many young people do think seriously along these lines. Instead of choosing college majors—and careers—according to their interests, they are channeling themselves into fields that promise to be profitable: business, engineering, computer science, allied health programs.

Introduction: anecdotal example of daughter juxtaposed to findings of Carnegie Foundation study.

Given the high cost of a college education, this trend is not surprising. A bachelor's degree now costs $40,000 at an average independent college. Can we expect students to major in the liberal arts when their starting salaries will be significantly lower than they are for business and professional majors? Shouldn't they get the best possible return on their investment?

Rhetorical Questions: these questions serve to set up Cheney's thesis.

They should, but I would suggest that there are better ways to calculate profit and loss than by looking at starting salaries. Consider, first of all, that very few people stay in the same line of work over a lifetime. They switch jobs, even change professions, and what is crucial for advancement is not specialized training but the ability to think critically and judge wisely. Given the difficulty of predicting which skills will be in demand even five years from now, let alone over a lifetime, a student's best career preparation is one that emphasizes general understanding and intellectual curiosity: a knowledge of how to learn and the desire to do it. Literature, history, philosophy and the social sciences—majors that students avoid today—are the ones traditionally believed to develop such habits of mind.

Thesis: Cheney claims that there are better ways to calculate a return on the investment of college costs than starting salaries.

Reason 1: Because people often switch jobs during their lifetimes, general understanding and intellectual curiosity are preferable to specialized skills.

I recently conducted an informal survey of successful Americans, and while several dozen phone calls aren't proof of the value of a liberal-arts major, the results are suggestive. The communications world, for example, is dominated by liberal-arts majors. Thomas H. Wyman, chairman of CBS, majored in English, as did Cathleen Black, publisher of USA Today. Washington Post columnist William Raspberry studied history;

NBC News anchorman Tom Brokaw, political science.

In public life, too, leaders more often than not were students of the liberal arts. They form a majority in the president's cabinet. Secretary of State George Shultz and Secretary of Energy John Herrington majored in economics. Interior Secretary Donald Hodel majored in government, and Transportation Secretary Elizabeth Dole, political science. Secretary of the Treasury James Baker read history with a minor in classics; Secretary of Education William Bennett studied philosophy.

Evidence for Reason 1: **Informal survey of notable figures in business and public life suggests that many successful leaders are products of the liberal-arts tradition.**

The president himself majored in economics and sociology. His communications director, Pat Buchanan, majored in English and philosophy. White House chief of staff (and former treasury secretary) Donald Regan was an English major and before he came to government had a remarkably successful business career as the head of Merrill Lynch. Secretary of Commerce Malcolm Baldrige headed Scovill Manufacturing, and now the former English major is leading a campaign for clear writing in government.

Executives like Regan and Baldrige are not unusual. According to a recent report in *Fortune* magazine, 38 percent of today's CEO's majored in the liberal arts, and a close reading of The New York Times shows that 9 of the top 13 executives at IBM are liberal-arts majors. At AT&T, a study showed social-science and humanities graduates moving into middle management faster than engineers and doing at least as well as their business and engineering counterparts in reaching top management levels.

Evidence for Reason 1: **a report in *Fortune* magazine, a close reading of *The New York Times*, and an AT&T study give further testimony to the success rate of liberal-arts graduates.**

For several years now, corporate executives have extolled the wide range of knowledge and interests that a study of the liberal arts encourages. And now under Tom Wyman's direction, CBS has funded an organization that investigates exactly why it is that liberal-arts training is valuable to the American corporation. "In an increasingly competitive, internationally oriented and technologically innovative society," Wyman recently wrote, "successful executives will be those who can understand — and interpret — complex relationships and who are capable of continually reconsidering assumptions underlying old operating practices."

Reason 2: **Corporate executives have praised the value of a liberal-arts education for people in American businesses.**

Testimony: **quotation by CBS Chairman supports Cheney's Reason 2.**

In the past, such top-level views did not always filter down to where entry-level hiring is done. But reports from that front are encouraging. A study by Northwestern University shows that many major companies plan to increase their hiring of liberal-arts graduates by some 20 percent in 1986. Or as one employer recently told "Today" show viewers, "Those that are involved in recruiting people to the company are looking for . . . broader skills . . . Then we will worry about teaching them terminology, specifics of the jobs."

Evidence for Reason 2: **Northwestern University study documents plans for the increased hiring of liberal-arts graduates.**

Testimony: **quotation by employer on "Today" show gives support for Reason 2.**

I don't mean to argue that liberal arts is the only road to success. The average starting salary for engineers remains impressively high, almost $30,000 compared to $21,000 for a liberal-arts graduate. In fact, my informal survey also shows that engineers are doing well in a variety of fields. Chrysler chairman Lee Iacocca was an engineering major, as was former Delaware Gov. Pete du Pont. My point is that there are many paths to suc-

Concessions: **Cheney acknowledges that there are successful people who did not major in the liberal arts. She goes on to explain how people like Iacocca and du Pont do not alter the thrust of her argument.**

cess and students shouldn't force themselves down any single one if their true interests lie elsewhere. College should be a time for intellectual enthusiasm, for trying to read one's way through the library, for heated debate with those who see the world differently. College should be a time for learning to enjoy the life of the mind rather than for learning to tolerate what one doesn't find interesting.

Students who follow their hearts in choosing majors will most likely end up laboring at what they love. They're the ones who will put in the long hours and intense effort that achievement requires. And they're the ones who will find the sense of purpose that underlies most human happiness.

Conclusion: **Cheney reiterates her thesis that there are better ways of measuring success than starting salaries: people who have an interest in and love for their work will find a sense of purpose and happiness in life.**

Our marginal notations provide an outline or quick overview of the structure of Cheney's essay. To better understand and interpret the arguments in the essays presented in *Controversies*, try annotating them in this way.

Writing Your Own Argument

Choose a Worthwhile Topic for Your Essay

The best place to start is with a topic that interests you and about which there is considerable difference of opinion. You would not, for example, find much disagreement about the fact that the Alaskan oil spill damaged the fishing industry in Valdez, or that AIDS poses a major health problem for the world, or that the Soviet political system is undergoing tremendous change as it enters the decade of the nineties. You would, however, find considerable disagreement about how to clean up the Alaskan oil spill, how to pay for it, and how to prevent future supertanker disasters. You would find people on both sides of the AIDS testing and identification question, how health-care workers can be protected from getting AIDS, and the government's obligations to work on a cure. And you would certainly find many different arguments on how America should respond to the needs of Eastern bloc countries struggling for their independence.

Developing a Thesis and Explaining Your Reasons for It

At the center of any argument is a controversial question for which there are at least two competing answers. As you read and think about your topic, you should identify the key issues or controversies that surround the topic. Next try to frame the essence of one of the issues that most interests you by putting it in the form of a question. There should be several possible answers, and your thesis statement will be the answer that you give to the question. At this point you should try to articulate your specific reasons for answering the issue question the way you did. One helpful way of thinking about each reason is to see it as beginning with the word *because*. Notice in the following example how students generated three thesis statements with reasons to support each using the process just described.

Topic:	The future of federal affirmative action programs.
Issue question:	What should be the future of federal affirmative action programs?
Thesis 1:	Affirmative action programs should be continued and expanded. (Pro position)
Reasons:	1. because color-sensitive and sex-sensitive policies ensure the long-range goal of equal opportunity.
	2. because the wrongs of the past need to be redressed.
	3. because women cannot be penalized as they move from working in the home to joining the work force at all levels.
Thesis 2:	Affirmative action programs should be abolished. (Con position)
Reasons:	1. because affirmative action programs have already had their maximum impact.

2. because people today should not have to be denied opportunities because of the wrongs of the past.
3. because affirmative action programs are discrimination in reverse in that they do not guarantee that the best people are hired.

Thesis 3: Affirmative action programs should be continued but be scaled down. (Intermediate or compromise position)

1. because federal funds are not available.
2. because employers have changed their hiring practices in accordance with equal opportunity principles.
3. because affirmative action programs have been largely successful but have not achieved their ultimate goals.

Presenting Evidence to Substantiate Your Reasons

While your reasons for arguing a particular point might be wholly true, reasons by themselves do not an argument make. You need to provide evidence for each reason or assertion you put forth to justify your claim. It is the evidence that you include that will both convince and persuade your readers of the validity of your position. Consider the following excerpt from Linda-Marie Delloff's article "Distorted Images: The Elderly and the Media," published in *The Christian Century* in January 1987. Delloff claims that in an age when the elderly are one of the fastest-growing elements of the total population their representation in the media is both inadequate and distorted. As evidence she summarizes a report given by Dr. Marsel Heisel, a gerontologist at Rutgers University.

Of the few elders who do appear on TV in one or another capacity, noted Marsel Heisel, almost all are male: only one in ten characters judged to be 65 or older is a woman. Thus, she said, if we assume that what has meaning and status for society finds its way onto televi-

Reference to authority and presentation of statistics

sion screens, the message conveyed seems to be that the elderly are not very important, and that among that population group, only men have significance. In referring to research of other gerontologists, Heisel also observed that when older persons do appear on screen, they tend to be "more comical, stubborn, eccentric, and foolish than other characters." She also cited a 1977 Annenberg School of Communication survey of more than 9,000 television characters, which determined that only 3.7 of them were elderly; moreover, compared to other groups, these individuals were portrayed as ineffective, unattractive and unhappy.

Quotation of authority

Reference to published study and data

You do not have to overwhelm your readers with evidence to convince them; more is not necessarily better. But do not skimp either. It is important that you show a command of your subject and a sensitivity to your audience by carefully choosing the most appropriate evidence at your disposal to make a compelling argument. As we have seen in the previous paragraph, evidence can take a variety of forms. Types of evidence you should know about and may wish to use to support your assertions include the following:

- examples from personal experience
- verifiable facts
- quotations and other testimony from experts
- statistical data
- analogies
- hypothetical cases
- experiments and case studies
- graphs, illustrations, photographs

Being Sensitive to the Needs of Your Audience

Perhaps in no other type of writing is an awareness of audience more important than when you argue or debate an issue. If you know that your readers are likely to be receptive, hostile, wavering, skeptical, or neutral, you will know what tone to establish, what diction to use, what types of evidence and how much of it to provide, and whether to organize your essay inductively or deductively. A quick and easy way to get a picture of your audience and its needs is to ask yourself some of the following questions:

- Who is my ideal reader?
- What common ground (beliefs, values, assumptions) do I and the reader share?
- What do I want my ideal reader to do?
- Is my ideal reader in a position to accomplish this?
- How much does my reader know and care about the issue?
- Are there any key terms or concepts that need to be defined and clarified?
- What is my reader's present attitude toward the issue?
- What is the most difficult part of the argument for my reader and why?

Your answers to these questions will help you make the crucial decisions that will ultimately determine the effectiveness of your argument. For example, suppose you were writing an argument against recently enacted tuition hikes at your college. Although you might find a sympathetic audience among your professors and fellow students, they are not really in a position to do much more than than agree with you or participate in an organized protest. If your intent is to get the tuition increase reconsidered or rescinded, then you should be directing your argument to your school's administrators or board of trustees. At all stages of thinking about and drafting your argument, it is helpful to keep your reader clearly in mind, almost as if you were carrying on a face-to-face exchange with that person.

Considering Counterarguments and Concessions

While developing your line of argument, you should try to see the argument from the opposition's point of view. In this way you will be able to anticipate the central points in his or her argument as well as see the weaknesses in your own reasoning. With these insights you should develop strong counterarguments to the opponent's central points and thus shore up your own position. For example, the argument that drugs such as marijuana, cocaine, and heroin should be legalized because drug users only harm themselves can be effectively countered by pointing to the number of drug-dependent babies that are born each year to drug-addicted mothers. If your opponent makes a valid point, however, it may help your own credibility to concede the reasonableness of that point and concentrate your efforts on counterarguing the more debatable points in your opponent's argument.

Organizing Your Argument

Once you have the claim and purpose of your argument clearly in mind, it is time to think about how you want to present or organize your supporting reasons and evidence. There are a number of strategies for logically organizing your essay; your job is to select the one that best suits your claim and purpose. For example, many arguments consist of identifying a specific problem and proposing one or more solutions for it. Let's see how one student handled this situation in her paper. Emma thought that parking was a problem on her campus and that more spaces were needed for commuter students. In her opening paragraphs she analyzed the complexities of the problem. Next she discussed a proposal for paving open spaces on campus but dismissed it as both aesthetically and environmentally unsound. Finally Emma offered two solutions—a shuttle to an off-campus parking lot and a multi-story parking garage—and argued vigorously for their implementation.

Other organizational strategies that reflect common patterns of thinking include illustrating with examples, defining controversial terms, comparing and contrasting to determine relative worth, determining causes and predicting effects, and analyzing a process. Let's look at two claims and a possible corresponding organizational pattern for each.

Illustration.   When using illustration it is always important to arrange your examples in an order that serves your purpose, is easy for readers to follow, and will be the most persuasive. On the simplest level you could arrange your examples chronologically or spatially. Other possible patterns include moving from the simplest example to the most complex, from the least to the most important, from the least to the most controversial, or from the most familiar to the least familiar. Notice how the writer used the principle of going from the least to the most offensive acts to organize the following:

> Claim: Film producers should reconsider the amount of violence in their films because they currently contain too much unnecessary violence.
>
> 1. films with verbal violence
> 2. films with beatings
> 3. films with shootings, stabbings
> 4. films with slashings, dismemberment, and other atrocities
>
> Conclusion: Violent acts of all sorts should be eliminated or sharply reduced in the making of films in the future.

Comparison and Contrast. Whenever you use this strategy you should begin with a list of the specific points that form the basis of your comparison. In our example we decided to compare professional basketball players Michael Jordan and Larry Bird on the basis of their ballhandling, shooting, and teamwork. A scratch outline for this argument might look something like the following:

> Claim: Michael Jordan is a better basketball player than Larry Bird.
>
> Michael Jordan
>
> Ball handling: Excellent
> Shooting: Excellent
> Teamwork: Excellent
>
> Larry Bird
>
> Ball handling: Good
> Shooting: Excellent
> Teamwork: Good
>
> Conclusion: Overall, Michael Jordan is a better basketball player than Larry Bird

Conclusion

It is important in any argument to end on a high note, to end forcefully. Besides briefly restating your position on the issue you may want to encourage some specific course of action on the part of your readers. Although it is sometimes tempting to conclude with a startling quotation or statistic, be careful that such new information serves to complement what you have already said rather than open a new discussion. Do not overstate your case in the conclusion; the reasons and evidence in your argument should speak for themselves and lead naturally to your conclusion. In other words, if your argument has failed to convince your readers, your conclusion can hardly be expected to do the job alone. On the other hand, you do not want to undermine the forcefulness of your argument by qualifying your conclusions.

Logical Fallacies

1. *Oversimplification:* to provide a simple solution to a complex problem ("We would be closer to a cure for AIDS if more money were spent on research.")

2. *Hasty Generalization:* a generalization based on inadequate or on unrepresentative evidence ("Running is the best exercise because other types of exercise don't give you a good workout.")

3. *Slippery Slope:* without evidence, a given action or decision is deemed capable of setting in motion a series of events that will end in catastrophe ("If we outlaw assault weapons, pretty soon all guns will be banned.")

4. *Post Hoc, Ergo Propter Hoc:* involves establishing a questionable causal relation; literally "after this, therefore because of this" ("Every time we take him fishing it rains.")

5. *Begging the Question:* assuming in a premise that which needs to be proven ("Using cocaine is wrong because it is against the law.")

6. *False Analogy:* a misleading association that is drawn between

logically unconnected ideas ("Of course she'll be a good mother. She takes good care of her two dogs.")

7. *Either/Or Thinking:* recognizing only two choices in any situation ("Either we legalize drugs or we fail to control violent crime in America.")

8. *Non Sequitur:* literally "it does not follow" ("My brother raises rabbits; therefore I am against wearing fur.")

9. *Ad Hominem:* literally "to the man" ("That economic policy is not surprising considering Bush was in favor of it.")

10. *Ad Populum:* literally "to the people" ("Chevrolet. The heartbeat of America.")

11. *Appeal to Pity:* irrelevant appeals to sentiments used to settle a factual matter ("He shouldn't be sent to jail. He's a single parent.")

12. *Appeal to Force:* a scare tactic ("If we don't ban the use of fluorocarbons we'll commit environmental suicide.")

13. *Red Herring:* a diversionary statement, a tangential comment ("Sure I use drugs, but so do a lot of other students.")

Annotated Student Paper

What Are Disposable Diapers?

Lisa Denis

I would like to call your attention to the children of today. I am speaking of the very young ones. Those who are dependent and innocent playing in their Oshkosh B'Gosh overalls and diapers. I would not suggest "Hugging," "Luving" or "Pampering" these kids. Picture yourself having to change a child's diaper. I bet that you didn't see yourself using a cloth diaper and pins. The use of disposable diapers has become the

norm in today's fast-paced society. The
fact is that we are doing great damage
to the environment by putting disposable diapers on our children. Enough
damage to say that we're putting their
future on the line. The time has come to
put an end to the use of disposable diapers. They are expensive, potentially
harmful to babies, and environmentally
unsound.

Disposable diapers came out in the
early 1970's and were looked upon by the
parents of newborns as not only a convenience but a technological advancement.
Throwaway diapers reduced the amount
of laundry, eased the task of traveling, and enabled friends or relatives
to take care of infants without the has-
sle of pinning and rinsing cloth diapers. Yes, I agree that disposable diapers can be easier to use and are more
convenient than their cloth counterparts. But that does not necessarily
make them better. Does the convenience
of these diapers override the immense
amount of non-biodegradable waste created each day?

Sixteen billion disposable diapers are dumped in U.S. landfills alone
each year. Cathy Spencer, writing in
the September 1989 issue of *Omni* magazine describes the amount as "enough
to stretch to the moon and back seven
times." Diapers are taking up an estimated 2% of the waste dumps, dumps that
are presently dwindling in our country. Over $300 million is spent each
year by taxpayers to rid our households of disposable diapers. Nan Scott,

Marginal annotations:

Claim

Reasons for claim

Concession

Reason 1: Environ-
mental problems

Citation of authority
with quotation

Counterargument

an owner of a California diaper service, estimates that a barge load of diapers are thrown away every six hours in the United States. A few companies claim they are making almost completely biodegradable diapers. The words "almost biodegradable" are the key, for these diapers can take three to five years to begin their breakdown process. One company's product breaks apart, but the tiny fragments haven't been declared "biodegradable." We're left with bits and pieces of plastic rather than a solid dense sheet. The manufacturer of another product, made from cornstarch, claims that its product will decompose in the same three to five years when exposed to direct sunlight. With current landfill practices, however, how much sun exposure can be received deep within the ground?

Continued discussion of environmental problems

The improper use of diapers can also lead to problems. Do you know that over 90% of parents of young children break the law daily? It is illegal to fill any waste site with human excretion. If you read the side of any diaper box, it will inform you, in small print, to empty the diaper in a toilet before disposal. The only legal way to dispose of human feces is through the sewer system. The problem with this is that the law is known by too few and is rarely enforced. Human waste from infants' diapers has been shown to expose sanitary workers to hepatitis and polio. Researchers have also linked diapers to high bacteria counts in drinking water.

Personal experience testimony

This past summer, back in the deep hills of Vermont, I worked as a live-in for a family that took advantage of a local diaper service. Each week the diaper service delivered six dozen freshly laundered, pressed, and neatly stacked diapers and picked up the soiled diapers in my diaper pail. I was with the kids daily and was responsible for keeping them freshly diapered.

Concessions

I will admit that there are some things that make reusable cloth diapers less convenient. They are heavier and need to be changed every time they become saturated. Occasionally they can leak causing wet clothes and discomfort.

Counterargument

While we didn't have the total convenience of disposables that we could throw in the trash when we went on day trips, we did have a biodegradable cotton insert, supplied by our service, that we could dispose of conveniently.

Testimony for cloth diapers

The diapers provided by the service weren't those old-fashioned cloth diapers, either. They were surprisingly easy-to-use, narrow four-ply strips of cotton cloth that fit easily within our diaper covers. These covers had elastic leg bands and Velcro waist fasteners that made for an easy change. The covers I used were made of attractive wool and cotton prints. They could be thrown in the washer and dryer and seemed so durable that a child would grow out of them before they would lose any stitching or see any wear and tear.

Reason 2: expense

The diaper service is consistently less expensive than purchasing disposables. Up to eight cents per changing could go to that child's future college fund instead of in the pocket of some company that doesn't care about our world.

That is a lot of money if you consider that the average child goes through 6,000 to 10,000 diapers in its early years. Proponents of disposable diapers claim that disposables need not be changed as often. Manufacturers claim that "ultra-absorbent" diapers can be left on for long periods of time. It is a fact, however, that diaper rash and urinary tract infections occur six times more often with the use of these diapers. In some cases, toxic shock syndrome has occurred when the skin was consistently wet for a long period of time. What happens is that the skin also re-absorbs urine through the pores. Often the urine mixes with chemicals in the diapers and this mixture can cause serious illness to the infant. This doesn't happen often, but why chance it? An added advantage of the diaper service is that you can have the diapers treated to achieve the right pH balance depending on the child's stage of growth. For example, a baby that is breast fed needs a different pH balance than that of a teething child. All that disposables offer are perfumes, dyes, and chemicals.

If I ever decide to have children, I would definitely use my own cloth diapers or a diaper service. Not only are the cloth diapers more economical, they are healthier, more comfortable, and

Reason 3: health hazards (margin note)

Restatement of thesis (margin note)

environmentally wise. Cloth diapers
can be used and re-used up to 200 times.
Theoretically, you could own as few as a
dozen diapers for the average two-and-
one-half years of your child's unpotty-
trained life. Also, at the most, cotton diapers take one to six months to
decompose if they are ever thrown away.
The use of disposable diapers symbol-
izes America's ignorance about and lack
of concern for the environment. Convenience and large publicity campaigns
from the manufacturers of disposable
diapers have been the major causes of
their general acceptance. The only way
caring Americans can make a difference
is to share the facts. Don't you think
that the softest of bottoms deserve
cotton, not to mention a clean and safe
Earth to play in?

Emotional appeal

1
Mirror, Mirror on the Wall: Looking at America

> *This is the world out of which grows the hope, for the first time in history, of a society where there will be freedom from want and freedom from fear. Our very anxiety is born of our knowledge of what is now possible for each and for all.*
>
> MARGARET MEAD

> *Our brave new world is one in which the basic social unit is the large, impersonal institution. . . . Today's young people are being forged into cogs in the corporate structure.*
>
> PHILIP G. ZIMBARDO

> *America has been a game show. Winning is all that matters. Cash prizes. Get rich quick. We are the captives of a culture that celebrates instant gratification and individual success no matter the larger costs.*
>
> NORMAN LEAR

> *Despite outbreaks of nativist frenzy, America has remained an immigrant country, open and true to itself.*
>
> RICHARD RODRIGUEZ

What is America? What is the American experience? And what does it mean to be American? Because we are living in America we take these questions lightly and overlook their complexity and importance. But they are puzzling questions, questions that lie at the heart of all the controversial social, ethical, moral, and philosophical issues now facing us as a people. How we look at problems—prejudice, our destruction of the environment, hunger and homelessness, abortion, capital punishment, the right to die, the AIDS epidemic, animal experimentation, violent crime, and substance abuse—to a large extent depends on how we define ourselves, our traditions, our ambitions, and our hopes and fears. In other words, we don't simply develop our attitudes and beliefs about issues in the abstract. Rather, they have been handed down to us by our parents and their parents before them, and our opinions and values have been shaped in turn by the schools we attended, the religious training we have had, and in a larger sense by what America was and still hopes to be.

It is popular in discussions of this sort to employ the phrase "inventing America" to label the process by which what we believe leads us to what we do and how what we do leads us yet again to what we believe. More appropriate, perhaps, is the phrase "re-inventing America," for the task is ongoing and never really completed. In reading and studying the essays in this first section of *Controversies* you will experience this process; you will be asked to question and re-examine your own assumptions and thoughts about our country and your place in it. The anthropologist Margaret Mead sees anxiety, or stress, as a positive emotion and a cause for hope. Psychologist Philip G. Zimbardo warns us of the possible negative effects of the endemic indifference that seems to isolate us from each other. Television writer and producer Norman Lear cautions us against our worship of the values of large corporations and the materialistic instincts they bring out in each of us. Finally, Richard Rodriguez, the child of immigrant parents, tells how America continues to embrace the immigrants of the world and find strength in its diversity. In reading these essays each of us will come to a better sense of who we are, what we believe, and how we can join forces to find solutions to the problems we face.

Margaret Mead

One Vote for This Age of Anxiety

Writer, educator, and anthropologist Margaret Mead (1901–1978) was born in Philadelphia, Pennsylvania. First enrolled at DePauw University, Mead graduated from Barnard College and Columbia University and was for many years professor of anthropology at Columbia. She devoted much of her professional life to the study of native cultures in the South Pacific, establishing herself as an expert on family structure, environmental problems, primitive societies, mental health, and the role of women in society. Several of her pioneering field studies carried out in the 1920s and 1930s are still considered classics in cultural anthropology. Later in life, Mead's work focused on the study of contemporary Western society. Her most important books include Coming of Age in Samoa *(1928),* Sex and Temperament in Three Primitive Societies *(1935),* Male and Female: A Study of the Sexes in a Changing World *(1949),* Continuities in Cultural Evolution *(1964), and* Culture and Commitment: A Study of the Generation Gap *(1970). After her retirement from the academic world, Mead worked at the American Museum of Natural History in New York and was a contributing editor to* Redbook.

In the following essay, which first appeared in The New York Times *on May 20, 1956, Mead explodes the myths associated with anxiety. Drawing upon her knowledge of primitive societies and their fears and terrors, she thinks that anxiety is not the negative emotion it was once supposed to be. In fact, she argues that it is anxiety that gives us "the hope, for the first time in history, of a society where there will be freedom from want and freedom from fear."*

1   When critics wish to repudiate the world in which we live today, one of their familiar ways of doing it is to castigate modern man because anxiety is his chief problem. This, they say, in W. H.

Auden's phrase, is the age of anxiety. That is what we have arrived at with all our vaunted progress, our great technological advances, our great wealth—everyone goes about with a burden of anxiety so enormous that, in the end, our stomachs and our arteries and our skins express the tension under which we live. Americans who have lived in Europe come back to comment on our favorite farewell which, instead of the old goodbye (God be with you), is now "Take it easy," each American admonishing the other not to break down from the tension and strain of modern life.

2   Whenever an age is characterized by a phrase, it is presumably in contrast to other ages. If we are the age of anxiety, what were the other ages? And here the critics and carpers do a very amusing thing. First, they give us lists of the opposites of anxiety: security, trust, self-confidence, self-direction. Then, without much further discussion, they let us assume that other ages, other periods of history, were somehow the ages of trust or confident direction.

3   The savage who, on his South Sea island, simply sat and let breadfruit fall into his lap, the simple peasant, at one with the fields he ploughed and the beasts he tended, the craftsman busy with his tools and lost in the fulfillment of the instinct of workmanship—these are the counter-images conjured up by descriptions of the strain under which men live today. But no one who lived in those days has returned to testify how paradisiacal they really were.

4   Certainly if we observe and question the savages or simple peasants in the world today, we find something quite different. The untouched savage in the middle of New Guinea isn't anxious; he is seriously and continually *frightened*—of black magic, of enemies with spears who may kill him or his wives and children at any moment, while they stoop to drink from a spring, or climb a palm tree for a coconut. He goes warily, day and night, taut and fearful.

5   As for the peasant populations of a great part of the world, they aren't so much anxious as hungry. They aren't anxious about whether they will get a salary raise, or which of the three colleges of their choice they will be admitted to, or whether to buy a Ford or Cadillac, or whether the kind of TV set they want is too expensive. They are hungry, cold and, in many parts of the world, they

dread that local warfare, bandits, political coups may endanger their homes, their meager livelihoods and their lives. But surely they are not anxious.

6   For anxiety, as we have come to use it to describe our characteristic state of mind, can be contrasted with the active fear of hunger, loss, violence and death. Anxiety is the appropriate emotion when the immediate personal terror—of a volcano, an arrow, the sorcerer's spell, a stab in the back and other calamities, all directed against one's self—disappears.

7   This is not to say that there isn't plenty to worry about in our world of today. The explosion of a bomb in the streets of a city whose name no one had ever heard before may set in motion forces which end up by ruining one's carefully planned education in law school, half a world away. But there is still not the personal, immediate, active sense of impending disaster that the savage knows. There is rather the vague anxiety, the sense that the future is unmanageable.

8   The kind of world that produces anxiety is actually a world of relative safety, a world in which no one feels that he himself is facing sudden death. Possibly sudden death may strike a certain number of unidentified other people—but not him. The anxiety exists as an uneasy state of mind, in which one has a feeling that something unspecified and undeterminable may go wrong. If the world seems to be going well, this produces anxiety—for good times may end. If the world is going badly—it may get worse. Anxiety tends to be without locus; the anxious person doesn't know whether to blame himself or other people. He isn't sure whether it is the current year or the Administration or a change in climate or the atom bomb that is to blame for this undefined sense of unease.

9   It is clear that we have developed a society which depends on having the *right* amount of anxiety to make it work. Psychiatrists have been heard to say, "He didn't have enough anxiety to get well," indicating that, while we agree that too much anxiety is inimical to mental health, we have come to rely on anxiety to push and prod us into seeing a doctor about a symptom which may indicate cancer, into checking up on that old life-insurance policy which may have out-of-date clauses in it, into having a conference with Billy's teacher even though his report card looks all right.

10   People who are anxious enough keep their car insurance up, have the brakes checked, don't take a second drink when they have to drive, are careful where they go and with whom they drive on holidays. People who are too anxious either refuse to go into cars at all—and so complicate the ordinary course of life—or drive so tensely and overcautiously that they help cause accidents. People who aren't anxious enough take chance after chance, which increases the terrible death toll of the roads.

11   On balance, our age of anxiety represents a large advance over savage and peasant cultures. Out of a productive system of technology drawing upon enormous resources, we have created a nation in which anxiety has replaced terror and despair, for all except the severely disturbed. The specter of hunger means something only to those Americans who can identify themselves with the millions of hungry people on other continents. The specter of terror may still be roused in some by a knock at the door in a few parts of the South, or in those who have just escaped from a totalitarian regime or who have kin still behind the Curtains.

12   But in this twilight world which is neither at peace nor at war, and where there is insurance against certain immediate, downright, personal disasters, for most Americans there remains only anxiety over what may happen, might happen, could happen.

13   This is the world out of which grows the hope, for the first time in history, of a society where there will be freedom from want and freedom from fear. Our very anxiety is born of our knowledge of what is now possible for each and for all. The number of people who consult psychiatrists today is not, as is sometimes felt, a symptom of increasing mental ill health, but rather the precursor of a world in which the hope of genuine mental health will be open to everyone, a world in which no individual feels that he need be hopelessly brokenhearted, a failure, a menace to others or a traitor to himself.

14   But if, then, our anxieties are actually signs of hope, why is there such a voice of discontent abroad in the land? I think this comes perhaps because our anxiety exists without an accompanying recognition of the tragedy which will always be inherent in human life, however well we build our world. We may banish hunger, and fear of sorcery, violence or secret police; we may bring up children who have learned to trust life and who have the spon-

taneity and curiosity necessary to devise ways of making trips to the moon; we cannot—as we have tried to do—banish death itself.

15   Americans who stem from generations which left their old people behind and never closed their parents' eyelids in death, and who have experienced the additional distance from death provided by two world wars fought far from our shores are today pushing away from them both a recognition of death and a recognition of the tremendous significance—for the future—of the way we live our lives. Acceptance of the inevitability of death, which, when faced, can give dignity to life, and acceptance of our inescapable role in the modern world, might transmute our anxiety about making the right choices, taking the right precautions, and the right risks into the sterner stuff and responsibility, which ennobles the whole face rather than furrowing the forehead with the little anxious wrinkles of worry.

16   Worry in an empty context means that men die daily little deaths. But good anxiety—not about the things that were left undone long ago, but which return to haunt and harry men's minds, but active, vivid anxiety about what must be done and that quickly—binds men to life with an intense concern.

17   This is still a world in which too many of the wrong things happen somewhere. But this is a world in which we now have the means to make a great many more of the right things happen everywhere. For Americans, the generalization which a Swedish social scientist made about our attitudes on race relations is true in many other fields: anticipated change which we feel is right and necessary but difficult makes us unduly anxious and apprehensive, but such change, once consummated, brings a glow of relief. We are still a people who—in the literal sense—believe in making good.

Analyzing the Writer's Argument

1. What is Mead arguing for in this essay? Identify the sentence(s) in which she states her thesis.
2. What do critics of the modern world see as the problems associated with anxiety? What is Mead's attitude toward these critics? What words or phrases in her essay led you to this conclusion?

3. According to Mead, what "amusing thing" do critics and carpers do when talking about "the age of anxiety"? Why do you suppose Mead finds their strategy amusing? Explain.

4. What contrast does Mead draw in paragraphs 3 through 6? How does this contrast function in the context of her argument? Did you find her discussion persuasive? Why, or why not?

5. What distinctions does Mead make between anxiety and fear? In what sense is "the kind of world that produces anxiety . . . actually a world of relative safety"?

6. What does Mead mean when she says, "we have developed a society which depends on having the *right* amount of anxiety to make it work"? Do her examples help to clarify her meaning? Why, or why not?

7. How does Mead differentiate between good and bad anxiety? Why does she find good anxiety a sign of hope?

8. If anxiety is supposed to be such a good emotion, how does Mead account for all the discontent in America? In what sense are Americans distanced from death? What does Mead believe we will gain if we accept the inevitability of death?

Exploring the Issues in This Essay

1. When Mead wrote this essay, the buzz word was *anxiety*. Today we hear people use the word *stress* and mostly in a negative context. Is *stress* simply a synonym for *anxiety*, or are there real differences that you see? Is it possible to see today's stress as a positive force in our lives in much the same way that Mead sees anxiety as a positive force? Discuss the possibilities using examples from your own experiences or observations.

2. Are you as optimistic about the future—about our ability "to make a great many more of the right things happen everywhere"—as Mead was when she wrote her essay? Discuss situations, events, and circumstances that bolster your spirits or ones that give you reason to be skeptical.

Philip G. Zimbardo

*The Age of Indifference**

> *Psychologist and Stanford University professor Philip G. Zimbardo was born in New York City on March 23, 1933. He received his A.B. from Brooklyn College and his M.S. and Ph.D. from Yale University. Zimbardo is perhaps best known to great numbers of college students for over two decades as the author (along with his wife Christina Maslach and Ebbe Ebbeson) of the introductory college-level psychology textbook* Psychology and Life *(12th edition, 1988). Zimbardo has also published many scholarly articles and books, among them* Shyness: What It Is, What to Do About It *(1977).*
>
> *In commenting on his research, Zimbardo writes: "All my work has as its original purpose improving the human condition by illuminating ways we can go wrong or have gone wrong. I try to show the power of situations to overwhelm people. It is important in my research and writing that I am of the people, learn from them, and give back to them all that I believe may help improve the human condition." The following essay was first published in* Psychology Today, *in August 1980.*

1   In some schools where computers are used as tutors, children have reported developing a closer, friendlier relationship with their ever-reliable machine than with Ms. Dove and her sundry personal idiosyncrasies. As these kiddies mature, some of them are likely to become "hackers," members of a new subculture of grown-up electronic whiz kids obsessed by interacting with computers. Hackers spend long hours at night or early in the morning, when "downtime" is shorter, playing with their programs and sending messages via electronic bulletin boards to hacker associates seated

at terminals a few feet away. Fascination with the computer becomes an addiction, and as with most addictions, the "substance" that gets abused is human relationships.

2   Not just in schools but in society as a whole, the hacker mentality is upon us, with or without the computer as a rationalization for putting other people at the bottom of our priority stack. There are forces at work in society increasing both the sense and the reality of our separateness from one another. It is as if we were suffering from a mysterious kind of "legionnaire's disease" of which the chief symptoms are isolation and a loss of naturalness in our relations with other people.

3   I used to believe that this separateness was the exclusive problem of the timid, introverted shys. For the past eight years I have been studying the personal and social dynamics of shyness, and I know that 40 percent of Americans quietly claim to be of that disposition. I also know that a surprising 25 percent of these sufferers became shy *after* leaving the universal self-concern and awkwardness of adolescence. I am aware, too, that self-help books for the shy are selling well; that shyness clinics are springing up; that social psychologists who used to be interested only in social affiliation are writing textbooks including chapters on loneliness, based on research and scientific meetings devoted to this fascinating phenomenon.

4   But shyness alone does not account for all of the isolation that marks contemporary society. My research team has surveyed, interviewed, observed, experimented upon, and done therapy with a vast number of shy people (reported in part in *Shyness: What It Is, What To Do About It*). While we were documenting their conversational awkwardness, passivity, reluctance to initiate social contact, and general social phobia, a curious discovery emerged—about a comparison group of nonshys. They do not show the same motivated avoidance and inhibition syndrome characteristic of their shy peers; theirs is an apparently unmotivated indifference. Unlike the shys, many of whom still *want* to connect, to have friends, date, marry, share intimate feelings, the nonshys often seem not to mind being isolated. Their conversations are rather banal and minimal, usually humorless, without signs of spontaneity, personal involvement, or joy in sharing ideas and feelings with friends. One gets the impression of watching a generation of clones of Mr. Spock from "Star Trek." Human speech is there, intelligence is evident,

but the executive command programming does not include feeling or affection. . . .

5   I have always believed that people can control their destinies by work, self-discipline, humor, love of life, concern for other people, and a sensitivity to the tactics of manipulation by the authorities. But tonight is different from all previous nights in America, and tomorrow will be even worse. As the father of three children, it is with sadness that I make such an assertion, and with the hope it will be shown to be a false alarm.

6   I believe that the basic quality of our social lives is being diluted, distorted, and demeaned by a host of profound structural changes in society. Because these new forces are systemic and not just transient developmental stages, they won't simply be outgrown but are likely to become permanent fixtures in our daily existence. The consequences are serious. I know of no more potent killer than isolation. There is no more destructive influence on physical and mental health than the isolation of you from me and of us from them. It has been shown to be a central agent in the etiology of depression, paranoia, schizophrenia, rape, suicide, mass murder, and a wide variety of disease states.

7   There is no dearth of research, anecdotes, and observations demonstrating the pervasiveness of the disorder I am talking about. A recently published report by Ralph Larkin, a sociologist, on the crises facing suburban youth underscores some aspects of this new malaise of the spirit. The children of American affluence are depicted as passively accepting a way of life that they view as empty and meaningless. The syndrome includes a constricted expression of emotions, a low threshold of boredom, and an apparent absence of joy in anything that is not immediately consumable; hence the significance of music, drugs, alcohol, sex, and status-symbol possessions.

8   According to a high school guidance counselor, the current generation of students differs in at least one way from the young people of their parents' day: "Kids hate school much more now than they did then. I mean the word *hate* and underline it." But this hatred is among the few strong emotions they allow themselves to feel about anything.

9   Where do we witness displays of strong emotion anymore, except at sports events and rock concerts? And even when we witness them, how many of us will acknowledge as much or dare to

share the emotion? On my way to visit my sister because she is dying of cancer, I explain the reason for my absence to student assistants.

10   "Have a nice trip!" chortles one. "See you when you get back," says another. And that is all they say. They haven't learned to extend comfort to another in distress. Too heavy.

11   Another anecdote, different but just as telling: "I hate myself for having this daydream, but I can't help enjoying it every time it pops into my head," confides Denny, a sophomore in my introductory psychology class of 680 students. "Everyone else fails the final exam, all hundreds upon hundreds of them, the nerds, the jocks, the freaks, and I get an A. Mine is the only A, floating high and dry in a sea of failure. Then somebody, everybody, would have to notice me, because I'd be special."

12   Assuming that the narcissism of shyness was fueling this fantasy, I launched into my counseling spiel of "shyness-can-be-over-come-if-you-work-at-it-and..." "Hold on, don't get me wrong," he objected. "I'm out-going, an extravert. I used to make friends easily, but it seems as if there's no value to that anymore. No one has time to go beyond the superficial level of 'How's it going?' 'Have a nice day!' 'See you around,' and stupid stuff like that. There must be something wrong with *me*, because I just can't seem to connect in any meaningful way to the people I live with. We are all working so hard to make it that maybe we don't have any energy left over for making it with each other."

13   The student health service at the university reassured this young man that his problem was a common psychiatric symptom of alienation and loneliness. In fact, it ranks near the top of the list of symptoms students present to this and similar clinics at other colleges when they seek professional help for their "attachment deficiencies."

14   Signs of alienation show up long before college. Visit the Serramonte Mall in San Francisco, the Smithtown Mall in Long Island, Florida's Broward County Mall, the Glendale Shopping Mall in Arizona. What you witness when school is out are mass minglings of kids too young to drive wandering about in the artificial air of a totally enclosed space amid artificial flowers, canned music, junk-food dispensers, and plastic twittering canaries. In smaller clusters are the elderly, keeping warm in winter and cool in summer, but

never talking with the youngsters, except when the generations become adversaries over a particular piece of Astroturf.

15   When the shopping-center kids get a little older, they escape the anxieties attendant on formal social dating (one-next-to-one) by dating in clusters. "We're all going for a pizza, wanna come along?" The tone seems to add, "No big deal if you say yes, no loss if you don't come."

16   Plenty of young adults who do date as couples find it less than satisfying. A handsome, successful television director tells me he has problems with women after the fifth date. He is concerned, wants help. For the first five innings, he has exciting, preprogrammed scripts for entertaining his dates. He strikes out when he runs out of scenarios and has to "be himself." Like many of his peers, he has never learned to be intimate, to relate closely to one other person, to make disclosures about his past, about his fears, frustrations, and future plans; in short, to reveal the private self behind the public facade. Disclosure presupposes trust, which in turn is nourished by sharing and gives substance and meaning to intimate contacts. But whom can you really trust these days?

17   If you yourself have switched from being a team player in life to going it alone more often, if you seek out your friends less often than you used to, it may be good for you, but it is a loss for the rest of us. Maybe you switched because we "weren't saying anything anyway," or because we "no longer turned you on," or because you had come to expect more of us while giving less of yourself. Or maybe, as a woman told me in Atlanta, 'There's times peoples just be tired of peoples." Or then again, the message might be the one that the mother of one of my shy freshmen passed along to him: "Do you realize how boring you are?" Better not to play the game at all than to be seen as boring by the other players?

18   Yet another sign of how alienated people are: not one of a dozen students in my wife's college seminar on sex roles could realistically imagine making a long-term commitment to one partner. "It would be nice if it happened, but it's not very realistic to expect it," a student said.

19   What about short-term commitments simply to pass the time of day with people occupying common space with you? Our world is becoming like an elevator: "No talking, smiling, or eye contact allowed without written consent of the management." Next time

you shop in a supermarket, do a study, make a work count of the conversations between shoppers in line or with the checkout person. Then try to use your data to prove that your subjects are not mute or deaf.

20   Our brave new world is one in which the basic social unit is the large, impersonal institution. In such institutions, authority is concentrated in the hands of a few remote power brokers. Decision making begins with concerns for cost-effectiveness, profitability margins, and efficient management of behavior, and ends with rules that must be followed—or else. If the rules are followed, everything runs smoothly, and the mark of impersonality is stamped on each product, each of us. Institutions can't do their thing unless they can count on the predictability and compliance of those they "serve." Thus there can be no spontaneity, impulsivity, strong emotion, dissent, opposition, time to think anything over, no time to be "just people." Today's young people are being forged into cogs in the corporate structure. And they are the ones who will eventually control our world.

21   Cult leaders and their management teams know all this. There they come, at least 2,000 strong, offering simple solutions to complex problems, love-bombing affection-starved youngsters. Cults attract a following not necessarily through political, religious, or economic ideology, but through offering the illusion of friendship, of noncontingent love. You exist, you are one of us, you get your fair share of our love and respect. (Wasn't that the message families once communicated?)

22   If there is a Devil, it is not through sin that he opposes God. The Devil's strategy for our times is to trivialize human existence in a number of ways: by isolating us from one another while creating the delusion that the reasons are time pressures, work demands, or anxieties created by economic uncertainty; by fostering narcissism and the fierce competition to be No. 1; by showing us the personal gains to be enjoyed from harboring prejudices and the losses from not moving out whenever the current situation is uncomfortable. Fostering in us the illusion of self-reliance, that sly Devil makes us mock the need for social responsibility and lets us forget how to go about being our brother's keeper—even if we were to want to.

23   Surely one cause of the growing sense of disengagement in our society is the rise in middle-class affluence since the 1950s, which has allowed an enormous number of people to buy space, privacy, and exclusive-use permits and services. The move to suburbia is a move away from too many people too close. The well-tended front lawn is the modern moat that keeps the barbarians at bay. Every occupant in a separate bedroom with private toilet, personal television, telephone, and hi-fi reduces hassles and conflicts. No need to share.

24   In the quest for upward mobility, moreover, the middle class sends its children away to prestigious colleges, moves to wherever its jobs demand, and does more and more of its business on the road. The consequence is a generation of children who have been uprooted time after time until, as one said to me, "I don't want to bother making friends. It's not worth the effort, because we'll be gone soon and it hurts more to leave good friends than casual acquaintances." The same is true of parents, who may find it even more difficult to make new friends in strange places. And as more of us take our paper-work jobs home or our jobs take us away from home, there is less time for family and neighborhood contacts.

25   Geographical mobility also strains the bonds of extended families. With relatives thousands of miles apart, ritual gatherings become rarer, and relatives become curious aliens to our children. The zero population growth movement has as one of its unintended consequences children with few siblings or cousins and eventually with few aunts or uncles. The paucity of relatives, coupled with a fact of delayed childbearing and the high divorce rate, mean there will be fewer of us with a sense of primal ties to many kin and of roots that run deep into one place, our "home."

26   By 1990, about one-third of all young people under 18 will have parents who have divorced at least once. Almost 60 percent of divorced couples have one or more children now under 18 years old. The number of children involved in divorce has risen from half a million in 1960 to 1.1 million now. Divorced mothers of children under 18 are increasingly likely to be in the labor force, which takes them away from home for long periods. I think a lasting legacy for the children of divorce is a deeply felt loss of trust in authorities (like parents, who have let them down) and in institutions (such

as marriage, whose for-better-or-worse slogan won't sell even in Peoria).

27 Finally, youthful cynicism has been fed by watching, on the evening news, or in some cases, "up close and personal," almost everyone going out on strike for better bucks—teachers, police, fire departments—all, apparently, in it for the money, not love of a profession. Widespread cynicism about institutions seems to be evident across the board. . . .

28 As corny and unsophisticated as it sounds, the only escape from hackerdom is to think of people as our most cherished resource. We need to work hard at reestablishing family rituals, such as family meals without TV and with meaningful conversation. Parents and teachers should show more concern for the social-emotional development of children and put less emphasis on intellectual competition. We must oppose systems and procedures that deny our uniqueness while spreading depersonalization and anonymity in the guise of efficiency.

29 Social-support networks provide emotional sustenance, informative feedback, and validation of self-worth. They have been shown to buffer the adverse impact of change on physical and mental health, and it is important to create enough of them for everyone to have a chance to become a valued part of a life-support system.

30 Maybe the economic downturn the nation is facing is a blessing in disguise. Parents will not be able to afford divorce as readily and may eventually discover that they have something of value in common—as many of our parents did. More children may return home after college, and communal living and expanding, elastic family structures may become necessities. Sharing instead of hoarding, and caring instead of flaunting, may even become fashionable.

31 While waiting for all that to happen, it is well to reevaluate the survival strategies that many of the poor—immigrants, blacks, and other minorities—have used to advantage in the past when their money was soft and times were hard. Without a false sense of personal invulnerability, and with an accurate appraisal of the power of the "system" to overwhelm all in its path, they maintained their dignity by reaffirming family values and by tightening the bonds

of friendship. Survival demands collective action; "alone" is for gravestones in hacker cemeteries.

Analyzing the Writer's Argument

1. What is Zimbardo arguing for in this essay? What does he find wrong with our society? What does he think ought to be changed? How does he think change ought to come about?
2. What kinds of evidence to support his argument does Zimbardo present? Give some examples of each type of evidence.
3. Explain how Zimbardo uses computers and computer-related terminology to further his argument. What does "hackerdom" represent for him?
4. Why does Zimbardo think that young couples who date "find it less than satisfying"?
5. Why does Zimbardo think that his study of shyness was helpful to him in developing his argument?
6. Does Zimbardo think cults are good, bad, or is he neutral about them? Why does he include a discussion of them in his argument?
7. Comment on Zimbardo's conclusion. Is it an appropriate one for his essay? Why, or why not?
8. Describe Zimbardo's tone. Is he angry, bemused, perplexed, nostalgic, reflective?
9. Zimbardo published his essay in *Psychology Today* in 1980. In what ways, if any, is today's society different from the one he describes? Have things gotten worse, improved, stayed the same? Explain.

Exploring the Issues in This Essay

1. Do the study that Zimbardo suggests: "Next time you are in a supermarket, do a study, make a word count of the conversations between shoppers in line or with the checkout person. Then try to use your data to prove that your subjects are not mute or deaf." Discuss your findings with your classmates.
2. Discuss how our very prosperity has tended "to trivialize our existence" and to engender in us all a sense of alienation and isolation. Do you agree with Zimbardo's solutions? What solutions do you have?

Norman Lear

Cashing in the Commonweal for the Commonwheel of Fortune

Writer, producer, director Norman Lear was born in New Haven, Connecticut, on July 27, 1922. After studying communications at Emerson College for two years, Lear enlisted in the Army Air Force, where he served with distinction during World War II. Several years after the war concluded, Lear started his long-time association with television and film as a comedy writer. During the 1960s he wrote and produced such films as Divorce American Style *and* The Night They Raided Minsky's. *But it is as the creator of the classic television comedy series "All in the Family," "Maude," "Sanford and Son," "The Jeffersons," "One Day at a Time," and "Hot L Baltimore" that Lear earned his reputation as a social satirist. Lear carried his commitment to social reform and public interest issues into public life. He founded People for the American Way in 1980 and has served as president of the American Civil Liberties Foundation in Southern California.*

In "Cashing in the Commonweal for the Commonwheel of Fortune" Lear criticizes what he calls "America's obsession with short-term success." By putting the modern corporation with its profit-statement mentality up on a pedestal, he fears we may be sacrificing our futures for today's gratification. This essay, an excerpt from a speech Lear delivered at the John F. Kennedy School at Harvard University in February 1987, was first published in the Washington Post *in April of that same year.*

1   The societal disease of our time, I am convinced, is America's obsession with short-term success, its fixation with the proverbial bottom-line. "Give me a profit statement this quarter larger than the last, and everything else be damned!" That is today's predom-

44

inant business ethic. It took root in the business community but has since spread beyond business and insinuated itself into the rest of our culture. In this climate, a quiet revolution in values has occurred, and it has not been for the better.

2   Short-term thinking, corrosive individualism, fixating on "economic man" at the expense of the human spirit, has taken an alarming toll. I focus on the business community for starters, not to make it a scapegoat—but because I believe business has become a fountainhead of values in our society.

3   If the church was the focal point for personal values and public mores in medieval times, that role in our time has been assumed, unwittingly perhaps, by the modern corporation.

4   For better or worse, traditional institutions such as the family, the churches and education are no longer as influential in molding moral-cultural values. There are, I suppose, dozens of reasons one could find: the disruptions of urbanization; the alarming increase of single-parent households; the rise of the mass media, especially television; the dizzy mobility of our car culture; the telecommunications revolution and the altered sense of time and distance it has created. As traditional families have come under stress and splintered, as education has come under siege, as churches and synagogues have become less influential in daily life, the modern corporation with the help of the media has stepped into the breach.

5   Mythologist Joseph Campbell has said that in medieval times, when one approached a city, one saw the cathedral and the castle. Now one sees the soaring tower of commerce. People build their lives around these towers. Communities take shape. Work skills are learned. Social relationships are formed. Attitudes and aspirations are molded. A dense matrix of values grow up around the towers of commerce and spread beyond.

6   Never before has the business of business been such a cultural preoccupation. If media attention is any indication of popular interest—and it is—today there is an unprecedented interest in business affairs. In recent years, a dozen new business programs have burst forth on commercial television, public television and cable. Americans once found their heroes, for the most part, in Congress or the entertainment world or sports; now more and

more people find them in business: Lee Iacocca; T. Boone Pickens; H. Ross Perot; Carl Icahn; until 10 minutes ago, Ivan Boesky; and until a moment ago, Martin A. Siegel.

7   If you grant me the possibility that American business is the preeminent force in shaping our culture and its values, what example are its leaders setting? What attitudes and behavior do they endorse and foster?

8   *The Wall Street Journal* recently took an overview of the American corporation and concluded: "Gone is talk of balanced, long-term growth; impatient shareholders and well-heeled corporate raiders have seen to that. Now anxious executives, fearing for their jobs or their companies, are focusing their efforts on trimming operations and shuffling assets to improve near-term profits, often at the expense of both balance and growth."

9   There are no two-legged villains in this "get-while-the-getting-is-good" atmosphere. Only victims. The villain is the climate which, like a house with a leaking gas pipe, is certain to see us all dead in our sleep one day, never knowing what hit us.

10   Sociologist Daniel Bell has argued that in promoting an ethic of "materialistic hedonism," the free enterprise system tends to subvert the very values that help to sustain it. If American business insists upon defining itself solely in terms of its market share, profitability and stock price—if its short-term material goals are allowed to prevail over all else—then business tends to subvert the moral-cultural values that undergird the entire system, such values as social conscience, pride in one's work, commitment to one's community, loyalty to one's company—in short, a sense of the commonweal.

11   This ethic breeds in a climate where leadership everywhere—in business, Congress, federal agencies, state legislatures, organized labor, the universities—refuses, through greed or myopia or weakness, to make provisions for the future. And in this climate, with this kind of short-sighted leadership, we have been raising generations of children to believe that there is nothing between winning and losing. The notion that life has anything to do with succeeding at the level of doing one's best, or that some of life's richest rewards are not monetary, is lost to these kids in this short-term, bottom-line climate.

12   America has become a game show. Winning is all that matters. Cash prizes. Get rich quick. We are the captive of a culture that celebrates instant gratification and individual success no matter the larger costs. George Will, in his book *Statecraft as Soulcraft*, argues that the country's future is imperiled unless our leaders can cultivate in citizens a deeper commitment to the commonweal. Yet rather than heed that admonition, we are turning the commonweal into the Commonwheel of Fortune.

13   Take a look at the Commonwheel of Fortune gameboard. It's not unlike the Monopoly gameboard—but instead of real estate, we've got just about every major American corporation represented, all up for grabs. For you latecomers to the game, Owens Corning, NBC, Texaco and TWA are off the board now—but Goodyear, USX, Union Carbide and many more have been in play recently. With a little roll of the dice and the junk bonds the game is played with, just watch the raiding and merging and acquisitioning! What fun!

14   The game produced 14 new billionaires last year—not to mention what it's done for foreign investors who, with their yens and deutschemarks, have caught on to our national lack of concern for the future. We are now selling them America as cheaply, under the circumstances, as the Indians sold us Manhattan.

15   On the surface, we seem to have accepted the selling of America just as we seem to have accepted the fact that we no longer make the best automobiles, the best radios and stereos and television sets and compact discs; the fact is we hardly make any of these products by ourselves today where we once were responsible for most of them. We've accepted that without a whimper.

16   There is a psychic, spiritual dimension to these changes that cannot be ignored. There is an open wound, a gash, on the American psyche that must be attended to.

17   Take the American motor car. Through all the years I was growing up, it was the standard of the world. "Keeping up with the Joneses" in those years meant only one thing: You were either trading up the General Motors line, the Ford line or the Chrysler line. My dad was a GM man. He got as far as the Oldsmobile; one year he almost made it to the Buick. But caring about your motor car was the universal family vocation. The American motor car

was the national, non-military symbol of America's macho—and one does not have to be a social scientist to know that when we lost that symbol, sometime in the past 25 years, it left a big dent in the American Dream.

18 The Big Three automakers failed to heed the handwriting on the wall and refused to innovate, to build small fuel-efficient cars; refused to sacrifice a current quarterly profit statement to invest in the future and meet the threat of imports from abroad.

19 There is the ailing steel industry, which refused to modernize and invest in its future. There are the labor unions in both industries, which fought only for added wages and benefits—and declined to fight to modernize and to protect their members' jobs in the long term. There is the U.S. consumer electronics industry, which surrendered the compact-disc technology to Japan and Holland, who were willing to make long-term investments in the fledgling technology.

20 There is a hurt and an emptiness and confusion in this nation to which attention must be paid. There is fear and resentment, which makes Americans ripe for extremists who offer promises of easy salvation. It can exacerbate social tensions and result in an escalation of the kind of racism we have witnessed around the country recently.

21 If you agree with me that our culture has been weaned from a respect for other values to the worshipping of money and success and the fruits of instant gratification—and that this is resulting in a spiritual and cultural crisis—what, then, do we do abut it? How can we reclaim the commonweal from the mindless game show it has become?

22 We can start by recognizing that government has a major responsibility here. I am a product of the free-enterprise system, and I cherish it. I am also a human being, and I cherish my humanity. But everything I know about human nature tells me we are innately selfish. We do look out for ourselves first. And then our family, our loved ones. Some of us, not enough, reach out beyond that. But when we, the people, talk about caring for things that are ours—our water, our air, our safety, our protection from the myriad harmful things we reasonable good people are capable of doing to each other—we have to know we can only rely on our

government! It is we, through government, who provide for the common welfare.

23   Business nurtures the conceit that its behavior is purely private— but take one look at the largess it receives from the government: It once accounted for 29 percent of federal tax revenues; it is now down to 6 percent. Take a look, too, at the role of corporate political action committees and the cultural values that business fosters— and it is clear why government must play a more influential role in protecting the commonweal from the Commonwheel of Fortune.

24   This, again, is a climate we are seeking to change—and there are thermostats that address that climate in every home, in every school, in every church, in every business in this country. We can start, perhaps, by establishing a new set of symbols and heroes. We have had Rambo and Oliver North and Ivan Boesky; corporate raiders and arbitrageurs; the "yuppie generation" and the culture of conspicuous consumption; we have had religious zealots who would abridge the First Amendment in the name of God and po- litical extremists who would censor books and condone racism.

25   But we have also had, and more attention must be paid to, people like Robert Hayes. An attorney with a top-flight New York law firm, he quit his lucrative job several years ago to start a new branch of legal practice: defending the right of the homeless. His initiative inspired dozens of other such legal practices around the country.

26   Attention must be paid to Eugene Lang, a New York millionaire who, while speaking at an elementary school graduation, spon- taneously offered to pay for the college expenses of some sixth graders of an inner city school if they would study hard and not drop out of school. His example has caught on in other cities, where individuals and businesses "adopt" students to help them succeed.

27   And attention must be paid to Warren Buffett, the Nebraska chairman of Berkshire-Hathaway, who has seen to it that a part of every single dollar among the millions of dollars earmarked for shareholders goes to a charity or a cause selected by the share- holder in advance.

28   We need to rehabilitate the idea of public service; to set new ethical standards for business; to harness the natural idealism of

young people; and to encourage leadership everywhere to assume a greater burden of responsibility to lead. As I said, the villain here is the climate. It needs changing.

29 Plant in your mind, if you will, the close-up actions of a man, as in a film. Savagely, he is cutting off the hands of another man. We are horrified; this action defies our understanding. Now pull back to examine the context, and learn that we are in a different culture—perhaps, but not necessarily, in an earlier time. Eyes can be gouged out here. Men are drawn and quartered—sometimes for sheer entertainment. We don't accept, but we understand better now that first savage act. Its perpetrators were behaving in the context of their time and culture.

30 Now look at Martin A. Siegel and gang, arrested recently for insider trading. A thief. Broke a trust. We don't understand. He was making $2 million. Why did he need another $7 million?

31 But let's pull back and see Siegel in the context of the culture I have been describing, and we must ask: In some perverse way, doesn't his story speak for the '80s?

32 Isn't Siegel's story an example in microcosm of the perverted values of our culture—where the making of money, not working hard, producing well, leaving something lasting behind—but the making of money has become the sole value?

33 The problem isn't Martin Siegel's alone. It is ours. We have found the Holy Grail, and it is the Bottom Line.

34 Do we want it?

35 Must we continue cashing in the commonweal for the Common-wheel of Fortune?

Analyzing the Writer's Argument

1. What is Lear's thesis, and where does he present it?
2. What does Lear believe has replaced the traditional institutions of family, church, and school in molding moral-cultural values. What evidence does he provide to support his belief? Did you find yourself agreeing with him? Why, or why not?
3. In paragraph 7 Lear asks two questions. How do these questions function in the context of his essay?

4. According to Lear, what are the predominate attitudes and behavior of America's corporate leaders? What examples does he use to illustrate business's short-term, bottom-line mentality? What should Americans learn from the example of the Big Three automakers?

5. What does Lear mean when he says, "we are turning the commonweal into the Commonwheel of Fortune"? Explain how his analogy of the Monopoly gameboard works. Did you find it effective? Why, or why not?

6. In paragraph 21 Lear again asks two questions. How are these two questions related to the ones he asked in paragraph 7 and how do they function within the context of his argument? Explain.

7. Lear cities the example of a film in which a man savagely cuts off the hands of another man. What is the point of this example, and how does Lear relate it to conditions in America?

8. What solutions does Lear offer to the problems he outlines in his argument? What, according to Lear, needs to be changed first? Does he give us any reason to be hopeful or optimistic that the situation will change?

Exploring the Issues in This Essay

1. Lear believes America has paid a tremendous price for its reliance on short-term thinking. What exactly have been the effects of such thinking on traditional American values and institutions? Do you believe that it is wrong to work for short-term benefits? Discuss the advantages and disadvantages of short-term thinking. Should it have a place in our culture?

2. Lear concludes his essay with a question for each one of us. How would you answer him? How do you suppose your friends and relatives would answer? Discuss what today's college students can do to bring about a change in our obsession with the "Bottom Line."

*"Religious freedom is my immediate goal,
but my long-range plan is to go into real estate."*

Richard Rodriguez

Does America Still Exist?

Like millions of Americans, Richard Rodriguez learned En-
glish as his second language. He was born in 1944 in San
Francisco, California, the son of Mexican parents, and Span-
ish was the language he grew up with at home. As a child,
Rodriguez learned English in the local Catholic schools. As an
adult he went on to Stanford and Columbia and did graduate
work at the Warburg Institute in London and the Univer-
sity of California at Berkeley, where he now teaches. In ad-
dition to writing essays and lecturing widely, Rodriguez has
published Hunger of Memory: The Education of Richard
Rodriguez *(1981), a collection of autobiographical essays.*

The following essay was first published in Harper's *in*
March 1984 as part of a group of essays responding to the
question "Does America still exist?" A child of immigrant
parents, a Mexican-American, Rodriguez recognizes "how in-
evitable the process of assimilation actually is" and chides us
"because we lack a vision of ourselves entire."

1   For the children of immigrant parents the knowledge comes easier. America exists everywhere in the city—on billboards, frankly
in the smell of French fries and popcorn. It exists in the pace: traffic lights, the assertions of neon, the mysterious bong-bong-bong
through the atriums of department stores. America exists as the
voice of the crowd, a menancing sound—the high nasal accent of
American English.

2   When I was a boy in Sacramento (California, the fifties), people
would ask me, "Where you from?" I was born in this country, but
I knew the question meant to decipher my darkness, my looks.

3   My mother once instructed me to say, "I am an American of
Mexican descent." By the time I was nine or ten, I wanted to say,
but dared not reply, "I am an American."

4   Immigrants come to America and, against hostility or mere loneliness, they recreate a homeland in the parlor, tacking up postcards

or calendars of some impossible blue—lake or sea or sky. Children of immigrant parents are supposed to perch on a hyphen between two countries. Relatives assume the achievement as much as anyone. Relatives are, in any case, surprised when the child begins losing old ways. One day at the family picnic the boy wanders away from their spiced food and faceless stories to watch other boys play baseball in the distance.

5   There is sorrow in the American memory, guilty sorrow for having left something behind—Portugal, China, Norway. The American story is the story of immigrant children and of their children—children no longer able to speak to grandparents. The memory of exile becomes inarticulate as it passes from generation to generation, along with wedding rings and pocket watches—like some mute stone in a wad of old lace. Europe. Asia. Eden.

6   But, it needs to be said, if this is a country where one stops being Vietnamese or Italian, this is a country where one begins to be an American. America exists as a culture and a grin, a faith and a shrug. It is clasped in a handshake, called by a first name.

7   As much as the country is joined in a common culture, however, Americans are reluctant to celebrate the process of assimilation. We pledge allegiance to diversity. America was born Protestant and bred Puritan, and the notion of community we share is derived from a seventeenth-century faith. Presidents and the pages of ninth-grade civics readers yet proclaim the orthodoxy: We are gathered together—but as individuals, with separate pasts, distinct destinies. Our society is as paradoxical as a Puritan congregation: We stand together, alone.

8   Americans have traditionally defined themselves by what they refused to include. As often, however, Americans have struggled, turned in good conscience at last to assert the great Protestant virtue of tolerance. Despite outbreaks of nativist frenzy, America has remained an immigrant country, open and true to itself.

9   Against pious emblems of rural America—soda fountain, Elks hall, Protestant church, and now shopping mall—stands the cold-hearted city, crowded with races and ambitions, curious laughter, much that is odd. Nevertheless, it is the city that has most truly represented America. In the city, however, the millions of singular lives have had no richer notion of wholeness to describe them than the idea of pluralism.

10   *"Where you from?" the American asks the immigrant child. "Mexico," the boy learns to say.*

11   Mexico, the country of my blood ancestors, offers formal contrast to the American achievement. If the United States was formed by Protestant individualism, Mexico was shaped by a medieval Catholic dream of one world. The Spanish journeyed to Mexico to plunder, and they may have gone, in God's name, with an arrogance peculiar to those who intend to convert. But through the conversion, the Indian converted the Spaniard. A new race was born, the *mestizo*, wedding European to Indian. José Vasconcelos, the Mexican philosopher, has celebrated this New World creation, proclaiming it the "cosmic race."

12   Centuries later, in a San Francisco restaurant, a Mexican-American lawyer of my acquaintance says, in English, over *salade niçoise*, that he does not intend to assimilate into gringo society. His claim is echoed by a chorus of others (Italian-Americans, Greeks, Asians) in this era of ethnic pride. The melting pot has been retired, clanking, into the museum of quaint disgrace, alongside Aunt Jemima and the Katzenjammer Kids. But resistance to assimilation is characteristically American. It only makes clear how inevitable the process of assimilation actually is.

13   For generations, this has been the pattern. Immigrant parents have sent their children to school (simply, they thought) to acquire the "skills" to survive in the city. The child returned home with a voice his parents barely recognized or understood, couldn't trust, and didn't like.

14   In Eastern cities—Philadelphia, New York, Boston, Baltimore—class after class gathered immigrant children to women (usually women) who stood in front of rooms full of children, changing children. So also for me in the 1950s. Irish-Catholic nuns. California. The old story. The hyphen tipped to the right, away from Mexico and toward a confusing but true American identity.

15   I speak now in the chromium American accent of my grammar school classmates—Billy Reckers, Mike Bradley, Carol Schmidt, Kathy O'Grady. . . . I believe I became like my classmates, became German, Polish, and (like my teachers) Irish. And because assimilation is always reciprocal, my classmates got something of me. (I mean sad eyes; belief in the Indian Virgin; a taste for sugar skulls on the Feast of the Dead.) In the blending, we became what

our parents could never have been, and we carried America one revolution further.

16 "Does America still exist?" Americans have been asking the question for so long that to ask it again only proves our continuous link. But perhaps the question deserves to be asked with urgency now. Since the black civil rights movement of the 1960s, our tenuous notion of a shared public life has deteriorated notably.

17 The struggle of black men and women did not eradicate racism, but it became the great moment in the life of America's conscience. Water hoses, bulldogs, blood—the images, rendered black, white, rectangular, passed into living rooms.

18 It is hard to look at a photograph of a crowd taken, say, in 1890 or in 1930 and not notice the absence of blacks. (It becomes an impertinence to wonder if America *still* exists.)

19 In the sixties, other groups of Americans learned to champion their rights by analogy to the black civil rights movement. But the heroic vision faded. Dr. Martin Luther King, Jr. had spoken with Pauline eloquence of a nation that would unite Christian and Jew, old and young, rich and poor. Within a decade, the struggles of the 1960s were reduced to a bureaucratic competition for little more than pieces of a representational pie. The quest for a portion of power became an end in itself. The metaphor for the American city of the 1970s was a committee: one black, one woman, one person under thirty. . . .

20 If the small town had sinned against America by too neatly defining who could be an American, the city's sin was a romantic secession. One noticed the romanticism in the antiwar movement— certain demonstrators who demonstrated a lack of tact or desire to persuade and seemed content to play secular protestants. One noticed the romanticism in the competition among members of "minority groups" to claim the status of Primary Victim. To Americans unconfident of their common identity, minority standing became a way of asserting individuality. Middle-class Americans—men and women clearly not the primary victims of social oppression— brandished their suffering with exuberance.

21 The dream of a single society probably died with *The Ed Sullivan Show*. The reality of America persists. Teenagers pass through bigcity high schools banded in racial groups, their collars turned up

to a uniform shrug. But then they graduate to jobs at the phone company or in banks, where they end up working alongside people unlike themselves. Typists and tellers walk out together at lunchtime.

22 It is easier for us as Americans to believe the obvious fact of our separateness—easier to imagine the black and white Americas prophesied by the Kerner report (broken glass, street fires)—than to recognize the reality of a city street at lunchtime. Americans are wedded by proximity to a common culture. The panhandler at one corner is related to the pamphleteer at the next who is related to the banker who is kin to the Chinese old man wearing an MIT sweatshirt. In any true national history, Thomas Jefferson begets Martin Luther King, Jr. who begets the Gray Panthers. It is because we lack a vision of ourselves entire—the city street is crowded and we are each preoccupied with finding our own way home—that we lack an appropriate hymn.

23 Under my window now passes a little white girl softly rehearsing to herself a Motown obbligato.

Analyzing the Writer's Argument

1. Why does Rodriguez believe that the answer to the question "Does America still exist?" comes easier to children of immigrant parents?

2. In paragraphs 4 through 6 Rodriguez describes the immigrant experience in America. How would you characterize the immigrants' transition from life in another country to life in the United States? What does he mean when he says, "Children of immigrant parents are supposed to perch on a hyphen between two countries"?

3. What does Rodriguez find paradoxical about Americans? How does he explain the paradox? Why does he believe "Americans are reluctant to celebrate the process of assimilation"?

4. What for Rodriguez are those values and characteristics that define America? What does he mean when he says, "America exists as a culture and a grin, a faith and a shrug. It is clasped in a handshake, called by a first name"?

5. In what ways, according to Rodriguez, has the city most truly represented America? What does the city have that, say, rural America does not? Explain.

6. Why does Rodriguez believe that the question "Does America still exist?" needs to be asked with urgency today? Do you share his sense of urgency? Explain. How does he ultimately answer the question contained in the title to his essay?

7. What is the meaning of Rodriguez's final paragraph? What idea in his essay does the example of a "little white girl softly rehearsing to herself a Motown obbligato" reinforce? In your opinion, does it provide a satisfactory conclusion to the essay as a whole?

Exploring the Issues in This Essay

1. Consider how you would answer the question Rodriguez addresses in his essay. Do you agree with him when he says, "The melting pot has been retired, clanking, into the museum of quaint disgrace, alongside Aunt Jemima and the Katzenjammer Kids"? Or when he suggests that "the dream of a single society probably died with *The Ed Sullivan Show*"? Finally, how do you react to Rodriguez's conclusion that "it is because we lack a vision of ourselves entire . . . that we lack an appropriate hymn"?

2. Rodriguez believes that "it is the city that has most truly represented America." However, there are millions of Americans for whom rural or small town America is the defining experience. For the first hundred or more years of her existence America was an agricultural society, but toward the end of the last century people started to move to the cities and industrial centers of our land. Do you think that the shift in population concentrations has brought with it a shift in America's identity? Are rural values and traditions viable in the 1990s, or are they simply memories of some long lost past? Discuss the changes that have occurred in America as a result of industrialization, immigration, computerization.

Writing Suggestions for
Mirror, Mirror on the Wall: Looking at America

1. Mead, Zimbardo, and Lear each offer their own perspectives on the present age. Write an essay in which you analyze where their views conflict and where they are in agreement.

2. Philip G. Zimbardo writes that one of the survival strategies of the poor and the minorities was that they did not have a "false sense of personal invulnerability." Write an essay in which you further develop his idea. Certainly you will want to include a definition of the concept and to give examples of it where appropriate.

3. Many of today's liberal arts undergraduates complain that their curriculum could be more career-oriented without compromising the integrity of the liberal arts tradition. Write an open letter to your classmates arguing either for or against career-oriented courses in the liberal arts curriculum. You may wish to restrict your argument to your own particular field of study.

4. Critics of higher education today point to the increasingly vocational emphasis of the curriculum. Some go so far as to state that college is simply a place to get the credentials to earn more money in the job market. Using examples from your own experience and reading, write an essay in which you argue for the intellectual, moral, and social benefits of a traditional college education.

5. Write an essay in which you argue either for or against the proposition that students would be better off taking the more than $40,000 a bachelor's degree now costs and starting a business of their own.

6. Argue that Philip G. Zimbardo in "The Age of Indifference" is simply, like a lot of Americans, growing older and more nostalgic about the good ol' days.

7. In his essay Norman Lear writes, "If the church was the focal point for personal values and public mores in medieval times, that role in our time has been assumed, unwittingly perhaps, by the modern corporation." Has religion lost its influential place in our lives? Write an essay in which you argue for or against the importance of religion in a person's life.

8. Are you an American? Or, are you, as Richard Rodriguez says, "perch[ed] on a hyphen between two countries": Irish-American, Italian-American, Asian-American, German-American, Mexican-American, African-American? Write an essay in which you ex-

plain how you regard yourself, where your sentiments lie, and for what reasons.

9. Write an article for your student newspaper in which you argue that students ought to be more concerned about their personal appearance.

10. If, as Louis Harris's opinion survey reveals, Americans are "close to be being obsessed with their physical appearance," what might this say about us as a people? Are we superficial, shallow, unconcerned about human values and worth? Or, is just the opposite true? Using examples from your own experience or reading, write an essay for or against the following proposition: Americans are concerned about each other's feelings and are deeply concerned about human values.

11. Richard Rodriguez wrote his essay in response to a question posed by the editors of *Harper's* magazine: "Does America still exist?" Write an essay in which you attempt to answer the question for yourself.

12. In order to explore, discuss, analyze, and make decisions about any issue or problem, each of us needs to have an understanding of who we are and what we believe and why. After reflecting on what the writers in this section have had to say, write an essay in which you explain what your basic beliefs are and how, in turn, these beliefs affect the decisions that you make.

13. Argue for or against Margaret Mead's thesis that anxiety (or stress) is a useful force in one's life.

14. Write an essay in which you argue for or against the sentiments expressed in the following statement by Norman Lear: "America has become a game show. Winning is all that matters. Cash prizes. Get rich quick. We are the captives of a culture that celebrates instant gratification and individual success no matter the larger costs."

15. All the essays in this section, in one way or another, turn on the question of how one balances self-interest with social responsibility. Recall a situation where your self-interest came into conflict with the greater public good. How did you resolve the conflict? In an essay, recount the event and explain what you learned both about yourself and human nature in general.

2

What's Happening to the American Family?

The family, not the individual, is the real molecule of society,
the key link in the social chain of being.

ROBERT NISBET

Of all our institutions perhaps none has fallen on harder times than the contemporary family. And perhaps no institution has been more analyzed, revered, and abused. Worn and weary from a journey that stretches back thousands of years and unable to cope with the vicissitudes of a rapidly changing social climate, the traditional family is now under attack. Torn apart by marital tensions and strife that very often lead to separation and divorce, unsettled by divergent values between the generations, buffeted by the demands of our fast-paced lifestyle, disoriented by our increasing mobility, diminished in size by single parenting and enlarged by family fragments coming together in new combinations, the family trudges on into a murky, uncertain future.

The simple or nuclear family exists in almost all societies. It is made up of a man and woman who are expected to have children, care for them, and nurture them in the ways of their culture. For centuries, religious, political, ethical, moral, intellectual, and philosophic values were transmitted from one generation to the next through the family. Although the traditional needs of the family in our post-industrial society have been met by a wide variety of institutions including schools, churches, offices, corporations, and by professionals including doctors, lawyers, and social and psychiatric counselors, the family remains the single most important group in providing love and affection in a society that has become increasingly specialized, depersonalized, and cold. Indeed, it might be argued that the contemporary family itself has become specialized by being a ready and reliable source of emotional support. Perhaps Warren in Robert Frost's "The Death of the Hired Man" immortalized the sentiment for all of us when he said, "Home is the place where, when you go there,/They have to take you in." Sadly, however, the family today frequently fails to offer the safe harbor it promises. Instead it becomes a repository of anguish, guilt, and misplaced hopes.

Most experts agree that the issue is not whether the family will survive, for it will surely do that, but rather how resilient and susceptible to change it will prove to be. What model will it follow, what shape will it take, what demands will be made of it, what problems will it create, and how will it meet our needs in the years ahead, these are the essential questions. And, more importantly, will the family unit be able to achieve stability within itself and within the larger community? In his book *In the Light of History*, Sir John Plumb describes a scene that set him to wondering about the future of the family:

> I was rather astonished when a minibus drove up to my house and out poured ten children. They had with them two parents, but not one child had them both in common as mother and father, and two of them belonged to neither parent, but to a former husband of the wife who had died. Both parents, well into middle age, had just embarked, one on his fourth, the other on her third marriage. The children, who came in all sizes, and ranged from blonde nordic to jet-haired Greek, bounded around the garden, young and old as happy as any children that I have seen. To them, as Californians, their situation was not particularly odd; most of their friends had multiple parents. Indeed to them perhaps the odd family was the one which Western culture has held up as a model for two thousand years or more—the lifelong union of man and wife. But it took me a very long time to believe that they could be either happy or adjusted. And yet, were they a sign of the future, a way the world was going?

George Gallup, Jr.

The Faltering Family

> *The president of the Gallup Poll, the research company that surveys public opinion, George Gallup, Jr. was born in Evanston, Illinois, in 1930, and educated at Princeton University. He is particularly interested in religion in American and has served as executive director of the Princeton Religion Research Center. In addition, Gallup has written widely on contemporary religious, political, and social issues. Among his books are* America's Search for Faith *(1980) with David Poling,* My Kid on Drugs *(1981) with Art Linkletter, and* Adventures in Immortality *(1982) with William Proctor.*
>
> *"The Faltering Family" is from* Forecast 2000 *(1985), a book Gallup wrote with Proctor. Using the results from several national opinion polls, Gallup examines the major cultural pressures that are impacting the American family today and foresees an uncertain future for our basic social unit.*

1   In a recent Sunday school class in a United Methodist Church in the Northeast, a group of eight- to ten-year-olds was in a deep discussion with their two teachers. When asked to choose which of ten stated possibilities they most feared happening, their response was unanimous. All the children most dreaded a divorce between their parents.

2   Later, as the teachers, a man and a woman in their late thirties, reflected on the lesson, they both agreed they'd been shocked at the response. When they were the same age as their students, they said, the possibility of their parents' being divorced never entered their heads. Yet in just one generation, children seemed to feel much less security in their family ties.

3   Nor is the experience of these two Sunday school teachers an isolated one. Psychiatrists revealed in one recent newspaper investigation that the fears of children definitely do change in different periods; and in recent times, divorce has become one of the most frequently mentioned anxieties. In one case, for example, a four-

year-old insisted that his father rather than his mother walk him to nursery school each day. The reason? He said many of his friends had "no daddy living at home, and I'm scared that will happen to me" (*The New York Times*, May 2, 1983).

4   In line with such reports, our opinion leaders expressed great concern about the present and future status of the American family. In the poll 33 percent of the responses listed decline in family structure, divorce, and other family-oriented concerns as one of the five major problems facing the nation today. And 26 percent of the responses included such family difficulties as one of the five major problems for the United States in the year 2000.

5   Historical and sociological trends add strong support to these expressions of concern. For example, today about one marriage in every two ends in divorce. Moreover, the situation seems to be getting worse, rather than better. In 1962, the number of divorces was 2.2 per 1,000 people, according to the National Center for Health Statistics. By 1982, the figure had jumped to 5.1 divorces per 1,000 people—a rate that had more than doubled in two decades.

6   One common concern expressed about the rise in divorces and decline in stability of the family is that the family unit has traditionally been a key factor in transmitting stable cultural and moral values from generation to generation. Various studies have shown that educational and religious institutions often can have only a limited impact on children without strong family support.

7   Even grandparents are contributing to the divorce statistics. One recent study revealed that about 100,000 people over the age of fifty-five get divorced in the United States each year. These divorces are usually initiated by men who face retirement, and the relationships being ended are those that have endured for thirty years or more (*The New York Times Magazine*, December 19, 1982).

8   What are the pressures that have emerged in the past twenty years that cause long-standing family bonds to be broken?

9   Many now agree that the sexual revolution of the 1960s worked a profound change on our society's family values and personal relationships. Certainly, the seeds of upheaval were present before that critical decade. But a major change that occurred in the mid-sixties was an explicit widespread rejection of the common values about sexual and family relationships that most Americans in the past had held up as an ideal.

10   We're just beginning to sort through all the changes in social standards that have occurred. Here are some of the major pressures that have contributed to those changes:

Pressure One: Alternative Lifestyles

11   Twenty years ago, the typical American family was depicted as a man and woman who were married to each other and who produced children (usually two) and lived happily ever after. This was the pattern that young people expected to follow in order to become "full" or "normal" members of society. Of course, some people have always chosen a different route—remaining single, taking many partners, or living with a member of their own sex. But they were always considered somewhat odd, and outside the social order of the traditional family.

12   In the last two decades, this picture has changed dramatically. In addition to the proliferation of single people through divorce, we also have these developments:

- Gay men and women have petitioned the courts for the right to marry each other and to adopt children. These demands are being given serious consideration, and there may even be a trend of sorts in this direction. For example, the National Association of Social Workers is increasingly supporting full adoption rights for gay people (*The New York Times*, January 10, 1983).

- Many heterosexual single adults have been permitted to adopt children and set up single-parent families. So being unattached no longer excludes people from the joys of parenthood.

- Some women have deliberately chosen to bear children out of wedlock and raise them alone. In the past, many of these children would have been given up for adoption, but no longer.

  A most unusual case involved an unmarried psychologist, Dr. Afton Blake, who recently gave birth after being artificially inseminated with sperm from a sperm bank to which Nobel Prize winners had contributed (*The New York Times*, September 6, 1983).

- In a recent Gallup Youth Poll, 64 percent of the teenagers questioned said that they hoped their lives would be different from those of their parents. This included having more money, pursuing a different kind of profession, living in a different area, having more free time—and staying single longer.

  Most surveys show increasing numbers of unmarried couples living together. Also, there are periodic reports of experiments in communal living, "open marriages," and other such arrangements. Although the more radical approaches to relationships tend to come and go and never seem to attract large numbers of people, the practice of living together without getting married seems to be something that's here to stay. The law is beginning to respond to these arrangements with awards for "palimony"—compensation for long-term unmarried partners in a relationship. but the legal and social status of unmarried people who live together is still quite uncertain—especially as far as any children of the union are concerned.

- Increasing numbers of married couples are choosing to remain childless. Planned Parenthood has even established workshops for couples to assist them in making this decision (*Los Angeles Herald-Examiner*, November 27, 1979).

13 So clearly, a situation has arisen during the last twenty years in which traditional values are no longer as important. Also, a wide variety of alternatives to the traditional family have arisen. Individuals may feel that old-fashioned marriage is just one of many options.

Pressure Two: Sexual Morality

14 The changes in attitudes toward sexual morality have changed as dramatically in the last two decades as the alternatives to traditional marriage. Hear what a widely used college textbook, published in 1953, said about premarital sex:

> The arguments against premarital coitus outweigh those in its favor. Except for the matter of temporary physical pleasure, all arguments

about gains tend to be highly theoretical, while the risks and unpleasant consequences tend to be in equal degree highly practical. . . .

The promiscuity of young men is certainly poor preparation for marital fidelity and successful family life. For girls it is certainly no better and sometimes leads still further to the physical and psychological shock of abortion or the more prolonged suffering of bearing an illegitimate child and giving it up to others. From the viewpoint of ethical and religious leaders, the spread of disease through unrestrained sex activities is far more than a health problem. They see it as undermining the dependable standards of character and the spiritual values that raise life to the level of the "good society."

(This comes from *Marriage and the Family* by Professor Ray E. Baber of Pomona College, California, which was part of the McGraw-Hill Series in Sociology and Anthropology and required reading for some college courses.)

15   Clearly, attitudes have changed a great deal in just three decades. Teenagers have accepted the idea of premarital sex as the norm. In one recent national poll, 52 percent of girls and 66 percent of boys favored having sexual relations in their teens. Ironically, however, 46 percent of the teenagers thought that virginity in their future marital partner was fairly important. Youngsters, in other words, display some confusion about what they want to do sexually, and what they expect from a future mate.

16   But of course, only part of the problem of defining sexual standards lies with young people and premarital sex. The strong emphasis on achieving an active and rewarding sex life has probably played some role in encouraging many husbands and wives into rejecting monogamy. Here's some of the evidence that's been accumulating:

- Half of the men in a recent nationwide study admitted cheating on their wives (*Pensacola Journal*, May 30, 1978).
- Psychiatrists today say they see more patients who are thinking about having an extramarital affair and who wonder if it would harm their marriage (*New York Post*, November 18, 1976).
- A psychiatrist at the Albert Einstein College of Medicine says, "In my practice I have been particularly struck by how many

women have been able to use an affair to raise their consciousness and their confidence."

17   So the desire for unrestrained sex now tends to take a place
among other more traditional priorities, and this can be expected
to continue to exert strong pressure on marriage relationships.

Pressure Three: The Economy

18   The number of married women working outside the home has
been increasing steadily, and most of these women are working out
of economic necessity. As a result, neither spouse may have time
to concentrate on the nurturing of the children or of the marriage
relationship.

19   One mother we interviewed in New Jersey told us about her
feelings when she was forced to work full time in a library after
her husband lost his job.

20   "It's the idea that I have no choice that really bothers me," she
said. "I have to work, or we won't eat or have a roof over our
heads. I didn't mind working part-time just to have extra money.
I suppose that it's selfish, but I hate having to work every day and
then to come home, fix dinner, and have to start doing housework.
Both my husband and I were raised in traditional families, where
the father went to work and the mother stayed home and took
care of the house and children. [My husband] would never think
of cooking or doing housework. I've raised my boys the same way,
and now I'm paying for it. Sometimes, I almost hate my husband,
even though I know it's not his fault."

21   Unfortunately, such pressures probably won't ease in the future.
Even if the economy improves and the number of unemployed
workers decreases, few women are likely to give up their jobs.
Economists agree that working-class women who have become
breadwinners during a recession can be expected to remain in the
work force. One reason is that many unemployed men aren't going
to get their old jobs back, even when the economy improves.

22   "To the extent that [the men] may have to take lower-paying service jobs, their families will need a second income," says Michelle
Brandman, associate economist at Chase Econometrics. "The trend

to two paycheck families as a means of maintaining family income is going to continue" (*The Wall Street Journal*, December 8, 1982).

23   In addition to the pressures of unemployment, the cost of having, rearing, and educating children is steadily going up. Researchers have found that middle-class families with two children *think* they're spending only about 15 percent of their income on their children. Usually, though, they *actually* spend about 40 percent of their money on them. To put the cost in dollars and cents, if you had a baby in 1977, the estimated cost of raising that child to the age of eighteen will be $85,000, and that figure has of course been on the rise for babies born since then (*New York Daily News*, July 24, 1977).

24   Another important factor that promises to keep both spouses working full time in the future is the attitude of today's teenagers toward these issues. They're not so much concerned about global issues like overpopulation as they are about the high cost of living. Both boys and girls place a lot of emphasis on having enough money so that they can go out and do things. Consequently, most teenage girls surveyed say they expect to pursue careers, even after they get married.

25   So it would seem that by the year 2000 we can expect to see more working mothers in the United States. The woman who doesn't hold down any sort of outside job but stays at home to care for her children represents a small percentage of wives today. By the end of the century, with a few exceptions here and there, she may well have become a part of America's quaint past.

26   As women have joined the work force in response to economic needs, one result has been increased emotional strains on the marriage and family relationships. But there's another set of pressures that has encouraged women to pursue careers. That's the power of feminist philosophy to permeate attitudes in grassroots America during the past couple of decades.

Pressure Four: Grassroots Feminist Philosophy

27   Many women may not agree with the most radical expressions of feminist philosophy that have arisen in the past decade or so. But most younger women—and indeed, a majority of women in

the United States—tend to agree with most of the objectives that even the radical feminist groups have been trying to achieve. The basic feminist philosophy has filtered down to the grass roots, and young boys and girls are growing up with feminist assumptions that may have been foreign to their parents and grandparents.

28 For example, child care and housework are no longer regarded strictly as "women's work" by the young people we've polled. Also, according to the Gallup Youth Poll, most teenage girls want to go to college and pursue a career. Moreover, they expect to marry later in life and to continue working after they're married. Another poll, conducted by *The New York Times* and CBS News, revealed that only 2 percent of the youngest age group interviewed— that is, those eighteen to twenty-nine years old—preferred "traditional marriage." By this, they meant a marriage in which the husband is exclusively a provider and the wife is exclusively a homemaker and mother.

29 If these young people continue to hold views similar to these into later life, it's likely that the changes that are occurring today in the traditional family structure will continue. For one thing, more day-care centers for children will have to be established. Consequently, the rearing of children will no longer be regarded as solely the responsibility of the family, but will become a community or institutional responsibility.

30 But while such developments may lessen the strain on mothers and fathers, they may also weaken the bonds that hold families together. Among other things, it may become psychologically easier to get a divorce if a person is not getting along with a spouse, because the divorcing spouses will believe it's less likely that the lives of the children will be disrupted.

31 So the concept of broadening the rights of women vis-á-vis their husbands and families has certainly encouraged women to enter the working world in greater numbers. They're also more inclined to seek a personal identity that isn't tied up so much in their homelife.

32 These grassroots feminist forces have brought greater benefits to many, but at the same time they've often worked against traditional family ties, and we remain uncertain about what is going to replace them. Feminists may argue that the traditional family caused its own demise—or else why would supposedly content wives and daughters have worked so hard to transform it? Whatever its theories, though, feminism is still a factor that, in its present form,

appears to exert a destabilizing influence on many traditional familial relationships among husbands, wives, and children.

33 As things stand now, our family lives are in a state of flux and will probably continue to be out of balance until the year 2000. The pressures we've discussed will continue to have an impact on our family lives in future years. But at the same time, counterforces, which tend to drive families back together again, are also at work.

34 One of these factors is a traditionalist strain in the large majority of American women. The vast majority of women in this country— 74 percent—continue to view marriage with children as the most interesting and satisfying life for them personally, according to a Gallup Poll for the White House Conference on Families released in June, 1980.

35 Another force supporting family life is the attitude of American teenagers toward divorce. According to a recent Gallup Youth Poll, 55 percent feel that divorces are too easy to get today. Also, they're concerned about the high rate of divorce, and they want to have enduring marriages themselves. But at the same time—in a response that reflects the confusion of many adult Americans on this subject—67 percent of the teens in this same poll say it's right to get a divorce if a couple doesn't get along together. In other words, they place little importance on trying to improve or salvage a relationship that has run into serious trouble.

36 There's a similar ambivalence in the experts we polled. As we've seen, 33 percent of them consider family problems as a top concern today, and 26 percent think these problems will be a big difficulty in the year 2000. But ironically, less than 3 percent suggest that strengthening family relationships is an important consideration in planning for the future! It's obvious, then, that we're confused and ambivalent in our feelings about marriage and the family. Most people know instinctively, without having to read a poll or a book, that happiness and satisfaction in life are rooted largely in the quality of our personal relationships. Furthermore, the most important of those relationships usually begin at home. So one of the greatest challenges we face before the year 2000, both as a nation and as individuals, is how to make our all-important family ties strong and healthy. It's only upon such a firm personal foundation that we can hope to venture forth and grapple effectively with more public problems.

Analyzing the Writer's Argument

1. Gallup begins his essay with the story about two Sunday school teachers and their students. What is the point of the story, and how does it work as an introduction to the essay as a whole? Explain.

2. What is Gallup's thesis, and where is it presented?

3. Gallup identifies four major pressures affecting American attitudes toward marriage and the family. According to Gallup, what effects has each of the pressures had on the family? Why do you suppose he chose to call these factors *pressures* instead of *causes* or *reasons*? Explain.

4. What kinds of evidence does he provide to document the impact that each pressure has had? Which of the four pressures did you find most convincingly presented? Explain.

5. According to Gallup, what new feminist assumptions about marriage and family are boys and girls growing up with? How do these assumptions differ from those of their parents or grandparents?

6. What are the forces Gallup identifies that are working "to drive families back together again"? In your opinion, are they strong enough to counter the destabilizing influences? Explain why, or why not.

7. What is Gallup's attitude toward the American family and toward the changes that have been occurring in the basic American values? What in the essay led you to this conclusion?

Exploring the Issues in This Essay

1. It would be difficult to ignore the influence that feminism has had on American life—both in the home and in the workplace—in the past twenty years. The controversy arises when people debate whether these changes have been for the good or not. How do you feel about the impact that feminism has had? How has it affected you personally?

2. Discuss the impact that alternative lifestyles have had on people you know at home or at school. Judging from your own experience, how widespread are divorce, single parenthood, communal living, so-called "open marriages," and other alternatives to the traditional family? Do you agree with Gallup's conclusion that "the practice of living together without getting married seems to be something that's here to stay"?

Margaret Mead

Can the American Family Survive?

> *Born in Philadelphia in 1901, Margaret Mead was an educator and writer, but it was as an anthropologist that she earned her lasting reputation. Several of her pioneering field studies carried out in the 1920s and 1930s are still considered classics in the area. First enrolled at DePauw University, Mead graduated from Barnard College and Columbia University and was for many years professor of anthropology at Columbia. She devoted much of her professional life to the study of native cultures in the South Pacific, establishing herself as an expert on family structure, environmental problems, and the role of women in society. Later in life, her work turned to the study of contemporary societies. Mead's best known books are* Coming of Age in Samoa *(1928),* Sex and Temperament *(1935),* Male and Female: A Study of the Sexes in a Changing World *(1949),* Continuities in Cultural Evolution *(1964), and* Culture and Commitment *(1970). After her retirement from the academic world, she was a contributing editor to* Redbook *until her death in 1978.*
>
> *Although Mead recognizes that the American family as an institution is in trouble, she maintains a firm belief in the value of family. In the following essay, which first appeared in the February 1977 issue of* Redbook, *she describes the problems confronting American families and calls for people to help each other make the family as an institution viable for future generations.*

1   All over the United States, families are in trouble. It is true that there are many contented homes where parents are living in harmony and raising their children responsibly, and with enjoyment in which the children share. Two out of three American households are homes in which a wife and husband live together, and almost seven out of ten children are born to parents living together in their first marriage.

2   However, though reassuring, these figures are deceptive. A great many of the married couples have already lived through one divorce. And a very large number of the children in families still intact will have to face the disruption of their parents' marriage in the future. The numbers increase every year.

3   It is also true that the hazards are much greater for some families than for others. Very young couples, the poorly educated, those with few skills and a low income, Blacks and members of other minority groups—particularly if they live in big cities—all these are in danger of becoming high-risk families for whose children a family breakdown is disastrous.

4   But no group, whatever its status and resources, is exempt. This in itself poses a threat to all families, especially those with young children. For how can children feel secure when their friends in other families so like their own are conspicuously lost and unhappy? In one way or another we all are drawn into the orbit of families in trouble.

5   Surely it is time for us to look squarely at the problems that beset families and to ask what must be done to make family life more viable, not only for ourselves now but also in prospect for all the children growing up who will have to take responsibility for the next generation.

The Grim Picture

6   There are those today—as at various times in the past—who doubt that the family can survive, and some who believe it should not survive. Indeed, the contemporary picture is grim enough.

- Many young marriages entered into with love and high hopes collapse before the first baby is weaned. The very young parents, on whom the whole burden of survival rests, cannot make it entirely on their own, and they give up.

- Families that include several children break up and the children are uprooted from the only security they have known. Some children of divorce, perhaps the majority, will grow up as stepchildren in homes that, however loving, they no longer dare to trust fully. Many—far too many—will grow up in single-parent homes. Still others will be moved, rootless as rolling stones, from foster family to foster family until at last they begin a rootless life on their own.

- In some states a family with a male breadwinner cannot obtain welfare, and some fathers, unable to provide adequately for their children, desert them so that the mothers can apply for public assistance. And growing numbers of mothers, fearful of being deserted, are leaving their young families while, as they hope and believe, they still have a chance to make a different life for themselves.

- As divorce figures have soared—today the proportion of those currently divorced is more than half again as high as in 1960, and it is predicted that one in three young women in this generation will be divorced—Americans have accepted as a truism the myth that from the mistakes made in their first marriage women and men learn how to do it better the second time around. Sometimes it does work. But a large proportion of those who have resorted to divorce once choose this as the easier solution again and again. Easily dashed hopes become more easily dashed.

- At the same time, many working parents, both of whom are trying hard to care for and keep together the family they have chosen to bring into being, find that there is no place at all where their children can be cared for safely and gently and responsibly during the long hours of their own necessary absence at their jobs. They have no relatives nearby and there is neither a daycare center nor afterschool care for their active youngsters. Whatever solution they find, their children are likely to suffer.

The Bitter Consequences

7   The consequences, direct and indirect, are clear. Thousands of young couples are living together in some arrangement and are wholly dependent on their private, personal commitment to each other for the survival of their relationship. In the years from 1970

to 1975 the number of single persons in the 25-to-34 year age group has increased by half. Some couples living together have repudiated marriage as a binding social relationship and have rejected the family as an institution. Others are delaying marriage because they are not sure of themselves or each other; still others are simply responding to what they have experienced of troubled family life and the effects of divorce.

8 At the end of the life span there are the ever-growing numbers of women and men, especially women, who have outlived their slender family relationships. They have nowhere to turn, no one to depend on but strangers in public institutions. Unwittingly we have provided the kind of assistance that, particularly in cities, almost guarantees such isolated and helpless old people will become the prey of social vultures.

9 And at all stages of their adult life, demands are made increasingly on women to earn their living in the working world. Although we prefer to interpret this as an expression of women's wish to fulfill themselves to have the rights that go with money earned and to be valued as persons, the majority of women who work outside their homes do so because they must. It is striking that ever since the 1950s a larger proportion of married women with children than of married but childless women have entered the labor force. According to recent estimates some 14 million women with children—four out of ten mothers of children under six years of age and more than half of all mothers of school-age children—are working, the great majority of them in full-time jobs.

10 A large proportion of these working women are the sole support of their families. Some 10 million children—more than one in six—are living with only one parent, generally with the mother. This number has doubled since 1960.

11 The majority of these women and their children live below the poverty level, the level at which the most minimal needs can be met. Too often the women, particularly the younger ones, having little education and few skills, are at the bottom of the paid work force. Though they and their children are in great need, they are among those least able to demand and obtain what they require merely to survive decently, in good health and with some hope for the future.

12   But the consequences of family trouble are most desperate as they affect children. Every year, all over the country, over 1 million adolescents, nowadays principally girls, run away from home because they have found life with their families insupportable. Some do not run very far and in the end a great many come home again, but by no means all of them. And we hear about only a handful whose terrifying experiences or whose death happens to come into public view.

13   In homes where there is no one to watch over them, elementary-school children are discovering the obliterating effects of alcohol; a growing number have become hard-case alcoholics in their early teens. Other young girls and boys, wanderers in the streets, have become the victims of corruption and sordid sex. The youngsters who vent their rage and desperation on others by means of violent crimes are no less social victims than are the girls and boys who are mindlessly corrupted by the adults who prey on them.

14   Perhaps the most alarming symptom of all is the vast increase in child abuse, which, although it goes virtually unreported in some groups, is not limited to any one group in our population. What seems to be happening is that frantic mothers and fathers, stepparents or the temporary mates of parents turn on the children they do not know how to care for, and beat them—often in a desperate, inarticulate hope that someone will hear their cries and somehow bring help. We know this, but although many organizations have been set up to help these children and their parents, many adults do not know what is needed or how to ask for assistance or whom they may expect a response from.

15   And finally there are the children who end their own lives in absolute despair. Suicide is now third among the causes of death for youngsters 15 to 19 years old.

What Has Gone Wrong?

16   In recent years, various explanations have been suggested for the breakdown of family life.

17   Blame has been placed on the vast movement of Americans from rural areas and small towns to the big cities and on the continual,

restless surge of people from one part of the country to another, so that millions of families, living in the midst of strangers, lack any continuity in their life-style and any real support for their values and expectations.

18   Others have emphasized the effects of unemployment and underemployment among Blacks and other minority groups, which make their families peculiarly vulnerable in life crises that are exacerbated by economic uncertainty. This is particularly the case where the policies of welfare agencies penalize the family that is poor but intact in favor of the single-parent family.

19   There is also the generation gap, particularly acute today, when parents and their adolescent children experience the world in such very different ways. The world in which the parents grew up is vanishing, unknown to their children except by hearsay. The world into which adolescents are growing is in many ways unknown to both generations—and neither can help the other very much to understand it.

20   Then there is our obvious failure to provide for the children and young people whom we do not succeed in educating, who are in deep trouble and who may be totally abandoned. We have not come to grips with the problems of hard drugs. We allow the courts that deal with juveniles to become so overloaded that little of the social protection they were intended to provide is possible. We consistently underfund and understaff the institutions into which we cram children in need of re-education and physical and psychological rehabilitation, as if all that concerned us was to get them—and keep them—out of our sight.

21   Other kinds of explanations also have been offered.

22   There are many people who, knowing little about child development, have placed the principal blame on what they call "permissiveness"—on the relaxing of parental discipline to include the child as a small partner in the process of growing up. Those people say that children are "spoiled," that they lack "respect" for their parents or that they have not learned to obey the religious prohibitions that were taught to their parents, and that all the troubles plaguing family life have followed.

23   Women's Liberation, too, has come in for a share of the blame. It is said that in seeking self-fulfillment, women are neglecting their homes and children and are undermining men's authority

and men's sense of responsibility. The collapse of the family is seen as the inevitable consequence.

24   Those who attribute the difficulties of troubled families to any single cause, whether or not it is related to reality, also tend to advocate panaceas, each of which—they say—should restore stability to the traditional family or, alternatively, supplant the family. Universal day care from birth, communal living, group marriage, contract marriage and open marriage all have their advocates.

25   Each such proposal fastens on some trouble point in the modern family—the lack of adequate facilities to care for the children of working mothers, for example, or marital infidelity, which, it is argued, would be eliminated by being institutionalized. Others, realizing the disastrous effects of poverty on family life, have advocated bringing the income of every family up to a level at which decent living is possible. Certainly this must be one of our immediate aims. But it is wholly unrealistic to suppose that all else that has gone wrong will automatically right itself if the one—but very complex—problem of poverty is eliminated.

A Look at Alternatives

26   Is there, in fact, any viable alternative to the family as a setting in which children can be successfully reared to become capable and responsible adults, relating to one another and a new generation of children as well as to the world around them? Or should we aim at some wholly new social invention?

27   Revolutionaries have occasionally attempted to abolish the family, or at least to limit its strength by such measures as arranging for marriages without binding force or for rearing children in different kinds of collectives. But as far as we know, in the long run such efforts have never worked out satisfactorily.

28   The Soviet Union, for instance, long ago turned away from the flexible, impermanent unions and collective child-care ideals of the early revolutionary days and now heavily emphasizes the values of a stable family life. In Israel the kibbutz, with its children's house and carefully planned, limited contact between parents and children, is losing out to social forms in which the family is both stronger and more closely knit. In Scandinavian countries, where

the standards of child care are very high, serious efforts have been made to provide a viable situation for unmarried mothers and the children they have chosen to bring up alone; but there are disturbing indices of trouble, expressed, for example, in widespread alcoholism and a high rate of suicide.

29   Experience suggests that we would do better to look in other directions. Two approaches may be rewarding. First we can look at other kinds of societies—primitive societies, peasant societies and traditional complex but unindustrialized societies (prerevolutionary China, for example)—to discover whether there are ways in which families are organized that occur in all societies. This can give us some idea of needs that must be satisfied for families to survive and prosper.

30   Second we can ask whether the problems that are besetting American families are unique or are instead characteristic of families wherever modern industrialization, a sophisticated technology and urban living are drawing people into a new kind of civilization. Placing our own difficulties within a wider context can perhaps help us to assess what our priorities must be as we attempt to develop new forms of stability in keeping with contemporary expressions of human needs.

31   Looking at human behavior with all that we know—and can infer—about the life of our human species from earliest times, we have to realize that the family, as an association between a man and a woman and the children she bears, has been universal. As far as we know, both primitive "group" marriage and primitive matriarchy are daydreams—or nightmares, depending on one's point of view—without basis in historical reality. On the contrary, the evidence indicates that the couple, together with their children, biological and adopted, are everywhere at the core of human societies, even though this "little family" (as the Chinese called the nuclear family) may be embedded in joint families, extended families of great size, clans, manorial systems, courts, harems or other institutions that elaborate on kin and marital relations.

32   Almost up to the present, women on the whole have kept close to home and domestic tasks because of the demands of pregnancy and the nursing of infants, the rearing of children and the care of the disabled and the elderly. They have been concerned primarily with the conservation of intimate values and human relations from one generation to another over immense reaches of time. In

contrast, men have performed tasks that require freer movement over greater distances, more intense physical effort and exposure to greater immediate danger; and everywhere men have developed the formal institutions of public life and the values on which these are based. However differently organized, the tasks of women and men have been complementary, mutually supportive. And where either the family or the wider social institutions have broken down; the society as a whole has been endangered.

33 In fact, almost everywhere in the world today societies *are* endangered. The difficulties that beset families in the United States are by no means unique. Families are in trouble everywhere in a world in which change—kinds of change that in many cases we ourselves proudly initiated—has been massive and rapid, and innovations have proliferated with only the most superficial concern for their effect on human lives and the earth itself. One difference between the United States and many other countries is that, caring so much about progress, Americans have moved faster. But we may also have arrived sooner at a turning point at which it becomes crucial to redefine what we most value and where we are headed.

34 Looking to the past does not mean that we should return to the past or that we can undo the experiences that have brought us where we are now. The past can provide us only with a base for judging what threatens sound family life and for considering whether our social planning is realistic and inclusive enough. Looking to the past is not a way of binding ourselves but of increasing our awareness, so that we are freer to find new solutions in keeping with our deepest human needs.

35 So the question is not whether women should be forced back into their homes or should have an equal say with men in the world's affairs. We urgently need to draw on the talents women have to offer. Nor is there any question whether men should be deprived of a more intimate family role. We have made a small beginning by giving men a larger share in parenting, and I believe that men and children have been enriched by it.

36 What we need to be sure of is that areas of caretaking associated in the past with families do not simply drop out of our awareness so that basic human needs go unmet. All the evidence indicates that this is where our greatest difficulties lie. The troubles that plague American families and families all over the industrialized

world are symptomatic of the breakdown of the responsible relationship between families and the larger communities of which they are part.

37   For a long time we have worked hard at isolating the individual family. This has increased the mobility of individuals; and by encouraging young families to break away from the older generation and the home community, we have been able to speed up the acceptance of change and the rapid spread of innovative behavior. But at the same time we have burdened every small family with tremendous responsibilities once shared within three generations and among a large number of people—the nurturing of small children, the emergence of adolescents into adulthood, the care of the sick and disabled and the protection of the aged. What we have failed to realize is that even as we have separated the single family from the larger society, we have expected each couple to take on a range of obligations that traditionally have been shared within a larger family and a wider community.

38   So all over the world there are millions of families left alone, as it were, each in its own box—parents faced with the specter of what may happen if either one gets sick, children fearful that their parents may end their quarrels with divorce, and empty-handed old people without any role in the life of the next generation.

39   Then, having pared down to almost nothing the relationship between families and the community, when families get into trouble because they cannot accomplish the impossible we turn their problems over to impersonal social agencies, which can act only in a fragmented way because they are limited to patchwork programs that often are too late to accomplish what is most needed.

40   Individuals and families do get some kind of help, but what they learn and what those who work hard within the framework of social agencies convey, even as they try to help, is that families should be able to care for themselves.

What Can We Do?

41   Can we restore family stability? Can we establish new bonds between families and communities? Perhaps most important of all, can we move to a firm belief that living in a family is worth a great effort? Can we move to a new expectation that by making

the effort, families can endure? Obviously the process is circular. Both optimism and action are needed.

42 We shall have to distinguish between the things that must be done at once and the relations between families and communities that can be built up only over time. We shall have to accept willingly the cost of what must be done, realizing that whatever we do ultimately will be less costly than our present sorry attempts to cope with breakdown and disaster. And we shall have to care for the failures too.

43 In the immediate future we shall have to support every piece of Federal legislation through which adequate help can be provided for families, both single-parent families and intact poor families, so that they can live decently and safely and prepare their children for another kind of life.

44 We shall have to support Federal programs for day care and afterschool care for the children of working mothers and working parents, and for facilities where in a crisis parents can safely leave their small children for brief periods; for centers where the elderly can be cared for without being isolated from the rest of the world; for housing for young families and older people in communities where they can actually interact as friendly grandparents and grandchildren might; and for a national health program that is concerned not with fleecing the Government but with health care. And we must support the plea of Vice-President Walter F. Mondale, who, as chairman of the Senate Subcommittee on Children and Youth, called for "family impact" statements requiring Government agencies to account for what a proposed policy would do for families—make them worse off or better able to take care of their needs.

45 Government-funded programs need not be patchwork, as likely to destroy as to save. We need to realize that problems related to family and community life—problems besetting education, housing, nutrition, health care, to name just a few—are interlocked. To solve them, we need awareness of detail combined with concern for the whole, and a wise use of tax dollars to accomplish our aims.

46 A great deal depends on how we see what is done—whether we value it because we are paying for it and because we realize that the protection given families in need is a protection for all families, including our own. Committing ourselves to programs of care—

instead of dissociating ourselves from every effort—is one step in the direction of reestablishing family ties with the community. But this will happen only if we accept the idea that each of us, as part of a community, shares in the responsibility for everyone, and thereby benefits from what is done.

47   The changes that are needed cannot be accomplished by Federal legislation alone. Over a longer time we must support the design and building of communities in which there is housing for three generations, for the fortunate and the unfortunate, and for people of many backgrounds. Such communities can become central in the development of the necessary support system for families. But it will take time to build such communities, and we cannot afford just to wait and hope they will happen.

48   Meanwhile we must act to interrupt the runaway belief that marriages must fail, that parents and children can't help but be out of communication, that the family as an institution is altogether in disarray. There still are far more marriages that succeed than ones that fail; there are more parents and children who live in trust and learn from one another than ones who are out of touch; there are more people who care about the future than we acknowledge.

49   What we need, I think, is nationwide discussion—in magazines, in newspapers, on television panel shows and before Congressional committees—of how people who are happily married can help those who are not, how people who are fortunate can help those who are not and how people who have too little to do can help those who are burdened by too much.

50   Out of such discussion can come a heightened awareness and perhaps some actual help, but above all, fresh thought about what must be done and the determination to begin to do it.

51   It is true that all over the United States, families are in trouble. Realizing this should not make us cynical about the family. It should start us working for a new version of the family that is appropriate to the contemporary world.

Analyzing the Writer's Argument

1. According to Mead, what are some of the telltale characteristics of families that are most prone to breaking down? Why do you suppose that these characteristics put families in the high-risk cat-

egory? Are any families ever really exempt from breakdown? Explain why, or why not.

2. For Mead the picture of contemporary American family life is grim. What have been the consequences of this situation for men, women, and children?

3. What significance does Mead see in the vast increase in child abuse?

4. According to Mead, what are some of the main reasons that people have offered for the breakdown of family life? Which of the reasons seem most persuasive to you? Why?

5. What is Mead's response to people who advocate "panaceas"? Do you agree with her position? Explain.

6. Mead believes that in America and in industrialized countries around the world people have tended to "separate the single family from the larger society." For what reasons does Mead think people have done this, and what have been the effects?

7. In paragraph 41 Mead asks a series of questions. Why do you suppose she chose to ask questions instead of making statements? How effective did you find this strategy?

8. What solutions does Mead offer to the problem of the endangered American family? Upon what assumptions about America does she base her solutions? Which of her solutions do you find most attractive? Explain why.

Exploring the Issues in This Essay

1. Is the family as an institution worth fighting for? What has been the importance of your family for you? Do you have an extended sense of family; are grandparents, aunts, uncles, and cousins, for example, a vital part of your family structure? Did you ever get the sense that your family was isolated from the larger community, as Mead suggests American families have become? Do you think that the American family is in trouble? Explain.

2. What are some of the innovative alternatives to the traditional family that have been proposed in recent years? What are the advantages and disadvantages of each, especially as compared to the traditional family? Discuss whether or not you believe that American society is ready to accept any of these alternatives on a large scale.

"Gerald, I'm switching to another channel."

Drawing by Joe Mirachi © 1989 *The New Yorker* Magazine, Inc.

Joseph L. White

*Black Family Life**

> *Born in Lincoln, Nebraska, on December 19, 1932, Joseph
> L. White received his B.A. from San Francisco State College
> and holds a Ph.D. from Michigan State University in clin-
> ical psychology. He taught at Washington University, Cali-
> fornia State College at Los Angeles, and San Francisco State
> College before coming to the University of California, Irvine,
> where he is currently professor of psychology and compar-
> ative cultures. White was active in the Civil Rights Move-
> ment in the 1960s and was instrumental in promoting and
> developing Black Studies programs and cultural awareness
> courses for schools in California. He believed that traditional
> deficiency-based theories failed to explain African-American
> behavior correctly and sought to give voice to an alternative
> viewpoint that would provide an adequate explanation. In "To-
> ward A Black Psychology," a seminal article that appeared in
> Ebony in 1970, White identifies a definitive Black ethos which
> African-Americans use as a frame of reference to interpret the
> world around them and calls for an integrated and conceptu-
> ally coherent psychological portrait of African-Americans.*
>
> *White's work in Black psychology culminated in the pub-
> lication of* The Psychology of Blacks: An Afro-American
> Perspective *in 1984. In "Black Family Life," an excerpt from
> chapter three of this book, White argues for a psychological
> model of African-American family life that "concentrates on
> the strengths of Afro-Americans and can be contrasted to the
> deficit-deficiency model of Black psychology which has been
> advanced by Euro-American psychologists."*

Introduction

1   The emerging view of Black family life is that its underlying
genotype, its basic structure, consists of an extended family group

made up of a number of legally related and nonlegally related adults and children who come together within a mutually support-ive social, psychological, and economic network to deal conjointly with the responsibilities of living (Stack, 1974). This pattern of fam-ily life with its emphasis on mutual solidarity, cooperation, and interdependence originated in Africa and has persisted despite its going through several cycles of formation, breakup, and reformu-lation brought about by slavery, a century of migration out of the rural South, and restrictive welfare codes (Nobles, 1978). During the periods of breakup and reformulation the extended family may take on a different surface or phenotypical appearance; however, if the Black family is observed across sufficient time and geographical space, its basic extended structure will reappear (Gutman, 1976).

The Deficit-Deficiency Model

2   The view of the core structure of the Black family as an ex-tended family grouping is not shared by all observers. The tradi-tional view of the Black family, which has evolved from the works of Frazier (1939), Elkins (1968), Moynihan (1965), and Rainwater (1970), is one of a disorganized, single-parent, subnuclear, female-dominated social system. This is essentially the deficit-deficiency model of Black family life. The deficit-deficiency model begins with the historical assumption that there was no carry-over from Africa to America of any sophisticated African-based form of family life and communal living. Viable patterns of family life either did not exist because Africans were incapable of creating them, or they were destroyed beginning with slavery and the separation of bio-logical parents and children, forced breeding, the master's sexual exploitation of Black women, and the accumulative effects of three hundred years of economic and social discrimination. As a re-sult of this background of servitude, deprivation, second-class cit-izenship, and chronic unemployment, Black adults have not been able to develop marketable skills, self-sufficiency, future orienta-tion, and planning and decision-making competencies, instrumen-tal behaviors thought to be necessary for sustaining a successful two-parent nuclear family while guiding the children through the socialization process.

3   In a society that placed a premium on decisive male leadership
in the family, the Black male was portrayed as lacking the masculine sex role behaviors characterized by logical thinking, willingness to take responsibility for others, assertiveness, managerial skills, achievement orientation, and occupational mastery. The
Black male in essence had been psychologically castrated and rendered ineffective by forces beyond his control. He is absent within
the family circle and unable to provide leadership and command
respect when he is present. After generations of being unable to
achieve the ideal male role in the family and in American society,
the Black male is likely to be inclined to compensate for his failure
by pursuing roles such as the pimp, player, hustler, and sweet
daddy, which are in conflict with the norms of the larger society.
The appearance of these roles in male behavior in the Black community, rather than being interpreted as a form of social protest,
reinforces the majority culture stereotypes of Black males as irresponsible, lazy, shiftless, and sociopathic.

4   The Black woman does not fare much better in terms of how she
is portrayed in the deficit-deficiency model of Black family life. She
is regarded as the head of the household, a matriarch who initially
received her power because the society was unwilling to permit
the Black male to assume the legal, economic, and social positions necessary to become a dominant force within the family and
community life. Having achieved this power by default, the Black
female is unwilling to share it. Her unwillingness to share her
power persists even when the Black male is present and willing
to assume responsibility in the family circle, since she is not confident of the male's ability to follow through on his commitments.
Confrontation over decision making and family direction is usually not necessary because the Black male is either not present in
the household on any ongoing basis or is regarded as ineffective
by the female when he is present.

5   The impact of the matriarchial family on the sex-role development of the children in relationship to the dominant social system,
which has a precedent for clearly distinguishing between acceptable male and female social roles, is considered to be devastating.
The Black male child has no adequate father figure to emulate
in acquiring the conventional masculine instrumental behaviors
typified by responsibility taking, resourcefulness, independence,

occupational preparation, and cool-headed, logical decision making. To make matters worse, the mother may ventilate her anger and disappointment with the father for not being able to fulfill his role as a provider on the male child by expressing an attitude that men are no good, irresponsible, and only interested in conquering women sexually. When trying to discourage behavior that she considers undesirable, the mother is likely to compare the child to his father by telling him that he is going to turn out to be a no-count man, just like his father. The effect of an absent role model, coupled with the negative image of masculinity that is being projected, prevents the male child from acquiring the confidence he needs to resolve successfully the issues associated with his identity and psychosexual development as he evolves through adolescence and early adulthood. The final outcome of this female-dominated socialization process is the creation of still another generation of Black males who will be unable to build the internal security and social role skills necessary to become heads of households, interact productively in relationships with women, and serve as sound role models for their own children.

6   The Black female child, on the other hand, is constantly exposed to a cadre of women in authority and decision-making roles within the family—not only her own mother, but a community of women made up of aunties, grandmothers, cousins, and other women neighbors who occupy the same positions in their families. Presented with this abundance of feminine role models without the balancing input from adult males in fatherlike roles, the Black female child is vulnerable to developing an exaggerated notion of her own role as a future adult and parent. She has no real idea of what male–female teamwork is all about, since she has had very little, if any, exposure to decision-making models where the male is part of the process. To further complicate matters, she has also heard her mother and other adult females bad-mouth Black males for their inability to take care of business. She has been admonished to learn to take care of herself and not to become dependent on some no-count man who would be unable to fulfill his responsibilities. In short, she has been told to "keep her pants up and her dress down," lest she fall victim to a situation where she will have a flock of children with no father to assist her in the child-rearing process.

7   When the offspring of these matriarchial families meet in the next generation as adults, it is difficult to conceive of how they could develop a mutually satisfying relationship. The male is confused, doesn't know who he is, and lacks the emotional maturity required for the ongoing responsibilities of family living. The Black female has an exaggerated sense of her own worth, doesn't have much confidence in the male's ability to meet his obligations over a prolonged period of time, and has very little preparation for the give-and-take of male–female relationships. These kinds of sisters have been known to sell their men "woof tickets" with statements to the effect "I was working and taking care of myself when I met you, I'm working and taking care of myself now, and I'll be working and taking care of myself when I leave you." Putting two people like these, who have been reared in matriarchial families, together in a conjugal union or marriage of their own would seem to represent the beginnings of another vicious, destructive, deficit-deficiency cycle with the "web and tangle of pathology" recreating itself.

8   The proponents of the pathology-oriented, matriarchial family model did not consider the possibility that a single-parent Black mother could serve as an adequate role model for the children of both sexes. The notion that the mother could reflect a balance of the traditional male and female roles, with respect to mental toughness and emotional tenderness, was largely ignored because of the rigid classification of psychosexual roles in American society. In the Black community, however, the categorization of social role behaviors based on gender is not as inflexible. It is conceivable that a Black mother could project a combination of assertive and nurturant behaviors in the process of rearing children of both sexes as nonsexist adults.

9   With the reality of accelerating divorce rates, in recent years the single-parent family headed by a woman has become a social reality in Euro-America. This reality has been accompanied by an attempt on the part of social scientists to legitimate family structures that represent alternatives to the nuclear family while reconceptualizing the social roles of males and females with less emphasis on exclusive behaviors. The concept of androgyny has been introduced to cover the vast pool of human personality traits that can be developed by either sex (Rogers, 1978). A well-balanced person

reflects a combination of both instrumental and expressive traits. The latter include feeling-oriented behaviors formerly considered feminine, such as tenderness, caring, and affection. Thus, it is conceptually possible for a white, single androgynous female parent to rear psychologically healthy, emotionally integrated children. It is interesting how the sociology of the times make available to white Americans psychological concepts designed to legitimatize changes in the family, in child-rearing patterns, and in relationships between the sexes. Yet, these same behaviors when first expressed by Afro-Americans were considered as pathological.

The Extended Family Model

10 The extended family, in contrast to the single-parent subnuclear family, consists of a related and quasi-related group of adults, including aunts, uncles, parents, cousins, grandparents, boyfriends, and girl friends linked together in a kinship or kinlike network. They form a cooperative interface with each other in confronting the concerns of living and rearing the children. This model of family life, which seems able to capture not only the strength, vitality, resilience, and continuity of the Black family, but also the essence of Black values, folkways, and life styles, begins with a different set of assumptions about the development and evolution of Black family life in America.

11 The Black extended family is seen as an outgrowth of African patterns of family and community life that survived in America. The Africans carried with them through the Mid-Atlantic passage and sale to the initial slave owners a well-developed pattern of kinship, exogamous mating, and communal values, emphasizing collective survival, mutual aid, cooperation, mutual solidarity, interdependence, and responsibility for others (Nobles, 1974; Blassingame, 1972). These values became the basis for the Black extended family in America. They were retained because they were familiar and they allowed the slaves to have some power over destiny by enabling them to develop their own styles for family interaction. A consciousness of closeness to others, belongingness, and togetherness protected the slave from being psychologically destroyed by feelings of despair and alienation and the extended family provided a vehicle to pass the heritage on to the children

(Fredrickson, 1976; Gutman, 1976). Slaves in essence created their own communal family space, regardless of whether the master was paternalistic or conducted a Nazilike concentration camp.

12   To understand the cultural continuity, it is necessary to depart from the traditional hypothesis that slave masters and their descendants exercised total psychological and social control over the development of Black family life and community institutions. The slaves were much more than empty psychological tablets on which the master imprinted an identity. These early Blacks were able to find ways of creating psychological space and implementing African cultural forms that whites were unaware of and did not understand. Once in the New World the African recreated a sense of tribal community within the plantation milieu through a series of extended kin and kinlike family networks that carried on the cultural values of responsibility for others, mutual aid and collective survival. First- and second-generation American slaves who were separated from biological kin by continued activity at the auction block and newly arriving slaves who were sold to different plantations were incorporated into the extended family structures of existing plantations. It was not essential for the survival of African conceptions of family life that biological or legal kinship ties be maintained. When a people share a philosophy of interdependence and collective survival, persons who are not biologically or legally related can become interwoven into newly created and existing kinlike networks. Cultural patterns once established seem to endure, especially if they work. The extended family survived because it provided Afro-Americans a support system within the context of a shared frame of reference. Along with other African customs and beliefs, an African family identity was passed along to the children as the link between generations through the oral tradition.

13   Once the philosophy of collective survival and interdependence was set into place as the foundation for community living, the extended family evolved through a series of cycles of formation, breakup, and reformation as the slaves who were without the recourse to legal rights to protect kinship structures and conjugal unions were transferred from place to place. Much later, with the beginnings of the Industrial Revolution after the Civil War, the pattern of Black family life based on combinations of kinship and kinlike networks continued, despite the emergence of the nuclear

family among Euro-Americans. The growth of the individual nuclear family in Euro-America seemed to correspond with the competitive and individualistic values of the market place. The cycles of formation, breakup, and reformation of the extended family continued as Blacks migrated farther north and west towards the cities at the turn of the century during the pre and post periods of the two world wars and into the modern age.

14   According to Gutman (1976), who in his extensive studies of the Black family used vital statistics of births, deaths, and conjugal unions kept in plantation ledgers, census bureau statistics, and regional and local population records, the true structure of the Black family only emerges when the Black family is observed over a period of at least two or three generations. It seems to go through four identifiable stages. The phenotypical structure may appear to be different at selected times during the transition periods, but the underlying genotype is one that involves a sense of communalism, interdependence, collective survival, and mutual aid.

15   The first stage, beginning in Africa or with a stable plantation population, involves an extended family composed of biologically related kin who are socially connected with similar groups to form a community. In the second stage the biological kin network becomes scattered as a result of trades or later by successive migrations. During the third stage the remaining individual and newly arriving Blacks come together in a combination of new kinship and kinlike structures. During this period the extended family is being rebuilt through new conjugal unions, marriages between young people, and the arrival of some folks who were members of the original family. In the fourth stage the extended family is completely visible again.

16   The Black extended family, with its grandparents, biological parents, conjugal partners, aunts, uncles, cousins, older siblings, boyfriends, girlfriends and quasi-kin, is an intergenerational group. The members of this three-generation family do not necessarily reside in the same household. Individual households are part of a sociofamilial network that functions like a minicommunity. The members band together to share information, resources, and communal concern (Stack, 1974). There is no central authority, matriarchial or patriarchial. Decisions are made on an equalitarian model with input and outcomes determined by who is available at a given time, who has expertise with reference to a given prob-

lem, and one's prior experience and track record in decision making. This is likely to give some edge to the tribal elders. They are looked up to within the extended family network as resource people and advisors because they have the life experience that is highly valued in the Black community. As in the past, the family is held together over time and across geographical space by a shared experience frame and a common set of values involving interdependence, mutual aid, resilience, communalism, and collective responsibility (Nobles, 1978). These values transcend sex roles and allow both men and women to participate in and contribute to the management of economic resources, child rearing, community activism, and other issues of family life without being categorically restricted on the basis of gender. The fluid distinction between social sex roles offers both men and women in the Black family network the opportunity to emerge as decision makers, influence molders, and household managers.

17   It could be argued that the Black extended family exists and persists primarily because Black people face the common fate of oppressive economic and social conditions, that it exists out of necessity as a way of surviving in an oppressive class system. Politically and economically oppressed people have historically banded together for survival, whether it be in internment camps, labor unions, or women's movements. It would follow from this argument that the Black extended family would disappear as Black people moved up the socioeconomic ladder. Yet the extended family does not appear to be disappearing with rising economic fortunes. McAdoo's (1979) work with upwardly mobile middle and upper-middle class Black families suggest that not only does the extended family model persist when Blacks move up the socioeconomic ladder but the Afro-American values of mutual aid, interdependence, and interconnectedness also remain as the guiding ethos of family existence.

18   Being part of a close-knit extended family group is a vital part of Afro-American life. Wherever Blacks appear in numbers of two or more, whether it be on predominately white college campuses, professional baseball teams, fraternal groups, street corners, storefront churches, automobile factories, or professional conferences, they soon seem to form a quasi-family network, share information and resources, get together, git down, rap, and party. White folks don't know what to make of this. The idea of sharing, close-

ness, and interdependence expressed in sociofamilial groups is so deeply ingrained in the fabric of the Afro-American ethos that it is not likely to give way to the nuclear family with its stress on isolation, competition, and independence. If anything, the traditional nuclear family may be moving toward becoming more like the Afro-American extended family.

19   To the extent that the extended family model represents a more accurate way of categorizing the Black family and capturing its strengths, the question arises as to why generations of the Black ghetto's Euro-American occupation army represented by sociologists, their graduate students, census takers, welfare workers, law-enforcement personnel, and bill collectors could only find broken, disorganized, single-parent, female-dominated families. The answer to this question involves several complex, interrelated reasons.

20   First, white observers may have been guided by a constricted cultural frame of reference where the only viable form of family life consisted of a two-parent family contained within the boundaries of a single household. When they didn't find this single household nuclear family operating in the Black community, their constricted model prevented them from being able to access correctly the differences they observed. They mistakenly labeled differences as deviant, therefore pathological.

21   Second, Black folks themselves have been known to be deceptive about the membership of their families when being questioned by authorities representing the white establishment whom they mistrust, such as law-enforcement personnel, bill collectors, and welfare workers. Given the restrictive nature of the welfare system, it is not hard to imagine why a Black woman would not be truthful to a public assistance worker about the nature of her conjugal relationships, regardless of whether they involve a legal husband, boyfriend, sweet daddy, or transient male friend. Carol Stack (1974) contends that the welfare system as it was traditionally structured worked against the emergence of stable conjugal unions within the extended family.

22   Third, the very nature of white institutions works against the Black extended family as it attempts to fulfill its collective responsibilities and functions within the context of Afro-American values (Nobles, 1978). Wade Nobles, a nationally recognized expert on the Black family, tells a story about moving his nephew, a high

school student, from the boy's mother's residence in Louisiana to his household in Berkeley, California. There were no major psychosocial adjustment problems associated with the nephew's making the transition from the Louisiana branch of the Nobles extended family to the Berkeley, California, branch. The problem came about when Dr. Nobles attempted to explain to the Internal Revenue Service how he came by an adolescent dependent in the space of one year with no legal papers to back him up. If Professor Nobles, who holds a Ph.D. from Stanford University, had difficulty explaining the composition of his extended family with the addition of this adolescent nephew, try to imagine what low-income Black aunties or grandmothers go through when they are trying to get aid for dependent children residing in their household who are not their biological or legal offspring, or for that matter what Black college freshmen go through trying to explain the income of their multiple extended-family parents divided by the number of dependent cousins, siblings, nieces, nephews, and fictional kin to college financial aid officers.

23 Finally, the true nature of the Black family may be clouded by confusing an observation of a phenotype at any given moment with the underlying or basic genotype as the Black family goes through periods of emergence and reemergence. A Black family moving through the rural to urban transition or following jobs from one urban environment to another may at any given observational point, while it is reforming by building new groupings and reestablishing old networks, appear to be a single-parent home, a nuclear family, or a partially developed extended family. All three models can coexist within the core structure and dynamics of the extended family.

24 The Black child growing up in the extended family is exposed to a variety of role models covering a wide age span whose social behaviors are not completely regulated by conventional sex roles. This offers the children a greater opportunity to incorporate a balanced pattern of expressive and instrumental behaviors. Since parents may not be equally effective as role models at every stage of the child's development, the presence of a range of role models allows the children a series of options at any stage of their development in terms of adults they might seek out for guidance. . . .

Conclusion

25   The deficit-deficiency model of Black family life in America represents a case where viewing Black family life through the inappropriate lens of the nuclear family contributed significantly to the perception of pathology and deviance. The emergence of the extended family model as a way of conceptualizing the Black family allows researchers greater freedom to move in the direction of understanding the strengths and coping strategies that the Black family has used to survive through successive cycles of formation and reformation, the family's role in preserving the Black heritage, and the way the supportive family network contributes to the growth and development of its members throughout the life cycle. At the applied level it is essential that social service agencies operating in the Black community reorganize their thinking about what constitutes a family in ways that will facilitate the delivery of a more comprehensive, well-coordinated package of services designed to strengthen the extended family and its support systems, rather than contributing to the breakup of the extended family by using a restrictive system of administrative rules based on the single-parent, subnuclear family.

26   Through discussion groups, workshops, and community forums, Black couples need to be provided with opportunities to look at the impact of cultural values on their relationship strategies, expectations, and goals, and to examine to what extent their values are congruent with the Afro-American ethos of genuineness, mutual aid, and interdependence. Finally, the nature of family life is changing in American society. With the advent of working mothers, rising divorce rates, and changing concepts of psychosexual roles, the family is moving outside the isolated nuclear framework for support systems and resource networks to assist with the concerns of living and child rearing. In developing alternative approaches to cope with the concerns of families in the contemporary era, a great deal can be learned from the cooperative and interdependent strategies that have been successful within the Black extended family.

References

BLASSINGAME, JOHN. *The Slave Community.* New York: Oxford University Press, 1972.

ELKINS, STANLEY. *Slavery: A Problem in American Institutions and Intellectual Life*. Chicago: University of Chicago Press, 1968.

FRAZIER, E. FRANKLIN. *The Negro Family in the United States*. Chicago: University of Chicago Press, 1939.

FREDRICKSON, GEORGE. "The Gutman Report," *The New York Review,* September 30, 1976, pp. 18–22, 27.

GUTMAN, HERBERT. *The Black Family in Slavery and Freedom, 1750–1925*. New York: Vintage Books, 1976.

MCADOO, HARRIET, "Black Kinship," *Psychology Today,* May 1979, pp. 67–69, 79, 110.

MOYNIHAN, DANIEL PATRICK. *The Negro Family: The Case for National Action*. Washington, D.C.: U.S. Government Printing Office, 1965.

NOBLES, WADE. "Africanity: Its Role in Black Families," *The Black Scholar,* June 1974, pp. 10–17.

———. "Toward an Empirical and Theoretical Framework for Defining Black Families," *Journal of Marriage and Family,* November 1978, pp. 679–688.

RAINWATER, LEE. *Behind Ghetto Walls: Black Family Life in a Federal Slum*. Chicago: Aldine, 1970.

ROGERS, DOROTHY. *Adolescence: A Psychological Perspective,* 2nd Edition. Monterey, Calif.: Brooks/Cole, 1978.

STACK, CAROL. *All Our Kin: Strategies for Survival in a Black Community*. New York: Harper & Row, 1974.

Analyzing the Writer's Argument

1. Up until recently what has been the prevailing or traditional view of the African-American family? According to White, what is the new model that some psychologists are offering as a way to view African-American family life of America?
2. What exactly is the "deficit-deficiency model" of African-American family life, and upon what assumptions is this model based? How do the assumptions of the "deficit-deficiency model" differ from those of the "extended family model"?
3. In what ways does the "rigid classification of psychosexual roles in American society" fail to give an accurate understanding or

picture of African-American men and women? In what ways is the African-American community more flexible in terms of social role behaviors based on gender?

4. How does White account for the presence and survival of the extended family structure among African-Americans? Why does he believe that it is necessary to observe African-American families over two or three generations in order to get an accurate picture of the true structure of the African-American family? Explain.

5. When did the nuclear family among Euro-Americans first emerge in America, and how does White explain the growth of the individual nuclear family as an ideal?

6. How does White answer those people who argue that "the Black extended family exists and persists primarily because Black people face the common fate of oppressive economic and social conditions, that it exists out of necessity as a way of surviving in an oppressive class system"? Did you find his counterargument convincing? Why, or why not?

7. How does White account for the fact that for years Euro-Americans "could only find broken, disorganized, single-parent, female-dominated families" in the African-American community? Does his explanation seem reasonable to you? Explain why, or why not.

Exploring the Issues in This Essay

1. At one point in his essay White suggests that "the traditional nuclear family may be moving toward becoming more like the Afro-American extended family." On what is he basing this assessment? Do you agree with his view? Finally, discuss the forces that are present in contemporary society that make the extended family model more attractive or realistic than the nuclear family model.

2. If, as White suggests, American society has been "viewing Black family life through the inappropriate lens of the nuclear family," what damage or injustice has been done to the African-American community? Discuss the implications of White's extended family model for research in the social sciences and for people working with various social service agencies in the African-American community.

Garrison Keillor

My Stepmother, Myself

> *Writer and broadcaster, Garrison Keillor was born in Anoka, Minnesota in 1942. After graduation from the University of Minnesota where he was a disc jockey at the campus radio station, Keillor went East to seek his fortune as a writer of humorous stories. He returned to Minnesota to host a classical music show on public radio when he failed to land a staff position with a major magazine. Keillor continued to write, however, and many of his early essays and stories appeared in* The New Yorker. *He is perhaps best known as the creator and host of "A Prairie Home Companion," the popular National Public Radio show broadcast live from Minnesota from 1974 until 1987. The show featured downhome music and Keillor's storytelling. Most of these humorous and sometimes poignant tales focused on the lives and adventures of the inhabitants of Lake Woebegon, the fictitious town that also serves as the setting for his best-selling books* Lake Woebegon Days *(1985) and* Leaving Home: A Collection of Lake Woebegon Stories *(1987).*
>
> *"My Stepmother, Myself" is taken from Keillor's first book* Happy to Be Here, *a collection of short, often humorous pieces. In this essay he uses parody to poke fun at the prevailing myths about the evil stepmother and our cultural tendency to find a sound psychological "excuse" for any behavior, no matter how "wicked."*

1   Recently in Weeseville, Pennsylvania, a woman was dismissed from her job as a human-resources coordinator and driven over a cliff by an angry mob of villagers carrying flaming torches and hurling sharp rocks after they learned that she was married to a man who had custody of his three children by a previous marriage.

2   In California, soon after her marriage to a prince (her first marriage, his seventh), a woman named Sharon Mittel was shut up in a dungeon under the provisions of that state's Cruel and Un-

natural Parent Act, which allows the immediate imprisonment of a stepparent upon the complaint of a stepchild. The prince's oldest daughter accused Sharon of slapping her. She was later freed after an appeal to a king, but she now faces a long series of tests to prove her innocence, such as finding a tree of pure gold and a seedless grapefruit. She also must answer some riddles.

3   Are these merely two isolated incidents? Or are they, as a new and exhaustive report on stepmothers clearly points out, fairly indicative?

4   "The myth of the evil stepmother is still with us," the report concludes. "Stepmothers are still associated with the words *cruel* and *wicked* which has made them easy targets for torture and banishment as well as severely limiting their employment, particularly in the so-called 'caring' professions such as nursing, social work, and education. The myth that stepmothers use poisons and potions has virtually barred them from the food and drug industries. In general, stepmothers are not only underpaid and underemployed but also feared and despised."

5   How cruel is the typical stepmother?

6   Not very, according to the report, which examines many cases of alleged cruelty and finds almost all of them untrue. "The media have jumped on every little misunderstanding, and have blown it up to outlandish proportions," the reports finds. Recently, three stepdaughters whose relationships with their stepmothers are well known agreed to speak out and set the record straight. Because each has suffered from publicity in the past and is trying to lead as normal a life as possible under the circumstances, only first names will be used.

Snow

7   The story the press told was that I was in a life-threatening situation as a child and that the primary causal factor was my stepmother's envy. I can see now that there were other factors and that *I* didn't giver *her* much reinforcement—but anyway, the story was that I escaped from her and was taken in by dwarves and she found me and poisoned me with an apple and I was dead and the prince fell in love with me and brought me back to life and we

got married, et cetera, et cetera. And that is what *I* believed right up to the day I walked out on him. I felt like I owed my life to Jeff because he had begged the dwarves for my body and carried it away and so the apple was shaken loose from my throat. That's why I married him. Out of gratitude.

8   As I look back on it, I can see that that was a very poor basis for a relationship. I was traumatized, I had been lying in a coffin under glass for *years*, and I got up and married the first guy I laid eyes on. The big prince. My hero.

9   Now I can see how sick our marriage was. He was always begging me to lie still and close my eyes and hold my breath. He could only relate to me as a dead person. He couldn't accept me as a living woman with needs and desires of my own. It is terribly hard for a woman to come to terms with the fact that her husband is a necrophiliac, because, of course, when it all starts, you aren't aware of what's going on—you're dead.

10   In trying to come to terms with myself, I've had to come to terms with my stepmother and her envy of my beauty, which made our relationship so destructive. She was a victim of the male attitude that prizes youth over maturity when it comes to women. Men can't dominate the mature woman, so they equate youth with beauty. In fact, she *was* beautiful, but the mirror (which, of course, reflected that male attitude) presented her with a poor self-image and turned her against me.

11   But the press never wrote the truth about me.

12   Or about the dwarves. All I can say is that they should have been named Dopey, Sleepy, Slimy, Sleazy, Dirty, Disgusting, and Sexist. The fact is that I *knew* the apple was poisoned. For me, it was the only way out.

Gretel

13   When Hansel and I negotiated the sale of book rights to Grimm Bros., he and I retained the right of final approval of the manuscript and agreed to split the proceeds fifty-fifty. We shook hands on it and I thought the deal was set, but then his lawyers put me under a spell, and when I woke up, they had rewritten the contract and the book too! I couldn't believe it! Not only did the new contract

cut me out (under the terms, I was to get ten shiny baubles out of the first fortune the book earned and three trinkets for each additional fortune) but the book was pure fiction.

14   Suddenly he was portrayed as the strong and resourceful one, a regular little knight, and I came off as a weak sister. Dad was shown as a loving father who was talked into abandoning us in the forest by Gladys, our "wicked" stepmother.

15   Nothing could be further from the truth.

16   My brother was a basket case from the moment the birds ate the bread crumbs. He lay down in a heap and whimpered, and I had to slap him a couple times *hard* to make him walk. Now the little wiener makes himself out to be the hero who kept telling me, "Don't cry, Gretel." Ha! The only crying I did was from sheer exhaustion carrying him on my back.

17   As for Dad, he was no bleeding heart. He was very much into the whole woodcutter/peasant/yeoman scene—cockfighting, bull-baiting, going to the village on Saturday to get drunk and watch a garroting or a boiling—don't kid yourself, Gladys couldn't send us to our *rooms* without his say-so. The truth is that he was in favor of the forest idea from the word go.

18   What I can't understand is why they had to lie about it. Many, *many* parents left their children in the forest in those days. It was nothing unusual.

19   Nowadays, we tend to forget that famine can be a very difficult experience for a family. For my parents, ditching the kids was not only a solution, it was an act of faith. They believed that ravens would bring morsels of food in their beaks, or that wolves would take care of the kids, or a frog would, or that the fairies would step in. Dwarves, a hermit, a band of pilgrims, a kindly shepherd, *somebody*. And they were right.

20   And that is why I was never seriously worried for one single moment while we were there. Deep down, I always knew we would make it.

21   I don't mean to say that it wasn't a trying experience, an *emotional* experience. It was. And yet there isn't a single documented case of a child left in the forest who suffered any lasting damage. You look at those children today and you will find they are better people for having gone through it. Except for my brother, that is. The little jerk. He and my father live in luxurious manors with beautiful

tapestries and ballrooms, and I live above an alchemist's shop in a tiny garret they call a condo. As for Gladys, she was kicked out without so much as a property settlement. She didn't even get half of the hut. I guess she is the one who suffered most. Her and the witch.

22   I often think about the witch—I ask myself, Why did I give her the shove? After all, it wasn't me she was after.

23   I guess that, back then, I wasn't prepared to understand her type of militance. I couldn't see that she was fattening up Hansel in order to make a very radical statement. If only I had. Not that I necessarily would have joined her in making that statement, but I would have seen that from her point of view it has validity and meaning.

24   And I would have seen that Gladys, in proposing the forest as a viable alternative, was offering me independence at a very early age.

25   I wish I had been able to thank her.

Cinderella

26   A woman in my position does not find it easy to "come out of the palace," so to speak, and to provide intimate details of her personal life. I do so only because I believe it is time to put the Cinderella myth to rest once and for all—the myth that one can escape housework by marrying a prince.

27   The truth is that I am busier than ever. Supervising a large household staff—cooks, maids, footmen, pages, ladies-in-waiting, minstrels and troubadours, a bard or two—is just plain hard work. Often I find myself longing for the "good old days" when my stepmother made me sweep the hearth.

28   We see each other almost every day—she comes up here and we play tennis or I go down there for lunch—and we often reminisce and laugh about our little disagreements. She is one of my best friends. Other people treat me like royalty but she treats me like a real person. My husband won't let me touch a broom, but I go to her house and she puts me to work! I love it. I tell her, "Mother, you're the only one who yells at me. Don't ever stop." And I mean it. Anger is real. It's honest.

29   Honesty is a rare commodity in a palace, and that is why so many "fairy-tale" marriages end up on the rocks. You wouldn't believe the amount of fawning and flattering that goes on! Between the courtiers bowing and scraping and the supplicants and petitioners wheedling and whining, and the scheming of bishops and barons, not to mention the sorcery and witchcraft, the atmosphere is such that it's terribly hard for a man and a woman to establish a loving, trusting, sharing type of relationship.

30   It's true that we lived happily ever after, but believe me, we have had to work at it!

Analyzing the Writer's Argument

1. Keillor begins his essay with two "real life" situations. Are these examples too farfetched? What attitudes about modern stepmothers do they reveal?

2. What is Keillor's thesis, and what kinds of examples does he use to make his point? What authority, if any, do these examples give to Keillor's argument about stepmother myths?

3. What clues suggest to you that this is not a serious essay? At what point did you begin to suspect Keillor might be kidding? At what point were you sure? What do you think Keillor's purpose is in this essay?

4. The second half of Keillor's essay is devoted to the testimony of three famous stepdaughters. Why does he refer to them by their first names only? What type of jargon does each one of them use? Why? How does their language compare with that in the stories at the beginning of the essay?

5. Keillor seems to be poking fun at much more than just our outrageous distrust of stepmothers. What else is he spoofing? Point to passages in the essay that led you to your conclusions.

6. What is a parody? Is Keillor's essay a parody? If so, what is being parodied and to what end?

7. What is the significance, if any, in Keillor's choice of a title for his essay?

8. Keillor uses a news format for his parody. Does this format lend an air of authenticity to his essay? How has he organized his essay? Why, for example, does he present Snow White's story first and Cinderella's last?

Exploring the Issues in This Essay

1. What myths about "evil" stepmothers does Keillor explode in this essay? What myths can you add to his list? Discuss why you think stepmothers—even more than mothers-in-law and stepfathers—are such easy targets for prejudicial stereotypes. Discuss if any such stereotypes exist for stepchildren.

2. How would you characterize the three celebrity stepmothers in Keillor's essay? What do they have in common? How are they different? Keillor has each of three stepdaughters offer psychological reasons for their stepmother's behavior. What is Keillor's attitude toward these contemporary psychological explanations? How do you feel about such explanations; are they helpful or simply "excuses"?

Barbara Ehrenreich

The "Playboy" Man and the American Family

Born in 1941, Barbara Ehrenreich graduated from Reed College and Rockefeller University, where in 1968 she earned her Ph.D. in biology. She taught courses in women's studies at New York University and State University of New York before launching a career as a writer on women's issues and social policy. Since 1982 Ehrenreich has been a fellow of the Institute for Policy Studies in Washington, D.C., and she is active in the women's movement and the Democratic Socialists of America. A regular contributor to Ms., Mother Jones, Esquire, *and* The New York Times, *she has made several important contributions to the literature of the feminist movement in America. Her books include* For Her Own Good: 150 Years of the Experts' Advice to Women *(1978) with Deirdre English,* The Hearts of Men: American Dreams and the Flight from Commitment *(1983), and* Re-Making Love: The Feminization of Sex *(1986) with Elizabeth Hess and Gloria Jacobs.*

In this essay, which first appeared in Ms. *in June 1983, Ehrenreich answers the charge that feminism has destroyed the family. To rebut this accusation, she traces the history of what she calls the male revolt against marriage starting with the appearance of Hugh Hefner's* Playboy *in 1953.*

1   As a scapegoat for social pathology, feminism ranks with creeping socialism, godless atheism, and other well-known historic threats to public order. We have, in the last decade alone, been accused of causing male impotence, encouraging sexual perversity, and undermining our colorful national tradition of sex roles. In most cases, we're happy to take the credit, but there's one charge that can still make strong women cringe: the accusation that fem-

inism "destroyed the family" or is deeply and wickedly "antifamily" even when we are talking about wholesome domestic issues
like child care for working parents or who folds the clothes.

2   The real issue in the debate over the family, it turns out, is
marriage (heterosexual, monogamous, and so on), and when the
critics charge feminists with being "antifamily," they mean we are
responsible for "broken" homes, the 50 percent divorce rate, un-
wed mothers, and sometimes the entire "me generation."

3   The notion that women, and feminists in particular, have been
waging war on matrimony departs so far from common experience and cultural memory as to deserve the status of whimsy.
True, many women initiate divorces, and not only because their
husbands are drunks and batterers. True, too, that a few brave
women, from Emma Goldman on, have taken a principled stand
against marriage as an unwelcome intrusion of government into
their private lives. But the truth is that if either sex has been in
revolt against marriage, it is men, and that the male revolt against
marriage started long before our own rebellion as feminists.

4   When I was growing up in the 1950s, male hostility to marriage
and the responsibilities of breadwinning was an accepted fact of
life. In the comics, Daisy Mae kept in training all year to catch L'il
Abner on Sadie Hawkins Day, and poor, beaten-down Dagwood
slaved away at the office to keep Blondie supplied with new hats.
From a male perspective, which was pretty much the only one
around, marriage was a "trap" for men and a lifelong sinecure for
women. Even after they were "caught," men tried to escape in
minor ways—into baseball, golf, hunting, bowling, poker games,
or the ideal, female-free world of Westerns.

5   This flight from "maturity," as concerned psychiatrists dubbed
it, is one of the most venerable themes in American literary culture. In American mythic tradition, women are the civilizers and
entrappers; men the footloose adventurers. Our heros chase across
the sea after great white whales, raft down the Mississippi, or ride
off into the sunset on horseback, Cooper's *Deerslayer* traveled light;
Davey Crockett didn't fuss over mortgage payments; and Rip Van
Winkle, not quite so enterprising, went to sleep for 20 years to
escape a nagging wife.

6   But it was in the 1950s that male hostility to marriage began
to take a more urgent and articulate tone. There were low rum-

blings against gray-flannel "conformity"—a code word for male acquiescence to marriage and breadwinning—but in an America that was busily purging itself of Communists, bohemians, and similar deviants, no viable alternative was offered. Until Hugh Hefner's *Playboy*, which began publication in 1953. From the first feature article in the very first issue, *Playboy's* writers railed against "gold-digging women"—wives, ex-wives, and would-be wives—all of them bent on crushing "man's adventurous, freedom-loving spirit." Marriage was an "estate in which the sexes . . . live half-slave and half-free," the slave-half being, of course, the husbands who toiled away while their wives spent their time "relaxing, reading, watching TV, playing cards, socializing. . . ." No man had to put up with this, *Playboy* told its readers: Why sign on for a life contract with one woman when there were so many Bunnies to sample? Why settle for "conformity, togetherness . . . and slow death" when you could have a bachelor apartment, a stereo, and a life of sybaritic thrills? By 1956, nearly a million loyal male readers were getting this manifesto of the male revolt.

7   All this, I emphasize, was going on at a time when there were fewer open feminists in the entire land than there are today in, say, the executive ranks of the Mormon Church. Married women by the thousands felt trapped and desperate too, but they weren't seething with a subversive zeal to "destroy the family" or smash the institution of marriage. In fact, when it came to marriage, Hefner was the radical; Friedan the conservative. Her manifesto of female discontent (*The Feminine Mystique*, published a full 10 years after the first issue of *Playboy*) argued that wider opportunities for women would strengthen marriage, since divorce reflected "the growing aversion and hostility that men have for the feminine millstones hanging around their necks. . . ." Friedan, and most of the feminists who followed, wanted a more equal, companionate marriage; Hefner and his followers simply wanted *out*.

8   There should be no mystery why, over the years, women have had a disproportionate investment in marriage. Women's earnings average out to a little more than $10,000 a year each—nowhere near enough to support a single in a swinging lifestyle, much less a single mother and her children. For most women, the obvious survival strategy has been to establish a claim on some man's more generous wage, i.e., to marry him. For men, on the other hand, as

Playboy's writers clearly saw, the reverse is true: not counting love, home-cooked meals, or other benefits of the married state, it makes more sense for a man to keep his paycheck for himself, rather than sharing it with an underpaid or unemployed woman and her no doubt unemployed children. A recent study by Stanford University sociologist Lenore J. Weitzman suggests the magnitude of men and women's divergent interests: upon divorce, a woman's standard of living falls, on the average, by 73 percent for the first year, while the standard of living of her ex-husband *rises* by 42 percent. For men, the alternative to marriage might be loneliness and TV dinners; for women it is, all too often, poverty.

9   By the standards of the 1950s, today's men are in many respects "free" at last: 7.3 million of them live alone (nearly half of them in the "never married" category) compared to 3.5 million in 1970. (The number of women living alone has also increased, but at a much lower rate, because single women are far more likely to live with children than single men.) If a man remains single until he is 28 or even 38, he may be criticized by girlfriends for his "fear of commitment," but he will no longer be suspected of an unhealthy attachment to his mother or a latent tendency to you-know-what. If he divorces his middle-aged wife for some sweet young thing, he may be viewed not as a traitor to the American way, but as a man who has a demonstrated capacity for "growth."

10   At the risk of sounding "antifamily," I must say that I do not think these changes, and the male revolt that inspired them, are an altogether bad thing. As feminists, we have always stood for men's as well as for women's liberation, which includes their right to be something other than husbands and breadwinners. As my son's mother, I know that I want him to grow up to be a loving and responsible adult, but I also know that it would be heartbreaking to see him "tied down," as the expression goes, to a lifetime of meaningless, uncreative jobs in order to support a family. So my purpose in recalling the recent history of men's revolt is not to say, "So there, blame *them!*"

11   The problem, and it is a big one, is that men may have won their freedom before we win our battle against sexism. Women might like to be free-spirited adventurers too, but the female equivalent of "playboy" does not work well in a culture still riddled with misogyny. We still earn less than men, whether or not we

have men to help support us. Which is only to say that the feminist agenda is as urgent as ever, and those who are concerned about "the family" should remember that we—and our sisters and daughters and mothers—are members of it also.

Analyzing the Writer's Argument

1. According to Ehrenreich, what is the real issue in the debate over family?
2. What is Ehrenreich's thesis in this essay, and where is it stated? What evidence does she provide to illustrate the male revolt against marriage? Did you find any of her examples more credible than the others? Explain.
3. Who is Ehrenreich's audience for this essay? To whom is she referring when she uses *we* in paragraphs 1, 2, and 11?
4. How would you describe Ehrenreich's tone in this essay? Did you think that her tone would be at all offensive to males? Why, or why not?
5. Betty Friedan was one of the early leaders of the women's movement in the late 1950s and early 1960s. In what way does Ehrenreich use Friedan's book *The Feminine Mystique* to further her argument?
6. On what grounds does Ehrenreich argue that "women have had a disproportionate investment in marriage"? Why does she consider today's men to be " 'free' at last"?
7. What is the function of paragraph 10 in the context of Ehrenreich's argument? If her purpose in tracing the history of men's revolt against marriage is not to say, "So there, blame *them*," what is her purpose?
8. Why, according to Ehrenreich, is there no female equivalent of "playboy"? What solution does she hold out for his problem? How did you interpret her closing sentence? Explain.

Exploring the Issues in This Essay

1. In her opening sentence, Ehrenreich claims that "as a scapegoat for social pathology, feminism ranks with creeping socialism, godless atheism, and other well-known historic threats to public order." Is this an exaggeration, or has feminism received more than its share

of bad raps? What has been your experience with feminists and feminism on your campus? Discuss what might be the reasons why people seem willing to blame feminism for any number of social ills during the last ten years.

2. Discuss the institution of marriage. What does traditional marriage have to offer men and women in the 1990s? What are women looking for in marriage today? What do men want from marriage? How do your views of marriage differ from those of your parents? What can two people do to improve the chances that their marriage will succeed?

Writing Suggestions for
*What's Happening to the
American Family?*

1. Both Margaret Mead and George Gallup claim that the American family is in trouble. In fact, they both wonder if the family can survive the pressures that are being exerted upon it today. Are they being alarmists, or are their assessments reasonable? Using materials from the articles in this section, write an essay arguing for or against the proposition that the American family of the 1990s is in desperate straits.

2. The 1980s have been called the "Age of Divorce." Perhaps no other single factor has had as much influence on the shape and definition of American families as divorce has had. Using materials from the essays by George Gallup and Margaret Mead and examples from your own experience or observation, write an essay in which you discuss the likely long-term effects of divorce on family structure, the post-divorce family, or on society at large.

3. How does your lifestyle compare with that of your parents and/or grandparents? What values, customs, and beliefs do you share? On what family issues do you have a difference of opinion? Write an essay in which you discuss the importance of family in preserving a culture's values, customs, and beliefs.

4. Has someone in your immediate family chosen one of the alternative lifestyles discussed by George Gallup, Jr. and Margaret Mead? What have been the effects—good and bad—on you, other members of your family, or your family's friends? In what ways has the person's choice strengthened or weakened relationships within your family? Write an essay in which you argue that such alternative lifestyles are or are not compatible with the notion of family.

5. Write an essay in which you argue that divorce is or is not a real solution to family problems.

6. Is the family unit worth saving? Should people take an active role in trying to preserve the nuclear family, or should the family be left at the mercy of contemporary social forces to adapt if it can? Write an essay in which you defend your position on this issue.

7. George Gallup, Jr. reports that "feminism... appears to exert a destabilizing influence on many traditional familial relationships among husbands, wives, and children." Barbara Ehrenreich, on the other hand, believes that this is just not the case. To what ex-

tent is feminism a factor in the changing American family? Write an essay in which you argue for or against feminism's destabilizing influence on traditional familial relationships.

8. Garrison Keillor exposes some of the widely held myths about stepmothers in "My Stepmother, Myself." In the process he reminds us that it is difficult for any group to escape being stereotyped. Don't myths exist about husbands, old men, wives, mothers-in-law, and teenagers to name just a few? In an essay describe the myths surrounding one of these groups, and then, by means of examples from your own experience or observation, argue for their elimination.

9. Write an essay in which you argue for at least one innovative alternative to the traditional nuclear family as the basic social unit.

10. For Barbara Ehrenreich, "the real issue in the debate over the family . . . is *marriage*. To what extent do think she is right? How do you and your peers feel about life-long commitments? What effect has the high divorce rate and the sexual revolution had on your thoughts about marriage? Write an essay in which you argue for or against the proposition that marriage is obsolete in the 1990s.

11. Using examples from your own experiences or reading, write an essay in which you discuss what for you are the "anti-family" forces present in American society.

12. Write an essay in which you discuss the importance of family for you. What are the benefits that your family gives you? What contributions to your family do you make in return?

13. Proponents of the "deficit-deficiency model" of African-American family life would have us believe that the African-American family is "a disorganized, single-parent, subnuclear, female-dominated social system." Using examples from your own reading or experience, write an essay in which you argue against this characterization.

14. Joseph White summarizes prevailing analyses of African-American family life, interprets how the ideology of an ideal nuclear family influenced these analyses and then offers another perspective. Write an essay in which you summarize and analyze contemporary stereotypes of the family unit in a particular racial or ethnic group. What values on the part of the observer do these stereotypes reveal? Can these family structures be reinterpreted?

3

Racial and
Gender Equality

*We hold these truths to be self-evident, that all men are created
equal, that they are endowed by their Creator with certain
unalienable Rights, that among these are Life, Liberty and the
pursuit of Happiness.*

THOMAS JEFFERSON, *The Declaration of Independence*

While our Declaration of Independence states as a "self-evident
truth" that all are created equal, it never bothers to define *equal*.
What exactly does it mean to be "equal"? For whom is equality
an issue? Should everyone be absolutely equal? Is true equality
even possible in the first place? These are provocative questions
that challenge a person's fundamental beliefs. To deny equality
is almost unthinkable. It doesn't take long to realize that there
are no easy answers to our questions. The subject of equality has
moved philosophers and thinkers alike to passion and eloquence
and reasoning of the highest order.

Equality is one of those seemingly simple concepts such as freedom, happiness, or progress that people think they know. But
definitions of equality always seem to elude us, and just when
we think we've got one, new questions and concerns arise. In his
article "We're Not Really 'Equal,'" economist Thomas Sowell provides some insight into the confusion and controversy surrounding *equal*:

> When we speak of "equal justice under law," we simply mean ap-
> plying the same rules to everybody. That has nothing whatsoever to do
> with whether everyone performs equally. A good umpire calls balls and

strikes by the same rules for everyone, but one batter may get twice as many hits as another.

We are a society that tends to think in terms of winners and losers. Even though we believe that everyone is equal, we also believe that everyone must compete to be the best that he or she can be. And this apparent contradiction is at the heart of the confusion created when equal opportunity does not create equal results.

The history of the present controversy over equality begins with Thomas Jefferson's famous claim about people being created equal. In 1868 the Fourteenth Amendment to the Constitution was ratified. It avows a further article of faith:

> No State shall make or enforce any law which shall abridge the privileges or immunities of citizens of the United States; nor shall any State deprive any person of life, liberty, or property, without due process of law; nor deny to any person within its jurisdiction the equal protection of the laws.

In 1920 the Nineteenth Amendment gave women the right to vote. Three years later Alice Paul of the National Women's party introduced the Equal Rights Amendment (ERA) in Congress. Intended to outlaw discrimination based on sex, the ERA states that "equality of rights under the law shall not be denied or abridged by the United States nor by any State on account of sex." Dormant for almost fifty years after first being introduced, the ERA was reintroduced to Congress in 1970 at the urging of the National Organization for Women. The House of Representatives approved the ERA in 1971, and the Senate followed suit a year later. Even though the deadline for ratification was extended in 1978, the ERA fell 3 states short of the 38 needed for ratification by June 30, 1982.

Although various other pieces of antidiscriminatory legislation have been passed by Congress since 1868, not until the beginning of the civil rights movement in 1957 and particularly the Civil Rights Act of 1964 and the establishment of the Equal Employment Opportunity Commission did prohibitions against discrimination in housing, public commerce, education, and employment become seriously enforceable. Programs and court rulings designed to counteract the ill effects of past discrimination soon followed.

Perhaps President Lyndon B. Johnson best expressed the spirit of so-called affirmative action in an address at Howard University in 1965:

> You do not take a person who, for years, has been hobbled by chains and liberate him, bring him up to the starting line of a race and then say, "you are free to compete with all the others."

This speech and indeed the concept of affirmative action reflect the most positive intentions to correct past injustices, to provide opportunities for the disadvantaged and the historically powerless. But, in its practical consequences, affirmative action can seem to be in conflict with the Fourteenth Amendment and to create a sort of discrimination in reverse. Here the broadest questions about the nature of equality are distilled into a more practical difficulty: when do the concessions granted one group infringe on the rights or the privacy of another, and how should the courts address such problems of enforcement and interpretation?

Our quest for equality has come to touch all aspects of American life and to involve all segments of American society. The subject is one that individuals must approach thoughtfully and without prejudice. Perhaps within our lifetime we'll realize Martin Luther King, Jr.'s dream of a nation where "all of God's children, Black men and white men, Jews and Gentiles, Protestants and Catholics, will be able to join hands and sing in the words of the old Negro spiritual: 'Free at last! Free at last! Thank God Almighty. We are free at last!'"

Martin Luther King, Jr.

I Have a Dream

> *Civil rights leader and 1964 Nobel Peace Prize winner, Martin Luther King, Jr. was born in Atlanta, Georgia, in 1929. King, the son of a Baptist minister, was ordained at the age of eighteen and later earned degrees from Morehouse College, Crozer Theological Seminary, Boston University, and Chicago Theological Seminary. Like India's Gandhi, he advocated the use of nonviolent resistance to achieve equality and racial integration. In 1955 he led a successful boycott against the segregated bus system in Montgomery, Alabama; this marked the beginning of his crusade against racial injustice in America and throughout the world. As the founder and first president of the Southern Christian Leadership Conference, King organized and led many civil rights demonstrations and spoke out against the military draft and the war in Vietnam. America lost a powerful and gifted leader when King was assassinated in Memphis, Tennessee, in 1968.*
>
> *"I Have a Dream," a classic in American oratory, was the keynote address at the March on Washington, August 28, 1963. King delivered his speech from the steps of the Lincoln Memorial to a crowd of more than 300,000 people who had traveled to our nation's capital to demonstrate for civil rights. In this unforgettable sermon, King assesses contemporary society's shortcomings and holds out his vision of what America can be, a vision that provides new inspiration each January when it is commemorated on Martin Luther King, Jr. Day.*

1   I am happy to join with you today in what will go down in history as the greatest demonstration for freedom in the history of our nation.

2   Five score years ago, a great American, in whose symbolic shadow we stand today, signed the Emancipation Proclamation. This momentous decree came as a great beacon light of hope to millions of Negro slaves who had been seared in the flames of

120

withering injustice. It came as a joyous daybreak to end the long night of their captivity. But one hundred years later, the Negro still is not free. One hundred years later, the life of the Negro is still sadly crippled by the manacles of segregation and the chains of discrimination. One hundred years later, the Negro lives on a lonely island of poverty in the midst of a vast ocean of material prosperity. One hundred years later, the Negro is still anguished in the corners of American society and finds himself in exile in his own land. And so we have come here today to dramatize a shameful condition.

3   In a sense we have come to our nation's capital to cash a check. When the architects of our republic wrote the magnificent words of the Constitution and the Declaration of Independence, they were signing a promissory note to which every American was to fall heir. This note was the promise that all men—yes, Black men as well as white men—would be guaranteed the inalienable rights of life, liberty, and the pursuit of happiness.

4   It is obvious today that America has defaulted on this promissory note insofar as her citizens of color are concerned. Instead of honoring this sacred obligation, America has given the Negro people a bad check, a check which has come back marked "insufficient funds." But we refuse to believe that the bank of justice is bankrupt. We refuse to believe that there are insufficient funds in the great vaults of opportunity of this nation; and so we have come to cash this check, a check that will give us upon demand the riches of freedom and the security of justice.

5   We have also come to this hallowed spot to remind America of the fierce urgency of *now*. This is no time to engage in the luxury of cooling off or to take the tranquilizing drug of gradualism. *Now* is the time to make real the promises of democracy. *Now* is the time to rise from the dark and desolate valley of segregation to the sunlit path of racial justice. *Now* is the time to lift our nation from the quicksands of racial injustice to the solid rock of brotherhood. *Now* is the time to make justice a reality for all of God's children.

6   It would be fatal for the nation to overlook the urgency of the moment. This sweltering summer of the Negro's legitimate discontent will not pass until there is an invigorating autumn of freedom and equality. Nineteen Sixty-three is not an end, but a beginning. And those who hope that the Negro needed to blow off steam

and will now be content will have a rude awakening if the nation returns to business as usual. There will be neither rest nor tranquility in America until the Negro is granted his citizenship rights. The whirlwinds of revolt will continue to shake the foundations of our nation until the bright day of justice emerges.

7   But there is something that I must say to my people who stand on the warm threshold which leads into the palace of justice. In the process of gaining our rightful place, we must not be guilty of wrongful deeds. Let us not seek to satisfy our thirst for freedom by drinking from the cup of bitterness and hatred. We must forever conduct our struggle on the high plane of dignity and discipline. We must not allow our creative protest to degenerate into physical violence. Again and again we must rise to the majestic heights of meeting physical force with soul force. And the marvelous new militancy which has engulfed the Negro community must not lead us to a distrust of all white people; for many of our white brothers, as evidenced by their presence here today, have come to realize that their destiny is tied up with our destiny, and they have come to realize that their freedom is inextricably bound to our freedom.

8   We cannot walk alone. And as we walk we must make the pledge that we shall always march ahead. We cannot turn back. There are those who are asking the devotees of civil rights, "When will you be satisfied?" We can never be satisfied as long as the Negro is the victim of the unspeakable horrors of police brutality. We can never be satisfied as long as our bodies, heavy with the fatigue of travel, cannot gain lodging in the motels of the highways and the hotels of the cities. We cannot be satisfied as long as the Negro's basic mobility is from a smaller ghetto to a larger one. We can never be satisfied as long as our children are stripped of their selfhood and robbed of their dignity by signs stating "For Whites Only." We cannot be satisfied as long as the Negro in Mississippi cannot vote and a Negro in New York believes he has nothing for which to vote. No, no, we are not satisfied, and we will not be satisfied until justice roles down like waters and righteousness like a mighty stream.

9   I am not unmindful that some of you have come here out of great trials and tribulations. Some of you have come fresh from narrow jail cells. Some of you have come from areas where your

quest for freedom left you battered by the storms of persecution and staggered by the winds of police brutality. You have been the veterans of creative suffering. Continue to work with the faith that unearned suffering is redemptive.

10   Go back to Mississippi, and go back to Alabama. Go back to South Carolina. Go back to Georgia. Go back to Louisiana. Go back to the slums and ghettos of our Northern cities, knowing that somehow this situation can and will be changed. Let us not wallow in the valley of despair.

11   I say to you today, my friends, even though we face the difficulties of today and tomorrow, I still have a dream. It is a dream deeply rooted in the American dream. I have a dream that one day this nation will rise up and live out the true meaning of its creed: "We hold these truths to be self-evident, that all men are created equal." I have a dream that one day, on the red hills of Georgia, sons of former slaves and the sons of former slave owners will be able to sit down together at the table of brotherhood. I have a dream that one day even the state of Mississippi, a state sweltering with the heat of injustice, sweltering with the heat of oppression, will be transformed into an oasis of freedom and justice. I have a dream that my four little children will one day live in a nation where they will not be judged by the color of their skin, but by the content of their character.

12   I have a dream today. I have a dream that one day down in Alabama—with its vicious racists, with its governor's lips dripping with the words of interposition and nullification—one day right there in Alabama, little Black boys and Black girls will be able to join hands with little white boys and white girls as sisters and brothers.

13   I have a dream today. I have a dream that one day every valley shall be exalted and every hill and mountain shall be made low, the rough places will be made plain and the crooked places will be made straight, and the glory of the Lord shall be revealed, and all flesh shall see it together.

14   This is our hope. This is the faith that I go back to the South with. And with this faith we will be able to hew out of the mountain of despair a stone of hope. With this faith we will be able to transform the jangling discords of our nation into a beautiful symphony of

brotherhood. With this faith we will be able to work together, to play together, to struggle together, to go to jail together, to stand up for freedom together, knowing that we will be free one day.

15   And this will be the day—this will be the day when all of God's children will be able to sing with new meaning:

> My country, 'tis of thee,
> Sweet land of liberty,
>   Of thee I sing;
> Land where my fathers died,
> Land of the Pilgrims' pride,
> From every mountainside
>   Let freedom ring.

And if America is to be a great nation, this must become true.

16   And so let freedom ring from the prodigious hilltops of New Hampshire. Let freedom ring from the mighty mountains of New York. Let freedom ring from the heightening Alleghenies of Pennsylvania. Let freedom ring from the snow-capped Rockies of Colorado. Let freedom ring from the curvaceous slopes of California.

17   But not only that. Let freedom ring from Stone Mountain of Georgia. Let freedom ring from Lookout Mountain of Tennessee. Let freedom ring from every hill and molehill of Mississippi. "From every mountainside let freedom ring."

18   And when this happens—when we allow freedom to ring, when we let it ring from every village and every hamlet, from every state and every city—we will be able to speed up that day when all of God's children, Black men and white men, Jews and Gentiles, Protestants and Catholics, will be able to join hands and sing in the words of the old Negro spiritual: "Free at last! Free at last! Thank God Almighty. We are free at last!"

Analyzing the Writer's Argument

1. To whom does King address his speech? What references in the speech reveal King's sensitivity to the occasion and the immediate experiences of his audience? What is his purpose in addressing these people?

2. How has King organized his speech? Identify the main sections of his speech and explain the purpose of each.
3. King begins the second paragraph with the words "Five score years ago." Why do you suppose he did not simply say "One hundred years ago"? Identify as many of King's references to great American documents and speeches, to the Bible, and to patriotic songs and Negro spirituals as you can. What do these allusions contribute to his speech? What effect would you expect these references to have on King's audience? Explain.
4. In paragraphs 3 and 4 King uses the analogy of the bad check to explain America's treatment of "her citizens of color." Did you find this analogy appropriate and effective? Explain why or why not.
5. King uses parallel constructions and repetition throughout his speech. Explain what these techniques add to the persuasiveness of his argument.
6. According to King, what are the specific grievances of black Americans? To what extent is King setting the agenda for the civil rights movement in 1963 in this speech? Explain.
7. In paragraph 11 King states that his dream is "a dream deeply rooted in the American dream." What exactly is this American dream to which he refers?
8. Explain King's choice of a title. Why does the word "dream" seem particularly appropriate given the context in which the speech was given? What else might he have called his speech?

Exploring the Issues in This Essay

1. Like John F. Kennedy's "Inaugural Address" and Abraham Lincoln's "Gettysburg Address," King's "I Have a Dream" has been acclaimed as one of the truly great speeches delivered by an American; it has lived on beyond the occasion for which it was written. Do you find King's speech deserving of such fame? What qualities of language and thought contribute to its lasting power? What phrases or lines do you find most memorable? Discuss those qualities that great speeches share.
2. Discuss King's assessment of the condition of African Americans in 1963. What changes have occurred in the years following King's speech? What still needs to be done to fulfill King's dream for America? What are the prospects for the future?

Elizabeth Cady Stanton

Declaration of Sentiments and Resolutions

Elizabeth Cady Stanton was an American reformer and an early leader of the women's rights movement. Together with Lucretia Mott, another reformer, she organized the first women's rights convention in the United States. Born in 1815 in Johnstown, New York, Stanton was educated at the all-male Johnstown Academy where she was admitted by special arrangement. An excellent student of Greek, she went on to study at the Troy Female Seminary (now the Emma Willard School) where she graduated in 1832. Later she studied law with her father, a prominent lawyer and judge, but because of her sex she was never able to gain admission to the New York bar. In 1840 shortly after her marriage to the abolitionist Henry B. Stanton, she was denied recognition as a delegate at the World Anti-Slavery Convention in London because she was a woman. As a result of these experiences, she became committed to eliminating the legal restrictions and outright discriminations against women that she saw around her. She also showed a strong interest in both the temperance and abolitionist movements. A lifelong leader in the fight for women's rights, Stanton was elected the first president of a newly formed National American Woman Suffrage Association in 1890. She also coauthored the History of Woman Suffrage *(1881–1896) and* The Woman's Bible *(1895). In 1898 she published* Eighty Years and More, *her reminiscences of a life of championing social reform. Stanton died in New York City in 1902.*

It is perhaps the Seneca Falls Convention held in July 1848 for which Elizabeth Cady Stanton is best remembered. Historians generally agree that this convention formally launched the women's rights movement. Using Thomas Jefferson's "Declaration of Independence" as her model, Stanton wrote her "Declaration of Sentiments and Resolutions," which she read to those attending the Seneca Falls Convention. In her "Declaration" she lists women's grievances against restrictive laws and customs and argues for woman suffrage.

Adopted by the Seneca Falls Convention, July 19–20, 1848

1   When, in the course of human events, it becomes necessary for one portion of the family of man to assume among the people of the earth a position different from that which they have hitherto occupied, but one to which the laws of nature and of nature's God entitle them, a decent respect to the opinions of mankind requires that they should declare the causes that impel them to such a course.

2   We hold these truths to be self-evident: that all men and women are created equal; that they are endowed by their Creator with certain inalienable rights; that among these are life, liberty, and the pursuit of happiness; that to secure these rights governments are instituted, deriving their just powers from the consent of the governed. Whenever any form of government becomes destructive of these ends, it is the right of those who suffer from it to refuse allegiance to it, and to insist upon the institution of a new government, laying its foundation on such principles, and organizing its powers in such form, as to them shall seem most likely to effect their safety and happiness. Prudence, indeed, will dictate that governments long established should not be changed for light and transient causes; and accordingly all experience hath shown that mankind are more disposed to suffer, while evils are sufferable, than to right themselves by abolishing the forms to which they were accustomed. But when a long train of abuses and usurpations, pursuing invariably the same object, evinces a design to reduce them under absolute despotism, it is their duty to throw off such government, and to provide new guards for their future security. Such has been the patient sufferance of the women under this government, and such is now the necessity which constrains them to demand the equal station to which they are entitled.

3   The history of mankind is a history of repeated injuries and usurpations on the part of man toward woman, having in direct object the establishment of an absolute tyranny over her. To prove this, let facts be submitted to a candid world.

4   He has never permitted her to exercise her inalienable right to the elective franchise.

5   He has compelled her to submit to laws, in the formation of which she had no voice.

6   He has withheld from her rights which are given to the most ignorant and degraded men—both natives and foreigners.

7   Having deprived her of this first right of a citizen, the elective franchise, thereby leaving her without representation in the halls of legislation, he has oppressed her on all sides.

8   He has made her, if married, in the eye of the law, civilly dead.

9   He has taken from her all right in property, even to the wages she earns.

10   He has made her, morally, an irresponsible being, as she can commit many crimes with impunity, provided they be done in the presence of her husband. In the covenant of marriage, she is compelled to promise obedience to her husband, he becoming to all intents and purposes, her master—the law giving him power to deprive her of her liberty, and to administer chastisement.

11   He has so framed the laws of divorce, as to what shall be the proper causes, and in case of separation, to whom the guardian-ship of the children shall be given, as to be wholly regardless of the happiness of women—the law, in all cases, going upon a false supposition of the supremacy of man, and giving all power into his hands.

12   After depriving her of all rights as a married woman, if single, and the owner of property, he has taxed her to support a govern-ment which recognizes her only when her property can be made profitable to it.

13   He has monopolized nearly all the profitable employments, and from those she is permitted to follow, she receives but a scanty remuneration. He closes against her all the avenues to wealth and distinction which he considers most honorable to himself. As a teacher of theology, medicine, or law, she is not known.

14   He has denied her the facilities for obtaining a thorough educa-tion, all colleges being closed against her.

15   He allows her in Church, as well as State, but a subordinate position, claiming Apostolic authority for her exclusion from the ministry, and, with some exceptions, from any public participation in the affairs of the Church.

16   He has created a false public sentiment by giving to the world a different code of morals for men and women, by which moral delinquencies which exclude women from society, are not only tolerated, but deemed of little account in man.

17   He has usurped the prerogative of Jehovah himself, claiming it as his right to assign for her a sphere of action, when that belongs to her conscience and to her God.

18   He has endeavored, in every way that he could, to destroy her confidence in her own powers, to lessen her self-respect, and to make her willing to lead a dependent and abject life.

19   Now, in view of this entire disfranchisement of one-half the people of this country, their social and religious degradation—in view of the unjust laws above mentioned, and because women do feel themselves aggrieved, oppressed, and fraudulently deprived of their most sacred rights, we insist that they have immediate admission to all the rights and privileges which belong to them as citizens of the United States.

20   In entering upon the great work before us, we anticipate no small amount of misconception, misrepresentation, and ridicule; but we shall use every instrumentality within our power to effect our object. We shall employ agents, circulate tracts, petition the State and National legislatures, and endeavor to enlist the pulpit and the press in our behalf. We hope this Convention will be followed by a series of Conventions embracing every part of the country.

[The following resolutions were discussed by Lucretia Mott, Thomas and Mary Ann McClintock, Amy Post, Catharine A. F. Stebbins, and others, and were adopted:]

21   Whereas, The great precept of nature is conceded to be, that "man shall pursue his own true and substantial happiness." Blackstone in his Commentaries remarks, that this law of Nature being coeval with mankind, and dictated by God himself, is of course superior in obligation to any other. It is binding over all the globe, in all countries and at all times; no human laws are of any validity if contrary to this, and such of them as are valid, derive all their force, and all their validity, and all their authority, mediately and immediately, from this original; therefore,

22 *Resolved*, That such laws as conflict, in any way, with the true and substantial happiness of woman, are contrary to the great precept of nature and of no validity, for this is "superior in obligation to any other."

23 *Resolved*, That all laws which prevent woman from occupying such a station in society as her conscience shall dictate, or which place her in a position inferior to that of man, are contrary to the great precept of nature, and therefore of no force or authority.

24 *Resolved*, That woman is man's equal—was intended to be so by the Creator, and the highest good of the race demands that she should be recognized as such.

25 *Resolved*, That the women of this country ought to be enlightened in regard to the laws under which they live, that they may no longer publish their degradation by declaring themselves satisfied with their present position, nor their ignorance, by asserting that they have all the rights they want.

26 *Resolved*, That inasmuch as man, while claiming for himself intellectual superiority, does accord to woman moral superiority, it is preeminently his duty to encourage her to speak and teach, as she has an opportunity, in all religious assemblies.

27 *Resolved*, That the same amount of virtue, delicacy, and refinement of behavior that is required of woman in the social state, should also be required of man, and the same transgressions should be visited with equal severity on both man and woman.

28 *Resolved*, That the objection of indelicacy and impropriety, which is so often brought against woman when she addresses a public audience, comes with a very ill-grace from those who encourage, by their attendance, her appearance on the stage, in the concert, or in feats of the circus.

29 *Resolved*, That woman has too long rested satisfied in the circumscribed limits which corrupt customs and a perverted application of the Scriptures have marked out for her, and that it is time she should move in the enlarged sphere which her great Creator has assigned her.

30 *Resolved*, That it is the duty of the women of this country to secure to themselves their sacred right of the elective franchise.

31 *Resolved*, That the equality of human rights results necessarily from the fact of the identity of the race in capabilities and responsibilities.

32   *Resolved, therefore,* That, being invested by·the Creator with the same capabilities, and the same consciousness of responsibility for their exercise, it is demonstrably the right and duty of woman, equally with man, to promote every righteous cause by every righteous means; and especially in regard to the great subjects of morals and religion, it is self-evidently her right to participate with her brother in teaching them, both in private and in public, by writing and by speaking, by any instrumentalities proper to be used, and in any assemblies proper to be held; and this being a self-evident truth growing out of the divinely implanted principles of human nature, any custom or authority adverse to it, whether modern or wearing the hoary sanction of antiquity, is to be regarded as a self-evident falsehood, and at war with mankind.

[At the last session Lucretia Mott offered and spoke to the following resolution:]

33   *Resolved,* That the speedy success of our cause depends upon the zealous and untiring efforts of both men and women, for the overthrow of the monopoly of the pulpit, and for the securing to woman an equal participation with men in the various trades, professions, and commerce.

Analyzing the Writer's Argument

1. Clearly Stanton has modeled her Seneca Falls declaration after Jefferson's "Declaration of Independence." Why do you suppose Stanton wished to associate her movement and its ideas with a document people respect and hold dear? Do you think her strategy was effective? Explain why or why not.
2. What is it that Stanton and the other women at the Seneca Falls Convention wanted to accomplish? You may find it helpful to make a list of their demands.
3. Stanton believes that a woman has an "inalienable right to the elective franchise." What does she mean by "inalienable right"? What is the "elective franchise"? And why is the "elective franchise" so important to her argument?
4. Stanton lists the abuses women suffer in paragraphs 4 through 18. Who is the "He" she refers to in each of these statements?

What is the effect of giving each grievance its own paragraph? Why do you suppose she starts most of these paragraphs with similar phrasing?

5. In paragraph 8 Stanton states that married women are, "in the eye of the law, civilly dead." What does she mean by "civilly dead"?

6. To what audience has Stanton directed her declaration? Point to specific words or phrases in the declaration that led you to this conclusion.

7. How would you describe Stanton's diction in this declaration? Does she use any language that might be considered "feminist"? Explain.

8. The "Declaration of Sentiments and Resolutions" can be roughly divided into two major parts: paragraphs 1–20 and 21–35. What is the main purpose of each part? How has Stanton organized her materials within each part? Finally, what would be lost or gained had the declaration ended with paragraph 20? Explain.

Exploring the Issues in This Essay

1. Make a list of the grievances presented by Stanton in her 1848 declaration. Which grievances, if any, have been resolved? Discuss what work still needs to be done. What new complaints have women voiced in the last three decades?

2. In paragraph 13 Stanton addresses the problems of jobs and pay. What does the job market look like today? Do women have access to professions that were formerly the domain of men? Are there still certain jobs that are filled predominately by women? By men? Do men and women receive equal pay for equal work today? Discuss what needs to be done to ensure more equality in the workplace.

Gloria Steinem

The Importance of Work

> *Gloria Steinem's name has become almost synonymous with the women's movement in this country during the last twenty years. A 1956 graduate of Smith College, she was born in Toledo, Ohio, in 1934. After college she studied in India before launching her multifaceted career as a political activist, lecturer, writer and editor. She is the cofounder of* New York *and* Ms., *two influential popular magazines, and the author of several books including* The Thousand Indias *(1957),* The Beach Book *(1963),* Outrageous Acts and Everyday Rebellions *(1983), and* Marilyn *(1986).*
>
> *For years American women who work outside the home have answered the question of why they work with the ready-made response "Womenworkbecausewehaveto." Gloria Steinem believes that such an answer is wrong-headed, because she believes that work is an inalienable human right. "Why Woman Work" first appeared in the March 1979 issue of* Ms. *and was later collected in* Outrageous Acts and Everyday Rebellions. *Here she argues that women should not be embarrassed when asked: "Why do women work, dear God, why do they work?" She knows that what most women are really thinking is: "Well, sometimes (even when we pretend not to), sometimes (don't say this too loud), sometimes we actually* want *to."*

1   Toward the end of the 1970s, *The Wall Street Journal* devoted an eight-part, front-page series to "the working woman"—that is, the influx of women into the paid-labor force—as the greatest change in American life since the Industrial Revolution.

2   Many women readers greeted both the news and the definition with cynicism. After all, women have always worked. If all the productive work of human maintenance that women do in the home were valued at its replacement cost, the gross national product of the United States would go up by 26 percent. It's just that we are

now more likely than ever before to leave our poorly rewarded, low-security, high-risk job of homemaking (though we're still trying to explain that it's a perfectly good one and that the problem is male society's refusal both to do it and to give it an economic value) for more secure, independent, and better-paid jobs outside the home.

3   Obviously, the real work revolution won't come until all productive work is rewarded—including child rearing and other jobs done in the home—and men are integrated into so-called women's work as well as vice versa. But the radical change being touted by the *Journal* and other media is one part of that long integration process: the unprecedented flood of women into salaried jobs, that is, into the labor force as it has been male-defined and previously occupied by men. We are already more than 41 percent of it—the highest proportion in history. Given the fact that women also make up a whopping 69 percent of the "discouraged labor force" (that is, people who need jobs but don't get counted in the unemployment statistics because they've given up looking), plus an official female unemployment rate that is substantially higher than men's, it's clear that we could expand to become fully half of the national work force by 1990.

4   Faced with this determination of women to find a little independance and to be paid and honored for our work, experts have rushed to ask: "Why?" It's a question rarely directed at male workers. Their basic motivations of survival and personal satisfaction are taken for granted. Indeed, men are regarded as "odd" and therefore subjects for sociological study and journalistic reports only when they *don't* have work, even if they are rich and don't need jobs or are poor and can't find them. Nonetheless, pollsters and sociologists have gone to great expense to prove that women work outside the home because of dire financial need, or if we persist despite the presence of a wage-earning male, out of some desire to buy "little extras" for our families, or even out of good old-fashioned penis envy.

5   Job interviewers and even our own families may still ask salaried women the big "Why?" If we have small children at home or are in some job regarded as "men's work," the incidence of such questions increases. Condescending or accusatory versions of "What's a nice girl like you doing in a place like this?" have not disappeared from the workplace.

6   How do we answer these assumptions that we are "working" out of some pressing or peculiar need? Do we feel okay about arguing that it's as natural for us to have salaried jobs as for our husbands—whether or not we have young children at home? Can we enjoy strong career ambitions without worrying about being thought "unfeminine"? When we confront men's growing resentment of women competing in the work force (often in the form of such guilt-producing accusations as "You're taking men's jobs away" or "You're damaging your children"), do we simply state that a decent job is a basic human right for everybody?

7   I'm afraid the answer is often no. As individuals and as a movement, we tend to retreat into some version of a tactically questionable defense: "Womenworkbecausewehaveto." The phrase has become one word, one key on the typewriter—an economic form of the socially "feminine" stance of passivity and self-sacrifice. Under attack, we still tend to present ourselves as creatures of economic necessity and familial devotion. "Womenworkbecausewehaveto" has become the easiest thing to say.

8   Like most truisms, this one is easy to prove with statistics. Economic need *is* the most consistent work motive—for women as well as men. In 1976, for instance, 43 percent of all women in the paid-labor force were single, widowed, separated, or divorced, and working to support themselves and their dependents. An additional 21 percent were married to men who had earned less than ten thousand dollars in the previous year, the minimum then required to support a family of four. In fact, if you take men's pension, stocks, real estate, and various forms of accumulated wealth into account, a good statistical case can be made that there are more women who "have" to work (that is, who have neither the accumulated wealth, nor husbands whose work or wealth can support them for the rest of their lives) than there are men with the same need. If we were going to ask one group "Do you really need this job?", we should ask men.

9   But the first weakness of the whole "have to work" defense is its deceptiveness. Anyone who has ever experienced dehumanized life on welfare or any other confidence-shaking dependency knows that a paid job may be preferable to the dole, even when the handout is coming from a family member. Yet the will and self-confidence to work on one's own can diminish as dependency and fear increase. That may explain why—contrary to the "have

to" rationale—wives of men who earn less than three thousand dollars a year are actually *less* likely to be employed than wives whose husbands make ten thousand dollars a year or more.

10 Furthermore, the greatest proportion of employed wives is found among families with a total household income of twenty-five to fifty thousand dollars a year. This is the statistical underpinning used by some sociologists to prove that women's work is mainly important for boosting families into the middle or upper middle class. Thus, women's incomes are largely used for buying "luxuries" and "little extras": a neat doublewhammy that renders us secondary within our families, and makes our jobs expendable in hard times. We may even go along with this interpretation (at least, up to the point of getting fired so a male can have our job). It preserves a husbandly ego-need to be seen as the primary breadwinner, and still allows us a safe "feminine" excuse for working.

11 But there are often rewards that we're not confessing. As noted in *The Two-Career Couple,* by Francine and Douglas Hall: "Women who hold jobs by choice, even blue-collar routine jobs, are more satisfied with their lives than are the full-time housewives."

12 In addition to personal satisfaction, there is also society's need for all its members' talents. Suppose that jobs were given out on only a "have to work" basis to both women and men—one job per household. It would be unthinkable to lose the unique abilities of, for instance, Eleanor Holmes Norton, the distinguished chair of the Equal Employment Opportunity Commission. But would we then be forced to question the important work of her husband, Edward Norton, who is also a distinguished lawyer? Since men earn more than twice as much as women on the average, the wife in most households would be more likely to give up her job. Does that mean the nation could do as well without millions of its nurses, teachers, and secretaries? Or that the rare man who earns less than his wife should give up his job?

13 It was this kind of waste of human talents on a society-wide scale that traumatized millions of unemployed or underemployed Americans during the Depression. Then, a one-job-per-household rule seemed somewhat justified, yet the concept was used to displace women workers only, create intolerable dependencies, and waste female talent that the country needed. That Depression experience, plus the energy and example of women who were finally allowed to work during the manpower shortage created by World

War II, led Congress to reinterpret the meaning of the country's full-employment goal in its Economic Act of 1946. Full employment was officially defined as "the employment of those who want to work, without regard to whether their employment is, by some definition, necessary. This goal applies equally to men and to women." Since bad economic times are again creating a resentment of employed women—as well as creating more need for women to be employed—we need such a goal more than ever. Women are again being caught in a tragic double bind: We are required to be strong and then punished for our strength.

14   Clearly, anything less than government and popular commitment to this 1946 definition of full employment will leave the less powerful groups, whoever they may be, in danger. Almost as important as the financial penalty paid by the powerless is the suffering that comes from being shut out of paid and recognized work. Without it, we lose much of our self-respect and our ability to prove that we are alive by making some difference in the world. That's just as true for the suburban woman as it is for the unemployed steel worker.

15   But it won't be easy to give up the passive defense of "weworkbecausewehaveto."

16   When a woman who is struggling to support her children and grandchildren on welfare sees her neighbor working as a waitress, even though that neighbor's husband has a job, she may feel resentful; and the waitress (of course, not the waitress's husband) may feel guilty. Yet unless we establish the obligation to provide a job for everyone who is willing and able to work, that welfare woman may herself be penalized by policies that give out only one public-service job per household. She and her daughter will have to make a painful and divisive decision about which of them gets that precious job, and the whole household will have to survive on only one salary.

17   A job as a human right is a principle that applies to men as well as women. But women have more cause to fight for it. The phenomenon of the "working woman" has been held responsible for everything from an increase in male impotence (which turned out, incidently, to be attributable to medication for high blood pressure) to the rising cost of steak (which was due to high energy costs and beef import restrictions, not women's refusal to prepare the cheaper, slower-cooking cuts). Unless we see a job as part of

every citizen's right to autonomy and personal fulfillment, we will continue to be vulnerable to someone else's idea of what 'need' is, and whose 'need' counts the most.

18 In many ways, women who do not have to work for simple survival, but who choose to do so nonetheless, are on the frontier of asserting this right for all women. Those with well-to-do husbands are dangerously easy for us to resent and put down. It's easier still to resent women from families of inherited wealth, even though men generally control and benefit from that wealth. (There is no Rockefeller Sisters Fund, no J. P. Morgan & Daughters, and sons-in-law may be the ones who really sleep their way to power.) But to prevent a woman whose husband or father is wealthy from earning her own living, and from gaining the self-confidence that comes with that ability, is to keep her needful of that unearned power and less willing to disperse it. Moreover, it is to lose forever her unique talents.

19 Perhaps modern feminists have been guilty of a kind of reverse snobbism that keeps us from reaching out to the wives and daughters of wealthy men; yet it was exactly such women who refused the restrictions of class and financed the first wave of feminist revolution.

20 For most of us, however, "womenworkbecausewehaveto" is just true enough to be seductive as a personal defense.

21 If we use it without also staking out the larger human right to a job, however, we will never achieve that right. And we will always be subject to the false argument that independence for women is a luxury affordable only in good economic times. Alternatives to layoffs will not be explored, acceptable unemployment will always be used to frighten those with jobs into accepting low wages, and we will never remedy the real cost, both to families and to the country, of dependent women and a massive loss of talent.

22 Worst of all, we may never learn to find productive, honored work as a natural part of ourselves and as one of life's basic pleasures.

Analyzing the Writer's Argument

1. What is Steinem's argument and where does she present it?
2. What seems to be the confusion about the phrase "working woman"? Why do you suppose women readers greeted *The Wall Street*

Journal's series on "the working woman" the way they did? According to Steinem, what social problems have been blamed on working women?

3. In answer to the question why they work, Steinem says many women respond defensively by saying "Womenworkbecausewehaveto." What does Steinem achieve by turning the sentence "Women work because we have to" into a single word?

4. What reasons does Steinem give for women resorting to the "have to work" defense when questioned why they work? What weaknesses does Steinem see in this defense?

5. In paragraph 6 Steinem asks several rhetorical questions. How do these questions function in the context of her essay?

6. What for Steinem are the rewards of working? Why does Steinem believe it is important that people recognize that "a job as a human right is a principle that applies to men as well as women"? What evidence does she present to persuade you to her way of thinking?

7. Who is Steinem's intended audience for this essay? What tone does she create by using the pronouns "we" and "our"? Is this tone appropriate for both her subject and her audience? Explain.

8. Why does Steinem believe that it will be difficult for women to relinquish the passive defense of "weworkbecausewehaveto"?

Exploring the Issue in This Essay

1. Consider your feelings about work. Be sure to touch on some of the following questions in your class discussion. What for you is work? What makes some work pleasurable and other work drudgery? Is there any intrinsic value in working? What would you like your life's work to be? Why? Will this work make any demands on you personally? Finally, try to draw some conclusions about your generation's attitudes toward work.

2. If, as Steinem believes, a job is a basic human right, why should "women have more cause to fight for it"? Has it been your experience that women have had to assert their right to work? What's wrong with a society that does not extend this right equally to men and women? What can each one of us do to remedy the situation? Discuss examples from your own experiences or reading that support Steinem's observations about women and work.

Drawing by Moreu, Copyright © 1990 College Press Service.

Judy Brady

Why I Want a Wife

Freelance writer and political activist, Judy Brady was born in San Francisco, California, in 1937. She married in 1960 and two years later was awarded her B.F.A. in painting from the University of Iowa. The mother of two daughters, Brady freelanced as a writer and editor and was active in the women's movement and other political causes. Now an "ex-wife," Brady is back in the San Francisco area working as a secretary. She continues to write on subjects to which she is personally committed. In recent years she has published articles on abortion, U.S. involvement in Central America, the role of women in society, and organizing labor unions.

"Why I Want a Wife" first appeared in the Spring 1971 issue of Ms. *magazine under the writer's married name, Judy Syfers. In using satire and wit to ridicule the unrealistic expectations of a wife, Brady calls into question the conventional social role of women and argues against the unfair distribution of labor in the modern marriage.*

1   I belong to that classification of people known as wives. I am A Wife. And, not altogether incidentally, I am a mother.

2   Not too long ago a male friend of mine appeared on the scene fresh from a recent divorce. He had one child, who is, of course, with his ex-wife. He is obviously looking for another wife. As I thought about him while I was ironing one evening, it suddenly occurred to me that I, too, would like to have a wife. Why do I want a wife?

3   I would like to go back to school so that I can become economically independent, support myself, and, if need be, support those dependent upon me. I want a wife who will work and send me to school. And while I am going to school I want a wife to take care of my children. I want a wife to keep track of the children's doctor and dentist appointments. And to keep track of mine, too. I want a wife to make sure my children eat properly and are kept

141

clean. I want a wife who will wash the children's clothes and keep them mended. I want a wife who is a good nurturant attendant to my children, who arranges for their schooling, makes sure that they have an adequate social life with their peers, takes them to the park, the zoo, etc. I want a wife who takes care of the children when they are sick, a wife who arranges to be around when the children need special care, because, of course, I cannot miss classes at school. My wife must arrange to lose time at work and not lose the job. It may mean a small cut in my wife's income from time to time, but I guess I can tolerate that. Needless to say, my wife will arrange and pay for the care of the children while my wife is working.

4   I want a wife who will take care of *my* physical needs. I want a wife who will keep my house clean. A wife who will pick up after me. I want a wife who will keep my clothes clean, ironed, mended, replaced when need be, and who will see to it that my personal things are kept in their proper place so that I can find what I need the minute I need it. I want a wife who cooks the meals, a wife who is a *good* cook. I want a wife who will plan the menus, do the necessary grocery shopping, prepare the meals, serve them pleasantly, and then do the cleaning up while I do my studying. I want a wife who will care for me when I am sick and sympathize with my pain and loss of time from school. I want a wife to go along when our family takes a vacation so that someone can continue to care for me and my children when I need a rest and change of scene.

5   I want a wife who will not bother me with rambling complaints about a wife's duties. But I want a wife who will listen to me when I feel the need to explain a rather difficult point I have come across in my course of studies. And I want a wife who will type my papers for me when I have written them.

6   I want a wife who will take care of the details of my social life. When my wife and I are invited out by my friends, I want a wife who will take care of the babysitting arrangements. When I meet people at school that I like and want to entertain, I want a wife who will have the house clean, will prepare a special meal, serve it to me and my friends, and not interrupt when I talk about the things that interest me and my friends. I want a wife who will have arranged that the children are fed and ready for bed before

my guests arrive so that the children do not bother us. I want a wife who takes care of the needs of my guests so that they feel comfortable, who makes sure that they have an ashtray, that they are passed the hors d'oeuvres, that they are offered a second helping of the food, that their wine glasses are replenished when necessary, that their coffee is served to them as they like it. And I want a wife who knows that sometimes I need a night out by myself.

7   I want a wife who is sensitive to my sexual needs, a wife who makes love passionately and eagerly when I feel like it, a wife who makes sure that I am satisfied. And, of course, I want a wife who will not demand sexual attention when I am not in the mood for it. I want a wife who assumes the complete responsibility for birth control, because I do not want more children. I want a wife who will remain sexually faithful to me so that I do not have to clutter up my intellectual life with jealousies. And I want a wife who understands that *my* sexual needs may entail more than strict adherence to monogamy. I must, after all, be able to relate to people as fully as possible.

8   If, by chance, I find another person more suitable as a wife than the wife I already have, I want the liberty to replace my present wife with another one. Naturally, I will expect a fresh, new life; my wife will take the children and be solely responsible for them so that I am left free.

9   When I am through with school and have a job, I want my wife to quite working and remain at home so that my wife can more fully and completely take care of a wife's duties.

10   My God, who *wouldn't* want a wife?

Analyzing the Writer's Argument

1. What is the point of Brady's essay? At what point in the essay did her purpose first become apparent? Explain.
2. What categories of wifely duties does Brady create in her description of a wife? What do these duties have in common? Has she failed to include any duties that are stereotypically associated with wives? If so, why do you suppose she has?
3. Although Brady never writes "A wife is . . . ," her essay is one of definition. What for her is a wife? What strategies does she use to define "wife"?

4. In your opinion does the wife Brady describes actually exist? Did you find any of the wife's duties unrealistic? Would you want to be the wife Brady wants? Explain.

5. According to Brady, what kind of man would expect a wife to behave the way her "perfect" wife does? How does the role of the husband differ from that of the wife?

6. Brady concludes paragraph 2 with the question "Why do I want a wife?" How is this question related to the one with which she ends the essay? How do the two questions function in the context of the essay?

7. Explain how Brady uses division and classification to organize her essay. First, what does she divide into specific categories, and then, what does she classify into these categories?

8. How would you describe Brady's tone in this essay? Did you find her tone appropriate for her subject and purpose? Can you surmise from this essay how Brady might have felt about her own role as a wife? Explain why or why not.

9. What is Brady's central argument in this essay? Identify her major premise, minor premise, and conclusion so as to see the syllogistic structure of her basic argument.

Exploring the Issues in This Essay

1. Consider what, if anything, has changed in the nearly twenty years since Brady wrote "Why I Want a Wife." Do you know any women who fit her definition of a wife or who aspire to be just such a wife? Discuss what you think today's men want in a wife, and conversely, what today's women want in a husband.

2. Think for a minute about the roles that each one of us plays each day (daughter, son, sister, brother, student, girlfriend, boyfriend, etc.). Is there one role that you particularly like or dislike? Why? Discuss how our own perceptions of the roles we play often do not coincide with the perceptions that others have of that role. What kinds of problems are created when such differences exist?

Bernard R. Goldberg

Television Insults Men, Too

Journalist and CBS news correspondent Bernard R. Goldberg was born in New York City on March 31, 1945. He grew up in the Bronx and attended high school in New Jersey. Four days after graduating from Rutgers University with a degree in journalism Goldberg joined Associated Press in New York City. In 1972 he joined the CBS news team, first for local television in Miami and later as correspondent in Atlanta and San Francisco. From 1981 through 1987 Goldberg worked as a news correspondent with Dan Rather and the CBS Evening News. Currently he is special correspondent for the CBS program "48 Hours," a news magazine show he has worked with since its inception in January 1988.

In "Television Insults Men, Too," an essay that first appeared on the Op-Ed page of The New York Times *on March 14, 1989, Goldberg strikes out against what he perceives as the new double standard. Using examples from popular television shows and advertisements, he argues against the current wave of men bashing.*

1   It was front page news and it made the TV networks. A mother from Michigan single-handedly convinces some of America's biggest advertisers to cancel their sponsorship of the Fox Broadcasting Company's "Married . . . With Children" because, as she put it, the show blatantly exploits women and the family.

2   The program is about a blue collar family in which the husband is a chauvinist pig and his wife is—excuse the expression—a bimbo.

3   These are the late 1980's, and making fun of people because of their gender—on TV no less, in front of millions of people—is déclassé. Unless, of course, the gender we're ridiculing is the male gender. Then it's O.K.

4   Take "Roseanne." (Please!) It's the season's biggest new hit show, which happens to be about another blue collar family. In this one, the wife calls her husband and kids names.

5   "Roseanne" is Roseanne Barr who has made a career saying such cute things as: "You may marry the man of your dreams, ladies, but 15 years later you are married to a reclining chair that burps." Or to her TV show son: "You're not stupid. You're just clumsy like your daddy."

6   The producer of "Roseanne" does not mince words either: "Men are slime. They say they're going to do 50 percent of the work around the house, but they never do."

7   I will tell you that the producer is a man, which does not lessen the ugliness of the remark. But because his target is men, it becomes acceptable. No one, to my knowledge, is pulling commercials from "Roseanne."

8   In matters of gender discrimination, it has become part of the accepted orthodoxy—of many feminists and a lot of the media anyway—that only women have the right to complain. Men have no such right. Which helps explain why there have been so many commercials ridiculing men—and getting away with it.

9   In the past year or so, I have seen a breakfast cereal commercial showing a husband and wife playing tennis. She is perky and he is jerky.

10   She is a regular Martina Navratilova of the suburbs and he is virtually dead (because he wasn't smart enough to eat the right cereal).

11   She doesn't miss a shot. He lets the ball hit him in the head. If he were black, his name would be Stepin Fetchitt.

12   I have seen a commercial for razor blades that shows a woman in an evening gown smacking a man in a tuxedo across the face, suggesting, I suppose, that the male face takes enough punishment to deserve a nice, smooth shave. If he hit her (an absolutely inconceivable notion, if a sponsor is trying to sell a woman something) he would be a batterer.

13   I have seen an airline commercial showing two reporters from competing newspapers. She's strong and smart. He's a nerd. He says to her: I read your story this morning; you scooped me again. She replies to him: I didn't know you could read.

14　I have seen a magazine ad for perfume showing a business woman patting a businessman's behind as they walk down the street. Ms. Magazine, the Journal of American feminism, ran the ad. The publisher told me there was nothing sexist about it.

15　A colleague who writes about advertising and the media says advertisers are afraid to fool around with women's roles. They know, as she puts it, they'll "set off the feminist emergency broadcast system" if they do. So, she concludes, men are fair game.

16　In 1987, Fred Hayward, who is one of the pioneers of the men's rights movement (yes, there is a men's rights movement) studied thousands of TV and print ads and concluded: "If there's a sleazy character in an ad, 100 percent of the ones that we found were male. If there's an incompetent character, 100 percent of them in the ads are male."

17　I once interviewed Garrett Epps, a scholar who has written on these matters, who told me: "The female executive who is driven, who is strong, who lives for her work, that's a very positive symbol in our culture now. The male who has the same traits—that guy is a disaster: He harms everybody around him; he's cold; he's unfeeling; he's hurtful."

18　The crusading mother from Michigan hit on a legitimate issue. No more cheap shots, she seems to have said. And the advertisers listened. No more cheap shots is what a lot of men are saying also. Too bad nobody is listening to *them*.

Analyzing the Writer's Argument

1. What is Goldberg's thesis, and where does he state it?
2. In paragraphs 4 through 7 Goldberg discusses "Roseanne," television's biggest new hit show in 1989. What point does he make with this example?
3. Goldberg claims that there are many commercials that ridicule men. What evidence does he supply to support this claim? Did you find his evidence convincing? Explain why or why not.
4. Who was Stepin Fetchitt? What does Goldberg gain by comparing the man in the cereal commercial to Stepin Fetchitt?
5. According to Goldberg, why are advertisers "afraid to fool around with women's roles"? Why does he believe that men are now considered "fair game"?

6. What do the statements by Fred Hayward and Garrett Epps contribute to Goldberg's argument? Did these quotes make the argument more persuasive for you? Explain.
7. Goldberg uses the example of the "crusading mother from Michigan" in his introductory paragraphs and again in his conclusion. Did you find this an effective beginning and ending to his argument? Why, why not?

Exploring the Issues in This Essay

1. In preparation for class discussion collect a dozen ads from your local newspapers and/or popular magazines. Analyze them for the way in which they present men and women. Do your ads tend to support Goldberg's claims or refute them? Do the ads for any particular product (cars, cereals, jeans, cigarettes, office equipment, etc.) tend to present a more negative picture of men than ads for other products? Discuss your findings in class.
2. Goldberg claims that "in matters of gender discrimination, it has become part of the accepted orthodoxy—of many feminists and a lot of the media anyway—that only women have the right to complain. Men have no such right." Do you agree with Goldberg's assessment of the current climate surrounding gender discrimination? Discuss the kinds of evidence that would need to argue against Goldberg's position. Be sure to consider his evidence and how you might discredit it.

Bernard E. Anderson

An Economic Defense of Affirmative Action

Born in Philadelphia, Pennsylvania, Bernard E. Anderson has received degrees from Livingstone College, Michigan State University, the University of Pennsylvania, and Shaw University. From 1964 to 1966 he was an economist for the U.S. Bureau of Labor Statistics, and later Anderson served as the director of the Social Sciences Division of the Rockefeller Foundation. Currently he is a senior economist at The Wharton School at the University of Pennsylvania. An active member of the Philadelphia Urban League and the NAACP, Anderson's special research interests involve the impact of economic policies on minorities in America. His books include Black Managers in American Business *(1980),* Youth Employment and Public Policy *(1981), and* The Changing American Economy *(1986).*

"An Economic defense of Affirmative Action" first appeared in the May 1982 issue of Black Enterprise *magazine. In this essay Anderson argues that affirmative action programs are necessary to ensure the continued economic advancement of minorities and women.*

1   Is affirmative action still necessary? Many critics argue that attitudes toward race relations have improved to a substantial degree and that discrimination is no longer a major factor in explaining employment and earnings disparities among minorities and others. According to these critics, economic growth and the expansion of jobs through unregulated, free market processes is all that is required to improve the economic status of minorities.

2   However, the available evidence suggests that just the reverse is true. Much of the progress achieved by minorities and women in some occupations and industries was either the direct result of or was substantially influenced by affirmative action remedies to employment discrimination.

149

Affirmative Action Is Necessary

3   The position of blacks and other minorities in the economy is like that of the caboose on a train. When the train speeds up, the caboose moves faster; when the train slows down, so does the caboose. No matter how fast the train goes, the caboose will never catch up with the engine unless special arrangements are made to change its position. So it is with minorities and the economy: Even during the best of times, there will be no change in the relative position of minorities unless affirmative action or other special measures are taken.

4   Policies designed to improve the relative position of minorities are justified by the continuing evidence of racial inequality in American economic life. In 1980, black unemployment was more than twice that of whites (13.2 percent vs. 6.3 percent). Unemployment among black teenagers, now officially reported at close to 50 percent, has been greater than 30 percent throughout the past decade, but has not reached that level among white youths in any year. Further, the employment/population ratio—for some purposes a more instructive measure of labor market participation than the unemployment rate—has steadily declined among black youths while increasing among whites. About 25 out of every 100 black youths had jobs in 1980, compared with 50 of every 100 whites.

5   Comparative income data also show continuing evidence of economic disparty between blacks and others. In 1979, the average black family had only $57 for every $100 enjoyed by whites. Even in families headed by persons fortunate enough to work year round, blacks have failed to achieve parity, earning only 77 percent of the income of comparable white families.

Effects of Past Discrimination

6   It would be incorrect to say that the continuing presence of such economic inequality is entirely the result of overt or systemic discrimination or that affirmative action alone would improve the economic position of minorities. But there is no question that much of the income and employment disadvantage of blacks and other

minorities reflects the accumulated impact of past discrimination. The continuing presence of many seemingly objective policies in the workplace have also had disproportionately unfavorable effects on the hiring, training and upgrading of minority-group workers. Affirmative action has an important role to play in correcting inequities.

7   In 1969, black workers represented 6.7 percent of the nearly 600,000 employees in the Bell System, mostly black women employed as telephone operators. Only 24 percent of Bell's black employees were in management (compared with 12 percent of whites), 7.2 percent were skilled craftsmen (compared with 26 percent of whites), and less than one percent were in professional jobs (compared with 8 percent of whites).

8   In 1971, the Equal Employment Opportunity Commission (EEOC) charged AT&T and its affiliates with discrimination against minorities and women. In 1975, after prolonged litigation and negotiations, EEOC and AT&T signed a consent decree designed to correct the inequities in the company's employment practices, and to provide back pay to many minority and female employees who had not enjoyed full equal opportunity in the past. In 1979, blacks and other minorities accounted for 14.4 percent of the Bell System's managerial employees, 18.7 percent of the outside craftsmen, 19.1 percent of the inside craftsmen, and 23.3 percent of the sales workers.

9   The consent decree was the catalyst necessary to spur the company toward many positive changes in personnel policies that top management today lauds as beneficial to the firm. The more efficient and equitable personnel selection and assessment system adopted by AT&T and its Bell operating affiliates puts the telephone company in a much stronger position to compete with other firms in the increasingly difficult and complex information systems markets. The experience of AT&T, and other firms specifically identified as subjects for affirmative action enforcement, is instructive for understanding the potential impact of affirmative action on the occupational status of minorities. For purposes of public policy formulation, such evidence may be more useful than inconclusive studies that attempt to show the relationship between affirmative action and minority employment opportunities.

Analyzing the Writer's Argument

1. Anderson starts his essay with the question: "Is affirmative action still necessary?" How does he answer his own question?
2. According to Anderson, what are the main arguments of those who are critical of affirmative action? What kinds of evidence does he provide to counter their objections?
3. In paragraph 3 Anderson uses the analogy of the caboose on a train to explain the position of African Americans and other minorities in the economy. Explain how this analogy works and whether or not you found it persuasive.
4. What evidence does Anderson give to demonstrate "racial inequality in American economic life"? Did you find his evidence convincing? Explain why or why not.
5. Explain how Anderson's example of AT&T illustrates his belief that "Affirmative action has an important role to play in correcting inequalities."
6. What importance does Anderson attach to the experience of AT&T and other firms where affirmative action policies have been enforced? What use can be made of these companies' experiences?

Exploring the Issues in This Essay

1. Many critics of affirmative action charge that it is a policy that "attempts to remedy past discrimination by creating new discrimination." How do you think Anderson would respond to such a charge? How do you respond? In what ways can affirmative action be considered "reverse discrimination"? Does the long-range goal of equal opportunity for minorities and women justify a policy that discriminates against white males today?
2. Suppose that your college has an affirmative action admissions policy, one that requires admissions personnel to make special efforts to recruit and admit students from groups that were formerly excluded. Make a list of the arguments in favor of such a policy and another list of arguments against it. What kinds of evidence would you need to marshal before arguing one side or the other of this issue? Where besides the library might you go on campus to locate the information you would need to argue your position?

Writing Suggestions for
Racial and Gender Equality

1. In an article for *Newsweek* entitled "We're Not Really 'Equal' " the African-American economist and teacher Thomas Sowell argues that "*Equality* is one of the great underfined terms underlying much current controversy and antagonism. This one confused word might even become the rock on which our civilization is wrecked. It should be worth defining." Write an essay in which you define *equality* and show why it is such a troublesome word today.

2. In 1963 Martin Luther King, Jr. had a dream of what America could be. In the more than twenty-five years that have passed since King delivered his famous speech in Washington, D.C., how much of what he envisioned for our country has come to pass? What remains unfulfilled to this day? Write an essay in which you urge your college classmates to rally behind King's vision of America and help bring his dream to reality.

3. Charles Osgood, the noted CBS correspondent, once said, "To hate somebody, to hate them enough to kill them, you must first dehumanize them in your mind. That is why racial and religious epithets are so evil. To call somebody a nigger or a kike or a spic or a wop is to rob a human being of his humanity. It is a form of hate, a form of murder." What racial, religious, and ethnic slurs have you heard? Have you ever been the object of such a slur? How did you feel? Using examples from your reading or experience, write an essay in which you argue against racial, religious, and ethnic slurs by clearly illustrating their dehumanizing effects.

4. Campuses across the country are torn by issues of sexual harassment, institutional racism, homophobia, and cultural diversity. Identify what you believe is the most pressing problem of equality facing students on your campus. Write an article for your school newspaper in which you identify the problem and persuade the campus community that it needs immediate attention.

5. Although progress has been made in the area of civil rights since landmark legislation was first passed in the 1960s, racism still exists in America. What exactly is racism? What do people mean when they talk about "institutional racism"? Is racism a problem on your campus? Write an essay in which you first define racism and then argue for a new course at your college that would help students understand the nature of racism and its effects on both blacks and whites in our country.

153

6. In recent years many studies have shown that both racist and sexist attitudes reveal themselves not only in our everyday talk, but in the language of textbooks, dictionaries, religion, and the media. Spend enough time in the library to learn about sexist (or racist) language and what is being done to eliminate such language from everyday use. Then write an essay in which you argue for or against the continued campaign to eradicate sexism (or racism) from English.

7. Bernard E. Anderson believes that affirmative action has made a difference and that such programs should be supported if minorities and women are to continue to make advances. Write an essay in which you argue that affirmative action programs are no longer needed.

8. Using Judy Brady's essay as a model, write an essay of your own on one of the following: "Why I Want a Husband," "Why I Want a Girlfriend," or "Why I Want a Boyfriend."

9. Write an essay in which you argue for or against Bernard R. Goldberg's claim that current television programs and advertisements openly engage in men bashing.

10. Write an essay in which you argue that your college admissions officers should actively recruit and admit minority students so as to achieve real cultural diversity on campus.

11. In "Why Women Work" Gloria Steinem argues that a decent job is every human being's birthright. Do you think she is being too idealistic or does our country have the obligation to ensure that every citizen that wants a job has one? Write an essay in which you argue that the United States government should (or should not) guarantee every citizen a job.

12. We are now living in the age of what has been dubbed the "two career family." If both partners in a marriage actively pursue careers outside the home, the question of how to divide the household duties immediately arises. Write an essay in which you propose a plan or strategy that a newly married couple could use to share the responsibilities of keeping a home together.

13. Historically, the vast majority of nurses, secretaries, and elementary school teachers have been women. Select one of these three job areas or one of your own choosing, and write an essay in which you argue the advantages of having more men working in these fields.

14. Using Elizabeth Cady Stanton's "Declaration" as a model, write a "Declaration of the Rights of College Students."

4

AIDS and Its Victims

Not since the great plague of the Middle Ages or the outbreak of smallpox among the American Indians has there been a public health crisis of the magnitude and seriousness of AIDS (acquired immune deficiency syndrome). Indeed, some people are already calling it a modern plague. Discovered in 1977 and first recognized in the United States in the early 1980s, AIDS is caused by the human immunodeficiency virus, or HIV virus. The disease attacks and destroys the body's immune system, rendering it incapable of fighting off infection and even certain types of cancer. The World Health Organization estimates that 6 million people worldwide may be infected with the HIV virus and that by the year 2000 the number will reach 15 to 20 million. At this time, 61,000 people in the United States have died from AIDS and, according to a report by the federal General Accounting Office, 480,000 people will have contracted the disease by the end of 1991. Presently, there is no cure for AIDS and no vaccine that can be administered to prevent the disease.

Unlike in the early stages of epidemics of the past, we know how people get AIDS and can take steps to prevent its spread. AIDS is conveyed in four ways: through sexual contact, through needle sharing (among drug users and in impoverished and poorly managed medical facilities), from infected mothers passing it to their fetuses and newborns, and by infected blood and blood products. A person *cannot* get AIDS by touching someone, casual kissing, drinking from someone else's glass, eating food processed by workers in restaurants, toilet seats, or from mosquito or other insect bites.

One can protect oneself from HIV infection and AIDS by avoiding multiple sexual partners, making sure that one's sexual partner is not a carrier or does not have AIDS, avoiding intercourse (vaginal, oral, or anal), using a condom (which reduces risk but does not guarantee protection) to prevent semen from coming into contact with vaginal secretions, and taking care not to share needles or other items (e.g., razors, toothbrushes) that could be contaminated with blood.

One of the most troublesome aspects of the epidemic is that it can be transmitted to others by those that carry the HIV virus and who do not know it. These "healthy carriers," it is now believed, can harbor the HIV virus for up to 12 years without showing any symptoms.

Not surprisingly, as with any major public health crisis, controversy has surrounded the AIDS epidemic. Fear, misinformation, indecisiveness, dismissal, accusations, moral pronouncements, self-righteousness, stigmatization, blame, alienation, prejudice, information, and questions about transmission, care, education, research, testing, and identification are but some of the emotions and issues that people have expressed and debated as people try to cope personally, to determine how best to manage the treatment of victims, and to stem the spread of the dreaded disease. Because AIDS was first associated with homosexuals, intravenous drug users, Haitians, and hemophiliacs who needed blood transfusions, most people saw AIDS as unfortunate but luckily not something that concerned them. For others, AIDS was seen as the moral retribution for being socially deviant, or merely different. For still others, showing compassion, determining how to act humanely and how to affirm the social contract was, and still is, the paramount issue. Concern has widened and heightened, however, as we have learned more about "healthy carriers" and the long latency period of the HIV virus, that it can be transmitted heterosexually, and that it can affect so-called average people—friends and members of one's family. Although a massive research effort is under way to find a cure for AIDS, one is not expected for some time, making it all the more necessary for each of us to be informed, to understand the issues, and to engage in the dialogue.

Bruce Lambert

Even You Can Get It

> *After the* New York Times *had done a number of stories about homosexuals and IV drug users who had contracted AIDS, Carol Gertz called Bruce Lambert at the* Times *and asked him to do a story she felt needed to be told. Her daughter Alison was a heterosexual AIDS victim who had become infected seven years earlier by a one-time sexual partner who has since died of the disease. Lambert was born in Albany, New York, in 1943 and attended Hamilton College before embarking on a career in journalism. After working as a reporter for several New York newspapers covering government and political issues, Lambert began in 1984 to focus on the developing AIDS story. In 1988 he became the first* Times *reporter to be assigned exclusively to cover AIDS.*
>
> *Lambert published his story on March 11 and 12, 1989, in the* Times. *The response to the article was extraordinary. As Lambert says, "We had published first-page stories on AIDS, but even though this one was in Section B, it drew hundreds of letters, phone calls, contributions, and offers of help from around the world." Readers clipped the article and mailed it to friends and relatives, tacked it on college dormitory bulletin boards, called AIDS hotlines and their doctors, warned their children, and reflected on their own sexual histories.*

1   Alison L. Gertz wasn't supposed to get AIDS.

2   She has never injected drugs or had a blood transfusion, and she describes herself as "not at all promiscuous." But she does say she had a single sexual encounter—seven years ago—with a male acquaintance who, she has since learned, has died of AIDS.

3   Though AIDS has hit hardest among gay men and poor intravenous drug users, it also afflicts people like Ms. Gertz.

4   "People think this can't happen to them," she said in an interview at her Manhattan apartment. "I never thought I could have AIDS."

Going Public

5 She is 23 years old, affluent, college-educated and a professional from a prominent family. She grew up on Park Avenue.

6 Now Ms. Gertz and her family are going public because they have a message. A message for heterosexuals who could make a potentially fatal mistake if they dismiss the threat of AIDS. A message for doctors who may miss a diagnosis; she spent three weeks undergoing exhaustive hospital tests for all other conceivable causes of her illness before AIDS was discovered. And a message asking for greater public support on AIDS issues.

7 "I decided when I was in the hospital I would give us much time as I can to help people who are going through this, and warn others of the danger," she said. "I want to make a condom commercial, do speaking engagements, whatever I can.

8 "All the AIDS articles are about homosexuals or poor people on drugs, and unfortunately a lot of people just flip by them," she said. "They think it doesn't apply to them."

9 But she added: "They can't turn the page on me. I could be one of them, or their daughter. They have to deal with this."

10 Statistics show that the number of AIDS cases is rising alarmingly among heterosexuals who get the virus by sharing needles for drugs and then pass it to their sex partners and babies.

11 Although there is no evidence that AIDS is spreading rampantly among other heterosexuals in this country—as it is in Haiti and parts of Africa—cases like Ms. Gertz's do exist. About four percent of all newly reported AIDS cases stem from heterosexual intercourse, and that rate has been remaining steady.

12 New York City has recorded 524 cases in which women got acquired immune deficiency syndrome through sexual intercourse. The men they were with were infected through either drug use or sexual contact with other men. Another 83 cases were of women from Haiti or Africa.

'It Took Only One Time for Me'

13 "I want to talk to these kids who think they're immortal," Ms. Gertz said. "I want to tell them: I'm heterosexual, and it took only one time for me."

14   Ms. Gertz is certain how it happened. "It was one romantic night," she said. "There were roses and champagne and everything. That was it. I only slept with him once."

15   Ms. Gertz has since learned that the man was bisexual and that he has died of AIDS. Had she known his past then, she said, she doubts it would have made a difference. "At that point they weren't publicizing AIDS," she said. "It wasn't an issue then."

16   AIDS is no respecter of wealth or social status. Ms. Gertz is a granddaughter of a founder of the old Gertz department stores in Queens and on Long Island. Her father, Jerrold E. Gertz, is a real-estate executive; her mother, Carol, is the co-founder of Tennis Lady, a national chain of high-fashion shops. Ms. Gertz went to Horace Mann, an exclusive private school in the Bronx, then studied art at Parsons School of Design in Manhattan.

'Probably Just a Bug'

17   When AIDS struck, Ms. Gertz said, "I was just, as they say, starting out in life." Her goals had been simple: "I wanted a house and kids and animals and to paint my paintings.

18   She had recently signed on with an art agent, embarking on a career as an illustrator. She had also quit her pack-a-day smoking habit and joined a health club "to get really healthy," she said.

19   Then fever and a spell of diarrhea hit last summer. A doctor told her it was "probably just a bug," she said. But the symptoms persisted, so she checked into Lenox Hill Hospital.

20   When her doctor told her the diagnosis, he had tears in his eyes. "I said 'Oh, my God. I'm going to die,' " she recalled. "And as I said it, I thought to myself, 'No I'm not. Why am I saying this?' I thought my life was over. 'I'm 22, I'm never going to have sex again. I'm never going to have children.' "

Determined to Keep Going

21   From that initial shock, Ms. Gertz bounced back with the ebullience so well known to her friends—they call her Ali for short—and with the fervor of activism that runs in the family. Recovering from her first treatment, she returned to her apartment, her pets

(a dog, Saki; a cat, Sambucca, and tropical fish) and a new course in life.

22 "It's a dreadful disease, but it's also a gift," she said. "I've always been positive, optimistic. I thought, 'What can I do with it? I like to think I'm here for a purpose. If I die, I would like to have left something, to make the world a little bit better before I go, to help people sick like me and prevent others from getting this. It would make it all worthwhile."

23 She and friends are organizing a fall theater performance and dinner-dance to raise money for an AIDS newsletter and other AIDS services. Her parents and their friends are planning a spring benefit for an organization they are forming called Concerned Parents and Friends for AIDS Research.

24 To keep her functioning normally, Ms. Gertz each day takes AZT, Acyclovir and Bactrim pills, which fight the virus and opportunistic diseases. "We just have to keep her healthy until there's a breakthrough and they find a cure," her mother said.

I Started to Cry Softly

25 "I'm not afraid of death, but I am afraid of pain," Ms. Gertz said. She is learning psychological and behavioral techniques to withstand it, and doctors have promised medication if she needs it. "As far as dying goes, it's okay," she said. "There's no point in thinking about it now."

26 But her frequent high spirits do not erase her pain. While watching a soap opera love scene one day, she said, "I started to cry softly."

27 "I've made a conscious effort not to cry in front of people," she added. "But I do give myself a certain amount of time each month to be miserable, to cry and to vent."

28 Ms. Gertz is an only child. Her illness "was an enormous shock," her father said. "AIDS was the furthest thing from my mind. I used to suspect they magnified the statistics to get research money." Now he's giving and raising money himself and feels "anger at AIDS happening to anyone."

29 "It certainly turned our lives around," Mrs. Gertz said. "It changes your perspective on what's important." For her, every day starts with a morning call to her daughter's apartment, a block away.

30   One of Ms. Gertz's first concerns was not for herself. "I was worried about my previous boyfriends." she said. "I didn't want them to be sick." Two past boyfriends have been tested, she said and "both of them are O.K."

31   Her current boyfriend "is wonderful," she said. "He's stood by me." But AIDS has changed their relationship. "Yes, you can have safe sex. I know all the facts, and so does he. But still, in the back of his mind, he is scared, so we don't sleep together any more, and that's rough."

32   Ms. Gertz has not felt ostracized as many AIDS patents have. But there have been a few exceptions.

33   "The nurses told me this one resident doctor, a woman, insisted that I must have used IV drugs or must have had anal sex," Ms. Gertz said. She interprets the doctor's own possible risk by regarding the patient as different.

Loss of a Friend

34   "And one friend I lost," Ms. Gertz said. "She left. She deserted me." That, too, she understands. "She was with me at Studio 54 during those earlier years, and she was much more sexually active than I was. It wasn't my mortality she was facing; it was her own. She just couldn't handle it."

35   Health insurance is a problem that has made her financially dependent on her parents. "I think the insurance company owes me about $50,000," she said. "I haven't gotten one dime. They're trying to prove I knew I had this before I signed up for the policy two years before."

36   That angers Ms. Gertz because of the dozens of exhaustive, sometimes painful, tests she underwent to find what was wrong.

37   The Gertz family praises the hospital staff and their doctors, but it does regret that AIDS wasn't checked earlier, Mrs. Gertz said, "Because of her background, nobody thought this was a possibility."

38   "It stands to reason you're going to see more people like Ali," her mother said, since AIDS symptoms may not show up for 10 or 12 years.

39   Indeed, such cases are appearing.

40   Dr. Jody Robinson, an internist in Washington who has written on AIDS, said that other cases like Ms. Gertz's are "out there."

41 "How many is a tremendous unknown," he said. "It may not be an overwhelming number, but what will it be five or six years from now?"

42 The danger, he said, is that because experts have said there has not been an explosive outbreak among heterosexuals, people have become complacent.

43 "The common wisdom has gone back to the idea that AIDS is really the gay plague and disease of IV drug users that it was set out to be in the first place, and the warning on heterosexual spread was a false alarm," he said.

44 Ailson Gertz struggles against AIDS with the benefit of a number of factors unknown to most patients–she has a determined optimism bolstered by the love of family and friends, financial aid and first-class medical care.

45 Gathered on a sofa for photographs, the Gertz family was all hugs and smiles. "I never felt from the beginning that this was anything to be hidden or ashamed of," Mrs. Gertz said. After a few pictures were taken, she wondered aloud. "Should we be looking so happy for such a serious subject?"

46 For a few seconds for family managed sober expressions for the camera. But soon, for at least one more day, the smiles broke through again.

Analyzing the Writer's Argument

1. Comment on Lambert's opening sentence. Is it an effective one in your opinion? Why, or why not?
2. What three messages does Alison Gertz hope to deliver? To whom does she hope to deliver these messages? Why?
3. How did Alison Gertz get AIDS? Why would the fact that she has AIDS be surprising to some people? Was it surprising to you?
4. What is significant about the fact that Alison carried the AIDS virus for seven years before being diagnosed as having AIDS?
5. Why does Alison consider her AIDS a "gift"?
6. How long can it take before AIDS symptoms manifest themselves?
7. If the number of people who have become infected with the HIV virus is not very high, why has Alison's case and her example received so much attention?
8. Is this article an argument? Why, or why not? What is Lambert's attitude toward AIDS? How do you know?

Exploring the Issues in This Essay

1. Some radio and television stations at the beginning of the AIDS epidemic refused to air public service announcements regarding the need to use condoms. Some still refuse to air such announcements. Why, do you suppose, have the media not always felt the urgency of the AIDS crisis? Discuss what can be done to convince radio and television stations that they have an obligation to the public and that the risk of AIDS is of far greater importance than any embarrassment or fears that such announcements would encourage promiscuity.

2. Discuss the attitudes and feelings that you and your classmates have concerning AIDS. Do you feel that you know the basic facts about AIDS and how it is transmitted? Do you think that your friends and acquaintances are concerned about AIDS? Have the media done a good job of informing the public: What work still needs to be done, especially on college campuses, to keep people informed, protected, reassured?

Stephen Jay Gould

The Terrifying Normalcy of AIDS

> *Stephen Jay Gould, a paleontologist and writer, has taught geology, biology, and the history of science at Harvard University since 1967. Born in New York City in 1941 and educated at Antioch College and Columbia University, Gould has gained a considerable reputation for his ability to explain scientific theories clearly and concisely. He writes a regular column in* Natural History *magazine and has collected many of his essays in* Ever Since Darwin *(1977),* The Panda's Thumb *(1980),* Hen's Teeth and Horse's Toes *(1983),* The Mismeasure of Man *(1981),* The Flamingo's Smile *(1985), and* An Urchin in the Storm, *among others.*
>
> *In almost all his writings Gould emphasizes the importance of understanding our evolution and our place in biological history. In "The Terrifying Normalcy of AIDS" he argues against the mistaken notion that technology will inevitably solve the AIDS epidemic and that rather than some grave moral pronouncement, "AIDS represents the ordinary workings of biology" and is no less terrifying for that reason. The essay was first published in the* New York Times Magazine, *April 19, 1987.*

1   Disney's Epcot center in Orlando, Fla., is a technological tour de force and a conceptual desert. In this permanent World's Fair, American industrial giants have built their versions of an unblemished future. These masterful entertainments convey but one message, brilliantly packaged and relentlessly expressed: progress through technology is the solution to all human problems. G.E. proclaims from Horizons: "If we can dream it, we can do it." A.T.&T. speaks from on high within its giant golf ball: We are now "unbounded by space and time." United Technologies bubbles from the depths of Living Seas: "With the help of modern technology, we feel there's really no limit to what can be accomplished."

2   Yet several of these exhibits at the Experimental Prototype Community of Tomorrow, all predating last year's space disaster, belie their stated message from within by using the launch of the shuttle as a visual metaphor for technological triumph. The Challenger disaster may represent a general malaise, but it remains an incident. The AIDS pandemic, as issue that may rank with nuclear weaponry as the greatest danger of our era, provides a more striking proof that mind and technology are not omnipotent and that we have not canceled our bond to nature.

3   In 1984, John Platt, a biophysicist who taught at the University of Chicago for many years, wrote a short paper for private circulation. At a time when most of us were either ignoring AIDS, or viewing it as a contained and peculiar affliction of homosexual men, Platt recognized that the limited data on the origin of AIDS and its spread in America suggested a more frightening prospect we are all susceptible to AIDS, and the disease has been spreading in a simple exponential manner.

4   Exponential growth is a geometric increase. Remember the old kiddy problem: if you place a penny on square one of a checkerboard and double the number of coins on each subsequent square—2, 4, 8, 16, 32 . . . —how big is the stack by the 64th square? The answer: about as high as the universe is wide. Nothing in the external environment inhibits this increase, thus giving to exponential processes their relentless character. In the real, noninfinite world, of course, some limit will eventually arise, and the process slows down, reaches a steady state, or destroys the entire system: the stack of pennies falls over, the bacterial cells exhaust their supply of nutrients.

5   Platt noticed that data for the initial spread of AIDS fell right on an exponential curve. He then followed the simplest possible procedure of extrapolating the curve unabated into the 1990's. Most of us were incredulous, accusing Platt of the mathematical gamesmanship that scientists call "curve fitting." After all, aren't exponential models unrealistic? Surely we are not all susceptible to AIDS. Is it not spread only by odd practices to odd people? Will it not, therefore, quickly run its short course within a confined group?

6   Well, hello 1987—worldwide data still match Platt's extrapolated curve. This will not, of course, go on forever. AIDS has probably

already saturated the African areas where it probably originated, and where the sex ratio of afflicted people is 1-to-1, male-female. But AIDS still has far to spread, and may be moving exponentially, through the rest of the world. We have learned enough about the cause of AIDS to slow its spread, if we can make rapid and fundamental changes in our handling of that most powerful part of human biology—our own sexuality. But medicine, as yet, has nothing to offer as a cure and precious little even for palliation.

7 This exponential spread of AIDS not only illuminates its, and our, biology, but also underscores the tragedy of our moralistic misperception. Exponential processes have a definite time and place of origin, an initial point of "inoculation"—in this case, Africa. We didn't notice the spread at first. In a population of billions, we pay little attention when 1 increases to 2, or 8 to 16, but when 1 million becomes 2 million, we panic, even though the *rate* of doubling has not increased.

8 The infection has to start somewhere, and its initial locus may be little more than an accident of circumstance. For a while, it remains confined to those in close contact with the primary source, but only by accident of proximity, not by intrinsic susceptibility. Eventually, given the power and liability of human sexuality, it spreads outside the initial group and into the general population. And now AIDS has begun its march through our own heterosexual community.

9 What a tragedy that our moral stupidity caused us to lose precious time, the greatest enemy in fighting an exponential spread, by downplaying the danger because we thought that AIDS was a disease of three irregular groups of minorities: minorities of life style (needle users), of sexual preference (homosexuals) and of color (Haitians). If AIDS had first been imported from Africa into a Park Avenue apartment, we would not have dithered as the exponential march began.

10 The message of Orlando—the inevitability of technological solutions—is wrong, and we need to understand why.

11 Our species has not won its independence from nature, and we cannot do all that we can dream. Or at least we cannot do it at the rate required to avoid tragedy, for we are not unbounded from time. Viral diseases are preventable in principle, and I suspect that an AIDS vaccine will one day be produced. But how will this discovery avail us if it takes until the millenium, and by then AIDS

has fully run its exponential course and saturated our population, killing a substantial percentage of the human race? A fight against an exponential enemy is primarily a race against time.

12   We must also grasp the perspective of ecology and evolutionary biology and recognize, once we reinsert ourselves properly into nature, that AIDS represents the ordinary workings of biology, not an irrational or diabolical plague with a moral meaning. Disease, including epidemic spread, is a natural phenomenon, part of human history from the beginning. An entire subdiscipline of my profession, paleopathology, studies the evidence of ancient diseases preserved in the fossil remains of organisms. Human history has been marked by episodic plagues. More native peoples died of imported disease than ever fell before the gun during the era of colonial expansion. Our memories are short, and we have had a respite, really, only since the influenza pandemic at the end of World War I, but AIDS must be viewed as a virulent expression of an ordinary natural phenomenon.

13   I do not say this to foster either comfort or complacency. The evolutionary perspective is correct, but utterly inappropriate for our human scale. Yes, AIDS is a natural phenomenon, one of a recurring class of pandemic diseases. Yes, AIDS may run through the entire population, and may carry off a quarter or more of us. Yes, it may make no *biological* difference to Homo sapiens in the long run: there will still be plenty of us left and we can start again. Evolution cares as little for its agents—organisms struggling for reproductive success—as physics cares for individual atoms of hydrogen in the sun. But we care. These atoms are our neighbors, our lovers, our children and ourselves. AIDS is both a natural phenomenon and, potentially, the greatest natural tragedy in human history.

14   The cardboard message of Epcot fosters the wrong attitudes; we must both reinsert ourselves into nature and view AIDS as a natural phenomenon in order to fight properly. If we stand above nature and if technology is all-powerful, then AIDS is a horrifying anomaly that must be trying to tell us something. If so, we can adopt one of two attitudes, each potentially fatal. We can either become complacent, because we believe the message of Epcot and assume that medicine will soon generate a cure, or we can panic in confusion and seek a scapegoat for something so irregular that it must have been visited upon us to teach us a moral lesson.

15 But AIDS is not irregular. It is part of nature. So are we. This should galvanize us and give us hope, not prompt the worst of all responses: a kind of "new-age" negativism that equates natural with what we must accept and cannot, or even should not, change. When we view AIDS as natural, and when we recognize both the exponential property of its spread and the accidental character of its points of entry into America, we can break through our destructive tendencies to blame others and to free ourselves of concern.

16 If AIDS is natural, then there is no *message* in its spread. But by all that science has learned and all the rationality proclaims, AIDS works by a *mechanism*—and we can discover it. Victory is not ordained by any principle of progress, or any slogan of technology, so we shall have to fight like hell, and be watchful. There is no message, but there is a mechanism.

Analyzing the Writer's Argument

1. Why does Gould begin his argument with a discussion of Disney's Epcot Center in Florida? How does his discussion of the technological message of the center figure into his argument?
2. What is Gould arguing for in his essay? What does he want us as readers to do with respect to AIDS, if anything?
3. Why does Gould define the terms "exponential growth" and "geometric increase" in paragraph 4? Do you feel that it was essential for you to have his explanation of these terms? Why, or why not?
4. What, according to Gould, is the greatest enemy in fighting the exponential spread of a disease like AIDS? Why does Gould think that this enemy was allowed to help the spread of AIDS?
5. Gould asserts that "if we stand above nature" with respect to AIDS that we will run the risk of adopting "One of two attitudes, each potentially fatal." What are those two attitudes? Why would they be "fatal"?
6. Assess the kinds of evidence Gould presents in support of his argument? Do you think that his evidence is convincing? Why, or why not?
7. Why does Gould tell us that there is "an entire subdiscipline" of his profession devoted to ancient diseases?
8. Explain Gould's title. Do you think it is an effective title for the essay? Why, or why not?

Exploring the Issues in This Essay

1. While much of the information concerning the AIDS epidemic is factual, there is also much that is myth and relies on perceptions. For example, how do we as Americans regard AIDS? Do you think that the people in other parts of the world see it as we do? How, for example, do the people in Africa afflicted with AIDS perceive the disease? There are some in our society who regard AIDS as a moral retribution for our sins. If you yourself do, why? If you don't, why do you suppose others see it that way?

2. Gould asserts that Epcot fosters the wrong attitudes? What does he mean? He claims that there is a mechanism for the discovery of a cure for AIDS and we will be able to discover it. In your opinion, will AIDS be susceptible to a "technological fix"? Is the mechanism he refers to part of a technological fix? Are you able to judge from the evidence Gould presents? What conditions in our way of life, do you think, have led us Americans always to expect a technological fix to our problems? Have we become the victims of our successes with technology?

William F. Buckley, Jr.

Identify All the Carriers

Best known as an articulate spokesman for the political right, William F. Buckley, Jr. was born in New York City in 1925. Upon graduating from Yale in 1950 Buckley published his first book, God and Man at Yale: The Superstitions of Academic Freedom *(1951). Since then Buckley has been editor-in-chief of* The National Review, *the country's leading conservative publication, has had a syndicated newspaper column, and has been the host of the popular television interview program, "Firing Line." On the show, as with his writings, Buckley exhibits an impressive grasp of pertinent facts as well as an ability to separate overriding principles from topical and practical considerations in the important political and social issues he addresses.*

In "Identify All the Carriers," first published in the New York Times *on March 8, 1986, Buckley argues for identifying all carriers of the AIDS virus. As he says in his concluding sentence, "Our society is generally threatened and in order to fight AIDS, we need the civil equivalent of universal military training."*

1   I have read and listened, and I think now that I can convincingly crystallize the thoughts chasing about in the minds of, first, those whose concern with AIDS victims is based primarily on a concern for them and for the maintenance of the most rigid standards of civil liberties and personal privacy, and, second, those whose anxiety to protect the public impels them to give subordinate attention to the civil amenities of those who suffer from AIDS and primary attention to the safety of those who do not.

2   Arguments used by both sides are sometimes utilitarian, sometimes moral, sometimes a little of each—and almost always a little elusive. Most readers will locate their own inclinations and priorities somewhere other than in the polar positions here put forward by design.

3   School A suspects, in the array of arguments of School B, a venture in ethical opportunism. Look, they say, we have made enormous headway in the matter of civil rights for all, dislodging the straight-laced from mummified positions, they inherited through eclectic superstitions ranging from the Bible's to Freud's. A generation ago, homosexuals lived mostly in the closet. Nowadays they take over cities and parade on Halloween and demand equal rights for themselves qua homosexuals, not merely as apparently disinterested civil libertarians.

4   Along comes AIDS, School A continues, and even though it is well known that the virus can be communicated by infected needles, known also that heterosexuals can transmit the virus, still it is both a fact and the popular perception that AIDS is the special curse of the homosexual, transmitted through anal sex between males. And if you look hard, you will discern that little smirk on the face of the man oh-so-concerned about public health. He is looking for ways to safeguard the public, sure, but he is by no means reluctant, in the course of doing so, to sound an invidious tocsin whose clamor is a call to undo all the understanding so painfully cultivated over a generation by those who have fought for the privacy of their bedroom. What School B is really complaining about is the extension of civil rights to homosexuals.

5   School A will not say all that in words quite so jut-jawed, but it plainly feels that no laws or regulations should be passed that have the effect of identifying the AIDS carrier. It isn't, School A concedes, as if AIDS were transmitted via public drinking fountains. But any attempt to segregate the AIDS carrier is primarily an act of moral ostracism.

6   School B does in fact tend to disapprove forcefully of homosexuality, but tends to approach the problem of AIDS empirically. It argues that acquired immune deficiency syndrome is potentially the most serious epidemic to have shown its face in this century. Summarizing currently accepted statistics, *The Economist* recently raised the possibility "that the AIDS virus will have killed more than 250,000 Americans in eight years' time." Moreover, if the epidemic extended to that point, it would burst through existing boundaries. There would then be "no guarantee that the disease will remain largely confined to groups at special risk, such as homosexuals, hemophiliacs, and people who inject drugs intra-

venously. If AIDS were to spread through the general population, it would become a catastrophe." Accordingly, School B says, we face a utilitarian imperative, and this requires absolutely nothing less than the identification of the million-odd people who, the doctors estimate, are carriers.

7   *How?*

8   Well, the military has taken the first concrete step. Two million soldiers will be given the blood test, and those who have AIDS will be discreetly discharged.

9   *Discreetly, you say!*

10   Hold on. I'm coming to that. You have the military making the first massive move designed to identify AIDS sufferers—and, bear in mind, an AIDS carrier today is an AIDS carrier on the day of his death, which day, depending on the viral strain, will be two years from now or when he is threescore and 10. The next logical step would be to require of anyone who seeks a marriage license that he present himself not only with a Wassermann test but also an AIDS test.

11   *But if he has AIDS, should he then be free to marry?*

12   Only after the intended spouse is advised that her intended husband has AIDS, and agrees to sterilization. We know already of children born with the disease, transmitted by the mother, who contracted it from the father.

13   *What then would School B suggest for those who are not in the military and who do not set out to get a marriage license? Universal testing?*

14   Yes, in stages. But in rapid stages. The next logical enforcer is the insurance company. Blue Cross, for instance, can reasonably require of those who wish to join it a physical examination that requires tests. Almost every American, making his way from infancy to maturity, needs to pass by one or another institutional turnstile. Here the lady will spring out, her right hand on a needle, her left on a computer, to capture a blood specimen.

15   *Is it then proposed by School B that AIDS carriers should be publicly identified as such?*

16   The evidence is not completely in as to the communicability of the disease. But while much has been said that is reassuring, the moment has not yet come when men and women of science are unanimously agreed that AIDS cannot be casually communicated. Let us be patient on that score, pending any tilt in the evidence. If

the news is progressively reassuring, public identification would not be necessary. If it turns in the other direction and AIDS develops among, say, children who have merely roughhoused with other children who suffer from AIDS, then more drastic segregation measures would be called for.

17 *But if the time has not come, and may never come, for public identification, what then of private identification?*

18 Everyone detected with AIDS should be tattooed in the upper forearm, to protect common-needle users, and on the buttocks, to prevent the victimization of other homosexuals.

19 *You have got to be kidding! That's exactly what we suspected all along! You are calling for the return of the Scarlet Letter, but only for homosexuals!*

20 Answer: The Scarlet Letter was designed to stimulate public obloquy. The AIDS tattoo is designed for private protection. And the whole point of this is that we are not talking about a kidding matter. Our society is generally threatened, and in order to fight AIDS, we need the civil equivalent of universal military training.

Analyzing the Writer's Argument

1. Buckley presents his argument in a quasi-debate style. Who is on each side of the debate? What views does each party have? To which side in the debate does Buckley belong?

2. Why do you think that Buckley chose to use A and B to represent the participants in his debate? Does Buckley gain anything by polarizing the arguments into two sides? Does he lose anything?

3. What does side A really fear that side B is after? How does B counter that argument?

4. Explain Buckley's use of the italicized questions and exclamations he uses in his essay. How does this format guide or limit the reader's interaction with the ideas?

5. What is your reaction to the methods Buckley offers for identifying AIDS carriers? What is the essential difference between using tattoos and the Puritans' use of the Scarlet Letter sewn onto the chest of an adulterer?

6. Are there issues to be raised or points to be made that Buckley has not accounted for in his essay? Explain.

7. Are you convinced by Buckley's argument as to the need for identifying AIDS carriers? Why, or why not?

8. How would you characterize Buckley's tone in this essay, calm, scarred, inflexible, conciliatory, reasoned, sure? Compare the one he creates for side A in the opening section with that of side B. Any difference?

Exploring the Issues in This Essay

1. Do you think AIDS carriers should be identified publicly, privately, or not at all? What are the risks to carriers of publicly identifying them? Are the risks of not identifying carriers greater than the risks of identifying as far as you are concerned?

2. AIDS is caused by the human immunodeficiency virus, or as it has come to be called, HIV. Ten to 30 percent of those who test positive for HIV develop AIDS within a five year period of time and the percentage is apparently increasing over time. HIV carriers are the "healthy carriers" because they may not know that they are infected and they may be unaware of the fact that they are transmitting the virus to others. Conservative estimates are that, by the year 2000, 15 to 20 million people will have been infected with the HIV virus. Discuss whether or not this information alters Buckley's case for identifying carriers. In other words, would we be wasting our time identifying carriers if there are many people who are unwittingly passing the virus on to others? Or, should all Americans be tested for the HIV virus and be somehow identified?

3. In the 1940s, the United States suffered under another sexually transmitted disease for which there was no cure: syphilis. Contemporary historians find that the premarital testing for the disease, the Wassermann test, remained relatively ineffective due to an unrealistic conception of marriage and American sexual practices. Argue for or against the feasibility of Buckley's pre-marital testing and sterilization laws in combatting the AIDS virus in contemporary America. Consider factors such as human rights, cost, modern marital and sexual practices as well as the possibility of developing a cure for the virus.

Richard Goldstein

*AIDS and the Social Contract**

Richard Goldstein was born in New York City in 1944 and earned his B.A. in 1965 from Hunter College and his M.S. in 1966 from Columbia University. He has worked in publishing, been an editor for US, *a quarterly magazine, and is now a writer and senior editor at* The Village Voice. *A provocative and engaging writer, Goldstein has written* One in Seven: Drugs on Campus *(1966) and* The Poetry of Rock *(1969).*

In "AIDS and the Social Contract," which first appeared in The Village Voice *on December 29, 1987, Goldstein argues that how we resolve the moral questions concerning the present AIDS epidemic will define who we are and who we hope to be. Because AIDS has the power to divide us as a people, to condemn millions to expendability, we must re-examine the social contract. AIDS, he argues, "demands that we renegotiate the terms, infusing the contract with an expanded sense of equity—and empathy."*

1   The first gay man I knew who died of AIDS did what no human being with a mortal sphincter should have done—or so I told myself. The second was an A-list achiever; he moved in "those circles"—no one who would ever pick me up. So it went. Every time I heard about another death, I would strain to find some basis for a distinction between the deceased and me: He was a clone, a Crisco queen, a midnight sling artist. Then Nathan died of AIDS, and Peter, and Ralph, to whom this piece is dedicated. When it moved in on my friends, the epidemic shattered my presumption of immunity. I, too, was vulnerable, and everything I thought and did about AIDS changed once I faced that fact.

2   Something like this process is going on in what the media call the "general public." There is a secret logic we apply to people with AIDS: they are sick because they are the Other, and they are the Other because they belong to groups that have always been stigmatized. Every now and then, we read about a woman or

---

*Reprinted by permission of the author and *The Village Voice*.

child with AIDS, but usually, they are black—another invitation to Otherness for the general public. The disease has brought all sorts of stigma to the surface, and made the fears that any deviance conjures up seen hyper-real. If anything, AIDS has made society less willing to confront those fears, because they suddenly seem so useful as a way to distinguish between people—and acts—that are "risky" or "safe." Rejecting partners who look like they run with junkies or queers is a lot less threatening than mastering the art of condoms. We would rather rely on stigma to protect us than on precautions that would force us to acknowledge that AIDS is not only among us, but of us.

3   The hot topic in AIDS discussions right now is how efficiently HIV virus can be transmitted during heterosexual intercourse. The medical answer is by no means clear: About a third of the sex partners of infected IV drug users have themselves become infected, but nearly all are women. To date, only six men in New York City have acquired the virus during heterosexual intercourse. Whether this ratio will change over time is anybody's guess. The point is that our sense of who is vulnerable to AIDS is based not on conclusive information about the disease, but on assumptions about its victims. Those who believe AIDS could permeate society tend to see carriers as ordinary people who were infected by specific practices. Any act that spreads the virus is potentially dangerous, regardless of its moral meaning. Those who are convinced the risk is low or nonexistent tend to see these acts, and the people who perform them, as isolated and perverse. Normal people don't do those things, and therefore, they will be spared. On the fringes of this scenario, AIDS is regarded as a natural process of eliminating the abominable.

4   Most of us are rationalists in the streets and moralists in the sheets. We look back on the past, when people flocked to their churches in times of plague, with pity and contempt for those who thought piety would spare them. Yet we act as if only corrupt acts performed by corrupt people can transmit AIDS. What's more, we proceed as if the corrupt and the virtuous never meet in bed. In this incantation of immunity, I hear echoes of my own denial. Every gay man alive is Ishmael, with a tale to tell about the infinite capacity of human beings to deny what they cannot feel or see. But the stigma that surrounds homosexuality makes it hard

for heterosexuals to act as if my witness applies to them. Few of my straight friends are compelled to ponder the question that has haunted me ever since I saw it plastered on a wall in Greenwich Village: "Why him and not me?"

5   That question must always be asked in regard to the sick, and it is never easy to answer. As Susan Sontag has observed, illness is made infinitely harder to bear by its affinity for metaphor. We pity the afflicted and simultaneously shun them, regardless of the actual danger they pose. In times of plague, the entire range of stigma is called into play in the service of public safety, and one is reminded that the word itself first entered our vocabulary as a description of the marks and signs of illness. For medieval Christians, lepers and victims of bubonic plague were literally *stigmatized*. This diagnosis persists in the contemporary notion that many illnesses—from cancer to ulcers—are expressions of a character flaw.

6   If the sick are often stigmatized, they are also, in many cases, dispensable. In the best of times, the temptation to ignore the vital interests of some patients is why we have an elaborate code of medical consent. But when plague strikes, we discover that there are no rights so inalienable that they cannot be subordinated to the greater good. Isolating the infected, which began with leprosy in the Middle Ages, soon became a standard public health measure, and once the concept of latent infection gained acceptance, the quarantine expanded to include anyone who might have been exposed. The pages of Defoe are filled with the howls of those locked up in their homes—healthy people trapped with dying relatives or spouses. Finally, the entire city is stigmatized. Murder is not uncommon, as refugees wander the countryside in search of food and shelter. In the plague zone, all the amenities of death— the rituals of nursing, praying, and memorializing—are sacrificed to the imperatives of corpse disposal. Merrymaking is banned, and the stench of gunpowder and vinegar hangs in the air.

7   So far, our response to AIDS has been governed by the distinctly modern assumption that epidemics can be contained. The periodic demands to crack down on commercial sex notwithstanding, very little has changed about the quality of public life in New York. The suffering of the afflicted, the fear and loathing of the well,

are artfully privatized. Visitors would hardly know that this city is in the grip of a health emergency. Partly, this response reflects the fact that AIDS is a plague in slow motion, and we are witnessing a protracted period of latency with no real idea of how far the infection will extend. But our obliviousness also derives from the conviction that AIDS is a disease of deviants. This image persists because, in America, the virus did initially appear to single out groups—and acts—regarded as contaminating. Many illnesses transform their victims into a stigmatized class, but AIDS is the first epidemic to take stigmatized classes and make them victims. Not even syphilis was so precise.

8   Worse still, AIDS is demonstrably infectious. So carriers are marked both by their Otherness and by the common humanity they are denied. They can infect anyone, though they themselves are infected because they are *not* just anyone. This paradox amplifies the fear and denial that always surround disease. AIDS is not just contagious; it is polluting. To catch this disease is to have your identity stolen; to be lowered, body and soul, into the pit of deviance. This is true even for an "innocent victim," since, once stigma attaches to an illness, it ceases to be about behavior. Anyone with AIDS becomes the Other. And since anyone can be otherized by this disease, deviance itself must be contagious. The most cherished components of personal identity an, irrationally and abruptly, be revoked. This may explain why, though a majority of Americans say they oppose discrimination against people with AIDS, 26 percent of those polled by Gallup last month still fear drinking from a glass or eating food prepared by an infected person. What people fear from casual contact is not so much the disease as its very real power to pollute.

9   Stigma is the reason an AIDS patient in North Carolina, being transferred from one hospital to another, arrived wrapped in a body bag with a small air tube protruding so he could breathe. Stigma is the reason a plane carrying demonstrators to the gay rights march on Washington was fumigated when the passengers departed. Stigma is the reason a social worker in the Bronx must regularly visit a healthy child whose parents have succumbed to AIDS, because no neighbor will comb her hair. All these incidents occurred within the last year—while, the polls tell us, people are becoming more "enlightened" about AIDS. What people are be-

coming enlightened about is transmission modes, but the impact of stigma remains poorly understood.

10   It is rarely mentioned in discussions of AIDS prevention, though the fear of being stigmatized is often the reason infected people have sex without revealing the danger to their partners. It is seldom raised in discussions of testing, though stigma plays a part in determining who will be screened—and why people resist screening in the first place. Stigma has always been a factor in mass detentions; the incarceration of Japanese-Americans during World War II had everything to do with their Otherness. Yet, opponents of proposals to isolate AIDS carriers often argue their case of the less contentious grounds of cost efficiency. To acknowledge that so much of what we fear stems from a conviction that AIDS is a disease of people with "spoiled identities" (Erving Goffman's phrase), would threaten the validity of these categories. So liberals try to separate AIDS the infection from AIDS the stigma, as if, by skirting the issue, they can transcend it. But in fact an unexamined stigma is free to expand.

11   Because it is not an objective condition, but a relationship between the normal and the deviant, stigma ripples out from the reviled to include their families, their friends, their neighborhoods, even the cities where they congregate. Whole zip codes have been marked by some insurance companies as AIDS zones, and when rumors about a famous fashion designer circulated, the concern was whether people would still be seen in clothing that bears his name. The stigma of AIDS has the capacity to reinvigorate ancient stereotypes, not just about sexuality but about race and urbanity. And no city in America is more vulnerable to this conjunction of biases than New York. Half its AIDS cases are among IV drug users, most of them heterosexual and nonwhite. Unless a treatment is found, the death toll in East Harlem and Bed-Stuy will eventually approach what it is today in Kinshasa. As the boundaries of infection extend, more and more of us will live in fear of being stigmatized. And in the end, it won't matter who is actually vulnerable. The entire city will bear the brand of AIDS.

12   And its cost. By 1991, the state health department estimates, one in 10 hospital beds in the city will be occupied by AIDS patients. Some administrators think that figure will be more like one in four—a prospect that terrifies them, since the city's hospitals

are already operating at 90 percent of capacity. Moreover, because so many AIDS patients in New York are IV users, they stay in the hospital longer than people with AIDS in other cities, and their infections are more expensive to treat. These patients are already putting an enormous strain on scarce medical resources. As the gap between supply and demand becomes acute, some form of triage could well emerge, along with violations of privacy, autonomy, and informed consent—concepts of medical ethics that were codified at the Nuremberg trials. The mounting despair of physicians in the face of demands that cannot be met from patients who cannot be saved is bound to affect the practice of medicine for all New Yorkers. The burnout is already leading to an exodus of medical residents and interns—as has often happened in cities besieged by plague.

13   But New York is only the focal point of an epidemic that will soon make its presence felt in every American city. A recent study sponsored by the Centers for Disease Control predicts that, by 1991, the bill for AIDS will be $8.5 billion in medical costs along—more money than is spent on any group of patients except for victims of automobile accidents. By 1991, the "indirect costs," in productivity, of a disease that kills people in their prime will be more than $55 billion—12 percent of the indirect cost of all illnesses. AIDS will be among the top 10 killers of Americans, and the leading killer of people between the ages of twenty-five and forty-four. "People don't seem to realize that, beyond compassion, there's a real self-interest in controlling AIDS, because we don't have the resources to handle this and all the other diseases," says medical ethicist Carol Levine, executive director of the Citizen's Commission on AIDS. "Everyone who gets sick will pay the price for thinking people can be separated."

14   Most of us still think AIDS is happening to someone else. It's not. AIDS is happening to some of us, and in some places, many of us. In the Bronx today, 6 percent of all women over 25 using a prenatal clinic, and 14 percent of all patients who had blood drawn in an emergency room, test positive for antibodies. Are they junkies? Are they faggots? Are they niggers? Are they us?

15   Where epidemics are concerned, the race, class, and sexuality of carriers has always played a major part in how they are cared for, and how dangerous they seem. Isolation, incarceration, the

destruction of whole neighborhoods—all were public health measures practiced in this country, almost exclusively against poor, nonwhite, or sexually disreputable people. AIDS hysteria is a throwback to a politics of public health we thought we'd put behind us—the "purity crusade" that flourished in the early part of this century, constructing the reality of prohibition and the ideal of abstinence. It turns out that the hygiene police have been lying in wait for a crisis like this.

16 One has only to ponder the thundering silence in the Senate whenever Jesse Helms rises to rail about "safe sodomy" to understand that this most social disease has occasioned a most political response. Every plan for prevention, every push for treatment and research funds, is guided by ideological assumptions, not just about the disease but about those who are vulnerable to it. The image of a person with AIDS determines who we think is guilty or innocent, where we fix blame for the epidemic, and whether we support a policy of education and volition or one of regulation and repression. As with all issues that arise from sexual politics, AIDS exhorts the right to fire and the left to platitudes. But beyond these reflexes, it taps our capacity for empathy, and so, AIDS transcends conventional divisions of left and right. *In These Times*, a socialist weekly with a profamily agenda, calls the president's program of routine testing, "by no means unreasonable." Nat Hentoff, an avowed advocate of minority rights, sees AIDS almost entirely as a threat to the majority. Some black activists regard the distribution of condoms as a "genocidal" act. In each case, one could argue that sexual conservatism is the driving force behind a paranoid agenda on AIDS. But C. Everett Koop, a reactionary on abortion, is a progressive on AIDS. Cardinal Kroll of Philadelphia may echo Vatican orthodoxy when he calls this epidemic "an act of vengeance against the sin of homosexuality," but the same tradition can encompass Sister Patrice, director of patient support services of Saint Vincent's, for whom AIDS is "an especially important time to live out reverence of the human being."

17 Where we place ourselves in relation to the stigma surrounding this disease determines what we think is necessary to protect ourselves; whether we think laws are needed to identify, and if necessary, isolate AIDS carriers; whether "innocent" people ought to take risks on their behalf. It isn't the extent of risk but its source that made a judge in California recently rule that a teacher of deaf

children could be removed from the classroom because he carries HIV antibodies. It's the image of the carrier that makes physicians and cops insist on taking extraordinary precautions. In both these cases, people who might ordinarily place themselves in considerable peril shrink from the relatively minor danger posed by those who carry the HIV virus. In some cities, police who risk their lives in pursuit of criminals wear rubber gloves during a gay rights demonstration. At some hospitals, surgeons who run a high risk of contracting hepatitis (a blood-borne virus that infects twenty-five thousand health workers–and kills three hundred– every year) refuse to operate on people with HIV. There's not a single reported case of AIDS being transmitted in the operating room; only doctors and nurses who care for AIDS patients day after day, and lab technicians who are constantly exposed to live virus, have been infected in the line of duty. Nevertheless, Dr. Ronald M. Abel, who has emerged as a spokesman for surgeons refusing to operate on AIDS carriers, calls such "personal, voluntary" decisions into question because they commit not only the physician but "dozens of operating-room assistants...to a high degree of risk." Though no policeman has ever been infected by a suspect, Phil Caruso, present of the Patrolmen's Benevolent Association, urges his members to "do whatever is necessary to protect your life and health in any police situation, be it a shootout or the handling of an AIDS sufferer, each of which is a potentially lethal proposition."

18   Carol Levine calls this refusal to deal with the relatively manageable hazards of AIDS "a disjunction of risk." She maintains that "what people are afraid of is not dying, but what happens before." A cop who is killed rescuing a baby from the ruins of a collapsed building becomes a hero. A doctor who risks his life to treat a victim of radiation poisoning, as happened recently in Brazil, makes the news-weeklies. But the HIV virus invests all its hosts with stigma. Doctors carrying AIDS have lost their practices; a policeman with AIDS could well imagine his peers abandoning him—and his family. Parents told that a classmate with AIDS poses no threat to their children might reason that, even if the children's safety is not at stake, their normalcy is. They may become bearers of a secondary stigma, shunned by other children even more insulated. And for what? "When you voluntarily assume a risk, it fits your self-image," says Levine. "But this is a risk you didn't

bargain for—and it's being brought to you by people you're not crazy about—so it's perceived as unacceptable."

19   Though AIDS has been dehomosexualized in the popular imagination, its origins as a "gay plague" continue to haunt the afflicted—and prevent us from acknowledging that, on a global scale, most people with AIDS are heterosexuals and their children. "What's the hardest thing about getting AIDS?" goes the joke among gay men. "Convincing your mother that you're Haitian." This is a nasty gag about the hierarchy of stigma, but few Haitians would be amused. Each stigma feels like the ultimate injustice, and each oppression seems unique. But the odium attached to race and sexuality actually reflects a single process, whose function is to organize and validate the norm. Anyone can fall prey to such a beast—the "innocent victim" along with the defiled. The irony about health workers demanding that their patients be tested for AIDS antibodies is that it will surely lead to a demand that doctors and nurses take the test—with penalties inevitable for those infected.

20   I was surprised by the anxiety testing provokes in heterosexuals, until I realized that nearly everyone I know has had a relationship with someone who might be infected. In any urban population, most people who take the test pass through a psychic rite that has less to do with fear of death than with the consequences of a positive result: guilt over the past, rage at the present, fear of the future. That fear must include not only the disease but disclosure—and the full range of rejection that might ensue. Yet it is seldom remarked that, for anyone in a vulnerable group, taking the test is an act of enormous courage. The only controversy is over whether such people should be forced to know their antibody status—and in this debate, the anguish of an AIDS "suspect" is easily subordinated to that great equalizer, the common good. Stigma determines whose interests are expendable. "You always assume the test will happen to someone else," says Levine. "Left to their own devices, most people don't want to know."

21   That may be wise. As *The New York Times* recently acknowledged, the potential for inaccuracy in the general population is high enough to make mass-testing a "treacherous paradox." Yet certain populations are expected to bear the uncertainty: soldiers, aliens applying for amnesty, Job Corps enrollees, and in some hospitals where state law permits, candidates for surgery. Just last month, at Jesse Helms's behest, the Senate voted to require all

veterans' hospitals to "mandatorily offer" antibody testing—an interesting euphemism, since patients who refuse the offer would risk being treated like a person with AIDS. (Turning down the test is, in itself, a stigmatizing experience, because it implies that you have reason to suspect . . . you may have had sex with . . . or might even be . . . !) What these groups have in common is not the danger they might pose to others, but the fact that they depend on public institutions. In America, everyone who relies on the government must expect to forfeit some basic rights. As the debate over testing heats up—and it will, once AIDS enters the arena of presidential politics—we may see this psychodrama acted out on other populations stigmatized by their dependence, such as welfare recipients. An old adage must be dusted off in the current crisis: "If you prick us, do we not bleed?"

22   This is the classic response to bigotry. Yet it takes a leap of consciousness to see the connection between one stigma and another. Gay men and IV drug users face each other across a vast behavioral divide. But both cultures are based on behavior—indeed, an act of penetration—deemed illicit. Both deviate from the norms of ecstasy, and invest their deviance with enormous significance, using it to foster intimate bonds and a "lifestyle" with its own slang and gait. Both exist as distinct groups within every class, though the drug culture flourishes in the ghetto, as a gory symbol of its vulnerability, and gay culture is most militant in bourgeois society. Of course, shooting heroin has profound implications for one's health and security, while homosexuality, per se, does not. And the drug culture is a violent, haunted environment. But it *is* a culture, and though we need to keep its damage in mind, we also must wonder how much the antisocial behavior associated with IV use stems from stigma and from the stranglehold of dealers. Freed from both these sources of oppression, the IV user might emerge as a citizen, and we might have to think about what the word "junkie" really conveys.

23   "It seems that some real change in the cultural norms is going to be necessary," says Don Des Jarlais, a behavioral researcher at the State Division of Substance Abuse Services. "Society will have to make a decision that the chance of spreading this virus is so great, and drug users play so crucial a part in that spread, that we

cannot simply allow them to die of AIDS, or make a rule that they must stop using drugs in order *not* to die of AIDS."

24 Rescuing the IV user may involve some of the same techniques that have worked in the gay community. The sharing of needles must be understood in the same context as anal sex—as an ecstatic act that enhances social solidarity. "Within the subculture, the running partner becomes the substitute for family," Des Jarlais writes. "It would be considered a major insult to refuse to use one's partner's works...[or] share one's own works....It would undermine the teamwork and synchronicity of intense experience that are the bases of the running-buddy relationship." One answer is to provide the IV equivalent of a condom: bleach kits or clean needles. Contrary to the assumption that drug users are oblivious to AIDS, Des Jarlais reports that the epidemic is "a topic of 'grave' concern among IV drug users" in several cities, and that they "want to learn how to protect themselves against exposure." Safe injection is as central to the humanistic AIDS agenda as safe sex.

25 Des Jarlais has observed much more ambivalence among drug users than among gay men about discussing AIDS prevention with their sexual partners. It may not be narcissism but fear of abandonment that stands in the way of candor. "Most IV users have their primary relationship with a non-drug-using partner," says Des Jarlais. The dependence for food, shelter, and money—not to mention emotional security—can be intense. "When you have a pair like that, there's no symmetricality of risk. To bring up the subject of AIDS points to the disparity in the relationship. Half the time, the partner using condoms gets abandoned by his female lover. So it's easier to practice safe sex with a casual partner than in a long-term relationship." Surveys have found the same phenomenon among gay men, but the likelihood that either partner could be carrying the virus makes mutual safety part of their bond.

26 Most gay men have other advantages—not just race and class, but organization. One has only to imagine what the response to AIDS would be like if the gay rights movement did not exist. There is no annual parade of drug users down Fifth Avenue, no press that circulates among them, and their advocacy organizations, such as ADAPT, are severely underfunded. This squad of

former and current addicts tours the shooting galleries, dispensing condoms and clean needles. But they are hardly as effective as the *junkiebonden* (drug users' unions) of Holland, because in that country, the need to fight stigma with community is imbedded in both the legal and social service traditions. Organizing IV users may enable their culture to preserve its members by altering the rituals of risk, much as gay men have altered theirs. It may empower users to strike back at oppressive dealers and lobby for access to meaningful treatment. But funding this liberation means overcoming what Des Jarlais calls "an empathy barrier."

27   So far, the support system for people with AIDS has done more to break down this barrier than any church or public agency. About a quarter of the clients at Gay Men's Health Crisis are non-gay, and many groups for "body positives" (as carriers now call themselves) are integrated. But most gay men and IV users still cannot imagine that each other's identities might spring from a shared perspective. As Erving Goffman writes: "Persons with different stigmas are in an appreciably similar situation, and respond in an appreciably similar way." AIDS forces us to confront this commonality. The "innocent" black woman infected by her lover, the gay man whose class has always insulated him, the addict abandoned in a hospital ward—all were victims of stigma before they became victims of disease. And though they may live (and die) in utter contempt for each other's deviations from the norm, they are implicated in each other's fate. What happens to the prostitute can happen to the amateur; what they do to the junkie they can do to the fag.

28 · In a hospital, everyone looks like the Other. An AIDS ward is no different, except that, in a public hospital, it might be filled with black people. I walked through one such ward on assignment, trying not to look too hard at the flesh bundles in the beds. Finally, I took a long peek at a black woman in her late thirties, propped up on pillows, surrounded by tissues and magazines. She had the gaunt intensity that people in the late stages of AIDS often get, as if her entire being were confined to the eyes. I stopped seeing her race and sex, both of which are, in some sense, alien to me. Instead, I saw my lover. She resembled him, not as he was but as he might be if he ever got AIDS. I walked on quickly, struggling to fight the welling up of tears.

29 That night, I dreamt I was leaving my apartment for work. There was a corpse outside the door.

30 "Love," writes Martin Buber, "is responsibility of an I for a thou." In social terms, this suggests that the bond between citizens is as essential to human development as the bond between lovers, or between parent and child. The social contract is a codification of that bond—an agreement to form a government that sustains us. There is a corollary obligation to protect each other, discharged through duties and limits on behavior which we accept as a fair price for the welfare of the community. Without this compact no individual can survive.

31 When a health crisis strikes, Buber's equation becomes demonstrable: the mutual obligation of the infected and the uninfected *is* the responsibility of an I for a thou. As we confront the limits of freedom, the ego becomes collectivized, and the community, an abstraction in ordinary times, becomes the tangible sum of its parts. An ethic of inclusiveness makes personal sacrifice not only bearable, but unremarkable. One simply does what is necessary, because, as Camus writes, "the only means of fighting a plague is common decency."

32 The gay community has gone through just such a process in the face of AIDS. It has reshaped itself to care for its own, and changed behavior once regarded as the mark of liberation. But the boundaries of the gay social contract are tightly drawn, for obvious reasons. The common good has always been enforced at their expense. For homosexuals, "public health" has been a euphemism for stigma. They are among the usual suspects rounded up in panics over sexually transmitted disease. AIDS threatens to revive this tradition of hygiene pogroms on a much more devastating scale. William Buckley's suggestion that people with AIDS be tatooed on the forearm and buttocks to warn the uninfected shows how easily the technocratic imagination can conjure up what Goffman calls a "stigma symbol." Every now and then, someone hatches a gothic variation on Buckley's scheme; the urge to literally stigmatize the infected will not die. A newly published tome called *AIDS in America: Our Chances, Our Choices* recommends "discreet genital tatooing"—just outside the urethra for men, just inside the labia minora for women. Such proposals are always couched in

the rhetoric of reason and equity, as if they would apply to anyone who happened to be infected. But in reality, they can only be enacted on people whose freedom is already precarious. IV users and prostitutes are eminently detainable, and the parole granted homosexuals can easily be revoked.

33   It's a mark of my generation to regard the social contract as fraught with bad faith. But AIDS can't be stopped without a compact among citizens, enforced by the government. It demands that we renegotiate the terms, infusing the contract with an expanded sense of equity—and empathy. "Our best weapon against AIDS," writes Dan Beauchamp, whose book, *The Health of the Republic*, will be published next year [1988 Temple University Press],

> would be a public health policy resting on the right to be different in fundamental choices and the democratic community as 'one body' in matters of the common health. This new policy would mean the right of every individual to fundamental autonomy, as in abortion and sexual orientation, while viewing health and safety as a common good whose protection (through restrictions on liberty) promotes community and the common health.

34   Under a new social contract, we could talk about the limits on personal freedom in a time of plague; the need for vulnerable people to know their antibody status or act as if they are seropositive; the duty to protect your partners and inform others at risk. But saving lives also means setting limits on moralism: confronting the full range of human sexuality, including its expression in the erotics of shooting up; promoting the use of any implement—condoms, needles—that slows the spread of AIDS (if anything, we will have to demand *better* implements); breaking down barriers of sexism that dispose women to infection and men to secrecy.

35   AIDS renders both the liberationist mentality and the moralistic world view obsolete. But so far, only the sexual revolution has been criticized—and in highly moralistic terms. The public health profession has beaten back the most savage proposals for dealing with AIDS, but it is neither powerful enough, nor militant enough, to stand up to political and social conservatism. Ethicists fill monographs with their vision of the social contract, while the

usual bad bargain is forged by church and state. And the epidemic goes on, as sexually transmitted diseases always have—stoked by shame and secrecy.

36   That's the usual progressive objection to stigma. But in the age of AIDS, social justice can't be promoted in purely pragmatic terms. It's too easy to imagine the majority protected by the erotic segregation that pervades American society. The danger is not that AIDS will wipe our species off the planet, but that it will wipe out people most of us already hate—and that is a moral as well as medical crisis. "My worst fear," says Beauchamp, "is not the concentration camps but a kind of paralysis, in which people will just be left to cope." As a professor of public health in Jesse Helms's home state, Beauchamp sees the epidemic not as an incarnation of the Holocaust (with which it is often wrongly compared), but as a "new civil war." The danger for him lies in "splitting off another chunk of the Republic," condemning millions of Americans to expendability. The wages of this sin is not only death, but "a kind of amnesia about who we are and who we want to be."

37   We are haunted by events that expose the gap between who we are and who we want to be. They may happen to other people, but they reveal us to ourselves. Hiroshima and Vietnam are watersheds in our culture because they were moral as well as military conflagrations. These two events shaped my generation. I believe AIDS will define the next.

Analyzing the Writer's Argument

1. In essence, Goldstein argues for us to reaffirm the social contract, but what is the meaning of the term "social contract"? Where, if at all, does Goldstein define the term and explain its importance?
2. Goldstein uses the terms "stigma" and "stigmatized" and uses Erving Goffman's phrase "spoiled identities" in his argument. What is the significance of these terms for Goldstein?
3. Why does Goldstein find it ironic that the police in some cities wear rubber gloves during a gay rights demostration? Is there a difference for the police in being harmed or killed in the line of duty and being accidentally infected by the HIV virus? Explain.

4. What does Goldstein find ironic about the demand of health workers that patients be tested for AIDS antibodies?
5. In paragraph 19, Goldstein refers to a "hierarchy of stigma." What does he mean by the term and why does he feel that it is important?
6. What is Goldstein's response to Buckley's proposal to identify people with AIDS by tattooing them? What does Goldstein see as the link between Buckley's proposal and Goffman's "stigma symbol"?
7. Describe what Goldstein would like to see "under a new social contract." Would you like to see America become the kind of society he envisions? Why, or why not?
8. Goldstein's argument was first published in *The Village Voice*, a liberal publication. Do you think that Goldstein makes the appropriate judgments about his subject and audience for this publication? Do you think that his essay could have appeared just as appropriately in *The New York Times*? Explain.
9. Does Goldstein argue inductively or deductively in this essay? Explain. Is he hoping to persuade us or is he hoping to convince us by reason and logic of the rightness of his views?

Exploring the Issues in This Essay

1. In paragraph 36, Goldstein writes, "The danger is not that AIDS will wipe our species off the planet, but that it will wipe out people most of us already hate—and that is a moral as well as a medical crisis." Discuss the implications of this statement so as to work toward a restatement, in your own words, of the issues he raises in his essay.
2. Discuss whether or not testing for AIDS should be mandatory. What's at risk? What would be gained? What would be lost?
3. Goldstein writes in his final paragraph, "Hiroshima and Vietnam are watersheds in our culture because they were moral as well as military conflagrations. These two events shaped my generation. I believe AIDS will define the next." Discuss the future of the AIDS epidemic as best you can given the evidence in this section, especially the ideas and information provided by Goldstein.

Writing Suggestions for
AIDS and Its Victims

1. Argue that all applicants for a marriage license should be tested for AIDS.

2. Before Alison Gertz was diagnosed as having AIDS, her father is quoted as having said, "I used to suspect that they magnified the statistics to get research money." How much money is the federal government currently spending on AIDS research? Where can you get reliable statistical data? Once you have the necessary information, argue for or against increasing our expenditures.

3. Argue against the tendency of many in our society to stigmatize those who are sick, and especially those that have AIDS. Before beginning to write you may want to review "AIDS and the Social Contract" by Richard Goldstein. It may also be helpful to you to review what sociologist Erving Goffman has to say about stigma in his book by the same title.

4. AIDS. Are we overreacting to the problem? Underreacting to it? Argue your point of view making sure to use appropriate examples, facts, and figures to substantiate your claims.

5. Should AIDS testing be made mandatory? Argue for or against passing laws that would require every citizen to be tested for AIDS.

6. Write an essay in which you argue for or against passing laws to require that the sexual partners of AIDS carriers be traced and notified that they may be HIV positive.

7. A number of programs to provide clean, safe IV needles to drug users in an effort to stop the spread of AIDS through needle sharing have come under intense public opposition. Investigate the reasons for this opposition and argue for or against the continuation of such programs.

8. Estimates vary, but it is believed that somewhere between 40,000 and 80,000 Americans who have carried on heterosexual relations with an infected person are carrying the AIDS virus. Because the latency period of AIDS is sometimes years long, these so-called healthy carriers may not know they are carrying the disease and may, in turn, have relations with others and pass the HIV virus to them. In light of this and other information you have gained from the articles in this section, write in favor of or against sexual abstinence, that is, that people should "just say no to sex" and not enter into sexual relations.

191

9. What are the drugs that are currently being used to help those that are HIV positive and those diagnosed as having AIDS? Write an essay in which you discuss these various drugs, what they are designed to do, and how effective they have been thus far. You will, of course, need to review the articles in this section for information as well as do some research in your school library.

10. AIDS is now being regarded as an epidemic and even a plague. In the belief that useful information about our present plight might be gained by an investigation of the circumstances of earlier plagues in the history of humankind (e.g., the Black Death of the fourteenth century and the Great Plague of London in 1664–1665), write an essay exploring how the plague you choose began and ended and what happened in between. What socio-political changes took place, how were the lives of individuals and society itself changed?

11. Write an essay in which you explain the process by which AIDS attacks the body's immune system. What are the signs and symptoms of AIDS? How does the disease progress from the HIV infection stage to its final stages?

12. No cure for AIDS has yet been found, nor do researchers expect to find one soon. Write an essay in which you explain why a cure for AIDS has proven to be especially difficult to find. What problems do researchers have to confront? What areas of research look promising? What is being done to comfort sufferers?

13. Write a letter for or against the distribution of condoms to students on your campus.

14. The issue of AIDS in the workplace is a difficult one and one on which people are divided. For example, can an employer fire an employee or refuse to hire someone who has AIDS? Does an AIDS victim come under the jurisdiction of the Federal Rehabilitation Act which provides protection for the handicapped? Charles J. Cooper, Assistant Attorney General with the United States Justice Department believes that while the disabling effects of AIDS qualifies as a handicap, an AIDS victim can be prevented from spreading the disease to others. Opponents of this view argue that it is highly unlikely that AIDS would be spread in the workplace, hence the law in effect allows for hiring and firing at the discretion of the employer with little or no regard for the employee. The law could easily allow for abuses. Investigate this issue further by looking into the policies of companies in your area and by researching the popular press for articles on the problem. Do local companies in your area have a policy for dealing with

HIV positive and AIDS afflicted workers? If so, what is it? What does the future hold in this respect? Will companies be able to cope with the problem if they do not plan for increased numbers of affected workers?

15. Write an argumentative essay that the nation's schools must do more than they have to inform their students of the risks of AIDS.

16. Argue against William F. Buckley, Jr.'s point of view in his essay "Identify All the Carriers."

5

Abortion: The Debate Continues

With the 1989 Supreme Court ruling in *Webster v. Reproductive Health Services* that put new restrictions on a woman's right to have an abortion, the battle over abortion escalated once again. The ruling set the stage for conflicts across the nation in legislative arenas between supporters and opponents of abortion. Clearly abortion seems destined to be the political and social issue of the 1990s. Martin Luther King, Jr. led the civil rights marches and anti-segregation sit-ins in the late 1950s and early 1960s which culminated in the passage of the Civil Rights Act in 1964, and the protests and demonstrations against the United States' involvement in the war in Vietnam led President Nixon to withdraw our troops in 1973. Now another issue, the question of abortion, has divided the nation. It would be an understatement to say that abortion is an emotional issue. The direct confrontation between the opposing forces has been frequent, and often these clashes have been marred by name-calling, shouting, and anger on both sides. Sometimes standoffs have deteriorated into pitched battle. And when the dust has cleared the result seem always to be the same: no agreement, no resolution, no compromise. It is not surprising then that many people find the abortion debate "all heat and no light."

Abortion has been a much debated subject for years. First, there is controversy whether a woman should be allowed by law to have an abortion and, if so, under what circumstances. And second, to what extent, if at all, should laws protect the unborn. People who believe that a woman should have the right to have an abortion have labeled themselves "Pro-Choice," while those who wish to legally restrict or outlaw abortion describe themselves as "Pro-Life." Both camps are firmly committed to their own beliefs and the issues surrounding these beliefs.

195

The "Pro-Choice" advocates see individual choice as the key issue in the debate. They believe that a woman should be able to end an unwanted pregnancy. If a woman is denied this choice, they believe she has been denied one of her most basic human rights. Pro-Choice people argue that a fetus is only a potential person and that its rights should never take precedence over the woman's. "Pro-Life" advocates, on the other hand, believe that a fetus, even as a fertilized ovum, is human and therefore deserving of the same rights as its mother. In their eyes, abortion is the unjustified killing of an unborn child.

Abortion is not a new issue. Although discouraged by many major religions, induced abortion has been practiced worldwide since ancient times. During the 19th century several countries passed restrictive legislation to protect women from the dangerous abortion procedures then being used. In the United States, state laws prohibiting abortion before the time the mother first feels the fetus move were passed in the years just prior to the Civil War. Until well into the 1800s the Roman Catholic Church had no specific doctrine against abortion before *animation*, that point—40 to 80 days after conception—at which a fetus became human. In 1869, the Catholic Church took a firm stand against all abortion. Starting in 1920 with Soviet Russia, many eastern European countries and later western ones liberalized their abortion statutes.

Up until the early 1970s abortion was generally illegal in the United States. Most states prohibited abortions except under certain medical circumstances. But that all changed in 1973 when the United States Supreme Court delivered its landmark decision on abortion in the now famous case of *Roe v. Wade*. Restrictive abortion laws were ruled unconstitutional because they violated the woman's right to privacy. In accordance with the Court's ruling, states could no longer restrict a woman from having an abortion during the first three months of her pregnancy. The ruling allowed states to regulate abortions during the second-trimester to ensure the woman's health and safety and to prohibit third-trimester abortions completely.

Since the *Roe v. Wade* decision was handed down, Congress passed the Hyde Amendment in 1976 restricting federal Medicaid funds for abortions except for medical reasons or when rape or incest was promptly reported. One year later the Supreme Court ruled that the government did not have to pay for abortions considered unnecessary for the woman's physical or mental health. The Hyde Amendment was revised in 1981 to eliminate rape and incest as grounds for a federally funded abortion. And in 1983 the Supreme Court struck down state and local laws limiting access to abortion—thus reaffirming *Roe v. Wade*—in *Akron v. Akron*. State and local regulations require parental notification in the case of an abortion for a minor and parental and judicial consent for females under age 15.

On July 3, 1989, in a sharply divided 5–4 decision, the Supreme Court put new limitations on a woman's right to have an abortion. In *Webster v. Reproductive Health Services* the Court upheld a Missouri law prohibiting public employees from performing abortions unless the mother's life was endangered, barring abortions in public buildings, and requiring medical tests on any fetus more than 20 weeks old to determine viability outside the womb. This decision unleashed a flurry of activity to enact new restrictive abortion laws and regulations in many states. And so the debate continues with "Pro-Choice" supporters arguing for safe, legal abortion as the right for every woman who chooses to have one and with "Pro-Life" advocates working to have *Roe v. Wade* overturned in this decade. The whole abortion question might well become a moot point if the new abortion-inducing drug RU 486, first developed in France, is made available in the United States.

Sallie Tisdale

We Do Abortions Here

Sallie Tisdale fondly remembers the day she took her first job in a nursing home as a nurse's aide. She was 17 and drawn to people who needed her, people she knew she could help. A writer and registered nurse, Tisdale was born in 1957. As a nurse, she daily witnessed the human drama, the life-and-death struggles of her patients. And in her writing she draws heavily on these experiences. Tisdale's first two books, The Sorcerer's Apprentice: Medical Miracles and Other Disasters *(1986) and* Harvest Moon: Portrait of a Nursing Home *(1987), are studies of the nursing profession at work in contemporary hospitals and nursing homes. Her third book,* Lot's Wife: Salt and the Human Condition, *appeared in 1988. Tisdale continues to write and to work as a part-time nurse.*

"We Do Abortions Here" first appeared in Harper's Magazine *in October 1987. She wrote this piece while working as a registered nurse in an abortion clinic. In her moving story she takes us inside the clinic where she worked and shows us the physical and psychological effects of abortion not only on the women who have them but also on the doctors and nurses who perform them.*

1   We do abortions here; that is all we do. There are weary, grim moments when I think I cannot bear another basin of bloody remains, utter another kind phrase of reassurance. So I leave the procedure room in the back and reach for a new chart. Soon I am talking to an eighteen-year-old woman pregnant for the fourth time. I push up her sleeve to check her blood pressure and find row upon row of needle marks, neat and parallel and discolored. She has been so hungry for her drug for so long that she has taken to using the loose skin of her upper arms; her elbows are already a permanent ruin of bruises. She is surprised to find herself nearly four months pregnant. I suspect she is often surprised, in a mild

way, by the blows she is dealt. I prepare myself for another basin, another brief and chafing loss.

2   "How can you stand it?" Even the clients ask. They see the machine, the strange instruments, the blood, the final stroke that wipes away the promise of pregnancy. Sometimes I see that too: I watch a woman's swollen abdomen sink to softness in a few stuttering moments and my own belly flip-flops with sorrow. But all it takes for me to catch my breath is another interview, one more story that sounds so much like the last one. There is a numbing sameness lurking in this job: the same questions, the same answers, even the same trembling tone in the voices. The worst is the sameness of human failure, of inadequacy in the face of each day's dull demands.

3   In describing this work, I find it difficult to explain how much I enjoy it most of the time. We laugh a lot here, as friends and as professional peers. It's nice to be with women all day. I like the sudden, transient bonds I forge with some clients: moments when I am in my strength, remembering weakness, and a woman in weakness reaches out for my strength. What I offer is not power, but solidness, offered almost eagerly. Certain clients waken in me every tender urge I have—others make me wince and bite my tongue. Both challenge me to find a balance. It is a sweet brutality we practice here, a stark and loving dispassion.

4   I look at abortion as if I am standing on a cliff with a telescope, gazing at some great vista. I can sweep the horizon with both eyes, survey the scene in all its distance and size. Or I can put my eye to the lens and focus on the small details, suddenly so close. In abortion the absolute must always be tempered by the contextual, because both are real, both valid, both hard. How can we do this? How can we refuse? Each abortion is a measure of our failure to protect, to nourish our own. Each basin I empty is a promise—but a promise broken a long time ago.

5   I grew up on the great promise of birth control. Like many women my age, I took the pill as soon as I was sexually active. To risk pregnancy when it was so easy to avoid seemed stupid, and my contraceptive success, as it were, was part of the promise of social enlightenment. But birth control fails, far more frequently than laboratory trials predict. Many of our clients take the pill; its failure to protect them is a shocking realization. We have clients

who have been sterilized, whose husbands have had vasectomies; each one is a statistical misfit, fine print come to life. The anger and shame of these women I hold in one hand, and the basin in the other. The distance between the two, the length I pace and try to measure, is the size of an abortion.

6   The procedure is disarmingly simple. Women are surprised, as though the mystery of conception, a dark and hidden genesis, requires an elaborate finale. In the first trimester of pregnancy, it's a mere few minutes of vacuuming, a neat tidying up. I give a woman a small yellow Valium, and when it has begun to relax her, I lead her into the back, into bareness, the stirrups. The doctor reaches in her, opening the narrow tunnel to the uterus with a succession of slim, smooth bars of steel. He inserts a plastic tube and hooks it to a hose on the machine. The woman is framed against white paper that crackles as she moves, the light bright in her eyes. Then the machine rumbles low and loud in the small windowless room; the doctor moves the tube back and forth with an efficient rhythm, and the long tail of it fills with blood that spurts and stumbles along into a jar. He is usually finished in a few minutes. They are long minutes for the woman; her uterus frequently reacts to its abrupt emptying with a powerful, unceasing cramp, which cuts off the blood vessels and enfolds the irritated, bleeding tissue.

7   I am learning to recognize the shadows that cross the faces of the women I hold. While the doctor works between her spread legs, the paper drape hiding his intent expression, I stand beside the table. I hold the woman's hands in mine, resting them just below her ribs. I watch her eyes, finger her necklace, stroke her hair. I ask about her job, her family; in a haze she answers me; we chatter, faces close, eyes meeting and sliding apart.

8   I watch the shadows that creep up unnoticed and suddenly darken her face as she screws up her features and pushes a tear out each side to slide down her cheeks. I have learned to anticipate the quiver of chin, the rapid intake of breath, and the surprising sobs that rise soon after the machine starts to drum. I know this is when the cramp deepens, and the tears are partly the tears that follow pain—the sharp, childish crying when one bumps one's head on a cabinet door. But a well of woe seems to open beneath many women when they hear that thumping sound. The antici-

pation of the moment has finally come to fruit; the moment has arrived when the loss is no longer an imagined one. It has come true.

9   I am struck by the sameness and I am struck every day by the variety here—how this commonplace dilemma can so display the differences of women. A twenty-one-year old woman, unemployed, uneducated, without family, in the fifth month of her fifth pregnancy. A forty-two-year-old mother of teenagers, shocked by her condition, refusing to tell her husband. A twenty-three-year-old mother of two having her seventh abortion, and many women in their thirties having their first. Some are stoic, some hysterical, a few giggle uncontrollably, many cry.

10   I talk to a sixteen-year-old uneducated girl who was raped. She has gonorrhea. She describes blinding headaches, attacks of breathlessness, nausea. "Sometimes I feel like two different people," she tells me with a calm smile, "and I talk to myself."

11   I pull out my plastic models. She listens patiently for a time, and then holds her hands wide in front of her stomach.

12   "When's the baby going to go up into my stomach?" she asks.

13   I blink. "What do you mean?"

14   "Well," she says, still smiling, "when women get so big, isn't the baby in your stomach? Doesn't it hatch out of an egg there?"

15   My first question in an interview is always the same. As I walk down the hall with the woman, as we get settled in chairs and I glance through her files, I am trying to gauge her, to get a sense of the words, and the tone, I should use. With some I joke, with others I chat, sometimes I fall into a brisk, business-like patter. But I ask every woman, "Are you sure you want to have an abortion?" Most nod with grim knowing smiles. "Oh, yes," they sigh. Some seek forgiveness, offer excuses. Occasionally a woman will flinch and say, "Please don't use that word."

16   Later I describe the procedure to come, using care with my language. I don't say "pain" any more than I would say "baby." So many are afraid to ask how much it will hurt. "My sister told me—" I hear. "A friend of mine said—" and the dire expectations unravel. I prick the index finger of a woman for a drop of blood to test, and as the tiny lancet approaches the skin she averts her eyes, holding her trembling hand out to me and jumping at my touch.

17   It is when I am holding a plastic uterus in one hand, a suction tube in the other, moving them together in imitation of the scrubbing to come, that women ask the most secret question. I am speaking in a matter-of-fact voice about "the tissue" and "the contents" when the woman suddenly catches my eye and asks, "How big is the baby now?" These words suggest a quiet need for a definition of the boundaries being drawn. It isn't so odd, after all, that she feels relief when I describe the growing bud's bulbous shape, its miniature nature. Again I gauge, and sometimes lie a little, weaseling around its infantile features until its clinging power slackens.

18   But when I look in the basin, among the curdlike blood clots, I see an elfin thorax, attenuated, its pencilline ribs all in parallel rows with tiny knobs of spine rounding upwards. A translucent arm and hand swim beside.

19   A sleepy-eyed girl, just fourteen, watched me with a slight and goofy smile all through her abortion. "Does it have little feet and little fingers and all?" she'd asked earlier. When the suction was over she sat up woozily at the end of the table and murmured, "Can I see it?" I shook my head firmly.

20   "It's not allowed," I told her sternly, because I knew she didn't really want to see what was left. She accepted this statement of authority, and a shadow of confused relief crossed her plain, pale face.

21   Privately, even grudgingly, my colleagues might admit the power of abortion to provoke emotion. But they seem to prefer the broad view and disdain the telescope. Abortion is a matter of choice, privacy, control. Its uncertainty lies in specific cases: retarded women and girls too young to give consent for surgery, women who are ill or hostile or psychotic. Such common dilemmas are met with both compassion and impatience; they slow things down. We are too busy to chew over ethics. One person might discuss certain concerns, behind closed doors, or describe a particularly disturbing dream. But generally there is to be no ambivalence.

22   Every day I take calls from women who are annoyed that we cannot see them, cannot do their abortion today, this morning, now. They argue the price, demand that we stay after hours to accommodate their job or class schedule. Abortion is so routine that one expects it to be like a manicure; quick, cheap, and painless.

23   Still, I've cultivated a certain disregard. It isn't negligence, but I don't always pay attention. I couldn't be here if I tried to judge each case on its merits; after all, we do over a hundred abortions a week. At some point each individual in this line of work draws a boundary and adheres to it. For one physician the boundary is a particular week of gestation; for another, it is a certain number of repeated abortions. But these boundaries can be fluid too: one physician overruled his own limit to abort a mature but severely malformed fetus. For me, the limit is allowing my clients to carry their own burden, shoulder the responsibility themselves. I shoulder the burden of trying not to judge them.

24   This city has several "crisis pregnancy centers" advertised in the Yellow Pages. They are small offices staffed by volunteers, and they offer free pregnancy testing, glossy photos of dead fetuses, and movies. I had a client recently whose mother is active in the anti-abortion movement. The young woman went to the local crisis center and was told that the doctor would make her touch her dismembered baby, that the pain would be the most horrible she could imagine, and that she might, after an abortion, never be able to have children. All lies. They called her at home and at work, over and over and over, but she had been wise enough to give a false name. She came to us a fugitive. We who do abortions are marked, by some, as impure. It's dirty work.

25   When a deliveryman comes to the sliding glass window by the reception desk and tilts a box toward me, I hesitate. I read the packing slip, assess the shape and weight of the box in the light of its supposed contents. We request familiar faces. The doors are carefully locked; I have learned to half glance around at bags and boxes, looking for a telltale sign. I register with security when I arrive, and I am careful not to bang a door. We are a little on edge here.

26   Concern about size and shape seem to be natural, and so is the relief that follows. We make the powerful assumption that the fetus is different from us, and even when we admit the similarities, it is too simplistic to be seduced by form alone. But the form is enormously potent—humanoid, powerless, palm-sized, and pure, it evokes an almost fierce tenderness when viewed simply as what it appears to be. But appearance, and even potential, aren't enough. The fetus, in becoming itself, can ruin others; its utter dependence

has a sinister side. When I am struck in the moment by the contents in the basin, I am careful to remember the context, to note the tearful teenager and the woman sighing with something more than relief. One kind of question, though, I find considerably trickier.

27 "Can you tell what it is?" I am asked, and this means gender. This question is asked by couples, not women alone. Always couples would abort a girl and keep a boy. I have been asked about twins, and even if I could tell what race the father was.

28 An eighteen-year-old woman with three daughters brought her husband to the interview. He glared first at me, then at his wife, as he sank lower and lower in the chair, picking his teeth with a toothpick. He interrupted a conversation with his wife to ask if I could tell whether the baby would be a boy or a girl. I told him I could not.

29 "Good," he replied in a slow and strangely malevolent voice, "'cause if it was a boy I'd wring her neck."

30 In a literal sense, abortion exists because we are able to ask such questions, able to assign a value to the fetus which can shift with changing circumstances. If the human bond to a child were as primitive and unflinchingly narrow as that of other animals, there would be no abortion. There would be no abortion because there would be nothing more important than caring for the young and perpetuating the species, no reason for sex but to make babies. I sense this sometimes, this wordless organic duty, when I do ultrasounds.

31 We do ultrasound, a sound-wave test that paints a faint, gray picture of the fetus, whenever we're uncertain of gestation. Age is measured by the width of the skull and confirmed by the length of the femur or thighbone; we speak of a pregnancy as being a certain "femur length" in weeks. The usual concern is whether a pregnancy is within the legal limit for an abortion. Women this far along have bellies which swell out round and tight like trim muscles. When they lie flat, the mound rises softly above the hips, pressing the umbilicus upward.

32 It takes practice to read an ultrasound picture, which is grainy and etched as though in strokes of charcoal. But suddenly a rapid rhythmic motion appears—the beating heart. Nearby is a soft oval, scratched with lines—the skull. The leg is harder to find, and then suddenly the fetus moves, bobbing in the surf. The skull turns away, an arm slides across the screen, the torso rolls. I know the

weight of a baby's head on my shoulder, the whisper of lips on ears, the delicate curve of a fragile spine in my hand. I know how heavy and correct a newborn cradled feels. The creature I watch in secret requires nothing from me but to be left alone, and that is precisely what won't be done.

33   These inadvertently made beings are caught in a twisting web of motive and desire. They are at least inconvenient, sometimes quite literally dangerous in the womb, but most often they fall somewhere in between—consequences never quite believed in come to roost. Their virtue rises and falls outside their own nature: they become only what we make them. A fetus created by accident is the most absolute kind of surprise. Whether the blame lies in a failed IUD, a slipped condom, or a false impression of safety, that fetus is a thing whose creation has been actively worked against. Its existence is an error. I think this is why so few women, even late in a pregnancy, will consider giving a baby up for adoption. To do so means making the fetus real—imagining it as something whole and outside oneself. The decision to terminate a pregnancy is sometimes so difficult and confounding that it creates an enormous demand for immediate action. The decision is a rejection; the pregnancy has become something to be rid of, a condition to be ended. It is a burden, a weight, a thing separate.

34   Women have abortions because they are too old, and too young, too poor, and too rich, too stupid, and too smart. I see women who berate themselves with violent emotions for their first and only abortion, and others who return three times, five times, hauling two or three children, who cannot remember to take a pill or where they put the diaphragm. We talk glibly about choice. But the choice for what? I see all the broken promises in lives lived like a series of impromptu obstacles. There are the sweet, light promises of love and intimacy, the glittering promise of education and progress, the warm promise of safe families, long years of innocence and community. And there is the promise of freedom: freedom from failure, from faithlessness. Freedom from biology. The early feminist defense of abortion asked many questions, but the one I remember is this: is biology destiny? And the answer is yes, sometimes it is. Women who have the fewest choices of all exercise their right to abortion the most.

35   Oh, the ignorance. I take a woman to the back room and ask her to undress; a few minutes later I return and find her positioned

discreetly behind a drape, still wearing underpants. "Do I have to take these off too?" she asks, a little shocked. Some swear they have not had sex, many do not know what a uterus is, how sperm and egg meet, how sex makes babies. Some late seekers do not believe themselves pregnant; they believe themselves *impregnable*. I was chastised when I began this job for referring to some clients as girls: it is a feminist heresy. They come so young, snapping gum, sockless and sneakered, and their shakily applied eyeliner smears when they cry. I call them girls with maternal benignity. I cannot imagine them as mothers.

36   The doctor seats himself between the woman's thighs and reaches into the dilated opening of a five-month pregnant uterus. Quickly he grabs and crushes the fetus in several places, and the room is filled with a low clatter and snap of forceps, the click of the tanaculum,[1] and a pulling, sucking sound. The paper crinkles as the drugged and sleepy woman shifts, the nurse's low, honey-brown voice explains each step in delicate words.

37   I have fetus dreams, we all do here: dreams of abortions one after the other; of buckets of blood splashed on the walls; trees full of crawling fetuses. I dreamed that two men grabbed me and began to drag me away: "Let's do an abortion," they said with a sickening leer, and I began to scream, plunged into a vision of sucking, scraping pain, of being spread and torn by impartial instruments that do only what they are bidden. I woke from this dream barely able to breathe and thought of kitchen tables and coat hangers, knitting needles striped with blood, and women all alone clutching a pillow in their teeth to keep the screams from piercing the apartment-house walls. Abortion is the narrowest edge between kindness and cruelty. Done as well as it can be, it is still violence—merciful violence, like putting a suffering animal to death.

38   Maggie, one of the nurses, received a call at midnight not long ago. It was a woman in her twentieth week of pregnancy; the necessarily gradual process of cervical dilation begun the day before had stimulated labor, as it sometimes does. Maggie and one of the doctors met the woman at the office in the night. Maggie helped her onto the table, and as she lay down the fetus was delivered into Maggie's hands. When Maggie told me about it the

[1] Type of sharp forceps used on bleeding arteries.

next day, she cupped her hands into a small bowl—"It was just like a little kitten," she said softly, wonderingly. "Everything was still attached."

39   At the end of the day I clean out the suction jars, pouring blood into the sink, splashing the sides with flecks of tissue. From the sink rises a rich and humid smell, hot, earthy, and moldering; it is the smell of something recently alive beginning to decay. I take care of the plastic tub on the floor, filled with pieces too big to be trusted to the trash. The law defines the contents of the bucket I hold protectively against my chest as "tissue." Some would say my complicity in filling that bucket gives me no right to call it anything else. I slip the tissue gently into a bag and place it in the freezer, to be burned at another time. Abortion requires of me an entirely new set of assumptions. It requires a willingness to live with conflict, fearlessness, and grief. As I close the freezer door, I imagine a world where this won't be necessary, and then return to the world where it is.

Analyzing the Writer's Argument

1. What do you think Tisdale's position on abortion is? Cite passages in her essay that led you to your conclusion. What does Tisdale mean when she says, "In abortion the absolute must always be tempered by the contextual, because both are real, both valid, both hard"?

2. Why do you suppose Tisdale wrote this descriptive narrative of her work in an abortion clinic? Is she trying to justify the work that she does? How do you think she wanted her intended audience to react?

3. What is Tisdale's job at the abortion clinic? What does she particularly like about her job? What doesn't she like? What "new assumptions" does abortion require of Tisdale?

4. In paragraph 6 Tisdale provides a graphic step-by-step description of the abortion procedure. Why do you think she included this description? Where else in her essay does Tisdale use explicitly graphic details? How did you react to these details when reading the essay? What insights do these graphic descriptions give you about the author's stance on abortion?

5. Tisdale uses a number of lengthy examples in her essay—the 16-year-old uneducated girl who was raped, a sleepy-eyed 14-

year-old girl, the 18-year-old woman with her husband, and her colleague Maggie. Being as specific as you can, explain what each of these examples contributes to the essay as a whole.

6. How do Tisdale's colleagues feel about their work in the clinic? What kinds of "boundaries" do they draw for themselves? Why do you suppose they need to draw such boundaries? What boundary does Tisdale draw?

7. Paragraph 24 is devoted to a retelling of experiences that one of Tisdale's clients had at a "crisis pregnancy center." Explain how this paragraph functions in the context of the essay as a whole.

8. Why, according to Tisdale, is the form of a fetus "enormously potent"? Why does she find questions about fetus gender tricky? What does she mean when she says, "abortion exists because we are able to ask such questions, able to assign a value to the fetus which can shift with changing circumstances"?

9. Why does Tisdale take such care in receiving packages from delivery men? What does this small detail tell you about the world of abortion clinics?

10. Tisdale uses the phrases "sweet brutality" and "merciful violence" to describe abortion. What do these phrases tell you about the nature of abortion and Tisdale's own attitude toward it?

11. Tisdale confesses that she and her colleagues sometimes have "fetus dreams." What did you make of the dream she recounts in paragraph 37?

Exploring the Issues in This Essay

1. For many who grew up during the "sexual revolution" of the 1970s, birth control offered great freedom. What, for Tisdale, was "the great promise of birth control"? And what is its downside? Discuss the range of current attitudes about birth control. How did you react when you heard Tisdale tell of the woman who came to the clinic for "her seventh abortion"?

2. Tisdale says, "Abortion is so routine that one expects it to be like a manicure; quick, cheap, and painless." Do you agree with this assessment of the attitude about abortion in America? If not, how do you think most Americans view abortion? Discuss what our feelings and attitudes about abortion say about us as a society.

Ellen Willis

*Putting Women Back into the Abortion Debate**

> *Ellen Willis was born on December 14, 1941, in New York City. After receiving her B.A. from Barnard College in 1962 and pursuing graduate studies at the University of California, Berkeley, Willis launched her successful career as a freelance writer in 1966. She was the rock music critic for* The New Yorker *and contributing editor to such magazines as* Us, Rolling Stone, *and* Ms. *A collection of her essays,* Beginning to See the Light, *appeared in 1981. The variety of topics she addresses in this book—rock music and musicians, politics, religion, and feminism—attest to her versatility and diverse interests. Since 1979 she has been a staff writer for* The Village Voice *in New York City.*
>
> *"Putting Women Back into the Abortion Debate" first appeared in* The Village Voice *in 1985. Is this essay she argues that abortion is not a "human life issue" but instead a "feminist issue."*

1   Some years ago I attended a New York Institute for the Humanities seminar on the new right. We were a fairly heterogeneous group of liberals and lefties, feminists and gay activists, but on one point nearly all of us agreed: the right-to-life movement was a dangerous antifeminist crusade. At one session I argued that the attack on abortion had significance far beyond itself, that it was the linchpin of the right's social agenda. I got a lot of supporting comments and approving nods. It was too much for Peter Steinfels, a liberal Catholic, author of *The Neoconservatives*, and executive editor of *Commonweal*. Right-to-lifers were not all right-wing fanatics, he protested. "You have to understand," he said plaintively, "that many of us see abortion as a *human life issue*." What I remember

*Reprinted by permission of the author and *The Village Voice*.

best was his air of frustrated isolation. I don't think he came back to the seminar after that.

2   Things are different now. I often feel isolated when I insist that abortion is, above all, a *feminist issue*. Once people took for granted that abortion was an issue of sexual politics and morality. Now, abortion is most often discussed as a question of "life" in the abstract. Public concern over abortion centers almost exclusively on fetuses; women and their bodies are merely the stage on which the drama of fetal life and death takes place. Debate about abortion — if not its reality — has become sexlessly scholastic. And the people most responsible for this turn of events are, like Peter Steinfels, on the left.

3   The left wing of the right-to-life movement is a small, seemingly eccentric minority in both "progressive" and antiabortion camps. Yet it has played a critical role in the movement: by arguing that opposition to abortion can be separated from the right's antifeminist program, it has given antiabortion sentiment legitimacy in left-symp and (putatively) profeminist circles. While left antiabortionists are hardly alone in emphasizing fetal life, their innovation has been to claim that a consistent "prolife" stand involves opposing capital punishment, supporting disarmament, demanding government programs to end poverty, and so on. This is of course a leap the right is neither able nor willing to make. It's been liberals–from Garry Wills to the Catholic bishops–who have supplied the mass media with the idea that prohibiting abortion is part of a "seamless garment" of respect for human life.

4   Having invented this counter-context for the abortion controversy, left antiabortionists are trying to impose it as the only legitimate context for debate. Those of us who won't accept their terms and persist in seeing opposition to abortion, antifeminism, sexual repression, and religious sectarianism as the real seamless garment have been accused of obscuring the issue with demagoguery. Last year *Commonweal* — perhaps the most important current forum for left antiabortion opinion — ran an editorial demanding that we shape up: "Those who hold that abortion is immoral believe that the biological dividing lines of birth or viability should no more determine whether a developing member of the species is denied or accorded essential rights than should the biological dividing lines of sex or race or disability or old age. This argument is open to challenge. Perhaps the dividing lines are sufficiently different.

Pro-choice advocates should state their reasons for believing so. They should meet the argument on its own grounds. . . . "

5   In other words, the only question we're allowed to debate—or the only one *Commonweal* is willing to entertain—is "Are fetuses the moral equivalent of born human beings?" And I can't meet the argument on its own grounds because I don't agree that this is the key question, whose answer determines whether one supports abortion or opposes it. I don't doubt that fetuses are alive, or that they're biologically human—what else would they be? I do consider the life of a fertilized egg less precious than the well-being of a woman with feelings, self-consciousness, a history, social ties; and I think fetuses get closer to being human in a moral sense as they come closer to birth. But to me these propositions are intuitively self-evident. I wouldn't know how to justify them to a "nonbeliever," nor do I see the point of trying.

6   I believe the debate has to start in a different place—with the recognition that fertilized eggs develop into infants inside the bodies of women. Pregnancy and birth are active processes in which a woman's body shelters, nourishes, and expels a new life; for nine months she is immersed in the most intimate possible relationship with another being. The growing fetus makes considerable demands on her physical and emotional resources, culminating in the cataclysmic experience of birth. And childbearing has unpredictable consequences; it always entails some risk of injury or death.

7   For me all this has a new concreteness: I had a baby last year. My much-desired and relatively easy pregnancy was full of what antiabortionists like to call "inconveniences." I was always tired, short of breath; my digestion was never right; for three months I endured a state of hormonal siege; later I had pains in my fingers, swelling feet, numb spots on my legs, the dread hemorrhoids. I had to think about everything I ate. I developed borderline glucose intolerance. I gained 50 pounds and am still overweight; my shape has changed in other ways that may well be permanent. Psychologically, my pregnancy consumed me—though I'd happily bought the seat on the roller coaster, I was still terrified to be so out of control of my normally tractable body. It was all bearable, even interesting—even, at times, transcendent—because I wanted a baby. Birth was painful, exhausting, and wonderful. If I hadn't wanted a baby it would only have been painful and exhausting—

or worse. I can hardly imagine what it's like to have your body and mind taken over in this way when you not only don't look forward to the result, but positively dread it. The thought appalls me. So as I see it, the key question is "Can it be moral, under any circumstances, to make a woman bear a child against her will?"

8   From this vantage point, *Commonweal's* argument is irrelevant, for in a society that respects the individual, no "member of the species" in *any* stage of development has an "essential right" to make use of someone else's body, let alone in such all-encompassing fashion, without that person's consent. You can't make a case against abortion by applying a general principle about everybody's human rights; you have to show exactly the opposite—that the relationship between fetus and pregnant woman is an exception, one that justifies depriving women of their right to bodily integrity. And in fact all antiabortion ideology rests on the premise— acknowledged or simply assumed—that women's unique capacity to bring life into the world carries with it a unique obligation; that women cannot be allowed to "play God" and launch only the lives they welcome.

9   Yet the alternative to allowing women this power is to make them impotent. Criminalizing abortion doesn't just harm individual women with unwanted pregnancies, it affects all women's sense of themselves. Without control of our fertility we can never envision ourselves as free, for our biology makes us constantly vulnerable. Simply because we are female our physical integrity can be violated, our lives disrupted and transformed, at any time. Our ability to act in the world is hopelessly compromised by our sexual being.

10   Ah, sex—it does have a way of coming up in these discussions, despite all. When pressed, right-to-lifers of whatever political persuasion invariably point out that pregnancy doesn't happen by itself. The leftists often give patronizing lectures on contraception (though some find only "natural birth control" acceptable), but remain unmoved when reminded that contraceptives fail. Openly or implicitly they argue that people shouldn't have sex unless they're prepared to procreate. (They are quick to profess a single standard—men as well as women should be sexually "responsible." Yes, and the rich as well as the poor should be allowed to sleep under bridges.) Which amounts to saying that if women want to lead heterosexual lives they must give up any claim to

self-determination, and that they have no right to sexual pleasure without fear.

11 Opposing abortion, then, means accepting that women must suffer sexual disempowerment and a radical loss of autonomy relative to men: if fetal life is sacred, the self-denial basic to women's oppression is also basic to the moral order. Opposing abortion means embracing a conservative sexual morality, one that subordinates pleasure to reproduction: if fetal life is sacred, there is no room for the view that sexual passion—or even sexual love—for its own sake is a human need and a human right. Opposing abortion means tolerating the inevitable double standard, by which men may accept or reject sexual restrictions in accordance with their beliefs, while women must bow to them out of fear . . . or defy them at great risk. However much *Commonweal's* editors and those of like mind want to believe their opposition to abortion is simply about saving lives, the truth is that in the real world they are shoring up a particular sexual culture, whose rules are stacked against women. I have yet to hear any left right-to-lifers take full responsibility for that fact or deal seriously with its political implications.

12 Unfortunately, their fuzziness has not lessened their appeal—if anything it's done the opposite. In increasing numbers liberals and leftists, while opposing antiabortion laws, have come to view abortion as an "agonizing moral issue" with some justice on both sides, rather than an issue—however emotionally complex—of freedom versus repression, or equality versus hierarchy, that affects their political self-definition. This above-the-battle stance is attractive to leftists who want to be feminist good guys but are uneasy or ambivalent about sexual issues, not to mention those who want to ally with "progressive" factions of the Catholic church on Central America, nuclear disarmament, or populist economics without that sticky abortion question getting in the way.

13 Such neutrality is a way of avoiding the painful conflict over cultural issues that continually smolders on the left. It can also be a way of coping with the contradictions of personal life at a time when liberation is a dream deferred. To me the fight for abortion has always been the cutting edge of feminism, precisely because it denies that anatomy is destiny, that female biology dictates women's subordinate status. Yet recently I've found it hard to focus on the issue, let alone summon up the militance needed to stop the antiabortion tanks. In part that has to do with second-

214 • *Putting Women Back into the Abortion Debate*

round weariness—do we really have to go through all these things twice—in part with my life now.

14   Since my daughter's birth my feelings about abortion—not as a political demand but as a personal choice—have changed. In this society, the difference between the situation of a childless woman and of a mother is immense; the fear that having a child will dislodge one's tenuous hold on a nontraditional life is excruciating. This terror of being forced into the seachange of motherhood gave a special edge to my convictions about abortion. Since I've made that plunge voluntarily, with consequences still unfolding, the terror is gone; I might not want another child, for all sorts of reasons, but I will never again feel that my identity is at stake. Different battles with the culture absorb my energy now. Besides, since I've experienced the primal, sensual passion of caring for an infant, there will always be part of me that does want another. If I had an abortion today, it would be with conflict and sadness unknown to me when I had an abortion a decade ago. And the antiabortionists' imagery of dead babies hits me with new force. Do many women—left, feminist women—have such feelings? Is this the sort of "ambivalence about abortion" that in the present atmosphere slides so easily into self-flagellating guilt?

15   Some left antiabortionists, mainly pacifists—Juli Loesch, Mary Meehan, and other "feminists for life"; Jim Wallis and various writers for Wallis's radical evangelical journal *Sojourners*—have tried to square their position with concern for women. They blame the prevalence of abortion on oppressive conditions—economic injustice, lack of child care and other social supports for mothers, the devaluation of childrearing, men's exploitative sexual behavior and refusal to take equal responsibility for children. They disagree on whether to criminalize abortion now (since murder is intolerable no matter what the cause) or to build a long-term moral consensus (since stopping abortion requires a general social transformation), but they all regard abortion as a desperate solution to desperate problems, and the women who resort to it as more sinned against than sinning.

16   This analysis grasps an essential feminist truth: that in a male-supremacist society no choice a woman makes is genuinely free or entirely in her interest. Certainly many women have had abortions they didn't want or wouldn't have wanted if they had any plausible means of caring for a child; and countless others wouldn't have

gotten pregnant in the first place were it not for inadequate contraception, sexual confusion and guilt, male pressure, and other stigmata of female powerlessness. Yet forcing a woman to bear a child she doesn't want can only add injury to insult, while refusing to go through with such a pregnancy can be a woman's first step toward taking hold of her life. And many women who have abortions are "victims" only of ordinary human miscalculation, technological failure, or the vagaries of passion, all bound to exist in any society, however utopian. There will always be women who, at any given moment, want sex but don't want a child; some of these women will get pregnant; some of them will have abortions. Behind the victim theory of abortion is the implicit belief that women are always ready to be mothers, if only conditions are right, and that sex for pleasure rather than procreation is not only "irresponsible" (i.e., bad) but something men impose on women, never something women actively seek. Ironically, left right-to-lifers see abortion as always coerced (it's "exploitation" and "violence against women"), yet regard motherhood—which for most women throughout history has been inescapable, and is still our most socially approved role—as a positive choice. The analogy to the feminist antipornography movement goes beyond borrowed rhetoric: the antiporners, too, see active female lust as surrender to male domination and traditionally feminine sexual attitudes as expressions of women's true nature.

17   This Orwellian version of feminism, which glorifies "female values" and dismisses women's struggles for freedom—particularly sexual freedom—as a male plot, has become all too familiar in recent years. But its use in the abortion debate has been especially muddleheaded. Somehow we're supposed to leap from an oppressive patriarchal society to the egalitarian one that will supposedly make abortion obsolete without ever allowing women to see themselves as people entitled to control their reproductive function rather than be controlled by it. How women who have no power in this most personal of areas can effectively fight for power in the larger society is left to our imagination. A "New Zealand feminist" quoted by Mary Meehan in a 1980 article in *The Progressive* says, "Accepting short-term solutions like abortion only delays the implementation of real reforms like decent maternity and paternity leaves, job protection, high-quality child care, community responsibility for dependent people of all ages, and recognition of the

economic contribution of childminders"—as if these causes were progressing nicely before legal abortion came along. On the contrary, the fight for reproductive freedom is the foundation of all the others, which is why antifeminists resist it so fiercely.

18   As "prolife" pacifists have been particularly concerned with refuting charges of misogyny, the liberal Catholics at *Commonweal* are most exercised by the claim that antiabortion laws violate religious freedom. The editorial quoted above hurled another challenge at the proabortion forces:

> It is time, finally, for the pro-choice advocates and editorial writers to abandon, once and for all, the argument that abortion [*sic*] is a religious "doctrine" of a single or several churches being imposed on those of other persuasions in violation of the First Amendment. . . . Catholics and their bishops are accused of imposing their "doctrine" on abortion, but not their "doctrine" on the needs of the poor, or their "doctrine" on the arms race, or their "doctrine" on human rights in Central America. . . .
>
> The briefest investigation into Catholic teaching would show that the church's case against abortion is utterly unlike, say, its belief in the Real Presence, known with the eyes of faith alone, or its insistence on a Sunday obligation, applicable only to the faithful. The church's moral teaching on abortion. . . . is for the most part like its teaching on racism, warfare, and capital punishment, based on ordinary reasoning common to believers and nonbelievers. . . .

19   This is one more example of right-to-lifers' tendency to ignore the sexual ideology underlying their stand. Interesting, isn't it, how the editorial neglects to mention that the church's moral teaching on abortion jibes neatly with its teaching on birth control, sex, divorce, and the role of women. The traditional, patriarchal sexual morality common to these teachings is explicitly religious, and its chief defenders in modern times have been the more conservative churches. The Catholic and evangelical Christian churches are the backbone of the organized right-to-life movement and—a few Nathansons and Hentoffs notwithstanding—have provided most of the movement's activists and spokespeople.

20   Furthermore, the Catholic hierarchy has made opposition to abortion a litmus test of loyalty to the church in a way it has done with no other political issue—witness Archbishop O'Connor's harassment of Geraldine Ferraro during her vice-presidential campaign.

It's unthinkable that a Catholic bishop would publicly excoriate a Catholic officeholder or candidate for taking a hawkish position on the arms race or Central America or capital punishment. Nor do I notice anyone trying to read William F. Buckley out of the church for his views on welfare. The fact is there is no accepted Catholic "doctrine" on these matters comparable to the church's absolutist condemnation of abortion. While differing attitudes toward war, racism, and poverty cut across religious and secular lines, the sexual values that mandate opposition to abortion are the bedrock of the traditional religious world view, and the source of the most bitter conflict with secular and religious modernists. When churches devote their considerable political power, organizational resources, and money to translating those values into law, I call that imposing their religious beliefs on me—whether or not they're technically violating the First Amendment.

21   Statistical studies have repeatedly shown that people's views on abortion are best predicted by their opinions on sex and "family" issues, not on "life" issues like nuclear weapons or the death penalty. That's not because we're inconsistent but because we comprehend what's really at stake in the abortion fight. It's the antiabortion left that refuses to face the contradiction in its own position: you can't be wholeheartedly for "life"—or for such progressive aspirations as freedom, democracy, equality—and condone the subjugation of women. The seamless garment is full of holes.

Analyzing the Writer's Argument

1. Willis starts her essay by recalling a seminar on the new right that she once attended. What is her purpose in recalling the discussion of the abortion issue at the seminar? Does this story serve as a fitting introduction to her essay? Explain why, or why not.
2. Why does Willis feel so alone when she insists that abortion is a feminist issue? What has changed since the time she attended the New York Institute for the Humanities seminar?
3. What intuitive beliefs does Willis have about fetuses? Why do you think she feels at a loss to justify these propositions to "nonbelievers"?
4. What for Willis is the "key question, whose answer determines whether one supports abortion or opposes it"? How does her question differ from that of the opposition?

5. In paragraph 7 Willis tells of her own pregnancy and the birth of her daughter. What, if anything, does this description of her pregnancy add to her argument?

6. On what premise does Willis believe all antiabortion ideology rests? How does she argue against this premise?

7. How according to Willis does the criminalization of abortion affect all women's sense of themselves? How does she respond to the right-to-lifers when they remind people that "pregnancy doesn't happen by itself"?

8. Willis believes that opposition to abortion is much more than simply saving lives. What for her does opposing abortion mean for women? What does Willis see as the contradiction in the antiabortion left's position on abortion?

9. Briefly summarize Willis's argument that antiabortion laws do indeed violate religious freedom. How does she respond to those who believe otherwise? Did you find her argument persuasive? Explain why, or why not.

Exploring the Issues in This Essay

1. For Willis the real debate concerning abortion centers on whether one considers it a human life issue or a feminist issue. Discuss the arguments for considering it a human life issue. A feminist issue. Where do you find yourself lining up in this debate? Explain why you feel the way you do.

2. Willis claims that "all antiabortion ideology rests on the premise— acknowledged or simply assumed—that women's unique capacity to bring life into the world carries with it a unique obligation that women cannot be allowed to 'play God' and launch only the lives they welcome." Is this an accurate assessment of antiabortion ideology as you understand it? Why, or why not? Is it possible to argue against abortion without relying on this premise? Explain.

3. On the basis of the fact that "fertilized eggs develop into infants inside the bodies of women," Willis believes that no woman should be made to bear a child "without that person's consent." Discuss what the phrase "without that person's consent" means to you. When should the consent for a pregnancy be given—before or after conception? Once pregnant by choice, should a woman be allowed to change her mind and withdraw consent? Explain why or why not.

Linda Bird Francke

The Ambivalence of Abortion

A nonfiction writer who specializes in issues of interest to women, Linda Bird Francke was born in New York City in 1939 and attended Bradford Junior College. She worked for eight years as an advertising copywriter before becoming an editor at New York *magazine and* Newsweek. *In 1980 Francke launched her career as a freelance writer and has since published* Fathers and Daughters *(1980) and* Growing Up Divorced *(1983).*

In 1973 Francke had an abortion; the decision to terminate her pregnancy had been made with her husband. As a result of the confusion and guilt she felt afterwards, she wrote the cathartic personal essay "There Just Wasn't Room in Our Lives for Another Baby" and published it anonymously on the Op-Ed page of the New York Times. *Hundreds of women were touched by her essay and wrote to the* Times, *many describing their guilt-ridden experiences with abortion. Prompted by this outpouring of letters, Francke interviewed other women and wrote* The Ambivalence of Abortion *(1978). She asks a great many painful yet necessary questions and concludes that "there are no neat answers to questions about abortions." The following excerpt from Francke's book includes the original* New York Times *essay together with her response to the letters received by the newspaper.*

1   "Jane Doe," thirty-eight, had an abortion in New York City in 1973. The mother of three children, then three, five, and eleven, Jane had just started a full-time job in publishing. She and her husband, an investment banker, decided together that another baby would add an almost unbearable strain to their lives, which were already overfull. What Jane had not anticipated was the guilt and sadness that followed the abortion. She wrote about the experience shortly thereafter and filed the story away. Three years later she reread it and decided it might be helpful to other women

219

who experience the ambivalence of abortion. The *New York Times* ran it on their Op-Ed page in May 1976. This is what she wrote:

2   We were sitting in a bar on Lexington Avenue when I told my husband I was pregnant. It is not a memory I like to dwell on. Instead of the champagne and hope which had heralded the impending births of the first, second and third child, the news of this one was greeted with shocked silence and Scotch. "Jesus," my husband kept saying to himself, stirring the ice cubes around and around. "Oh, Jesus."

3   Oh, how we tried to rationalize it that night as the starting time for the movie came and went. My husband talked about his plans for a career change in the next year, to stem the staleness that fourteen years with the same investment-banking firm had brought him. A new baby would preclude that option.

4   The timing wasn't right for me either. Having juggled pregnancies and child care with what freelance jobs I could fit in between feedings, I had just taken on a full-time job. A new baby would put me right back in the nursery just when our youngest child was finally school age. It was time for *us*, we tried to rationalize. There just wasn't room in our lives now for another baby. We both agreed. And agreed. And agreed.

5   How very considerate they are at the Women's Services, known formally as the Center for Reproductive and Sexual Health. Yes, indeed, I could have an abortion that very Saturday morning and be out in time to drive to the country that afternoon. Bring a first morning urine specimen, a sanitary belt and napkins, a money order or $125 cash—and a friend.

6   My friend turned out to be my husband, standing awkwardly and ill at ease as men always do in places that are exclusively for women, as I checked in at nine A.M. Other men hovered around just as anxiously, knowing they had to be there, wishing they weren't. No one spoke to each other. When I would be cycled out of there four hours later, the same men would be slumped in their same seats, locked downcast in their cells of embarrassment.

7   The Saturday morning women's group was more dispirited than the men in the waiting room. There were around fifteen of us, a mixture of races, ages and backgrounds. Three didn't speak English at all and a fourth, a pregnant Puerto Rican girl around eighteen, translated for them.

8   There were six black women and a hodge-podge of whites, among them a T-shirted teenager who kept leaving the room to throw up and a puzzled middle-aged woman from Queens with three grown children.

9   "What form of birth control were you using?" the volunteer asked each one of us. The answer was inevitably "none." She then went on to describe the various forms of birth control available at the clinic, and offered them to each of us.

10   The youngest Puerto Rican girl was asked through the interpreter which she'd like to use: the loop, diaphragm, or pill. She shook her head "no" three times. "You don't want to come back here again, do you?" the volunteer pressed. The girl's head was so low her chin rested on her breastbone. "Si," she whispered.

11   We had been there two hours by that time, filling out endless forms, giving blood and urine, receiving lectures. But unlike any other group of women I've been in, we didn't talk. Our common denominator, the one which usually floods across language and economic barriers into familiarity, today was one of shame. We were losing life that day, not giving it.

12   The group kept getting cut back to smaller, more workable units, and finally I was put in a small waiting room with just two other women. We changed into paper bathrobes and paper slippers, and we rustled whenever we moved. One of the women in my room was shivering and an aide brought her a blanket.

13   "What's the matter?" the aide asked her. "I'm scared," the woman said. "How much will it hurt?" The aide smiled. "Oh, nothing worse than a couple of bad cramps," she said. "This afternoon you'll be dancing a jig."

14   I began to panic. Suddenly the rhetoric, the abortion marches I'd walked in, the telegrams sent to Albany to counteract the Friends of the Fetus, the Zero Population Growth buttons I'd worn, peeled away, and I was all alone with my microscopic baby. There were just the two of us there, and soon, because it was more convenient for me and my husband, there would be one again.

15   How could it be that I, who am so neurotic about life that I step over bugs rather than on them, who spend hours planting flowers and vegetables in the spring even though we rent out the house and never see them, who make sure the children are vaccinated and inoculated and filled with vitamin C, could so arbitrarily decide that this life shouldn't be?

16   "It's not a life," my husband had argued, more to convince himself than me. "It's a bunch of cells smaller than my fingernail."

17   But any woman who has had children knows that certain feeling in her taut, swollen breasts, and the slight but constant ache in her

uterus that signals the arrival of a life. Though I would march myself into blisters for a woman's right to exercise the option of motherhood, I discovered there in the waiting room that I was not the modern woman I thought I was.

18 When my name was called, my body felt so heavy the nurse had to help me into the examining room. I waited for my husband to burst through the door and yell "stop," but of course he didn't. I concentrated on three black spots in the acoustic ceiling until they grew in size to the shape of saucers, while the doctor swabbed my insides with antiseptic.

19 "You're going to feel a burning sensation now," he said, injecting Novocaine into the neck of the womb. The pain was swift and severe, and I twisted to get away from him. He was hurting my baby, I reasoned, and the black saucers quivered in the air. "Stop," I cried. "Please stop." He shook his head, busy with his equipment. "It's too late to stop now," he said. "It'll just take a few more seconds."

20 What good sports we women are. And how obedient. Physically the pain passed even before the hum of the machine signaled that the vacuuming of my uterus was completed, my baby sucked up like ashes after a cocktail party. Ten minutes start to finish. And I was back on the arm of the nurse.

21 There were twelve beds in the recovery room. Each one had a gaily flowered draw sheet and a soft green or blue thermal blanket. It was all very feminine. Lying on these beds for an hour or more were the shocked victims of their sex, their full wombs now stripped clean, their future less encumbered.

22 It was very quiet in that room. The only voice was that of the nurse, locating the new women who had just come in so she could monitor their blood pressure, and checking out the recovered women who were free to leave.

23 Juice was being passed about, and I found myself sipping a Dixie cup of Hawaiian Punch. And older woman with tightly curled bleached hair was just getting up from the next bed. "That was no goddamn snap," she said, resting before putting on her miniskirt and high white boots. Other women came and went, some walking out as dazed as they had entered, others with a bounce that signaled they were going right back to Bloomingdale's.

24 Finally then, it was time for me to leave. I checked out, making an appointment to return in two weeks for a IUD insertion. My husband was slumped in the waiting room, clutching a single yellow rose wrapped in a wet paper towel and stuffed into a baggie.

25 We didn't talk the whole way home, but just held hands very tightly. At home there were more yellow roses and a tray in bed for me and the children's curiosity to divert.

26 It had certainly been a successful operation. I didn't bleed at all for two days just as they had predicted, and then I bled only moderately for another four days. Within a week my breasts had subsided and the tenderness vanished, and my body felt mine again instead of the eggshell it becomes when it's protecting someone else.

27 My husband and I are back to planning our summer vacation and his career switch.

28 And it certainly does make more sense not to be having a baby right now—we say that to each other all the time. But I have this ghost now. A very little ghost that only appears when I'm seeing something beautiful, like the full moon on the ocean last weekend. And the baby waves at me. And I wave at the baby. "Of course, we have room," I cry to the ghost. "Of course, we do."

29 I am "Jane Doe." Using a pseudonym was not the act of cowardice some have said it was, but rather an act of sympathy for the feelings of my family. My daughters were too young then to understand what an abortion was, and my twelve-year-old son (my husband's stepson) reacted angrily when I even broached the subject of abortion to him. Andrew was deeply moralistic, as many children are at that age, and still young enough to feel threatened by the actions of adults; his replies to my "suppose I had an abortion" queries were devastating. "I think abortion is okay if the boy and girl aren't married, and they just made a mistake," he said. "But if you had an abortion, that would be different. You're married, and there is no reason for you not to have another baby. How could you just kill something—no matter how little it is—that's going to grow and have legs and wiggle its fingers?

30 "I would be furious with you if you had an abortion. I'd lose all respect for you being so selfish. I'd make you suffer and remind you of it all the time. I would think of ways to be mean. Maybe I'd give you the silent treatment or something.

31 "If God had meant women to have abortions, He would have put buttons on their stomachs."

32 I decided to wait until he was older before we discussed it again.

33 There were other considerations as well. My husband and I had chosen not to tell our parents about the abortion. My mother was

very ill at the time and not up to a barrage of phone calls from her friends about "what Linda had written in the newspaper." And there were my parents-in-law, who had always hoped for a male grandchild to carry on the family name. So I avoided the confessional and simply wrote what I thought would be a helpful piece for other women who might have shared my experience.

34   The result was almost great enough to be recorded on a seismograph. Interpreting the piece as anti-abortion grist, the Right-to-Lifers reproduced it by the thousands and sent it to everyone on their mailing lists. In one Catholic mailing, two sentences were deleted from the article: one that said I was planning to return to the clinic for an IUD insertion, and the other the quote from a middle-aged woman, "That was no goddamn snap." Papers around the country and in Canada ran it, culminating in its appearance in the Canadian edition of the *Reader's Digest*, whose staff took it upon their editorial selves to delete the last paragraph about the "little ghost" because they considered it "mawkish." They also changed the title from "There Just Wasn't Room in Our Lives for Another Baby" to "A Successful Operation" in hopes that it would change their magazine's pro-abortion image.

35   Hundreds of letters poured into the *New York Times*, some from Right-to-Lifers, who predictably called me a "murderer," and others from pro-choice zealots who had decided the article was a "plant" and might even have been written by a man. Women wrote about their own abortions, some of which had been positive experiences and some disastrous. One woman even wrote that she wished her own mother had had an abortion instead of subjecting her to a childhood that was "brutal and crushing." Many of the respondents criticized me, quite rightly, for not using birth control in the first place. I was stunned, and so was the *New York Times*. A few weeks later they ran a sampling of the letters and my reply, which follows:

36   The varied reactions to my abortion article do not surprise me at all. They are all right. And they are all wrong. There is no issue so fundamental as the giving of life, or the cessation of it. These decisions are the most personal one can ever make and each person facing them reacts in her own way. It is not black-and-white as the laws governing abortion are forced to be. Rather it is the gray area whose core touches

our definition of ourselves that produces "little ghosts" in some, and a sense of relief in others.

37   I admire the woman who chose not to bear her fourth child because she and her husband could not afford to give that child the future they felt necessary. I admire the women who were outraged that I had failed to use any form of contraception. And I ache for the woman whose mother had given birth to her even though she was not wanted, and thus spent an empty, lonely childhood. It takes courage to take the life of someone else in your own hands, and even more courage to assume responsibility for your own.

38   I had my abortion over two years ago. And I wrote about it shortly thereafter. It was only recently, however, that I decided to publish it. I felt it was important to share how one person's abortion had affected her, rather than just sit by while the pro and con groups haggled over legislation.

39   The effect has indeed been profound. Though my husband was very supportive of me, and I, I think, of him, our relationship slowly faltered. As our children are girls, my husband anguished at the possibility that I had been carrying a son. Just a case of male macho, many would argue. But still, that's the way he feels, and it is important. I hope we can get back on a loving track again.

40   Needless to say, I have an IUD now, instead of the diaphragm that is too easily forgotten. I do not begrudge my husband his lack of contraception. Condoms are awkward. Neither do I feel he should have a vasectomy. It is profoundly difficult for him to face the possibility that he might never have that son. Nor do I regret having the abortion. I am just as much an avid supporter of children by choice as I ever was.

41   My only regret is the sheer irresponsibility on my part to become pregnant in the first place. I pray to God that it will never happen again. But if it does, I will be equally thankful that the law provides women the dignity to choose whether to bring a new life into the world or not.

Analyzing the Writer's Argument

1. How does Francke's husband react to the news that she is pregnant? What reason does he give for not wanting another child? What are Francke's own reasons?

2. What is Francke's attitude toward the other women at the center that morning?

3. What does Francke mean when she says, "I discovered there in the waiting room that I was not the modern woman I thought I was"? What exactly for Francke is a modern woman?

4. Had you read only the essay that originally appeared in the *New York Times*, would you think Francke was for or against abortion? Point to specific words, phrases, or passages that led you to your conclusion. Now, having read her reply to the letters, what is her position on the question of abortion?

5. According to Francke, why did she write her personal essay for the *New York Times* in the first place? Why did she publish it using the pseudonym "Jane Doe"?

6. How would you characterize the responses to Francke's original essay? Did any of the responses surprise you? Explain.

7. The story of Francke's abortion and her reply to the hundreds of letters were written for the *New York Times*. How does the style of the newspaper account and reply differ from the surrounding text? What conclusions about newspaper style can you draw from your comparison?

Exploring the Issues in This Essay

1. Francke is not the least bit ambivalent about the issue of birth control. What is your own attitude toward birth control? Discuss your feelings about abortion being used as birth control.

2. Did you sympathize with the Franckes' decision for Linda to have an abortion? Or did you find it difficult to agree with their decision because it just seemed "more convenient" for the two of them not to have a new baby? Discuss the various reasons that a woman might have for seeking an abortion. Do some reasons seem more acceptable than others? Explain.

George F. Will

*Discretionary Killing**

> *Pulitzer Prize winning journalist George F. Will was born in Champaign, Illinois, in 1941. He studied political science at Trinity College in Hartford, Connecticut, and Princeton University before going on to teach at Michigan State University and the University of Toronto. But it has been as a syndicated newspaper columnist that he earned a reputation for his insightful social and political commentary. His column appears in nearly 400 newspapers and he has a biweekly column in* Newsweek. *Will's essays have been collected in* The Pursuit of Happiness and Other Sobering Thoughts *(1979),* The Pursuit of Virtue and Other Tory Notions *(1982), and* The Morning After: American Successes and Excesses, 1981–1986 *(1986).* Statecraft as Soulcraft: What Government Does *(1983), Will's fourth book concerns itself with politics and political theory.*
>
> *"Discretionary Killing" first appeared in* Newsweek *on September 20, 1976. Here, three years after the famous* Roe vs. Wade *decision, Will expresses his alarm about the abortion epidemic and argues, in the words of Dr. Leon R. Kass, that "we are already witnessing the erosion of our idea of man as something splendid or divine, as a creature with freedom and dignity."*

1   It is neither surprising nor regrettable that the abortion epidemic alarms many thoughtful people. Last year there were a million legal abortions in the U.S. and 50 million worldwide. The killing of fetuses on this scale is a revolution against the judgment of generations. And this revolution in favor of discretionary killing has not run its course.

2   That life begins at conception is not disputable. The dispute concerns when, if ever, abortion is a *victimless* act. A nine-week-old

fetus has a brain, organs, palm creases, fingerprints. But when, if ever, does a fetus acquire another human attribute, the right to life?

3   The Supreme Court has decreed that *at no point* are fetuses "persons in the whole sense." The constitutional status of fetuses is different in the third trimester of pregnancy. States constitutionally can, but need not, prohibit the killing of fetuses after "viability" (24 to 28 weeks), which the Court says is when a fetus can lead a "meaningful" life outside the womb. (The Court has not revealed its criterion of "meaningfulness.") But states cannot ban the killing of a viable fetus when that is necessary to protect a woman's health from harm, which can be construed broadly to include "distress." The essence of the Court's position is that the "right to privacy" means a mother (interestingly, that is how the Court refers to a woman carrying a fetus) may deny a fetus life in order that she may lead the life she prefers.

4   Most abortions kill fetuses that were accidentally conceived. Abortion also is used by couples who want a child, but not the one gestating. Chromosome studies of fetal cells taken from amniotic fluid enable prenatal diagnosis of genetic defects and diseases that produce physical and mental handicaps. Some couples, especially those who already have handicapped children, use such diagnosis to screen pregnancies.

5   New diagnostic techniques should give pause to persons who would use a constitutional amendment to codify their blanket opposition to abortion. About fourteen weeks after conception expectant parents can know with virtual certainty that their child, if born, will die by age 4 of Tay–Sachs disease, having become deaf, blind and paralyzed. Other comparably dreadful afflictions can be detected near the end of the first trimester or early in the second. When such suffering is the alternative to abortion, abortion is not obviously the greater evil.

6   Unfortunately, morals often follow technologies, and new diagnostic and manipulative skills will stimulate some diseased dreams. Geneticist Bentley Glass, in a presidential address to the American Association for the Advancement of Science, looked forward to the day when government may require what science makes possible: "No parents will in that future time have a right to burden society with a malformed or a mentally incompetent child."

7   At a 1972 conference some eminent scientists argued that infants with Down's syndrome (Mongolism) are a social burden and

should be killed, when possible, by "negative euthanasia," the denial of aid needed for survival. It was the morally deformed condemning the genetically defective. Who will they condemn next? Old people, although easier to abandon, can be more inconvenient than unwanted children. Scientific advances against degenerative diseases will enable old people to (as will be said) "exist" longer. The argument for the discretionary killing of these burdensome folks will be that "mere" existence, not "meaningful" life, would be ended by euthanasia.

8   The day is coming when an infertile woman will be able to have a laboratory-grown embryo implanted in her uterus. Then there will be the "surplus embryo problem." Dr. Donald Gould, a British science writer, wonders: "What happens to the embryos which are discarded at the end of the day—washed down the sink?" Dr. Leon R. Kass, a University of Chicago biologist, wonders: "Who decides what are the grounds for discard? What if there is another recipient available who wishes to have the otherwise unwanted embryo? Whose embryos are they? The woman's? The couple's? The geneticist's? The obstetrician's? The Ford Foundation's?... Shall we say that discarding laboratory-grown embryos is a matter solely between a doctor and his plumber?"

9   But for now the issue is abortion, and it is being trivialized by cant about "a woman's right to control her body." Dr. Kass notes that "the fetus simply is not a mere part of a woman's body. One need only consider whether a woman can ethically take thalidomide while pregnant to see that this is so." Dr. Kass is especially impatient with the argument that a fetus with a heartbeat and brain activity brain activity "is indistinguishable from a tumor in the uterus, a wart on the nose, or a hamburger in the stomach." But that argument is necessary to justify discretionary killing of fetuses on the current scale, and some of the experiments that some scientists want to perform on live fetuses.

10   Abortion advocates have speech quirks that may betray qualms. Homeowners kill crabgrass. Abortionists kill fetuses. Homeowners do not speak of "terminating" crabgrass. But Planned Parenthood of New York City, which evidently regards abortion as just another form of birth control, has published an abortion guide that uses the word "kill" only twice, once to say what some women did to themselves before legalized abortion, and once to describe what some contraceptives do to sperm. But when referring to the killing

of fetuses, the book, like abortion advocates generally, uses only euphemisms, like "termination of potential life."

11 Abortion advocates become interestingly indignant when opponents display photographs of the well-formed feet and hands of a nine-week-old fetus. People avoid correct words and object to accurate photographs because they are uneasy about saying and seeing what abortion is. It is *not* the "termination" of a hamburger in the stomach.

12 And the casual manipulation of life is not harmless. As Dr. Kass says: "We have paid some high prices for the technological conquest of nature, but none so high as the intellectual and spiritual costs of seeing nature as mere material for our manipulation, exploitation and transformation. With the powers for biological engineering now gathering, there will be splendid new opportunities for a similar degradation of our view of man. Indeed, we are already witnessing the erosion of our idea of man as something splendid or divine, as a creature with freedom and dignity. And clearly, if we come to see ourselves as meat, then meat we shall become."

13 Politics has paved the way for this degradation. Meat we already have become, at Ypres and Verdun, Dresden and Hiroshima, Auschwitz and the Gulag. Is it a coincidence that this century, which is distinguished for science and war and totalitarianism, also is the dawn of the abortion age?

Analyzing the Writer's Argument

1. What is Will's thesis, and where is it stated?
2. What does Will mean when he states, "The dispute concerns when, if ever, abortion is a *victimless* act"? On what assumption is this statement based?
3. In paragraph 3 Will discusses the Supreme Court's decision on abortion. What is his attitude toward this decision? What is the purpose of his parenthetical comments?
4. What evidence does Will provide to document his claim that "most abortions kill fetuses that were accidentally conceived"?
5. New diagnostic techniques permit doctors to screen fetuses for genetic defects and diseases. What is Will's position on these new scientific advances? Does he believe abortion should be permitted if a positive diagnosis is made in such a case?

6. In paragraphs 7 and 8 Will introduces the subjects of "euthanasia" and "surplus embryos." How are these two paragraphs related to Will's argument, or are they simply digressions designed to "scare"?

7. Will quotes a number of medical experts, notably geneticist Bentley Glass, Dr. Donald Gould, and Dr. Leon R. Kass. What does the use of these authorities add to Will's argument? Explain your conclusions with reference to specific quotations.

8. Will claims that "abortion advocates have speech quirks that may betray qualms." Identify several examples of these "speech quirks." How would you characterize Will's own diction? How does it differ from that of the abortion advocates? Did you find Will's language persuasive or abrasive? Explain.

Exploring the Issues in This Essay

1. Writing in 1976, George Will foresaw the problems that innovative reproductive technology could produce. The process of *in vitro* fertilization has indeed given the world "laboratory-grown embryos." How do you feel about such technology? Discuss the ethical dimensions of both *in vitro* fertilization and the "surplus embryo problem."

2. Reread Will's last two paragraphs. Is he being fair when he compares abortion to the human slaughter and atrocities at "Ypres and Verdun, Dresden and Hiroshima, Auschwitz and the Gulag"? Several commentators on the issue have gone so far as to call abortion the new holocaust. Do you agree with Will when he says, "the casual manipulation of life is not harmless"? Discuss the "intellectual and spiritual costs," if there are indeed any, that Americans will have to pay for abortion.

What every man should know about abortion.

It's easy for men to have an opinion about abortion. We can always pretend it's not our problem.

But for many women, abortion involves more than an opinion. They face a *decision* about abortion. And that's harder and lonelier. They have to live with the consequences.

This doesn't make abortion a "woman's issue" any more than birth control is. Because no woman ever made herself pregnant. Men are responsible, too.

So the public controversy over keeping abortion safe and legal concerns your freedom as well. To marry when and if you want. To decide with your partner to have children when you want them. If you want them.

Yet an increasingly vocal, violent minority wants to outlaw abortion.

For all women. Regardless of circumstances. Even if her life or health is endangered by a pregnancy. Even if she's a victim of rape or incest. Even if she's too young to be a mother.

But outlawing abortion won't stop it. Women have always had abortions when they've felt there's no other way. Even at the risk of being maimed or killed with a back-alley abortion.

Ironically, it's mostly men who want to outlaw abortion — men in the White House, Congress, the courts. Many of them even want to ban contraceptives and sex education.

These people must know there's a man intimately involved in every unwanted pregnancy. Why don't they ever mention it?

Maybe they're hoping to buy your silence until it's too late. And think

you're too selfish to care. Prove them wrong by returning the coupon below.

Take action! The President has urged the Supreme Court to take away our right to decide for ourselves. I'm writing him to tell him to respect every woman's personal privacy. I enclose my contribution to support Planned Parenthood's Campaign to Keep Abortion Safe and Legal, 810 Seventh Avenue, New York, NY 10019-5882

NAME _____ NY 12-25

ADDRESS _____

CITY _____ STATE _____ ZIP _____

Don't wait until women are dying again.

Planned Parenthood®
Federation of America

Reprinted by permission, Planned Parenthood® Federation of America, Inc.

232

Jean Seligmann

The Medical Quandary*

>   *Jean Seligmann was born in New York City in 1944, and educated at Bryn Mawr where she majored in classical Greek. Shortly after graduation she went to work at* Newsweek *as a news researcher. In 1971 she joined* Newsweek's *editorial staff where today she is a general editor. For almost twenty years she has reported and written about health and medicine in the United States, specializing in women's medical and reproductive issues.*
>
>   *In "The Medical Quandary," first published as part of* Newsweek's *cover story on America's abortion dilemma in the January 14, 1985 issue, Seligmann discusses the new abortion policy questions that have arisen with advances in medical technology. Physicians continue to hold different opinions about the point in a pregnancy after which abortions should no longer be performed, and what their responsibilities are if a fetus should survive an abortion attempt.*

1   The ultimate Hippocratic dilemma, the nightmare that unsettles a good doctor's sleep: a pregnant patient, after much agony, has chosen an abortion and the doctor performs the procedure by injecting prostaglandins (hormonelike substances that induce labor) into her amniotic sac. But when, some hours later, the fetus is expelled from the woman's uterus, it is not the 22-week-old creature he had anticipated. It is 26 weeks old—and alive.

2   This is an unlikely scenario; 90 percent of abortions in the United States are performed before the 13th week of pregnancy, and only 1 percent, or about 13,000 procedures a year, take place after the 20th week (the start of gestation is calculated from the onset of the last menstrual period). But the branch of medicine known as neonatology—the special care of newborns—now routinely saves the lives of preemies who would have died a decade ago. Today, a

premature delivery can lead to heroic—and sometimes successful—attempts to save mid-trimester babies. Increasingly, survival is possible for fetuses that can legally be aborted. At the same time, the growing ability to treat fetuses in *utero*—shunts to correct hydrocephalus or bladder blockage, drugs to alter metabolism—deepen the quandary. "When you do things to a child in the womb, you're acknowledging that you're dealing with a patient," says medical ethicist Thomas Murray of the University of Texas Medical School at Galveston. "It's hard to do that and then turn around and abort a child of the same developmental age."

3   While the numbers of late abortions are relatively small, the moral implications are substantial. As a result, physicians and hospitals are taking new and searching looks at their policies on abortion. Across the United States, many hospitals skirt the issue by simply refusing to perform most abortions after 20 weeks; some physicians have adopted an even earlier "personal cutoff" of 10 or 12 weeks. And when doctors do administer late abortions, they are much more likely to employ the techniques certain to kill the developing child before it leaves the womb—anything to forestall the possibility of a live birth in the operating room.

4   Dr. Sherwood Lynn, an obstetrician and gynecologist at Houston's Hermann Hospital, used to perform many more abortions that he does now. Today, he refers most requests to area clinics set up expressly for abortions. He does them himself only when a clear-cut medical problem jeopardizes the fetus or mother—for example, if the woman has been taking potent cancer drugs that could cause a fatal maternal hemorrhage during labor and would almost certainly kill the baby. Still, he says, "I don't like to do abortions. It's not a moral question—I just have a bad feeling about it. It's always a strain." One reason for the strain, says Dr. Paul Blumenthal, director of ambulatory care at Chicago's Michael Reese Hospital, is that one of the most widely used techniques for late abortions, dilatation and evacuation (D & E) requires the physician to crush and kill the fetus while it is still in the womb. It's one thing when a physician injects a drug to induce labor and walks away, says Blumenthal, "and another thing to actively take part in the procedure. The physician can't see what he's doing in the uterus. It's bloody and a little frightening."

5   No woman deliberately plans a late abortion, and most of those who end up having them belong to well-recognized categories. Forty-four per cent of abortions done after the 21st week of gestation are performed on teen-agers, who may not realize that they are pregnant until they feel the baby kicking. Or they may deny the evidence of their own bodies. In states like Massachusetts, where a minor must have the consent of both parents for an abortion, "a young girl may be well into her second trimester before she gets the nerve to tell her momma, who may in turn hesitate to tell daddy," explains Dr. Phillip Stubblefield, chief of obstetrics and gynecology at Mount Auburn Hospital in Cambridge. Or, refusing to confess at all, a teen-ager may shop for a friendlier jurisdiction, delaying the procedure still further.

6   Other typical recipients of late abortions include poor women, who may find it difficult to scrape up $200 for the procedure or do not know how to find out where to go for the operation; women with histories of irregular menses, and women approaching menopause who attribute missed periods to their impending change of life.

7   Perhaps the most agonizing late abortions, however, are those that result from yet another product of modern technology. Amniocentesis, the withdrawal and analysis of amniotic fluid to identify possible genetic abnormalities like Down's syndrome in an unborn child, cannot be done until the 14th to 17th week of pregnancy. Moreover, the results of the test may not be ready until the 21st week or even later. Thus, most abortions performed because of amniocentesis findings necessarily take place in the gestation period's problematic zone. But Dr. John Carpenter, director of the prenatal diagnostic center at the Baylor College of Medicine in Houston, says he has no reservations about abortions under such circumstances. However, "I don't do it as a cold-blooded killer," he explains. "I have a great deal of empathy and sympathy for these families. They suffer grief and I suffer grief, too. But I have no qualms because I've seen the impact a seriously impaired child can have on a family."

8   Within the next five years, amniocentesis and its unsatisfactory timetable may be supplemented by a newer research tool: chorionic villus biopsy. This procedure, in which a small sample of the tissue lining the amniotic sac is removed and analyzed for abnor-

malities, can be done as early as eight weeks into pregnancy, with results at 12 weeks. In an abortion at that stage, of course, fetal viability is out of the question. But chorionic villus biopsy is more risky to the fetus than amniocentesis, and some researchers doubt that it will ever be safe enough for routine screening.

9 The most disturbing late abortions, of course, are those that result in live births. Although rare, they sometimes occur because the age of the fetus has been underestimated. The woman may not remember the date of her last menstrual period—or she may deliberately lie about it if she is determined to get an abortion despite an advanced pregnancy. Relying on a physical examination alone, explains Dr. Michael Burnhill, an obstetrician and gynecologist at the College of Medicine and Dentistry of New Jersey, a doctor can miscalculate fetal age by more than a month. For that reason, many physicians routinely perform an ultrasound scan for abortions after the 12th week of pregnancy. This visual image of the fetus enables a skilled practitioner to estimate its age with a high degree of accuracy.

10 But even when the age can be determined precisely, doctors don't always agree on when the fetus should be considered "viable," or indeed on exactly what viability means. In neonatal intensive-care units, doctors treat 24- to 26-week-old fetuses weighing as little as 1 pound 10 ounces, and 28-week preemies stand a good chance of surviving to lead healthy lives. But these are babies whose births are intended, and for whom major life-sustaining efforts are made during both labor and delivery. By contrast, observes Dr. Richard Stavis, director of the neonatal unit at Bryn Mawr Hospital in Bryn Mawr, Pa., "when you do an abortion, you're obviously not doing it in the interest of the baby's viability." Stavis considers that viability begins "in the range of 24 weeks," noting that the likelihood of survival before that point is close to zero. But even at 26 weeks, he explains, survival rates are low because the baby is born with immature lungs, skin so fragile it can be torn by surgical tape, and blood vessels that may be too minuscule for the introduction of needles and tubes necessary for monitoring and nutrition.

11 New Jersey's Burnhill, who has performed abortions at 26 weeks in cases of severe birth defects, believes it is unrealistic to speak of viability before that point, when the baby still weighs less than

two pounds. "I don't think a 24-week fetus can ever have an independent existence," he observes, "though you can keep some of them alive on assisted ventilation for a while." Fetuses weighing less than 35 ounces, he notes, are often born with serious defects: learning disabilities, poor vision and impaired hearing. "Technological advances have been keeping them alive, not keeping them intact," says Burnhill, "and the heartbreak for the parents later is staggering."

12   In most cases of late abortion, physicians try to prevent such tragedies by using one of the two methods that nearly always result in fetal death. One is the relatively new D&E, in which the fetus is literally dismembered by a forceps within the uterus, limb by limb, and the "pieces" are withdrawn through the vagina. Although a D&E is safe for the mother, it can be devastating for the hospital staff; many doctors simply won't do advanced D&E's Burnhill refuses to perform them later than 14 or 15 weeks into pregnancy, at least in part, he says, because "I have trouble getting nurses and anesthesiologists to work with me." (It may have been this technique that President Reagan was referring to when he asserted last winter that the fetus experiences pain during an abortion. However, while even a 10-week-old embryo will shrink from an instrument poked into the uterus, researchers argue that the neurological pathways necessary for pain perception are not well developed until very late in pregnancy and perhaps not until after birth.)

13   In the other method, the physician administers substances that first kill the fetus, then induce the labor that will expel it. Saline solution, for example, injected in small quantities into the amniotic sac, usually performs both functions. However, this procedure carries some risk to the woman; the saline may find its way into her bloodstream, causing hemorrhage or lung and kidney damage. Another procedure calls for introducing a small amount of urea into the sac, or injecting it directly into the fetus itself. At some medical centers, the heart drug digoxin is administered to the fetus before labor is induced, resulting in a fatal cardiac arrhythmia.

14   One of the safest methods for inducing labor in a late abortion is the "instillation" of prostaglandins, which cut off the fetus's oxygen supply. Still, there are occasional live births. Some states

and hospitals require doctors to treat such a baby like any other "live" birth from premature labor, but this does not mean that extraordinary, "heroic" efforts are necessarily made to save its life. "If we had an aborted baby below the age of viability that was technically live-born," says Stavis of Bryn Mawr, "we'd put it in an Isolette [incubator], keep it warm, give it oxygen and observe it. But we would not actively intervene to protect that baby from dying." To place tubes in a fetus that has no chance of survival, Stavis believes, is abusive. "It is subjecting the fetus to an experiment," he declares. "To me, that is cruel."

15 "Nobody who provides abortions wants to kill babies," adds Stubblefield. "Nobody is in favor of infanticide. The question is, where do you draw the line? In my morality, an abortion prior to 24 weeks is a reasonable thing to do; after that it is not." And if a fetus should survive an abortion attempt, Stubblefield says, "if it looks as if it might have a chance—not just for an hour or two, but for survival to leave the hospital—then you give it everything you've got."

Analyzing the Writer's Argument

1. Late abortions are, according to Seligmann, the "ultimate Hippocratic dilemma" facing obstetricians and gynecologists today. What for her are the "substantial" moral implications of such late abortions?

2. What is "neonatology"? In what ways has this branch of medicine deepened the quandary for physicians?

3. How have doctors and hospitals attempted to skirt the issue of late abortions?

4. Seligmann identifies four groups of women—teen-agers, poor women, women with histories of irregular menses, and women approaching menopause—who have late abortions. Explain how each of these groups of women help support her claim, "No woman deliberately plans a late abortion."

5. According to Seligmann, why are abortions performed after the result of amniocentesis are returned often so agonizing? What hope, if any, does the new research tool chorionic villus biopsy promise for alleviating the problem?

6. Why are some physicians reluctant to do advanced D&E's What other methods do physicians have available when performing late

abortions? Are there any problematic side-effects or complications associated with these procedures?

7. Seligmann directly quotes a number of people from the medical community in her essay. What do these citations of authorities contribute to her essay? In your opinion, has Seligmann managed to give equal time to the opposing viewpoints, or does she reveal a personal bias on the issue? Explain.

Exploring the Issues in This Essay

1. What are the options available to a physician when a late abortion results in a live birth? Is there a consensus among physicians about how best to proceed in such a situation? Discuss what you would do if you were the physician in the scenario Seligmann describes in paragraph 1.

2. According to Seligmann, the largest percentage of abortions (41 percent) "done after the 21st week of gestation are performed on teen-agers." Discuss what parents, schools, and the community at large can do to help to see that teenage females have abortions earlier or do not get pregnant in the first place.

Writing Suggestions for
Abortion: The Debate Continues

1. What is your position on abortion? What are the most compelling arguments against your position? Write an essay in which you argue for your position, being careful to refute the arguments of the opposition.

2. In an essay consider the reasons why abortion as a topic has received so much attention in the media. What are the major arguments both for and against abortion? Do some arguments seem to be more rational than others? Why do emotions seem to run high for participants in the abortion debate?

3. Tisdale claims, "Women who have the fewest choices of all exercise their right to abortion the most." Write an essay in which you argue for or against this thesis.

4. Spend enough time in the library to learn what you can about Planned Parenthood Federation of America, Inc. When was the organization founded? What are its goals? What role has it been playing in the abortion debate? Write an essay in which you report your findings.

5. After reading the essays in this section, do you believe that abortion is a human life issue (the sanctity of life) or a feminist issue (a woman's right to control her own body)? Using materials from your reading in this section, write an essay in which you argue for your position.

6. Write an essay in which you argue for or against the father's right to have a say in the decision to abort a fetus.

7. There is hardly a discussion of reproductive rights in which the subject of birth control is not mentioned. How is birth control related to the issue of abortion? Is abortion sometimes used as a method of birth control? If so, is there any way to restrict its use as such? Write an essay in which you argue for or against birth control.

8. Imagine you have just read Linda Bird Francke's original essay for *The New York Times*. What was your response to her story? Write a letter to the editor of the *Times* in which you articulate your reaction.

9. Using information from the readings in this section, write an essay in which you evaluate the weaknesses or shortcomings in both the "pro-life" and "pro-choice" arguments.

10. Write an essay in which you analyze the "pro-choice" position. How would you defend the "pro-choice" position from critics who charge that it is really a "pro-abortion" position?

11. Today, new technologies allow doctors to "routinely save the lives of preemies who would have died a decade ago." At the same time, doctors are treating fetuses *in utero*. The bottom line is, we live in an age when "survival is possible for fetuses that can be legally aborted." When medical technology and law collide, new moral and ethical questions often result. What are some of the questions now being asked, and how is the medical profession answering them?

6

Animal Experimentation: Unwarranted Cruelty?

Animal experimentation is the study of animal anatomy and physiology in order to increase our knowledge, especially of human biology. Animals are used in research and teaching and to test the safety and effectiveness of various commercial products, including drugs, cosmetics, sundries, weapons, toys, and safety equipment. The kinds of animals used in such research range from frogs and turtles to guinea pigs, rabbits, cats, dogs, and monkeys. And, of course, no animals are more widely used in this context than the proverbial and almost ubiquitous white laboratory mice and rats, which some experts estimate number 75–100 million in any given year.

In health-care research, animals are used to test experimental surgical procedures and mechanical devices, the toxicity or irritation risk of new drugs and chemicals, the effectiveness of vitamins, the adaptability of living organisms to physical and psychological impairment, the side effects of contraceptives, the responses to various kinds of cancer therapy, and the effects of radiation on endurance. Without the aid of the monkey, the now familiar heart-lung machine used in all open-heart surgery would not have been developed. Without the use of the Syrian hamster, efforts to understand kala-azar, a disease of Mediterranean area and Asian children, would not have taken place; and, without the use of many dogs, insulin would not have been discovered and the lives of millions of diabetics would be considerably shortened.

Although a small portion of what we as humans learn about ourselves from animals goes to help the animals themselves, there is no question that this research is overwhelmingly for human benefit. Opponents of animal research, then, are faced with a moral dilemma. Do humans have a right to use other species in often

243

painful, disfiguring, and deadly experiments? The philosophical basis for the debate stems from a long English tradition of antivivisection (the argument against the dissection of live animals in experiments) and the very influential work of Australian philosopher Peter Singer, who in his book *Animal Liberation* (1975) advanced the notion that each animal species has a right to its biological destiny and that no one species, no matter how intelligent or powerful, should be allowed to infringe on the rights of another. Such arrogance he termed "speciesism," and since the publication of his book the world has witnessed a crescendo of public concern about the uses and abuses of animals. Articles and books have been published, revelations of abuses have appeared in films and on radio and television, and financially devastating guerrilla and terrorist-like raids on animal laboratories have been carried out in order to liberate animals held captive by researchers.

In response, the medical community has done little to convince the public of its need for animal experimentation. Instead, it has shown outrage and has charged animal rights advocates and liberationists with ignorance of the role of science, the nature of research, soft-headed sentimentality, and a callousness toward the welfare of humans. Although some doctors and researchers admit that charges of animal abuses in research settings have some legitimacy, they also contend that these have been very much overplayed and publicized and that the research community will be crippled if animal rights groups succeed in their drive not only to make sure animals are treated humanely but ultimately to prohibit the use of any animals for medical purposes.

In 1966 the federal government passed the Animal Welfare Act, legislation aimed at protecting animals but with no power to police; various other scientific groups and educational institutions have instituted somewhat stricter regulations governing the use of animals. Yet the debate continues, and it is not likely to quiet as the animal rights groups gather strength and diversify their interests, examining such questions as the use of animals for their skins, hides, tusks, fur, and meat, the treatment of animals in pet shops, and even the rationale for zoos and animal preserves.

Patricia Curtis

The Argument Against Animal Experimentation

> *Born in Orange, New Jersey, in 1924, Patricia Curtis received her B.A. degree from the University of Missouri. She has been an editor for various popular magazines and since 1979 has worked as a free-lance writer, publishing books chiefly for children and young adults. Her best known work is* Animal Rights: Stories of People Who Defend the Rights of Animals *(1980), which Mary Matthews described in* The Washington Post *as "an overview of the horrifying things done to animals when they are raised in factory farms, hunted, trapped, experimented on, used by rodeos, circuses, moviemakers and television shows, and kept in second-rate zoos or as pets by second-rate people."*
>
> *"I write as an advocate, a defender of the non-human animals we share the planet with. While I try to interest, inform, and entertain my readers, I hope to make messages come through about the rights, the dignity, and the plight of animals," says Curtis. This she has done well in "The Argument Against Animal Experimentation" which was first published in* The New York Times Magazine *December 31, 1978.*

1   The professor was late leaving the medical school because he'd had to review papers by his third-year students in experimental surgery. It was well after 11 when he wearily drove his car into the garage. The house was dark except for a hall light left on for him. His wife and youngsters were already asleep, he realized, and the professor suddenly felt lonely as he fit his key in the lock. But even as he pushed open the door, Sabrina was there to welcome him. She was always waiting for him, lying on the rug just inside the door.

2   The little dog leaped up ecstatically, wagging her tail and licking the professor's hand. The professor stroked her affectionately. She

245

flopped on her back and grinned at him as he tickled her chest and belly; then she jumped to her feet and danced around his legs as he walked into the kitchen to get something to eat. Sabrina's exuberant joy at his return never failed to cheer him.

3   Early next morning, the professor drove back to the medical school and entered the laboratory. He noticed that a dog on which one of his students had operated the previous afternoon still had an endotracheal tube in its throat and obviously had not received pain medication. He must be more strict in his orders, he thought to himself. Another dog had bled through its bandages and lay silently in a pool of blood. Sloppy work, the professor thought— must speak to that student. None of the dogs made any sounds, because new arrivals at the laboratory were always subjected to an operation called a ventriculocordectomy that destroyed their vocal cords so that no barks or howls disturbed people in the medical school and surrounding buildings.

4   The professor looked over the animals that would be used that day by his surgery students. He came across a new female dog that had just been delivered by the dealer. Badly frightened, she whined and wagged her tail ingratiatingly as he paused in front of her cage. The professor felt a stab. The small dog bore an amazing resemblance to Sabrina. Quickly he walked away. Nevertheless, he made a note to remind himself to give orders for her vocal cords to be destroyed and for her to be conditioned for experimental surgery.

5   American researchers sacrifice approximately 64 million animals annually. Some 400,000 dogs, 200,000 cats, 33,000 apes and monkeys, thousands of horses, ponies, calves, sheep, goats and pigs, and millions of rabbits, hamsters, guinea pigs, birds, rats and mice are used every year in experiments that often involve intense suffering. The research establishment has generally insisted that live animals provide the only reliable tests for drugs, chemicals and cosmetics that will be used by people. Researchers also believe that animal experiments are necessary in the search for cures for human illnesses and defects. There is no question that many important medical discoveries, from polio vaccine to the physiology of the stress response, have indeed been made through the use of animals. Thus universities, medical and scientific institutions, pharmaceutical companies, cosmetics manufacturers and the mil-

itary have always taken for granted their right to use animals in almost any way they see fit.

6 But increasing numbers of scientists are beginning to ask themselves some hard ethical questions and to re-evaluate their routine use of painful testing tools such as electric shock, stomach tubes, hot plates, restraining boxes and radiation devices. A new debate has arisen over whether all such experiments are worth the suffering they entail.

7 Strongly opposing curtailment of animal experimentation are groups such as the National Society for Medical Research, which insists that any such reduction would jeopardize public safety and scientific progress. The N.S.M.R. was formed to resist what it considers the threat of Government regulation of animal research and to refute the charges of humane societies. Many scientists, however, although they firmly believe that some animal research is necessary, no longer endorse such an absolutist approach to the issue.

8 "Some knowledge can be obtained at too high a price," writes British physiologist Dr. D. H. Smyth in his recent book *Alternatives to Animal Experiments*.

9 "The lives and suffering of animals must surely count for something," says Jeremy J. Stone, director of the Washington-based Federation of American Scientists, which has devoted an entire newsletter to a discussion of the rights of animals.

10 According to physiologist Dr. F. Barbara Orlans of the National Institutes of Health, "Within the scientific community there's a growing concern for animals that has not yet had a forum." Dr. Orlans is president of the newly formed Scientists' Center for Animal Welfare, which hopes to raise the level of awareness on the part of fellow scientists and the public about avoidable suffering inflicted on lab animals, wildlife, and animals raised for meat. "We will try to be a voice of reason. We can perhaps be a link between scientists and the humane organizations," Dr. Orlans explains. "We hope also to provide solid factual data on which animal-protection decisions can be based."

11 Another link between researchers and humane organizations is a new committee comprising more than 400 doctors and scientists that has been formed by Friends of Animals, a national animal-welfare group. Headed by eight M.D.'s, the committee is mak-

ing a survey of Federally funded animal-research projects. Friends of Animals hopes that the study will expose not only needless atrocities performed on animals, but also boondoggles involving taxpayers' money.

12   One reason scientists are no longer so indifferent to the suffering they inflict on animals is the discoveries that science itself has made. We now know that many animals feel, think, reason, communicate, have sophisticated social systems, and even, on occasion, behave altruistically toward each other. Communication by sign language with higher primates, demonstrations of the intelligence of dolphins and whales, observations of the complex societies of wolves and other animals, and many other investigations have narrowed the gap between ourselves and the rest of the animal kingdom, making it more difficult to rationalize inhumane experiments. Dr. Dallas Pratt, author of *Painful Experiments on Animals*, points out that "among the rats and mice, the computers and oscilloscopes, there is Koko"—referring to the young gorilla whom a California primatologist has taught a working vocabulary of 375 words and concepts in sign language and who has even learned to take snapshots with a Polaroid camera. It's hard not to feel squeamish about subjecting animals to inhumane experiments when they possess almost-human intelligence.

13   The thinking of researchers is also beginning to be affected by the growing movement for animal rights. The rising concern for the welfare of animals is seen by some people as a natural extension of contemporary movements promoting civil rights, women's rights, homosexual rights, human rights, and children's rights. Public interest in preserving endangered species is based first on an increasing awareness of the complexity and fragility of ecosystems, and second on the notion, still much debated, that any species of plant or animal, from the lowly snail darter to the blue whale, has the right to continue to exist. From here it is only a short logical step to the belief that animals have the right to exist without suffering unnecessarily.

14   Near the top of the list of animal-welfare activists' causes is putting an end to inhumane experiments on laboratory animals. In Great Britain, where a vigorous antivivisection movement has existed for more than a century, a clandestine group called the Animal Liberation Front conducts commando-style raids on laboratories, liberating animals and sabotaging research equipment.

A.L.F. members have also been known to slash tires and pour sugar in the gas tanks of trucks used by animal dealers who supply labs. To be sure, this group of zealots hasn't made much of a dent in England's vast research community, but it does appeal to a gut reaction on the part of many Britons against animal research.

15 Animal-rights activists are not merely sentimental do-gooders and pet-lovers. They have mounted a philosophical attack on the traditional Western attitude toward animals, branding it as "speciesist" (like racist or sexist), a term derived from the word "speciesism," coined by psychologist and author Dr. Richard Ryder. The Australian philosopher Peter Singer, in his influential 1975 book *Animal Liberation*, argued that the "speciesist" rationalization, "Human beings come first," is usually used by people who do nothing for either human or nonhuman animals. And he pointed out the parallels between the oppression of blacks, women, and animals: Such oppression is usually rationalized on the grounds that the oppressed group is inferior.

16 In 1977, when outraged antivivisectionists heard about some highly unpleasant electric-shock and burn experiments conducted on young pigs in Denmark, they wasted no time in pointing out the irony that the tests were being conducted by Amnesty International, the human-rights organization. Amnesty International was attempting to prove that human prisoners could be tortured without leaving any marks, and pigs were used because of the similarity of their skin to ours. (The tests were subsequently discontinued.)

17 Paradoxically, the public tends to be "speciesist" in its reaction to animal experimentation: For many people, a test is permissible when it inflicts pain on a "lower" animal like a hamster, but not when the victim is a dog. When it was discovered in the summer of 1976 that the American Museum of Natural History was damaging the brains of cats and running painful sex experiments on them, hundreds of people picketed in protest. The museum's Animal Behavior Department defended itself on the grounds that the research was intended to gain a better understanding of human sexual responses. Animal-rights groups, scientists among them, were not convinced of the necessity of the tests, which came to an end only when the chief researcher retired. But the protesters made no stir about the pigeons, doves, and rats that suffered in the same laboratory.

18   If United States Army researchers had used guinea pigs instead of beagles when they tried out a poison gas, they probably would not have provoked the public outcry that resulted in the curtailment of their funding in 1974. When a few Avon saleswomen quit their jobs last spring after reading about painful eye-makeup tests the company conducts on rabbits, they did not complain about the thousands of guinea pigs and rats Avon routinely puts to death in acute-toxicity tests.

19   It is not known whether any single vertebrate species is more or less immune to pain than another. A neat line cannot be drawn across the evolutionary scale dividing the sensitive from the insensitive. Yet the suffering of laboratory rats and mice is regarded as trivial by scientists and the public alike. These rodents have the dubious honor of being our No. 1 experimental animals, composing possibly 75 percent of America's total lab-animal population. As Russell Baker once wrote, "This is no time to be a mouse."

20   Rats and mice are specifically excluded from a Federal law designed to give some protection to laboratory animals. The Animal Welfare Act, passed in 1966 and amended in 1970, is administered by the Department of Agriculture and covers only about 4 percent of laboratory animals. Animal advocates worked hard for the bill, which sets some standards for the housing of animals in laboratories and at the dealers' facilities from which many of them are obtained. But the law places no restrictions on the kinds of experiments to which animals may be subjected. It does indicate that pain-relieving drugs should be used on the few types of animals it covers—but it includes a loophole so as not to inhibit researchers unduly. If a scientist claims that pain is a necessary part of an experiment, anesthetics or analgesics may be withheld.

21   One standard test conducted on rats by drug companies is called the "writhing test" because of the agonized way the animals react to irritants injected into their abdomens. Paradoxically, this test assesses the efficacy of pain-killers, which are administered only after the rats show signs of acute suffering.

22   Equally common are psychological experiments in "learned helplessness" that have been conducted on rats, dogs, and other kinds of animals. In some of these tests, caged animals are given painful electric shocks until they learn certain maneuvers to obtain their food. As they become adept at avoiding the shocks, the researchers

keep changing the rules so that the animals have to keep learning more and more ways to avoid shocks. Ultimately no way remains to escape, and the animals simply give up and lie on the floors of their cages, passively receiving shock after shock. Researchers have attempted to draw parallels between "learned helplessness" and depression in human beings, but some critics have difficulty perceiving their necessity. "What more are we going to learn about human depression by continuing to produce immobility in animals?" asks former animal experimenter Dr. Roger Ulrich, now a research professor of psychology at Western Michigan University.

23   Electric shock is widely used on many different kinds of animals in various types of research. In one experiment typical of a series that has been under way since 1966 at the Armed Forces Radiobiology Research Institute in Bethesda, Md., 10 rhesus monkeys were starved for 18 hours and then "encouraged" with electric prods to run rapidly on treadmills. This went on for several weeks before the monkeys were subjected to 4,600 rads of gamma-neutron radiation. Then they were retested on the treadmills for six hours, and subsequently for two hours each day until they died. Mean survival time for the vomiting, incapacitated monkeys was recorded in A.F.R.R.I.'s report as 37 hours. Dogs have been used in similar experiments, whose purpose is to get an idea of the effects of radiation on human endurance.

24   Now A.F.R.R.I. and other American research facilities are having to look for new sources of monkeys. In March 1978, the Government of India banned further export of rhesus monkeys to the United States. The native population was dwindling and Prime Minister Morarji R. Desai cited violations of a previous agreement that restricted the use of rhesus monkeys to medical research under humane conditions. "There is no difference between cruelty to animals and cruelty to human beings," the ascetic Prime Minister stated. The International Primate Protection League, a four-year-old watchdog group whose members include many scientists and especially primatologists (Jane Goodall, for one), had spread word in the Indian press that American scientists were using rhesus monkeys in grisly trauma experiments. According to the Primate Protection League, these tests included dipping monkeys in boiling water at the University of Kansas, shooting them in the face with high-powered rifles at the University of Chicago, and slam-

ming them in the stomach with a cannon-impactor traveling at a speed of 70 miles per hour at the University of Michigan.

25   "I feel justified in stating that fully 80 percent of the experiments involving rhesus monkeys are either unnecessary, represent useless duplication of previous work, or could utilize nonanimal alternatives," wrote Illinois Wesleyan University biologist Dr. John E. McArdle, a specialist in primate functional anatomy, in a letter to Prime Minister Desai, who so far has held firm despite pressure from the American scientific community to rescind the ban. In the meantime, researchers are making do with non-Indian rhesus monkeys and a close relative, the crab-eating macaque.

26   One of the arguments in favor of animal tests is that under the controlled circumstances of the experimental laboratory they are likely to be objective and consistent. But the results of the same tests conducted on the same kinds of animals often differ from one laboratory to the next. When 25 cooperating companies, including Avon, Revlon, and American Cyanamid, conducted a comprehensive study of eye- and skin-irritation tests using rabbits, the results varied widely. The study concluded that these tests "should not be recommended as standard procedures in any new regulations" because they yielded "unreliable results."

27   One of these tests, the Draize Ophthalmic Irritancy Test, is used to evaluate the effect upon the eyes of household and aerosol products, shampoos, and eye makeup. Rabbits are used because their eyes do not have effective tear glands and thus cannot easily flush away or dissolve irritants. The animals are pinioned in stocks and their eyes are exposed to a substance until inflammation, ulceration, or gross damage occurs.

28   Many investigators concede that the data provided by such experiments are often inconsistent and that the stresses caused by crowded cages, callous treatment, pain, and fear can affect animals' metabolisms and thus confuse test results. "Since there is hardly a single organ or biochemical system in the body that is not affected by stress," says Dr. Harold Hillman, a British physiologist, "it is almost certainly the main reason for the wide variation reported among animals on whom painful experiments have been done."

29   Very often, different species respond differently to substances or situations. The rationale for many animal tests is that they predict human reactions, but thalidomide, for example, did not produce

deformities in the fetuses of dogs, cats, monkeys, and hamsters. On the other hand, insulin has been proved harmful to rabbits and mice although it saves human lives.

30   Researchers are becoming increasingly dubious about the efficacy of the LD/50, a test for acute toxicity that consists of force-feeding a group of animals a specific substance until half of them die, ostensibly providing a quantitative measure of how poisonous the substance is. In *Painful Experiments on Animals,* Dr. Pratt asks what we learn from forcing hair dye or face powder into a dog or rat through a stomach tube until its internal organs rupture.

31   One small victory for animal-welfare activists that was hailed by many American scientists was the 1975 Canadian ban on the use of vertebrate animals by students participating in science fairs. Children had been awarded prizes for attempting heart-transplant surgery on unanesthetized rabbits, amputating the feet of lizards, performing Caesarean operations on pregnant mice, bleeding dogs into a state of shock and blinding pigeons. Remarking that such "experiments" were a distortion of the spirit of research, science fair officials ruled out all such projects except observations of the normal living patterns of wild or domestic animals.

32   In this country, the search for adequate substitutes for laboratory animals was officially launched last summer when the year-old American Fund for Alternatives to Animal Research made its first grant—$12,500 to a biology professor at Whitman College in Walla Walla, Wash. The award to Dr. Earl William Fleck will help finance his development of a test substituting one-celled organisms called tetrahymena for animals in screening substances for teratogens, agents that can cause birth defects. It is expected that the test, if and when perfected, will be cheaper, quicker, more accurate, and certainly more humane than putting thousands of pregnant animals to death.

33   According to veterinarian Thurman Grafton, executive director of the National Society for Medical Research, people who talk about alternatives to animals are creating false hopes. "These new technologies can only be adjuncts to the use of animals," he claims. "While they serve a purpose in furnishing clues as to what direction a type of research might take, you will always ultimately need an intact animal with all its living complications and interchanging biochemical functions to properly assay a drug."

34 "Not so," says Ethel Thurston, administrator of the American Fund for Alternatives. "Enough progress has already been made to indicate that certain techniques can completely replace animals."

35 Several of these techniques have been developed over the last five years in Great Britain, where the Lord Dowding Fund for Humane Research has given grants totaling more than $400,000 to dozens of scientists engaged in research aimed at finding experimental substitutes for animals. Dowding is currently financing several developmental studies of the Ames Test, a promising technique invented by a Berkeley biochemistry professor, Dr. Bruce Ames, that uses salmonella bacteria rather than animals to determine the carcinogenic properties of chemicals. (It was the Ames Test that recently revealed the possible carcinogenic dangers of certain hair dyes.) Another Dowding Fund recipient, research physician Dr. John C. Petricciani, now with the Food and Drug Administration, has devised a method of assessing how tumors grow by inoculating the tumor cells into skin from 9-day-old chicken embryos instead of into living animals.

36 Animal tests are frequently replaced by other methods discovered and developed by scientists like Dr. Ames who are not trying to avoid the use of animals per se but are simply searching for simpler and more cost-efficient ways to achieve their goals. Dr. Hans Stich, a Canadian cancer researcher, for example, has devised a new test for detecting carcinogenicity in chemicals; it uses human cells, takes one week and costs only about $260. The traditional method, using rats and mice, takes three years and costs approximately $150,000.

37 In addition to egg embryos, bacteria, and simple organisms, possible substitutes for animals include tissue cultures, human and other mammal cells grown in test tubes, and organ banks. Preserved human corneas, for instance, might be used to spare rabbits the agony of the Draize test. Computers could also play a role if researchers used them fully to analyze experimental data, predict the properties of new drugs, and test theoretical data. Computers can even be programmed to simulate living processes. Mechanical models and audio-visual aids can and do substitute for animals as teaching instruments. Simulated human models could provide valid information in car-crash tests.

38 Last winter, Representative Robert F. Drinan, Democrat of Massachusetts, introduced a bill authorizing the Department of Health,

Education and Welfare to fund projects aimed at discovering research methods that would reduce both the numbers of animals used in laboratories and the suffering to which they are subjected.

39 Meanwhile, medical and military research and an unending stream of new pharmaceutical, cosmetic, and household products are resulting in an ever-increasing use of animals in the laboratory.

40 The most recent and thorough exploration of alternatives is Dr. D. H. Smyth's book *Alternatives to Animal Experiments*, which examines every option and weighs its pros and cons. He concludes that there is certainly reason to hope that the numbers of laboratory animals can be drastically reduced, but also warns that it is unlikely a complete phasing out of animal experimentation will happen soon. "By the time we can produce complete alternatives to living tissue," Dr. Smyth writes, "we will not need those alternatives because we will already understand how living tissues work."

41 Still, Dr. Smyth asks, "Does this mean we can perpetrate any cruelty on animals to satisfy scientific curiosity in the hope that it will one day be useful? To me it certainly does not. . . . Everyone has a right to decide that certain procedures are unacceptable."

42 Richard Ryder calls animal experimenters to task for trying to have it both ways: Researchers defend their work scientifically on the basis of the *similarities* between human beings and animals, but defend it morally on the basis of the *differences*.

43 And there's the rub: The differences aren't as reassuringly clear-cut as they once were. We now know that some animals have a more highly developed intelligence than some human beings—infants, for example, or the retarded and the senile. Dr. Ryder asks, "If we were to be discovered by some more intelligent creatures in the universe, would they be justified in experimenting on us?"

Analyzing the Writer's Argument

1. In the first four paragraphs of her essay, Curtis tells the story of the professor's activities. Why do you think she begins her essay this way? What points does she make about animal experimentation?

2. If important medical discoveries have resulted from research on animals, as Curtis admits in paragraph 5, what is her problem with animal research?

3. Curtis makes the point that we now have information about animals that we did not have only a few decades ago. What do we

now know and how has that information changed our thinking about the role of animals in an experimenter's laboratory?

4. Define "speciesism." What does the concept have to do with the present argument? What does it have to do with the rights of minorities and women? How does speciesism color our view of the experiments done on animals?

5. What, according to Curtis, are the provisions of the Animal Welfare Act of 1966? What are its shortcomings, as she sees it?

6. Why did the government of India ban the export of rhesus monkeys to the United States?

7. Explain what the Draize test and the LD/50 tests are and how they are conducted.

8. Curtis explains that there may be alternatives to the use of animals in the laboratory. What are those alternatives?

Exploring the Issues in This Essay

1. In the conclusion of her essay, Curtis refers to Richard Ryder's claim that animal researchers want to have it both ways: "Researchers defend their work scientifically on the basis of the *similarities* between human beings and animals, but defend it morally on the basis of the *differences*." Discuss the meaning of this statement and its implications for the future of research involving animals.

2. Curtis writes at the end of paragraph 12: "It's hard not to feel squeamish about subjecting animals to inhumane experiments when they possess almost-human intelligence." In her final paragraph, she writes: "We now know that some animals have a more highly developed intelligence than some human beings—infants, for example, or the retarded or the senile." What is the relationship between animals and humans for Curtis? Does she think animals are inferior, equal to, or superior to humans? Do animals have language? Do they have intelligence? Is her comparison to infants and the retarded or senile a fair one? Discuss these questions in an attempt to come to a deeper understanding of the views of those seeking to protect animals from undue cruelty.

Jack Rosenberger

Whose Life Is It, Anyway?

A free-lance writer, Jack Rosenberger was born in 1958 in Maquon, Wisconsin. In 1981 he received his B.A. degree in literature from Macalester College in St. Paul, Minnesota. His interest in the plight of animals used for experimental purposes was sparked after seeing The Animals Film, *a British documentary, and he has since that time devoted his attention to writing articles for popular magazines about the issue. Those articles have appeared in such publications as* Penthouse, American Health, The Village Voice, Premiere, *and the animals rights advocacy magazine* Animals' Agenda.*

Currently, Rosenberger is working on an article for The Village Voice *on toy companies that test their products by killing animals. In the following article, taken from the January 15, 1990, issue of* New York Magazine, *Rosenberger provides basic information about the key figures and organizations in the animals rights movement, as well as brings us up to date on their thinking and activities.*

1   According to animal-rights activists, the suffering endured by laboratory animals in the United States is staggering—beyond human comprehension. Seventy million animals, they contend, are killed in this country's research labs every year.

2   Traditional animal-welfare organizations, writes Australian philosophy professor Peter Singer, have emphasized "safe activities like collecting stray dogs and prosecuting individual acts of wanton cruelty." But the newer animal-rights groups have a much broader goal: They aim to stop *all* animal experimentation.

3   "Animal rights is not a matter of charity but of justice," says Tom Regan, author of *The Case for Animal Rights.* "What's wrong with animal research is not that the cages are too small but that the animals are in cages at all."

4   If the movement has a bible, it's Singer's 1975 book, *Animal Liberation.* In it, he recounts his conversation with a fellow Oxford

257

student at lunchtime one day in 1970: "I asked him why he did not eat meat, and he began to tell me about the conditions in which the animal whose body I was eating had lived." The answer changed Singer's life. "Although I had specialized in moral and social philosophy," he writes, "it had not occurred to me—any more than it occurs to most people—that our relations with animals raised a serious moral issue."

5   Singer calls human beings' attitude toward other animals speciesism. He knows the word is awkward, "but I can think of no better term [for] a prejudice . . . toward the interests of members of one's own species and against those of members of other species." In other words, all animals are equal.

6   Singer bases part of his argument on the utilitarian philosophy of Jeremy Bentham, who said, "The question is not 'Can they reason?' nor 'Can they talk?' but *'Can they suffer?'* " All animals, including mice and rats (which are used in most animal experiments), feel anger and fear, pleasure and pain, just like human beings.

7   What sort of rights does Singer have in mind? "Concern for the well-being of a child . . . ," he writes, "would require that we teach him to read; concern for the well-being of a pig may require no more than that we leave him alone with other pigs in a place where there is adequate food and room to run freely."

8   Concern for the well-being of a child, of course, is one of the most compelling arguments that those who use animals in research can make. What the animal-rights advocates tend to leave out of their discussions is an acknowledgment of the other side of the story: the thousands of human lives saved, the human pain assuaged, as a result of experiments on animals. Health and Human Services Secretary Louis W. Sullivan has declared the use of laboratory animals "crucial" for research on life-threatening illnesses, including AIDS, cancer and Alzheimer's disease. The benefits humanity has reaped from animal experiments include our understanding of the human nervous system; the development of insulin, antibiotics, and vaccines against hepatitis and polio, skin grafts; the transplantation of corneas and internal organs; and the development of open-heart surgery and other advanced surgical techniques. A mother of a child whose life has been saved by these discoveries can make a case as heart-rending as any animal-rights advocate's. But, of course, Singer would call that speciesism—the

assumption that a child's life is worth more than a rat's or a monkey's.

9   There are some 7,000 groups in the United States concerned with the plight of animals, and their cause—once viewed as oddball—is winning more and more converts. In the year after the Humane Farming Association initiated its advertising campaign against cruelty to calves being raised for veal, the group's strength rose from 22,000 to 45,000 members. Indeed, animal-rights activists have put their case so persuasively that for the past few years Congress has gotten more mail about animal research than about any other topic. (The letters have run 100 to 1 against the use of animals in experiments).

10   And the movement has claimed some tangible victories. By June of last year, several large cosmetics companies, including Avon and Revlon, had agreed to stop—and Mary Kay cosmetics had declared a moratorium on—animal testing. (The companies don't acknowledge, though, that pressure from the activists led them to these decisions). And People for the Ethical Treatment of Animals (PETA), the nation's largest animal-rights group, which has 250,000 members, believes its efforts were responsible for persuading toy companies like Mattel and Tonka to stop animal testing.

11   Even so, the number of animals killed in laboratories every year has hardly lessened. Therefore, to get the media attention that forces change, activists are using confrontational tactics. PETA members have demonstrated outside researchers' houses on Halloween, bombarded the Gillette Company with calls protesting its animal-testing policy, and picketed the American International Fur Fair in Las Vegas. PETA also publicizes the activities of the Animal Liberation Front, which since 1979 has broken into research institutions 24 times, "liberated" more than 3,000 animals, and caused nearly $4 million worth of damage. PETA sells videotapes "consisting of actual footage of conditions in laboratories," says Carol L. Burnett, a spokeswoman. "A picture is worth a thousand words, and the tapes show exactly what we say."

12   The hard-core activists divide their lives into two halves: Life Before Animal Rights and Life Now. Steve Siegel, 40, director of Trans-Species Unlimited's New York regional office (a windowless lower Broadway room about the size of a studio apartment), was a fund-raiser, wrote fiction and poetry, and worked part-time as a

high-school teacher in New York public schools before he joined the group as full-time director. He calls himself "a fairly intelligent and well-read person." But, he says, "I don't know where I was the first 35 years of my life. I mean, I didn't know what was going on in labs."

13   What opened his eyes was a viewing of *The Animals Film*, a British documentary with a shocking segment about a burn experiment whose subject is a live pig. "The animal is fully conscious and squealing throughout the whole thing," says Siegel. He learned, much to his surprise, that gruesome experiments like the film's burn-research scenes are common. (Anne St. Laurent, of United Action for Animals, says her organization has collected hundreds of recent research papers about burn experiments, and though the animals were anesthetized during the experiments, "only a few papers mention giving painkillers after they wake up.")

14   Like PETA, Trans-Species is employing the activists' newest technique—challenging the *scientific merit* of a researcher's work. Three years ago, the group managed to derail Cornell University researcher Michiko Okamoto's studies of barbiturate addiction in cats. First Trans-Species turned for advice to the Medical Research Modernization Committee, a group of health professionals (half of them doctors) highly critical of current animal testing standards; when the committee said it did not consider Okamoto's research critically relevant to human patients, Trans-Species went to the public. Its relentless picketing, demonstrations, and letter writing campaigns generated such pressure (the National Institute on Drug Abuse—NIDA—got 10,000 letters and postcards and 75 to 80 congressional-office inquiries about the matter) that Okamoto—who had been using cats in her research for fourteen years—gave up and returned her grant to NIDA.

15   Now Trans-Species is targeting Ronald Wood, a researcher at New York University Medical Center who is using macaque monkeys in researching crack addiction and the effects of inhaling an ingredient used in glue and paint-thinner. Is Wood a reasonable target? Not according to Charles Schuster, NIDA's director. "Wood's research is one of the very few projects we support that study the behaviors of animals self-administering inhalants," he says. "The proper question is not why we're supporting Dr. Wood but how we can get other scientists to study this problem as well."

16 Ironically, Trans-Species' success against Okamoto may prove to be the strongest barrier to its triumph at NYU, for that victory woke up the biomedical community. NYU has held three press conferences stressing the legitimacy of its research on animals; the last, held this past April, included leading officials of federal health agencies, New York State medical schools, and a patient-advocacy group.

17 "After we won at Cornell," Siegel says, "I thought animal researchers would take a look around and start cleaning house on their own. But I don't know of any animal experiments that have been stopped."

18 "Animals have a need to breathe, not to feel pain, and to experience enjoyment in life," says PETA's national director, Ingrid Newkirk. "We have very selfishly denied animals those needs for our own whims and peripheral interests. Animals are not handbags and hamburgers. They're living beings like ourselves."

Analyzing the Writer's Argument

1. What does Rosenberger see as the difference between the goals of the animal rights groups of old and the newer ones operating today?

2. What did Peter Singer mean when he said, "it had not occurred to me—any more than it occurs to most people—that our relations with animals raised a serious moral issue"?

3. What is "speciesism"? What are its implications for those who believe in the concept?

4. What, according to Rosenberger, is the latest technique of groups like PETA and Trans-Species for eliminating animal research? How successful has that technique been?

5. Rosenberger is an avowed animal rights advocate. Does he show his bias in this essay or does he present a balanced view? Should he have gone into greater detail regarding the benefits that we have derived from animal research or has he said enough? Explain.

6. What does Rosenberger's title mean? Is it a good title for his essay? Why or why not?

7. Mail to Congress has run 100 to 1 against experiments using animals. How does this fact influence, if at all, your position on the animal rights issue?

Exploring the Issues in This Essay

1. Rosenberger writes that Singer would call the placing of a child's life above that of a rat's or a monkey's speciesism. Discuss the concept. What is your position with regard to it? If you believe that humans practice speciesism, what are the implications for you? For example, is some kind of action required on your part? Have you, or would you change your behavior in any way?

2. The question of the legitimacy of Okamoto's research raises some interesting questions about the freedom that researchers have to pursue their research goals. Does a researcher have total freedom in this regard? Should a researcher have total freedom? What role do funding agencies have in directing the activities of researchers? Under what circumstances, if any, should research be monitored?

Bumper stickers, pins, and print ads from the pro- and anti-fur factions.

From *New York Magazine*, January 15, 1990, Reprinted by permission.

Teresa K. Rye

How I Benefited from Animal Research

Teresa K. Rye was born in Minneapolis, Minnesota, in 1955 and holds a B.S. degree in Nursing from Boston University. Currently, she is a nurse with the Boston Visiting Nurses Association, where she works administering intravenous infusion therapy to AIDS and cancer victims in their homes. She has made a number of appearances on radio and television talk shows, including NBC Nightly News, explaining why she believes that biomedical research using animals must continue.

In 1984 she gave the following testimony at a symposium on animal experimentation held at the National Academy of Science. Rye argues in favor of the continuation of biomedical research from a highly personal viewpoint. Simply put, she believes she is alive and healthy today because of surgical procedures that were developed in the laboratory on live animals.

1   As I am listening to these proceedings and talking to you today, my emotions are of deep gratitude for the work that has been done by medical researchers and practitioners. Had I been born 20 years earlier I would not be alive now. Had the research not been performed to develop the knowledge base and sophisticated techniques to support the surgery that I had, I would have only a short life to look forward to.

2   I was asked to come and speak at this symposium as I have directly received the benefits of animal research. A year-and-a-half ago I had open-heart surgery at the Brigham and Women's Hospital in Boston performed by Doctor Cohn. I am 28 years old. I am a registered nurse and an instructor for nursing education and research at University Hospital at Boston University Medical Center. In October 1982 I underwent surgery for repair of a very

rare congenital heart defect called the scimitar syndrome. In spite of my education as a nurse, I had never heard of this syndrome. The name is derived from the appearance of the chest X-ray which shows the veins connecting the lungs to the heart in a semi-curved pattern around the right side of the heart.

3   The very name "scimitar syndrome" frightened me. I felt doomed. My cardiologist said this defect is so rare, he would be surprised if he saw three or four more cases of this type in his entire career. I was told I would need open-heart surgery. The alternative would have been to develop pulmonary artery hypertension and almost certain death around age 35.

4   My operation was unique. Part of my surgery required the heart-lung bypass machine to be turned off. It was a chilling experience for me to learn my body was frozen to 15° centigrade and that I had been clinically dead for 30 minutes during the operation. I hope that legislators, lobbyists, and research agencies appreciate that these kinds of procedures would be impossible to perform had there not been an animal research model. No number of mathematical, statistical, analytical, and engineering techniques could replace the animal model in my case. I am deeply fortunate to have the opportunity of a normal life expectancy now. Death at 35 seems much too close for me.

5   I was admitted for surgery and stayed in the hospital for 11 days. I recuperated at home and returned to work 6 weeks after my surgery, working 4 hours a day. Two weeks later, just 2 months after the operation, I was working full-time.

6   Not only was my successful surgery due to the techniques developed form animal research, but also the diagnostic testing was possible because of animal modeling. I required a cardiac catheterization as well as a nuclear scan with injections of dye to diagnose my abnormality.

7   It was by chance that this problem was discovered. I had begun a new job and had a routine chest X-ray as a pre-employment screen to rule out tuberculosis. I was called to the employee health department to discuss the findings of my film. The physician told me my right heart was enlarged and the blood vessels over my right lung were quite prominent. He said the film suggested that I had a congenital heart defect with signs of an abnormal left to right shunting of blood. He urged me to see a cardiologist.

8   I was shocked, confused, and scared. At the time I was working as a surgical intensive care unit nurse. I felt absolutely fine and lead a physically active life. I had no other symptoms of cardiac disease aside from what had been described as a benign heart murmur that I had known about since age 12. As a surgical intensive care unit nurse I was familiar with the battery of tests I would have to undergo. I was aware of the life-threatening risks that could arise during a cardiac catheterization as well as from open-heart surgery. As a nurse I was caring for patients who did, indeed, develop serious—sometimes fatal—complications. I found myself experiencing maximum stress.

9   Once again, animal research had a direct benefit for me. I was able to use medication to ease my anxiety and continue to be productive at work while I waited 6 weeks between my cardiac catheterization and my open-heart surgery.

10   The first day after my surgery I developed a life-threatening complication. My left lung collapsed from positive pressure on the mechanical ventilator. I needed a chest tube emergently inserted into my lung to re-expand it. This procedure also could not have been performed without prior animal testing.

11   At times I experienced intense pain. One of my friends, also a nurse, came to visit me in the intensive care unit and asked me "How is the pain?" I did not remember this, but later she told me I said "It's killing me. I don't want to move." She asked, "Does the medication help?" I said, "Yes, it does." I am thankful for the amnesia of some of my experience. I sincerely hope and have to believe that animals are given the same kind of relief.

12   Six years ago I adopted a kitten from the Boston Animal Shelter. She has grown into a beautiful affectionate cat. She has given me much happiness and feelings of love. Her picture was on my bedside table at the hospital. Even though I am a pet owner and animal lover, there is no question in my mind that animal research must be continued.

13   I have tremendous appreciation for the advances in science, the skill and care from my doctors and nurses and the gift of life from animals that allow my continued good health.

14   Ten years ago, Lane Potter, in the *Proceedings of the Royal Society of Medicine*, posed five questions for animal researchers: Is the animal the best experimental system for the problem? Must the

animal be conscious at any time throughout the experiment? Can pain or discomfort associated with the experiment be lessened or eliminated? Could the number of animals be reduced? Is the problem worth solving anyhow?

15   For me, it is clear that some research involving the use of animals similar to man must continue if mankind is to continue to advance and survive. For me, it is clear that these animals deserve the utmost respect and care that we can give them. They give so much to us. Antivivisectionist legislation which, in some cases, would absolutely prohibit animal research, would cause irreparable damage to the advancement of medical science. If these measures were in place 20 years ago, surgery involving an open chest and heart would not be possible. I would probably be experiencing the beginning signs and symptoms of chronic pulmonary artery hypertension. I would be unable to work in my early thirties. I would have high medical care costs and would be facing almost certain death at age 35.

16   But today I am looking forward to turning 29 next week and intend to have a big celebration when I turn 35. I hope that research using animals continues so that children who are presently in life-threatening situations will also have a chance to look forward to birthdays, anniversaries and a healthy, productive life.

Analyzing the Writer's Argument

1. Why was Rye asked to speak at the symposium? Why did she become a patient in the hospital? Is the perspective she brings as a surgical intensive care unit nurse a useful one for her argument? Why or why not?

2. Review the references Rye makes to how animal research has made possible the pre-operation, operation, and post-operation care and procedures used on her. Has she explained to your satisfaction the exact nature of the research on animals and its relationship to her care? Is it important that she do so?

3. In paragraph 4, Rye dismisses the alternatives to animal research as a model for the heart-lung bypass machine used in her operation. What are those alternatives? Do you feel you know enough about these alternatives from the essay to judge whether or not Rye is correct in her assertion? Explain.

4. Why does Rye refer to the five questions that Lane Potter has posed in *Proceedings of the Royal Society of Medicine?* Do you think that they are necessary questions? Why or why not? Does she want her listeners to use these questions in any particular way?

5. Rye tells us that she adopted a cat from the Boston Animal Shelter, that she had a picture of her cat at her bedside when she was in the hospital, and that she is a pet owner and animal lover. Why does she feel that it is important to give us these details of her personal life?

6. Who is Rye's intended audience? Do you think that there were many animal rights advocates in that audience?

Exploring the Issues in This Essay

1. Discuss the value of personal testimony to argumentation. Is it more effective than other types of evidence in your opinion? Less effective? Why? Are there any special problems with personal testimony? Is Rye an authority on the question of the use of animals in biomedical research?

2. Rye suggests that she is both an animal lover and an advocate for animal research. Is this a realistic position, in your view? What is your own philosophy with regard to this question? Do you feel comfortable with it? Why or why not?

An AMA White Paper

Use of Animals in Biomedical Research

Founded in Philadelphia in 1847 by a group of 250 physicians, the American Medical Association (AMA) seeks "to promote the science and art of medicine and the betterment of public health." The AMA is based in Chicago, Illinois, and is very active in all matters relating to medicine ranging from the ongoing education of physicians and the encouragement of pure research, to lobbying efforts in matters relating to food, drugs, automobile safety, water pollution control, mental health, rural health care, nursing, aging, and exercise and fitness.

In 1989, the AMA issued its "white paper," or official position, on the use of animals in biomedical research because as it stated in its Preface, "Recently, the animal rights movement has been making substantial inroads in obtaining philosophic and financial support for legislative and regulatory changes that would compromise the future of biomedical research." Too long to include in its entirety, the AMA report has been shortened for inclusion in Controversies.

1   Animals have been used in experiments for at least 2,000 years, with the first reference made in the third century B.C., in Alexandria, Egypt, when the philosopher and scientist, Erisistratus, used animals to study body functions.

2   Five centuries later, the Roman physician Galen used apes and pigs to prove his theory that veins carry blood rather than air. In succeeding centuries, animals were employed to discover how the body functions or to confirm or disprove theories developed through observation. Advances in knowledge made through these experiments included Harvey's demonstration of the circulation of blood in 1622, the effect of anesthesia on the body in 1846, and the relationship between bacteria and disease in 1878.

3   Today, animals are used in experiments for three general purposes: (1) biomedical and behavioral research, (2) education, (3) drug and product testing.

4   Biomedical research increases understanding of how biological systems function and advances medical knowledge. Biomedical experiments are conducted in accordance with the principles of the scientific method developed by the French physiologist, Claude Bernard, in 1865. This method established two requirements for the conduct of a valid experiment: (1) control of all variables so that only one factor or set of factors is changed at a time, and (2) the replication of results by other laboratories. Unless these requirements are met, an experiment is not considered scientifically valid. Behavioral research is a type of biomedical research that is directed toward determining the factors that affect behavior and how various organisms and organs respond to different stimuli. Much behavioral research is environmental in nature but some involves the study of responses to physical stimuli or manipulation of biological systems or organs, such as the brain.

5   Educational experiments are conducted to educate and train students in medicine, veterinary medicine, physiology, and general science. In many instances, these experiments are conducted with dead animals.

6   Animals also are employed to determine the safety and efficacy of new drugs or the toxicity of chemicals to which humans or animals may be exposed. Most of these experiments are conducted by commercial firms to fulfill government requirements. . . .

7   A basic assumption of all types of research is that man should relieve human and animal suffering. One objection to the use of animals in biomedical research is that the animals are used as surrogates for human beings. This objection presumes the equality of all forms of life; animal rights advocates argue that if the tests are for the benefit of man, then man should serve as the subject of the experiments. There are limitations, however, to the use of human subjects both ethically, such as in the testing of a potentially toxic drug or chemical, and in terms of what can be learned. The process of aging, for instance, can best be observed through experiments with rats, which live an average of two to three years, or with some types of monkeys, which live 15 to 20 years. Some experiments require numerous subjects of the same weight or genetic makeup or require special diets or physical environments; these conditions

make the use of human subjects difficult or impossible. By using animals in such tests, researchers can observe subjects of uniform age and background in sufficient numbers to determine if findings are consistent and applicable to a large population.

8   Animals are important in research precisely because they have complex body systems that react and interact with stimuli much as humans do. The more true this is with a particular animal, the more valuable that animal is for a particular type of research. One important property to a researcher is discrimination—the extent to which an animal exhibits the particular quality to be investigated. The greater the degree of discrimination, the greater the reliability and predictability of the information gathered from the experiment.

9   For example, dogs have been invaluable in biomedical research because of the relative size of their organs compared to humans. The first successful kidney transplant was performed in a dog and the techniques used to save the lives of "blue babies," and babies with structural defects in their hearts, were developed with dogs. Open heart surgical techniques, coronary bypass surgery and heart transplantation all were developed using dogs.

10   Another important factor is the amount of information available about a particular animal. Mice and rats play an extensive role in research and testing, in part because repeated experiments and controlled breeding have created a pool of data to which the findings from a new experiment can be related and given meaning. Their rapid rate of reproduction also has made them important in studies of genetics and other experiments that require observation over a number of generations. Moreover, humans cannot be bred to produce "inbred strains" as can be done with animals; therefore, humans cannot be substituted for animals in studies where an inbred strain is essential. . . .

11   One demonstration of the critical role that animals play in medical and scientific advances is that 54 of 76 Nobel Prizes awarded in physiology or medicine since 1901 have been for discoveries and advances made through the use of experimental animals. Among these have been the Prize awarded in 1985 for the studies (using dogs) that documented the relationship between cholesterol and heart disease; the 1966 Prize for the studies (using chickens) that linked viruses and cancer; and the 1960 Prize for studies (using cattle, mice, and chicken embryos) that established that a body

can be taught to accept tissue from different donors if it is inoculated with different types of tissue prior to birth or during the first year of life, a finding expected to help simplify and advance organ transplants in the future. Studies using animals also resulted in successful culture of the poliomyelitis virus; a Nobel Prize was awarded for this work in 1954. The discovery of insulin and treatment of diabetes, achieved through experiments using dogs, also earned the Prize in 1923.

12 In fact, virtually every advance in medical science in the 20th century, from antibiotics and vaccines to antidepressant drugs and organ transplants, has been achieved either directly or indirectly through the use of animals in laboratory experiments. The result of these experiments has been the elimination or control of many infectious diseases—smallpox, poliomyelitis, measles—and the development of numerous life-saving techniques—blood transfusions, burn therapy, open-heart and brain surgery. This has meant a longer, healthier, better life with much less pain and suffering. For many, it has meant life itself. Often forgotten in the rhetoric is the fact that humans *do* participate in biomedical research in the form of clinical trials. They experience pain and are injured and in fact, some of them die from this participation. Hence, scientists are not asking animals to be "guinea pigs" alone for the glory of science. Some medical breakthroughs accomplished through research with animals are described below.

PRE-1900	Treatment of rabies, anthrax, beriberi (thiamine deficiency), and smallpox
	Principles of infection control and pain relief
	Management of heart failure
EARLY 1900s	Treatment of histamine shock, pellagra (niacin deficiency), and rickets (Vitamin D deficiency)
	Electrocardiography and cardiac catheterization
1920s	Discovery of thyroxin
	Intravenous feeding
	Discovery of insulin—diabetes control
1930s	Therapeutic use of sulfa drugs
	Prevention of tetanus
	Development of anticoagulants, modern anesthesia and neuro-muscular blocking agents

1940s   Treatment of rheumatoid arthritis and whooping cough
Therapeutic use of antibiotics, such as penicillin, aureomycin and streptomycin
Discovery of Rh factor
Treatment of leprosy
Prevention of diphtheria

1950s   Prevention of poliomyelitis
Development of cancer chemotherapy
Open heart surgery and cardiac pacemaker

1960s   Prevention of rubella
Corneal transplant and coronary bypass surgery
Therapeutic use of cortisone
Development of radioimmunoassay for the measurement of minute quantities of antibodies, hormones and other substances in the body

1970s   Prevention of measles
Modern treatment of coronary insufficiency
Heart transplant
Development of non-addictive pain killers

1980s   Use of cyclosporin and other anti-rejection drugs
Artificial heart transplantation
Identification of psychophysiological factors in depression, anxiety and phobias
Development of monoclonal antibodies for treating disease

13   Scientists feel that it is essential for the public to understand that had scientific research been restrained in the first decade of the 20th century as antivivisectionists and activists were then, and are today urging, many millions of Americans alive and healthy today would never have been born or would have suffered a premature death. Their parents or grandparents would have died from diphtheria, scarlet fever, tuberculosis, diabetes, appendicitis, and countless other diseases and disorders. . . .

14   Behavioral research has also been of immense benefit to humans. For example, fundamental information on how people learn was discovered by experiments on animals in laboratories; the learning principles and behavior modification therapies discovered

or developed through such experiments are today being used to treat conditions such as anuresis (bed-wetting), addictive behaviors (tobacco, drugs, alcohol), and compulsive behaviors such as anorexia nervosa.

15   Biofeedback techniques that have become a major means of treatment for a number of conditions were developed through behavioral research with animals. The use of biofeedback enables people to control what are normally automatic body functions, such as blood pressure, heart rate, and muscle tension. Biofeedback helps cardiac patients reduce the risk of heart attack by controlling their blood pressure, assists persons paralyzed with spinal injuries to raise their blood pressure and permit them to sit up, and relieves the discomfort of migraine headaches, insomnia, and low back pain. Many of these afflictions had no effective treatment before biofeedback, which was developed through studies of the nervous system of the rat.

16   Experiments on cats have enhanced the understanding of the corpus callosum, a band of fibers that connects the left and right sides of the brain needed for transfer of information from one side to another. This finding, for which a Nobel Prize was awarded in 1981, led directly to the development of new treatments for patients with strokes, language disorders, brain damage, intractable epilepsy, and other neurologic conditions.

17   One objection of animal rights advocates to behavioral research is their belief that many tests are conducted merely to confirm or prove long accepted or obvious concepts, such as that a child will suffer when deprived of love or a parenting figure. However, what appears to be an obvious truth often proves to be false when subjected to close scrutiny in experiments. This includes the idea that all animals suffer when separated from a parent. In tests conducted over a number of years with rhesus monkeys, scientists discovered that, whereas some infants became withdrawn and anxious, others grew stronger and showed fewer stress-related symptoms when exposed to new or threatening situations. This has prompted new research into possible genetic and physiologic reasons why people react differently to stress and which types of persons are more likely to develop conditions such as depression.

18   Other behavioral research utilizing animals is leading to a deeper understanding of links between the mind and the body that may

have important ramifications for the prevention and treatment of disease. Studies conducted with mice and monkeys have helped to establish and explore the relationship between stress and conditions such as heart disease, hypertension, and breakdowns in the immune system that leave individuals vulnerable to disease. Such studies may lead to an understanding of the nature of psychosomatic illnesses in humans. . . .

19   Criticism by animal rights adherents is directed at three types of experiments: those that are conducted for educational purposes; those that are conducted merely to "prove the obvious"; and those that repeat experiments already conducted.

20   Fewer animals are used for education than for any other purpose. They are used either to instruct students in courses such as physiology or to teach techniques, such as surgery. The use of animals in education varies from school to school and from program to program, even within medical schools. Educators generally agree, however, that students are better trained and patients better served when the students are given "hands-on" experience with living tissue, especially for training in surgery. Even the British, who otherwise ban the use of animals for educational purposes, accept the necessity of using animals under anesthesia to teach the techniques of microsurgery.

21   Animal rights activists also object to the duplication of experiments including those conducted for educational purposes and those that have failed elsewhere. The performance of experiments when the result is known in advance is a sound educational technique and is employed in many fields that do not involve animals, such as mathematics, physics, and chemistry. By utilizing an experiment in which the result is known in advance, it can be determined whether the experiment is performed correctly or incorrectly.

22   The criticism relating to the repetition of failed experiments has some merit, scientists agree, and emphasizes the need to improve communication among scientists in both the research and testing communities. Commercial firms that perform many of the testing experiments, such as drug and chemical companies, have taken steps both directly and through their trade associations to respond to this need by establishing mechanisms for sharing of data and results among firms. The creation of a comprehensive data bank

for all research and testing is a far more complex undertaking, however, and an attempt by a private firm to establish a limited system failed earlier this decade.

23   A third reason for duplication of experiments is the requirement of the scientific method for a new finding to be verified by scientists in other laboratories before the finding can be considered valid. Such replication is necessary and quite often uncovers a mistake in technique or design or some other flaw in the original experiments that will render it invalid.

24   Both economic pressure and the peer review process used to evaluate research proposals make the conduct of unnecessary experiments unlikely. Research today involves intense competition for funding; for example, only about 25% of studies proposed to, and approved by, federal agencies each year are actually funded. Therefore, scientists on research evaluation committees are not likely to approve redundant or unnecessary experiments. Also, given the competition for funds, scientists are unlikely to waste valuable time and resources conducting unnecessary or duplicative experiments. . . .

25   The emotional appeals made by animal rights activists are often directed toward the use of apes and monkeys in experiments, the pain and death associated with animal experimentation, and what they assert is the abuse that animals are subjected to by scientists.

26   Although animal rights activists object to the use of all animals in experiments, they make a special plea and have shown a particular interest on behalf of the nonhuman primates. Many of the sit-ins, demonstrations, and raids on laboratories have been directed at primate research centers. The argument they advance is that, because apes and monkeys are so much like man, they experience suffering much as man does and this should exempt them from use in experiments, just as it does man. Even keeping them in cages for long periods or isolating them from others of their kind is both cruel and destructive to psychological well-being, the activists argue.

27   Scientists argue that it is this very factor—their similarity to man—that makes apes and monkeys so valuable to research and their use in some experiments indispensable. Apes and monkeys have both strong physiologic and strong behavioral similarities to man. They are susceptible to many of the same diseases and have similar immune systems. They also possess intellectual, cognitive,

and social organizational skills far above those of other animals, and these characteristics have made them invaluable in research related to language, perception, and visual and spatial skills. Primates are used in experiments in relatively few numbers—approximately one-half of 1% of all animals used. However, their contributions to both biological and behavioral sciences have been numerous, significant, and in some cases crucial, as with poliomyelitis and hepatitis.

28   Primates played three different roles in the development of the poliomyelitis vaccines, all of them essential. Although many studies on poliomyelitis in humans were conducted in the late 19th century, the cause of the disease remained unknown until scientists were able to transmit the virus to monkeys in 1908. There followed many years of research with primates until scientists were able, in the early 1950s, to grow the virus in human cell cultures and development of a vaccine became possible. At that point, to ensure the safety and effectiveness of the vaccines, tests were conducted with monkeys. To produce the vaccines in pure form in great quantities, it was necessary to use kidney tissue taken from monkeys. Today, the use of the monkey kidney tissue is no longer necessary because vaccines now are produced through self-propagating cells—an alternative to the use of animals developed through appropriate research. . . .

29   The chimpanzees may play a critical role in developing a therapy for AIDS. Medical researchers note that, in contemporary medicine, AIDS is the first infectious disease that is virtually 100% fatal. The chimpanzees has been the only animal that scientists have been able to infect with the AIDS virus. To date, none have developed the disease, leading some animal rights activists and even some scientists to question its value in the research. However, the fact that chimpanzees do not become ill may in itself provide a clue to combating the disease if the reason can be discovered through research. Primates will be vitally important in the development and testing of vaccines for AIDS. Recently a prominent AIDS researcher at the National Institutes of Health commented that the difficulty of procuring animals for experiments with the AIDS virus may significantly slow the development of effective drugs and vaccines. He attributes these problems directly to the efforts of animal rights groups. . . .

30 Among all the issues raised by animal rights activists, that of "alternatives" has probably caused the most confusion. The reason for that, say scientists, is the misrepresentation and misunderstanding that has been created regarding what is possible. The concept of alternatives was first introduced in 1959 by two British scientists and was defined in terms of what has become known as the Three R's—refinement, reduction and replacement. In their book, *The Principles of Humane Experimental Techniques*, W.M.S. Russell and R.L. Burch contended that humane research techniques require scientists to work toward refinement of techniques to reduce potential suffering, toward reduction in the number of animals needed, and, where possible, toward replacement of animals by non-animal techniques.

31 In the present debate, the focus is on the last of these—replacement—as animal rights activists have insisted that certain experimental methods that investigators have developed can be used in lieu of animal experiments. Thus, as used in the debate, the word "alternatives" has become virtually synonymous with the word "substitutes" and animal rights activists have tended to focus on two: *in vitro* research (cell, tissue, and organ cultures) and computer simulation of biological systems in the form of mathematical models.

32 Both of these methods play important roles in biomedical research and have allowed the performance of experiments not possible with animals. In addition, both have avoided the need to use animals in some stages of research. However, they cannot serve, either individually or in combination with any other research method, as total replacement for use of live animals in experiments, for they cannot reproduce exactly the intact biological system provided by live animals. Each method suffers from at least some inherent deficiency.

33 The technology and use of cell cultures has grown dramatically during the past 20 years, making possible the performance of experiments that were previously impossible. Cells in isolation, however, do not act or react the same as cells in an intact system. As the Congressional Office of Technology Assessment noted in a report it prepared for Congress, *Alternatives to Animal Use in Research, Testing, and Education:* "... isolated systems give isolated results that may bear little relation to results obtained from the integrated systems of whole animals."

34   The same is true of tissues and organs placed in cultures. In addition, scientists point out, tissue and organs are difficult to nourish and maintain and tend to disintegrate automatically or lose their ability to function when maintained in cultures for long periods.

35   Computer simulations, often promoted as the great hope of the future by animal rights activists, have been invaluable in developing or suggesting new lines of scientific inquiry and in developing new mechanisms or techniques. However, both computers and computer simulations have inherent limitations that make it unlikely that they will ever totally replace animals in experiments. One of these limitations is the nature of simulation. The validity of any model depends on how closely it resembles the original in every respect. Much about the body and the various biological systems of humans and animals is not known. For example, how the body breaks down each chemical or drug or the manner in which brain cells transmit the sensory signals that create vision are not known; therefore, they cannot be programmed into any model. Until full knowledge of a particular biological system is developed, no model can be constructed that will in every case predict or accurately represent the reaction of the system to a given stimulus. . . .

36   No other method of study can exactly reproduce the characteristics and qualities of a living intact biological system or organism. Therefore, in order to understand how much a system or organism functions in a particular set of circumstances or how it will react to a given stimulus, it becomes necessary at some point to conduct an experiment or test to find out. There simply is no alternative to this approach and therefore no alternative to using animals for most types of health related research. . . .

37   The American people should not be misled by emotional appeals and philosophic rhetoric on this issue. Biomedical research using animals is essential to continued progress in clinical medicine. Animal research holds the key for solutions to AIDS, cancer, heart disease, aging and congenital defects. In discussing legislation concerning animal experimentation, the prominent physician and physiologist, Dr. Walter B. Cannon, stated in 1896 that ". . . the antivivisectionists are the second of the two types Theodore Roosevelt described when he said, 'Common sense without conscience may lead to crime, but conscience without common sense may lead to folly, which is the handmaiden of crime.'"

38   The American Medical Association has been an outspoken proponent of biomedical research for over 100 years, and that tradition continues today. The Association believes that research involving animals is absolutely essential to maintaining and improving the health of the American people. The Association is opposed to any legislation or regulation that would inappropriately limit such research, and actively supports all legislative efforts to ensure the continued use of animals in research, while providing for their humane treatment.

Analyzing the Writer's Argument

1. Why, according to the authors of the "white paper," is it not always possible for researchers to use human subjects in their research?
2. The authors of the "white paper" write that "one important property to a researcher is discrimination. . . ." What do they mean? Why is discrimination important?
3. Why are mice and rats so frequently used in biomedical research?
4. Give at least six examples of research using animals that has benefited humans. Give several examples of research using animals that has helped animals themselves.
5. Is this essay an argument? How do you know? If it is an argument, what is the thesis and where is it stated?
6. The authors claim that humans have also been used in biomedical research to show that animals are not the only subjects used. Does this information add or detract from their argument? Explain.
7. What argument do animal rights advocates put forth against the use of primates in research? How do the authors of the "white paper" answer their argument?
8. What kind of evidence have the authors put forth in defense of their position? Give an example of each type of evidence.

Exploring the Issues in This Essay

1. If, as some claim, animal rights advocates want a total ban on the use of animals in biomedical research, and scientists claim that there are no real alternatives to the use of a "living intact biological system or organism," what resolution(s) is possible? What ways out of these apparently irreconcilable differences can you suggest?

2. Scientists claim that computer simulations, while being immensely helpful so far in their work, will not offer immediate alternatives to the use of animals in the laboratory. They believe that living organisms represent the interplay of too many variables for a computer to handle and that if we knew how to program in the range of variables we would already have many of the answers that the research is actually pursuing. From your experience with computers and from what you know from your reading and study of the complexity of living organisms, does this objection seem justified to you? Are computer programs really incapable of handling immense complexities? How do scientists deal with such complexities now, without the aid of computers?

Michael E. DeBakey, M.D.

Holding Human Health Hostage

Michael DeBakey was born in Lake Charles, Louisiana, in 1908. He received his B.S., M.S., and M.D. from Tulane University. A world-renowned surgeon, he has been instrumental in the development of techniques and procedures essential to successful cardiovascular or open-heart surgery. For example, he pioneered procedures for the resectioning or removal of a portion of an artery damaged as a result of an aneurysm, the ballooning out of a weakened wall of the artery. He also invented a special pump used in the heart-lung machine now essential to successful heart surgery. Currently DeBakey is the Director of The DeBakey Heart Center at Baylor University.

Dr. DeBakey is a widely respected member of the medical community and feels strongly that if efforts to curb or eliminate animal experimentation in our scientific laboratories are successful, hundreds of thousands of victims of disease in this country will have to be abandoned.

1   As a patient-advocate, both in and out of the operating room, I feel a responsibility to protect the rights of patients to medical advances resulting from animal research. Had the animal legislation now pending in Congress been enacted when I began my career, it would have prevented me from developing a number of life-saving procedures in my research laboratory. Instead of restoring thousands of patients to a normal life and a return to productive work, my colleagues and I would have been helpless to offer many of our patients any real hope at all. This legislation, known as the Mrazek bill, seeks to ban the use of pound animals for any research supported by the National Institutes of Health, the chief source of funds for biomedical research in this country. Are we now to hold human health hostage to the rights of abandoned animals to be killed in pounds?

2   Even with today's technology, I could not have developed on a computer the roller pump that made open-heart surgery possible

or the artificial artery that restored to health previously doomed patients with aneurysms. Nor could we have attempted the first successful coronary artery bypass or implanted the first temporary mechanical heart with which we saved a patient's life two decades ago. Would animal-rights activists have objected to the first kidney, heart, or liver transplant? Would they forego the protection humanity enjoys today against poliomyelitis, tetanus, diphtheria, and whooping cough or the treatment for strep throat, ear infections, bronchitis, and pneumonia—all the products of animal research? Would they have denied the 11 million diabetics the right to life that insulin has given them—or victims of cancer the help they have received from radiation and chemotherapy? It was in monkeys that the deadly AIDS virus was isolated, and that isolation is the initial step in the ultimate development of a vaccine. Would the animal-rights activists halt that research and allow an epidemic to rage unopposed? The truth is that there are no satisfactory insentient models at present for certain types of biomedical research and testing. A computer is not a living system and would not have produced the dramatic medical advances of the past few decades.

3   Only about 1% of abandoned dogs are released for research. If pounds are such a meager source of research animals, you may ask, why am I concerned about losing that source? My reasons are well-founded, I believe: not only are pound animals of particular value in research on heart and kidney disease, brain injury, stroke, blindness, and deafness, but a ban on their use could have grave and far-reaching consequences for human and animal health. In addition, such a ban would impose an extra burden on taxpayers and could price many important research projects out of existence. Each dog and cat bred specifically for research costs hundreds of dollars more than a pound animal. The Mrazek bill makes no accommodation in appropriations for this substantial rise in cost. For many of our most productive researchers, the additional expense would shut down their laboratories. Critical work on inducing tolerance in organ grafts, for example, and on minimizing damage to cardiac muscles after heart attacks has been halted in some research laboratories because of soaring costs of dogs.

4   Moreover, eliminating the use of pound animals in research would, paradoxically, cause even more animals to die. According

to the American Humane Society, 7 million pet dogs are abandoned to pounds or shelters each year, 5 million of which are killed—600 "trusting pets" killed hourly. Yet some would have you believe that killing animals in a pound is more virtuous than having them help to advance medical knowledge and ultimately benefit human and animal health. I don't like to see life taken from any species unnecessarily, and that would happen if this law is enacted. Every year we would have to breed an additional 138,000 dogs and 50,000 cats for research to replace the pound animals, which would then be put to death anyway because no one wants them. With the current overpopulation of dogs and cats, the logic of such a policy escapes me.

5   It was humane concerns that led me into medicine. I strongly disapprove of cruelty to animals as well as humans. Medical scientists are not engaged in cockfighting, bullfighting, bull-dogging, calf-roping, or any other "sport" imposing stress or violence on animals. Rather, they are searching for ways to relieve suffering and preserve life. Unquestionably, every precaution should be taken, and enforced, to ensure that laboratory animals are treated humanely. Responsible scientists observe humane guidelines, not only because their search for new medical knowledge is motivated by compassion for the suffering, but because they know that improper treatment adversely affects the quality of their research. Scientists are also obligated to use insentient models when these are satisfactory, but again, no responsible scientist would incur the substantial expense and devote the considerable space required for housing and caring for animals when other equally satisfactory models were available.

6   If scientists abandon cat and dog experiments for other models that are not as suitable or as well understood, many potential medical breakthroughs may be severely crippled or halted. Grave diseases such as AIDS, cancer, heart disease, muscular dystrophy, Alzheimer's disease, and other serious conditions will, however, continue to plague our families, friends, and fellow citizens, and those patients will properly expect to receive effective treatments and cures.

7   Remember, too, that pets have also profited from animal research. It is doubtful that animals could be treated today for heart or kidney disease, leukemia, or other serious disorders if animal research had been prohibited previously. If an animal is seriously

ill or injured, would the animal-rights activists deny him a form of treatment potentially beneficial but never used before—and therefore experimental? Until one is faced with a life-threatening condition of a loved one—human or animal—it is difficult to answer that question truthfully.

8   We have aggressive advocates of the rights of trees, sharks, bats, whales, seals, and other mammals, but what about the rights of ailing humans? Shrill attacks against speciesism are difficult to defend when one observes pit bulldogs mauling and killing children, wolves killing deer, cats consuming rats and birds, and birds consuming worms. And even vegetarians destroy living plants for consumption. Self-preservation is a primary instinct of all members of the animal kingdom, and patients with that instinct deserve our compassion, protection, and assistance as much as other species.

9   Some animal-rights zealots have been quoted as regarding "the right to human life as a perversion," meat-eating as "primitive, barbaric, and arrogant," and pet ownership as an "absolutely abysmal situation brought about by human manipulation." It is difficult to believe that many animal lovers would embrace such an extreme position. There is a difference, moreover, between animal welfare and antisciencism. Infiltrating laboratories surreptitiously by posing as volunteer workers, destroying research records, vandalizing research facilities, bombing, and threatening scientists are all irrational methods of persuasion. At one research institution, damages amounted to more than a half million dollars when computers were destroyed, blood was poured on files, and liberationist slogans were painted on laboratory walls. Research on infant blindness was halted for eight months while claims of animal abuse were investigated, only to be found baseless. Such harassment, demoralization, and interference divert funds from productive research to security and discourage bright young people from entering research. Once the manpower chain is broken, it will not be easily restored. And where will we then turn for answers to devastating human diseases? Guerilla tactics, lurid pictures, and sensational headlines may inflame emotions, but they do not lead to rational judgments. More important, should we condone harassment, terrorism, and violence masquerading as concern for animal rights?

10   As a physician, my greatest concern is, of course, the suffering human beings who will be denied effective treatment because we

took action that seems superficially humane but may ultimately render us powerless against certain diseases. What do I tell dying patients who are waiting for the medical advances that these threatened investigations may produce—that there is no hope because we have been prevented from acquiring the new knowledge needed to correct their conditions? As a human being and physician, I cannot conceive of telling parents their sick child is doomed because we cannot use all the tools at our disposal. Surely those who object to animals in research laboratories must be equally distressed at seeing sick children hooked up to tubes. How will those parents feel about a society that legislates the rights of animals above those of humans?

11   Through research, we have made remarkable advances in medicine, but we still do not have all the answers. If the animal-rights activists could witness the heartbreaking suffering of patients and families that I encounter daily, I doubt that they would deliberately pose a direct threat to human and animal health by demanding that we abandon some of our most fruitful methods of medical investigation. The American public must decide: Shall we tell hundreds of thousands of victims of heart attacks, cancer, AIDS, and numerous other dread diseases that the right of abandoned animals to die in a pound supersedes the patient's rights to relief from suffering and premature death? In making that decision, let us use not anger and hatred but reason and good will.

Analyzing the Writer's Argument

1. What are the "pound animals" DeBakey is referring to in paragraph 1?
2. In paragraph 2, DeBakey cites a number of diseases that would not have been cured if researchers had been prevented from using animals in their work. How convincing for you is his list of examples?
3. What does DeBakey mean when he says that there are "no satisfactory insentient models at present for biomedical research and testing"?
4. Reread DeBakey's fourth paragraph and explain his claim that "eliminating the use of pound animals in research would, paradoxically, cause even more animals to die." He charges that animal rights advocates believe that it is more virtuous for animals to die

in pounds than in laboratories. Does he offer any proof for this claim? Is he putting words in their mouths? Do animals die more "virtuously" in biomedical research labs?

5. DeBakey seems to be concerned about the cost of buying specially bred dogs for research should the use of pound animals be prohibited by law. Is cost a factor in the animals rights issue? Explain.

6. In paragraph 7, DeBakey asks the following question: "If an animal is seriously ill or injured, would the animal-rights activists deny him a form of treatment potentially beneficial but never used before—and therefore experimental?" He goes on to say that you'd have to be faced with the situation before you could answer truthfully. Does one, in fact, have to be directly faced with the question to answer it truthfully? Explain.

7. DeBakey asks, finally, if we should tell sick patients that their rights are superseded by the rights of abandoned animals who are condemned to die in pounds. Is this the real issue in the animal rights debate, as you understand it? Where has, for example, DeBakey considered the suffering of animals in what are sometimes thought to be redundant and poorly designed research experiments?

Exploring the Issues in This Essay

1. Discuss what you would do if you knew that you might be able to help many people who were suffering from a horrible and ultimately deadly disease by performing painful and, at times, gruesome experiments on a great number of dogs and cats. Could you rationalize the certain inhumane treatment for an uncertain triumph over the disease? Discuss the factors that you need to consider before arriving at this very difficult decision.

2. To what extent should cost be a factor in an ethical debate? Is it simply realistic to include the cost of a solution because it will have to be met and does the price of a course of action cloud the issue, blur the essential philosophic points of the debate? Should one favor an inexpensive but not totally satisfactory solution over an expensive but acceptable one?

Writing Suggestions for
Animal Experimentation: Unwarranted Cruelty?

1. Let's assume that you are not happy about the present situation with respect to the use of animals for biomedical research. Write a short statement and offer some guidelines for the proper care and treatment of research animals. You may want to start with the questions posed by Lane Potter in the *Proceedings of the Royal Society of Medicine* as cited in the selection by Teresa Rye (p. 266). You may then wish to discuss the subject with several classmates or even interview them to ascertain how they feel in preparation for writing.

2. Write an essay in which you argue that if animal rights advocates get their way, all biomedical research using animals will be halted and human suffering will be the inevitable result.

3. What alternatives are there to using live animals for research? What progress, if any, has been made with them? You may wish to consult Dr. D. H. Smyth's *Alternatives to Animal Experiments*, a work cited by Patricia Curtis (p. 247). Write an essay in which you argue for or against the use of such alternatives, giving ample evidence of your research into the question.

4. In "The Facts About Animal Research," an article which appeared in the March 1988 issue of *Reader's Digest*, Dr. Robert J. White, M.D., writes, "It is not hard to understand why opponents of research with animals have received such a sympathetic response. The idea conjures up images of experiments on beloved family pets. But the fact is that over 90 percent of the more than 20 million animals used annually in medical research are mice, rats and other rodents" (p. 128). Does Dr. White exhibit speciesism in his comment? Does it make a difference to you if the animals in question are rodents or dogs and cats? At this writing, there is a bill in Congress (H.R. 2766) that would include mice, rats, and birds under the provisions of the Animal Welfare Act. Argue for or against such a change in the Animal Welfare Act.

5. Argue for the continuation of animal research basing your argument on a detailed examination of the use of laboratory animals in developing a cure for a dreaded disease or specific surgical procedures necessary to saving human lives or restoring patients' health. The history of the heart-lung machine and the discovery

of insulin may be good cases to investigate but these are rather well-known ones and you may wish to range further afield in your investigations. Check the list of achievements included in the essay by Jack Rosenberger (p. 257), and Dr. Michael E. De-Bakey (p. 282).

6. Some argue that if we concede to the wishes of animal rights activists, they will next want us to refrain from killing animals for other reasons. As the ad on p. 263 puts it, "Today fur. Tomorrow leather, Then wool. Then meat." This is, of course, a "slippery slope" argument. Argue for or against this eventuality.

7. Dr. Michael DeBakey writes, "according to the American Humane Society, 7 million pet dogs are abandoned to pounds or shelters each year, 5 million of which are killed—600 'trusting' pets killed hourly." Can we do something about abandoned pets, something to stem the tide of unwanted pets in this country? Write a proposal for the elimination of unwanted pets. What would you do? How would you go about doing it? How much would your solution cost?

8. Argue in favor of or against the animal rights position in areas other than biomedical research (e.g., hunting, so-called factory farming, pet shops, zoos, rodeos, circuses, etc.). A good starting place for information is *Animal Rights: Stories of People Who Defend the Rights of Animals* (1980).

9. If you are for animal rights, does it follow that you must be a vegetarian? Argue for or against vegetarianism that is based on the refusal to take the life of animals for meat.

10. It is now an almost universally recognized fact among scientists that there is not the clear line between animals and humans that we once thought existed, especially in pre-Darwinian times. Instead, we believe that various species are arrayed along a spectrum from the lowest forms of life to the so-called higher primates, animals that are believed to possess almost-human intelligence. Write an essay in which you argue that the very investigations of scientists, especially ethologists or those that study animal behavior, have made it more difficult morally to use animals for human benefit. A good place to start your work is Dr. Dallas Pratt's *Painful Experiments on Animals*, a work discussed by Patricia Curtis (p. 248).

11. Argue not for more or fewer laboratory experiments using live animals but for much stricter monitoring of research proposals to prevent duplication, poor research design, ill-conceived objectives, and the unnecessary use of animals.

12. Argue for or against the boycotting of cosmetics and toy companies that use animals in their product safety research. You will need to consult the *Reader's Guide to Periodical Literature* for articles in this area to learn what the issues are before taking a stand of your own.

7

America's Dependency on Drugs

When we think about substance abuse today, we naturally turn to the stories played up in the media: the relationship between drugs and crime, the Columbian cocaine connection, addiction among the newborn, infected needles and public health, the addictive powers of newly created designer drugs, the money spent by law enforcement agencies at all levels of government to combat drug abuse, the financial lure of drug dealing, and the efforts of communities to make their neighborhoods drug free. In short, the emphasis of the media has been overwhelmingly on the trafficking and use of illegal drugs and the economic toll they take on our society. According to Dorothy Rice, a former director of national health statistics at the Federal Department of Health and Human Services, "It's clear that for 1989, the cost of drugs on society is tremendous, far more than $60 billion."

In focusing our attention on this war against drugs, we seem too willing to place the blame on others. Unless we are personally involved in the sale or use of these drugs, we tend to objectify the problem and to remove or isolate ourselves from it. The problem of substance abuse is more complex and more pervasive, however, than any of us is willing to admit. In fact, many experts believe we are a nation of substance abusers—a nation of drinkers, smokers, and pill poppers. The statistics, too, are staggering, and the consequences devastating:

- Alcohol is a factor in over 50% of fatal automobile accidents.
- Alcohol is the most often cited contributing factor in divorce.
- Over 60% of violent crimes are alcohol related.
- The American Heart Association claims that tobacco contributes to over 300,000 deaths each year.

291

- Alcohol-related deaths are estimated from 50–200,000.
- Forty percent of suicide attempts are alcohol related.

While these statistics are alarming, they do not begin to suggest the tremendous grief and suffering that substance abuse leaves in its wake. Loved ones are killed, relationships are fractured, children are abandoned, productivity in the work place falters, the dreams of children are snuffed out, and the social fabric is stretched and torn in ways that statistics could not possibly measure.

These are not stories of high-adventure drug busts, of powerful drug cartels, or of corrupt foreign leaders, but they are our stories and the stories of our neighbors, and they need to be told. And it's in telling these stories that we will begin to understand America's addictions and the kinds of problems these addictions cause. Most importantly, with this knowledge each of us will be better able to participate in the debate about driving while intoxicated, driving while drugged, smoking in public places, the legalization of drugs, and the use and abuse of painkillers. As we search for solutions to our substance abuse problems, we need to develop approaches that get at the heart of the problem rather than merely address its symptoms.

Linda Weltner

Every 23 Minutes...

Linda Weltner was born in Worcester, Massachusetts, in 1938. After graduating from Wellesley, she began a career as a freelance writer and has been a columnist in the Boston Globe *since 1981. She has written* Beginning to Feel the Magic *(1981) and* The New Voice *(1981), both novels for young adults, and* No Place Like Home *(1989), a collection of her essays.*

Like most of us, Weltner knew that drunk driving was a serious problem, but it took the chance meeting of an acquaintance to bring the horror of it all home to her. She realized that "in one minute this woman's whole life had been turned upside-down." In "Every 23 Minutes..." she makes us aware of the living victims of drunk driving accidents. And she uses their stories to make an emotional appeal against drinking and driving. Her essay first appeared in the Boston Globe *on June 6, 1986.*

1   My husband and I went to a funeral a few weeks ago. The man we honored had not been ill and will never grow old. He was killed in his car on a Sunday night, driving home along a divided highway.

2   It was an ordinary evening, no blacker than any other, when a car coming in the other direction jumped the median strip, broke through the guard rail, and hit two other cars before smashing head on into his. According to the newspaper, the driver, who was returning from a wedding, seemed puzzled. "I only had two bottles of beer and two glasses of champagne," she is reported to have said.

3   A wedding.

4   Followed by a funeral.

5   I wish she could have been there to see all the lives her act has changed forever, the wife, and four children, the extended family, the hundreds and hundreds of friends who sat in numbed silence, listening to words which barely touched the depths of their grief.

293

6   Strange to think that, according to the National Highway Traffic Safety Administration, this happens in America every 23 minutes.

7   Somebody drinks.

8   Somebody drives.

9   Somebody dies.

10   And other lives are altered forever, though sometimes the changes may be invisible to a casual observer. By chance, the day before the funeral I ran into a longtime acquaintance while shopping. He commented on my crutches. I asked if he had ever broken his leg.

11   "Uh, I have a long rod in this thigh," he said, "from an automobile accident two weeks after I came back from Vietnam."

12   "That's ironic. To leave a war zone and get injured," I teased him. "You're lucky it wasn't worse."

13   "Well, my wife was killed in the crash and so was the wife of the driver," he said uncomfortably. "We were hit by a drunk."

14   I've known this man for years, yet suddenly I realized there was a whole chapter of his life he never mentioned. I asked and discovered he'd remained in the hospital seven weeks, and that all that time he'd known his wife was dead. It was hard to know where to go from there, for there are questions you can't put to someone in a casual conversation, like "How could you bear it?" or "What did you do about wanting revenge?"

15   I wish I knew the answers to those questions. I wish I could offer those answers to the woman who, overwhelmed by grief, could barely walk as she followed her husband's coffin from the synagogue.

16   My friend Lynn saw a movie at the high school where she teaches in which the young male narrator recounted how he'd killed someone while driving drunk. "He said he didn't know how he'd stand it if he'd killed someone he loved," Lynn told me. "That really bothered me. Isn't everyone someone that somebody loves?"

17   Every 23 minutes, who dies?

18   A mother who will never comfort the child who needs her. A woman who will never know how very much her friends depended on her. A man whose contributions to his community would have made a difference. A wife whose husband cannot picture the future without her.

19 Every 23 minutes, who dies?

20 A son who involuntarily abandons his parents in their old age. A father who can never acknowledge his children's accomplishments. A daughter who can never take back her angry words in parting. A sister who will never be her sister's maid of honor.

21 Every 23 minutes, who dies?

22 A brother who will not be there to hold his newborn nephew. A friend whose encouragement is gone forever. A bride-to-be who will never say her vows. An aunt whose family will fragment and fall apart.

23 Every 23 minutes, who dies?

24 A child who will never fulfill his early promise. An uncle who leaves his children without guidance and support. A grandmother whose husband must now grow old alone. A lover who never had a chance to say how much he cared.

25 *Every 23 minutes.*

26 A void opens.

27 Someone looks across the table at a vacant chair, climbs into an empty bed, feels the pain of no voice, no touch, no love. Where there was once intimacy and contact, now there is only absence and despair.

28 *Every 23 minutes.*

29 A heart breaks.

30 Someone's pain shatters the confines of her body, leaking out in tears, exploding in cries, defying the healing power of tranquilizers and Seconal. Sleep offers no escape from the nightmare of awakening. And morning brings only the irreversibility of loss.

31 *Every 23 minutes.*

32 A dream ends.

33 Someone's future blurs and goes blank as anticipation fades into nothingness. The phone will not ring, the car will not pull into the driveway. The weight of tomorrow becomes unbearable in a world in which all promises have been forcibly broken.

34 *Every 23 minutes.*

35 Somebody wants to run. Somebody wants to hide.

36 Someone is left with hate. Somebody wants to die.

37 And we permit this to go on.

38 *Every 23 minutes.*

Analyzing the Writer's Argument

1. What is Weltner's stance on drinking? Drinking and driving? Explain.
2. Weltner provides very little personal information about the drunken driver or the man this driver killed. Do you feel the need for more information? Does the lack of more specific information help or hinder Weltner in making her point? Explain.
3. What point is Weltner trying to make with the example of the Vietnam veteran? Why is the information he provides the author even more ironic than she at first realized?
4. Why is Weltner's friend so "bothered" by the narrator of the film she watched? What do the narrator's words tell us about him? How does this paragraph help to structure the rest of Weltner's essay?
5. How do you respond to Weltner's repetition of the phrase, "Every 23 minutes"? Did it make you more aware of the startling reality of this statistic? Or did it seem melodramatic?
6. What do you think Weltner wants her readers to do after reading this essay? How do you know?

Exploring the Issues in This Essay

1. Weltner concludes her essay with the simple statement: "And we permit this to go on." Our obvious response is that we can't let it go on, but what, in fact, can we do? Can society make people more responsible for their own behavior?
2. Have you known someone who died in an alcohol-related automobile accident? Discuss how that person's death affected the community, the person's family, the person responsible for the accident? Why does public attention always seem to focus on the accident itself and not on the people whose lives have been forever changed?

Joseph Califano and Paul Screvane

Pro/Con: Restrict Smoking in Public Places?*

In 1986, as part of its coverage of the debate over smoking in public places in New York City, U.S. News and World Report *conducted pro/con interviews with Joseph Califano, former Secretary of Health, Education and Welfare under Jimmy Carter, and Paul Screvane, former president of the New York City Council. Both men are outspoken in their opposing viewpoints on this subject. To this debate, Califano brings his experience as a public health official while Screvane reflects his experience in business and city politics. This set of interviews clearly illustrates the controversies that arise when questions of public policy collide with those of individual rights.*

PRO

Interview with Joseph Califano, former Secretary of Health, Education and Welfare

Q Mr. Califano, why do you favor restricting smoking in public?

1 People—whether they're children, workers or pregnant women—should not be forced to breathe other people's smoke. Maybe you can drink alone or eat alone, but it is not possible to smoke alone in an enclosed space with other people.

2 Studies show that 5,000 Americans die each year because of secondhand smoke. A Japanese report concluded that nonsmoking wives of heavy smokers had an 80 percent higher risk of lung cancer than women married to nonsmokers. Study after study has associated involuntary smoking and lung cancer, pneumonia, asthma and bronchitis. A recent study has linked secondhand smoke to heart disease.

Q Where do you think smoking should be banned?

3   In schools, hospitals, sports arenas and convention halls, theaters, banks or other public places where people have to stand and
wait. Sections of theater lobbies and other areas could be set aside
for smokers. Smoking should not be permitted in stores. Restaurants should be required to provide smoke-free space. Employers
should provide a smoke-free workplace for employees who wish
it. I support the efforts to restrict smoking to designated areas in
federal buildings. Virtually all assembly lines now prohibit smoking, and most large companies with large workroom areas have
restrictions. Businesses that permit smoking at work can provide
a room for smoking or segregate smokers in one part of a room
with proper ventilation.

4   The commission I worked with to propose a New York City
antismoking law recommended no restrictions for bars, private
residences, hotel and motel rooms or tobacco stores.

Q Many restaurants already have no-smoking areas. Why should
merchants and employers be forced to separate smokers?

5   Because the last five surgeons general have concluded that this
is a public-health problem with heavy costs to our society. Why
should the nonsmoker have to protect himself against breathing
smoke any more than a customer should have to inspect the kitchen
of a restaurant to see if it is sanitary?

Q Businesses argue that such measures are costly—

6   It costs no more than a sign that says "No-Smoking Section."
Employers will save money in terms of reduced illness and absen-
teeism and increased productivity.

Q Is the real goal to force people to stop smoking altogether?

7   Not at all. That is their choice. I'm only trying to protect nonsmokers. But I do support employers who fund programs to help
workers quit smoking if they want to. Smoking is slow-motion
suicide. The point here is to prevent secondhand smoking from
becoming slow-motion murder.

CON

Interview with Paul Screvane, former president, New York City
Council

Q Mr. Screvane, why do you oppose banning or restricting smoking in public places?

8 Because such laws would set up two classes of citizens—smokers and nonsmokers—and would be very confrontational. They give the nonsmoker virtual dictatorial power to determine where smoking may not be permitted.

9 And such laws are unenforceable. Health departments and the police are already overworked.

Q What about studies that link smoke-filled rooms to lung cancer in nonsmokers?

10 I can find no evidence that secondary smoke is a danger. At three separate workshops on this very issue, scientists concluded that health hazards to nonsmokers could not be established.

Q Why then are cancer doctors among those pressing to ban smoking in public places?

11 Passive smoke is a subterfuge. They are really trying to make it difficult to smoke in public. They think many young people will say: "Well, if it's that inconvenient, why even get started on it? Forget it." They can't point to any scientific danger to nonsmokers. It's a sham, a fraud.

Q Don't you think restaurant patrons, for instance, have the right to dine without smoke if they wish?

12 If enough people came into a restaurant and said, "We will not patronize your place because you don't have a no-smoking section," they'd have one. Restaurants aren't required by law to provide sugar substitutes, but because of the pressures of the marketplace, most do.

Q What about the workplace? Shouldn't all workers have the right to a smoke-free environment?

13 The workplace is not always a big room in which you can segregate smokers and nonsmokers. What if 10 people work in a section and two are smokers? Can you put a wall around them? If they need to communicate with their fellow workers, I think you're depriving them of their livelihood.

14 Also, segregating smokers costs money. An AFL-CIO study estimated that an antismoking law would cost $265 million a year in New York City.

Q How would such laws cost employers money?

15 Besides reorganizing the office and putting up partitions, a company would suffer from time lost.

16 I smoke three packs a day, which means I smoke three or four cigarettes an hour. As president of Federal Metal Maintenance, Inc., I have my own office. But if I did not, I would have to absent myself from my workplace and go to a designated area to smoke. That's time—and time is money.

Analyzing the Writers' Argument

1. What does Califano say is the difference between smoking and eating and drinking? Why is this an important distinction for him to make?

2. Califano refers to a number of studies that point to the negative effects of secondhand smoke. How do you react to these references? Would you have reacted differently had he named them? Why or why not?

3. Califano refers to smoking as "slow-motion suicide" and to secondhand smoking as "slow-motion murder." Is there some truth in his statements or is he merely being sensational? Explain.

4. Both Califano and Screvane use analogies to argue their respective positions. Identify these analogies and compare their effectiveness.

5. Screvane admits that he is a three-pack-a-day smoker. How does this admission affect your response to his argument?

6. Screvane assumes that the natural response to the needs of smokers and nonsmokers is segregation in the workplace. Is this a reasonable assumption?

7. Is the establishment of a smoke-free workplace as much an economic issue as Screvane would like us to believe? Explain.

Exploring the Issues in This Essay

1. To what extent is smoking a public health issue? To what extent is it a question of individual rights? How do you resolve the controversy when these two positions vie for control?

2. In a 1985 article in *The Washington Monthly*, David Owen states that "in the United States, smoking now causes 85 percent of lung cancer cases, 30 percent of all cancer cases, and a total of 350,000

premature deaths every year, including deaths form emphysema, bronchitis, pneumonia, and heart disease (but not including 2,000 deaths from house fires caused by careless smoking or as many as 5,000 deaths among nonsmokers who breathe in smoke that others exhale). Smoking, in the words of the surgeon general, is the 'chief single avoidable cause of death in our society.' " In light of these statistics, why do you suppose smokers continue to smoke? Discuss what can be done to curb their addiction. Is there any justification for considering smokers' rights when setting policies concerning smoking in public places?

3. Collect several cigarette advertisements from a variety of popular magazines and examine them. Do they carry similar messages? What are the hidden messages of the ads? What advantages are attributed to smoking that have nothing to do with the product? What conclusions can you draw from your analysis?

Norman Cousins

Pain Is Not the Ultimate Enemy

> *Norman Cousins is perhaps best known as the former editor of the* Saturday Review, *a position he held for more than three decades. Under Cousins' direction, the* Saturday Review *became one of the most influential magazines in America, defining our country's cultural tastes and identifying major social issues. Born in Union Hill, New Jersey, in 1915, Cousins attended Columbia University before embarking on his career as an educator, journalist, and writer. In later life, an experience with a near-fatal illness provided the basis for his controversial* Anatomy of an Illness as Perceived by the Patient: Reflections on Healing and Regeneration *(1979), a book in which Cousins argues that the will to live and capacity for self-healing have been neglected by the medical profession. Cousins has also written* The Healing Heart: Antidotes to Panic and Helplessness *(1983) and* The Pathology of Power *(1987). His most recent book* Head First: The Biology of Hope *(1989) explores the scientific evidence for his conviction that the mind can help mobilize the body's healing resources. Currently, he is Professor of Medical Humanities at UCLA.*
>
> *During his illness, Cousins discovered that his reliance on the pain-killing drugs given to him by his doctor were actually making his condition worse. He stopped taking the drugs and substituted large doses of laughter by watching old Marx brothers movies. In "Pain Is Not the Ultimate Enemy" a selection taken from* Anatomy of an Illness, *he argues that Americans have little tolerance for, or understanding of, pain and have, therefore, turned to pain-killing drugs for relief. Cousins believes that Americans' use of such drugs has become addictive.*

1   Americans are probably the most pain-conscious people on the face of the earth. For years we have had it drummed into us— in print, on radio, over television, in everyday conversation—that

any hint of pain is to be banished as though it were the ultimate evil. As a result, we are becoming a nation of pill grabbers and hypochondriacs, escalating the slightest ache into a searing ordeal.

2   We know very little about pain and what we don't know makes it hurt all the more. Indeed, no form of illiteracy in the United States is so widespread or costly as ignorance about pain—what it is, what causes it, how to deal with it without panic. Almost everyone can rattle off the names of at least a dozen drugs that can deaden pain from every conceivable cause—all the way from headaches to hemorrhoids. There is far less knowledge about the fact that about 90 percent of pain is self-limiting, that it is not always an indication of poor health, and that, most frequently, it is the result of tension, stress, worry, idleness, boredom, frustration, suppressed rage, insufficient sleep, overeating, poorly balanced diet, smoking, excessive drinking, inadequate exercise, stale air, or any of the other abuses encountered by the human body in modern society.

3   The most ignored fact of all about pain is that the best way to eliminate it is to eliminate the abuse. Instead, many people reach almost instinctively for the painkillers—aspirins, barbiturates, codeines, tranquilizers, sleeping pills, and dozens of other analgesics or desensitizing drugs.

4   Most doctors are profoundly troubled over the extent to which the medical profession today is taking on the trappings of a pain-killing industry. Their offices are overloaded with people who are morbidly but mistakenly convinced that something dreadful is about to happen to them. It is all too evident that the campaign to get people to run to a doctor at the first sign of pain has boomeranged. Physicians find it difficult to give adequate attention to patients genuinely in need of expert diagnosis and treatment because their time is soaked up by people who have nothing wrong with them except a temporary indisposition or a psychogenic ache.

5   Patients tend to feel indignant and insulted if the physician tells them he can find no organic cause for the pain. They tend to interpret the term "psychogenic" to mean that they are complaining of nonexistent symptoms. They need to be educated about the fact that many forms of pain have no underlying physical cause but are the result, as mentioned earlier, of tension, stress, or hostile factors in the general environment. Sometimes a pain may be a manifestation of "conversion hysteria," as mentioned earlier, the

name given by Jean Charcot to physical symptoms that have their origins in emotional disturbances.

6   Obviously, it is folly for an individual to ignore symptoms that could be a warning of a potentially serious illness. Some people are so terrified of getting bad news from a doctor that they allow their malaise to worsen, sometimes past the point of no return. Total neglect is not the answer to hypochondria. The only answer has to be increased education about the way the human body works, so that more people will be able to steer an intelligent course between promiscuous pill-popping and irresponsible disregard of genuine symptoms.

7   Of all forms of pain, none is more important for the individual to understand than the "threshold" variety. Almost everyone has a telltale ache that is triggered whenever tension or fatigue reaches a certain point. It can take the form of a migraine-type headache or a squeezing pain deep in the abdomen or cramps or a pain in the lower back or even pain in the joints. The individual who has learned how to make the correlation between such threshold pains and their cause doesn't panic when they occur; he or she does something about relieving the stress and tension. Then, if the pain persists despite the absence of apparent cause, the individual will telephone the doctor.

8   If ignorance about the nature of pain is widespread, ignorance about the way pain-killing drugs work is even more so. What is not generally understood is that many of the vaunted pain-killing drugs conceal the pain without correcting the underlying condition. They deaden the mechanism in the body that alerts the brain to the fact that something may be wrong. The body can pay a high price for suppression of pain without regard to its basic cause.

9   Professional athletes are sometimes severely disadvantaged by trainers whose job it is to keep them in action. The more famous the athlete, the greater the risk that he or she may be subjected to extreme medical measures when injury strikes. The star baseball pitcher whose arm is sore because of a torn muscle or tissue damage may need sustained rest more than anything else. But his team is battling for a place in the World Series; so the trainer or team doctor, called upon to work his magic, reaches for a strong dose of butazolidine or other powerful pain suppressants. Presto, the pain disappears! The pitcher takes his place on the mound and

does superbly. That could be the last game, however, in which he is able to throw a ball with full strength. The drugs didn't repair the torn muscle or cause the damaged tissue to heal. What they did was to mask the pain, enabling the pitcher to throw hard, further damaging the torn muscle. Little wonder that so many star athletes are cut down in their prime, more the victims of overzealous treatment of their injuries than of the injuries themselves.

10   The king of all painkillers, of course, is aspirin. The U.S. Food and Drug Administration permits aspirin to be sold without prescription, but the drug, contrary to popular belief, can be dangerous and, in sustained doses, potentially lethal. Aspirin is self-administered by more people than any other drug in the world. Some people are aspirin-poppers, taking ten or more a day. What they don't know is that the smallest dose can cause internal bleeding. Even more serious perhaps is the fact that aspirin is antagonistic to collagen, which has a key role in the formation of connective tissue. Since many forms of arthritis involve disintegration of the connective tissue, the steady use of aspirin can actually intensify the underlying arthritic condition.

11   The reason why aspirin is prescribed so widely for arthritic patients is that it has an antiinflammatory effect, apart from its pain-deadening characteristics. In recent years, however, medical researchers have suggested that the antiinflammatory value of aspirin may be offset by the harm it causes to the body's vital chemistry. Doctors J. Hirsh, D. Street, J. F. Cade, and H. Amy, in the March 1973 issue of the professional journal *Blood*, showed that aspirin impedes the interaction between "platelet release" and connective tissue. In the *Annals of Rheumatic Diseases*, also in March 1973, Dr. P. N. Sperryn reported a significant blood loss in patients who were on heavy daily doses of aspirin. (It is not unusual for patients suffering from serious rheumatoid arthritis to take as many as twenty-four aspirin tablets a day.)

12   Again, I call attention to the article in the May 8, 1971 issue of *Lancet*, the English medical journal. Dr. M. A. Sahud and Dr. R. J. Cohen stated that the systematic use of aspirin by rheumatoid patients produces abnormally low plasma-ascorbic-acid levels. The authors reported that aspirin blocks the "uptake of ascorbic acid into the blood platelets." Since vitamin C is essential in collagen formation, its depletion by aspirin would seem to run directly

counter to the body's need to combat connective tissue breakdown in arthritic conditions. The *Lancet* article concludes that, at the very least, ascorbic acid should be administered along with aspirin to counteract its harmful effects.

13   Aspirin is not the only pain-killing drug, of course, that is known to have dangerous side effects. Dr. Daphne A. Roe, of Cornell University, at a medical meeting in New York City in 1974, presented startling evidence of a wide range of hazards associated with sedatives and other pain suppressants. Some of these drugs seriously interfere with the ability of the body to metabolize food properly, producing malnutrition. In some instances, there is also the danger of bone-marrow depression, interfering with the ability of the body to replenish its blood supply.

14   Pain-killing drugs are among the greatest advances in the history of medicine. Properly used, they can be a boon in alleviating suffering and in treating disease. But their indiscriminate and promiscuous use is making psychological cripples and chronic ailers out of millions of people. The unremitting barrage of advertising for pain-killing drugs, especially over television, has set the stage for a mass anxiety neurosis. Almost from the moment children are old enough to sit up-right in front of a television screen, they are being indoctrinated into the hypochondriac's clamorous and morbid world. Little wonder so many people fear pain more than death itself.

15   It might be a good idea if concerned physicians and educators could get together to make knowledge about pain an important part of the regular school curriculum. As for the populace at large, perhaps some of the same techniques used by public-service agencies to make people cancer-conscious can be used to counteract the growing terror of pain and illness in general. People ought to know that nothing is more remarkable about the human body than its recuperative drive, given a modicum of respect. If our broadcasting stations cannot provide equal time for responses to the pain-killing advertisements, they might at least set aside a few minutes each day for common-sense remarks on the subject of pain. As for the Food and Drug Administration, it might be interesting to know why an agency that has so energetically warned the American people against taking vitamins without prescriptions is doing

so little to control over-the-counter sales each year of billions of pain-killing pills, some of which can do more harm than the pain they are supposed to suppress.

Analyzing the Writer's Argument

1. If "pain is not the ultimate enemy," what does Cousins believe is?
2. Why does Cousins believe that America has become "a nation of pill-grabbers and hypochondriacs"? What evidence does he provide for this claim? Do you agree with his assessment that we are "the most pain-conscious people on the face of the earth"? Why or why not?
3. What is "threshold pain," and why does Cousins think that an understanding of it is essential to one's well-being? What does he think we need to know about the nature of pain and the way pain-killing drugs work?
4. In paragraph 9, Cousins introduces the example of the star baseball pitcher who was suffering with a sore arm. What point does he make with this example and what does it contribute to the overall persuasiveness of his argument?
5. What does Cousins see as the relationships among education, ignorance, and the nature of pain? Present these relationships in the form of a syllogism.
6. In paragraphs 10–12, Cousins discusses our use of aspirin. For what purpose does he single out aspirin? How does Cousins support his claim that aspirin is overused and potentially dangerous?
7. How would you describe Cousins' tone, his attitude toward his subject and audience, in this essay? What is the value for Cousins of using the first person "we"? How does his tone affect your response to his argument?
8. What does Cousins want the American public to do? After reading his argument, are you convinced we ought to do this? Why or why not?

Exploring the Issues in This Essay

1. Look through recent issues of several popular magazines for advertisements promoting over-the-counter pain remedies. If possible, bring several of these ads to class with you. How would you

characterize these ads? What, if any, warnings do these ads carry? What emotional appeals are they making? Do the ads substantiate Cousins' claim that Americans fear pain?

2. Cousins mentions the Food and Drug Agency on several occasions in his essay. What is his attitude toward this government agency? Establish a basis for assessing this agency. What is the role of the FDA, as you understand it? In your opinion, is it fulfilling its function?

William Bennett

*Should Drugs Be Legalized?**

The current leader of America's "war on drugs," William Bennett was born on July 31, 1943. As an undergraduate at Williams College, Bennett played football, joined a fraternity, and played guitar in the rock band Plato and the Guardians. *It was at Williams that he "first fell in love with the world of ideas." Bennett went on to earn his Ph.D. in philosophy at the University of Texas and his J.D. at Harvard Law School. A classroom teacher by inclination, Bennett taught philosophy at the University of Southern Mississippi, the University of Wisconsin, and Boston University and coauthored the book* Counting by Race: Equality in American Thought from the Founding Fathers to Bakke. *He served as chairperson of The National Endowment for the Humanities from 1981–1985 before becoming U.S. Secretary of Education in the Reagan administration. In 1989 he was appointed the first director of the National Drug Control Policy by President Bush and charged with the task of commanding our war on drugs.*

Bennett is committed to the war on drugs. "It's essential that we win," he said in a recent interview for Newsweek. *"This stuff is destroying the lives of millions of Americans, and it is virtually eliminating the possibility of upward mobility for an awful lot of people. These are American citizens, and they're dying, they're shooting each other. Whatever we may think of their merit as individuals, they are part of* us." *In the following essay written for the March 1990 issue of* Reader's Digest, *Bennett answers critics who believe that our fight against drugs is "flawed, fatalistic, hopeless, bankrupt!" He argues that the plea to legalize drugs is nothing short of an outright call to surrender.*

1   Since I took command of the war on drugs, I have learned from former Secretary of State George Shultz that our concept of fight-

* Reprinted with permission from the March 1990 *Reader's Digest*. Copyright © 1990 by The Reader's Digest Assn., Inc.

ing drugs is "flawed." The only thing to do, he says, is to "make it possible for addicts to buy drugs at some regulated place." Conservative commentator William F. Buckley, Jr., suggests I should be "fatalistic" about the flood of cocaine from South America and simply "let it in." Syndicated columnist Mike Royko contends it would be easier to sweep junkies out of the gutters "than to fight a hopeless war" against the narcotics that send them there. Labeling our efforts "bankrupt," federal judge Robert W. Sweet opts for legalization, saying, "If our society can learn to stop using butter, it should be able to cut down on cocaine."

2 Flawed, fatalistic, hopeless, bankrupt! I never realized surrender was so fashionable until I assumed this post.

3 Though most Americans are overwhelmingly determined to go toe-to-toe with the foreign drug lords and neighborhood pushers, a small minority believe that enforcing drug laws imposes greater costs on society than do drugs themselves. Like addicts seeking immediate euphoria, the legalizers want peace at any price, even though it means the inevitable proliferation of a practice that degrades, impoverishes and kills.

4 I am acutely aware of the burdens drug enforcement places upon us. It consumes economic resources we would like to use elsewhere. It is sometimes frustrating, thankless and often dangerous. But the consequences of *not* enforcing drug laws would be far more costly. Those consequences involve the intrinsically destructive nature of drugs and the toll they exact from our society in hundreds of thousands of lost and broken lives . . . human potential never realized . . . time stolen from families and jobs . . . precious spiritual and economic resources squandered.

5 That is precisely why virtually every civilized society has found it necessary to exert some form of control over mind-altering substances and why this war is so important. Americans feel up to their hips in drugs now. They would be up to their necks under legalization.

6 Even limited experiments in drug legalization have shown that when drugs are more widely available, addiction skyrockets. In 1975 Italy liberalized its drug law and now has one of the highest heroin-related death rates in Western Europe. In Alaska, where marijuana was decriminalized in 1975, the easy atmosphere has increased usage of the drug, particularly among children. Nor does

it stop there. Some Alaskan schoolchildren now tout "coca puffs," marijuana cigarettes laced with cocaine.

7 Many legalizers concede that drug legalization might increase use, but they shrug off the matter. "It may well be that there would be more addicts, and I would regret that result," says Nobel laureate economist Milton Friedman. The late Harvard Medical School psychiatry professor Norman Zinberg, a longtime proponent of "responsible" drug use, admitted that "use of now illicit drugs would certainly increase. Also, casualties probably would increase."

8 In fact, Dr. Herbert D. Kleber of Yale University, my deputy in charge of demand reduction, predicts legalization might cause "a five-to-sixfold increase" in cocaine use. But legalizers regard this as a necessary price for the "benefits" of legalization. What benefits?

9 1. *Legalization will take the profit out of drugs.* The result supposedly will be the end of criminal drug pushers and the big foreign drug wholesalers, who will turn to other enterprises because nobody will need to make furtive and dangerous trips to his local pusher.

10 But what, exactly, would the brave new world of legalized drugs look like? Buckley stresses that "adults get to buy the stuff at carefully regulated stores." (Would you want one in *your* neighborhood?) Others, like Friedman, suggest we sell the drugs at "ordinary retail outlets."

11 Former City University of New York sociologist Georgette Bennett assures us that "brand-name competition will be prohibited" and that strict quality control and proper labeling will be overseen by the Food and Drug Administration. In a touching egalitarian note, she adds that "free drugs will be provided at government clinics" for addicts too poor to buy them.

12 Almost all the legalizers point out that the price of drugs will fall, even though the drugs will be heavily taxed. Buckley, for example, argues that somehow federal drugstores will keep the price "low enough to discourage a black market but high enough to accumulate a surplus to be used for drug education."

13 Supposedly, drug sales will generate huge amounts of revenue, which will then be used to tell the public not to use drugs and to treat those who don't listen.

14 In reality, this tax would only allow government to *share* the drug profits now garnered by criminals. Legalizers would have to

tax drugs heavily in order to pay for drug education and treatment programs. Criminals could undercut the official price and still make huge profits. What alternative would the government have? Cut the price until it was within the lunch-money budget of the average sixth-grade student?

15   *2. Legalization will eliminate the black market.* Wrong. And not just because the regulated prices could be undercut. Many legalizers admit that drugs such as crack or PCP are simply too dangerous to allow the shelter of the law. Thus criminals will provide what the government will not. "As long as drugs that people very much want remain illegal, a black market will exist," says legalization advocate David Boaz of the libertarian Cato Institute.

16   Look at crack. In powdered form, cocaine was an expensive indulgence. But street chemists found that a better and far less expensive—and far more dangerous—high could be achieved by mixing cocaine with baking soda and heating it. Crack was born, and "cheap" coke invaded low-income communities with furious speed.

17   An ounce of powdered cocaine might sell on the street for $1200. That same ounce can produce 370 vials of crack at $10 each. Ten bucks seems like a cheap hit, but crack's intense ten- to 15-minute high is followed by an unbearable depression. The user wants more crack, thus starting a rapid and costly descent into addiction.

18   If government drugstores do not stock crack, addicts will find it in the clandestine market or simply bake it themselves from their legally purchased cocaine.

19   Currently crack is being laced with insecticides and animal tranquilizers to heighten its effect. Emergency rooms are now warned to expect victims of "sandwiches" and "moon rocks," life-threatening smokable mixtures of heroin and crack. Unless the government is prepared to sell these deadly variations of dangerous drugs, it will perpetuate a criminal black market by default.

20   And what about children and teen-agers? They would obviously be barred from drug purchases, just as they are prohibited from buying beer and liquor. But pushers will continue to cater to these young customers with the old, favorite come-ons—a couple of free fixes to get them hooked. And what good will anti-drug education be when these youngsters observe their older brothers and sisters, parents and friends lighting up and shooting up with government permission?

21   Legalization will give us the worst of both worlds: millions of *new* drug users *and* a thriving criminal black market.

22   *3. Legalization will dramatically reduce crime.* "It is the high price of drugs that leads addicts to robbery, murder and other crimes," says Ira Glasser, executive director of the American Civil Liberties Union. A study by the Cato Institute concludes: "Most, if not all, 'drug-related murders' are the result of drug prohibition."

23   But researchers tell us that many drug-related felonies are committed by people involved in crime *before* they started taking drugs. The drugs, so routinely available in criminal circles, make the criminals more violent and unpredictable.

24   Certainly there are some kill-for-a-fix crimes, but does any rational person believe that a cut-rate price for drugs at a government outlet will stop such psychopathic behavior? The fact is that under the influence of drugs, normal people do not act normally, and abnormal people behave in chilling and horrible ways. DEA agents told me about a teen-age addict in Manhattan who was smoking crack when he sexually abused and caused permanent internal injuries to his one-month-old daughter.

25   Children are among the most frequent victims of violent, drug-related crimes that have nothing to do with the cost of acquiring the drugs. In Philadelphia in 1987 more than half the child-abuse fatalities involved at least one parent who was a heavy drug user. Seventy-three percent of the child-abuse deaths in New York City in 1987 involved parental drug use.

26   In my travels to the ramparts of the drug war, I have seen nothing to support the legalizers' argument that lower drug prices would reduce crime. Virtually everywhere I have gone, police and DEA agents have told me that crime rates are highest where crack is cheapest.

27   *4. Drug use should be legal since users only harm themselves.* Those who believe this should stand beside the medical examiner as he counts the 36 bullet wounds in the shattered corpse of a three-year-old who happened to get in the way of his mother's drug-crazed boyfriend. They should visit the babies abandoned by cocaine-addicted mothers—infants who already carry the ravages of addiction in their own tiny bodies. They should console the devastated relatives of the nun who worked in a homeless shelter and was stabbed to death by a crack addict enraged that she would not stake him to a fix.

28   Do drug addicts only harm themselves? Here is a former co-caine addict describing the compulsion that quickly draws even the most "responsible" user into irresponsible behavior: "Everything is about getting high, and any means necessary to get there becomes rational. If it means stealing something from somebody close to you, lying to your family, borrowing money from people you know you can't pay back, writing checks you know you can't cover, you do all those things—things that are totally against everything you have ever believed in."

29   Society pays for this behavior, and not just in bigger insurance premiums, losses from accidents and poor job performance. We pay in the loss of a priceless social currency as families are destroyed, trust between friends is betrayed and promising careers are never fulfilled. I cannot imagine sanctioning behavior that would increase that toll.

30   In find no merit in the legalizers' case. The simple fact is that drug use is wrong. And the moral argument, in the end, is the most compelling argument. A citizen in a drug-induced haze, whether on his back-yard deck or on a mattress in a ghetto crack house, is not what the founding fathers meant by the "pursuit of happiness." Despite the legalizers' argument that drug use is a matter of "personal freedom," our nation's notion of liberty is rooted in the ideal of a self-reliant citizenry. Helpless wrecks in treatment centers, men chained by their noses to cocaine—these people are slaves.

31   Imagine if, in the darkest days of 1940, Winston Churchill had rallied the West by saying, "This war looks hopeless, and besides, it will cost too much. Hitler can't be *that* bad. Let's surrender and see what happens." That is essentially what we hear from the legalizers.

32   This war *can* be won. I am heartened by indications that education and public revulsion are having an effect on drug use. The National Institute on Drug Abuse's latest survey of current users shows a 37-percent *decrease* in drug consumption since 1985. Cocaine is down 50 percent; marijuana use among young people is at its lowest rate since 1972. In my travels I've been encouraged by signs that Americans are fighting back.

33   I am under no illusion that such developments, however hopeful, mean the war is over. We need to involve more citizens in the fight, increase pressure on drug criminals and build on anti-

drug programs that have proved to work. This will not be easy. But the moral and social costs of surrender are simply too great to contemplate.

Analyzing the Writer's Argument

1. What is Bennett's thesis, and where is it stated?
2. Bennett starts his essay by citing some formidable people who favor the legalization of drugs. Why do you suppose he chose to start this way? Bennett attempts to disarm these people by calling their solution to the problem a "surrender" and likening them to "addicts seeking immediate euphoria." Did you find these strategies effective? Why or why not?
3. What does Bennett see as the consequences or cost of not rigorously enforcing our drug laws?
4. In paragraph 6 Bennett cites several experiments in drug legalization that have ended in failure. Did you find his evidence convincing, or would you have liked to see more examples?
5. Although legalizers readily admit that drug legalization would likely mean increased use, they believe that benefits to be derived would far outweigh any negatives. What are the benefits that the legalization of drugs would bring?
6. Briefly summarize Bennett's counterarguments to each of the benefits that legalizers see. Which of his arguments did you find most convincing? Least convincing? How might he have made his argument stronger? Explain.
7. How has Bennett organized his argument? Could he have organized his material more effectively? For example, is there a logic to the order in which he discusses the four benefits of legalization, or could these benefits have been presented in any sequence?
8. In the end, what does Bennett see as the most compelling argument against the legalization of drugs?
9. Bennett, America's "drug czar," is an optimist. He believes that the war on drugs can be won. What does he think Americans need to do to help insure our eventual success?

Exploring the Issues in This Essay

1. Novelist Gore Vidal, himself a proponent of legalizing drugs, readily concedes that "some people will always become drug addicts

just as some people will always become alcoholics, and that is just too bad." But Vidal, like other legalizers, believes that each person has the right to do what he or she wants with his or her own life as long as it doesn't interfere with a neighbor's pursuit of happiness. Do you agree? How would Bennett respond to this argument? Discuss what role or responsibility, if any, society has in protecting the addicted from themselves.

2. In March of 1989 William Bennett took command of America's war on drugs and immediately launched a campaign both at home and abroad to get at the heart of our drug problem. Always cautiously optimistic, he knows that there are no easy answers to this complex problem, and that solutions might take as long as fifteen or twenty years to be fully realized. But it is a war that he believes we must fight. Is Bennett being realistic in waging his war on drugs or is he a man with a mission many people think is impossible? Discuss whether or not you believe America can win its war on drugs. What progress has been made since Bennett fired his first shots in 1989? What alternative courses of action can we realistically undertake?

3. Many of those who want to legalize drugs hold up our experience with alcohol during prohibition as a warning to us regarding our laws against drug use. Are the two situations analogous? Do you find this a convincing argument in favor of legalization? Discuss why or why not.

Cocaine lies.

After nearly a decade of being America's glamour drug, researchers are starting to uncover the truth about cocaine.

It's emerging as a very dangerous substance.

No one thinks the things described here will ever happen to them.

But you can never be certain. Whenever and however you use cocaine, you're playing Russian roulette.

You can't get addicted to cocaine.

Cocaine was once thought to be non-addictive, because users don't have the severe *physical* withdrawal symptoms commonly associated with heroin—delirium, muscle-cramps, and convulsions.

However, cocaine is intensely addicting *psychologically.*

In animal studies, monkeys with unlimited access to cocaine self-administer until they die. One monkey pressed a bar 12,800 times to obtain a single dose of cocaine. Rhesus monkeys won't smoke tobacco or marijuana, but 100% will smoke cocaine, preferring it to sex and to food—even when starving.

Like monkey, like man.

If you take cocaine, you run a 10% chance of addiction. The risk is higher the younger you are, and may be as high as 50% for those who smoke cocaine. (Some crack users say they felt addicted from the *first time* they smoked.)

When you're addicted, all you think about is getting and using cocaine. Family, friends, job, home, possessions, and health become unimportant.

Because cocaine is expensive, you end up doing what all addicts do. You steal, cheat, lie, deal, sell anything and everything, including yourself. All the while you risk imprisonment. Because, never forget, cocaine is illegal.

There's no way to tell who'll become addicted. But one thing is certain.

No one who is an addict, set out to become one.

Sex with coke is amazing.

Cocaine's powers as a sexual stimulant have never been proved or disproved. However, the evidence seems to suggest that the drug's reputation alone serves to heighten sexual feelings. (The same thing happens in Africa, where natives swear by powdered rhinoceros horn as an aphrodisiac.)

What is certain is that continued use of cocaine leads to impotence and finally complete loss of interest in sex.

C'mon, just once can't hurt you.

Cocaine hits your heart before it hits your head. Your pulse rate rockets and your blood pressure soars. Even if you're only 15, you become a prime candidate for a heart attack, a stroke, or an epileptic-type fit.

In the brain, cocaine mainly affects a primitive part where the emotions are seated. Unfortunately, this part of the brain also controls your heart and lungs.

A big hit or a cumulative overdose may interrupt the electrical signal to your heart and lungs. They simply stop. That's how basketball player Len Bias died.

If you're unlucky the first time you do coke, your body will lack a chemical that breaks down the drug. In which case, you'll be a first time O.D. Two lines will kill you.

It'll make you feel great.

Cocaine makes you feel like a new man, the joke goes. The only trouble is, the first thing the new man wants is more cocaine.

It's true. After the high wears off, you may feel a little anxious, irritable, or depressed. You've got the coke blues. But fortunately, they're easy to fix, with a few more lines or another hit on the pipe.

Of course, sooner or later you have to stop. Then— for days at a time—you may feel lethargic, depressed, even suicidal.

Says Dr. Arnold Washton, one of the country's leading cocaine experts: "It's impossible for the non-user to imagine the deep, vicious depression that a cocaine addict suffers from."

Partnership for a Drug-Free America

Courtesy of DDB Needham Worldwide, Inc. 1987

318

Writing Suggestions for
America's Dependency on Drugs

1. Write an essay in which you argue for or against the following statement: the fight against drugs is as big a business as the drug business itself.
2. When we think of addiction we most often think of marijuana, cocaine, heroin, and alcohol abuse. Surprisingly, a large portion of our population are addicts and they don't even know that they are. These are the people who are hooked on caffeine in coffee, soft drinks, and chocolate, or who take one of many over-the-counter sleeping pills each night. Write an essay in which you analyze the causes and effects of such legal addictions.
3. Imagine that you yourself are a smoker and are being restricted in your activities by an ever-increasing number of smoke-free environments. You feel that nonsmokers are dictating your lifestyle. After reviewing the information in the Califano/Screvane debate, write an essay arguing for smokers' rights.
4. Smoking, drinking, and drugs are only three of America's more widely publicized addictions. Today, therapists and counselors tell us that Americans are particularly prone to addictive/compulsive behavior. We tend to be excessive about things that we feel are good for us or that make us happy. Why do we eat too much, exercise too hard, stay in abusive relationships too long, or work too hard? How do you explain such behavior? Write an essay in which you explore reasons for why we seem to be excessive in our behavior and articulate a solution for this problem. Use examples from your own experience or reading to document your essay.
5. Gore Vidal was one of the first people to advocate legalization as the solution to the drug problem. Is that argument more compelling today than when he first proposed it in 1970? Why or why not? Write an essay arguing either for or against the legalization of drugs.
6. What is your college or university's policy regarding the consumption of alcohol on campus? How strictly is this policy enforced? How widely disregarded? Can colleges and universities be considered training grounds for drinking? Write a guest editorial for your school newspaper in which you argue for either a stronger alcohol policy or for stricter enforcement of the existing rules.
7. What kinds of drug and alcohol abuse problems did you observe in high school? How were these problems addressed by

the school administration, parents, and the community? Now that you have graduated from high school, write a proposal for a mandatory drug and alcohol awareness course for your high school.

8. Alcohol and smoking-related diseases are such pressing health problems that we assume that the government and society at large should do something about them. To what extent, however, do attempts, no matter how well-intended and effective, infringe upon an individual's personal liberties? In an essay, explore the pros and cons of this issue.

9. Spend enough time in the library to become familiar with the issue of mandatory drug testing in the workplace. Write an essay in which you synthesize the major arguments for and against drug testing by employers.

10. Since 1964 health warnings have been mandated on all tobacco products and tobacco advertising, and many claim that these warnings have contributed significantly to the successes of the antismoking movement in recent decades. Do you believe that similar health warnings should be placed on alcohol products and alcohol advertising. What do you think about such warning labels? Write an essay arguing your point of view.

11. In the debate between smokers and nonsmokers about smoking in public places, both parties claim that their rights are being infringed upon. Who has the right to do what? When individual rights come into conflict, by what principles are resolutions reached? Using information contained in the essays in this section, write an essay in which you propose a method for the resolution of such a conflict.

12. Do some research on the question of the harmful effects of secondhand smoke. Is it, in fact, harmful, as the antismoking lobby argues? Write an essay in which you summarize the main points of your reading and draw a conclusion about the question of secondhand smoke and the need for smoke-free environments.

13. Normal Cousins believes that Americans are a nation of pill-poppers as a result of being bombarded by advertisements for over-the-counter painkillers. We have lost our tolerance for pain to the point where even the thought of discomfort or pain sends us scurrying to the drugstore. Are the various addictions we succumb to a way of dealing with the pain—not only the physical but also the psychological and spiritual pain—in our lives? Present your answer to this question using your own personal experiences as well as information from the essays in this section.

8

Hunger and Homelessness: Our National Disgrace?

The other America, the America of poverty, is hidden today in a way it never was before. . . . The poor are increasingly slipping out of the vast experience and consciousness of the nation.

MICHAEL HARRINGTON

In comparison to other parts of the world, Mexico, India, and Africa, for example, America does not have widespread poverty. That we are the richest and most technologically advanced of all nations, however, makes the poverty we have seem all the more surprising and incongruous. As the great historian Arnold Toynbee so succinctly said: "The worst country to be poor in is America." We have poor people among the elderly, the minorities, the mentally ill, and among our children. Some of these people have clothing, appliances, radios, televisions, furniture, and housing that would make the poor of other countries envious. And we have the poor who are homeless (some by their own choosing) and without adequate food.

No matter at what level of concern or from what perspective we begin to consider the questions of poverty, we are immediately confronted by the fundamental problem of definition. Here is a formal definition: poverty is a state in which one lacks the material possessions and services necessary to maintain an adequate standard of living. The word *adequate* is, of course, troublesome because it points to the problem of relativity when discussing poverty and it, too, needs to be defined. What is considered inadequate by some might be thought more or less adequate by

321

others. What might be considered adequate in the United States might be considered comfortable by those living in another part of the world. What was considered adequate in 1950 might be thought insufficient and unacceptable in the 1990s.

Statistical information provided by the United States government adds another dimension and helps to round out the picture. In 1987, for example, the official poverty level for a single person was set at $5,778 and for a family of four at $11,611. In 1987 the number of people at or below the poverty level was determined to be 32,546,000 or 13.5% of the population.

Poverty is an abstract term, though. Because it affects humans, it needs to be made personal and to be defined in concrete and specific terms so that we can grasp its full meaning. In the following excerpt from her essay "What Is Poverty?" Jo Goodwin Parker offers just such an anecdotal, or personal, definition of poverty:

> Poverty is dirt. You say in your clean clothes coming from your clean house, "Anybody can be clean." Let me explain about housekeeping with no money. For breakfast I give my children grits with no oleo or cornbread without eggs and oleo. This does not use up many dishes. What dishes there are, I wash in cold water and with no soap. Even the cheapest soap has to be saved for the baby's diapers. Look at my hands, so cracked and red. Once I saved for two months to buy a jar of Vaseline for my hands and the baby's diaper rash. When I had saved enough, I went to buy it and the price had gone up two cents. The baby and I suffered on. I have to decide every day if I can bear to put my cracked, sore hands into the cold water and strong soap. But you ask, why not hot water? Fuel costs money. If you have a wood fire it costs money. If you burn electricity, it costs money. Hot water is a luxury. I do not have luxuries. I know you will be surprised when I tell you how young I am. I look so much older. My back has been bent over the wash tubs for so long, I cannot remember when I ever did anything else. Every night I wash every stitch my school age child has on and just hope her clothes will be dry by morning.

Beyond the questions of what constitutes poverty in both an absolute and relative sense and how many poor people we have in this country, lies the question of the causes and cures of poverty. Is the individual responsible for his or her economic failures or does blame rest with society? What responsibility does each of us have to our fellow citizens and what should society do about the poor? Is the problem of poverty capable of solution? Will money solve it? Do we need to subsidize the poor with provisions rather than money? Are more jobs the answer? Can more jobs be created? How our society views the poor, how our government policies and programs address the problem, and how each of us attempts to come to terms with the poor are sources of debate that are colored by strong emotions ranging from prejudice to compassion.

Some people fear and despise the poor, as Michael Harrington revealed in his ground-breaking study *The Other America* (1962): "Here is the most familiar version of social blindness: 'The poor are that way because they are afraid of work. And anyway they all have big cars. If they were like me they could pay their own way. But they prefer to live on the dole and cheat the taxpayers.' " Fortunately, not all Americans felt this way. In part because of Harrington's study, President Lyndon Johnson began his "War on Poverty," a national program which substantially reduced poverty in America during the 1960s. Johnson's program offered convincing proof that poverty could be alleviated and that the American people were willing to answer the call and help those less fortunate than themselves. Perhaps now that superpower tensions have eased considerably, we will redirect our national resources away from military spending and once again develop programs designed to help the nation's poor people.

Jon D. Hull

Slow Descent into Hell

Born in 1960, Jon D. Hull has written widely on two of America's most pressing problems in the 1990s: homelessness and drugs. He has for some time been associated with Time *magazine, serving first as its Los Angeles correspondent and currently as the bureau chief in Jerusalem.*

When preparing to write about the homeless in Philadelphia, Hull knew that he wanted to get beyond the economic statistics that were becoming commonplace. In order to meet the homeless and to feel what they experienced everyday, he knew that he would have to live with them. So during the winter of 1986–87, Hull spent a week living among the homeless of Philadelphia. His research resulted in "Slow Descent into Hell," which first appeared in Time *magazine in February 1987. Here Hull adds a new dimension to the issue of homelessness when he introduces us to the real people who call the streets and subway stations of Philadelphia home.*

1   A smooth bar of soap, wrapped neatly in a white handkerchief and tucked safely in the breast pocket of a faded leather jacket, is all that keeps George from losing himself to the streets. When he wakes each morning from his makeshift bed of newspapers in the subway tunnels of Philadelphia, he heads for the rest room of a nearby bus station or McDonald's and begins an elaborate ritual of washing off the dirt and smells of homelessness: first the hands and forearms, then the face and neck, and finally the fingernails and teeth. Twice a week he takes off his worn Converse high tops and socks and washes his feet in the sink, ignoring the cold stares of well-dressed commuters.

2   George, twenty-eight, is a stocky, round-faced former high school basketball star who once made a living as a construction worker. But after he lost his job just over a year ago, his wife kicked him out of the house. For a few weeks he lived on the couches of friends, but the friendships soon wore thin. Since then he has been on

the street, starting from scratch and looking for a job. "I got to get my life back," George says after rinsing his face for the fourth time. He begins brushing his teeth with his forefinger. "If I don't stay clean," he mutters, "the world ain't even going to look me in the face. I just couldn't take that."

3 George lives in a world where time is meaningless and it's possible to go months without being touched by anyone but a thug. Lack of sleep, food, or conversation breeds confusion and depression. He feels himself slipping but struggles to remember what he once had and to figure out how to get it back. He rarely drinks alcohol and keeps his light brown corduroy pants and red-checked shirt meticulously clean. Underneath, he wears two other shirts to fight off the cold, and he sleeps with his large hands buried deep within his coat pockets amid old sandwiches and doughnuts from the soup kitchens and garbage cans.

4 Last fall he held a job for six weeks at a pizza joint, making $3.65 an hour kneading dough and cleaning tables. Before work, he would take off two of his three shirts and hide them in an alley. It pleases him that no one knew he was homeless. Says George: "Sure I could have spent that money on some good drink or food, but you gotta suffer to save. You gotta have money to get out of here and I gotta get out of here." Some days he was scolded for eating too much of the food. He often worked without sleep, and with no alarm clock to wake him from the subways or abandoned tenements, he missed several days and was finally fired. He observes, "Can't get no job without a home, and you can't get a home without a job. They take one and you lose both."

5 George had sixty-four dollars tucked in his pocket on the evening he was beaten senseless in an alley near the Continental Trailways station. "Those damn chumps," he says, gritting his teeth, "took every goddam penny. I'm gonna kill 'em." Violence is a constant threat to the homeless. It's only a matter of time before newcomers are beaten, robbed, or raped. The young prey on the old, the big on the small, and groups attack lonely individuals in the back alleys and subway tunnels. After it's over, there is no one to tell about the pain, nothing to do but walk away.

6 Behind a dumpster sits a man who calls himself Red enjoying the last drops of a bottle of wine called Wild Irish Rose. It's 1 A.M., and the thermometer hovers around 20 degrees with a biting wind. His nickname comes from a golden retriever his family once had

back in Memphis, and a sparkle comes to his eyes as he recalls examples of the dog's loyalty. One day he plans to get another dog, and says, "I'm getting to the point where I can't talk to people. They're always telling me to do something or get out of their way. But a dog is different."

7   At thirty-five, he looks fifty, and his gaunt face carries discolored scars from the falls and fights of three years on the streets. An upper incisor is missing, and his lower teeth jut outward against his lower lip, giving the impression that he can't close his mouth. His baggy pants are about five inches too long and when he walks, their frayed ends drag on the ground. "You know something?" he asks, holding up the bottle. "I wasn't stuck to this stuff until the cold got to me. Now I'll freeze without it. I could go to Florida or someplace, but I know this town and I know who the creeps are. Besides, it's not too bad in the summer."

8   Finishing the bottle, and not yet drunk enough to sleep out in the cold, he gathers his blanket around his neck and heads for the subways beneath city hall, where hundreds of the homeless seek warmth. Once inside, the game of cat-and-mouse begins with the police, who patrol the maze of tunnels and stairways and insist that everybody remain off the floor and keep moving. Sitting can be an invitation to trouble, and the choice between sleep and warmth becomes agonizing as the night wears on.

9   For the first hour, Red shuffles through the tunnels, stopping occasionally to urinate against the graffiti-covered walls. Then he picks a spot and stands for half an hour, peering out from the large hood of his coat. In the distance, the barking of German shepherds echoes through the tunnels as a canine unit patrols the darker recesses of the underground. Nearby, a young man in a ragged trench coat stands against the wall, slapping his palms against his sides and muttering, "I've got to get some paperwork done. I've just got to get some paperwork done!" Red shakes his head. "Home sweet home," he says. Finally exhausted, he curls up on the littered floor, lying on his side with his hands in his pockets and his hood pulled all the way over his face to keep the rats away. He is asleep instantly.

10   Whack! A police baton slaps his legs and a voice booms, "Get the hell up, you're outta here. Right now!" Another police officer

whacks his night-stick against a metal grating as the twelve men sprawled along the tunnel crawl to their feet. Red pulls himself up and walks slowly up the stairs to the street, never looking back.

11   Pausing at every pay phone to check the coin-return slots, he makes his way to a long steam grate whose warm hiss bears the acrid smell of a dry cleaner's shop. He searches for newspaper and cardboard to block the moisture but retain the heat. With his makeshift bed made, he curls up again, but the rest is short-lived. "This s.o.b. use to give off more heat," he says, staring with disgust at the grate. He gathers the newspapers and moves down the block, all the while muttering about the differences among grates. "Some are good, some are bad. I remember I was getting a beautiful sleep on this one baby and then all this honking starts. I was laying right in a damn driveway and nearly got run over by a garbage truck."

12   Stopping at a small circular vent shooting jets of steam, Red shakes his head and curses: "This one is too wet, and it'll go off sometimes, leaving you to freeze." Shaking now with the cold, he walks four more blocks and finds another grate, where he curls up and fishes a half-spent cigarette from his pocket. The grate is warm, but soon the moisture from the steam has soaked his newspapers and begins to gather on his clothes. Too tired to find another grate, he sets down more newspapers, throws his blanket over his head, and sprawls across the grate. By morning he is soaked.

13   At the St. John's Hospice for Men, close to the red neon marquees of the porno shops near city hall, a crowd begins to gather at 4 P.M. Men and women dressed in ill-fitting clothes stamp their feet to ward off the cold and keep their arms pressed against their sides. Some are drunk; others simply talk aloud to nobody in words that none can understand. Most are loners who stand in silence with the sullen expression of the tired and hungry.

14   A hospice worker lets in a stream of women and old men. The young men must wait until 5 P.M., and the crowd of more than two hundred are asked to form four rows behind a yellow line and watch their language. It seems an impossible task. A trembling man who goes by the name Carper cries, "What goddam row am I in!" as he pulls his red wool hat down until it covers his eyebrows. Carper has spent five to six years on the streets, and thinks he

may be thirty-three. The smell of putrid wine and decaying teeth poisons his breath; the fluid running from his swollen eyes streaks his dirty cheeks before disappearing into his beard. "Am I in a goddam row? Who the hell's running the rows?" he swears. An older man with a thick gray beard informs Carper he is in Row 3 and assures him it is the best of them all. Carper's face softens into a smile; he stuffs his hands under his armpits and begins rocking his shoulders with delight.

15   Beds at the shelters are scarce, and fill up first with the old, the very young, and women. Young men have little hope of getting a bed, and some have even come to scorn the shelters. Says Michael Brown, twenty-four: "It stinks to high heaven in those places. They're just packed with people and when the lights go out, it's everybody for themselves." Michael, a short, self-described con man, has been living on the streets three years, ever since holding up a convenience store in Little Rock. He fled, fearing capture, but now misses the two young children he left behind. He says he is tired of the streets and plans to turn himself in to serve his time.

16   Michael refuses to eat at the soup kitchens, preferring to pan-handle for a meal: "I don't like to be around those people. It makes you feel like some sort of crazy. Before you know it, you're one of them." He keeps a tear in the left seam of his pants, just be-low the pocket; when he panhandles among commuters, he tells them that his subway fare fell out of his pants. When that fails, he wanders past fast-food outlets, waiting for a large group eating near the door to get up and leave. Then he snatches the remaining food off the table and heads down the street, smiling all the more if the food is still warm. At night he sleeps in the subway stations, catnapping between police rounds amid the thunder of the trains. "Some of these guys sleep right on the damn floor," he says. "Not me. I always use two newspapers and lay them out neatly. Then I pray the rats don't get me."

17   It was the last swig of the bottle, and the cheap red wine con-tained flotsam from the mouths of three men gathered in a vacant lot in northeast Philadelphia. Moments before, a homeless and dy-ing man named Gary had vomited. The stench and nausea were dulled only by exhaustion and the cold. Gary, wheezing noisily, his lips dripping with puke, was the last to drink from the half-

gallon jug of Thunderbird before passing it on, but no one seemed to care. There was no way to avoid the honor of downing the last few drops. It was an offer to share extended by those with nothing, and there was no time to think about the sores on the lips of the previous drinkers or the strange things floating in the bottle or the fact that it was daybreak and time for breakfast. It was better to drink and stay warm and forget about everything.

18   Though he is now dying on the streets, Gary used to be a respectable citizen. His full name is Gary Shaw, forty-eight, and he is a lifelong resident of Philadelphia and a father of three. He once worked as a precision machinist, making metal dies for casting tools. "I could work with my eyes closed," he says. "I was the best there was." But he lost his job and wife to alcohol. Now his home is an old red couch with the springs exposed in a garbage-strewn clearing amid abandoned tenements. Nearby, wood pulled from buildings burns in a fifty-five-gallon metal drum while the Thunderbird is passed around. When evening falls, Gary has trouble standing, and he believes his liver and kidneys are on the verge of failing. His thighs carry deep burn marks from sleeping on grates, and a severe beating the previous night has left bruises on his lower back and a long scab across his nose. The pain is apparent in his eyes, still brilliant blue, and the handsome features of his face are hidden beneath a layer of grime.

19   By 3 A.M., Gary's back pains are unbearable, and he begins rocking back and forth while the others try to keep him warm. "Ah, please God help me. I'm f—ing dying, man. I'm dying." Two friends try to wave down a patrol car. After forty-five minutes, a suspicious cop rolls up to the curb and listens impatiently to their plea: "It's not drugs, man, I promise. The guy was beat up bad and he's dying. Come on, man, you've got to take us to the hospital." The cop nods and points his thumb toward the car. As Gary screams, his two friends carefully lift him into the back seat for the ride to St. Mary Hospital.

20   In the emergency room, half an hour passes before a nurse appears with a clipboard. Address: unknown. No insurance. After an X ray, Gary is told that a bone in his back may be chipped. He is advised to go home, put some ice on it and get some rest. "I don't have a goddam home!" he cries, his face twisted in pain. "Don't you know what I am? I'm a goddam bum, that's what, and

I'm dying!" After an awkward moment, he is told to come back tomorrow and see the radiologist. The hospital pays his cab fare back to the couch.

21   Gary returns in time to share another bottle of Thunderbird, and the warm rush brings his spirits up. "What the hell are we doing in the city?" asks Ray Kelly, thirty-seven, who was one a merchant seaman. "I know a place in Vermont where the fishing's great and you can build a whole damn house in the woods. There's nobody to bother you and plenty of food." Gary interrupts to recall fishing as a boy, and the memories prior to his six years on the street come back with crystal clarity. "You got it, man, we're all getting out of here tomorrow," he says with a grin. In the spirit of celebration, King, a thirty-four-year-old from Puerto Rico, removes a tube of glue from his pocket with the care of a sommelier, sniffs it and passes it around.

22   When the sun rises, Ray and King are fast asleep under a blanket on the couch. Gary is sitting at the other end, staring straight ahead and breathing heavily in the cold air. Curling his numb and swollen fingers around the arm of the couch, he tries to pull himself up but fails. When another try fails, he sits motionless and closes his eyes. Then the pain hits his back again and he starts to cry. He won't be getting out of here today, and probably not tomorrow either.

23   Meanwhile, somewhere across town in the washroom of a Mc-Donald's, George braces for another day of job hunting, washing the streets from his face so that nobody knows where he lives.

Analyzing the Writer's Argument

1. In the opening paragraphs of Hull's essay, we meet George. What is George's situation? In what ways is a bar of soap "all that keeps George from losing himself to the streets"?

2. What does George have in common with the other homeless men whom Hull introduces us to in the essay? How is George different? What does each portrait—George, Red, Carper, Michael Brown, Gary Shaw, Ray Kelly, and King—contribute to the picture that Hull paints of homelessness?

3. What does George mean when he says, "Can't get no job without a home, and you can't get a home without a job. They take one and you lose both"?

4. How has Hull organized his essay? Does there seem to be any reason for introducing the homeless men in the order that Hull does? Is this order in any way related to Hull's title? Explain. In the end, Hull returns to George, washing the "streets from his face" in a McDonald's washroom. Is this an effective conclusion? Why, or why not?

5. What are some of the dangers that the homeless encounter every night? What is the unexpected danger of sleeping on heated grates?

6. What does Red mean when he says, "Home sweet home"? Is Red being serious? How do you know? What does this comment tell us about Red?

7. How would you describe Hull's tone in this essay? What is his attitude toward the homeless men? What is his attitude toward the problem of homelessness? Explain.

Exploring the Issues in This Essay

1. George realizes what will happen if he gives up trying and loses himself to the streets. But he also knows that it's an almost impossible battle. Is it only a matter of time before homelessness traps George? Or is there cause for hope that America can break the vicious cycle of unemployment, homelessness, poverty, unemployment . . . , and save the people of the streets from their "slow descent into hell"?

2. There are no simple solutions to America's problem of homelessness; at least none have been proposed. Because the problem is so large and there are so many variables involved, our leaders need to initiate some long-term solutions and stop looking for the politically advantageous "quick fixes." But with elections every four years and with public concern—and dollars—being drawn in many different directions, how can we make any progress? At the close of the decade of the 1980s, homelessness was in the spotlight. Already it seems to have taken a back seat to other social issues. Have Americans become inured to the homeless men, women, and children who inhabit our streets?

Peter Marin

Helping and Hating the Homeless

> *Peter Marin is an activist, poet, and educator with an inter-*
> *est in young people and social issues such as drugs and home-*
> *lessness. Born in 1936, he received degrees from Swarthmore*
> *College and Columbia University. After graduation, Marin*
> *"took to the road, hitchhiking and traveling on freights, doing*
> *odd jobs here and there, crisscrossing the country. . . . I felt at*
> *home on the road." Marin has drawn upon these experiences*
> *in serving as director of an experimental high school in Palo*
> *Alto, California, in 1967–68, working as a visiting fellow at*
> *the Center for the Study of Democratic Institutions in 1968–*
> *69, and teaching and lecturing at a number of colleges and*
> *universities in California. He is the coauthor of* Understand-
> ing Drug Use *(1971), author of* In a Man's Time *(1974),*
> *and coauthor of* The Limits of Schooling *(1975). A con-*
> *tributing editor to* Harper's Magazine, *Marin has written*
> *articles on education and other issues for a variety of popular*
> *magazines.*
>
> *In the mid-1980s the plight of the homeless was front-page*
> *copy in newspapers and magazines across the country. Social*
> *workers, politicians, and activists debated a variety of strate-*
> *gies that could be used to solve this problem. Peter Marin,*
> *in the following article, which first appeared in a somewhat*
> *longer version in* Harper's Magazine, *examines the nature*
> *of homelessness and delineates what he believes are society's*
> *obligations to the homeless.*

1   When I was a child, I had a recurring vision of how I would end
as an old man: alone, in a sparsely furnished second-story room
I could picture quite precisely, in a walk-up on Fourth Avenue in
New York, where the second-hand bookstores then were. It was
not a picture that frightened me. I liked it. The idea of anonymity
and solitude and marginality must have seemed to me, back then,
both inviting and inevitable.

2   Later, out of college, I took to the road, hitchhiking and traveling on freights, doing odd jobs here and there, crisscrossing the country. I liked that too: the anonymity and the absence of constraint and the rough community I sometimes found. I felt at home on the road, perhaps because I felt at home nowhere else, and periodically, for years, I would return to that world, always with a sense of relief and release.

3   I have been thinking a lot about that these days, now that transience and homelessness have made their way into the national consciousness, and especially since the town I live in, Santa Barbara, has become well known because of the successful campaign last year to do away with the meanest aspects of its "sleeping ordinances"—a set of foolish laws making it illegal for the homeless to sleep at night in public places.

4   During that campaign I got to know many of the homeless men and women in Santa Barbara, who tend to gather, night and day, in a small park at the lower end of town, not far from the tracks and the harbor, under the rooflike, overarching branches of a gigantic fig tree. There one enters much the same world I thought, as a child, I would die in, and the one in which I traveled as a young man: a marginal world inhabited by all those unable to find a place in "our" world.

5   Late last summer, the Santa Barbara city council was meeting to vote on the repeal of the sleeping ordinances, though not out of any sudden sense of compassion or justice. Council members had been pressured into it by the threat of massive demonstrations— "The Selma of the '80s" was the slogan one heard among the homeless.

6   But this threat that frightened the council enraged the town's citizens. Hundreds of them turned out for the meeting. One by one they filed to the microphone to curse the council and castigate the homeless. Drinking, doping, loitering, panhandling, defecating, urinating, molesting, stealing—the litany went on and on, accompanied by fantasies of disaster; the barbarian hordes at the gates, civilization ended.

7   What astonished me about the meeting was not what was said; one could have predicted that. It was the power and depth of the emotion revealed: the mindlessness of the fear, the vengefulness of the fury. Also, almost none of what was said had anything to do

with the homeless people I know—not the ones I traveled with, not the ones in town. They, the actual homeless men and women, might not have existed at all.

8   In the last few months I have visited several cities around the country, and in each of them I have found the same thing: more and more people in the streets, more and more suffering. (There are at least 350,000 homeless people in the country, perhaps as many as 3 million.) And, in talking to the good citizens of these cities, I found, almost always, the same thing: confusion and ignorance, or simple indifference, but anger, too, and fear.

9   Homelessness, in itself, is nothing more than a condition visited upon men and women (and, increasingly, children) as the final stage of a variety of problems about which the word *homelessness* tells us almost nothing. Or, to put it another way, it is a catch basin into which pour all of the people disenfranchised or marginalized or scared off by processes beyond their control, those that lie close to the heart of American life. Here are the groups packed into the single category of "the homeless":

- Veterans, mainly from the war in Vietnam. In many American cities, vets make up close to 50 percent of all homeless males.
- The mentally ill. In some parts of the country, roughly a quarter of the homeless would, a couple of decades ago, have been institutionalized.
- The physically disabled or chronically ill, who do not receive any benefits or whose benefits do not enable them to afford permanent shelter.
- The elderly on fixed incomes whose funds are no longer sufficient for their needs.
- Men, women, and whole families pauperized by the loss of a job. Some 28 percent of the homeless population is composed of families with children, and 15 percent are single women.
- Single parents, usually women, without the resources or skills to establish new lives.
- Runaway children, many of whom have been abused.
- Alcoholics and those in trouble with drugs (whose troubles often begin with one of the other conditions listed here).

- Immigrants, both legal and illegal, who often are not counted among the homeless because they constitute a "problem" in their own right.
- Traditional tramps, hobos and transients, who have taken to the road or the streets for a variety of reasons and who prefer to be there.

10   You can quickly learn two things about the homeless from this list. First, you can learn that many of the homeless, before they were homeless, were people more or less like ourselves: members of the working or middle class. And you can learn that the world of the homeless has its roots in various policies, events and ways of life for which some of us are responsible and from which some of us actually prosper.

11   We decide, as a people, to go to war, we ask our children to kill and to die, and the result, years later, is grown men homeless on the street.

12   We change, with the best intentions, the laws pertaining to the mentally ill and then, without intention, neglect to provide them with services; and the result, in our streets, drives some of us crazy with rage.

13   We cut taxes and prune budgets, we modernize industry and shift the balance of trade, and the result of all these actions and errors can be read, sleeping form by sleeping form, on our city streets.

14   The liberals cannot blame the conservatives. The conservatives cannot blame the liberals. Homelessness is the sum total of our dreams, policies, intentions, errors, omissions, cruelties, kindnesses, all of it recorded, in flesh, in the life of the streets.

15   The homeless can be roughly divided into two groups: those who have had homelessness forced upon them and want nothing more than to escape it; and those who have at least in part chosen it for themselves, and now accept it, or in some cases embrace it.

16   I understand how dangerous it is to introduce the idea of choice into a discussion of homelessness. It can all too easily be used to justify indifference or brutality toward the homeless, or to argue that they are only getting what they "deserve." And yet it seems to me that it is only by taking choice into account, in all of the intricacies of its various forms and expressions, that one can really understand certain kinds of homelessness.

17   The fact is, many of the homeless are not only hapless victims but voluntary exiles, "domestic refugees," people who have turned not against life itself but against us, our life, American life. Look for a moment at the vets. The price of returning to America was to forget what they had seen or learned in Vietnam, to "put it behind them." But some could not do that, and the stress of trying showed up as alcoholism, broken marriages, drug addiction, crime. And it showed up too as life on the street, which was for some vets a desperate choice made in the name of life—the best they could manage.

18   We must learn to accept that there may indeed be people, and not only vets, who have seen so much of our world, or seen it so clearly, that to live in it becomes impossible. Here, for example, is the story of Alice, a homeless middle-aged woman in Los Angeles, where there are perhaps 50,000 homeless people, a 50 percent increase over the previous year. It was set down last year by one of my students at the University of California at Santa Barbara, where I taught for a semester. I had encouraged them to go find the homeless and listen to their stories. And so, one day, when this student saw Alice foraging in a dumpster outside a McDonald's, he stopped and talked to her:

> She told me she had led a pretty normal life as she grew up and eventually went to college. From there she went on to Chicago to teach school. She was single and lived in a small apartment.
>
> One night, after she got off the train after school, a man began to follow her to her apartment building. When she got to her door she saw a knife and the man hovering behind her. She had no choice but to let him in. The man raped her.
>
> After that, things got steadily worse. She had a nervous breakdown. She went to a mental institution for three months, and when she went back to her apartment she found her belongings gone. The landlord had sold them to cover the rent.
>
> She had no place to go and no job because the school had terminated her employment. She slipped into depression. She lived with friends until she could muster enough money for a ticket to Los Angeles. She said she no longer wanted to burden her friends, and that if she had to live outside, at least Los Angeles was warmer than Chicago.

19   This is, in essence, the same story one hears over and over again on the street. You begin with an ordinary life; then an event occurs—traumatic, catastrophic; smaller events follow, each one deepening the original wound; finally, homelessness becomes inevitable, or begins to seem inevitable to the person involved—the only way out of an intolerable situation.

20   We like to think, in America, that everything is redeemable, that everything broken can be magically made whole again, and that what has been "dirtied" can be cleansed. Yes, many of those on the streets could be transformed, rehabilitated. But there are others whose lives have been irrevocably changed, damaged beyond repair, and who no longer want help, who no longer recognize the need for help, and whose experience in our world has made them want only to be left alone.

21   How, for instance, would one restore Alice's life, or reshape it in a way that would satisfy our notion of what a life should be? What would it take to return her to the fold? How to erase the four years of homelessness, which have become as familiar to her, and as much a home, as her "normal" life once was? Whatever we think of the way in which she has resolved her difficulties, it constitutes a sad peace made with the world. Intruding ourselves upon it in the name of redemption is by no means as simple or as justifiable a task as one might think.

22   It is important to recognize the immensity of the changes that have occurred in the marginal world in the past 20 years. Whole sections of many cities—the Bowery in New York, the Tenderloin in San Francisco—were once ceded to the transient. In every skid-row area in America you could find what you needed to survive: hash houses, saloons offering free lunches, pawnshops, surplus-clothing stores and, most important of all, cheap hotels and flop-houses and two-bit employment agencies specializing in seasonal labor. It was by no means a wonderful world. But it was a world.

23   But things have changed. There began to pour into the marginal world—slowly in the '60s, a bit faster in the '70s, and then faster still in the '80s—more and more people who neither belonged nor knew how to survive there. The '60s brought the counterculture

and drugs; the streets filled with young dropouts. Changes in the law loosed upon the streets mentally ill men and women. Inflation took its toll, then recession. Working-class and even middle-class men and women—entire families—began to fall into a world they did not understand.

24   At the same time, the marginal world's landscape and its economy was shrinking radically. Jobs became harder to find. Modernization had something to do with it; machines took the place of men and women. And the influx of workers from Mexico and points farther south created a class of semipermanent transient workers. More important, perhaps, was the fact that the forgotten parts of many cities began to attract attention. Downtown areas were redeveloped, reclaimed. The skid-row sections of smaller cities were turned into "old townes." The old hotels that once catered to transients were upgraded or torn down or became warehouses for welfare families—an arrangement far more profitable to the owners. The mentally ill, who once could afford to house themselves in cheap rooms, the alcoholics, who once would drink themselves to sleep at night in their cheap hotels, were out on the street—exposed to the weather and to danger, and also in plain and public view: "problems" to be dealt with.

25   The homeless, simply because they are homeless, are strangers, alien—and therefore a threat. Their presence, in itself, comes to constitute a kind of violence; it deprives us of our sense of safety. Let me use myself as an example. If I walk through the park near my home and see strangers bedding down for the night, my first reaction, if not fear, is a sense of annoyance and intrusion, of worry and alarm. I think of my teenage daughter, who often walks through the park, and then of my house, a hundred yards away, and I am tempted—only tempted, but tempted, still—to call the "proper" authorities to have the strangers moved on. Out of sight, out of mind.

26   Notice: I do not bring them food. I do not offer them shelter or a shower in the morning. I do not even stop to talk. Instead, I think: my daughter, my house, my privacy. What moves me is not the threat of danger—nothing as animal as that. Instead there pops up inside of me, neatly in a row, a set of anxieties, ones you might arrange in a dollhouse living room and label: Family of

bourgeois fears. Our response to the homeless is fed by a complex set of cultural attitudes, habits of thought and fantasies and fears so familiar to us, so common, that they have become second nature. And it is by no means easy to untangle this snarl of responses.

27   If you look to the history of Europe you find that homelessness first appears (or is first acknowledged) at the very same moment that bourgeois culture begins to appear. The same process produced them both: the breakup of feudalism, the rise of commerce and cities, the combined triumphs of capitalism, industrialism and individualism. The historian Fernand Braudel, in the "Wheels of Commerce," describes, for instance, the armies of impoverished men and women who began to haunt Europe as far back as the 11th century. And the makeup of these masses? Essentially the same then as it is now: " . . . widows, orphans, cripples . . . journeymen who had broken their contracts, out-of-work labourers, homeless priests with no living, old men, fire victims . . . war victims, deserters, discharged soldiers, would-be vendors of useless articles, vagrant preachers without licenses. . . . "

28   Then, as now, distinctions were made between the "homeless" and the supposedly "deserving" poor, those who knew their place and willingly sustained, with their labors, the emergent bourgeois world.

29   And just as the distinctions made about these masses were the same then as they are now, so too was the way society saw them. They seemed to bourgeois eyes (as they still do) the one segment of society that remained resistant to progress, unassimilable and incorrigible, inimical to all order.

30   With the Victorians we begin to see the entangling of self-protection with social obligation, the strategy of masking self-interest and the urge to control as moral duty. Order, ordure—this, in essence, was the tension at the heart of bourgeois culture, and it was the singular genius of the Victorians to make it the main component of their medical, aesthetic and moral systems. It was not a sense of justice or even empathy that called for charity or new attitudes toward the poor; it was hygiene.

31   All of this is still true in America. Here, for instance, is part of a paper a student of mine wrote about her first visit to a Rescue Mission on skid row.

The sermon began. The room was stuffy and smelly. The mixture of body odors and cooking was nauseating. I remember thinking: How can these people share this facility? They must be repulsed by each other. They had strange habits and dispositions. They were a group of dirty, dishonored, weird people to me.

When it was over I ran to my car, went home and took a shower. I felt extremely dirty. Through the day I would get flashes of that disgusting smell.

32 Our policies toward the homeless, our spontaneous sense of disgust and horror, our wish to be rid of them—all of this has hidden in it, close to its heart, our feelings about excrement.

33 What I am getting at here is the nature of the desire to help the homeless—what is hidden behind it and why it so often does harm. Every government program, almost every private project, is geared as much to the needs of those giving help as it is to the needs of the homeless.

34 Santa Barbara is as good an example as any. There are three main shelters in the city—all of them private. Between them they provide fewer than 100 beds a night for the homeless. Two of three shelters are religious in nature: the Rescue Mission and the Salvation Army. In the mission, as in most places in the country, there are elaborate and stringent rules. Beds go first to those who have not been there for two months, and you can stay for only two nights in any two-month period. No shelter is given to those who are not sober.

35 Even if you go to the mission only for a meal, you are required to listen to sermons and participate in prayer, and you are regularly proselytized. There are obligatory, regimented showers. You go to bed precisely at 10: lights out, no reading, no talking. After the lights go out you will find 15 men in a room with double-decker bunks. As the night progresses the room grows stuffier and hotter. Men toss, turn, cough and moan. In the morning you are awakened precisely at 5:45. Then breakfast. At 7:30 you are back on the street.

36 The town's newest shelter was opened almost a year ago by a consortium of local churches. Families and those who are employed have first call on the beds—a policy that excludes the congenitally homeless. Alcohol is not simply forbidden in the shelter; those with a history of alcoholism must sign a "contract" pledging

to remain sober and chemical-free. Finally, in a paroxysm of therapeutic bullying, the shelter has added a new wrinkle: If you stay more than two days you are required to fill out and then discuss with a social worker a complex form listing what you perceive as your personal failings, goals and strategies—all of this for men and women who simply want a place to lie down out of the rain!

37   We are moved either to "redeem" the homeless or to punish them. Perhaps there is nothing consciously hostile about it. Perhaps it is simply that as the machinery of bureaucracy cranks itself up to deal with these problems, attitudes assert themselves automatically. But whatever the case, the fact remains that almost every one of our strategies for helping the homeless is simply an attempt to rearrange the world cosmetically, in terms of how it looks and smells to us. Compassion is little more than the passion for control.

38   The central question emerging from all this is, What does a society owe to its members in trouble, and how is that debt to be paid? It is a question that must be answered in two parts: first, in relation to the men and women who have been marginalized against their will, and then, in a slightly different way, in relation to those who have chosen (or accept or even prize) their marginality.

39   As for those who have been marginalized against their wills, the general answer is obvious: A society owes its members whatever it takes for them to regain their places in the social order. And when it comes to specific remedies, one need only read backward the various processes that have created homelessness and then figure out where help is likely to do the most good.

40   But the real point here is not the specific remedies required—affordable housing, say—but the basis upon which they must be offered, the necessary underlying ethical notion we seem in this nation unable to grasp: that those who are the inevitable casualties of modern industrial capitalism and the free-market system are entitled, by right, and by the simple virtue of their participation in that system, to whatever help they need. They are entitled the help to find and hold their places in the society whose social contract they have, in effect, signed and observed.

41   But those marginalized against their will are only half the problem. There remains, still, the question of whether we owe anything

to those who are voluntarily marginal. What about them: the street people, the rebels and the recalcitrants, those who have torn up their social contracts or returned them unsigned?

42 I was in Las Vegas last fall, and I went out to the Rescue Mission at the lower end of town, on the edge of the black ghetto, where I first stayed years ago on my way west. It was twilight, still hot; in the vacant lot next-door to the mission 200 men were lining up for supper. There were elderly alcoholics in line, and derelicts, but mainly the men were the same sort I had seen here years ago: youngish, out of work, restless and talkative, the drifters and wanderers for whom the word "wanderlust" was invented.

43 At supper—long communal tables, thin gruel, stale sweet rolls, ice water—a huge black man in his twenties, fierce and muscular, sat across from me. "I'm from the Coast, man," he said. "Never been away from home before. Ain't sure I like it. Sure don't like *this* place. But I lost my job back home a couple of weeks ago and figured, why wait around for another. I thought I'd come out here, see me something of the world."

44 After supper, a squat Portuguese man in his mid-thirties, hunkered down against the mission wall, offered me a smoke and told me: "Been sleeping in my car, up the street, for a week. Had my own business back in Omaha. But I got bored, man. Sold everything, got a little dough, came out here. Thought I'd work construction. Let me tell you, this is one tough town."

45 In a world better than ours, I suppose, men (or women) like this might not exist. Conservatives seem to have no trouble imagining a society so well disciplined and moral that deviance of this kind would disappear. And leftists envision a world so just, so generous, that deviance would vanish along with inequity. But I suspect that there will always be something at work in some men and women to make them restless with the systems others devise for them, and to move them outward toward the edges of the world, where life is always riskier, less organized, and easier going.

46 Do we owe anything to these men and women? We owe them, I think, at least a place to exist, a way to exist. That may not be a moral obligation, in the sense that our obligation to the involuntarily marginal is clearly a moral one, but it is an obligation nevertheless, one you might call an existential obligation.

47 I think we as a society need men like these. A society needs its margins as much as it needs art and literature. It needs holes and

gaps, breathing spaces, let us say, into which men and women can escape and live, when necessary, in ways otherwise denied them. Margins guarantee to society a flexibility, an elasticity, and allow it to accommodate itself to the natures and needs of its members. When margins vanish, society becomes too rigid, too oppressive by far and therefore inimical to life.

48 What we see on the streets of our cities are two dramas, both of which cut to the troubled heart of the culture and demand from us a response we may not be able to make. There is the drama of those struggling to survive by regaining their place in the social order. And there is the drama of those struggling to survive outside it.

49 The resolution of both struggles depends on a third drama occurring at the heart of the culture: the tension and contention between the magnanimity we owe to life and the darker tendings of the human psyche: our fear of strangeness, our hatred of deviance, our love of order and control. How we mediate by default or design between those contrary forces will determine not only the destinies of the homeless, but also something crucial about the nation, and perhaps—let me say it—about our own souls.

Analyzing the Writer's Argument

1. How does Marin define "homelessness"? What groups of people does he see lumped together as "the homeless"? How have the armies of the homeless changed in 900 years? Explain.

2. What gives Marin the authority to write about homelessness?

3. When Marin attended the meeting of the Santa Barbara city council concerning the sleeping ordinances, he was not surprised to hear what the citizens had to say. What did surprise him? Did it surprise you? Explain.

4. What does Marin mean when he says that he learned that "the world of the homeless has its roots in various policies, events and ways of life for which some of us are responsible, and from which some of us actually prosper"? What examples does he provide to illustrate this claim? Did you find them convincing?

5. Into what two large groups does Marin divide the homeless? Do you believe his claim that there are people who have actually chosen to be homeless? Are his examples of the Vietnam vet and Alice convincing? Does the idea of choice have a place in discussions of homelessness? Explain.

6. What changes, according to Marin, have occurred in the marginal world? How do these changes help to explain why homelessness emerged as a problem in the 1980s?
7. How does Marin explain the fear with which society reacts to the homeless? Does he find the fear justified? Do you agree with his position? Why or why not?
8. According to Marin, what are society's obligations to the people who have been "marginalized" against their wills? To those who are voluntarily marginal? Why does Marin think that society needs the men and women who have chosen to live in the marginal world?

Exploring the Issues in This Essay

1. Marin claims that "every government program, almost every private project, is geared as much to the needs of those giving help as it is to the needs of the homeless." Does Marin's discussion of Santa Barbara's missions adequately illustrate his point? What has been your experience with or observations about efforts to help the homeless in your area? How do they compare with Marin's? To what extent can Marin's assertion that "compassion is little more than the passion for control" be extended to relief efforts in general? Explain.
2. Marin argues that society needs its margins. Just how important are these margins? What do they offer society that society can't get for itself? Is there a "marginal world" on your campus? If so, who inhabits this world, and how does the rest of the campus community benefit from their presence? What are your reactions to Marin's claim that "when margins vanish, society becomes too rigid, too oppressive by far and therefore inimical to life"? Discuss.

Garrett Hardin

Lifeboat Ethics: The Case Against Helping the Poor

> *A biologist by training, Garrett Hardin has for over four decades warned Americans of the human tragedy and natural disasters that await them if they don't stop to consider the moral, social, and ecological implications of the decisions they're now making. Born in Dallas, Texas, in 1915, Hardin received his training at the University of Chicago and at Stanford University. He was Professor of Human Ecology at the University of California, Santa Barbara, from 1946 until his retirement in 1978. A prolific writer and lecturer, Hardin likes to explore those areas where biological and ecological issues interface with social and moral ones, and his books speak to this fact. They include* Nature and Man's Fate *(1959),* Exploring New Ethics for Survival: The Voyage of the Spaceship Beagle *(1972),* Mandatory Motherhood: The True Meaning of "Right to Life" *(1974),* The Limits of Altruism: An Ecologist's View of Survival *(1977), and* Filters Against Folly: How to Survive Despite Economists, Ecologists, and the Merely Eloquent *(1985).*
>
> *While studying biology at Stanford in the 1940s, Hardin first came to believe that the solution to the world's population problem was not increased food production. In searching for long-term, workable ways to deal with poverty and hunger, he discovered that many people were not ready to listen to his solutions. In the following essay, which first appeared in* Psychology Today *in 1974, Hardin argues that to save the world from environmental ruin we must stop trying to share the world's natural resources equitably and adopt his ethics of the lifeboat.*

1   Environmentalists use the metaphor of the earth as a "spaceship" in trying to persuade countries, industries and people to

345

stop wasting and polluting our natural resources. Since we all share life on this planet, they argue, no single person or institution has the right to destroy, waste, or use more than a fair share of its resources.

2   But does everyone on earth have an equal right to an equal share of its resources? The spaceship metaphor can be dangerous when used by misguided idealists to justify suicidal policies for sharing our resources through uncontrolled immigration and foreign aid. In their enthusiastic but unrealistic generosity, they confuse the ethics of a spaceship with those of a lifeboat.

3   A true spaceship would have to be under the control of a captain, since no ship could possibly survive if its course were determined by committee. Spaceship Earth certainly has no captain; the United Nations is merely a toothless tiger, with little power to enforce any policy upon its bickering members.

4   If we divide the world crudely into rich nations and poor nations, two thirds of them are desperately poor, and only one third comparatively rich, with the United States the wealthiest of all. Metaphorically each rich nation can be seen as a lifeboat full of comparatively rich people. In the ocean outside each lifeboat swim the poor of the world, who would like to get in, or at least to share some of the wealth. What should the lifeboat passengers do?

5   First, we must recognize the limited capacity of any lifeboat. For example, a nation's land has a limited capacity to support a population and as the current energy crisis has shown us, in some ways we have already exceeded the carrying capacity of our land.

6   So here we sit, say 50 people in our lifeboat. To be generous let us assume it has room for 10 more, making a total capacity of 60. Suppose the 50 of us in the lifeboat see 100 others swimming in the water outside, begging for admission to our boat or for handouts. We have several options: we may be tempted to try to live by the Christian ideal of being "our brother's keeper," or by the Marxist ideal of "to each according to his needs." Since the needs of all in the water are the same, and since they can all be seen as "our brothers," we could take them all into our boat, making a total of 150 in a boat designed for 60. The boat swamps, everyone drowns. Complete justice, complete catastrophe.

7   Since the boat has an unused excess capacity of 10 more passengers, we could admit just 10 more to it. But which 10 do we let in? How do we choose? Do we pick the best 10, the neediest

10, "first come, first served"? And what do we say to the 90 we exclude? If we do let an extra 10 into our lifeboat, we will have lost our "safety factor," an engineering principle of critical importance. For example, if we don't leave room for excess capacity as a safety factor in our country's agriculture, a new plant disease or a bad change in the weather could have disastrous consequences.

8   Suppose we decide to preserve our small safety factor and admit no more to the lifeboat. Our survival is then possible although we shall have to be constantly on guard against boarding parties.

9   While this last solution clearly offers the only means of our survival, it is morally abhorrent to many people. Some say they feel guilty about their good luck. My reply is simple: "Get out and yield your place to others." This may solve the problem of the guilt-ridden person's conscience, but it does not change the ethics of the lifeboat. The needy person to whom the guilt-ridden person yields his place will not himself feel guilty about his good luck. If he did, he would not climb aboard. The net result of conscience-stricken people giving up their unjustly held seats is the elimination of that sort of conscience from the lifeboat.

10   This is the basic metaphor within which we must work out our solutions. Let us now enrich the image, step by step, with substantive additions from the real world, a world that must solve real and pressing problems of overpopulation and hunger.

11   The harsh ethics of the lifeboat become even harsher when we consider the reproductive differences between the rich nations and the poor nations. The people inside the lifeboats are doubling in numbers every 87 years: those swimming around outside are doubling on the average, every 35 years, more than twice as fast as the rich. And since the world's resources are dwindling, the difference in prosperity between the rich and the poor can only increase.

12   As of 1973, the U.S. had a population of 210 million people, who were increasing by 0.8 percent per year. Outside our lifeboat, let us imagine another 210 million people (say the combined populations of Colombia, Ecuador, Venezuela, Morocco, Pakistan, Thailand and the Philippines), who are increasing at a rate of 3.3 percent per year. Put differently, the doubling time for this aggregate population is 21 years, compared to 87 years for the U.S.

13   Now suppose the U.S. agreed to pool its resources with those seven countries, with everyone receiving an equal share. Initially the ratio of Americans to non-Americans in this model would be

one-to-one but consider what the ratio would be after 87 years, by which time the Americans would have doubled to a population of 420 million. By then, doubling every 21 years, the other group would have swollen to 354 billion. Each American would have to share the available resources with more than eight people.

14   But, one could argue, this discussion assumes that current population trends will continue, and they may not. Quite so. Most likely the rate of population increase will decline much faster in the U.S. than it will in the other countries, and there does not seem to be much we can do about it. In sharing with "each according to his needs," we must recognize that needs are determined by population size, which is determined by the rate of reproduction, which at present is regarded as a sovereign right of every nation, poor or not. This being so, the philanthropic load created by the sharing ethic of the spaceship can only increase.

15   The fundamental error of spaceship ethics, and the sharing it requires, is that it leads to what I call "the tragedy of the commons." Under a system of private property, the men who own property recognize their responsibility to care for it, for if they don't they will eventually suffer. A farmer, for instance, will allow no more cattle in a pasture than its carrying capacity justifies. If he overloads it, erosion sets in, weeds take over, and he loses the use of the pasture.

16   If a pasture becomes a commons open to all, the right of each to use it may not be matched by a corresponding responsibility to protect it. Asking everyone to use it with discretion will hardly do, for the considerate herdsman who refrains from overloading the commons suffers more than a selfish one who says his needs are greater. If everyone would restrain himself all would be well; but it takes only one less than everyone to ruin a system of voluntary restraint. In a crowded world of less than perfect human beings, mutual ruin is inevitable if there are no controls. This is the tragedy of the commons.

17   One of the major tasks of education today should be the creation of such an acute awareness of the dangers of the commons that people will recognize its many varieties. For example, the air and water have become polluted because they are treated as commons. Further growth in the population or per-capita conversion of natural resources into pollutants will only make the problem worse. The same holds true for the fish of the oceans. Fishing fleets have

nearly disappeared in many parts of the world, technological improvements in the art of fishing are hastening the day of complete ruin. Only the replacement of the system of the commons with a responsible system of control will save the land, air, water and oceanic fisheries.

18   In recent years there has been a push to create a new commons called a World Food Bank, an international depository of food reserves to which nations would contribute according to their abilities and from which they would draw according to their needs. This humanitarian proposal has received support from many liberal international groups, and from such prominent citizens as Margaret Mead, U.N. Secretary General Kurt Waldheim, and Senators Edward Kennedy and George McGovern.

19   A world food bank appeals powerfully to our humanitarian impulses. But before we rush ahead with such a plan, let us recognize where the greatest political push comes from, lest we be disillusioned later. Our experience with the "Food for Peace program," or Public Law 480, gives us the answer. This program moved billions of dollars worth of U.S. surplus grain to food-short, population-long countries during the past two decades. But when P.L. 480 first became law, a headline in the business magazine *Forbes* revealed the real power behind it: "Feeding the World's Hungry Millions: How It Will Mean Billions for U.S. Business."

20   And indeed it did. In the years 1960 to 1970, U.S. taxpayers spent a total of $7.9 billion on the Food for Peace program. Between 1948 and 1970, they also paid an additional $50 billion for other economic-aid programs, some of which went for food and food-producing machinery and technology. Though all U.S. taxpayers were forced to contribute to the cost of P.L. 480, certain special interest groups gained handsomely under the program. Farmers did not have to contribute the grain; the Government, or rather the taxpayers, bought it from them at full market prices. The increased demand raised prices of farm products generally. The manufacturers of farm machinery, fertilizers and pesticides benefited by the farmers' extra efforts to grow more food. Grain elevators profited from storing the surplus until it could be shipped. Railroads made money hauling it to ports, and shipping lines profited from carrying it overseas. The implementation of P.L. 480 required the creation of a vast Government bureaucracy, which then acquired its own vested interest in continuing the program regardless of its merits.

21 Those who proposed and defended the Food for Peace program in public rarely mentioned its importance to any of these special interests. The public emphasis was always on its humanitarian effects. The combination of silent selfish interests and highly vocal humanitarian apologists made a powerful and successful lobby for extracting money from taxpayers. We can expect the same lobby to push now for the creation of a World Food Bank.

22 However great the potential benefit to selfish interests, it should not be a decisive argument against a truly humanitarian program. We must ask if such a program would actually do more good than harm, not only momentarily but also in the long run. Those who propose the food bank usually refer to a current "emergency" or "crisis" in terms of world food supply. But what is an emergency? Although they may be infrequent and sudden, everyone knows that emergencies will occur from time to time. A well-run family, company, organization or country prepares for the likelihood of accidents and emergencies. It expects them, it budgets for them, it saves for them.

23 What happens if some organizations or countries budget for accidents and others do not? If each country is solely responsible for its own well-being, poorly managed ones will suffer. But they can learn from experience. They may mend their ways, and learn to budget for infrequent but certain emergencies. For example, the weather varies from year to year, and periodic crop failures are certain. A wise and competent government saves out of the production of the good years in anticipation of bad years to come. Joseph taught this policy to Pharoah in Egypt more than 2,000 years ago. Yet the great majority of the governments in the world today do not follow such a policy. They lack either the wisdom or the competence, or both. Should those nations that do manage to put something aside be forced to come to the rescue each time an emergency occurs among the poor nations?

24 "But it isn't their fault!" Some kind-hearted liberals argue, "How can we blame the poor people who are caught in an emergency? Why must they suffer for the sins of their governments?" The concept of blame is simply not relevant here. The real question is, what are the operational consequences of establishing a world food bank? If it is open to every country every time a need develops, slovenly rulers will not be motivated to take Joseph's advice.

Someone will always come to their aid. Some countries will deposit food in the world food bank, and others will withdraw it. There will be almost no overlap. As a result of such solutions to food shortage emergencies, the poor countries will not learn to mend their ways, and will suffer progressively greater emergencies as their populations grow.

25   On the average, poor countries undergo a 2.5 percent increase in population each year; rich countries, about 0.8 percent. Only rich countries have anything in the way of food reserves set aside, and even they do not have as much as they should. Poor countries have none. If poor countries received no food from the outside, the rate of their population growth would be periodically checked by crop failures and famines. But if they can always draw on a world food bank in time of need, their population can continue to grow unchecked, and so will their "need" for aid. In the short run, a world food bank may diminish that need, but in the long run it actually increases the need without limit.

26   Without some system of worldwide food sharing, the proportion of people in the rich and poor nations might eventually stabilize. The overpopulated poor countries would decrease in numbers, while the rich countries that had room for more people would increase. But with a well-meaning system of sharing, such as a world food bank, the growth differential between the rich and the poor countries will not only persist, it will increase. Because of the higher rate of population growth in the poor countries of the world, 88 percent of today's children are born poor, and only 12 percent rich. Year by year the ratio becomes worse, as the fast-reproducing poor outnumber the slow-reproducing rich.

27   A world food bank is thus a commons in disguise. People will have more motivation to draw from it than to add to any common store. The less provident and less able will multiply at the expense of the abler and more provident, bringing eventual ruin upon all who share in the commons. Besides, any system of "sharing" that amounts to foreign aid from the rich nations to the poor nations will carry the taint of charity, which will contribute little to the world peace so devoutly desired by those who support the idea of a world food bank.

28   As past U.S. foreign-aid programs have amply and depressingly demonstrated, international charity frequently inspires mistrust

and antagonism rather than gratitude on the part of the recipient nation [see "What Other Nations Hear When the Eagle Screams," by Kenneth J. and Mary M. Gergen, *Psychology Today*, June 1974].

29   The modern approach to foreign aid stresses the export of technology and advice, rather than money and food. As an ancient Chinese proverb goes: "Give a man a fish and he will eat for a day; teach him how to fish and he will eat for the rest of his days." Acting on this advice, the Rockefeller and Ford Foundations have financed a number of programs for improving agriculture in the hungry nations. Known as the "Green Revolution," these programs have led to the development of "miracle rice" and "miracle wheat," new strains that offer bigger harvests and greater resistance to crop damage. Norman Borlaug, the Nobel Prize winning agronomist who, supported by the Rockefeller Foundation, developed "miracle wheat," is one of the most prominent advocates of a world food bank.

30   Whether or not the Green Revolution can increase food production as much as its champions claim is a debatable but possibly irrelevant point. Those who support this well-intended humanitarian effort should first consider some of the fundamentals of human ecology. Ironically, one man who did was the late Alan Gregg, a vice president of the Rockefeller Foundation. Two decades ago he expressed strong doubts about the wisdom of such attempts to increase food production. He likened the growth and spread of humanity over the surface of the earth to the spread of cancer in the human body, remarking that "cancerous growths demand food, but, as far as I know, they have never been cured by getting it."

31   Every human born constitutes a draft on all aspects of the environment: food, air, water, forests, beaches, wildlife, scenery and solitude. Food can, perhaps, be significantly increased to meet a growing demand. But what about clean beaches, unspoiled forests, and solitude? If we satisfy a growing population's need for food, we necessarily decrease its per capita supply of the other resources needed by men.

32   India, for example, now has a population of 600 million, which increases by 15 million each year. This population already puts a huge load on a relatively impoverished environment. The country's forests are now only a small fraction of what they were three centuries ago, and floods and erosion continually destroy the in-

sufficient farmland that remains. Every one of the 15 million new lives added to India's population puts an additional burden on the environment, and increases the economic and social costs of crowding. However humanitarian our intent, every Indian life saved through medical or nutritional assistance from abroad diminishes the quality of life for those who remain, and for subsequent generations. If rich countries make it possible, through foreign aid, for 600 million Indians to swell to 1.2 billion in a mere 28 years, as their current growth rate threatens, will future generations of Indians thank us for hastening the destruction of their environment? Will our good intentions be sufficient excuse for the consequences of our actions?

33   My final example of a commons in action is one for which the public has the least desire for rational discussion—immigration. Anyone who publicly questions the wisdom of current U.S. immigration policy is promptly charged with bigotry, prejudice, ethnocentrism, chauvinism, isolationism or selfishness. Rather than encounter such accusations, one would rather talk about other matters, leaving immigration policy to wallow in the crosscurrents of special interests that take no account of the good of the whole, or the interests of posterity.

34   Perhaps we still feel guilty about things we said in the past. Two generations ago the popular press frequently referred to Dagos, Wops, Polacks, Chinks and Krauts, in articles about how America was being "overrun" by foreigners of supposedly inferior genetic stock [see "The Politics of Genetic Engineering: Who Decides Who's Defective?" *Psychology Today*, June 1974]. But because the implied inferiority of foreigners was used then as justification for keeping them out, people now assume that restrictive policies could only be based on such misguided notions. There are other grounds.

35   Just consider the numbers involved. Our Government acknowledges a net inflow of 400,000 immigrants a year. While we have no hard data on the extent of illegal entries, educated guesses put the figure at about 600,000 a year. Since the natural increase (excess of births over deaths) of the resident population now runs about 1.7 million per year, the yearly gain from immigration amounts to at least 19 percent of the total annual increase, and may be as much as 37 percent if we include the estimate for illegal immigrants. Considering the growing use of birth-control devices, the

potential effect of educational campaigns by such organizations as Planned Parenthood Federation of America and Zero Population Growth, and the influence of inflation and the housing shortage, the fertility rate of American women may decline so much that immigration could account for all the yearly increase in population. Should we not at least ask if that is what we want?

36   For the sake of those who worry about whether the "quality" of the average immigrant compares favorably with the quality of the average resident, let us assume that immigrants and native born citizens are of exactly equal quality, however one defines that term. We will focus here only on quantity; and since our conclusions will depend on nothing else, all charges of bigotry and chauvinism become irrelevant.

37   World food banks *move food to the people,* hastening the exhaustion of the environment of the poor countries. Unrestricted immigration, on the other hand, *moves people to the food,* thus speeding up the destruction of the environment of the rich countries. We can easily understand why poor people should want to make this latter transfer, but why should rich hosts encourage it?

38   As in the case of foreign-aid programs, immigration receives support from selfish interests and humanitarian impulses. The primary selfish interest in unimpeded immigration is the desire of employers for cheap labor, particularly in industries and trades that offer degrading work. In the past, one wave of foreigners after another was brought into the U.S. to work at wretched jobs for wretched wages. In recent years the Cubans, Puerto Ricans and Mexicans have had this dubious honor. The interests of the employers of cheap labor mesh well with the guilty silence of the country's liberal intelligentsia. White Anglo-Saxon Protestants are particularly reluctant to call for a closing of the doors to immigration for fear of being called bigots.

39   But not all countries have such reluctant leadership. Most educated Hawaiians, for example, are keenly aware of the limits of their environment, particularly in terms of population growth. There is only so much room on the islands, and the islanders know it. To Hawaiians, immigrants from the other 49 states present as great a threat as those from other nations. At the recent meeting of Hawaiian government officials in Honolulu, I had the ironic delight of hearing a speaker, who like most of his audience was of

Japanese ancestry, ask how the country might practically and constitutionally close its doors to further immigration. One member of the audience countered: "How can we shut the doors now? We have many friends and relatives in Japan that we'd like to bring here some day so that they can enjoy Hawaii too." The Japanese-American speaker smiled sympathetically and answered: "Yes, but we have children now, and someday we'll have grandchildren too. We can bring more people here from Japan only by giving away some of the land that we hope to pass on to our grandchildren some day. What right do we have to do that?"

40   At this point, I can hear U.S. liberals asking: "How can you justify slamming the door once you're inside? You say that immigrants should be kept out. But aren't we all immigrants, or the descendants of immigrants? If we insist on staying, must we not admit all others?" Our craving for intellectual order leads us to seek and prefer symmetrical rules and morals: a single rule for me and everybody else; the same rule yesterday, today and tomorrow. Justice, we feel, should not change with time and place.

41   We Americans of non-Indian ancestry can look upon ourselves as the descendants of thieves who are guilty morally, if not legally, of stealing this land from its Indian owners. Should we then give back the land to the now living American descendants of those Indians? However morally or logically sound this proposal may be, I, for one, am unwilling to live by it and I know no one else who is. Besides, the logical consequence would be absurd. Suppose that, intoxicated with a sense of pure justice, we should decide to turn our land over to the Indians. Since all our other wealth has also been derived from the land, wouldn't we be morally obliged to give that back to the Indians too?

42   Clearly, the concept of pure justice produces an infinite regression to absurdity. Centuries ago, wise men invented statutes of limitations to justify the rejection of such pure justice, in the interest of preventing continual disorder. The law zealously defends property rights. Drawing a line after an arbitrary time has elapsed may be unjust, but the alternatives are worse.

43   We are all the descendants of thieves, and the world's resources are inequitably distributed. But we must begin the journey to tomorrow from the point where we are today. We cannot remake the past. We cannot safely divide the wealth equitably among all peo-

ples so long as people reproduce at different rates. To do so would guarantee that our grandchildren, and everyone else's grandchildren, would have only a ruined world to inhabit.

44 To be generous with one's own possessions is quite different from being generous with those of posterity. We should call this point to the attention of those who, from a commendable love of justice and equality, would institute a system of the commons, either in the form of a world food bank, or of unrestricted immigration. We must convince them if we wish to save at least some parts of the world from environmental ruin.

45 Without a true world government to control reproduction and the use of available resources, the sharing ethic of the spaceship is impossible. For the foreseeable future, our survival demands that we govern our actions by the ethics of a lifeboat, harsh though they may be. Posterity will be satisfied with nothing less.

Analyzing the Writer's Argument

1. According to Hardin, environmentalists talk of the earth as a "spaceship" when discussing the need to conserve and not pollute our natural resources. Explain how their metaphor of the "spaceship" works. What does Hardin find wrong with the spaceship metaphor? Explain.

2. Hardin believes that a lifeboat is a more appropriate and accurate metaphor when talking about sharing the resources of the earth. Why? Explain how his lifeboat metaphor works. How does he deal with the problem of guilt?

3. Why, according to Hardin, do the ethics of the lifeboat become even harsher when the reproductive differences between rich and poor nations are factored in? Does the example he presents in paragraphs 12 and 13 convincingly illustrate his point? Explain.

4. What does Hardin mean by "the tragedy of the commons"? What examples does he use to illustrate this concept? Do you agree with Hardin that spaceship ethics inevitably leads to the tragedy of the commons? Why or why not?

5. What does Hardin see as the main problems with immigration? Where does he see support for immigration coming from in America? What is his attitude toward this support? How do you know?

6. How does Hardin respond to questions U.S. liberals would raise about immigration restrictions: "How can you justify slamming

the door once you're inside? You say that immigrants should be kept out. But aren't we all immigrants, or the descendants of immigrants?"

7. Hardin grants the fact that the world resources are inequitably distributed. Why does he believe that today "we cannot safely divide the wealth equitably among all peoples"? Do you agree with his thinking? Why or why not?

Exploring the Issues in This Essay

1. In this essay Hardin juxtaposes his "ethics of the lifeboat" to the environmentalists' "ethics of the spaceship." Hardin continually calls his lifeboat ethics "harsh." What makes them so much harsher than the spaceship ones? Is there no middle ground? What would be needed to make the sharing ethic of the spaceship work? Discuss.

2. Hardin believes that the issue of population control is inextricably tied to the issue of sharing the world's resources. How are the two issues related? Does one of these issues need to be addressed before we can move on to the other? What are the advantages and disadvantages for the United States in controlling its population? What related issues need to be studied while considering population controls?

358

Shelley List

Each Starving Child Is Your Child

An essayist and novelist, Shelley List lives in Los Angeles, California, and works as a writer-producer for television. In 1985 she traveled to famine-stricken Ethiopia with Operation California, a relief group whose president believes that "we can feed and doctor the world with what we discard, through surplus goods." List and her partner Jonathan Estrin were filming a television documentary about the relief group and its efforts in Makelle, Ethiopia.

It was a time when network evening news showed us pictures of the millions of malnourished and starving children throughout Africa, and we responded with donations to the popular "Live Aid" concert and other relief organizations or by purchasing the USA for Africa recording of "We Are the World." But even these pictures did not prepare List for what she found in the primitive hospital and refugee camp in Makelle. In "Each Starving Child Is Your Child," first published in the Los Angeles Times *in 1985, Shelley List graphically describes the human devastation she witnessed and argues for a worldwide human conscience and commitment to our hungry brothers and sisters.*

1   MAKELLE, Ethiopia—The mother holds the shriveled child in her arms. I cannot look her in the eye. My children are healthy.

2   Does she know? Does she know that my daughters' legs can support their bodies when they stand, that their bellies do not protrude like balloons?

3   I cannot look her in the eye. But there is nowhere to look, for at every turn, a face presses into my vision, a beautiful face like hers. And a body withered by malnutrition.

4   I have come here with Operation California, the relief group that collected close to $1 million worth of donated medical supplies. My partner, Jonathan Estrin, and I are working on a film for television about the group and its founders.

359

5   Richard Walden, the enterprising president of the private aid organization, works out of a one-room office in Los Angeles. He believes that we can feed and doctor the world with what we discard, through surplus goods. He has accompanied the cargo to make sure it reaches its destination.

6   In the primitive hospital near the feeding center, there are several children to a bed, ragged blankets covering their wasted bodies. Their immature immune systems are defenseless against the ravages of the famine.

7   Clinically, with some dispassion, a young Ethiopian doctor displays the children to us. "This boy is 8," he says of a child who does not look more than 2.

8   He implores the child to stand; his mother (or sister, or aunt) moves to help. The doctor waves her away. The child must show the visitors himself.

9   He is naked, his buttocks only bone. He cannot stand by himself. He begins to fall. The doctor picks him up, and the child's legs shake, quiver like a telephone wire in a storm. The child tries. He tries so hard. He looks as if he is dying.

10   The doctor continues on his grim grand rounds.

11   A strikingly beautiful girl is told to stand. She has dark eyes like me. She could be my daughter.

12   He picks up her gray shroud of a dress. She is naked underneath. Her dignity has already been lost somewhere on the road where she walked for days after her village was abandoned. Her thighs are prepubescent, child-like, her eyes oversized in her small face. She looks at us apologetically, as if to say, If only I were not so weak, I could stand and show you that I will not die. She is 20, the doctor says.

13   How can he see this day after day? It's not fair. But there is no fair. But for an accident of geography, it could be me there, naked under my dress, being asked to show the visitors how hard it is to stand.

14   We move from the hospital into the camp itself. Like billowing sails on a pale parched sea, like air-filled sheets blowing on a clothesline, the tents come into view. Hundreds and hundreds of white tents hugging against one another. The cracked earth is covered with them, white on beige; green does not live here.

15   We hold onto our hearts, they will melt in this heat, they will disappear from our bodies in the face of such suffering. It is a

scene out of the Bible. We see plague. We see pestilence. Jehovah unleashing his mighty fury. We see thousands and thousands and thousands of people who have arrived at this place to get food.

16   We walk in and among the milling throng. An old man takes a switch and beats the children away as they crowd around us. Touch me, notice me, look at me. They grasp our fingers, our hands, spill out a hello, a word learned from previous awestruck visitors hiding behind their notebooks and cameras.

17   We pass stone graves, hundreds of them. Diggers are at work burying shrouded forms of all sizes.

18   We see cows whose bones strain at their mangy coats. There is no flesh on them. A cow should be fat. A baby should be fat.

19   My heart is pounding. It is very hot, but I am still wearing my heavy jacket because I am chilled. And I wonder how to process such tragedy. I wonder where to put such masses of people, such grandiose suffering, into my memory.

20   We have all known loss—a parent, a grandparent, a friend, a relative, or, the worst, a child. Each time, a light goes out. But to watch one's entire family, village, world, starve is an extravagance of darkness. It is an obscenity. One can get through anything, I suppose, but how does one endure devastation on such a scale that the tears do not dry before there is another body over which to weep?

21   The relief people from all donor groups now fear that the conscience of the world will wane, that photos of gaunt children with flies crusting their eyelids will lose their impact, that people will become inured to the images and stop giving.

22   One hopes that this will not happen to the people of Ethiopia. One prays not. This is only the beginning; by next year many other African nations will be afflicted by the famine. Already Chad, Mali, the Sudan and Somalia are suffering from the drought. The world must continue to donate funds and food and medical supplies. It is predicted that millions—yes millions—will die. And each death will diminish us all. Many pieces of me already have died here.

23   What happens in a place like this is that each mother's child becomes your child. My child. When my children had a cough, I would put them to bed with tea and honey and a story and M & Ms and a present from the toy store. "Cool hands when you're hot, warm hands when you're cold, that's what mothers are for," my daughter said once when she was sick.

24   I would tuck my children in and take their temperatures and read to them and hold them and fuss over them. The mothers here have no time, no energy to fuss, no place to fuss, no chance to do "what mothers are for."

25   If their children are our children, and we can't tuck them in and lay on a cool hand and give them M & Ms and tell them a story, if we can't look these mothers in the eye, then what do we do? Turn away?

26   We do what we can do, what we must do if we are to feel whole.

27   As for me, a part of my heart has indeed melted, and I will never be the same.

Analyzing the Writer's Argument

1. What is List's purpose in this essay? How do you know? What does she want her readers to do after hearing her story?
2. List tells us that she cannot look the Ethiopian mother "in the eye." Why do you suppose she can't? As a mother, how does List respond emotionally to the ravages of famine?
3. List chooses to depict the mass starvation by focusing our attention on two vivid examples, those of the 8-year-old boy and the 20-year-old girl. How did you respond to these two examples? Why? What did these examples contribute to the persuasiveness of her argument? Explain.
4. What, according to List, did most of the relief people fear most? In your opinion, have their fears been borne out since this essay was written in 1985?
5. List contrasts the children of Ethiopia to her own children. What does this contrast contribute to her argument? Explain.
6. What is the meaning of List's title? Does she manage to develop this point in a convincing manner in the essay? Explain why or why not.

Exploring the Issues in This Essay

1. What responsibility do we as Americans have to starving people throughout the world? How do Americans usually respond to human tragedies like the famine in Africa? Do we tend to "become inured to the images [of mass starvation] and stop giving"? Do

we have a responsibility to feed and house our own citizens first before we attempt to become the world's caretaker?

2. How do you react to the popular fundraising efforts of the 1980s like "Live Aid"? Benefit concerts have been able to raise large sums of money in the past, but have they always worked in the best long-term interest of the cause? Could it be argued that they contribute to our wane in conscience because they create the feeling that the problem has been addressed or that enough money has been raised to solve the problem? What strategies need to be used to sustain the necessary long-term interest and support of the public in a cause?

Jonathan Swift

A Modest Proposal

> *Jonathan Swift, one of the world's greatest satirists, was born in Dublin, Ireland, in 1667. He was educated at Trinity College, and when his early attempts at a literary career ended in disappointment, Swift returned to Ireland and was ordained an Anglican priest. He served as Dean of Dublin's St. Patrick's Cathedral from 1713 until he died in 1745. A successful pamphleteer on political and religious issues, Swift is best known today as the author of* Gulliver's Travels *(1726) and the following essay, "A Modest Proposal" (1729).*
>
> *During the 1720s the Irish people suffered through several famines. The landowners, mostly absentee Englishmen, did nothing to assist the tenant farmers and their families, and the English government refused to intervene. A number of people wrote pamphlets in which they proposed solutions to the problems of poverty and starvation in Ireland. "A Modest Proposal," published anonymously, was Swift's ironic contribution to the heated and controversial debate.*

> *A Modest Proposal for Preventing the Children of Poor People in Ireland from Being a Burden to Their Parents or Country, and for Making Them Beneficial to the Public*

1   It is a melancholy object to those who walk through this great town, or travel in the country, when they see the streets, the roads and cabin-doors crowded with beggars of the female sex, followed by three, four, or six children, all in rags, and importuning every passenger for an alms. These mothers, instead of being able to work for their honest livelihood, are forced to employ all their time in strolling, to beg sustenance for their helpless infants, who, as they grow up, either turn thieves for want of work, or leave their dear native country to fight for the Pretender in Spain, or sell themselves to the Barbadoes.

364

2   I think it is agreed by all parties that this prodigious number of children, in the arms, or on the backs, or at the heels of their mothers, and frequently of their fathers, is in the present deplorable state of the kingdom a very great additional grievance; and therefore whoever could find out a fair, cheap, and easy method of making these children sound and useful members of the commonwealth would deserve so well of the public as to have his statue set up for a preserver of the nation.

3   But my intention is very far from being confined to provide only for the children of professed beggars; it is of a much greater extent, and shall take in the whole number of infants at a certain age who are born of parents in effect as little able to support them as those who demand our charity in the streets.

4   As to my own part, having turned my thoughts for many years upon this important subject, and maturely weighed the several schemes of other projectors, I have always found them grossly mistaken in their computation. It is true a child just dropped from its dam may be supported by her milk for a solar year with little other nourishment, at most not above the value of two shillings, which the mother may certainly get, or the value in scraps, by her lawful occupation of begging, and it is exactly at one year old that I propose to provide for them, in such a manner as, instead of being a charge upon their parents, or the parish, or wanting food and raiment for the rest of their lives, they shall, on the contrary, contribute to the feeding and partly to the clothing of many thousands.

5   There is likewise another great advantage in my scheme, that it will prevent those voluntary abortions, and that horrid practice of women murdering their bastard children, alas, too frequent among us, sacrificing the poor innocent babes, I doubt, more to avoid the expense than the shame, which would move tears and pity in the most savage and inhuman breast.

6   The number of souls in Ireland being usually reckoned one million and a half, of these I calculate there may be about two hundred thousand couples whose wives are breeders, from which number I subtract thirty thousand couples who are able to maintain their own children, although I apprehend there cannot be so many under the present distresses of the kingdom, but this being granted, there will remain an hundred and seventy thousand breeders. I again subtract fifty thousand for those women who miscarry, or

whose children die by accident or disease within the year. There only remain an hundred and twenty thousand children of poor parents annually born: the question therefore is, how this number shall be reared, and provided for, which as I have already said, under the present situation of affairs is utterly impossible by all the methods hitherto proposed, for we can neither employ them in handicraft or agriculture; we neither build houses (I mean in the country), nor cultivate land: they can very seldom pick up a livelihood by stealing until they arrive at six years old, except where they are of towardly parts, although I confess they learn the rudiments much earlier, during which time they can however be properly looked upon only as probationers, as I have been informed by a principal gentleman in the County of Cavan, who protested to me that he never knew above one or two instances under the age of six, even in a part of the kingdom so renowned for the quickest proficiency in that art.

7   I am assured by our merchants that a boy or girl before twelve years old, is no saleable commodity, and even when they come to this age, they will not yield above three pounds, or three pounds and half-a-crown at most on the Exchange, which cannot turn to account either to the parents or the kingdom, the charge of nutriment and rags having been at least four times that value.

8   I shall now therefore humbly propose my own thoughts, which I hope will not be liable to the least objection.

9   I have been assured by a very knowing American of my acquaintance in London, that a young healthy child well nursed is at a year old a most delicious, nourishing and wholesome food, whether stewed, roasted, baked, or boiled, and I make no doubt that it will equally serve in a fricassee, or a ragout.

10   I do therefore humbly offer it to public consideration, that of the hundred and twenty thousand children already computed, twenty thousand may be reserved for breed, whereof only one fourth part to be males, which is more than we allow to sheep, black-cattle, or swine, and my reason is that these children are seldom the fruits of marriage, a circumstance not much regarded by our savages, therefore one male will be sufficient to serve four females. That the remaining hundred thousand may at a year old be offered in sale to the persons of quality, and fortune, through the kingdom, always advising the mother to let them suck plentifully in the last month, so as to render them plump, and fat for a good table. A

child will make two dishes at an entertainment for friends, and when the family dines alone, the fore or hind quarter will make a reasonable dish, and seasoned with a little pepper or salt will be very good boiled on the fourth day, especially in winter.

11   I have reckoned upon a medium, that a child just born will weigh twelve pounds, and in a solar year if tolerably nursed increaseth to twenty-eight pounds.

12   I grant this food will be somewhat dear, and therefore very proper for landlords, who, as they have already devoured most of the parents, seem to have the best title to the children.

13   Infant's flesh will be in season throughout the year, but more plentiful in March, and a little before and after, for we are told by a grave author, an eminent French physician, that fish being a prolific diet, there are more children born in Roman Catholic countries about nine months after Lent than at any other season; therefore reckoning a year after Lent, the markets will be more glutted than usual, because the number of Popish infants is at least three to one in this kingdom, and therefore it will have one other collateral advantage by lessening the number of Papists among us.

14   I have already computed the charge of nursing a beggar's child (in which list I reckon all cottagers, labourers, and four-fifths of the farmers) to be about two shillings *per annum*, rags included, and I believe no gentleman would repine to give ten shillings for the carcass of a good fat child, which, as I have said, will make four dishes of excellent nutritive meat, when he hath only some particular friend of his own family to dine with him. Thus the Squire will learn to be a good landlord and grow popular among his tenants, the mother will have eight shillings net profit, and be fit for work until she produces another child.

15   Those who are more thrifty (as I must confess the times require) may flay the carcass; the skin of which artificially dressed, will make admirable gloves for ladies, and summer boots for fine gentlemen.

16   As to our city of Dublin, shambles may be appointed for this purpose, in the most convenient parts of it, and butchers we may be assured will not be wanting, although I rather recommend buying the children alive, and dressing them hot from the knife, as we do roasting pigs.

17   A very worthy person, a true lover of his country, and whose virtues I highly esteem was lately pleased, in discoursing on this

matter to offer a refinement upon my scheme. He said that many gentlemen of this kingdom, having of late destroyed their deer, he conceived that the want of venison might be well supplied by the bodies of young lads and maidens, not exceeding fourteen years of age, nor under twelve, so great a number of both sexes in every county being now ready to starve, for want of work and service: and these to be disposed of by their parents if alive, or otherwise by their nearest relations. But with due deference to so excellent a friend, and so deserving a patriot, I cannot be altogether in his sentiments. For as to the males, my American acquaintance assured me from frequent experience that their flesh was generally tough and lean, like that of our schoolboys, by continual exercise, and their taste disagreeable, and to fatten them would not answer the charge. Then as to the females, it would, I think with humble submission, be a loss to the public, because they soon would become breeders themselves: and besides, it is not improbable that some scrupulous people might be apt to censure such a practice (although indeed very unjustly) as a little bordering upon cruelty, which I confess, hath always been with me the strongest objection against any project, howsoever well intended.

18   But in order to justify my friend, he confessed that this expedient was put into his head by the famous Psalmanazar, a native of the island Formosa, who came from thence to London, above twenty years ago, and in conversation told my friend that in his country when any young person happened to be put to death, the executioner sold the carcass to persons of quality, as a prime dainty, and that, in his time, the body of a plump girl of fifteen, who was crucified for an attempt to poison the emperor, was sold to his Imperial Majesty's Prime Minister of State, and other great Mandarins of the Court, in joints from the gibbet, at four hundred crowns. Neither indeed can I deny that if the same use were made of several plump young girls in this town who, without one single groat to their fortunes, cannot stir abroad without a chair, and appear at the playhouse and assemblies in foreign fineries, which they never will pay for, the kingdom would not be the worse.

19   Some persons of a desponding spirit are in great concern about that vast number of poor people, who are aged, diseased, or maimed, and I have been desired to employ my thoughts what course may be taken to ease the nation of so grievous an encum-

brance. But I am not in the least pain upon that matter, because it is very well known that they are every day dying, and rotting, by cold, and famine, and filth, and vermin, as fast as can be reasonably expected. And as to the younger labourers they are now in almost as hopeful a condition. They cannot get work, and consequently pine away from want of nourishment, to a degree that if at any time they are accidentally hired to common labour, they have not strength to perform it; and thus the country and themselves are in a fair way of being soon delivered from the evils to come.

20 I have too long digressed, and therefore shall return to my subject. I think the advantages by the proposal which I have made are obvious and many, as well as of the highest importance.

21 For first, as I have already observed, it would greatly lessen the number of Papists, with whom we are yearly over-run, being the principal breeders of the nation, as well as our most dangerous enemies, and who stay at home on purpose with a design to deliver the kingdom to the Pretender, hoping to take their advantage by the absence of so many good Protestants, who have chosen rather to leave their country than stay at home and pay tithes against their conscience to an idolatrous Episcopal curate.

22 Secondly, the poorer tenants will have something valuable of their own, which by law may be made liable to distress, and help to pay their landlord's rent, their corn and cattle being already seized, and money a thing unknown.

23 Thirdly, whereas the maintenance of an hundred thousand children, from two years old, and upwards, cannot be computed at less than ten shillings a piece *per annum,* the nation's stock will be thereby increased fifty thousand pounds *per annum,* besides the profit of a new dish, introduced to the tables of all gentlemen of fortune in the kingdom, who have any refinement in taste, and the money will circulate among ourselves, the goods being entirely of our own growth and manufacture.

24 Fourthly, the constant breeders, besides the gain of eight shillings sterling *per annum,* by the sale of their children, will be rid of the charge of maintaining them after the first year.

25 Fifthly, this food would likewise bring great custom to taverns, where the vintners will certainly be so prudent as to procure the best receipts for dressing it to perfection, and consequently have their houses frequented by all the fine gentlemen, who justly value

themselves upon their knowledge in good eating; and a skilful cook, who understands how to oblige his guests, will contrive to make it as expensive as they please.

26 Sixthly, this would be a great inducement to marriage, which all wise nations have either encouraged by rewards, or enforced by laws and penalties. It would increase the care and tenderness of mothers towards their children, when they were sure of a settlement for life, to the poor babes, provided in some sort by the public to their annual profit instead of expense. We should soon see an honest emulation among the married women, which of them could bring the fattest child to the market. Men would become as fond of their wives, during the time of their pregnancy, as they are now of their mares in foal, their cows in calf, or sows when they are ready to farrow, nor offer to beat or kick them (as it is too frequent a practice) for fear of a miscarriage.

27 Many other advantages might be enumerated. For instance, the addition of some thousand carcasses in our exportation of barrelled beef; the propagation of swine's flesh, and improvement in the art of making good bacon, so much wanted among us by the great destruction of pigs, too frequent at our tables, are no way comparable in taste or magnificence to a well-grown, fat yearling child, which roasted whole will make a considerable figure at a Lord Mayor's feast, or any other public entertainment. But this and many others I omit, being studious of brevity.

28 Supposing that one thousand families in this city would be constant customers for infants' flesh, besides others who might have it at merry meetings, particularly weddings and christenings; I compute that Dublin would take off annually about twenty thousand carcasses, and the rest of the kingdom (where probably they will be sold somewhat cheaper) the remaining eighty thousand.

29 I can think of no one objection that will possibly be raised against this proposal, unless it should be urged that the number of people will be thereby much lessened in the kingdom. This I freely own, and it was indeed one principal design in offering it to the world. I desire the reader will observe, that I calculate my remedy *for this one individual Kingdom of* Ireland, *and for no other that ever was, is, or, I think, ever can be upon earth.* Therefore let no man talk to me of other expedients: *Of taxing our absentees at five shillings a pound: Of using neither clothes, nor household furniture except what is of our own growth and manufacture: Of utterly rejecting the materials*

and instruments that promote foreign luxury: Of curing the expensiveness of pride, vanity, idleness, and gaming in our women: Of introducing a vein of parsimony, prudence, and temperance: Of learning to love our country, wherein we differ even from Laplanders, *and the inhabitants of* Topinamboo: *Of quitting our animosities and factions, nor act any longer like the* Jews, *who were murdering one another at the very moment their city was taken: Of being a little cautious not to sell our country and consciences for nothing: Of teaching landlords to have at least one degree of mercy towards their tenants.* Lastly, *of putting a spirit of honesty, industry, and skill into our shopkeepers, who, if a resolution could now be taken to buy only our native goods, would immediately unite to cheat and exact upon us in the price, the measure and the goodness, nor could ever yet be brought to make one fair proposal of just dealing, though often and earnestly invited to it.*

30   Therefore I repeat, let no man talk to me of these and the like expedients, till he hath at least a glimpse of hope that there will ever be some hearty and sincere attempt to put them in practice.

31   But as to myself, having been wearied out for many years with offering vain, idle, visionary thoughts, and at length utterly despairing of success, I fortunately fell upon this proposal, which as it is wholly new, so it hath something solid and real, of no expense and little trouble, full in our own power, and whereby we can incur no danger in disobliging England. For this kind of commodity will not bear exportation, the flesh being of too tender a consistence to admit a long continuance in salt, *although perhaps I could name a country which would be glad to eat up our whole nation without it.*

32   After all I am not so violently bent upon my own opinion as to reject any offer, proposed by wise men, which shall be found equally innocent, cheap, easy and effectual. But before some thing of that kind shall be advanced in contradiction to my scheme, and offering a better, I desire the author, or authors, will be pleased maturely to consider two points. First, as things now stand, how they will be able to find food and raiment for a hundred thousand useless mouths and backs? And secondly, there being a round million of creatures in human figure, throughout this kingdom, whose whole subsistence put into a common stock would leave them in debt two millions of pounds sterling; adding those who are beggars by profession, to the bulk of farmers, cottagers, and laborers with their wives and children, who are beggars in effect; I

desire those politicians who dislike my overture, and may perhaps be so bold to attempt an answer, that they will first ask the parents of these mortals whether they would not at this day think it a great happiness to have been sold for food at a year old, in the manner I prescribe, and thereby have avoided such a perpetual scene of misfortunes as they have since gone through, by the oppression of landlords, the impossibility of paying rent without money or trade, the want of common sustenance, with neither house nor clothes to cover them from the inclemencies of weather, and the most inevitable prospect of entailing the like, or greater miseries upon their breed for ever.

33   I profess in the sincerity of my heart that I have not the least personal interest in endeavoring to promote this necessary work, having no other motive than the *public good of my country, by advancing our trade, providing for infants, relieving the poor, and giving some pleasure to the rich.* I have no children by which I can propose to get a single penny; the youngest being nine years old, and my wife past child-bearing.

Analyzing the Writer's Argument

1. What is the problem that Swift addresses in this essay? What is Swift's solution for this problem?

2. Swift dismisses a number of other "expedients" because they are "vain, idle, visionary thoughts." How do you react to these other solutions, especially in comparison to Swift's "modest proposal"? What does your answer tell you about Swift's purpose in this essay?

3. How would you characterize the speaker in this essay? What type of person is he? What does Swift do to make his speaker sound like an authority on the subject? Why do you think Swift created such a persona to make this proposal? Finally, what is the purpose of the final sentence?

4. Is the argument presented in this essay reasoned and logical? Explain. For example, how did the calculations presented in paragraph 6 strike you?

5. Irony is the use of words to suggest something different from their meaning. Swift is being ironic when he talks of making Irish "children sound and useful members of the commonwealth" in paragraph 2. Identify other examples of Swift's irony in this essay. What does his irony contribute to his argument?

6. What words does Swift use to refer to Irish women, their children, and the poor people of Ireland in general? In terms of his proposal, is his diction appropriate and effective? Explain.
7. At what point in the essay were you first aware that Swift did not intend his proposal to be taken literally? What tipped you off?

Exploring the Issues in This Essay

1. The issues of poverty, hunger, and starvation, as Swift's essay clearly illustrates, are often much more than they appear. It would be a wonderful world if, without hesitating, people responded to other people's needs in a humanitarian way. But then prejudice, politics, and religion always seem to get in the way. What similarities, if any, do you see between Swift's Ireland and America today?
2. Why do you think that Swift chose to make his "A Modest Proposal" ironic? Explain why irony is such an effective strategy for dealing with difficult, perhaps even long-standing, social problems. What do you see as the advantages and the potential disadvantages of such a strategy? How easy is irony to use? Explain. In what types of writing situations might you find it useful?

Writing Suggestions for
Hunger and Homelessness:
Our National Disgrace?

1. Part of the controversy surrounding many social issues involves defining the problem in terms that are acceptable to others. What exactly is hunger, or homelessness, or poverty? After reviewing Marin's argument, write an essay in which you define one of these concepts. Use examples from your reading or observation to illustrate your definition.

2. Jon Hull makes it clear that after a person loses himself or herself to the streets homelessness seems to be the end of the line. Are there any preventative measures that can be taken to assist people before they start the slow slide into homelessness? Write an essay in which you explore several of the causes of homelessness and argue for some measure or program that might help eliminate this problem.

3. Using the articles that you read in this section, write an essay in which you argue that America should solve its own problems of hunger and homelessness before it tries to feed and shelter the world.

4. Peter Marin believes that we as a society have an obligation to those people who have been made homeless against their wills. Do you agree? If not, why? If so, what exactly do you think our obligations are? What kinds of programs should be set up to assist the involuntarily homeless? Write an essay in which you argue your position on this question.

5. Spend enough time in the library to learn about the relief efforts that were intended to aid famine-stricken Africa in the mid-1980s. How successful were these efforts? Were some more successful than others? What types of problems did relief groups encounter? Does the problem of famine and starvation still exist? Has Shelley List's "fear that the conscience of the world will wane" become reality? Write an essay in which you come to some conclusions about the merit or worth of our recent relief efforts.

6. Write an essay in which you argue either for or against Garrett Hardin's "lifeboat ethics." Use materials from the other essays in this section to illustrate your argument.

7. Peter Marin believes that "compassion is little more than the passion for control." Using examples of efforts to help the hungry and homeless from your reading or observations, write an essay in which you either support or refute Marin's statement.

8. Garrett Hardin argues that the issue of world hunger is inevitably tied to the issue of population control. To what extent do you believe this is true for the United States? Write an essay in which you explore the ways in which population control—including immigration policies—might help solve the issue of hunger/poverty in our country.

9. Over the summer months a number of homeless people have located in your community. Now that winter is approaching, their numbers have become very visible and their well-being has become cause for real concern. Imagine yourself serving on a community commission charged with the task of writing policy guidelines for addressing the "problem" of homeless people in the community. Does a community have the right to create laws or ordinances that would protect city or town property against uses for which it was not intended? For example, can "camping out" in the city park be prohibited? What accomodations or programs should the community make available to the homeless? Write an essay in which you propose what your community should do both for and about the homeless people within the city limits.

10. What in your opinion is the most compelling answer or solution to the problem of homelessness in America? Using materials from the essays in this section, write an essay in which you argue for this approach.

11. Write your own "modest proposal" for the problem of hunger or homelessness in America today.

9

Gun Control:
The Right to
Bear Arms

- June 12, 1963, civil rights leader Medgar Evers is gunned down in front of his home in Jackson, Mississippi.
- November 23, 1963, President John F. Kennedy is slain by a sniper's bullet in Dallas, Texas.
- February 21, 1965, Black Muslim Malcom X is assassinated at a rally in New York City.
- April 4, 1968, civil rights leader Martin Luther King, Jr. is killed by a sniper's bullet in Memphis, Tennessee.
- June 6, 1968, Senator Robert F. Kennedy is assassinated in a Los Angeles hotel.
- May 15, 1972, Alabama Governor George Wallace is shot and paralyzed in Laurel, Maryland, while campaigning for the Democratic nomination for president.
- September 23, 1975, President Gerald Ford is shot at by a would-be assassin in San Francisco.
- March 30, 1981, President Ronald Reagan is shot as he leaves a Washington, D.C. hotel. Jim Brady, his press secretary, receives a near-fatal head wound.

With each of these assassinations and attempts on the lives of public figures came calls for stricter gun-control laws. On the heels of the assassinations of King and Kennedy, Congress passed the 1968 Gun Control Act. This legislation, commonly called the nation's handgun law, prohibits convicted felons, minors, drug addicts, fugitives from justice, and those adjudicated mentally incompetent from purchasing handguns. This law has proven largely ineffective because there are no checks as to the honesty of the purchaser in filling out the required federal forms. For example, in Florida, Arthur Kane, a convicted felon, lied on the federal handgun purchase form and less than an hour later shot and killed a Merrill Lynch stockbroker and wounded another before ending his own life. Could this tragedy have been avoided if the authorities were able to discover that Kane was a convicted felon? Perhaps. The Brady Handgun Violence Prevention Act, now before Congress, calls for a seven-day waiting period which would allow authorities to do the necessary background checks.

No one can deny that there is a problem. Each year in America, more than 25,000 people die of gunshot wounds. But people can't agree on a solution. The National Rifle Association (NRA) and other pro gun groups believe that the right to bear arms is guaranteed by the Second Amendment of the United States Constitution and that law abiding citizens should not have their rights restricted. Their popular slogan, "Guns don't kill people—criminals do," highlights their belief that in America guns are not the real culprit, criminals are. The NRA would like to see more money spent on upgrading law enforcement agencies and a toughening of our judicial and correctional systems.

On the other side of the controversy, Handgun Control Inc., the leading antigun lobby, campaigns to keep guns out of the wrong hands. They argue with the NRA's literal interpretation of the Second Amendment and believe that a national seven-day waiting period for the purchase of handguns is a reasonable and necessary compromise. In addition, they contend that assault weapons, such as the AK-47 used in the massacre of children in a Stockton, California, school yard in 1989, have no place in the hands of ordinary citizens.

The controversy continues as people search for a solution, a common ground that will safeguard the public safety while not unduly diminishing the rights of the individual.

Edward M. Kennedy

The Need for Handgun Control

Born in 1932, Edward M. Kennedy, the younger brother of President John F. Kennedy and Senator Robert F. Kennedy, graduated from Harvard in 1956 and received his law degree from the University of Virginia in 1959. When his brother was elected president, "Teddy" was elected to finish out his term as senator from Massachusetts. A leader of the liberal Democrats in the Senate since that time, Kennedy challenged incumbent President Jimmy Carter for the presidential nomination in 1980, was defeated in most of the primaries but chose to stay in the race, hoping that the ever-increasing dissatisfaction with Carter would lead to an open convention. That contingency did not materialize, however, and Kennedy eventually gave his support to Carter.

When President Kennedy and Senator Kennedy were struck down by assassins' bullets, the nation mourned the loss of two of its most dynamic and forward-looking leaders, and Ted Kennedy felt the loss even more deeply. Since that time, he has become a vigorous advocate of gun control, arguing that the ready availability of guns in this country represents an enemy within our society that is as great a threat to our safety as any enemy from without. Shortly after President Ronald Reagan was shot by John Hinckley in 1981, Kennedy wrote "The Need for Handgun Control" for The Los Angeles Times.

1   The wounding of President Reagan has stunned the world and stirred a vast reaction. Yet he is only the most famous casualty of an endless guerrilla war inside this country waged with a growing arsenal of handguns in the wrong hands. Every day others less famous are wounded or killed; their families worry and suffer. They weep and, too often, they mourn.

2   Every 50 minutes an American is killed by a handgun; 29 Americans who are alive today will be shot dead tomorrow. In the streets of our cities, the arms race of Saturday-night specials and

cheap handguns will take 10,000 lives this year and will threaten or wound another 250,000 citizens. In the past year alone, we have seen a 13 percent rise in violent crime, the greatest increase in a decade.

3   Today the clear and present danger to our society is the midnight mugger and the deranged assassin. And their weapons are as close as the nearest pawnshop. There are 55 million handguns in circulation. The lethal number rises by two and a half million each year. By the year 2000, there will be 100 million handguns in America.

4   The shooting of President Reagan was frightening, but not surprising. Are we now too accustomed to the repeated carnage of our national leaders? Are we ready to accept the neighborhoods of our cities as permanent free-fire zones? That sort of fatalism insures more fatalities.

5   But handgun control is hardly the whole answer to lawlessness. That is why we must adopt other measures as well.

6   We can, and we must, set more stringent conditions on bail, because no suspect charged with violent crime should be free to rape or to rob again. We can, and we must, demand that juveniles who shoot, stab and assault should not be allowed to misuse their youth as an automatic excuse for their offenses. We can, and we must, provide sufficient resources for law enforcement. No police officer should ever have to jeopardize his life for a subsistence salary that cannot support his family.

7   All of this is important—but none of it is enough. In the truest sense, law enforcement is part of our national defense. And in the effort to defend ourselves, we must not duck the question of gun control. No sane society should stand by while its enemies arm themselves—whether those enemies are adversaries abroad or criminals and assassins at home.

8   For America in 1981, crime control means gun control. This is not an easy issue for any officeholder or candidate. In 1980, in the presidential primaries, I constantly met voters who opposed me because they thought I favored confiscation of hunting rifles, shotguns and sporting pistols. It was not true, but it was believed— because the gun lobby had repeated it over and over.

9   Other senators and representatives faced a similar assault in 1980. The political action committees opposing gun control spent $2.2 million for their candidates, while those on the other side had

less than a tenth as much to contribute. This is why we cannot control the plague of handguns even though two-thirds of the American people have favored such control ever since 1963.

10 Perhaps this latest tragedy will challenge us to put away past apprehensions and appeals which have treated handgun control as a sinister plot or a subversion of civil liberties. I hope we can now agree that the first civil liberty of all citizens is freedom from fear of violence and sudden death on the streets of their communities.

11 In this session of congress, I will join again with Rep. Peter Rodino (D-N.J.) to introduce a bill to control handguns. It will be a moderate bill. It will be a sensible bill. It is all I will seek on this issue—and it is something all Americans should be able to support.

12 All Americans, including sportsmen and hunters, should be able to support a ban on Saturday-night specials and cheap handguns. Those guns are not accurate beyond a range of 10 or 15 feet. They are meant to maim or kill another human being. Saturday-night specials can be purchased now because of a loophole in the law that allows their lethal parts to be imported from abroad, to be assembled and sold in this country. And last week, one of those weapons almost killed our President.

13 All Americans, including all liberals, should be able to support a mandatory minimum prison sentence for any felon who commits a crime with a handgun. And all Americans, including the National Rifle Assn., should be able to support a waiting period for the purchase of handguns to prevent them from falling into the hands of criminals and psychopaths.

14 The question is not whether we will disarm honest citizens, as some gun lobbyists have charged. The question is whether we will make it harder for those who break the law to arm themselves.

15 Gun control is not an easy issue. But, for me, it is a fundamental issue. My family has been touched by violence; too many others have felt the same terrible force. Too many children have been raised without a father or a mother. Too many widows have lived out their lives alone. Too many people have died.

16 We all know the toll that has been taken in this nation. We all know the leaders of our public life and of the human spirit who have been lost or wounded year after year: My brother, John Kennedy, and my brother, Robert Kennedy; Medgar Evers, who died so that others could live free; Martin Luther King, the apostle

of nonviolence who became the victim of violence; George Wallace, who has been paralyzed for nearly nine years, and George Moscone, the mayor of San Francisco, who was killed in his office. Last year alone, we lost Allard Lowenstein and we almost lost Vernon Jordan. Four months ago, we lost John Lennon, that gentle soul who challenged us in song to "give peace a chance." We had two attacks on President Ford and now the attack on President Reagan.

17   It is unacceptable that all these good men have been shot down. They all sought, each in their own way, to make ours a better world. And, too often, too soon, their own world came to an end.

18   It is unacceptable that a man who has been arrested before, who has been apprehended carrying loaded guns through an airport security check, who apparently has psychiatric problems as well as a criminal record should be able to go to a pawnshop and buy a cheap handgun imported because of a loophole in the law, and then use that gun to attempt murder against the President of the United States.

19   It is unacceptable that there are states in the American union where the accused attacker of President Reagan could today buy another Saturday night special.

20   The day after Martin Luther King's assassination, Robert Kennedy said: "The victims of violence are black and white, rich and poor, young and old, famous and unknown. They are, most important of all, human beings whom other human beings loved and needed. No one, no matter where he lives or what he does, can be certain who next will suffer from some senseless act of bloodshed. And yet it goes on, and on, and on, in this country of ours. Why?"

21   Thirteen years later, that same tragic question must be raised again.

22   It is for us to answer it. We must resolve that the next generation of Americans will not have to witness the carnage next time and ask—"Why?"

Analyzing the Writer's Argument

1. Kennedy makes it clear that he is not for tighter controls on the sale of all types of weapons. What kinds of guns is he opposed to? Why?

2. What does Kennedy, an influential senator, believe have been the major obstacles to passing gun-control legislation in the United States Congress?

3. Opponents of gun-control legislation argue that passing stricter gun-control laws will do nothing to curb crime, that there are insufficient funds for law enforcement, and that the judicial system is too lenient with convicted criminals. Where in his argument does Kennedy make concessions to those points of view?

4. Kennedy might have begun his essay with his reactions to the death of his two brothers, as well as those of friends and associates struck down by assassins' bullets. Why does he delay mention of them to a later point in his essay?

5. Kennedy anticipates the following arguments:
   a. handgun control would be a subversion of civil liberties
   b. law-abiding hunters and sportspeople would not be able to pursue their sports.
   How does he answer these arguments?

6. According to Kennedy's statistics, annually 10,000 people are killed and another 250,000 are wounded in the United States. Has Kennedy explained to your satisfaction the casual relationship between these deaths and woundings and the availability of cheap handguns? Why or why not?

7. Politicians are fond of using repetition and parallelism in their speech and writings. They find these rhetorical devices useful in making their ideas more emphatic and memorable which, in turn, can make their argument more persuasive. Where in his essay has Kennedy used repetition and parallelism? Do you find his use of these devices effective? Why or why not?

Exploring the Issues in This Essay

1. There are some that argue that instead of trying to make guns more difficult to purchase, we should by trying to find out what makes people seek out guns as a way of solving their difficulties in the first place. They argue that guns are, in effect, a symptom and not a cause. Discuss the validity of this argument.

2. What is your personal attitude toward guns? You may find it helpful to consider the following questions in exploring the reasons behind your current attitude: Do you or members of your family own guns? If so, why? Have you ever used a gun? Were you allowed to own and play with toy guns as a child? Did your childhood experiences in any way shape your current attitude toward guns? Have you ever felt the need to own a gun?

Barry Goldwater

Why Gun-Control Laws Don't Work

Former U.S. Senator Barry Goldwater was born in Phoenix,
Arizona, in 1909. A staunch conservative, he was first elected
to the Senate in 1952, and he soon became a spokesman for
right-wing Republicans. Goldwater left the Senate in 1964
to wage a bid for the presidency against Lyndon B. Johnson.
Because of his outspoken views, Democrats labeled him an
"extremist," particularly on nuclear issues and relations with
the Soviet Union, and made it stick. Goldwater was soundly
rejected by voters at the polls. In 1968 the people of Arizona
returned Goldwater to the Senate, and, after serving three
exemplary terms, he retired in 1986.

"Why Gun-Control Laws Don't Work" first appeared in
the pages of Reader's Digest *in 1976. Experience had shown*
Goldwater that gun-control legislation was not the answer.
Such laws were simply not getting the job done. Therefore, he
argues that we need to "control not the weapon but the user."

1   Let me say immediately that if I thought more gun-control laws
would help diminish the tragic incidence of robberies, muggings,
rapes and murders in the United States, I would be the first to
vote for them. But I am convinced that making more such laws
approaches the problem from the wrong direction.

2   It is clear, I think, that gun legislation simply doesn't work. There
are already some 20,000 state and local gun laws on the books, and
they are no more effective than was the prohibition of alcoholic
beverages in the 1920s. Our most recent attempt at federal gun legislation was the Gun Control Act of 1968, intended to control the
interstate sale and transportation of firearms and the importation
of uncertified firearms; it has done nothing to check the availability of weapons. It has been bolstered in every nook and cranny of

the nation by local gun-control laws, yet the number of shooting homicides per year has climbed steadily since its enactment, while armed robberies have increased 60 percent.

3   Some people, even some law-enforcement officials, contend that "crimes of passion" occur because a gun just happens to be present at the scene. I don't buy that. I can't equate guns with the murder rate, because if a person is angry enough to kill, he will kill with the first thing that comes to hand—a gun, a knife, an ice pick, a baseball bat.

4   I believe our *only* hope of reducing crime in this country is to control not the weapon but the user. We must reverse the trend toward leniency and permissiveness in our courts—the plea bargaining, the pardons, the suspended sentences and unwarranted paroles—and make the lawbreaker pay for what he has done by spending time in jail. We have plenty of statutes against killing and maiming and threatening people with weapons. These can be made effective by strong enforcement and firm decisions from the bench. When a man knows that if he uses a potentially deadly object to rob or do harm to another person he is letting himself in for a mandatory, unparolable stretch behind bars, he will think twice about it.

5   Of course, no matter what gun-control laws are enacted—including national registration—the dedicated crook can always get a weapon. So, some people ask, even if national registration of guns isn't completely airtight, isn't it worth trying? Sure, it would cause a little inconvenience to law-abiding gun owners. And it certainly wouldn't stop all criminals from obtaining guns. But it might stop a few, maybe quite a few. What's wrong with that?

6   There are several answers. The first concerns enforcement. How are we going to persuade the bank robber or the street-corner stickup artist to register his means of criminal livelihood? Then there is the matter of expense. A study conducted eight years ago showed a cost to New York City of $72.87 to investigate and process one application for a pistol license. In mid-1970 dollars, the same procedure probably costs over $100. By extrapolation to the national scale, the cost to American taxpayers of investigating and registering the 40 to 50 million handguns might reach $4 billion or $5 billion. On top of that, keeping the process in operation year after year would require taxpayer financing of another sizable

federal bureau. We ought to have far better prospects of success before we hobble ourselves with such appalling expenditures.

7   Finally, there are legal aspects based on the much-discussed Second Amendment to the Bill of Rights, which proclaims, that "A well regulated Militia, being necessary to the security of a free State, the right of the people to keep and bear Arms, shall not be infringed." The anti-gun faction argues that this right made sense in the days of British oppression but that it has no application today. I contend, on the other hand, that the Founding Fathers conceived of an armed citizenry as a necessary hedge against tyranny from within as well as from without, that they saw the right to keep and bear arms as basic and perpetual, the one thing that could spell the difference between freedom and servitude. Thus I deem most forms of gun control unconstitutional in intent.

8   Well, then, I'm often asked, what kind of gun laws *are* you for? I reply that I am for laws of common sense. I am for laws that prohibit citizen access to machine guns, bazookas and other military devices. I am for laws that are educational in nature. I believe that before a person is permitted to buy a weapon he should be required to take a course that will teach him how to use it, to handle it safely and keep it safely about the house.

9   Gun education, in fact, can actually reduce lawlessness in a community, as was demonstrated in an experiment conducted in Highland Park, Mich. City police launched a program to instruct merchants in the use of handguns. The idea was to help them protect themselves and their businesses from robbers, and it was given wide publicity. The store-robbery rate dropped from an average of 1.5 a day to none in four months.

Where do we go from here? My answer to this is based on the firm belief that we have a crime problem in this country, not a gun problem, and that we must meet the enemy on his own terms. We must start by making crime as unprofitable for him as we can. And we have to do this, I believe, by getting tough in the courts and corrections systems.

10   A recent news story in Washington, D.C., reports that, of 184 persons convicted of gun possession in a six-month period, only 14 received a jail sentence. Forty-six other cases involved persons who had previously been convicted of a felony or possession of a gun. Although the maximum penalty for such repeaters in the

District of Columbia is ten years in prison, half of these were not jailed at all. A study last year revealed that in New York City, which has about the most prohibitive gun legislation in the country, only one out of six people convicted of crimes involving weapons went to jail.

11 This sorry state of affairs exists because too many judges and magistrates either don't know the law or are unwilling to apply it with appropriate vigor. It's time to demand either that they crack down on these criminals or be removed from office. It may even be time to review the whole system of judicial appointments, to stop weakening the cause of justice by putting men on the bench who may happen to be golfing partners of Congressmen and too often lack the brains and ability for the job. In Arizona today we elect our judges, and the system is working well, in part because we ask the American and local bar associations to consider candidates and make recommendations. In this way, over the last few years, we have replaced many weaklings with good jurists.

12 We have long had all the criminal statutes we need to turn the tide against the crime wave. There is, however, one piece of proposed legislation that I am watching with particular interest. Introduced by Sen. James McClure (R., Idaho), it requires that any person convicted of a federal crime in which a gun is used serve five to ten years in jail automatically on top of whatever penalty he receives for the crime itself. A second conviction would result in an extra ten-year-to-life sentence. These sentences would be mandatory and could not be suspended. It is, in short, a "tough" bill. I think that this bill would serve as an excellent model for state legislation.

13 And so it has in California which, last September, signed into law a similar bill requiring a mandatory jail sentence for any gun-related felony.

14 Finally, it's important to remember that this is an area of great confusion; an area in which statistics can be juggled and distorted to support legislation that is liable to be expensive, counterproductive or useless. The issue touches upon the freedom and safety of all of us, whether we own firearms or not. The debate over gun control is an adjunct to the war against crime, and that war must be fought with all the intelligence and tenacity we can bring to it.

Analyzing the Writer's Argument

1. What is Goldwater's position on the issue of gun-control legislation? What reasons does he give for maintaining this position?
2. What does Goldwater believe is necessary to "turn the tide against the crime wave" in America? Do you agree? Why or why not?
3. What does Goldwater see as the drawbacks to a program of national gun registration? How convincing is his reasoning? Explain.
4. On what grounds does Goldwater consider "most forms of gun control unconstitutional in intent"? In your opinion, is the constitutional argument against gun-control legislation convincing? Explain.
5. What kinds of evidence does Goldwater use to document his argument? Does his admission that "statistics can be juggled and distorted" affect your reaction to his documentation? If so, how?
6. What is Goldwater's attitude toward America's judicial system? Is he digressing from the point of his argument to suggest that more states would be better off if they followed Arizona's lead and elected their judges? Why or why not?
7. How would you describe Goldwater's tone in this essay? Is it that of a man who has gained a reputation over the years as a straight-talking, honest politician? Is his tone appropriate for his argument?

Exploring the Issues in This Essay

1. Goldwater is convinced that America has a "crime problem" and not a "gun problem." What is the relationship between crime and guns? Is it possible to separate the two issues? Are there any gun problems that are not related to crime? Explain.
2. In response to questions about the types of laws he favors, Goldwater states that "I am for laws of common sense. I am for laws that prohibit citizen access to machine guns, bazookas and other military devices." It's difficult to argue with such a common sense position. But if such a position seems so reasonable, why is it so difficult to get restrictions placed on assault rifles and other similar weapons today? What are the arguments in favor of restricting these "military-type" weapons? What seems to be hampering legislation in this area?

Reprinted courtesy of Handgun Control, Inc.

389

Reprinted courtesy of the National Rifle Association of America.

Adam Smith

Fifty Million Handguns

George Goodman, Harvard graduate and Rhodes Scholar whose pen name is Adam Smith, earned his reputation as a financial analyst. He began his career as a journalist, eventually becoming an editor at Time *and* Fortune *magazines. After a stint in Los Angeles as a screenwriter, he returned to writing about business and finance, achieving widespread success with the popular and topical* The Money Game *(1968),* Supermoney *(1972), and* Paper Money *(1981). In recent years, Smith's editorial column "Unconventional Wisdom" has been a regular feature of* Esquire *magazine.*

The following essay originally appeared in the April 1981 issue of Esquire. *Outraged at the violent death of his friend and college classmate Michael Halberstam and the senseless murder of John Lennon, Smith researched the arguments both for and against gun control in preparation for this essay. In the process, he learned that violence is infecting our society and threatening our personal safety. Smith's solution to this problem is handgun registration.*

1   "You people," said my Texas host, "do not understand guns or gun people." By "you people" he meant not just me, whom he happened to be addressing, but anyone from a large eastern or midwestern city. My Texas host is a very successful businessman, an intelligent man. "There are two cultures," he said, "and the nongun culture looks down on the gun culture."

2   My Texas host had assumed—correctly—that I do not spend a lot of time with guns. The last one I knew intimately was a semi-automatic M-14, and, as any veteran knows, the Army bids you call it a weapon, not a gun. I once had to take that weapon apart and reassemble it blindfolded, and I liked it better than the heavy old M-1. We were also given a passing introduction to the Russian Kalashnikov and the AK-47, the Chinese copy of that automatic weapon, presumably so we could use these products of our Rus-

sian and Chinese enemies if the need arose. I remember that you could drop a Kalashnikov in the mud and pick it up and it would still fire. I also remember blowing up a section of railroad track using only an alarm clock, a primer cord, and a plastic called C-4. The day our little class blew up the track at Fort Bragg was rather fun. These experiences give me some credibility with friends from the "gun culture." (Otherwise, they have no lasting social utility whatsoever.) And I do not share the fear of guns—at least of "long guns," rifles and shotguns—that some of my college-educated city-dweller friends have, perhaps because of my onetime intimacy with that Army rifle, whose serial number I still know.

3   In the gun culture, said my Texas host, a boy is given a .22 rifle around the age of twelve, a shotgun at fourteen, and a .30-caliber rifle at sixteen. The young man is taught to use and respect these instruments. My Texas host showed me a paragraph in a book by Herman Kahn in which Kahn describes the presentation of the .22 as a rite of passage, like a confirmation or a bar mitzvah. "Young persons who are given guns," he wrote," go through an immediate maturing experience because they are thereby given a genuine and significant responsibility." Any adult from the gun culture, whether or not he is a relative, can admonish any young person who appears to be careless with his weapon. Thus, says Kahn, the gun-culture children take on "enlarging and maturing responsibilities" that their coddled upper-middle-class counterparts from the nongun culture do not share. The children of my Texas host said "sir" to their father and "ma'am" to their mother.

4   I do not mean to argue with the rite-of-passage theory. I am quite willing to grant it. I bring it up because the subjects of guns and gun control are very emotional ones, and if we are to solve the problems associated with them, we need to arrive at a consensus within and between gun and nongun cultures in our country.

5   Please note that the rite-of-passage gifts are shotguns and rifles. Long guns have sporting uses. Nobody gives a child a handgun, and nobody shoots a flying duck with a .38 revolver. Handguns have only one purpose.

6   Some months ago, a college friend of mine surprised a burglar in his home in Washington, D.C. Michael Halberstam was a cardiologist, a writer, and a contributor to this magazine. The burglar shot Halberstam, but Halberstam ran him down with his car on the street outside before he died, and the case received

widespread press. I began to work on this column, in high anger, right after his death. A few days later, John Lennon was killed in New York. These two dreadful murders produced an outpouring of grief, followed immediately by intense anger and the demand that something be done, that Congress pass a gun-control law. The National Rifle Association was quick to point out that a gun-control law would not have prevented either death; Halberstam's killer had already violated a whole slew of existing laws, and Lennon's was clearly sufficiently deranged or determined to kill him under any gun law. The National Rifle Association claims a million members, and it is a highly organized lobby. Its Political Victory Fund "works for the defeat of antigun candidates and for the support and election of progun office seekers." Let us grant the National Rifle Association position that the accused killers in these two recent spectacular shootings might not have been deterred even by severe gun restrictions.

7   In the course of researching this column, I talked to representatives of both the progun and the antigun lobbies. Anomalies abound. Sam Fields, a spokesman for the National Coalition to Ban Handguns, is an expert rifleman who was given a gun at age thirteen by his father, a New York City policeman. The progun banner is frequently carried by Don Kates Jr., who describes himself as a liberal, a former civil rights worker, and a professor of constitutional law. Fields and Kates have debated each other frequently. Given their backgrounds, one might expect their positions to be reversed.

8   Some of the progun arguments run as follows:

9   Guns don't kill people, people kill people. Gun laws do not deter criminals. (A 1976 University of Wisconsin study of gun laws concluded that "gun-control laws have no individual or collective effect in reducing the rate of violent crime.") A mandatory sentence for carrying an unlicensed gun, says Kates, would punish the "ordinary decent citizens in high-crime areas who carry guns illegally because police protection is inadequate and they don't have the special influence necessary to get a 'carry' permit." There are fifty million handguns out there in the United States already; unless you were to use a giant magnet, there is no way to retrieve them. The majority of people do not want guns banned. A ban on handguns would be like Prohibition—widely disregarded, un-

enforceable, and corrosive to the nation's sense of moral order. Federal registration is the beginning of federal tyranny; we might someday need to use those guns against the government.

10 Some of the antigun arguments go as follows:

11 People kill people, but handguns make it easier. When other weapons (knives, for instance) are used, the consequences are not so often deadly. Strangling or stabbing someone takes a different degree of energy and intent than pulling a trigger. Registration will not interfere with hunting and other rifle sports but will simply exercise control over who can carry handguns. Ordinary people do not carry handguns. If a burglar has a gun in his hand, it is quite insane for you to shoot it out with him, as if you were in a quick-draw contest in the Wild West. Half of all the guns used in crimes are stolen; 70 percent of the stolen guns are handguns. In other words, the supply of handguns used by criminals already comes to a great extent from the households these guns were supposed to protect.

12 "I'll tell you one thing," said a lieutenant on the local police force in my town. "You should never put that decal in your window, the one that says THIS HOUSE IS PROTECTED BY AN ARMED CITI-ZEN. The gun owners love them, but that sign is just an invitation that says 'Come and rob my guns.' Television sets and stereos are fenced at a discount; guns can actually be fenced at a premium. The burglar doesn't want to meet you. I have had a burglar tell me, 'If I wanted to meet people, I would have been a mugger.'"

13 After a recent wave of burglaries, the weekly newspaper in my town published a front-page story. "Do not buy a gun—you're more likely to shoot yourself than a burglar," it said. At first the police agreed with that sentiment. Later, they took a slightly different line. "There is more danger from people having accidents or their kids getting hold of those guns than any service in defending their houses; but there was a flap when the paper printed that, so now we don't say anything," said my local police lieutenant. "If you want to own a gun legally, okay. Just be careful and know the laws."

14 What police departments tell inquiring citizens seems to depend not only on the local laws but also on whether or not that particular police department belongs to the gun culture.

15 Some of the crime statistics underlying the gun arguments are surprising. Is crime-ridden New York City the toughest place in the

country? No: your chances of being murdered are higher in Columbus, Georgia, in Pine Bluff, Arkansas, and in Houston, Texas, among others. Some of the statistics are merely appalling: we had roughly ten thousand handgun deaths last year. The British had forty. In 1978, there were 18,714 Americans murdered. Sixty-four percent were killed with handguns. In that same year, *we had more killings with handguns by children ten years old and younger than the British had by killers of all ages.* The Canadians had 579 homicides last year; we had more than twenty thousand.

16   H. Rap Brown, the Sixties activist, once said, "Violence is as American as apple pie." I guess it is. We think fondly of Butch Cassidy and the Sundance Kid; we do not remember the names of the trainmen and the bank clerks they shot. Four of our Presidents have died violently; the British have never had a prime minister assassinated. *Life* magazine paid $8,000 to Halberstam's accused killer for photos of his boyhood. Now he will be famous, like Son of Sam. The list could go on and on.

17   I am willing to grant to the gunners a shotgun in every closet. Shotguns are not used much in armed robberies, or even by citizens in arguments with each other. A shotgun is a better home-defense item anyway, say my police friends, if only because you have to be very accurate with a handgun to knock a man down with one. But the arguments over which kinds of guns are best only demonstrate how dangerously bankrupt our whole society is in ideas on personal safety.

18   Our First Lady has a handgun.

19   Would registry of handguns stop the criminal from carrying the unregistered gun? No, and it might afflict the householder with some extra red tape. However, there is a valid argument for registry. Such a law might have no immediate effect, but we have to begin somewhere. We license automobiles and drivers. That does not stop automobile deaths, but surely the highways would be even more dangerous if populated with unlicensed drivers and uninspected cars. The fifty million handguns outstanding have not caused the crime rate to go down. Another two million handguns will be sold this year, and I will bet that the crime rate still does not go down.

20   Our national behavior is considered close to insane by some of the other advanced industrial nations. We have gotten so accus-

tomed to crime and violence that we have begun to take them for granted; thus we are surprised to learn that the taxi drivers in Tokyo carry far more than five dollars in cash, that you can walk safely around the streets of Japan's largest cities, and that Japan's crime rate is going *down*. I know there are cultural differences; I am told that in Japan the criminal is expected to turn himself in so as not to shame his parents. Can we imagine that as a solution to crime here?

21 In a way, the tragic killings of Michael Halberstam and John Lennon have distracted us from a larger and more complex problem. There is a wave of grief, a wave of anger—and then things go right on as they did before. We become inured to the violence and dulled to the outrage. Perhaps, indeed, no legislation could stop murders like these, and perhaps national gun legislation would not produce overnight change. The hard work is not just to get the gunners to join in; the hard work is to do something about our ragged system of criminal justice, to shore up our declining faith in the institutions that are supposed to protect us, and to promote the notion that people should take responsibility for their own actions.

22 What makes us so different from the Japanese and the British and the Canadians? They are not armed, as we are, yet their streets and houses are far safer. Should we not be asking ourselves some sober questions about whether we are living the way we want to?

Analyzing the Writer's Argument

1. In his opening paragraph, Smith develops the theme that there are two cultures in America—the gun culture and the nongun culture. What characterizes these two cultures? What does Smith believe the two cultures need to do in order to solve the problems associated with guns and gun control?
2. What qualifies Smith to write about the gun-control issue? How important do you consider these qualifications?
3. Why does Smith make a point of distinguishing between long guns and handguns? What does Smith mean when he says that "handguns have only one purpose"?
4. What, according to Smith, are the popular progun arguments? The antigun arguments? What are some of the surprises he found

while doing his research? What, if anything, does this information contribute to his argument?

5. What concessions is he willing to make to the "gunners"? Why? How does Smith feel about arguments over which kinds of guns are best for home-defense?

6. Smith uses four very brief paragraphs in his essay. Explain the function of each. What impact did they have on you?

7. Smith believes that America is inherently a violence-loving society. What problems has this love of violence created? Is handgun registration the answer to our problems, or does Smith believe that other important issues need to be addressed?

8. Has Smith organized his argument inductively or deductively? Explain.

Exploring the Issues in This Essay

1. Smith believes that in order to solve the problem of violence in America we as a society must "do something about our ragged system of criminal justice, to shore up our declining faith in the institutions that are supposed to protect us, and to promote the notion that people should take responsibility for their own actions." How effective have police been in controlling crime and protecting citizens from criminals? What, if anything, has hampered them in their efforts? Why have the people in certain communities taken to arming themselves?

2. Discuss the issues that would have to be addressed when drafting a law that would either call for the registration of handguns or prohibit private citizens from owning handguns. For example, how would you get people to register guns they currently own, or how would you take those same guns completely out of circulation? How would you enforce the law? And what would be an appropriate penalty for violation of the law?

Robert Hughes

The NRA in a Hunter's Sights

A native of Sydney, Australia, Robert Hughes studied art and architecture at the University of Sydney during the late 1950s. Since 1970, Hughes has been an art critic for Time *magazine and the author of several books of art criticism, most notably* Heaven and Hell in Western Art *(1970) and* The Shock of the New *(1981). Hughes, however, is probably best known for his critically acclaimed* The Fatal Shore *(1987), an epic volume that recounts the colonization of Australia in carefully researched and dramatic detail.*

Given his first hunting rifle at the age of 11 by his father, Hughes has been a hunter ever since. He knows first hand the destructive power of guns and the respect that must be given them to ensure their proper use. Surprisingly Hughes, in the following essay which first appeared in Time *in 1989, strikes out against the National Rifle Association, an organization traditionally thought to be the hunter's friend and advocate.*

1   Like George Bush and thousands of other people, I am a Small White Hunter. Which means that, two or three times a year, one scrambles into one's brush pants and jacket, pulls on a pair of snake boots and goes ambling off on a sedate horse with friends and dogs in pursuit of quail in a pine forest in southern Georgia. Or spends cold predawn hours in a punt on Long Island Sound, or a damp blind on a California marsh, waiting for the gray light to spread and the ducks to come arrowing in.

2   In have done this at intervals most of my life, ever since I was eleven years old in Australia and my father first issued me a single-shot .22 and two bullets and told me to bring back one rabbit. I hope to keep doing it as long as I can walk and see.

3   I don't shoot deer anymore; the idea of large-game trophy hunting repels me. But I have never thought there was anything wrong with killing as much small game in one day as I and a few friends could eat in the evening—no more than that and always within

the limits. On a good day I can break 24 targets out of 25 at trap-shooting and 22 or so at skeet, which is O.K. for an art critic.

4   In short, I am supposed—if you believe the advertisements of the National Rifle Association—to be exactly the kind of person whose rights the N.R.A. claims to want to protect. Why, then, have I never joined the N.R.A.? And why do I think of this once omnipotent though now embattled lobby as the sportsman's embarrassment and not his ally?

5   The answer, in part, goes back to the famous Second Amendment of the American Constitution, which the N.R.A. keeps brandishing like Holy Writ. "A well-regulated militia, being necessary to the security of a free State," it reads, "the right of the people to keep and bear arms shall not be infringed."

6   The part the N.R.A. quotes is always the second half. The first half is less convenient because it undermines the lobby's propaganda for universal weaponry.

7   The Founding Fathers, in their wisdom—and more pointedly, their experience—distrusted standing armies. They associated British ones with tyranny and lacked the money and manpower to create their own. Without a citizens' militia, the Revolution would have failed. Does the Constitution let you have the second half of the Second Amendment, the right to keep and bear arms, without the first part, the intended use of those arms in the exercises and when necessary, the campaigns of a citizens' militia to which the gun owner belongs—as in Switzerland today? That is still very much a subject for legal debate.

8   The constitutional framers no more had in mind the socially psychotic prospect of every Tom, Dick and Harriet with a barnful of MAC–10s. Saturday night specials and AK–47s than, in writing the First Amendment, they had in mind the protection of child-porn video, which did not exist in the 18th century either. Nowhere does the Constitution say the right to bear arms means the right to bear any or all arms. *Which* arms is the real issue. At present, firepower has outstripped the law's power to contain it within rational limits.

9   Where the N.R.A. has always revealed its nature as a paranoid lobby, a political anachronism, is in its rigid ideological belief that *any* restriction on the private ownership of *any* kind of hand-held gun leads inexorably to *total* abolition of *all* gun ownership—that, if today the U.S. Government takes the Kalashnikov from the hands of the maniac on the school playground, it will be coming for my

Winchester pump tomorrow. There is no evidence for this absurd belief, but it remains an article of faith. And it does so because the faith is bad faith: the stand the N.R.A. takes is only nominally on behalf of recreational hunters. The people it really serves are gun manufacturers and gun importers, whose sole interest is to sell as many deadly weapons of as many kinds to as many Americans as possible. The N.R.A. never saw a weapon it didn't love. When American police officers raised their voices against the sale of "cop-killer" bullets—Teflon-coated projectiles whose sole purpose is to penetrate body armor—the N.R.A. mounted a campaign to make people believe this ban would infringe on the rights of deer hunters as though the woods of America were full of white-tails in Kevlar vests. Now that the pressure is on to restrict public ownership of semiautomatic assault weapons, we hear the same threadbare rhetoric about the rights of hunters. No serious hunter goes after deer with an Uzi or an AK–47; those weapons are not made for picking off an animal in the woods but for blowing people to chopped meat at close-to-medium range, and anyone who needs a banana clip with 30 shells in it to hit a buck should not be hunting at all. These guns have only two uses: you can take them down to the local range and spend a lot of money blasting off 500 rounds an afternoon at silhouette targets of the Ayatullah, or you can use them to off your rivals and create lots of police widows. It depends on what kind of guy you are. But the N.R.A. doesn't care—underneath its dumb incantatory slogans ("Guns don't kill people: people kill people"), it is defending both guys. It helps ensure that cops are outgunned right across America. It preaches hunters' rights in order to defend the distribution of weapons in what is, in effect, a drug-based civil war.

10   But we who love hunting have much more to fear from the backlash of public opinion caused by the N.R.A.'s pigheadedness than we do from the Government. Sensible hunters see the need to follow the example of other civilized countries. All fireable guns should be licensed: delays and stringent checks should be built into their purchase, right across the board: and some types, including machine guns and semiautomatic assault weapons, should not be available to the civilian public at all. It is time, in this respect, that America enter the 20th century, since it is only a few years away from the 21st.

Analyzing the Writer's Argument

1. In the first three paragraphs, Hughes gives us some information about himself. What bearing, if any, does this information have on his argument?

2. The N.R.A. regularly invokes the Second Amendment of the Constitution when arguing against gun control. Why, according to Hughes, does the N.R.A. refuse to quote the entire Second Amendment?

3. Does the information Hughes provides in paragraph 9 support his claim that the N.R.A. is a "paranoid lobby, a political anachronism"? Explain.

4. In paragraph 4, Hughes asks several questions. How do these questions function in the context of his argument and how does he answer them?

5. Hughes freely uses emotionally charged language in his essay. For example, in paragraph 10, he refers to the N.R.A.'s 'pigheadedness" and in paragraph 9 he calls its slogans "dumb." Locate several other examples of such language. Collectively, what do they add or detract from the forcefulness of his argument? Explain.

6. Paragraph 9 is an extremely long paragraph. How is the paragraph organized? What would be gained or lost if the paragraph had been divided into several shorter paragraphs?

7. Hughes claims that the N.R.A. "helps ensure that cops are outgunned right across America. It preaches hunters' rights in order to defend the distribution of weapons in what is, in effect, a drug-based civil war." How does he document these claims?

Exploring the Issues in This Essay

1. Hughes claims that the N.R.A. is, in effect, hiding behind the nation's hunters, while actually promoting the profit motives of gun merchants. Who has the most to lose if gun-control legislation is enacted? Will gun merchants really suffer? Will hunters really be restricted by such laws?

2. Consider the advertisement for the National Rifle Association that appears on p. 390. Discuss what messages the ad conveys about N.R.A. membership. Does the ad surprise you in any way? Explain.

Gerald Nachman

Biting the Bullets

A graduate of San Jose State, Gerald Nachman was born in Oakland, California, in 1938. Nachman got his start in the newspaper business with the San Jose Mercury *as a humorist and television critic. Most recently, he has written an entertainment column for the* San Francisco Chronicle. *His newspaper writing has been recognized with the Page One Award in 1965 and the Associated Press Feature-Writing Award in 1974. Nachman is the author of two books,* Playing House *(1977) and* Out on a Whim: Some Very Close Brushes With Life *(1983).*

Nachman is equally at home writing about politics, social issues, and fashion. But he's at his best when he brings his humor to bear on a serious topic. In "Biting the Bullets," taken from Out on a Whim, *Nachman takes aim at the gun-control debate, and none of the participants in the fray escapes his humorous and sometimes not-so-gentle satire.*

1   After a seventeen-year study, my sub-subcommittee on gun control has come up with a compromise solution: bullet control.

2   By banning the large-scale sale of bullets, gun owners may keep their weapons, the average person (or squirrel) will be safe and criminals won't have to go around empty-handed.

3   It will, of course, still be possible to get conked over the head with a gun butt, but this is just a first step. The agreement should satisfy everyone except perhaps the hard-to-please National Bullet Association and its 728 members.

4   The ban on bullets will work this way: Starting in 1984, all cartridges fired by "Saturday-night specials" will be illegal—however, so as not to annoy the powerful pro-ammo lobby and collectors of antique bullets, all other ammunition will still be readily available.

5   By 1990, all bullets fired by "Sunday-through-Tuesday-night specials" will be outlawed (except in woodsy states).

6   Bullet control is designed to mollify the rifle groups whose favorite slogan is "Guns don't kill people—people kill people." When the committee looked into this, it found that, in actual (target) practice, bullets kill people.

7   The committee also discovered that, to inflict any real damage, the bullet should be inside a gun. To test this, several marksmen tried to pick off a moving target by *throwing* bullets at it. Results showed that the bullets merely ricocheted off the man and he escaped with only a few nicks.

8   When the same test was tried using bullets fired from a gun, however, the fellow died (presumably from the bullets). The committee concluded that guns and bullets can be hazardous to your health when "used in connection with each other," as our report phrases it. To be on the safe side, though, the committee temporarily recommends a twenty-minute "cooling off" period for people purchasing bullets.

9   As it now stands, any nut can walk into a gun shop and buy enough lead to wipe out a small town. Until the new law goes into effect, a ruling will require "all nuts to be registered and forced to cool their heels for half an hour."

10   Another popular riflemen's slogan—"When guns are outlawed, only outlaws will have guns"—is true enough, the committee agreed, but many outlaws who testified before the committee said they're willing to give bullet control a try.

11   "Look," said one gangster, "we hate to be unreasonable about this, but we'd look pretty dumb wandering around the streets without a gun. We can be every bit as terrifying with an empty .38 and then at least we won't be booked for carrying a loaded weapon."

12   Sub-subcommittee members foresee a day when Congress may pass a measure banning guns with handles and, eventually, triggers. Gradually, the entire gun will be phased out of existence, a part at a time. Remarks one congressman, "There's no reason to rush into this gun-control thing helter-skelter."

Analyzing the Writer's Argument

   1. What is Nachman's purpose in this essay? How do you know? Explain.

2. Why do you suppose Nachman chose to treat a serious issue like gun control in the way that he did? How did you react to his humor? Did it make his argument more or less effective for you? Explain.

3. According to Nachman, who are the participants in the gun-control debate? What criticism does he level at each of them?

4. Analyze Nachman's humor in this essay. What passages are particularly funny for you? Why did you find them funny? What are the sources of Nachman's humor?

5. What audience do you think Nachman had in mind when he wrote this essay? The N.R.A.? The antigun lobby? A general readership? A politically savvy readership? How do you know?

Exploring the Issues in This Essay

1. Two of the slogans used by progun groups become the butt of Nachman's humor in this essay. What other "gun-control" slogans have you heard or seen on bumper stickers lately? Analyze each of these slogans. What does each seem to be saying? How much truth is contained in each, or are they all "near truths" or "half truths"? What do you think gives them their persuasive power?

2. What is the place of humor in the arena of serious issues? When is it appropriate? When isn't it? What makes a humorous approach to a serious topic more persuasive or more effective than a straightforward, practical one? Does humor make criticism more palatable? Explain.

Writing Suggestions for
Gun Control: The Right to Bear Arms

1. Assume that you are a member of the N.R.A. Write an essay in which you argue against Hughes' criticism.

2. One of the sticking points in the gun-control debate involves the interpretation of the language of our Constitution's Second Amendment. Using information provided by Kennedy, Goldwater, and Smith, write an essay in which you argue for either a strict literal interpretation or a looser interpretation that takes into account the fact that the Amendment was written over two hundred years ago.

3. In a recent article entitled "The Right to Bear Arms" (*Parade Magazine*, January 14, 1990), Warren E. Burger, Chief Justice of the United States (1969–86), uses the following analogy to argue for the regulation of guns: "Is there any question that a citizen has the right to own and keep an automobile? Yet we accept the state's power to regulate its purchase and to license the vehicle and its driver. Should guns be any different?" Write an essay in which you argue for the registration and licensing of firearms. Be sure to consider arguments to the contrary presented in the Goldwater selection.

4. Jim Brady received a near fatal wound to the head when, along with President Reagan, he was shot by John Hinckley on March 30, 1981. The Brady Handgun Violence Prevention Act, popularly known as the Brady Bill in honor of Jim and Sarah Brady was introduced to the 100th Congress and came close to passage. The bill requires a seven-day waiting period for handgun purchases from gun dealers. The waiting period would give local police the opportunity to run a background check on the purchases and provide a "cooling off" period for individuals seeking to settle heated disputes with handguns or for those who in a moment of despondency decide to buy a handgun to take their own lives. Write an essay in which you consider the benefits of such legislation. Be sure to consider why someone might find the legislation a restriction on his or her freedom.

5. Spend enough time in the library to collect current information about the success or failure experienced by countries that have enacted gun-control legislation. On the basis of what you find in the library and what you have read in this section, write an argument for or against such national legislation in this country.

6. Review the gun laws in your state. If you believe that they are inadequate, what would you propose to strengthen them? Write a letter to your state legislator(s) arguing for your proposal.

7. A recent survey in *The Wall Street Journal* indicated that police chiefs favor stricter gun-control measures. Seventy-two percent favored legislation banning the manufacture, sale, and possession of semi-automatic assault guns, such as the AK-47. Interview a member of your local police force in order to learn what he or she thinks about such weapons and gun control in general. How, for example, do these military weapons affect the way the police go about their jobs. Summarize in writing what you have learned from your interview and share it with the members of your class. Do the views of Goldwater and Smith reflect what you have learned from your interview?

8. Using the selections presented in this unit, write an essay in which you argue your own stance on the gun-control issue. What for you is the heart of the problem? What would you like to see done? Why, and how would you go about doing it?

9. All the attention in the gun-control debate is focused on handguns? Why handguns? What differentiates them from other kinds of guns? Are handguns inherently more dangerous? Using the articles in this section, write a position paper arguing for restrictions on the sale of handguns but not other types of guns commonly used for hunting or sport.

10

Crime, Criminals, and Victims

In July, 1988, writer Robert James Bidinotto wrote "Getting Away with Murder," a compelling article about prison furlough programs. The article recounted the story of Willie Horton who had been convicted for the brutal murder of 17-year-old Joey Fournier in 1974. In 1986 Horton was released on furlough from prison and on the evening of April 3, 1987, he assaulted Clifford Barnes for seven hours. After brutally punching, pistol-whipping, and lacerating his midsection, he bound and gagged him. Angela Miller, Barnes's fiancee, arrived home later that night and, according to Bidinotto, "Cliff listened in helpless horror to Angi's screams as Horton savagely attacked her. For four hours, she was assaulted, tied up, and twice raped." The Willie Horton story subsequently became the cornerstone of the Republican party's controversial but successful television ad campaign against Massachusetts Governor Michael Dukakis, a strong advocate of the furlough program. Some people believe that Bidinotto's article changed the course of the presidential race by dramatically tapping a major public concern.

On March 11, 1989, the *New York Times* ran a retrospective story on the celebrated murder of Catherine "Kitty" Genovese. Twenty-five years earlier in an article entitled "38 Who Saw Murder Didn't Call Police" (pp. 482–484) *Times* reporter Martin Gansberg began his coverage of the murder with this sentence: "For more than half an hour 38 respectable law-abiding citizens in Queens watched a killer stalk and stab a woman in three separate attacks in Kew Gardens." The story stunned New Yorkers and people around the world and has since achieved almost mythic stature. Kitty Genovese's name is still invoked whenever and wherever people lament the loss of public decency. Her murder has become synonymous with the apathy of modern urban life.

The two stories are revealing. The Horton story shows that people are angry about crime, they are fed up with the leniency of the criminal justice system in releasing hardened criminals, and they want their public officials to do something. The Kitty Genovese story shows us that people are, as well, understandably afraid to take action themselves, or, worse yet, they are sadly apathetic about those whose lives are in danger. Simply put, people just don't want to get involved.

By its very nature, crime is not meant to be public. Many crimes go undetected and unreported. Frequently victims are too terrified or embarrassed to go to the authorities. As a result crime statistics are incomplete at best and therefore difficult to interpret. Nonetheless, the FBI Uniform Crime Report can give some indication of the size of the crime problem in the United States. In 1988, for example, 13.9 million crimes were reported, a 2.1 percent increase over 1987. Overall violent crimes increased by 4.5 percent and property crimes increased by 1.8 percent over 1987 statistics. Perhaps it is easier to grasp the enormity of the problem from the Report's 1988 "Crime Clock" which gives some idea of the frequency with which crimes are committed on average in the United States:

- One violent crime every 20 seconds
- One property crime every 3 seconds
- One murder every 25 minutes
- One forcible rape every 6 minutes
- One robbery every minute
- One aggravated assault every 35 seconds
- One larceny theft every 4 seconds
- One motor vehicle theft every 22 seconds

The high rate of crime is a clear problem. Not so clear, however, is how to resolve the controversies that surround crime in America. Debates continue on whether heredity or environment is the cause of crime, how to reduce the incidence of crime, how best to punish criminals, who should be incarcerated, what attempts should be made to rehabilitate offenders, what role drugs play in violent crimes, what should be done about violence directed toward women, how big a problem date rape is and what should be done about it, what methods should be used to curtail teenage offenses, and what role law enforcement should play in cases of domestic violence. Each year we have to struggle with more criminal activity and greater complexity growing from it.

Brent Staples

A Brother's Murder

Brent Staples was born in 1951 in Chester, Pennsylvania, an industrial city southwest of Philadelphia. He earned his B.A. degree in 1973 from Widener University in Chester and his Ph.D. in Psychology from the University of Chicago in 1982. He has taught school, been a reporter for the Chicago Sun-Times, *an editor of the* New York Times Book Review, *and is currently assistant metropolitan editor of the* New York Times. *His first book,* Parallel Time, *is scheduled for publication early in 1991. Staples now lives in Brooklyn.*

In the following essay, first published in the New York Times Magazine, *Staples poignantly reflects on the power of the black male machismo world that he was fortunate to escape but that so tragically destroyed his younger brother.*

1   It has been more than two years since my telephone rang with the news that my younger brother Blake—just twenty-two years old—had been murdered. The young man who killed him was only twenty-four. Wearing a ski mask, he emerged from a car, fired six times at close range with a massive .44 Magnum, then fled. The two had once been inseparable friends. A senseless rivalry—beginning, I think, with an argument over a girlfriend—escalated from posturing, to threats, to violence, to murder. The way the two were living, death could have come to either of them from anywhere. In fact, the assailant had already survived multiple gunshot wounds from an accident much like the one in which my brother lost his life.

2   As I wept for Blake I felt wrenched backward into events and circumstances that had seemed light-years gone. Though a decade apart, we both were raised in Chester, Pennsylvania, an angry, heavily black, heavily poor, industrial city southwest of Philadelphia. There, in the 1960s, I was introduced to mortality, not by the old and failing, but by beautiful young men who lay wrecked after sudden explosions of violence. The first, I remembered from

410

my fourteenth year—Johnny, brash lover of fast cars, stabbed to death two doors from my house in a fight over a pool game. The next year, my teenage cousin, Wesley, whom I loved very much, was shot dead. The summers blur. Milton, an angry young neighbor, shot a crosstown rival, wounding him badly. William, another teenage neighbor, took a shotgun blast to the shoulder in some urban drama and displayed his bandages proudly. His brother, Leonard, severely beaten, lost an eye and donned a black patch. It went on.

3   I recall not long before I left for college, two local Vietnam veterans—one from the Marines, one from the Army—arguing fiercely, nearly at blows about which outfit had done the most in the war. The most killing, they meant. Not much later, I read a magazine article that set that dispute in a context. In the story, a noncommissioned officer—a sergeant, I believe—said he would pass up any number of affluent, suburban-born recruits to get hard-core soldiers from the inner city. They jumped into the rice paddies with "their manhood on their sleeves," I believe he said. These two items—the veterans arguing and the sergeant's words— still characterize for me the circumstances under which black men in their teens and twenties kill one another with such frequency. With a touchy paranoia born of living battered lives, they are desperate to be *real* men. Killing is only machismo taken to the extreme. Incursions to be punished by death were many and minor, and they remain so: they include stepping on the wrong toe, literally; cheating in a drug deal; simply saying "I dare you" to someone holding a gun; crossing territorial lines in a gang dispute. My brother grew up to wear his manhood on his sleeve. And when he died, he was in that group—black, male and in its teens and early twenties—that is far and away the most likely to murder or be murdered.

4   I left the East Coast after college, spent the mid- and late 1970s in Chicago as a graduate student, taught for a time, then became a journalist. Within ten years of leaving my hometown, I was overeducated and "upwardly mobile," ensconced on a quiet, tree-lined street where voices raised in anger were scarcely ever heard. The telephone, like some grim umbilical, kept me connected to the old world with news of deaths, imprisonings and misfortune. I felt emotionally beaten up. Perhaps to protect myself, I added a

psychological dimension to the physical distance I had already achieved. I rarely visited my hometown. I shut it out.

5   As I fled the past, so Blake embraced it. On Christmas of 1983, I traveled from Chicago to a black section of Roanoke, Virginia, where he then lived. The desolate public housing projects, the hopeless, idle young men crashing against one another—these reminded me of the embittered town we'd grown up in. It was a place where once I would have been comfortable, or at least sure of myself. Now, hearing of my brother's forays into crime, his scrapes with police and street thugs, I was scared, unsteady on foreign terrain.

6   I saw that Blake's romance with the street life and the hustler image had flowered dangerously. One evening that late December, standing in some Roanoke dive among drug dealers and grim, hair-trigger losers, I told him I feared for his life. He had affected the image of the tough he wanted to be. But behind the dark glasses and the swagger, I glimpsed the baby-faced toddler I'd once watched over. I nearly wept. I wanted desperately for him to live. The young think themselves immortal, and a dangerous light shone in his eyes as he spoke laughingly of making fools of the policemen who had raided his apartment looking for drugs. He cried out as I took his right hand. A line of stitches lay between the thumb and index finger. Kickback from a shotgun, he explained, nothing serious. Gunplay had become part of his life.

7   I lacked the language simply to say: Thousands have lived this for you and died. I fought the urge to lift him bodily and shake him. This place and the way you are living smells of death to me, I said. Take some time away, I said. Let's go downtown tomorrow and buy a plane ticket anywhere, take a bus trip, anything to get away and cool things off. He took my alarm casually. We arranged to meet the following night—an appointment he would not keep. We embraced as though through glass. I drove away.

8   As I stood in my apartment in Chicago holding the receiver that evening in February 1984, I felt as though part of my soul had been cut away. I questioned myself then, and I still do. Did I not reach back soon enough or earnestly enough for him? For weeks I awoke crying from a recurrent dream in which I chased him, urgently trying to get him to read a document I had, as though reading it would protect him from what had happened in waking

life. His eyes shining like black diamonds, he smiled and danced just beyond my grasp. When I reached for him, I caught only the space where he had been.

Analyzing the Writer's Argument

1. How and where was Staples introduced to mortality?
2. What point does Staples attempt to make with the story of the two Vietnam veterans and the sergeant? What is the "touchy paranoia" that he refers to in paragraph 3? What does he mean when he writes that "killing is only machismo taken to the extreme"?
3. What made Staples' life different from his brother's? What was he able to do in order to survive? Is there a survival lesson in what he did?
4. In paragraph 7 Staples writes that he wished he had said to his brother, "Thousands have lived this for you and died." What does he mean?
5. Staples' title contains a thought-provoking ambiguity. What is it? Discuss the effectiveness of the various meanings of the word *brother*, especially in the black community.
6. In his dream, Staples said that he tried to get his brother to read a document. What do you think that document was?
7. What is the meaning of Staples' last line? Does he mean to imply that there was nothing he could have done for Blake? Explain.

Exploring the Issues in This Essay

1. What is machismo? How does it develop? Is it inherently and inevitably violent? Is it a cultural trait or something individually determined? Why do you think that Brent was able to escape it, but Blake unable to do so? Is machismo a sign of something wrong with the society in which it develops?
2. What responsibility does each of us have in society's response to crime? Can we somehow work with individuals in society who are misguided or susceptible to the "romance of street life and the hustler image," as Staples puts it, or is intervention of this sort futile? Do we need, instead, to approach the problem of crime on a social level? Staples claims the community in which he and his brother grew up was angry and poor, and that Roanoke reminded

him of Chester. Can we solve the crime problem by providing jobs and reducing poverty, by revitalizing areas that seem to encourage bitterness and violent behavior?

3. One classic debate on crime centers on whether it is heredity or environment that prompts criminal behavior. Discuss the extent to which Staples in his essay sheds light on this question? Of presumably the same parentage and certainly of the same background (there was a ten-year difference in age), these two men turned out very differently. What are your own thoughts and feelings about the heredity/environment controversy in this particular context?

Martin Gansberg

38 Who Saw Murder Didn't Call the Police

The New York Times *published the following article on March 17, 1964, two weeks after the events described in it actually occurred. Since that time this newspaper story has been reprinted many times, and the name Kitty Genovese has become almost synonymous with the issue of public apathy with regard to street crime. The account is an argument, in story form and in simple terms, for people to take notice of what is happening in their neighborhoods and to take appropriate action if a fellow citizen is in trouble and needs help.*

Martin Gansberg was born in Brooklyn, New York, in 1920 and graduated from St. John's University. A long-time editor and reporter for the Times, *he has written for a number of popular magazines and served on the faculty of Fairleigh Dickinson University in New Jersey.*

1   For more than half an hour 38 respectable, law-abiding citizens in Queens watched a killer stalk and stab a woman in three separate attacks in Kew Gardens.

2   Twice their chatter and the sudden glow of their bedroom lights interrupted him and frightened him off. Each time he returned, sought her out, and stabbed her again. Not one person telephoned the police during the assault; one witness called after the woman was dead.

3   That was two weeks ago today.

4   Still shocked is Assistant Chief Inspector Frederick M. Lussen, in charge of the borough's detectives and a veteran of 25 years of homicide investigations. He can give a matter-of-fact recitation on many murders. But the Kew Gardens slaying baffles him—not because it is a murder, but because the "good people" failed to call the police.

5   "As we have reconstructed the crime," he said, "the assailant had three chances to kill this woman during a 35-minute period. He returned twice to complete the job. If we had been called when he first attacked, the woman might not be dead now."

6   This is what the police say happened beginning at 3:20 A.M. in the staid, middle-class, tree-lined Austin Street area:

7   Twenty-eight-year-old Catherine Genovese, who was called Kitty by almost everyone in the neighborhood, was returning home from her job as manager of a bar in Hollis. She parked her red Fiat in a lot adjacent to the Kew Gardens Long Island Rail Road Station, facing Mowbray Place. Like many residents of the neighborhood, she had parked there day after day since her arrival from Connecticut a year ago, although the railroad frowns on the practice.

8   She turned off the lights of her car, locked the door, and started to walk the 100 feet to the entrance of her apartment at 82–70 Austin Street, which is in a Tudor building, with stores in the first floor and apartments on the second.

9   The entrance to the apartment is in the rear of the building because the front is rented to retail stores. At night the quiet neighborhood is shrouded in the slumbering darkness that marks most residential areas.

10   Miss Genovese noticed a man at the far end of the lot, near a seven-story apartment house at 82–40 Austin Street. She halted. Then, nervously, she headed up Austin Street toward Lefferts Boulevard, where there is a call box to the 102nd Police Precinct in nearby Richmond Hill.

11   She got as far as a street light in front of a bookstore before the man grabbed her. She screamed. Lights went on in the 10-story apartment house at 82–67 Austin Street, which faces the bookstore. Windows slid open and voices punctuated the early-morning stillness.

12   Miss Genovese screamed: "Oh, my God, he stabbed me! Please help me! Please help me!"

13   From one of the upper windows in the apartment house, a man called down: "Let that girl alone!"

14   The assailant looked up at him, shrugged, and walked down Austin Street toward a white sedan parked a short distance away. Miss Genovese struggled to her feet.

15 Lights went out. The killer returned to Miss Genovese, now trying to make her way around the side of the building by the parking lot to get to her apartment. The assailant stabbed her again.

16 "I'm dying!" she shrieked. "I'm dying!"

17 Windows were opened again, and lights went on in many apartments. The assailant got into his car and drove away. Miss Genovese staggered to her feet. A city bus, Q-10, the Lefferts Boulevard line to Kennedy International Airport, passed. It was 3:35 A.M.

18 The assailant returned. By then, Miss Genovese had crawled to the back of the building, where the freshly painted brown doors to the apartment house held out hope for safety. The killer tried the first door; she wasn't there. At the second door, 82–62 Austin Street, he saw her slumped on the floor at the foot of the stairs. He stabbed her a third time—fatally.

19 It was 3:50 by the time the police received their first call, from a man who was a neighbor of Miss Genovese. In two minutes they were at the scene. The neighbor, a 70-year-old woman, and another woman were the only persons on the street. Nobody else came forward.

20 The man explained that he had called the police after much deliberation. He had phoned a friend in Nassau County for advice and then he had crossed the roof of the building to the apartment of the elderly woman to get her to make the call.

21 "I didn't want to get involved," he sheepishly told the police.

22 Six days later, the police arrested Winston Moseley, a 29-year-old business-machine operator, and charged him with homicide. Moseley had no previous record. He is married, has two children and owns a home at 133–19 Sutter Avenue, South Ozone Park, Queens. On Wednesday, a court committed him to Kings County Hospital for psychiatric observation.

23 When questioned by the police, Moseley also said that he had slain Mrs. Annie May Johnson, 24, of 146–12 133rd Avenue, Jamaica, on Feb. 29 and Barbara Kralik, 15, of 174–17 140th Avenue, Springfield Gardens, last July. In the Kralik case, the police are holding Alvin L. Mitchell, who is said to have confessed that slaying.

24 The police stressed how simple it would have been to have gotten in touch with them. "A phone call," said one of the detectives, "would have done it." The police may be reached by dialing "0" for operator or SPring 7-3100.

25 Today witnesses from the neighborhood, which is made up of one-family homes in the $35,000 to $60,000 range with the exception of the two apartment houses near the railroad station, find it difficult to explain why they didn't call the police.

26 A housewife, knowingly if quite casually, said, "We thought it was a lovers' quarrel." A husband and wife both said, "Frankly, we were afraid." They seemed aware of the fact that events might have been different. A distraught woman, wiping her hands in her apron, said, "I didn't want my husband to get involved."

27 One couple, now willing to talk about that night, said they heard the first screams. The husband looked thoughtfully at the bookstore where the killer first grabbed Miss Genovese.

28 "We went to the window to see what was happening," he said, "but the light from our bedroom made it difficult to see the street." The wife, still apprehensive, added: "I put out the light and we were able to see better."

29 Asked why they hadn't called the police, she shrugged and replied: "I don't know."

30 A man peeked out from a slight opening in the doorway to his apartment and rattled off an account of the killer's second attack. Why hadn't he called the police at the time? "I was tired," he said without emotion. "I went back to bed."

31 It was 4:25 A.M. when the ambulance arrived to take the body of Miss Genovese. It drove off. "Then," a solemn police detective said, "the people came out."

Analyzing the Writer's Argument

1. What do you think Gansberg's purpose is in this news account? Do you think he accomplished it?
2. Review the reasons the victim's neighbors gave for not helping her and for not calling the police. What do these comments tell us about crime and about the way people in an urban area view their obligations to the community?
3. Gansberg uses narration to get his point across. Is narration an effective strategy for argumentation in this selection? Explain.
4. The author uses quite a bit of dialogue in this article. What does he accomplish by using it?
5. Does Gansberg tell us what he thinks about the situation he reports? Explain.

6. Discuss Gansberg's tone in this article? Is it sentimental? Distanced? Concerned? How do you know?
7. Is Gansberg's conclusion an effective one? Why or why not?
8. Why do you think that the criminal returned several times to the scene of the crime? Did he fear getting caught? Why or why not?

Exploring the Issues in This Essay

1. Gansberg's account of the murder of Kitty Genovese is about public apathy. What is wrong with apathy? Do you think our present society is still apathetic or have things changed? Explain.
2. Gansberg said the police stressed how easy it would have been for someone to call them. Do people generally place a lot of faith in the ability of the police to safeguard them? Why or why not? Is involvement with the police "simple," or is it often more complicated than we might think? Have you had any experiences as a good samaritan in reporting dangerous situations to the police? How have they turned out? Were there ever situations that you wish you did report to the police? Explain.
3. To what extent is a crime such as the one Gansberg reports a matter of geographic location? In other words, do you think such a thing could happen in small-town America? In a "well-to-do" suburb?

"It's people like you, young man, who ruin it for everyone else!"

Drawing by Ziegler; © 1990 *The New Yorker* Magazine, Inc.

Ellen Sweet

Date Rape: The Story of an Epidemic and Those Who Deny It

Ellen Sweet was born in 1942 in Newark, New Jersey. A freelance writer and editor specializing in family and parenting issues she earned her B.A. from Smith College and her M.A. from Yale University, both in English. Following college she taught high school English for several years before becoming an editor at Ms. *Magazine. While in that capacity Sweet oversaw the* Ms. *Magazine Campus Project on Sexual Assault and was a consulting editor of* I Never Called It Rape *(1988), a book on date rape. Sweet's own writing has appeared in* Ms., Redbook, *and the family magazine,* Special Reports. *She is currently the managing editor of the magazine* New Choices for the Best Years.*

In the following article, Sweet explores the subject of date, or acquaintance, rape with the hope of making people aware of its existence, especially on the nation's campuses. She defines it, gives examples, and attempts to uncover its causes, as well as suggests some possible ways in which men and women can begin to remedy the dangerous attitudes and behavior it represents.

1   Let's call this Yale graduate Judy. Her experience and her disbelief, as she describes them, are not unique. Gretchen, another student victim of date rape (or acquaintance rape, as it is also called), had known for five years the man who invited her to an isolated vacation cabin and then raped her. "I considered him my best friend," she says on a Stanford University videotape used in discussions of the problem. "I couldn't believe it. *I couldn't believe it was actually happening to me.*"

2   Such denial, the inability to believe that someone they know could have raped them, is a common reaction of victims of date

421

rape, say psychologists and counselors who have researched the topic and treated these women. In fact, so much silence surrounds this kind of crime that many women are not even aware that they have been raped. In one study, Mary P. Koss, a psychology professor at Kent State University, Ohio, asked female students if they had had sexual intercourse against their will through use of or threat of force (the minimal legal definition of rape). Of those who answered yes, only 57 percent went on to identify their experience as rape. Koss also identified the other group (43 percent) as those who hadn't even acknowledged the rape to themselves.

3   "I can't believe it's happening on our campus," is usually the initial response to reports such as Koss's. She also found that one in eight women students had been raped, and another one in four were victims of attempted rape. Since only 4 percent of all those reported the attack, Koss concluded that "at least ten times more rapes occur among college students than are reflected in official crime statistics." (Rape is recognized to be the most underreported of all crimes, and date rape is among the least reported, least believed, and most difficult to prosecute, second only to spouse rape.)

4   Working independently of Koss, researchers at Auburn University, Alabama, and more recently, University of South Dakota and St. Cloud State University, Minnesota, all have found that one in five women students were raped by men they knew.

5   Koss also found a core group of highly sexually aggressive men (4.3 percent) who use physical force to compel women to have intercourse but who are unlikely to see their act as rape. These "hidden rapists" have "oversubscribed" to traditional male roles, she says. They believe that aggression is normal and that women don't really mean it when they say no to sexual advances. Such men answer "True" to statements like "most women are sly and manipulating when they want to attract a man," "a woman will only respect a man who will lay down the law to her," and "a man's got to show the woman who's boss right from the start or he'll end up henpecked."

6   In Koss's current study, one respondent who answered yes to a question about obtaining intercourse through physical force, wrote in the comment, "I didn't rape the chick, she was enjoying it and responding," and later, "I feel that sex is a very pleasant way to relieve stress. Especially when there are no strings attached."

7   "He acted like he had a right, like he *didn't believe me*," says a coed from Auburn University on a videotaped dramatization of data rape experiences. And several weeks later, when she confronts him, saying he forced her, he says no, she wanted it. "You raped me," she finally tells him. And the picture freezes on his look of incredulity.

8   Barry Burkhart, a professor of psychology at Auburn, who has also studied sexual aggression among college men, found that 10 percent had used physical force to have intercourse with a woman against her will, and a large majority admitted to various other kinds of aggression. "These are ordinary males operating in an ordinary social context," he says. "So what we conclude is that there's something wrong with that social context."

9   The something wrong is that our culture fosters a "rape supportive belief system," according to social psychologist Martha Burt. She thinks that "there's a large category of 'real' rapes, and a much smaller category of what our culture is willing to call a 'real' rape. The question is, how does the culture manage to write off all those other rapes?" The way is done, says Burt, currently director of the Social Services Research Center at the Urban Institute in Washington, D.C., is by believing in a series of myths about rape, including:

- It didn't really happen (the woman was lying);
- Women like rape (so there's no such thing as rape);
- Yes, it happened, but no harm was done (she wasn't a virgin; she wasn't white);
- Women provoke it (men can't control themselves);
- Women deserve it anyway.

10   It's easy to write off date rapes with such myths, coupled with what Burt calls our culture's "adversarial sexual beliefs": the gamesmanship theory that everybody is out for what they can get, and that all sexual relationships are basically exploitive and predatory. In fact, most victims of date rape initially blame themselves for what happened, and almost none report it to campus authorities. And most academic institutions prefer to keep it that way, judging from the lack of surveys on date rape—all of which makes one wonder if they don't actually blame the victim, too.

11   As long as such attacks continue to be a "hidden" campus phenomenon, unreported and unacknowledged by many college administrators, law enforcement personnel, and students, the problem will persist. Of course, the term has become much better
known in the three years since *Ms.* reported on the prevalence
of experiences such as Judy's and Gretchen's. (See "Date Rape: A
Campus Epidemic?" September 1982.) It has been the subject of
talk shows such as "The Donahue Show" and TV dramas ("Cagney
and Lacey"). But for most people it remains a contradiction in
terms. "Everybody has a stake in denying that it's happening so
often," says Martha Burt. "For women, it's self-protective . . . if only
bad girls get raped, then I'm personally safe. For men, it's the denial that 'nice' people like them do it."

12   The fault has not entirely been that of the institutions. "Ten years
ago, we were telling women to look over your shoulder when you
go out at night and lock your doors," says Py Bateman, director of
a nationally known rape education program in Seattle, Alternatives
to Fear. The prevailing myth was that most rapes were committed
by strangers in dark alleys.

13   "If you have to think that sixty to eighty percent of rape is by
people you know—that's hard to deal with," says Sylvia Callaway,
who directed the Austin, Texas, Rape Crisis Center for more than
eight years before leaving last July. "No rape center in a university
community would be surprised that the university is not willing
to deal with the problem."

14   Statistics alone will not solve the problem of date rape, but they
could help bring it out into the open. Which is why *Ms.* undertook
the first nationwide survey on college campuses. The *Ms.* Magazine Campus Project on Sexual Assault, directed by Mary P. Koss
at Kent State and funded by the National Center for the Prevention
and Control of Rape, reached more than seven thousand students
at a nationally representative sample of thirty-five schools, to find
out how often, under what circumstances, and with what after-
effects a wide range of sexual assaults, including date rape, took
place.

15   Preliminary results are now ready, and the information is no
surprise. Participating schools were promised anonymity, but each
will receive the results applying to its student body. Our hope is
that the reaction of "we can't believe it's happening on our campus" will be followed by "what can we do about it—now."

16 Just how entrenched is denial of this problem today? One gauge might be the difficulty our own researchers had in persuading schools to let us on campus. For every college that approved our study, two others rejected it. Their reasons (in writing and in telephone conversations) were themselves instructive: "we don't want to get involved," "limited foreseeable benefit," "too volatile a topic," "have not had any problems in this area," "worried about publicity," "can't allow surveys in classroom," "just can't invest the time now," "would be overintrusive," "don't want to be left holding the bag if something goes wrong."

17 Several schools rejected the study on the basis that filling out the questionnaire might upset some students, and that we were not providing adequate follow-up counseling. (Researchers stayed on campus for at least a day after the distribution of the questionnaire, gave students listings of counselors or rape crisis centers to consult if anything upset them, and offered to meet with school personnel to brief them.) But isn't it less upsetting for a student to recognize and admit that she has been the victim of an acquaintance rape than to have buried the trauma of that rape deep inside herself?

18 "It's a Catch-22 situation. You want a survey to publicize a problem that has tremendous psychological implications. And the school says, 'Don't do it, because it will get people psychologically upset,'" admits John Jung, who heads the human subjects review committee at California State University/Long Beach (a school that declined our study).

19 One wonders just who are the "people" who will get most psychologically upset: the students, or their parents who pay for their educations, or the administrators who are concerned about the school's image. "There may have been an episode here," said John Hose, executive assistant to the president of Brandeis University, "but there is no cause célèbre surrounding the issue. In such cases, the reaction of Student Affairs is to encourage the student to be in touch with her parents and to take legal action."

20 "Student Affairs" at Brandeis is headed by Rodger Crafts, who moved to this post about a year ago from the University of Rhode Island. "I don't think we have a significant problem here because we have a sophisticated and intelligent group of students," said Dean Crafts. As for the University of Rhode Island, more students there are "first generation college attenders," as he put it, and therefore have "less respect" for other people. Vandalism and

physical harm are more likely to occur with "lower educational levels." Respect for other people goes along with "intelligence level."

21   Back at the University of Rhode Island, the counseling center is sponsoring a twelve-week support and therapy group this fall for male students who are coercive and abusive in their relationships with women. Even though Nancy Carlson, director of Counseling and Career Services, is enthusiastic about such programs and workshops she notes, "the awareness about date rape has been a long time coming."

22   Another school where administrators were the last to confront the challenge to their school's self-image is Yale. Last year, two student publications reported instances of date rape on campus that surprised students, faculty, and administration. "There are no full statistics available on rape between students at Yale anywhere. . . . There is no mention of rape in the 1983–1984 Undergraduate Regulations. There is no procedure for a victim to file a formal complaint of rape with the university. But there is rape between students at Yale," wrote Sarah Oates in the *Yale Daily News*. Partly in response to such charges, current Yale undergraduate regulations now list "sexual harassment" under "offenses that are subject to disciplinary action"—but still no mention of rape.

23   Yale students brave enough to bring a charge of sexual harassment may go before the Yale College Executive Committee, a specially convened group of faculty, administrators, and students that can impose a series of penalties, graduated in severity, culminating in expulsion. All its hearings and decisions are kept secret (but can in theory be subpoenaed in a court of law). But Michael McBride, current chair of the committee, told me that cases of date rape have come up during the past year, leading in one instance to a student being asked to "resign" from the university, and in another, the conclusion that there was not "sufficient evidence." (In Judy's case, described at the beginning of this article, the senior she charged was penalized by being denied the privilege of graduating with his class. But she claims that after he demanded that the case be reconsidered, he was fully exonerated.) Said McBride, "What surprised me the most was how complicated these cases are. It's only one person's word against another's. It's amazing how different their perceptions can be."

24   Judy chose to take her case before the Executive Committee

rather than report it to the local police, because she felt she would have complete confidentiality and quick action. Actually, there were many delays. And then, because the man she accused hired a lawyer, she was forced to hire one too. As a result, the meeting felt very much like a jury trial to her, complete with cross-examinations that challenged her truthfulness and raised excruciatingly embarrassing questions.

25 Judy's lawyer felt that such painful questions were necessary. But it seems as if the lesson feminists in the sixties and seventies worked so hard and successfully to make understood—not to blame the victim for stranger rape—is one that will have to be learned all over again in the case of acquaintance rape. Only this time, the woman who reports the rape suffers a triple victimization. Not only is she attacked and then not believed, but she carries the added burden of losing faith in her own judgment and trust in other people.

26 In a recently published study of jurors in rape trials, University of Illinois sociologist Barbara Reskin found that jurors were less likely to convict a man if the victim knew him. "Consent is the preferred rape defense and gets the highest acquittal rates," Reskin observes. "In a date rape situation, I would think the jury would assume that the woman had already accepted his invitation in a romantic sense. It would be a matter of how *much* did she consent to."

27 Personal characteristics also influence jurors, Reskin says. Those she studied couldn't imagine that certain men would commit a rape: if they were attractive, had access to sexual partners such as a girlfriend or a wife. More often than not, they'd say, "But he doesn't look like a rapist." Reskin imagines that this pattern would be "magnified in date rape, because these are men who could get a date, they're not complete losers."

28 It may turn out that solutions to the problem will turn up at places with a less genteel image to protect. Jan Strout, director of Montana State, Women's Resource Center, wonders if schools such as hers, which recognize that they are dealing with a more conservative student body and a "macho cowboy image," aren't more willing to take the first step toward acknowledging the problem. A group called Students Against Sexual Assault was formed there two-and-a-half years ago after several students who were raped or resisted an attempted rape "went public." With men and women

sharing leadership, this group is cosponsored by the Women's Resource Center and the student government.

29   Admitting to the problem isn't easy even when data is available, as doctoral student Genny Sandberg found at University of South Dakota. Last spring, she announced the results of a dating survey she coauthored with psychologists Tom Jackson and Patricia Petretic-Jackson. The most shocking statistic: 20 percent of the students (most from rural backgrounds and living in a rural campus setting) had been raped in a dating situation. The state board of regents couldn't believe it. "I just think that that's absolutely ridiculous," former regent Michael Rose said, according to the Brookings *Daily Register*, "I can't believe we would allow that to occur. If it is true, it's a very serious problem." Regent William Srstka agreed, "If this is true it's absolutely intolerable."

30   Following testimony by one of the researchers, the board changed its tune. Members are now discussing how to begin a statewide education and prevention program.

31   An inspiring example of how an administration can be led to new levels of consciousness took place at the University of Michigan earlier this year. Spurred by an article in *Metropolitan Detroit* magazine, a group of students staged a sit-in at the office of a university vice-president who had been quoted as saying that "Rape is a red flag word. . . . [The university] wants to present an image that is receptive and palatable to the potential student cohort," and also that "Rape is an issue like Alzheimer's disease or mental retardation [which] impacts on a small but sizable part of the population . . . Perhaps it has to become a crisis that is commonly shared in order to get things done."

32   The students who spent the entire day in Vice-President Henry Johnson's office claimed that rape had already become a crisis on their campus. They presented a list of twelve demands, ranging from a rape crisis center on campus to better lighting and installation of outdoor emergency phones. By the end of the day, Johnson had started to change his mind. Although he insisted that he had been misquoted and quoted out of context in the press, he told me that "I did not realize [before that] acquaintance rape was so much of a problem, that it was the most prevalent type of rape. There is a heightened awareness now on this campus. Whether we as a faculty and administration are as sensitive as we should be is another issue—and that will take some time."

33   In the meantime, members of the Michigan Student Assembly Women's Issues Committee (one of the groups active in organizing the protest) took their demands before the school's board of regents. The result: a $75,000 program for rape prevention and education on campus, directly reporting to Johnson's office. "We'll now be in a position to document the problem and to be proactive," says Johnson. Jennifer Faigel, an organizer of the protest, acknowledges a change in the administration's awareness but says the students themselves, disappointed in the amount of funding promised for the program, have already formed a group (Students Organized Against Rape) to develop programs in the dorms.

34   In just the three years since *Ms.* first reported on date rape [in 1982], several new campus organizations have sprung up and other ongoing programs have surfaced.

35   But the real measure of a school's commitment to dealing with this problem is the range of services it provides, says Mary Harvey, who did a nationwide study of exemplary rape programs for the National Center for the Prevention and Control of Rape. "It should have preventive services, crisis intervention, possibilities for long-term treatment, advocacy, and women's studies programs that educate about violence. The quality of a university's services to rape victims can be measured by the degree to which these other things are in place."

36   Minimally, rape counselors and educators feel, students need to be exposed to information about date rape as soon as they enter college. Studies show that the group most vulnerable to acquaintance rape are college freshmen, followed by high school seniors. In Koss's original survey, or example, the average age of the victim was eighteen.

37   "I'd like a program where no first-year students could finish their starting week at college without being informed about the problem of acquaintance rape," says Andrea Parrot, a lecturer in human service studies at Cornell University, who is developing a program to train students and dorm resident advisers as date rape awareness counselors. Parrot and others admit that this would be a bare minimum. Handing out a brochure to read, even conducting a workshop on the subject during the busy orientation week and counting on students voluntarily attending, needs to be followed up with sessions in dormitories or other living units. These are the most common settings for date rapes, according to a study by Parrot and Robin Lynk.

38 So how do we go about changing attitudes? And how do we do it without "setting student against student?" asks Gretchen Mieszkowski, chair of the Sexual Assault Prevention Committee at the University of Houston/Clear Lake. Chiefly a commuter campus, with a majority of married women students, Clear Lake nevertheless had seventeen acquaintance rapes reported to the local crisis hot line last year. "We had always focused on traditional solutions like lighting and escort services at night," Mieszkowski says. "But changing lighting in the parking lot is easy; it's only money."

39 Many who have studied the problem of rape education believe it has to begin with college-age women and men talking to each other more frankly about their beliefs and expectations about sex. Py Bateman of Alternatives to Fear thinks it has to start earlier, among teenagers, by developing rudimentary dating skills at the lower end of the sexual activity scale. "We need to learn more about holding hands than about sexual intercourse."

40 Bateman continues: "We've got to work on both sides. Boys don't know what they want any more than girls do. The way our sexual interaction is set up is that boys are supposed to push. Their peers tell them that scoring is what counts. They're as divorced from intimacy as girls."

41 Gail Abarbanel of the Rape Treatment Center at Santa Monica Hospital agrees. Her center conducts educational programs for schools in Los Angeles County. In a recent survey of more than five thousand teenagers, she found a high degree of misconception and lack of information about rape: "Most boys say yes to the question, 'If a girl goes back to a guy's house when she knows no one is home, is she consenting to sex?' And most boys believe that girls don't mean no when they say it."

42 Women clearly need to get more convincing, and men clearly need to believe them more. But until that ideal time, Montana State's Jan Strout warns, "Because men have been socialized to hear yes when women say no, we have to scream it."

Analyzing the Writer's Argument

1. Why, according to Sweet, is the date rape or acquaintance rape so difficult for women to deal with? Why is date rape reported less often than rape in general?
2. Who are the "hidden rapists"? What false beliefs are they operating under?
3. Why do academic institutions prefer to ignore the question of date rape? What kinds of responses did academic institutions give for why they did not want to participate in the *Ms.* magazine survey? What underlying beliefs do these responses reveal?
4. What role does denial play in the dynamics of date rape? What do women deny? What do men deny?
5. What problems are encountered with jurors who sit on date rape trials?
6. Why does Sweet think that solutions to the date rape problem may turn up at institutions with a "less genteel image to protect"?
7. What solutions to the problem of date rape have been proposed by researchers? Do these solutions seem reasonable to you? Why or why not?

Exploring the Issues in This Essay

1. Discuss the different conceptions of rape held by men and women. What, in your opinion, are the reasons for these differing views? What information about rape is lacking? What misconceptions still prevail? How is your college or university dealing with the problem? Were you made aware of the problem when you first arrived on campus? If so, how helpful was the information you received?
2. What myths prevail concerning date rape or acquaintance rape? How do such myths arise? Why do they persist? What can be done to reveal them as myths?

Ethan A. Nadelmann

Shooting Up

> *Although still a young man, Ethan Nadelmann has built an*
> *impressive career as a political scientist who has specialized in*
> *the areas of crime and the legislation of drugs. He has written*
> *numerous articles and has spoken to groups both here and*
> *abroad about our national drug policy. Nadelmann was born*
> *in 1957 in New York City and received his B.A. from McGill*
> *University in Montreal, his M.S. from the London School*
> *of Economics, and his law degree and Ph.D. from Harvard*
> *University. He is presently on the faculty of the Woodrow*
> *Wilson School of Public and International Affairs at Princeton*
> *University.*
>
> *The argument for the legalization of drugs is not a new*
> *one, of course, but it has gained renewed popularity in the*
> *late 80s. In this essay, first published in* The New Republic
> *in 1988, Nadelmann breathes new life into the idea by drawing*
> *an important connection between drugs and crime.*

1   Hamburgers and ketchup. Movies and popcorn. Drugs and
crime.

2   Drugs and crime are so thoroughly intertwined in the public
mind that to most people a large crime problem seems an inevitable consequence of widespread drug use. But the historical
link between the two is more a product of drug laws than of drugs.
There are four clear connections between drugs and crime, and
three of them would be much diminished if drugs were legalized.
This fact doesn't by itself make the case for legalization persuasive,
of course, but it deserves careful attention in the emerging debate
over whether the prohibition of drugs is worth the trouble.

3   The first connection between drugs and crime—and the only
one that would remain strong after legalization—is the commission of violent and other crimes by people under the influence
of illicit drugs. It is this connection that most infects the popular imagination. Obviously some drugs do "cause" people to com-

mit crimes by reducing normal inhibitions, lessening the sense of responsibility, and unleashing aggressive and other antisocial tendencies. Cocaine, particularly in the form of "crack," has earned such a reputation in recent years, just as heroin did in the 1960s and 1970s and marijuana did in the years before that.

4   Crack's reputation may or may not be more deserved than those of marijuana and heroin. Reliable evidence isn't yet available. But no illicit drug is as widely associated with violent behavior as alcohol. According to Justice Department statistics, 54 percent of all jail inmates convicted of violent crimes in 1983 reported having used alcohol just prior to committing the offense. The impact of drug legalization on this drug-crime connection is hard to predict. Much would depend on overall rates of drug abuse and changes in the nature of consumption, both imponderables. It's worth noting, though, that any shift in consumption from alcohol to marijuana would almost certainly reduce violent behavior.

5   This connection between drugs and antisocial behavior—which is inherent and may or may not be substantial—is often confused with a second link between the two that is definitely substantial and not inherent: many illicit drug users commit crimes such as robbery, burglary, prostitution, and numbers-running to earn enough money to buy drugs. Unlike the millions of alcoholics who support their habits for modest amounts, many cocaine and heroin addicts spend hundreds, maybe even thousands, of dollars a week. If these drugs were significantly cheaper—if either they were legalized or drug laws were not enforced—the number of crimes committed by drug addicts to pay for their habits would drop dramatically. Even if the drugs were taxed heavily to discourage consumption, prices probably would be much lower than they are today.

6   The third drug-crime link—also a byproduct of drug laws—is the violent, intimidating, and corrupting behavior of the drug traffickers. Illegal markets tend to breed violence, not just because they attract criminally minded people but also because there are no legal institutions for resolving disputes. During Prohibition violent struggles between bootlegging gangs and hijackings of booze-laden trucks were frequent and notorious. Today's equivalents are the booby traps that surround marijuana fields; the pirates of the

Caribbean, who rip off drug-laden vessels en route to the United States; and the machine-gun battles and executions of the more sordid drug mafias—all of which occasionally kill innocent people. Most authorities agree that the dramatic increase in urban murder rates over the past few years is almost entirely due to the rise in drug-dealer killings, mostly of one another.

7 Perhaps the most unfortunate victims of drug prohibition laws have been the residents of America's ghettos. These laws have proved largely futile in deterrring ghetto-dwellers from becoming drug abusers, but they do account for much of what ghetto residents identify as the drug problem. Aggressive, gun-toting drug dealers often upset law-abiding residents far more than do addicts nodding out in doorways. Meanwhile other residents perceive the drug dealers as heroes and successful role models. They're symbols of success to children who see no other options. At the same time the increasingly harsh criminal penalties imposed on adult drug dealers have led drug traffickers to recruit juveniles. Where once children started dealing drugs only after they had been using them for a few years, today the sequence is often reversed. Many children start using drugs only after working for older drug dealers for a while.

8 The conspicuous failure of law enforcement agencies to deal with the disruptive effect of drug traffickers has demoralized inner-city neighborhoods and police departments alike. Intensive crackdowns in urban neighborhoods, like intensive anti-cockroach efforts in urban dwellings, do little more than chase the menace a short distance away to infect new areas. By contrast, legalization of drugs, like legalization of alcohol in the early 1930s, would drive the drug-dealing business off the streets and out of apartment buildings and into government regulated, tax-paying stores. It also would force many of the guntoting dealers out of the business and convert others into legitimate businessmen. Some, of course, would turn to other types of criminal activities, just as some of the bootleggers did after Prohibition's repeal. Gone, though, would be the unparalleled financial gains that tempt people from all sectors of society into the drug-dealing business.

9 Gone, too, would be the money that draws police into the world of crime. Today police corruption appears to be more pervasive than at any time since Prohibition. In Miami dozens of law enforcement officials have been charged with accepting bribes, rip-

ping off drug dealers, and even dealing drugs themselves. In small towns and rural communities in Georgia, where drug smugglers from the Caribbean and Latin America pass through, dozens of sheriffs have been implicated in corruption. In one New York police precinct, drug-related corruption has generated the city's most far-reaching police scandal since the late 1960s. Nationwide, over 100 cases of drug-related corruption are now prosecuted each year. Every one of the federal law enforcement agencies with significant drug enforcement responsibilities has seen an agent implicated.

10   It isn't hard to explain the growth of this corruption. The financial temptations are enormous relative to other opportunities, legitimate or illegitimate. Little effort is required. Many police officers are demoralized by the scope of drug traffic, the indifference of many citizens, a frequent lack of appreciation for their efforts, and the seeming futility of it all; even with the regular jailing of drug dealers, thee always seem to be more to fill their shoes. Some police also recognize that their real function is not so much to protect victims from predators as to regulate an illicit market that can't be suppressed but that much of society prefers to keep underground. In every respect, the analogy to Prohibition is apt. Repealing drug prohibition laws would dramatically reduce police corruption. By contrast, the measures currently being proposed to deal with the growing problem, including more frequent and aggressive internal inspection, offer little promise and cost money.

11   The final link between drugs and crime is the tautological connection: producing, selling, buying, and consuming drugs is a crime in and of itself that occurs billions of times each year nationwide. Last year alone, about 30 million Americans violated a drug law, and about 750,000 were arrested, mostly for mere possession, not dealing. In New York City almost half of the felony indictments were on drug charges, and in Washington, D.C., the figure was more than half. Close to 40 percent of inmates in federal prisons are there on drug-dealing charges, and that population is expected to more than double within 15 years.

12   Clearly, if drugs were legalized, this drug-crime connection— which annually accounts for around $10 billion in criminal justice costs—would be severed. (Selling drugs to children would, of course, continue to be prosecuted.) And the benefits would run deeper than that. We would no longer be labeling as criminals the

tens of millions of people who use drugs illicitly, subjecting them to the risk of arrest, and inviting them to associate with drug dealers (who may be criminals in many more senses of the word). The attendant cynicism toward the law in general would diminish, along with the sense of hostility and suspicion that otherwise law-abiding citizens feel toward police. It was costs such as these that strongly influenced many of Prohibition's more conservative opponents. As John D. Rockefeller wrote in explaining why he was withdrawing his support of Prohibition:

> That a vast array of lawbreakers has been recruited and financed on a colossal scale; that many of our best citizens, piqued at what they regarded as an infringement of their private rights, have openly and unabashedly disregarded the 18th Amendment; that as an inevitable result respect for all law has been greatly lessened; that crime has increased to an unprecedented degree—I have slowly and reluctantly come to believe.

Analyzing the Writer's Argument

1. What are the four connections between drugs and crime that Nadelmann makes in his essay? Which of these connections would not change even if drugs were made legal?
2. What evidence does Nadelmann provide to substantiate his argument that "no illicit drug is as widely associated with violent behavior as alcohol"?
3. On which drugs-crime link does Nadelmann write most extensively? Why do you suppose he gives it so much of his attention?
4. Nadelmann makes the analogy between the present drug-crime link and the alcohol-crime link that he says existed during Prohibition when it was against the law to manufacture and sell alcoholic beverages. How much do you know about Prohibition? Is the analogy a convincing one for you? Why or why not?
5. What does Nadelmann mean by writing that his fourth connection is a tautological one? Do you find it easy to follow his reasoning at this point? Can you restate this point in your own words?
6. Does Nadelmann believe that the legalization of drugs will help to reduce violent behavior? Why or why not? Does he know? Can he know?
7. Do you think that Nadelmann's use of statistics, of facts and figures, is helpful to his argument? Why or why not?

Exploring the Issues in This Essay

1. If the American people decided to legalize drugs that we now consider illicit, would we simply be giving up, saying in effect, "okay, you win," to the drug users and traffickers? Would we simply be calling by another name that which we now call illegal and dangerous? In other words, would anything change? Why was Prohibition repealed? Did we give in at that point when we perhaps should not have? Is there an equally important lesson to be learned from the analogy between Prohibition and the present violence-alcohol connection that even Nadelmann admits in his essay? Does repealing the prohibition against alcohol justify the argument to legalize drugs?

2. Does Nadelmann concern himself with what would happen to the people who would legally buy drugs and use them regularly if drugs were made legal? Is he concerned about addiction? Why or why not? Is Nadelmann looking at only one part of the problem, the drug-crime connection, and ignoring other aspects of it? Why would he want to prohibit the sale of drugs to children?

Note: You may also wish to read William Bennett's essay against the legalization of drugs in *America's Dependency on Drugs* (pp.310–317).

Jean Harris

Inside Story

Jean Harris is currently serving a prison term in the Bedford Hills Correctional Facility in New York for the murder of Dr. Hyman Tarnower, her lover. As the author of the best-selling The Complete Scarsdale Medical Diet *Tarnower had become an international celebrity. Jean Harris was born in 1923 in Cleveland, Ohio, and is a 1945 magna cum laude graduate of Smith College. Bright, industrious, and ambitious, Harris had worked in business and in education, and was at the time of the murder the headmistress of the Madeira School for Girls in Virginia. The trial of Mrs. Harris attracted world-wide media attention for two major reasons: the celebrity status of its victim, the question of Mrs. Harris' guilt (she claimed that she intended to commit suicide and that the murder was an accident). Beyond these issues, however, was a feminist concern: Harris was distraught over the fact that Tarnower, an intense womanizer, had "dumped" her for a younger woman. Among the articles and books that the Harris case generated was a book by the highly respected writer and critic, Diana Trilling. She ends her book,* Mrs. Harris, *with conjectures on what imprisonment might bring to Harris' life: "Her gifts of mind may now be put to use as they never were before. There is work to be done in the sphere of prison education, serious work of a kind for which she has the training, energy, and intelligence. She may now be splendid in a way that she never knew how to be or dared to be." Since that time Harris has lived out Trilling's prophecy.*

In the following article, which first appeared in New York *magazine in 1983, Jean Harris gives us a rare look "inside" a prison and what goes on there. She is highly critical of our criminal justice system and argues for reforms that would reduce the cost to society of housing and rehabilitating prisoners without the risk to society.*

1   Come at me, Harris!" The woman said. "Come at me! Wanna hit me, Harris? Why 'ncha hit me? Hit me here!" The woman was a correction officer at Bedford Hills Correctional Facility, and I was being "corrected," at society's expense. For months, this woman—who earns more than many good teachers—had been trying to get me to hit her so she could charge me with assault and have me sent to segregation. She'd just finished strip-searching me following a meeting with friends in the visiting room. Her search went on for twelve minutes while I stood naked. She slowly caressed the seams of each piece of my clothing, presumably to make sure I hadn't sewn away any drugs during the visit. Her specialty is "squats," and that day she outdid herself. "That ain't a good squat. Squat again, and this time cough. Cough harder." Finally, under her goading I started to shriek and howl and shake, until people came from all around and tried to quiet me. That day, I thought I could never go through it again and remain sane. I was wrong. I am still reasonably sane, and I went through it many more times before the woman was finally removed—not fired but transferred to another facility, where she now helps to "correct" other unfortunates.

2   My point in describing the "squat lady" is not to shock or arouse pity but to raise questions about a growing part of society's tax bill—the part that goes to pay for prisons. Are taxpayers getting their money's worth? The people of New York spend over $3 billion a year on the many-headed monster called the criminal-justice system. Nearly half a billion goes for prisons alone. The cost of keeping one prisoner for one year is about $20,000—for far less than that the state could send the inmate to Smith.

3   This money is being spent at a time when essential social programs are being canceled, thousands of New Yorkers are homeless, old people are afraid they'll live longer than they can afford, and school budgets are being dangerously shortchanged. According to the Ford Foundation, 64 million Americans—28 out of every 100—are functionally illiterate. Many of these people are doomed to fail unless they can be educated. But education is competing for the same dollars as corrections—and corrections is clearly a growth industry.

4   In the past ten years, New York's prison population has risen from 12,000 to an overcrowded 30,000, prison personnel have increased from 6,500 to almost 16,000, an nineteen additional prisons

have been opened or reopened. Even with that, three more prisons are being planned—including one in New York City. Yet, despite this increase in the number of cells, the police estimate that as many as 200,000 criminals are walking the streets of New York today, and New Yorkers are as apt to be victimized by crime as ever. Americans spend $26 billion a year on the criminal-justice system. For all that, only 5 percent of all serious reported crimes end in conviction and a prison sentence. Common sense indicates that the system isn't working in society's best interest.

5   Last September, the Correctional Association of New York, a private group that examines criminal justice, issued a report on current conditions in New York State prisons. Called "Attica 1982," the report focused on that supposedly representative institution. Many of the same tensions and frustrations that sparked the tragic uprising of 1971 exist today, the report said. The results are predictable. Reported assaults by prisoners on prisoners, and by prisoners on guards, are far higher than three years ago. The number of assaults by guards on prisoners is not recorded, but they happen, too. The January uprising at Sing Sing came as no surprise to anyone who knows about conditions there.

6   Though Bedford Hills, where I am imprisoned, and Attica are different in many ways, certain issues and problems exist in all prisons. Bedford can't always find room in the reception area for arriving inmates, so newcomers get jammed into any available space—the medical unit, for example, or even the protective-custody unit, a section of the prison that's part of the segregation building, where the inmates with the most serious behavior problems are held. Some women in segregation are more mentally ill than criminal. They cry all night, scream obscenities, set their beds on fire, throw feces on the guards and on one another, and generally behave as if the place were Bedlam, not Bedford.

7   I spoke recently with a young woman who had spent the first week of her stay at Bedford in protective custody. Her eyes were still wide with fright. "This isn't prison, it's a crazy house," she said. Prison administrations—even enlightened ones, as here at Bedford—have no control over the number of inmates sent to them. Bodies are delivered, and a place must be found for them.

8   As more and more prisoners are packed into existing facilities, the opportunity to work and take part in rehabilitation programs

declines. At Attica, more than 500 men have no jobs to go to, and spend 20 to 23 hours a day locked in 50-square-foot-cells. They get little exercise, no job training, no education, and virtually no responsibility. Recidivism is born of this kind of costly neglect. The average prison inmate is about 27 years old, with an active sexual drive, and cut off from legitimate avenues of sex. The constant ferment of prison life isn't hard to understand.

9   Motivation almost vanishes in prison. Getting to work on time, for example, is never applauded—impossible. Every day for two years, I have spent time waiting at as many as 76 locked doors: 18 doors to and from meals, 24 to and from work, 8 to and from medication, 12 to and from a visit, and 14 to and from my volunteer job on Fridays. I began knitting mittens during those waits to help salve the utter frustration that comes with throwing away time needlessly. By now, I have knitted more than a hundred pairs. If every door were opened in a minute—and it usually takes longer than that—the time spent standing in front of a locked door would still add up to more than six hours per week, or thirteen days per year. Is that preparation to face the world with drive, energy, and a new attitude? Or is that the sort of thing that creates an embittered, uninterested zombie? One fights to stay whole in prison.

10   The people opening and closing those doors (it seems to be their principal activity) aren't known as "guards." The law insists that they be called "correction officers"—which has to rank among the state's most blatant hypocrisies, considering their style of correcting. These officers receive minimal training, often only a few weeks, though their own union says that sixteen weeks of training should be required. To be fair, there are some correction officers who live up to the title—decent people with sound values, good judgment, self-respect, and common sense. But there aren't enough of them. Twice I've seen new C.O.'s ask an inmate to come to the officer's station to show how to open and close the cell doors. I've tried with other inmates to hold down a prisoner having a seizure, to keep her from pounding her head open on the floor and swallowing her tongue, while a C.O. stood by, hands on hips, and said. "She just does that to get attention." I've heard someone shout "Fire!" and seen the C.O. panic and lock all the doors with inmates inside.

11   The day an inmate in the cell next to mine set her bed on fire, a C.O. immediately locked her cell, and the inmate sat happily on her toilet, watching the fire burn closer. It took screams from other inmates to get the door open, and it was inmates who ran in and pulled her out. The woman is in prison for arson, she is mentally confused, and three times during the previous night a C.O. had brought her matches "because she asked for them."

12   The same woman will be released in the next few months, "if I can find a place to stay when I go out." Mentally ill and without money, marketable skills, family help, or friends, she spends her days writing sad, rather lovely poetry. If she is let out, almost as surely as the morning follows the night she will return someday to prison, unless she dies first. Is prison the place she should be?

13   The nature of prison life seems to be written into the rules of medical care. The seriously ill are sometimes overlooked, while the doctors' and nurses' time is wasted on nonsense. I had to make an appointment and get written permission from the doctor to wear a flimsy little pantie girdle. The reason? "Well, you know, if a woman is pregnant, it isn't good to wear a tight girdle." I'm 60 years old, and a nurse said this to me with a straight face. I had to go to the doctor to get a "prescription" for a one-a-day vitamin pill, and the doctor told me, in his most pontifical tone. "I cannot prescribe a one-a-day vitamin for you until you are examined and have blood tests." Should I have cared? Though I was supplying the girdle and the vitamins, I wasn't paying for the doctor's time or for the tests—the state was.

14   Taxpayers pay when harm is done—when a prisoner is injured or the law is ignored. Six years ago, inmates won a class-action suit against Bedford, challenging the medical procedures then in effect. Two years ago, they won $125,000 in a suit over disciplinary proceedings at the prison. Both cases dragged on for years, running up legal fees for the state. But today the risk of a lawsuit doesn't seem to frighten C.O.'s and middle management at all. "Go ahead and sue. It ain't my money" is a familiar comment.

15   There are many legitimate ways to help lift the burden of crime from taxpayers' shoulders, while still punishing the guilty and even making some restitution to victims—something that prison doesn't accommodate. Even if society has given up trying to improve criminals, there's no reason to work at making them worse.

Immediate steps can be taken to reduce the cost of prison without increasing the risk to society.

16 One such step was recently taken at Bedford Hills, with the opening of Fiske Cottage, an honor house for 26 inmates—myself among them. Fiske was built almost 70 years ago as a separate building at Westfield Farms, a women's facility that was Bedford's predecessor. When the law was changed to require that each locked cell contain running water and a toilet, Fiske was closed down. It had been shuttered for fifteen years when the new Bedford administration, headed by Superintendent Frank R. Headley, decided to make use of it. Installing plumbing in each room would have been exorbitantly expensive, but Headley took another approach: He turned it into an honor cottage in which none of the rooms is locked. Total renovation, including the installation of a new heating system and the addition of prison-made furniture, cost $44,000. Building 26 cells would have cost more than $2 million. Of course, in addition to a reasonable price, Fiske has another, immeasurable benefit: 26 women have been given the opportunity to prove that they can govern themselves and make intelligent decisions.

17 There are dangerous, repeat offenders who must be kept in top-security cells, but officials should be far more selective about the use of these expensive obscenities, especially in a women's prison. Many women would be adequately contained by the twelve-foot-high fences—topped with row after row of razor-sharp wire—that circle Bedford Hill. For these women, a steel cage is wasteful overkill. More than half the women in Fiske have been convicted of homicide, yet they were chosen by staff members to handle special privileges because of their contributions to the prison community. Of the 500 or so women at Bedford, there are far more than 26 who could live the same way. To build another honor cottage large enough for 26 women would cost less than it would to construct four top-security cells.

18 The surest way to avoid prison waste is to release some prisoners sooner, or not to put them there in the first place. Work-release programs are probably the most constructive alternative to too much caging. No program better eases the transition from inside to outside.

19 Intensive probation for nonviolent first offenders is another good alternative to prison. Under that system, the offender remains out

of prison, under close supervision. He or she may be independently employed, or may be working in the community to make restitution. In some instances, weekends are spent in prison for a certain number of months. Mothers are allowed to stay with their children, thus eliminating the added expense of foster-care services. The Correctional Association of New York estimates that $21 million could be saved this year alone if intensive probation replaced imprisonment in such cases. In the past four years, New York has incarcerated more than 8,000 probation-eligible people.

20   A higher release rate for inmates who are eligible for parole and have a good institutional record would also free cells and save money. Of course, as crime stories attest every week, careful judgment has to be used to decide who gets out. In some states, parole boards have been replaced by the people in the system who know the inmate best—the judge who tried him and the prison staff that kept him. Their decision on release is probably wiser than that of an overworked, underinformed parole board. In 1972, New York's parole board released 72 percent of those inmates who became eligible for parole for the first time. In 1982, the figure had dropped to 52 percent, and 5,000 potential parolees were still in prison. If even 60 percent of those first eligible were released or put in halfway houses this year, the state would save up to $41.5 million and open up more than 2,000 cells.

21   Parole violators are another group filling too many top-security cells. They are people who have been released and have not committed new crimes but have failed to adhere to the strict rules that parole properly lays down. A parolee may be returned to prison for getting drunk and disorderly, for using drugs, for being seen with the wrong people (though usually "the wrong people" are the only friends an ex-prisoner has), for getting married without the parole officer's consent, or even for getting pregnant. Alternative sanctions, such as halfway houses or extended parole periods, could save as much as $6 million a year and free as many as 350 top-security cells.

22   Using these three widely advocated alternatives alone—intensive probation, increased parole, and non-prison sanctions for parole violators—New York could save as much as $65 million this year and free 3,500 cells for violent criminals. Building that many cells this year would cost up to $350 million.

23   There is one short-term saving—at long-term expense—that the public should also look at when assessing the cost of the criminal justice system. It's called plea bargaining. Americans are proud of the jury system in this country, but 85 to 90 percent of the people in prison did not go to trial. They pleaded guilty to a lesser time than the one they had been charged with and arranged for a lighter sentence. Thus is revolving door justice created. And what about the innocent, and those untutored in "jail house smarts"? They put years of their lives on the line and go to trial. I know rather well three women who were urged to plea-bargain: Two were offered probation, and one was offered "one to three." All professed their innocence and insisted on a trial. All three were found guilty by their juries and sentenced to fifteen years to life in prison. One of them was granted clemency last year after serving almost five years. The other two are still here, and there are more than a few other women like them. If it is safe and just for a person to be given probation and sent back into the world, by what standards of human decency can you cage the person for fifteen years? The one unforgivable error in the criminal-justice system is to be innocent. Young Americans are taught that trial by jury is a right, freely given, but that is not so. It is enormously expensive for the innocent, and casually sidestepped by the guilty. Plea bargaining with career criminals is false economy, but one of the few economies the system practices enthusiastically.

24   America is a violent and crime-ridden country. There are more homicides per year in New York City than in France and Britain combined. Yet most Americans live out their lives believing the myth that they are the good guys. American prison sentences are the longest in the Western World, and only South Africa and the Soviet Union have more prisoners per 100,000 people than the United States does.

25   Incarceration is a violent act. Violence is a response to violence, but not a solution to it. The hypocrisy that masquerades as criminal justice has done little to make the country safer, to compensate crime victims, or to prepare wrongdoers to re-enter the community. The system clearly doesn't work, and it costs a fortune—two of the best possible arguments for change.

Analyzing the Writer's Argument

1. Does Harris develop her argument inductively or deductively? Explain.
2. Harris uses many statistics in her essay. What effect do these statistics have on you as a reader?
3. What does the author mean when she says that "the nature of prison life seems to be written into the rules of medical care"?
4. How does Harris propose to reduce the cost of prison without increasing the risk to society? Do you agree with her proposals?
5. What does Harris mean when she condemns the criminal justice system by claiming that "the one unforgivable error in the criminal-justice system is to be innocent"? Does she substantiate that claim to your satisfaction? Explain.
6. Harris claims that if her suggestions were followed, various sums of money would be saved. Does she explain how these savings will actually occur?
7. Are the arguments that Harris puts forth self-serving? Is she just complaining about having to be in prison? Why or why not?

Exploring the Issues in This Essay

1. Harris claims that "incarceration is a violent act." Do you agree with that assessment from what you have read? Do you have any reason to doubt her? Should society worry about how criminals are treated in prison? Why or why not? Should we worry about the cost-effectiveness of incarceration?
2. Why is the criminal justice system in this country so difficult to reform? Is it fundamentally archaic thinking about the nature of punishment and incarceration? Is it the invisibility of the problem for most Americans? Do most people believe that criminals deserve what they get? Or is there something else at work when we try to find ways of modernizing and making more efficient the means of achieving the purposes of imprisonment? Discuss ideas that you have to reform the nation's criminal justice system.

Writing Suggestions for
Crime, Criminals, and Victims

1. "38 Who Saw Murder Did Not Call Police" is a classic example of public apathy toward a fellow citizen's distress. Certainly no one would argue that we should not help someone in need, but is the question of what to do quite so simple? For example, several years ago in Burlington, Vermont, a public garage attendant witnessed a man snatch a woman's purse from her. The attendant pursued the man only to have the assailant turn and shoot him. The garage attendant is now paralyzed as a result of his good samaritan act. The attendant claims he would do it all over again, but is the price he paid worth the risk he took? Write an essay in which you argue that those who witness a crime should take certain actions but not others. Had the garage attendant called the police, for example, he might not be crippled today.

2. Write an argument in favor of regarding rape as an act of violence rather than a sexual act. Be sure to take into consideration why the distinction is an important one to make.

3. Jean Harris points out some of the inadequacies of our prison system in "Inside Story." Write an argument in favor of new strategies for prison reform. You may wish to start by spending some time in your library with books and articles on the subject.

4. Research in your library the "victim compensation" proposals that have been put forth in recent years. Write an argument for or against such proposals.

5. Date or acquaintance rape is an "invisible" crime because the public and often the victims and perpetrators do not understand what is happening. Argue that public attention should be similarly focused on other "invisible crimes," such as computer white-collar crime, or corporate crime involving negligence and dangerous products.

6. Argue that drug addiction is a major cause of crime and offer a proposal to decrease the availability of illicit drugs.

7. Argue that our judicial and correctional systems are too lenient and, therefore, do not adequately deter the commission of crimes in this country.

8. Argue for or against the results of recent studies which are attempting to establish a genetic basis for criminal behavior. You will, of course, need to research in your school library the recent literature that advances such theories.

9. Write an essay in which you argue that frequently victims of violent behavior are doubly victims: first they are harmed by the perpetrator and then wronged by an apathetic public.

10. Investigate how domestic violence is handled by the police and the courts in your area. One common complaint of battered and abused women is that the police do nothing and the courts issue restraining orders which go unheeded. The result is that those who are battered or abused can only prove they are endangered by being further abused or, worse yet, killed. Write an essay in which you argue for a change in police practices and/or stiffer penalties for those who disobey the court's orders.

11. Is poverty a cause of crime? If a person can make more money stealing and dealing drugs than working a regular job, isn't crime an economic necessity? Write an essay in which you argue that crime will be lessened if we can solve the economic problems of those on the bottom rungs of the economic ladder, and give them decent jobs with the potential for personal growth and responsibility.

12. Because frequently a connection is made between drug users and violent behavior, some have proposed legalizing drugs as a means of reducing the incidence of violent crimes. Argue for or against the decriminalization of drugs as a means of reducing crime.

13. The treatment of prisoners in our nation's correctional facilities is a difficult matter for the public to assess. Most of us would agree that the life of a prisoner is not a happy one and would probably further agree that it should not be. But what if, as Jean Harris claims, the taxpayers are not getting their money's worth because the system is simply not working and prisoners are poorly treated and cared for? Should we listen to the complaints of prisoners (those that have already proven themselves antisocial), should we simply ignore the question, or should we try to investigate further? Argue for a particular course of action and put forth a proposal for carrying it out.

11

Capital Punishment

On January 17, 1977, Gary Mark Gilmore was executed by a firing squad in the state of Utah. Having spent more than half of his thirty-five years in prison, Gilmore had been freed, and shortly thereafter had shot two men in cold blood. He was the first person to be executed in this country in more than ten years and, as such, his case received worldwide press coverage. In *The Executioner's Song,* novelist Norman Mailer, who befriended Gilmore as the case moved through the courts, chronicled the life and death of Gilmore in an attempt to come to a better understanding of his criminal mind and the way the judicial system dealt with him. Gilmore's death not only marked the end of the moratorium on capital punishment, it began a new era of executions and renewed the debate over the death penalty. Today, thirty-seven states permit the death penalty and over 1200 people condemned to die are awaiting execution.

In 1972, after more than five years of public debate during which no one was executed in the United States, the Supreme Court in a narrow 5–4 decision declared capital punishment in violation of the constitutional prohibition against cruel and unusual punishment because state statutes could be applied capriciously and without discernible standards. The *Furman v. Georgia* decision, however, left the door open, because several of the justices did not say that capital punishment was inherently unconstitutional. Instead of going along with the Supreme Court's ruling and striking down their laws on capital punishment, many state legislatures revised their capital punishment statutes to bring them more in line with the Constitution.

In another test of the constitutionality of state capital punishment laws, *Gregg v. Georgia,* the Supreme Court, in July of 1976, upheld the death penalty for certain carefully defined types of murder. In doing so, the court banned the so-called mandatory capital punishment laws and stated that judges and juries should be given complete information and adequate guidance in determining the appropriateness of the punishment. Less than six months later, Gilmore went to his death and Americans were once again embroiled in the death penalty dilemma—is capital punishment a necessary deterrent to serious crimes against society or but the sad reminder that we are not yet as civilized as we would like to believe?

George Orwell

A Hanging

George Orwell (1903–1950) was an English novelist and essayist and one of the most brilliant social critics of the twentieth century. Orwell, whose real name was Eric Blair, was born in Bengal, India, educated at Eton in England, and served for five years with the Imperial Police in Burma. He returned to Europe in the 1930s where he began his writing career and served with the Loyalist forces during the Spanish Civil War. Seeing firsthand the destruction of war, he developed a fierce hatred of totalitarianism. Settling finally in England, Orwell wrote Animal Farm *(1945) and* 1984 *(1949). Both novels, which continue to be very popular, satirize the excesses of the totalitarian system.*

"A Hanging," first published in the British journal The Adelphi *in 1931 and later included in Orwell's collection* Shooting an Elephant and Other Essays *(1950), recounts an execution Orwell witnessed while serving in Burma. His account is much more than a newspaper story about an execution, however. Having witnessed the event and realizing the inhumanity of capital punishment, he writes about what he has seen in a way that appeals to our emotions and in the process thus subtly persuades us to his position.*

1   It was in Burma, a sodden morning of the rains. A sickly light, like yellow tinfoil, was slanting over the high walls into the jail yard. We were waiting outside the condemned cells, a row of sheds fronted with double bars, like small animal cages. Each cell measured about ten feet by ten and was quite bare within except for a plank bed and a pot for drinking water. In some of them brown silent men were squatting at the inner bars, with their blankets draped around them. These were the condemned men, due to be hanged within the next week or two.

2   One prisoner had been brought out of his cell. He was a Hindu, a puny wisp of a man, with a shaven head and vague liquid eyes.

451

He had a thick, sprouting moustache, absurdly too big for his body, rather like the moustache of a comic man on the films. Six tall Indian warders were guarding him and getting him ready for the gallows. Two of them stood by with rifles and fixed bayonets, while the others handcuffed him, passed a chain through his handcuffs and fixed it to their belts, and lashed his arms tight to his sides. They crowded very close about him, with their hands always on him in a careful, caressing grip as though all the while feeling him to make sure he was there. It was like men handling a fish which is still alive and may jump back into the water. But he stood quite unresisting, yielding his arms limply to the ropes, as though he hardly noticed what was happening.

3 Eight o'clock struck and a bugle call, desolately thin in the wet air, floated from the distant barracks. The superintendent of the jail, who was standing apart from the rest of us, moodily prodding the gravel with his stick, raised his head at the sound. He was an army doctor, with a gray toothbrush moustache and a gruff voice. "For God's sake hurry up, Francis," he said irritably. "The man ought to have been dead by this time. Aren't you ready yet?"

4 Francis, the head jailer, a fat Dravidian in a white drill suit and gold spectacles, waved his black hand. "Yes sir, yes sir," he bubbled. "All iss satisfactorily prepared. The hangman iss waiting. We shall proceed."

5 "Well, quick march, then. The prisoners can't get their breakfast till this job's over."

6 We set out for the gallows. Two warders marched on either side of the prisoner, with their rifles at the slope; two others marched close against him, gripping him by arm and shoulder, as though at once pushing and supporting him. The rest of us, magistrates and the like, followed behind. Suddenly, when we had gone ten yards, the procession stopped short without any order or warning. A dreadful thing had happened—a dog, come goodness knows whence, had appeared in the yard. It came bounding among us with a loud volley of barks, and leapt round us wagging its whole body, wild with glee at finding so many human beings together. It was a large woolly dog, half Airedale, half pariah. For a moment it pranced round us, and then, before anyone could stop it, it had made a dash for the prisoner and, jumping up, tried to lick his face. Everyone stood aghast, too taken aback even to grab at the dog.

7 "Who let that bloody brute in here?" said the superintendent angrily. "Catch it, someone!"

8 A warder, detached from the escort, charged clumsily after the dog, but it danced and gamboled just out of his reach, taking everything as part of the game. A young Eurasian jailer picked up a handful of gravel and tried to stone the dog away, but it dodged the stones and came after us again. Its yaps echoed from the jail walls. The prisoner, in the grasp of the two warders, looked on incuriously, as though this was another formality of the hanging. It was several minutes before someone managed to catch the dog. Then we put my handkerchief through its collar and moved off once more, with the dog still straining and whimpering.

9 It was about forty yards to the gallows. I watched the bare brown back of the prisoner marching in front of me. He walked clumsily with his bound arms, but quite steadily, with that bobbing gait of the Indian who never straightens his knees. At each step his muscles slid neatly into place, the lock of hair on his scalp danced up and down, his feet printed themselves on the wet gravel. And once, in spite of the men who gripped him by each shoulder, he stepped slightly aside to avoid a puddle on the path.

10 It is curious, but till that moment I had never realized what it means to destroy a healthy, conscious man. When I saw the prisoner step aside to avoid the puddle I saw the mystery, the unspeakable wrongness, of cutting a life short when it is in full tide. This man was not dying, he was alive just as we are alive. All the organs of his body were working—bowels digesting food, skin renewing itself, nails growing, tissues forming—all toiling away in solemn foolery. His nails would still be growing when he stood on the drop, when he was falling through the air with a tenth of a second to live. His eyes saw the yellow gravel and the gray walls, and his brain still remembered, foresaw, reasoned—reasoned even about puddles. He and we were a party of men walking together, seeing, hearing, feeling, understanding the same world; and in two minutes, with a sudden snap, one of us would be gone—one mind less, one world less.

11 The gallows stood in a small yard, separate from the main grounds of the prison, and overgrown with tall prickly weeds. It was a brick erection like three sides of a shed, with planking on top, and above that two beams and a crossbar with the rope dangling. The hangman, a gray-haired convict in the white uniform of the prison,

was waiting beside his machine. He greeted us with a servile crouch as we entered. At a word from Francis the two warders, gripping the prisoner more closely than ever, half led half pushed him to the gallows and helped him clumsily up the ladder. Then the hangman climbed up and fixed the rope round the prisoner's neck.

12   We stood waiting, five yards away. The warders had formed in a rough circle round the gallows. And then, when the noose was fixed, the prisoner began crying out to his god. It was a high, reiterated cry of "Ram! Ram! Ram! Ram"[1] not urgent and fearful like a prayer or cry for help, but steady, rhythmical, almost like the tolling of a bell. The dog answered the sound with a whine. The hangman, still standing on the gallows, produced a small cotton bag like a flour bag and drew it down over the prisoner's face. But the sound, muffled by the cloth, still persisted, over and over again: "Ram! Ram! Ram! Ram! Ram!"

13   The hangman climbed down and stood ready, holding the lever. Minutes seemed to pass. The steady, muffled crying from the prisoner went on and on, "Ram! Ram! Ram!" never faltering for an instant. The superintendent, his head on his chest, was slowly poking the ground with his stick; perhaps he was counting the cries, allowing the prisoner a fixed number—fifty, perhaps, or a hundred. Everyone had changed color. The Indians had gone gray like bad coffee, and one or two of the bayonets were wavering. We looked at the lashed, hooded man on the drop, and listened to his cries—each cry another second of life; the same thought was in all our minds: oh, kill him quickly, get it over, stop that abominable noise!

14   Suddenly the superintendent made up his mind. Throwing up his head he made a swift motion with his stick. "Chalo!"[2] he shouted almost fiercely.

15   There was a clanking noise, and then dead silence. The prisoner had vanished, and the rope was twisting on itself. I let go of the dog, and it galloped immediately to the back of the gallows; but when it got there it stopped short, barked, and then retreated into a corner of the yard, where it stood among the weeds, looking timorously out at us. We went round the gallows to inspect the

[1] In the Hindu religion, Rama is the incarnation of the god Vishnu.
[2] *"Let go,"* in Hindi.

prisoner's body. He was dangling with his toes pointed straight downward, very slowly revolving, as dead as a stone.

16 The superintendent reached out with his stick and poked the bare brown body: it oscillated slightly. "*He's* all right," said the superintendent. He backed out from under the gallows, and blew out a deep breath. The moody look had gone out of his face quite suddenly. He glanced at his wrist watch. "Eight minutes past eight. Well, that's all for this morning, thank God."

17 The warders unfixed bayonets and marched away. The dog, sobered and conscious of having misbehaved itself, slipped after them. We walked out of the gallows yard, past the condemned cells with their waiting prisoners, into the big central yard of the prison. The convicts, under the command of warders armed with lathis,[3] were already receiving their breakfast. They squatted in long rows, each man holding a tin pannikin, while two warders with buckets marched round ladling out rice; it seemed quite a homely, jolly scene, after the hanging. An enormous relief had come upon us now that the job was done. One felt an impulse to sing, to break into a run, to snigger. All at once everyone began chattering gaily.

18 The Eurasian boy walking beside me nodded toward the way we had come, with a knowing smile: "Do you know, sir, our friend [he meant the dead man] when he heard his appeal had been dismissed, he pissed on the floor of his cell. From fright. Kindly take one of my cigarettes, sir. Do you not admire my new silver case, sir? From the boxwalah, two rupees eight annas.[4] Classy European style."

19 Several people laughed—at what, nobody seemed certain.

20 Francis was walking by the superintendent, talking garrulously: "Well, sir, all hass passed off with the utmost satisfactoriness. It was all finished—flick! like that. It iss not always so—oah, no! I have known cases where the doctor wass obliged to go beneath the gallows and pull the prisoner's legs to ensure decease. Most disagreeable!"

21 "Wriggling about, eh? That's bad," said the superintendent.

22 "Ach, sir, it iss worse when they become refractory! One man, I recall, clung to the bars of hiss cage when we went to take him out.

---

[3] Wooden batons.

[4] Indian currency worth less than 50 cents. *Boxwalah*: in Hindi, a seller of boxes.

You will scarcely credit, sir, that it took six warders to dislodge him, three pulling at each leg. We reasoned with him. 'My dear fellow,' we said, 'think of all the pain and trouble you are causing to us!' But no, he would not listen! Ach, he wass very troublesome!"

23 I found that I was laughing quite loudly. Everyone was laughing. Even the superintendent grinned in a tolerant way. "You'd better all come out and have a drink," he said quite genially. "I've got a bottle of whisky in the car. We could do with it."

24 We went through the big double gates of the prison into the road. "Pulling at his legs!" exclaimed a Burmese magistrate suddenly, and burst into a loud chuckling. We all began laughing again. At that moment Francis' anecdote seemed extraordinarily funny. We all had a drink together, native and European alike, quite amicably. The dead man was a hundred yards away.

Analyzing the Writer's Argument

1. Orwell spends a considerable amount of time describing the prisoner and telling of the preparations for the hanging. Why do you think that the author included these details? How did you react to them?

2. The dog seems to intrude upon the proceedings. Review the passages in the essay dealing with the dog. What is the dog's reaction to the prisoner? To the execution? What, if anything, does the dog contribute to Orwell's purpose in this essay?

3. Why does Orwell make note of the fact that the prisoner stepped around the puddle in paragraphs 9 and 10? How did the prisoner's behavior strike you? Explain.

4. As a writer, Orwell has a reputation for using words purposefully. Select four or five examples of Orwell's diction that illustrate how he chooses words for their emotional and persuasive appeal.

5. Identify several metaphors and similes and explain how each works to further Orwell's purpose in this essay.

6. One of the risks an author runs when writing about an emotionally charged event is sentimentality. How would you describe Orwell's tone in this essay? Does Orwell become sentimental at any point?

7. We know how Orwell feels about capital punishment. Does the Superintendent share Orwell's discomfort? Does the laughter of the group at the end of the essay contradict these feelings? Explain.

Exploring the Issues in This Essay

1. Orwell never tells us what the man's crime was. In fact, he makes it seem that it doesn't matter. Why do you think Orwell presents the situation in this manner? What questions does it raise for you regarding the political situation in Burma in the 1930s, the appropriateness of the punishment for the crime, and the issue of capital punishment?

2. As a member of the Imperial Police force, it was Orwell's duty to escort the prisoner to the gallows and to witness the execution. The experience causes Orwell to question his duty because "till that moment I had never realized what it means to destroy a healthy, conscious man." Despite the "unspeakable wrongness" that Orwell felt, he did not let his conscience override his sense of duty at the time. What options did he have? What do you think you would have done if you had been in Orwell's position? Why?

Clarence Darrow

The Futility of the Death Penalty

> *Clarence Seward Darrow (1857–1938) is perhaps best re-*
> *membered for his skillful, though unsuccessful, defense of the*
> *evolutionist John L. Scopes in the now-famous "Monkey Trial"*
> *in Dayton, Tennessee, in 1925. Darrow was born in Kinsman,*
> *Ohio, and attended Allegheny College and the University of*
> *Michigan Law School before being admitted to the Ohio bar*
> *in 1878. After years of work on celebrated labor cases in-*
> *volving the likes of union activist Eugene Debs and the defen-*
> *dants in the Los Angeles* Times *dynamiting case, he redirected*
> *his practice to cases of criminal law. In 1924 Darrow saved*
> *Richard Loeb and Nathan Leopold from the death sentence for*
> *the murder of Bobby Franks in Chicago.*
>
> *Throughout his life, Darrow was a popular lecturer and*
> *debater, and he wrote a number of books on crime, criminals,*
> *and punishment. "The Futility of the Death Penalty" was*
> *first published in* The Forum, *a monthly magazine of articles*
> *debating national and international questions. Here, Darrow*
> *argues against capital punishment because he believes that it*
> *does not act as deterrent and that the "state continues to kill*
> *its victims not so much to defend society from them—for it*
> *could do that equally well by imprisonment—but to appease*
> *the mob's emotions of hatred and revenge."*

1   Little more than a century ago, in England, there were over two
hundred offenses that were punishable with death. The death sentence was passed upon children under ten years old. And every
time the sentimentalist sought to lessen the number of crimes punishable by death, the self-righteous said no, that it would be the
destruction of the state; that it would be better to kill for more
transgressions rather than for less.

2   Today, both in England and America, the number of capital offenses has been reduced to a very few, and capital punishment
would doubtless be abolished altogether were it not for the self-

righteous, who still defend it with the same old arguments. Their major claim is that capital punishment decreases the number of murders, and hence, that the state must retain the institution as its last defense against the criminal.

3   It is my purpose in this article to prove, first, that capital punishment is no deterrent to crime; and second, that the state continues to kill its victims, not so much to defend society against them—for it could do that equally well by imprisonment—but to appease the mob's emotions of hatred and revenge.

4   Behind the idea of capital punishment lie false training and crude views of human conduct. People do evil things, say the judges, lawyers, and preachers, because of depraved hearts. Human conduct is not determined by the causes which determine the conduct of other animal and plant life in the universe. For some mysterious reason human beings act as they please; and if they do not please to act in a certain way, it is because, having the power of choice, they deliberately choose to act wrongly. The world once applied this doctrine to disease and insanity in men. It was also applied to animals, and even inanimate things were once tried and condemned to destruction. The world knows better now, but the rule has not yet been extended to human beings.

5   The simple fact is that every person starts life with a certain physical structure, more or less sensitive, stronger or weaker. He is played upon by everything that reaches him from without, and in this he is like everything else in the universe, inorganic matter as well as organic. How a man will act depends upon the character of his human machine, and the strength of the various stimuli that affect it. Everyone knows that this is so in disease and insanity. Most investigators know that it applies to crime. But the great mass of people still sit in judgment, robed with self-righteousness, and determine the fate of their less fortunate fellows. When this question is studied like any other, we shall then know how to get rid of most of the conduct that we call "criminal," just as we are now getting rid of much of the disease that once afflicted mankind.

6   If crime were really the result of wilful depravity, we should be ready to concede that capital punishment may serve as a deterrent to the criminally inclined. But it is hardly probable that the great majority of people refrain from killing their neighbors because they are afraid; they refrain because they never had the inclination. Human beings are creatures of habit; and, as a rule, they are not

in the habit of killing. The circumstances that lead to killings are manifold, but in a particular individual the inducing cause is not easily found. In one case, homicide may have been induced by indigestion in the killer; in another, it may be traceable to some weakness inherited from a remote ancestor; but that it results from *something* tangible and understandable, if all the facts were known, must be plain to everyone who believes in cause and effect.

7   Of course, no one will be converted to this point of view by statistics of crime. In the first place, it is impossible to obtain reliable ones; and in the second place, the conditions to which they apply are never the same. But if one cares to analyze the figures, such as we have, it is easy to trace the more frequent causes of homicide. The greatest number of killings occur during attempted burglaries and robberies. The robber knows that penalties for burglary do not average more than five years in prison. He also knows that the penalty for murder is death or imprisonment. Faced with this alternative, what does the burglar do when he is detected and threatened with arrest? He shoots to kill. He deliberately takes the chance of death to save himself from a five-year term in prison. It is therefore as obvious as anything can be that fear of death has no effect in diminishing homicides of this kind, which are more numerous than any other type.

8   The next largest number of homicides may be classed as "sex murders." Quarrels between husbands and wives, disappointed love, or love too much requited cause many killings. They are the result of primal emotions so deep that the fear of death has not the slightest effect in preventing them. Spontaneous feelings overflow in criminal acts, and consequences do not count.

9   Then there are cases of sudden anger, uncontrollable rage. The fear of death never enters into such cases; if the anger is strong enough, consequences are not considered until too late. The old-fashioned stories of men deliberately plotting and committing murder in cold blood have little foundation in real life. Such killings are so rare that they need not concern us here. The point to be emphasized is that practically all homicides are manifestations of well-recognized human emotions, and it is perfectly plain that the fear of excessive punishment does not enter into them.

10   In addition to these personal forces which overwhelm weak men and lead them to commit murder, there are also many social and economic forces which must be listed among the causes of homi-

cides, and human beings have even less control over these than over their own emotions. It is often said that in America there are more homicides in proportion to population than in England. This is true. There are likewise more in the United States than in Canada. But such comparisons are meaningless until one takes into consideration the social and economic differences in the countries compared. Then it becomes apparent why the homicide rate in the United States is higher. Canada's population is largely rural; that of the United States is crowded into cities whose slums are the natural breeding places of crime. Moreover, the population of England and Canada is homogeneous, while the United States has gathered together people of every color from every nation in the world. Racial differences intensify social, religious, and industrial problems, and the confusion which attends this indiscriminate mixing of races and nationalities is one of the most fertile sources of crime.

11   Will capital punishment remedy these conditions? Of course it won't; but its advocates argue that the fear of this extreme penalty will hold the victims of adverse conditions in check. To this piece of sophistry the continuance and increase of crime in our large cities is a sufficient answer. No, the plea that capital punishment acts as a deterrent to crime will not stand. The real reason why this barbarous practice persists in a so-called civilized world is that people still hold the primitive belief that the taking of one human life can be atoned for by taking another. It is the age-old obsession with punishment that keeps the official headsman busy plying his trade.

12   And it is precisely upon this point that I would build my case against capital punishment. Even if one grants that the idea of punishment is sound, crime calls for something more—for careful study, for an understanding of causes, for proper remedies. To attempt to abolish crime by killing the criminal is the easy and foolish way out of a serious situation. Unless a remedy deals with the conditions which foster crime, criminals will breed faster than the hangman can spring his trap. Capital punishment ignores the causes of crime just as completely as the primitive witch doctor ignored the causes of disease, and, like the methods of the witch doctor, it is not only ineffective as a remedy, but is positively vicious in at least two ways. In the first place, the spectacle of state executions feeds the basest passions of the mob. And in the second

place, so long as the state rests content to deal with crime in this barbaric and futile manner, society will be lulled by a false sense of security, and effective methods of dealing with crime will be discouraged.

13   It seems to be a general impression that there are fewer homicides in Great Britain than in America because in England punishment is more certain, more prompt, and more severe. As a matter of fact, the reverse is true. In England the average term for burglary is eighteen months; with us it is probably four or five years. In England, imprisonment for life means twenty years. Prison sentences in the United States are harder than in any country in the world that could be classed as civilized. This is true largely because, with us, practically no official dares to act on his own judgment. The mob is all-powerful and demands blood for blood. That intangible body of people called "the public" vents its hatred upon the criminal and enjoys the sensation of having him put to death by the state—this without any definite idea that it is really necessary.

14   For the last five or six years, in England and Wales, the homicides reported by the police range from sixty-five to seventy a year. Death sentences meted out by jurors have averaged about thirty-five, and hangings, fifteen. More than half of those convicted by juries were saved by appeals to the Home Office. But in America there is no such percentage of lives saved after conviction. Governors are afraid to grant clemency. If they did, the newspapers and the populace would refuse to re-elect them.

15   It is true that trials are somewhat prompter in England than America, but there no newspaper dares publish the details of any case until after the trial. In America the accused is often convicted by the public within twenty-four hours of the time a homicide occurs. The courts sidetrack all other business so that a homicide that is widely discussed may receive prompt attention. The road to the gallows is not only opened but greased for the opportunity of killing another victim.

16   Thus, while capital punishment panders to the passions of the mob, no one takes the pains to understand the meaning of crime. People speak of crime or criminals as if the world were divided into the good and the bad. This is not true. All of us have the same emotions, but since the balance of emotions is never the same, nor the inducing causes identical, human conduct presents

a wide range of differences, shading by almost imperceptible degrees from that of the saint to that of the murderer. Of those kinds of conduct which are classed as dangerous, by no means all are made criminal offenses. Who can clearly define the difference between certain legal offenses and many kinds of dangerous conduct not singled out by criminal statute? Why are many cases of cheating entirely omitted from the criminal code, such as false and misleading advertisements, selling watered stock, forestalling the market, and all the different ways in which great fortunes are accumulated to the envy and despair of those who would like to have money but do not know how to get it? Why do we kill people for the crime of homicide and administer a lesser penalty for burglary, robbery, and cheating? Can anyone tell which is the greater crime and which is the lesser?

17   Human conduct is by no means so simple as our moralists have led us to believe. There is no sharp line separating good actions from bad. The greed for money, the display of wealth, the despair of those who witness the display, the poverty, oppression, and hopelessness of the unfortunate—all these are factors which enter into human conduct and of which the world takes no account. Many people have learned no other profession but robbery and burglary. The processions moving steadily through our prisons to the gallows are in the main made up of these unfortunates. And how do we dare to consider ourselves civilized creatures when, ignoring the causes of crime, we rest content to mete out harsh punishments to the victims of conditions over which they have no control?

18   Even now, are not all imaginative and humane people shocked at the spectacle of a killing by the state? How many men and women would be willing to act as executioners? How many fathers and mothers would want their children to witness an official killing? What kind of people read the sensational reports of an execution? If all right-thinking men and women were not ashamed of it, why would it be needful that judges and lawyers and preachers apologize for the barbarity? How can the state censure the cruelty of the man who—moved by strong passions, or acting to save his freedom, or influenced by weakness or fear—takes human life, when everyone knows that the state itself, after long premeditation and settled hatred, not only kills, but first tortures, and bedevils its victims for weeks with the impending doom?

19   For the last hundred years the world has shown a gradual tendency to mitigate punishment. We are slowly learning that this way of controlling human beings is both cruel and ineffective. In England the criminal code has consistently grown more humane, until now the offenses punishable by death are reduced to practically one. There is no doubt whatever that the world is growing more humane and more sensitive and more understanding. The time will come when all people will view with horror the light way in which society and its courts of law now take human life; and when that time comes, the way will be clear to devise some better method of dealing with poverty and ignorance and their frequent byproducts, which we call crime.

Analyzing the Writer's Argument

1. In the first three paragraphs of his essay Darrow makes reference to "the self-righteous" and the "mob." Who are these people? Are they separate groups or are they one and the same? Explain.

2. As Darrow sees it, are criminals different from other people? Why or why not?

3. What reasons does Darrow give for why he believes that capital punishment does not deter crime? Do you find his reasons convincing? Why or why not?

4. Review Darrow's comments about the way crime is handled in England and Wales. Why does he compare our situation in America to that of the people in those countries? Is the comparison helpful to you in your understanding of the issues? Explain.

5. At the end of paragraph 16, Darrow writes: "Why do we kill people for the crime of homicide and administer a lesser penalty for burglary, robbery, and cheating? Can anyone tell which is the greater crime and which is the lesser?" Is Darrow's question naive or is there something more to it? Explain.

6. Who is Darrow's intended audience? How do you know? Does he hope to change the thinking of those he criticizes in the essay, fellow lawyers and other members of the judicial system, thoughtful and sensitive people in general, or yet some other group that is interested in the question of capital punishment? Explain.

7. What does Darrow find offensive about the state's carrying out of the death sentence? What does he believe that the state should be doing instead? Do you agree with him on this point?

Exploring the Issues in This Essay

1. Are you convinced by Darrow's argument that criminals do not think of the consequences of their actions and therefore would not be deterred by the knowledge that if they are caught and convicted they would be executed? Why or why not?

2. What changes have occurred in American life and culture between the time that Darrow wrote and published his essay and the present that affect the way we regard capital punishment? What do most Americans believe regarding capital punishment? Would they like to see capital punishment laws upheld, done away with, modified? Where could information concerning our current attitudes be found?

H. L. Mencken

The Penalty of Death

> *Born in Baltimore, Henry Louis Mencken (1880–1956) brought a boisterous irreverence to American letters in the early years of this century. He was contemptuous of politics and highly skeptical of democracy, once saying that "democracy is the theory that the common people know what they want, and deserve to get it good and hard." Fresh out of high school, Mencken began his career as a journalist with the Baltimore* Herald; *at twenty-five, he was its editor-in-chief. He achieved a national audience as a columnist for the Baltimore* Sun, *literary critic for* The Smart Set, *and co-founder and editor of the* American Mercury, *for which he wrote on everything from American lifestyles to social issues.*
>
> *Many of his best articles are collected in the six-volume* Prejudices *(1919–1927). In "The Penalty of Death," taken from* Prejudices, Fifth Series, *Mencken in his inimitable style rebuts the two most common arguments of the 1920s against capital punishment.*

1   Of the arguments against capital punishment that issue from uplifters, two are commonly heard most often, to wit:

    1. That hanging a man (or frying him or gassing him) is a dreadful business, degrading to those who have to do it and revolting to those who have to witness it.

    2. That it is useless, for it does not deter others from the same crime.

2   The first of these arguments, it seems to me, is plainly too weak to need serious refutation. All it says, in brief, is that the work of the hangman is unpleasant. Granted. But suppose it is? It may be quite necessary to society for all that. There are, indeed, many other jobs that are unpleasant, and yet no one thinks of abolishing them—that of the plumber, that of the soldier, that of the

garbage-man, that of the priest hearing confessions, that of the sand-hog, and so on. Moreover, what evidence is there that any actual hangman complains of his work? I have heard none. On the contrary, I have known many who delighted in their ancient art, and practiced it proudly.

3   In the second argument of the abolitionists there is rather more force, but even here, I believe, the ground under them is shaky. Their fundamental error consists in assuming that the whole aim of punishing criminals is to deter other (potential) criminals—that we hang or electrocute A simply in order to so alarm B that he will not kill C. This, I believe, is an assumption which confuses a part with a whole. Deterrence, obviously, is *one* of the aims of punishment, but it is surely not the only one. On the contrary, there are at least a half dozen, and some are probably quite as important. At least one of them, practically considered, is *more* important. Commonly, it is described as revenge, but revenge is really not the word for it. I borrow a better term from the late Aristotle: *katharsis. Katharsis,* so used, means a salubrious discharge of emotions, a healthy letting off of steam. A school-boy, disliking his teacher, deposits a tack upon the pedagogical chair; the teacher jumps and the boy laughs. This is *katharsis.* What I contend is that one of the prime objects of all judicial punishments is to afford the same grateful relief (*a*) to the immediate victims of the criminal punished, and (*b*) to the general body of moral and timorous men.

4   These persons, and particularly the first group, are concerned only indirectly with deterring other criminals. The thing they crave primarily is the satisfaction of seeing the criminal actually before them suffer as he made them suffer. What they want is the peace of mind that goes with the feeling that accounts are squared. Until they get that satisfaction they are in a state of emotional tension, and hence unhappy. The instant they get it they are comfortable. I do not argue that this yearning is noble; I simply argue that it is almost universal among human beings. In the face of injuries that are unimportant and can be borne without damage it may yield to higher impulses; that is to say, it may yield to what is called Christian charity. But when the injury is serious Christianity is adjourned, and even saints reach for their sidearms. It is plainly asking too much of human nature to expect it to conquer so natural an impulse. A keeps a store and has a bookkeeper, B. B steals $700, employs it in playing at dice or bingo, and is cleaned out. What is

A to do? Let B go? If he does so he will be unable to sleep at night. The sense of injury, of injustice, of frustration will haunt him like pruritus. So he turns B over to the police, and they hustle B to prison. Thereafter A can sleep. More, he has pleasant dreams. He pictures B chained to the wall of a dungeon a hundred feet underground, devoured by rats and scorpions. It is so agreeable that it makes him forget his $700. He has got his *katharsis*.

5   The same thing precisely takes place on a larger scale when there is a crime which destroys a whole community's sense of security. Every law-abiding citizen feels menaced and frustrated until the criminals have been struck down—until the communal capacity to get even with them, and more than even, has been dramatically demonstrated. Here, manifestly, the business of deterring others is no more than an afterthought. The main thing is to destroy the concrete scoundrels whose act has alarmed everyone, and thus made everyone unhappy. Until they are brought to book that unhappiness continues; when the law has been executed upon them there is a sigh of relief. In other words, there is *katharsis*.

6   I know of no public demand for the death penalty for ordinary crimes, even for ordinary homicides. Its infliction would shock all men of normal decency of feeling. But for crimes involving the deliberate and inexcusable taking of human life, by men openly defiant of all civilized order—for such crimes it seems, to nine men out of ten, a just and proper punishment. Any lesser penalty leaves them feeling that the criminal has got the better of society— that he is free to add insult to injury by laughing. That feeling can be dissipated only by a recourse to *katharsis*, the invention of the aforesaid Aristotle. It is more effectively and economically achieved, as human nature now is, by wafting the criminal to realms of bliss.

7   The real object to capital punishment doesn't lie against the actual extermination of the condemned, but against our brutal American habit of putting it off so long. After all, every one of us must die soon or late, and a murderer, it must be assumed, is one who makes that sad fact the cornerstone of his metaphysic. But it is one thing to die, and quite another thing to lie for long months and even years under the shadow of death. No sane man would choose such a finish. All of us, despite the Prayer Book, long for a swift and unexpected end. Unhappily, a murderer, under the ir-

rational American system, is tortured for what, to him, must seen a whole series of eternities. For months on end he sits in prison while his lawyers carry on their idiotic buffoonery with writs, injunctions, mandamuses, and appeals. In order to get his money (or that of his friends) they have to feed him with hope. Now and then, by the imbecility of a judge or some trick of juridic science, they actually justify it. But let us say that, his money all gone, they finally throw up their hands. Their client is now ready for the rope or the chair. But he must still wait for months before it fetches him.

8   That wait, I believe, is horribly cruel. I have seen more than one man sitting in the death-house, and I don't want to see any more. Worse, it is wholly useless. Why should he wait at all? Why not hang him the day after the last court dissipates his last hope? Why torture him as not even cannibals would torture their victims? The common answer is that he must have time to make his peace with God. But how long does that take? It may be accomplished, I believe, in two hours quite as comfortably as in two years. There are, indeed, no temporal limitations upon God. He could forgive a whole herd of murderers in a millionth of a second. More, it has been done.

Analyzing the Writer's Argument

1. Why do you suppose Mencken starts his essay by presenting two arguments against capital punishment? What would he have gained or lost had he presented these arguments after stating his own position?
2. Mencken labels those opposed to capital punishment as "uplifters." What is your reaction to this label? How do you think Mencken wanted his contemporaries to react? Explain.
3. On what grounds does Mencken refute the argument that capital punishment functions as a deterrent?
4. Mencken believes that the primary aim of capital punishment is *katharsis*. What is *katharsis*, and how does it differ from revenge? Did Mencken's hypothetical examples of the schoolboy and the storekeeper effectively illustrate this concept for you?
5. For what types of crimes does Mencken feel there is a public demand for the death penalty? Do you agree with Mencken? Explain.

6. Mencken claims that he has known many hangmen and more than one man on death row. Do you believe him? Does it make any difference to you that he has known these people?
7. Mencken earned a reputation for saying the most outrageous things about almost any topic conceivable. What, if anything, in Mencken's style or approach to this very serious topic do you find shocking?

Exploring the Issues in This Essay

1. Mencken cites two arguments against capital punishment. What other arguments have you heard? How do you think Mencken would have responded to those arguments? Be specific.
2. What does Mencken find wrong with America's judicial system? To what extent is the way that capital punishment is administered from conviction to execution "horribly cruel"? Are there any good reasons for having the process stretch out over a period of time?

Edward I. Koch

Death and Justice: How Capital Punishment Affirms Life

> *Born in New York City in 1924, Edward I. Koch graduated from City College and New York University Law School. He became active in Democratic politics in 1962, served as a member of Congress from 1969 to 1976, and was elected mayor of New York City in 1977, an office he held until 1989. Famous for his good humor, tough talk, and up-front manner, Koch led New York through a period of economic and social change characterized by strikes, a rising crime rate, and unemployment. Koch's three books* Mayor *(1985),* Politics *(1986), and* His Eminence and Hizzoner *(with John Cardinal O'Connor) (1989) attest to his willingness to publicly engage the issues and to share his beliefs.*
>
> *"Death and Justice: How Capital Punishment Affirms Life" was first published in* The New Republic *in 1985. As the mayor of a city with one of the highest crime rates in the nation, Koch takes a strong law-and-order stance with regard to capital punishment, and in this essay he argues against those who seek the abolishment of the death penalty.*

1   Last December a man named Robert Lee Willie, who had been convicted of raping and murdering an 18-year-old woman, was executed in the Louisiana state prison. In a statement issued several minutes before his death, Mr. Willie said: "Killing people is wrong. . . . It makes no difference whether it's citizens, countries, or governments. Killing is wrong." Two weeks later in South Carolina, an admitted killer named Joseph Carl Shaw was put to death for murdering two teenagers. In an appeal to the governor for clemency, Mr. Shaw wrote: "Killing is wrong when I did it. Killing is wrong when you do it. I hope you have the courage and moral strength to stop the killing."

2   It is a curiosity of modern life that we find ourselves being lectured on morality by cold-blooded killers. Mr. Willie previously

had been convicted of aggravated rape, aggravated kidnapping, and the murders of a Louisiana deputy and a man from Missouri. Mr. Shaw committed another murder a week before the two for which he was executed, and admitted mutilating the body of the 14-year-old girl he killed. I can't help wondering what prompted these murderers to speak out against killing as they entered the death-house door. Did their newfound reverence for life stem from the realization that they were about to lose their own?

3   Life is indeed precious, and I believe the death penalty helps to affirm this fact. Had the death penalty been a real possibility in the minds of these murderers, they might well have stayed their hand. They might have shown moral awareness before their victims died, and not after. Consider the tragic death of Rosa Velez, who happened to be home when a man named Luis Vera burglarized her apartment in Brooklyn. "Yeah, I shot her," Vera admitted. "She knew me, and I knew I wouldn't go to the chair."

4   During my 22 years in public service, I have heard the pros and cons of capital punishment expressed with special intensity. As a district leader, councilman, congressman, and mayor, I have represented constituencies generally thought of as liberal. Because I support the death penalty for heinous crimes of murder, I have sometimes been the subject of emotional and outraged attacks by voters who find my position reprehensible or worse. I have listened to their ideas. I have weighed their objections carefully. I still support the death penalty. The reasons I maintain my position can be best understood by examining the arguments most frequently heard in opposition.

5   1. *The death penalty is "barbaric."* Sometimes opponents of capital punishment horrify with tales of lingering death on the gallows, of faulty electric chairs, or of agony in the gas chamber. Partly in response to such protests, several states such as North Carolina and Texas switched to execution by lethal injection. The condemned person is put to death painlessly, without ropes, voltage, bullets, or gas. Did this answer the objections of death penalty opponents? Of course not. On June 22, 1984, *The New York Times* published an editorial that sarcastically attacked the new "hygienic" method of death by injection, and stated that "execution can never be made humane through science." So it's not the method that really troubles opponents. It's the death itself they consider barbaric.

6   Admittedly, capital punishment is not a pleasant topic. However, one does not have to like the death penalty in order to support it any more than one must like radical surgery, radiation, or chemotherapy in order to find necessary these attempts at curing cancer. Ultimately we may learn how to cure cancer with a simple pill. Unfortunately, that day has not yet arrived. Today we are faced with the choice of letting the cancer spread or trying to cure it with the methods available, methods that one day will almost certainly be considered barbaric. But to give up and do nothing would be far more barbaric and would certainly delay the discovery of an eventual cure. The analogy between cancer and murder is imperfect, because murder is not the "disease" we are trying to cure. The disease is injustice. We may not like the death penalty, but it must be available to punish crimes of cold-blooded murder, cases in which any other form of punishment would be inadequate and, therefore, unjust. If we create a society in which injustice is not tolerated, incidents of murder—the most flagrant form of injustice—will diminish.

7   *2. No other major democracy uses the death penalty.* No other major democracy—in fact, few other countries of any description—are plagued by a murder rate such as that in the United States. Fewer and fewer Americans can remember the days when unlocked doors were the norm and murder was a rare and terrible offense. In America the murder rate climbed 122 percent between 1963 and 1980. During that same period, the murder rate in New York City increased by almost 400 percent, and the statistics are even worse in many other cities. A study at M.I.T. showed that based on 1970 homicide rates a person who lived in a large American city ran a greater risk of being murdered than an American soldier in World War II ran of being killed in combat. It is not surprising that the laws of each country differ according to differing conditions and traditions. If other countries had our murder problem, the cry for capital punishment would be just as loud as it is here. And I daresay that any other major democracy where 75 percent of the people supported the death penalty would soon enact it into law.

8   *3. An innocent person might be executed by mistake.* Consider the work of Hugo Adam Bedau, one of the most implacable foes of capital punishment in this country. According to Mr. Bedau, it is

"false sentimentality to argue that the death penalty should be abolished because of the abstract possibility that an innocent person might be executed." He cites a study of the 7,000 executions in this country from 1893 to 1971, and concludes that the record fails to show that such cases occur. The main point, however, is this. If government functioned only when the possibility of error didn't exist, government wouldn't function at all. Human life deserves special protection, and one of the best ways to guarantee that protection is to assure that convicted murderers do not kill again. Only the death penalty can accomplish this end. In a recent case in New Jersey, a man named Richard Biegenwald was freed from prison after serving 18 years for murder; since his release he has been convicted of committing four murders. A prisoner named Lemuel Smith, who while serving four life sentences for murder (plus two life sentences for kidnapping and robbery) in New York's Green Haven Prison, lured a woman corrections officer into the chaplain's office and strangled her. He then mutilated and dismembered her body. An additional life sentence for Smith is meaningless. Because New York has no death penalty statute, Smith has effectively been given a license to kill.

9   But the problem of multiple murder is not confined to the nation's penitentiaries. In 1981, 91 police officers were killed in the line of duty in this country. Seven percent of those arrested in the cases that have been solved had a previous arrest for murder. In New York City in 1976 and 1977, 85 persons arrested for homicide had a previous arrest for murder. Six of these individuals had two previous arrests for murder, and one had four previous murder arrests. During those two years the New York police were arresting for murder persons with a previous arrest for murder on the average of one every 8.5 days. This is not surprising when we learn that in 1975, for example, the median time served in Massachusetts for homicide was less than two-and-a-half years. In 1976 a study sponsored by the Twentieth Century Fund found that the average time served in the United States for first-degree murder is ten years. The median time served may be considerably lower.

10   4. *Capital punishment cheapens the value of human life.* On the contrary, it can be easily demonstrated that the death penalty strengthens the value of human life. If the penalty for rape were lowered,

clearly it would signal a lessened regard for the victims' suffering, humiliation, and personal integrity. It would cheapen their horrible experience, and expose them to an increased danger of recurrence. When we lower the penalty for murder, it signals a lessened regard for the value of the victim's life. Some critics of capital punishment, such as columnist Jimmy Breslin, have suggested that a life sentence is actually a harsher penalty for murder than death. This is sophistic nonsense. A few killers may decide not to appeal a death sentence, but the overwhelming majority make every effort to stay alive. It is by exacting the highest penalty for the taking of human life that we affirm the highest value of human life.

11   5. *The death penalty is applied in a discriminatory manner.* This factor no longer seems to be the problem it once was. The appeals process for a condemned prisoner is lengthy and painstaking. Every effort is made to see that the verdict and sentence were fairly arrived at. However, assertions of discrimination are not an argument for ending the death penalty but for extending it. It is not justice to exclude everyone from the penalty of the law if a few are found to be so favored. Justice requires that the law be applied equally to all.

12   6. *Thou Shalt Not Kill.* The Bible is our greatest source of moral inspiration. Opponents of the death penalty frequently cite the sixth of the Ten Commandments in an attempt to prove that capital punishment is divinely proscribed. In the original Hebrew, however, the Sixth Commandment reads, "Thou Shalt Not Commit Murder," and the Torah specifies capital punishment for a variety of offenses. The biblical viewpoint has been upheld by philosophers throughout history. The greatest thinkers of the 19th century— Kant, Locke, Hobbes, Rousseau, Montesquieu, and Mill—agreed that natural law properly authorizes the sovereign to take life in order to vindicate justice. Only Jeremy Bentham was ambivalent. Washington, Jefferson, and Franklin endorsed it. Abraham Lincoln authorized executions for deserters in wartime. Alexis de Tocqueville, who expressed profound respect for American institutions, believed that the death penalty was indispensable to the support of social order. The United States Constitution, widely admired as one of the seminal achievements in the history of humanity, condemns cruel and inhuman punishment, but does not condemn capital punishment.

13   7. *The death penalty is state-sanctioned murder.* This is the defense with which Messrs. Willie and Shaw hoped to soften the resolve of those who sentenced them to death. By saying in effect, "You're no better than I am," the murderer seeks to bring his accusers down to his own level. It is also a popular argument among opponents of capital punishment, but a transparently false one. Simply put, the state has rights that the private individual does not. In a democracy, those rights are given to the state by the electorate. The execution of a lawfully condemned killer is no more an act of murder than is legal imprisonment an act of kidnapping. If an individual forces a neighbor to pay him money under threat of punishment, it's called extortion. If the state does it, it's called taxation. Rights and responsibilities surrendered by the individual are what give the state its power to govern. This contract is the foundation of civilization itself.

14   Everyone wants his or her rights, and will defend them jealously. Not everyone, however, wants responsibilities, especially the painful responsibilities that come with law enforcement. Twenty-one years ago a woman named Kitty Genovese was assaulted and murdered on a street in New York. Dozens of neighbors heard her cries for help but did nothing to assist her. They didn't even call the police. In such a climate the criminal understandably grows bolder. In the presence of moral cowardice, he lectures us on our supposed failings and tries to equate his crimes with our quest for justice.

15   The death of anyone—even a convicted killer—diminishes us all. But we are diminished even more by a justice system that fails to function. It is an illusion to let ourselves believe that doing away with capital punishment removes the murderer's deed from our conscience. The rights of society are paramount. When we protect guilty lives, we give up innocent lives in exchange. When opponents of capital punishment say to the state: "I will not let you kill in my name," they are also saying to murderers: "You can kill in your *own* name as long as I have an excuse for not getting involved."

16   It is hard to imagine anything worse than being murdered while neighbors do nothing. But something worse exists. When those same neighbors shrink back from justly punishing the murderer, the victim dies twice.

Analyzing the Writer's Argument

1. Where is Koch's thesis and where is it stated?
2. How has Koch organized his essay? What are the advantages of his organizational strategy? Could he have organized it differently without loss of effectiveness?
3. What is the function of paragraph 4 in the context of Koch's argument?
4. In paragraph 6, Koch draws an analogy between cancer and murder. How does he use this analogy to argue against the notion that the death penalty is barbaric?
5. What kinds of examples does Koch use to argue each of his points? Did you find them convincing? Why or why not?
6. In paragraph 9, Koch discusses both the median and the average time served for first degree murder. What is the difference between median and average? Is one term more useful than the other? Explain.
7. Of all the arguments against the death penalty that Koch presents, which do you find the strongest? Why? Is Koch successful in his refutation of this particular argument?

Exploring the Issues in This Essay

1. In paragraph 14, Koch cites the case of Kitty Genovese, a woman who was murdered outside her own apartment while her neighbors watched and did nothing (see Martin Gansberg's "38 Who Saw Murder Didn't Call the Police," pp. 415–419). Discuss the relationship that Koch sees between the Kitty Genovese case and capital punishment. If we do not support capital punishment are we really saying to murderers, as Koch says in paragraph 15, "You can kill in your *own* name as long as I have an excuse for not getting involved"?
2. Consider Koch's title for his essay. In what ways can the death penalty, the taking of a human life, actually affirm that which it so blatantly denies? Explain.

Marvin L. Coan

Let the Convicted Person Decide

A graduate of the University of Indiana, Marvin L. Coan was born in Louisville, Kentucky, in 1948. While studying law at the University of Kentucky, Coan first became intrigued by the issue of capital punishment and subsequently wrote an article about it for the school's law review. Coan has served with the Justice Department in Washington and is currently a practicing attorney in Louisville.

Coan's essay "Let the Convicted Person Decide" first appeared during the heated debate surrounding the celebrated execution of Gary Gilmore by a firing squad. Sensitive to the pain and anguish suffered by all the parties in a capital punishment case—"from judge to jury to the respective families and the condemned person," Coan first proposed the following solution in the Louisville Courier-Journal *in 1980.*

1   The time has come when American society should begin to resolve some of the seemingly insoluble ethical and legal problems that divert our attention from achieving loftier goals such as attaining energy independence and raising the standard of living for all citizens.

2   Since the 1979 execution of Gary Gilmore in Utah ended the 12-year moratorium on carrying out the death penalty, every case involving the possible execution of an individual has become circus-like.

3   Each imposition of the death penalty—a highly charged emotional issue—causes attorneys to race between state and federal courthouses seeking a stay of execution. Meanwhile, the family of the victim curses the delays inherent in such legal maneuvering. Furthermore, members of the condemned person's family are often left with open anguish over whether and when their loved one is going to be put to death.

4   The psychological dilemma imposed upon all the actors in this drama—from judge to jury to the respective families and the con-

demned person—is severely in need of being resolved. The process has become even more complicated since in many instances the condemned person is either unaware of or indifferent to the issue of whether or not the appeal process is worthwhile and may even be totally opposed to further legal action to save him from execution.

5   My proposed solution to the death penalty dilemma would involve amending Kentucky laws (and hopefully pertinent federal statutes) so that all crimes now punishable by death would be changed to carry a punishment of life imprisonment without privilege of parole.

6   In this respect, society would be adequately protected from those individuals who deserve such severe punishment and there still would be a great deterrent to others who might be inclined to perform heinous acts. Our only sacrifice as a society would be the elimination of any possible "benefit" to be derived from retribution for the sake of revenge alone.

7   The next and perhaps most revolutionary step in this proposed solution to the death-penalty dilemma would entail a decision made solely by the condemned person facing life imprisonment without privilege of parole. That person, *as opposed to society,* would be permitted to elect self-imposition of death as a sentence alternative with government authorities simply serving to see that death occurred in the most humane way available to medical science.

8   For instance, if the administration of a deadly drug could cause instant death, it would be made available at a specified time, with witnesses chosen by the prisoner available to observe the self-administration of the drug by the condemned person.

9   Society's moral and ethical dilemma will be greatly eased, if not totally eliminated, since the condemned person would make the ultimate freedom-of-choice decision—a life of imprisonment without parole or death self-administered in the most humane fashion known.

10   This proposed solution is not at all unrealistic or farfetched, since so many individuals sentenced to death throughout the nation since the Gilmore execution have openly expressed the preference for death when balanced against the option of life imprisonment without parole.

11   The only pre-condition that would need to be satisfied when allowing self-imposed death would entail a determination of com-

petency. This, however, would be largely resolved when the question of competency to stand trial for the crime is made by the trial court. Only in rare instances would it be necessary to have a second "competency hearing" upon election of self-imposed death by the person—for example, when a pattern of abnormal behavior presented itself after completion of the trial proceedings.

12 My proposal could effectively eliminate the moralistic debate by pro- and anti-capital punishment factions. Society will have fulfilled its duty to protect the citizenry through life imprisonment without parole while doing away with the unenviable task placed upon judges, juries and state officials who have in the past been required to recommend, impose and carry out the death penalty.

13 Even those who base their opposition to the death penalty on the Constitution's Eighth Amendment "cruel-and-unusual-punishment" clause should respect this proposal, since it bestows absolute freedom of choice in death-penalty cases solely upon the convicted person. Since state and/or federal officials would participate in the actual imposition of death *only* by making the means of carrying out the penalty available to the convicted person, their roles would no longer be subject to endless controversy.

14 Seemingly insoluble issues such as the death penalty, abortion and ending discrimination but causing reverse discrimination in the process, must be solved practically and more expeditiously than has been the case in the last several decades. As a nation of multitudinous special-interest groups, we must begin to realize that resolution of such problems cannot be accomplished until there is a relaxation of absolutist principles by opposing factions. Only in this manner can a workable consensus be achieved.

15 Until the various factions on both sides of moral and ethical problems of contemporary American society realize that there will never be a true winner or true loser emergent from the fray, real progress in advancing the living standards of all Americans will remain an elusive goal.

Analyzing the Writer's Argument

1. What, according to Coan, is the death penalty dilemma in America? What does he mean when he says "every case involving the possible execution of an individual has become circus-like"?

2. What is Coan's solution to the death penalty dilemma? To what extent does his solution meet the objectives of capital punishment? In what ways is his proposal better?
3. If we adopted Coan's solution, what "sacrifice" would we have to make? Is this a real sacrifice in your opinion? Explain.
4. What possible objections to his proposal does Coan anticipate? Did you find his refutations convincing? Why or why not?
5. Does Coan's proposal "effectively eliminate the moralistic debate by pro- and anti-capital punishment factions" as he claims in paragraphs 12 and 13? Explain.
6. Why does Coan believe that it is time for Americans to resolve the ethical and legal problems associated with capital punishment?

Exploring the Issues in This Essay

1. Many would argue that allowing a condemned person "to elect self-imposition of death" raises yet another moral issue. Do you have any reservations about allowing a convicted person to choose death? In effect, wouldn't this legalize suicide? Finally, what about the person who has a change of heart, electing life imprisonment initially and later wanting to take his or her own life?
2. Coan never addresses the issue of the cost of life imprisonment without benefit of parole. Is this an extraneous issue or is it something that ought to be factored into his proposal? In your opinion, what standard of living is society required to provide those in prison for life?

Writing Suggestions for
Capital Punishment

1. What has been the history of capital punishment in your state? Does your state have statutes that permit capital punishment? Has this always been the case? If your state does have, or has had, such laws, when were they first enacted? What types of crimes are punishable by death? What major changes in the laws governing capital punishment have occurred since they were first enacted? Write an essay in which you argue either for the retention of the present laws in your state or for their modification or abolishment.

2. Executions today are rarely witnessed by large numbers of people. Historically, however, this has not always been so. If, as many believe, capital punishment has a deterrent effect, does it make sense for executions to be made private? If the state has the right to execute people, and if by extension we are the state, does not each one of us have the right to witness those executions? Write an essay in which you argue for or against public executions, either televised or publicly attended.

3. Imagine that you have just been convicted of first degree murder in a state where Coan's proposal has been made law. You are now faced with the choice of life in prison without benefit of parole or self-imposition of death. What would you decide? Why? Write an essay in which you defend your decision.

4. Using the seven arguments presented by Koch in his essay for capital punishment, write an essay in which you argue against Coan's proposal that the convicted person be allowed to decide between life in prison or self-imposed death.

5. Clarence Darrow believes that governments continue to carry out capital punishment "to appease the mob's emotions of hatred and revenge." While we perhaps assume that executions are carried out as humanely as possible, history gives us a different picture. Persons convicted of capital crimes have, for example, been boiled in oil, thrown to wild beasts, crucified, torn apart, smothered, and disemboweled. After researching the diverse methods of inflicting death that have been used by various cultures over the centuries, write an essay supporting Darrow's thesis.

6. Using any or all of the essays on capital punishment, write an essay arguing for or against the proposition that the death penalty is nothing more than legalized murder.

7. A relative of yours was brutally murdered and a person has been arrested, tried, convicted, and is now awaiting sentencing. What

would you like to see happen to the person convicted of the crime? Write a letter to the prosecutor or the editor of your local newspaper in which you argue for either life imprisonment or the death penalty.

8. Argue for or against the creation of a federal law that would standardize the treatment of people convicted of serious crimes in this country. What would be the advantages of such a law? What possible objections might individual states have to the creation of a national capital punishment statute?

9. Starting in the middle of the nineteenth century, many countries have abolished the death penalty. Their ranks now include Netherlands, Portugal, Norway, Sweden, Denmark, Switzerland, Austria, West Germany, Italy, Britain, New Zealand, and France among others. Research the situation in any one of the countries that has abolished capital punishment to determine what has been its experience. What does the information you gather add to the debate about capital punishment here in America? Should America abolish capital punishment? Write an essay in which you argue for your position.

10. Much of the controversy surrounding the Supreme Court's decisions in the 1970s regarding capital punishment had to do with interpretations of the phrase "cruel and unusual punishment" in the Constitution. When does punishment become cruel and unusual? Are there situations in which the death penalty is cruel and usual? In a brief essay, define the phrase "cruel and unusual punishment" as it applies to capital punishment. Use quotations from the essays in this section to illustrate your definition.

12

Censorship

CAUTION!

SOME PEOPLE CONSIDER THESE BOOKS DANGEROUS

AMERICAN HERITAGE DICTIONARY • THE BIBLE • ARE YOU THERE, GOD? IT'S ME, MARGARET • OUR BODIES, OURSELVES • TARZAN ALICE'S ADVENTURES IN WONDERLAND • THE EXORCIST • THE CHOCOLATE WAR • CATCH-22 • LORD OF THE FLIES • ORDINARY PEOPLE • SOUL ON ICE • RAISIN IN THE SUN • OLIVER TWIST • A FAREWELL TO ARMS • THE BEST SHORT STORIES OF NEGRO WRITERS • FLOWERS FOR ALGERNON • ULYSSES • TO KILL A MOCKINGBIRD • ROSEMARY'S BABY • THE FIXER • DEATH OF A SALESMAN • MOTHER GOOSE • CATCHER IN THE RYE • THE MERCHANT OF VENICE • ONE DAY IN THE LIFE OF IVAN DENISOVICH • GRAPES OF WRATH • THE ADVENTURES OF HUCKLEBERRY FINN • SLAUGHTERHOUSE-FIVE • GO ASK ALICE

BANNED BOOKS WEEK—CELEBRATING THE FREEDOM TO READ

Courtesy of the American Library Association.

Censorship is the suppression of information, ideas, or artistic expression by private citizens, church officials, government authorities, school and community leaders. It may even be self-imposed as in the case of an artist or writer who does not want to incur public sanction or punishment.

485

In America, we have come to take freedom of speech for granted. After all, it is guaranteed by the First Amendment of our Constitution: "Congress shall make no law respecting an establishment of religion, or prohibiting the free exercise thereof; or abridging the freedom of speech, or of the press, or the right of the people peaceably to assemble, and to petition the Government for a redress of grievances." Therefore, if you asked Americans if they were in favor of censorship most would probably answer "No." Yet you are likely to get a different response if you ask those same people whether they are in favor of making readily available such books as: *The Terrorist's Handbook, How to Commit Suicide, The Do-It-Yourself Guide to Making an Atomic Bomb, How to Overthrow the Government*, or *Quick Profits in Designer Drugs*. The titles are fictional, but it may surprise you to learn that real books with similar titles are, in fact, legally available today.

In spite of First Amendment rights, censorship exists. In a society that is based upon the free exchange of ideas and beliefs, there will always be people who are not satisfied to just promote their own ideas but who also wish to suppress those ideas that are not to their liking. In the United States today, censorship knows no geographical or political bounds. Censorship debates currently center on the content of school newspapers, the explicit sex and violence in rock lyrics and video, obscenity and pornography in the film and magazine industries, and the perennial targets of censorship, books, especially the classics. Some censorship is carried out with the best of intentions, to protect the defenseless, the young, the government, and society at large. But as Henry Steele Commager has observed, "Censorship always defeats its own purpose, for it creates in the end, the kind of society that is incapable of exercising real discretion. In the long run it will create a generation incapable of appreciating the difference between independence of thought and subservience."

If Commager is right and censorship is essentially self-defeating, what then is the controversy? The controversy grows out of differences of opinion or belief. Today, for example, many Americans believe for one reason or another that our society is tending to become morally degenerate and valueless. Thinking that the way to reverse that trend is to suppress ideas and forms of expression that eat away at America's traditional values, concerned citizens have called for tighter controls on the types of information, ideas, and artistic expression made available to the public.

Nat Hentoff

When Nice People Burn Books

A columnist for The Washington Post *and a writer for liberal publications like* The Progressive, *Nat Hentoff was born in Boston, Massachusetts, on June 10, 1925. He has written more than 25 books of fiction and nonfiction, among them* The First Freedom: The Tumultuous History of Free Speech in America. *A self-described advocacy writer, Hentoff says his interest in human rights grew out of his love of jazz and the world it embraces. His articles on racism, the military draft, educational reform, abortion, and police spying have earned Hentoff his reputation as a spokesperson for the Left.*

Despite his liberal persuasions, Hentoff, in the following essay taken from the February 1983 issue of The Progressive, *argues that the far right does not have a monopoly on censorship. He fears those well-meaning people who champion the cause of civil rights while at the same time justifying censorship when it advances their ideas of what is good.*

1   It happened one splendid Sunday morning in a church. Not Jerry Falwell's Baptist sanctuary in Lynchburg, Virginia, but rather the First Unitarian Church in Baltimore. On October 4, 1981, midway through the 11 A. M. service, pernicious ideas were burned at the altar.

2   As reported by Frank P. L. Somerville, religion editor of the *Baltimore Sun*, "Centuries of Jewish, Christian, Islamic, and Hindu writings were 'expurgated'—because of sections described as 'sexist.'

"Touched off by a candle and consumed in a pot on a table in front of the altar were slips of paper containing 'patriarchal' excerpts from Martin Luther, Thomas Aquinas, the Koran, St. Augustine, St. Ambrose, St. John Chrysostom, the Hindu Code of Manu V., an anonymous Chinese author, and the Old Testament." Also hurled into the purifying fire were works by Kierkegaard and Karl Barth.

4   The congregation was much exalted: "As the last flame died in the pot, and the organ pealed, there was applause," Somerville wrote.

5   I reported this news of the singed holy spirit to a group of American Civil Liberties Union members in California, and one woman was furious. At me.

6   "We did the same thing at our church two Sundays ago," she said. "And long past time, too. Don't you understand it's just *symbolic?*"

7   I told this ACLU member that when the school board in Drake, North Dakota, threw thirty-four copies of Kurt Vonnegut's *Slaughterhouse Five* into the furnace in 1973, it wasn't because the school was low on fuel. That burning was symbolic, too. Indeed, the two pyres—in North Dakota and in Baltimore—were witnessing to the same lack of faith in the free exchange of ideas.

8   What an inspiring homily for the children attending services at a liberated church: They now know that the way to handle ideas they don't like is to set them on fire.

9   The stirring ceremony in Baltimore is just one more illustration that the spirit of the First Amendment is not being savaged only by malign forces of the Right, whether private or governmental. Campaigns to purge school libraries, for example, have been conducted by feminists as well as by Phyllis Schlafly. Yet, most liberal watchdogs of our freedom remain fixed on the Right as *the* enemy of free expression.

10   For a salubrious change, therefore, let us look at what is happening to freedom of speech and press in certain enclaves—some colleges, for instance—where the New Right has no clout at all. Does the pulse of the First Amendment beat more vigorously in these places than where the Yahoos are?

11   Well, consider what happened when Eldridge Cleaver came to Madison, Wisconsin, last October to savor the exhilarating openness of dialogue at the University of Wisconsin. Cleaver's soul is no longer on ice; it's throbbing instead with a religious conviction that is currently connected financially, and presumably theologically, to the Reverend Sun Myung Moon's Unification Church. In Madison, Cleaver never got to talk about his pilgrim's progress from the Black Panthers to the wondrously ecumenical Moonies. In the Humanities Building—*Humanities*—several hundred students and others outraged by Cleaver's apostasy shouted, stamped their feet, chanted "Sieg Heil," and otherwise prevented him from being heard.

12   After ninety minutes of the din, Cleaver wrote on the black-board, "I regret that the totalitarians have deprived us of our constitutional rights to free assembly and free speech. Down with communism. Long live democracy."

13   And, raising a clenched fist while blowing kisses with his free hand, Cleaver left. Cleaver says he'll try to speak again, but he doesn't know when.

14   The University of Wisconsin administration, through Dean of Students Paul Ginsberg, deplored the behavior of the campus totalitarians of the Left, and there was a fiercely denunciatory editorial in the Madison *Capital Times:* "These people lack even the most primitive appreciation of the Bill of Rights."

15   It did occur to me, however, that if Eldridge Cleaver had not abandoned his secularist rage at the American Leviathan and had come to Madison as the still burning spear of black radicalism, the result might have been quite different if he had been shouted down that night by young apostles of the New Right. That would have made news around the country, and there would have been collectively signed letters to the *New York Review of Books* and *The Nation* warning of the prowling dangers to free speech in the land. But since Cleaver has long since taken up with bad companions, there is not much concern among those who used to raise bail for him as to whether he gets to speak freely or not.

16   A few years ago, William F. Buckley Jr., invited to be commencement speaker at Vassar, was told by student groups that he not only would be shouted down if he came but might also suffer some contusions. All too few liberal members of the Vassar faculty tried to educate their students about the purpose of a university, and indeed a good many faculty members joined in the protests against Buckley's coming. He finally decided not to appear because, he told me, he didn't want to spoil the day for the parents. I saw no letters on behalf of Buckley's free-speech rights in any of the usual liberal forums for such concerns. After all, he had not only taken up with bad companions; he was an original bad companion.

17   During the current academic year, there were dismaying developments concerning freedom for bad ideas in the college press. The managing editor of *The Daily Lobo*, the University of New Mexico's student newspaper, claimed in an editorial that Scholastic Aptitude Test scores show minority students to be academically in-

ferior. Rather than rebut his facile misinterpretation of what those scores actually show—that class, not race, affects the results—black students and their sympathizers invaded the newspaper's office.

18   The managing editor prudently resigned, but the protesters were not satisfied. They wanted the head of the editor. The brave Student Publications Board temporarily suspended her, although the chairman of the journalism department had claimed the suspension was a violation of her First Amendment rights. She was finally given her job back, pending a formal hearing, but she decided to quit. The uproar had not abated, and who knew what would happen at her formal hearing before the Student Publications Board?

19   When it was all over, the chairman of the journalism department observed that the confrontation had actually reinforced respect for First Amendment rights on the University of New Mexico campus because infuriated students now knew they couldn't successfully insist on the firing of an editor because of what had been published.

20   What about the resignations? Oh, they were free-will offerings.

21   I subscribe to most of the journalism reviews around the country, but I saw no offer of support to those two beleaguered student editors in New Mexico from professional journalists who invoke the First Amendment at almost any public opportunity.

22   Then there was a free-speech war at Kent State University, as summarized in the November 12, 1982, issue of *National On-Campus Report*. Five student groups at Kent State are vigorously attempting to get the editor of the student newspaper fired. They are: "gay students, black students, the undergraduate and graduate student governments, and a progressive student alliance."

23   Not a reactionary among them. Most are probably deeply concerned with the savaging of the free press in Chile, Uruguay, Guatemala, South Africa, and other such places.

24   What had this editor at Kent State done to win the enmity of so humanistic a grand alliance? He had written an editorial that said that a gay student group should not have access to student-fee money to sponsor a Hallowe'en dance. Ah, but how had he gone about making his point?

25   "In opening statements," says the *National On-Campus Report*, "he employed words like 'queer' and 'nigger' to show that prej-

udice against any group is undersirable." Just like Lenny Bruce. Lenny, walking on stage in a club, peering into the audience, and asking, "Any spics here tonight? Any kikes? Any niggers?"

26 Do you think Lenny Bruce could get many college bookings today? Or write a column for a college newspaper?

27 In any case, the rest of the editorial went on to claim that the proper use of student fees was for educational, not social, activities. The editor was not singling out the Kent Gay/Lesbian Foundation. He was opposed to *any* student organization using those fees for dances.

28 Never mind. He had used impermissible words. Queer. Nigger. And those five influential cadres of students are after his head. The editor says that university officials have assured him, however, that he is protected at Kent State by the First Amendment. If that proves to be the case, those five student groups will surely move to terminate, if not defenestrate, those university officials.

29 It is difficult to be a disciple of James Madison on campus these days. Take the case of Phyllis Schlafly and Wabash College. The college is a small, well-regarded liberal arts institution in Crawfordsville, Indiana. In the spring of 1981, the college was riven with discord. Some fifty members of the ninety-odd faculty and staff wrote a stiff letter to the Wabash Lecture Series Committee, which had displayed the exceedingly poor taste to invite Schlafly to speak on campus the next year.

30 The faculty protesters complained that having the Sweetheart of the Right near the Wabash River would be "unfortunate and inappropriate." The dread Schlafly is "an ERA opponent . . . a far-right attorney who travels the country, being highly paid to tell women to stay at home fulfilling traditional roles while sending their sons off to war."

31 Furthermore, the authors wrote, "The point of view she represents is that of an ever-decreasing minority of American women and men, and is based in sexist mythology which promulgates beliefs inconsistent with those held by liberally educated persons, and this does not merit a forum at Wabash College under the sponsorship of our Lecture Series."

32 This is an intriguing document by people steeped in the traditions of academic freedom. One of the ways of deciding who gets invited to a campus is the speaker's popularity. If the speaker

appeals only to a "decreasing minority of American women and men," she's not worth the fee. So much for Dorothy Day, were she still with us.

33 And heaven forfend that anyone be invited whose beliefs are "inconsistent with those held by liberally educated persons." Mirror, mirror on the wall. . . .

34 But do not get the wrong idea about these protesting faculty members: "We subscribe," they emphasized, "to the principles of free speech and free association, of course."

35 All the same, "it does not enhance our image as an all-male college to endorse a well-known sexist by inviting her to speak on our campus." If Phyllis Schlafly is invited nonetheless, "we intend not to participate in any of the activities surrounding Ms. Schlafly's visit and will urge others to do the same."

36 The moral of the story: If you don't like certain ideas, boycott them.

37 The lecture committee responded to the fifty deeply offended faculty members in a most unkind way. The committee told the signers that "William Buckley would endorse your petition. No institution of higher learning, he told us on a visit here, should allow to be heard on its campus any position that it regards as detrimental or 'untrue'.

38 "Apparently," the committee went on, "error is to be refuted not by rational persuasion, but by censorship."

39 Phyllis Schlafly did come to Wabash and she generated a great deal of discussion—most of it against her views—among members of the all-male student body. However, some of the wounded faculty took a long time to recover. One of them, a tenured professor, took aside at a social gathering the wife of a member of the lecture committee that had invited Schafly. Both were in the same feminist group on campus.

40 The professor cleared her throat, and said to the other woman, "You are going to leave him, aren't you?"

41 "My husband? Why should I leave him?"

42 "Really, how can you stay married to someone who invited Phyllis Schlafly to this campus?"

43 And really, should such a man even be allowed visitation rights with the children?

44 Then there is the Ku Klux Klan. As Klan members have learned in recent months, both in Boston and in Washington, their First

Amendment right peaceably to assemble—let alone actually to speak their minds—can only be exercised if they are prepared to be punched in the mouth. Klan members get the same reception that Martin Luther King Jr. and his associates used to receive in Bull Conner's Birmingham.

45 As all right-thinking people know, however, the First Amendment isn't just for anybody. That presumably is why the administration of the University of Cincinnati has refused this year to allow the KKK to appear on campus. Bill Wilkerson, the Imperial Wizard of the particular Klan faction that has been barred from the University of Cincinnati, says he's going to sue on First Amendment grounds.

46 Aside from the ACLU's, how many *amicus* briefs do you think the Imperial Wizard is likely to get from liberal organizations devoted to academic freedom?

47 The Klan also figures in a dismaying case from Vancouver, Washington. There, an all-white jury awarded $1,000 to a black high school student after he had charged the Battle Ground School District (including Prairie High School) with discrimination. One of the claims was that the school had discriminated against this young man by permitting white students to wear Ku Klux Klan costumes to a Hallowe'en assembly.

48 Symbolic speech, however, is like spoken or written speech. It is protected under the First Amendment. If the high school administration had originally forbidden the wearing of the Klan costumes to the Hallowe'en assembly, it would have spared itself that part of the black student's lawsuit, but it would have set a precedent for censoring symbolic speech which would have shrunken First Amendment protections at Prairie High School.

49 What should the criteria be for permissible costumes at a Hallowe'en assembly? None that injure the feelings of another student? So a Palestinian kid couldn't wear a PLO outfit. Or a Jewish kid couldn't come as Ariel Sharon, festooned with maps. And watch out for the wise guy who comes dressed as that all-around pain-in-the-ass, Tom Paine.

50 School administrators might say the best approach is to have no costumes at all. That way, there'll be no danger of disruption. But if there were real danger of physical confrontation in the school when a student wears a Klan costume, is the school so powerless that it can't prevent a fight? And indeed, what a compelling

opportunity the costumes present to teach about the Klan, to ask those white kids who wore Klan costumes what they know of the history of the Klan. To get black and white kids *talking* about what the Klan represents, in history—and right now.

51   Such teaching is too late for Prairie High School. After that $1,000 award to the black student, the white kids who have been infected by Klan demonology will circulate their poison only among themselves, intensifying their sickness of spirit. There will be no more Klan costumes in that school, and so no more Klan costumes to stimulate class discussion.

52   By the way, in the trial, one offer of proof that the school district had been guilty of discrimination was a photograph of four white boys wearing Klan costumes to that Hallowe'en assembly. It's a rare picture. It was originally printed in the school yearbook but, with the lawsuit and all, the picture was cut out of each yearbook before it was distributed.

53   That's the thing about censorship, whether good liberals or bad companions engage in it. Censorship is like a greased pig. Hard to confine. You start trying to deal with offensive costumes and you wind up with a blank space in the yearbook. Isn't that just like the Klan? Causing decent people to do dumb things.

Analyzing the Writer's Argument

1. What is Hentoff's thesis in this essay and where does he present it?

2. In the opening paragraphs of his essay, Hentoff describes two book burnings, one in Baltimore, Maryland, and the other in Drake, North Dakota. In what ways were these burnings different? How were they alike?

3. How does Hentoff respond to the woman who believes that the Baltimore book burning was "just *symbolic*"? What does he see as the flaw in her reasoning?

4. The body of Hentoff's essay contains a number of examples— Phyllis Schlafly, Eldridge Cleaver, William F. Buckley, Jr., and the managing editor of the University of New Mexico's student newspaper, to name just a few. What specifically does each of these examples add to his argument? Did he need to include so many examples of left-wing violations of free-speech rights? Explain.

5. What does Hentoff mean when he says that Buckley "had not only taken up with bad companions; he was an original bad companion"?
6. What, according to Hentoff, is "symbolic speech"? Why does it need to be protected the same way spoken and written speech are? How does Hentoff use the Prairie High School incident to illustrate his point?
7. Who is Hentoff's audience for this essay? How do his diction and examples support your conclusion? How do you interpret his last two sentences? Explain.

Exploring the Issues in This Essay

1. In paragraph 16 Hentoff refers to "the purpose of a university" while discussing students who have refused freedom of speech to people with whom they strongly disagree. What does Hentoff see as the purpose of a university? Do you agree with him? Why or why not? Have incidents like the ones Hentoff describes occurred on your campus? If so, how did you and your peers react?
2. In discussing symbolic speech, Hentoff asks two very basic questions: "What should the criteria be for permissible costumes at a Hallowe'en assembly? None that injure the feelings of another student?" What are your feelings about these questions? Have you ever found the appearance of someone whose views differ from yours offensive? If you were a high school principal what would be your policy on symbolic speech? How would you enforce your policy?

PUZZLED BY BANNED BOOKS?

ACROSS
1. *American Heritage* _____
4. Dorian's creator
10. Bogart/Bacall film
11. *Go Ask* _____
15. *Emma* _____
17. *Boston Collective's book*
20. *O'Hara's War*
21. *Naked* _____
22. Sue Lyon role
26. Diary author
28. _____ *de Maupin*
30. Word from Salinger title
32. *The Living*
33. Author of *Soup*
35. Kurt _____
37. Matthew, Mark, Luke and

John each wrote
39. Hemingway character's milieu
41. Gervaise's daughter
43. Eugene _____
44. Plath's jar
46. Lara's lover
47. *Adam Bede* author
50. One flew over it
51. Part of E.B. Browning title
52. Darwin's theory

DOWN
1. Charles B. _____
2. "A _____," Kubrick film
3. Author of *Human Body*

5. _____ *Story*
6. Jay _____
7. Goethe bestseller
8. Woman with the scarlet letter
9. Maya _____
12. Michigan-born author
13. Gave us *The Giving Tree*
14. *Are You There* _____, *It's Me Margaret*
15. *Decameron* author
16. Studs Terkel's labor
18. Author of *Candide*
19. Loman's profession
23. Orwell's farm
24. Robinson's last name
25. _____ *Tragedy*
27. Erica's fear

29. Alias for Doris Kappelhoff
31. Where Alice had her adventures
33. Corleone's creator
34. Infamous place in early soap
36. *Bridge to* _____
37. Rabelais' largest title
38. Below Benchley's gums
39. Sex education book for children
40. _____ Zola
42. _____ *Fishing in America*
44. Royko title
45. *Little Black* _____
48. Hardy character
49. _____ *Flanders*

Puzzle by Nita Krygier-Fox, Sue Gordan, Dave Bowman, and Michael Hirsch.
Reprinted with permission of the American Library Association, from *Banned Books Week 1987: Celebrating the Freedom to Read*, produced by the Office for Intellectual Freedom, pp. 49–50; copyright ©ALA 1987.

496

ANSWERS TO BANNED BOOKS PUZZLE

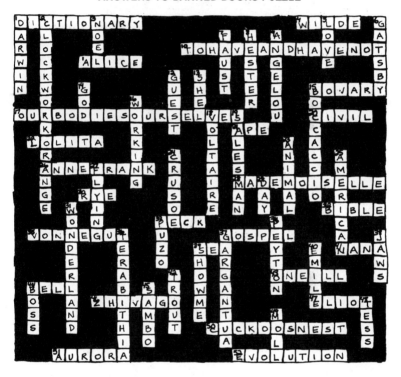

Phyllis Schlafly

Citizens' Bill of Rights
About Schools and Libraries

> *Phyllis Schlafly has built a grass roots following over the years*
> *as a spokesperson for conservative women in this coun-*
> *try. She has had an extremely active career as an author,*
> *commentator, organizer, and agitator. Born in 1924 in St.*
> *Louis, Missouri, she was raised in a Depression-era family*
> *that would have nothing to do with welfare. She went on to*
> *earn her B. A. from Washington University in 1944, her M. A.*
> *from Radcliffe College in 1945, and her law degree from*
> *Niagara University over 30 years later. A staunch Catholic*
> *conservative, she saw the Equal Rights Amendment as a reli-*
> *gious issue, and she successfully fought the forces of NOW and*
> *the many politicians, including President Carter, who sup-*
> *ported it. She has published a number of books, most recently*
> The Power of the Positive Woman *(1977), her conserva-*
> *tive response to the women's movement. When not lecturing*
> *or writing, Schlafly directs the activities of the Eagle Forum,*
> *a conservative women's group.*
>
> *In 1967 Schlafly founded* The Phyllis Schlafly Report, *a*
> *newsletter through which she continues to keep her followers*
> *informed. "The Citizens' Bill of Rights About Schools and*
> *Libraries" first appeared as part of the February 1983 issue*
> *which was devoted to censorship.*

1   All those who spend taxpayers' money are accountable to the
public. (The "public" includes citizens, parents, private groups,
and the media.) The public has a right to exercise its right of free
speech on how taxpayers' funds are spent and on what standards,
to second-guess the judgment of the persons doing the spending,
and to remove from office those responsible for any misuse of
tax funds. Public supervision and criticism may be annoying, but
they must be endured by all those spending tax funds, whether
they be Presidents, Congressmen, bureaucrats, military, teachers,
librarians, or others.

498

2   Since parents have the primary responsibility for the education of their own children, schools should have a decent respect for the parents' beliefs and attitudes. Schools should make every possible effort to avoid offending the religious, ethical, cultural or ethnic values of school children and their parents. Since presumably all educators would agree that *Playboy* and *Penthouse* magazines are not suitable reading materials for school children, it is clear that the issue over any particular book is one of appropriateness (which is a value judgment), not the First Amendment or "academic freedom."

3   Since thousands of good books and hundreds of important, educational books are easily available, and since a child can read only a small number of books prior to high school graduation, it is highly unreasonable and intolerant for a school or teacher to force a child to read a particular book as a precondition to graduation or to passing a course. When a book selected as course material or supplementary reading offends the religious, ethical, cultural or ethnic values of a child or his parents, an alternate book should be assigned or recommended which does not so offend. This substitution should be made without embarrassing the child.

4   This same respect for parental values and the assignment of alternate books should apply when the question is raised as to the assignment of a book at a particular grade level. Many books are appropriate in the upper grades which are not at all appropriate for younger children. Parental decisions about the maturity of their own children should be respected by the schools without embarrassing the child.

5   Public libraries should adhere to a standard like the Fairness Doctrine which governs television and radio broadcasters; i.e., they have the obligation to seek out and make available books on all sides of controversial issues of public importance. For example, libraries should present a balanced selection of book titles on sensitive current issues such as the morality of nuclear war, women's liberation, basic education, evolution/creationism, Reaganomics, and the Equal Rights Amendment.

6   Child pornography (i.e., the use of children in pictures, books or films to perform sex acts or to pose in lewd positions or circumstances) should be absolutely prohibited. In 1982, the U.S. Supreme Court held in *New York v. Ferber* that child pornography is not protected by the First Amendment because the prevention

of sexual abuse of children is "a governmental objective of surpassing importance." Laws against child pornography, therefore, must apply equally to everyone including bookstores, theaters, schools, and libraries.

7   No library buys every book published. Every day in the week, librarians, teachers and school administrators are making decisions to select some books for library shelves and school classrooms while excluding (censoring) other books. These select-and-exclude decisions can be called "preemptive censorship."

8   The selection of reading materials is a major responsibility of school and library personnel. Most such personnel have the historical knowledge, fairness, and mature judgment which are necessary to make those decisions. However, the public always has the right to question whether any preemptive censorship is carried out on the basis of the personal political biases of the librarian or teacher, or results from a genuine attempt to give students and the public the wisdom of the ages through time-tested "great books" plus fairness on current controversies.

9   The public clearly has a First Amendment right to investigate, evaluate and critique the selections and the criteria. If the school board or the library board does not reflect the values of the citizens in the area of its jurisdiction, the voters have the right to change the board members through the political process. That's an important part of our free, democratic society.

Analyzing the Writer's Argument

1. What is Schlafly's thesis in this essay? Where in the essay does she give the clearest statement of it?
2. Schlafly writes that the public has the right to "remove from office those responsible for any misuse of tax funds." In Schlafly's view, what actions or decisions made by librarians would constitute "misuse of tax funds"?
3. Schlafly believes that "the issue over any particular book is one of appropriateness (which is a value judgment), not the First Amendment or 'academic freedom.'" How does she propose, if at all, that differences of opinion over "appropriateness" be resolved?
4. In paragraph 6, Schlafly cites *New York v. Ferber*, a case that involved conflicting rights. How did the court rule in the case? What is the meaning of the ruling?

5. What, for Schlafly, is "preemptive censorship"? Is she for it, against it, or does she reveal no attitude toward it?

6 Does Schlafly think that librarians don't know what they are doing? Does she believe that they like to push their own ideas onto others, that they fail to be fair, impartial, and balanced in their acquisitions? Explain.

7. Is Schlafly's tone in her "Bill of Rights" reasonable, angry, bitter, mediating, legalistic? How do you know? Point to examples of her word usage to support your view.

Exploring the Issues in This Essay

1. Schlafly places the responsibility for decision with respect to libraries and schools with the voters in the community. While it would seem difficult to argue with the democratic process, with those who pay for the services of a librarian, do you see any problems with her proposal? Discuss the implications of a democratically achieved community vote which prohibits the purchase of books by liberals or blacks or women. Might minorities see themselves under-represented or even not represented at all?

2. Schlafly seems very concerned about reassuring her audience that they have a First Amendment right to question, challenge, and argue with responsible public servants. Discuss the reasons why she may have felt compelled to so reassure her readers. Do you think that she may have seen the fear of censorship overshadowing freedom of speech? Did she perhaps fear that people were being intimidated? If so, by whom or what?

Tipper Gore

The Smut and Sadism of Rock

In recent years Tipper Gore's name has become synonymous with the Parents Music Resource Center (PMRC) which she helped establish in 1983. The PMRC addresses issues of obscenity and pornography in today's rock lyrics. Tipper Gore was born in Washington, D. C., in 1948 and grew up in Arlington, Virginia. She graduated from Boston University with a degree in psychology in 1970 and pursued her studies in psychology at the master's level at George Peabody College in Nashville, Tennessee. Gore's colleagues describe her as tireless in her dedicated work for the causes that concern her. An advocate for the homeless in America, Gore is cofounder of Families for the Homeless and is chairperson of Homeless in America: A Photographic Exhibit, *a traveling exhibit currently making the rounds of museums in the United States. In 1987 she published her book* Raising PG Kids in an X-Rated Society, *an exposé of the sex, violence, and obscenity in contemporary music, television, and film.*

Since the early 1980's Tipper Gore has waged a campaign against the exploitation of children by the music industry. "Porno rock," she believes, "is not only sexually explicit; songs and videos celebrate torture, incest and even suicide and murder. The music business should clean up its act." In the following essay, which first appeared in Newsday *just prior to the Senate Commerce Committee hearings on pornographic rock music in September 1985, Gore argues for a rating system that would include an "industrywide uniform standard defining what constitutes explicit and violent material."*

1   Sexual innuendo or rebellion has always been a part of rock 'n' roll, but nowadays, sex is described explicitly, complete with moans and groans. Moreover, sadomasochism, bondage, incest and rape are out of the closet and into the lyrics. Whips, chains, handcuffs and leather masks are being popularized in songs and as images in videos and on album covers. Lyrics glorify forced sex, videos depict thrill killings.

2   "Eat Me Alive" from Judas Priest's double platinum album (2 million copies sold) "Defenders of the Faith" depicts forcing oral sex at gunpoint.

3   Motley Crue, a heavy metal band increasingly popular with young teens, sings this in "Live Wire":

> I'll either break her face
> Or take down her legs
> Get my ways at will
> Go for the throat, never let loose.
> Going in for the kill

4   Or consider this from "Too Young to Fall in Love" from "Shout at the Devil".

> Not a woman, but a whore
> I can taste the hate.
> Well, now I'm killing you.
> Watch your face turning blue.

5   Twisted Sister, a group often in the Top 40, has these lyrics on their "Under the Blade" album:

> Your hands are tied,
> Your legs are strapped
> You're going under the blade.

6   My 11-year-old bought Prince's 10-million-seller "Purple Rain" album because she heard an innocuous song, "Let's Go Crazy," on the radio. But once we got our purchase home, we were also treated to "Darling Nikki." The song describes "Nikki" as " a sex fiend" who spends her time "in a hotel lobby, masturbating."

7   Another example of Prince's work comes in the song "Sister" from the "Dirty Mind" album. The lyrics describe a 16-year-boy making love to his "lovely and loose" sister. The song concludes that "incest is everything it's said to be."

8   I feel that these songs, and others like them, are inappropriate for my children. Yet I find it very difficult to protect them from their twisted themes.

9   Studies indicate that the listening, buying and viewing audience for music is growing younger. To those who say, "Just turn

it off," I submit that it is unrealistic to believe parents can control everything a child listens to.

10   It's time to remember that radio stations are licensed to broadcast "in the public interest," using a precious natural resource that belongs to all of us. And it isn't just radio anymore. Music videos, which are used to sell records to kids, come into our homes via broadcast TV and via cable on MTV, a 24-hour music channel, reaching 26 million homes.

11   Graphic sex, sadomasochism and violence, particularly toward women, are rampant on MTV. Its executives need to respond to the public outcry and curb the excesses, especially since MTV is an industry trend-setter. Jay Durbin, a music video director, has been quoted as saying he doesn't let his young children watch MTV because of the "incredible sadism."

12   Thomas Radechi of the National Coalition on Television Violence warns that more than half of music videos are violent. For example:

- Def Leppard's video "Photograph" shows the strangling of a Marilyn Monroe look-alike, and ends with her body wrapped in barbed wire.

- Twisted Sister's "We're Not Going to Take It Anymore" shows a son destroying his father, smashing him with doors, dragging him by the hair and eventually blasting him through a plate-glass window.

- Billy Idol's "Dancing with Myself" has a naked woman struggling in chains behind a transparent sheet. The Jacksons' "Torture" shows women whipping skeletons and attacking men with claws and swords. Images of devil worship abound.

- Van Halen's "Hot for Teacher" features a schoolteacher doing a striptease on top of desks while elementary schoolboys ogle at her. When my 8-year-old asked me, "Why is the teacher taking off her clothes in school," I started paying attention to the videos my children watch.

13   Children process reality differently from adults, a fact we too often forget. These images have powerful and terrifying effects on young minds.

14   In another disconcerting development, some rock artists promote and glorify suicide. Ozzy Osbourne sings "Suicide Solu-

tion"; Blue Oyster Cult sings "Don't Fear the Reaper"; AC/DC sings "Shoot to Thrill." Every year half a million teenagers attempt suicide. More than 6,000 succeed. Yet too many of the executives of the rock record industry apparently don't care.

15 No one should want a return to Victorian hypocrisy about sex. It was repressive at worst and unrealistic at best. But now the pendulum has swung too far toward the hedonistic and materialistic philosophy of: If it feels good, do it; if you want it, take it.

16   The time has come for concerned parents and consumers to demand a choice. Recently, 19 record companies offered to apply a warning label to albums containing explicit and sexual material. However, each company would have its own standard as to what lyrics warranted a label. The effect in the marketplace would be to confuse the consumer.

17 The Parents Music Resource Center has asked the record executives to create an industrywide uniform standard defining what constitutes explicit and violent material. We of the PMRC are not trying to ban any songs, and we oppose censorship or government regulation. Instead, we believe that the music industry itself and its media outlets should voluntarily cut down on violent and sexually explicit material.

18 We have proposed a rating system for records, tapes and videos that the industry could administer itself.

19 The national PTA (National Congress of Parents and Teachers) has also been calling for records to be rated. And some responsible voices within the industry have called for restraint. George David Weiss, president of the Songwriters Guild of America, called for the music industry to tone down. "There is enough violence without glorifying it in music aimed at youngsters," he wrote in Billboard.

20 Even Sting, formerly of the rock group The Police, is on record as saying "to write pornography is to display a lack of imagination."

21 On Sept. 19, the Senate Commerce Committee will hold hearings on pornographic rock music.

22 That's the good news. The bad news is that most purveyors of porno rock think they can get by with anything by simply accusing their critics of advocating censorship.

23 To market explicit sex and graphic and sadistic violence to an audience of preteens and teens is a secondary form of child abuse. A society whose mass media peddles these themes unchallenged

is abdicating its responsibility to an entire generation of young Americans. I believe in the First Amendment, but freedom always involves responsibilities.

24   It's not easy being a parent these days, but it's even tougher being a kid. It's about time the record industry gave us all a break.

Analyzing the Writer's Argument

1. What, according to Gore, differentiates today's rock from traditional rock 'n' roll? What examples does she use to illustrate her point? Did you find her examples convincing? Explain.
2. What does Gore's example of her 11-year-old daughter buying Prince's album *Purple Rain* add to her argument?
3. What is it that Gore and the Parents Music Resource Center want the music industry to do? Does their proposal seem reasonable to you? Why or why not?
4. How does Gore answer the opposition who claim that it is a parent's responsibility to monitor what his or her children listen to or watch? Whom does she believe must share this responsiblity with parents?
5. Gore either quotes or makes reference to a number of people and organizations including Jay Durbin, Parents Music Resource Center, National Congress of Parents and Teachers, George David Weiss, and Sting. Explain what her use of each of these quotes or references adds to her argument.
6. Gore claims that some "rock artists promote and glorify suicide." Is she justified in making the link between rock music and the teen suicide problem? Did she convince you that such a link exists? Why or why not?

Exploring the Issues in This Essay

1. What role should government play in a controversy such as the one surrounding rock music? Would the government be justified in banning or censoring certain songs or artists? Or would it be more reasonable to have the music industry regulate itself by imposing standards that would "cut down on violent and sexually explicit material"? And, finally, what would be the impact of these standards or regulations on composers and recording artists?

2. In an age when we are bombarded with terrible stories of child abuse, do you believe, as Tipper Gore does, that "to market explicit sex and graphic and sadistic violence to an audience of preteens and teens is a secondary form of child abuse"? In what way can explicit rock music and music videos be considered "child abuse"? Do you think that there is a cause-and-effect link between such music and the high incidence of physical child abuse? Explain what you think the connections, if any, are.

Caryl Rivers

What Should Be Done
About Rock Lyrics?

Novelist and Professor of Journalism, Caryl Rivers was born in December 1937. After graduating from Trinity College in Washington, D.C. and receiving a master's degree from Columbia University, Rivers launched a career in journalism as the family editor for the Middletown Record (New York). *She was the Washington correspondent for the* Puerto Rico based El Mundo *before becoming a Professor of Journalism at Boston University, a position she has held since 1966. Over the years she has been a frequent contributor to* Saturday Review, New York Times Magazine, Glamour, McCall's *and* Boston Magazine. *In her fiction and nonfiction Rivers draws heavily upon her experiences growing up in the 1950s. Her nonfiction includes* Aphrodite at Midcentury: Growing up Female and Catholic in Postwar America (1973), Beyond Sugar and Spice: How Women Grow, Learn, and Thrive *(1979) with Rosalind Barnett and Grace Baruch, and* For Better, For Worse *(1981) with her husband Alan Lupo. She has also authored* Virgins *(1984) and* Girls Forever Brave and True *(1986), two punchy novels about the exploits of Catholic girls in the 1950s. Rivers is currently working on* Intimate Enemies, *a novel about a Vietnam vet and a 1960s ex-radical.*

Rivers' essay "What Should Be Done About Rock Lyrics?" first appeared in the Boston Globe *on September 15, 1985. Here she identifies the serious problem of explicit violence against women in some of today's popular rock lyrics and music videos. She concludes by encouraging people to take an active part in addressing the issue of what amounts to pornographic rock lyrics and helping reduce and ultimately eliminating the incidence of violence against women in America.*

508

1 After a grisly series of murders in California, possibly inspired by the lyrics of a rock song, we are hearing a familiar chorus: don't blame rock and roll. Kids will be kids. They love to rebel, and the more shocking the stuff, the better they like it.

2 There's some truth in this, of course. I loved to watch Elvis shake his torso when I was a teenager, and it was even more fun when Ed Sullivan wouldn't let the cameras show him below the waist. I snickered at the forbidden "Rock with Me, Annie" lyrics by a black rhythm and blues group, which were deliciously naughty. But I am sorry, rock fans, that is not the same thing as hearing lyrics about how a man is going to force a woman to perform oral sex on him at gunpoint in a little number called "Eat Me Alive." It is not in the same league with a song about the delights of slipping into a woman's room while she is sleeping and murdering her, the theme of an AC/DC ballad that allegedly inspired the California slayer.

3 Make no mistake, it is not sex we are talking about here, but violence. Violence against women. Most rock songs are not violent— they are funky, sexy, rebellious, and sometimes witty. Please do not mistake me for a Mrs. Grundy. If Prince wants to leap about wearing only a purple jock strap, fine. Let Mick Jagger unzip his fly as he gyrates, if he wants to. But when either one of them starts garroting, beating, or sodomizing a woman in their number, that is another story.

4 I always find myself annoyed when "intellectual" men dismiss violence against women with a yawn, as if it were beneath their dignity to notice. I wonder if the reaction would be the same if the violence were directed against someone other than women. How many people would yawn and say, "Oh, kids will be kids" if a rock group did a nifty little number called "Lynchin," in which stringing up and stomping on black people were set to music? Who would chuckle and say, "Oh, just a little adolescent rebellion" if a group of rockers went on MTV dressed as Nazis, desecrating synagogues and beating up Jews to the beat of twanging guitars?

5 I'll tell you what would happen. Prestigious dailies would thunder on editorial pages; senators would fall over each other to get denunciations into the *Congressional Record*. The president would appoint a commission to clean up the music business.

6 But violence against women is greeted by silence. It shouldn't be.

7   This does not mean censorship, or book (or record) burning. In a society that protects free expression, we understand a lot of stuff will float up out of the sewer. Usually, we recognize the ugly stuff that advocates violence against any group as the garbage it is, and we consider its purveyors as moral lepers. We hold our nose and tolerate it, but we speak out against the values it proffers.

8   But images of violence against women are not staying on the fringes of society. No longer are they found only in tattered, paper-covered books or in movie houses where winos snooze and the scent of urine fills the air. They are entering the mainstream at a rapid rate. This is happening at a time when the media, more and more, set the agenda for the public debate. It is a powerful legitimizing force—especially television. Many people regard what they see on TV as the truth; Walter Cronkite once topped a poll as the most trusted man in America.

9   Now, with the advent of rock videos and all-music channels, rock music has grabbed a big chunk of legitimacy. American teenagers have instant access, in their living rooms, to the messages of rock, on the same vehicle that brought them Sesame Street. Who can blame them if they believe that the images they see are accurate reflections of adult reality, approved by adults? After all, Big Bird used to give them lessons on the same little box. Adults, by their silence, sanction the images. Do we really want our kids to think that rape and violence are what sexuality is all about?

10   This is not a trivial issue. Violence against women is a major social problem, one that's more than a cerebral issue to me. I teach at Boston University, and one of my most promising young journalism students was raped and murdered. Two others told me of being raped. Recently, one female student was assaulted and beaten so badly she had $5,000 worth of medical bills and permanent damage to her back and eyes.

11   It's nearly impossible, of course, to make a cause-and-effect link between lyrics and images and acts of violence. But images have a tremendous power to create an atmosphere in which violence against certain people is sanctioned. Nazi propagandists knew that full well when they portrayed Jews as ugly, greedy, and powerful.

12   The outcry over violence against women, particularly in a sexual context, is being legitimized in two ways: by the increasing movement of these images into the mainstream of the media in TV, films, magazines, albums, videos, and by the silence about it.

13   Violence, of course, is rampant in the media. But it is usually set in some kind of moral context. It's usually only the bad guys who commit violent acts against the innocent. When the good guys get violent, it's against those who deserve it. Dirty Harry blows away the scum, he doesn't walk up to a toddler and say, "Make my day." The A team does not shoot up suburban shopping malls.

14   But in some rock songs, it's the "heroes" who commit the acts. The people we are programmed to identify with are the ones being violent, with women on the receiving end. In a society where rape and assaults on women are endemic, this is no small problem, with millions of young boys watching on their TV screens and listening on their Walkmans.

15   I think something needs to be done. I'd like to see people in the industry respond to the problem. I'd love to see some women rock stars speak out against violence against women. I would like to see disc jockeys refuse air play to records and videos that contain such violence. At the very least, I want to see the end of the silence. I want journalists and parents and critics and performing artists to keep this issue alive in the public forum. I don't want people who are concerned about this issue labeled as bluenoses and bookburners and ignored.

16   And I wish it wasn't always just women who were speaking out. Men have as large a stake in the quality of our civilization as women do in the long run. Violence is a contagion that infects at random. Let's hear something, please, from the men.

Analyzing the Writer's Argument

1. What does Rivers object to about some of today's rock lyrics? What examples does she provide to illustrate what she means? How do these examples differ from the "deliciously naughty" lyrics that Rivers heard growing up?

2. In paragraphs 2 and 3, Rivers admits that she "loved to watch Elvis shake his torso when [she] was a teenager" and that it is just fine for "Prince . . . to leap about wearing only a purple jock strap" or for "Mick Jagger [to] unzip his fly as he gyrates." What do these admissions tell you about the type of person Rivers is, and what do they add to her argument? Where does Rivers draw the line; when are rock songs and videos no longer "funky, sexy, rebellious, and sometimes witty"?

3. Who is Rivers' audience for this essay? What in the essay led you to this conclusion?
4. What does Rivers see as the importance of television in contemporary society? According to her, how has television enabled rock music to grab "a big chunk of legitimacy"?
5. Rivers states that "violence against women is a major social problem, one that's more than a cerebral issue to me." What does she mean by "cerebral issue," and how does she show how violence has touched her own life?
6. Paragraph 6 is a two-sentence paragraph. How does it function in the context of Rivers' argument?
7. What does Rivers gain by using such words and phrases as "garbage," "ugly stuff," "sewer," and "moral lepers" when talking about materials and people who advocate violence? What other examples of such diction can you identify in her essay?
8. How, according to Rivers, is violence against women being legitimized today? What distinctions about types of violence is Rivers attempting to draw in paragraphs 13 and 14? Do you agree with her? Explain.
9. If Rivers, as she says in paragraph 7, is not for "censorship, or book (or record) burning," what is she arguing for? What specific suggestions for action does she make? Did you find her appeal persuasive? Why or why not?

Exploring the Issues in This Essay

1. Rivers claims that "violence against women is greeted by silence." Do you agree with her perception, or has the scene changed since Rivers wrote this article in 1985? Why does she believe people do not speak out? Why do you suppose people seem quite willing to speak out against the injustices and prejudices directed at African-Americans and Jews, for example, but not women? What can be done to break further silence? What can be done to get more men involved in the fight to eliminate violence against women? Make a list of specific steps that might be taken. Finally, discuss the responsibilities to speak out and make our own views known that each of us has as a member of a society that cherishes the free expression of ideas.
2. Rivers admits that it's almost impossible to establish a cause-and-effect link between rock lyrics and images on music videos on the one hand and acts of violence on the other. Do you think such a link exists? How would you go about documenting such a rela-

tionship? Discuss the tremendous power of images in America's popular media both to dictate certain behavior and to create an atmosphere that condones if not encourages violent behavior.

3. Voltaire once said, "I disapprove of what you say, but I will defend to the death your right to say it." Does the sentiment of Voltaire's statement hold true for most Americans today? How far, for example, are you willing to go to defend your First Amendment rights? What are you willing to do in defense of that right for others? What if they disagree with you?

Frank Zappa

The Wives of Big Brother

Musician, composer Frank Zappa was born on December 21, 1940, in Baltimore, Maryland. After graduating from Chaffrey Junior College, he founded the musical group Mothers of Invention in 1964. Zappa's compositions achieved widespread popularity during the late 1960s, and he was named "Pop Musician of the Year" by Down Beat *magazine in 1970 and again in 1971 and 1972. His solo recordings include "Apostrophe," "Chunga's Revenge," "Hot Rats," "Zoot Allures," "Joe's Garage," and "You Are What You Is."*

In September 1985, Frank Zappa testified at the Senate Commerce Committee hearings on record labeling. Zappa, quite naturally, was vehemently opposed to the labeling proposal from the Parents Music Resource Center, and he voiced his disagreement in no uncertain terms. The following is the text of the prepared statement that Zappa gave the committee.

1   These are my personal observations and opinions. They are addressed to the PMRC as well as this committee. I speak on behalf of no group or professional organization.

2   The PMRC proposal is an ill-conceived piece of nonsense which fails to deliver any real benefits to children, infringes the civil liberties of people who are not children and promises to keep the courts busy for years, dealing with the interpretational and enforcemental problems inherent in the proposal's design.

3   It is my understanding that, in law, First Amendment Issues are decided with a preference for the least restrictive alternative. In this context, the PMRC's demands are the equivalent of treating dandruff by decapitation.

4   No one has forced Mrs. Baker or Mrs. Gore to bring Prince or Sheena Easton into their homes. Thanks to the Constitution, they are free to buy other forms of music for their children. Apparently they insist on purchasing the works of contemporary recording artists in order to support a personal illusion of aerobic sophisti-

cation. Ladies, please be advised: the $8.98 purchase price does not entitle you to a kiss on the foot from the composer or performer in exchange for a spin on the family Victrola. Taken as a whole, the complete list of PMRC demands reads like an instruction manual for some sinister kind of "toilet training program" to house-break all composers and performers because of the lyrics of a few. Ladies, how dare you?

5   The ladies' shame must be shared by the bosses at the major labels who, through the RIAA, chose to bargain away the rights of composers, performers, and retailers in order to pass H. R. 2911, The Blank Tape Tax: A private tax, levied by an industry on consumers, for the benefit of a select group within that industry. Is this a "consumer issue"? You bet it is. PMRC spokesperson, Kandy Stroud, announced to millions of fascinated viewers on last Friday's ABC Nightline debate that Senator Gore, a man she described as "A friend of the music industry," is co-sponsor of something she referred to as "anti-piracy legislation." Is this the same tax bill with a nicer name?

6   The major record labels need to have H. R. 2911 whiz through a few committees before anybody smells a rat. One of them is chaired by Senator Thurmond. Is it a coincidence that Mrs. Thurmond is affiliated with the PMRC? I can't say she's a member, because the PMRC has no members. Their secretary told me on the phone last Friday that the PMRC has no members . . . only founders. I asked how many other D. C. wives are non-members of an organization that raises money by mail, has a tax-exempt status, and seems intent on running the Constitution of the United States through the family paper-shredder. I asked her if it was a cult. Finally, she said she couldn't give me an answer and that she had to call their lawyer.

7   While the wife of the Secretary of Treasury recites "Gonna drive my love inside you . . . ", and Senator Gore's wife talks about "Bondage!" and "oral sex at gunpoint," on the CBS Evening News, people in high places work on a tax bill that is so ridiculous, the only way to sneak it through is to keep the public's mind on something else: 'Porn Rock.'

8   The PMRC practices a curious double standard with these fervent recitations. Thanks to them, helpless young children all over America get to hear about oral sex at gunpoint on network TV several nights a week. Is there a secret FCC dispensation here? What

sort of end justifies THESE means? PTA parents should keep an eye on these ladies if that's their idea of 'good taste'.

9 Is the basic issue morality? Is it mental health? Is it an issue at all? The PMRC has created a lot of confusion with improper comparisons between song lyrics, videos, record packaging, radio broadcasting, and live performances. These are all different mediums, and the people who work in them have a right to conduct their business without trade-restraining legislation, whipped up like an instant pudding by The Wives of Big Brother.

10 Is it proper that the husband of PMRC non-member/founder/person sits on any committee considering business pertaining to the Blank Tape Tax or his wife's lobbying organization? Can any committee thus constituted 'find facts' in a fair and unbiased manner? This committee has three. A minor conflict of interest?

11 The PMRC promotes their program as a harmless type of consumer information service providing 'guidelines' which will assist baffled parents in the determination of the 'suitability' of records listened to by 'very young children'. The methods they propose have several unfortunate side effects, not the least of which is the reduction of all American Music, recorded and live, to the intellectual level of a Saturday morning cartoon show.

12 Teen-agers with $8.98 in their pocket might go into a record store alone, but 'very young children' do not. Usually there is a parent in attendance. The $8.98 is in the parent's pocket. The parent can always suggest that the $8.98 be spent on a book.

13 If the parent is afraid to let the child read a book, perhaps the $8.98 can be spent on recordings of instrumental music. Why not bring jazz or classical music into your home instead of Blackie Lawless or Madonna? Great music with no words at all is available to anyone with sense enough to look beyond this week's platinum-selling fashion plate.

14 Children in the 'vulnerable' age bracket have a natural love for music. If, as a parent, you believe they should be exposed to something more uplifting than sugar walls, support Music Appreciation programs in schools. Why haven't you considered your child's need for consumer information? Music Appreciation costs very little compared to sports expenditures. Your children have a right to know that something besides pop music exists.

15 It is unfortunate that the PMRC would rather dispense governmentally sanitized Heavy Metal Music, than something more

'uplifting'. Is this an indication of PMRC's personal taste, or just another manifestation of the low priority this administration has placed on education for The Arts in America? The answer, of course, is neither. You can't distract people from thinking about an unfair tax by talking about Music Appreciation. For that you need sex . . . and lots of it.

16 Because of the subjective nature of the PMRC ratings, it is impossible to guarantee that some sort of 'despised concept' won't sneak through, tucked away in new slang or the overstressed pronunciation of an otherwise innocent word. If the goal here is total verbal/moral safety, there is only one way to achieve it: watch no TV, read no books, see no movies, listen to only instrumental music, or buy no music at all.

17 The establishment of a rating system, voluntary or otherwise, opens the door to an endless parade of Moral Quality Control Programs based on "Things Certain Christians Don't Like." What if the next bunch of Washington Wives demands a large yellow "J" on all material written or performed by Jews, in order to save helpless children from exposure to 'concealed Zionist doctrine'?

18 Record ratings are frequently compared to film ratings. Apart from the quantitative difference, there is another that is more important: People who act in films are hired to 'pretend'. No matter how the film is rated, it won't hurt them personally. Since many musicians write and perform their own material and stand by it as their art (whether you like it or not), an imposed rating will stigmatize them as individuals. How long before composers and performers are told to wear a festive little PMRC arm band with their Scarlet Letter on it?

19 The PMRC rating system restrains trade in one specific musical field: Rock. No ratings have been requested for Comedy records or Country Music. Is there anyone in the PMRC who can differentiate infallibly between Rock and Country Music? Artists in both fields cross stylistic lines. Some artists include comedy material. If an album is part Rock, part Country, part Comedy, what sort of label would it get? Shouldn't the ladies be warning everyone that inside those Country albums with the American Flags, the big trucks, and the atomic pompadours there lurks a fascinating variety of songs about sex, violence, alcohol, and the devil, recorded in a way that lets you hear every word, sung for you by people who have been to prison and are proud of it.

20   If enacted, the PMRC program would have the effect of protectionist legislation for the Country Music Industry, providing more security for cowboys than it does for children. One major retail outlet has already informed the Capitol Records sales staff that it would not purchase or display an album with any kind of sticker on it.

21   Another chain with outlets in shopping malls has been told by the landlord that if it racked "hard-rated albums" they would lose their lease. That opens up an awful lot of shelf space for somebody. Could it be that a certain Senatorial husband and wife team from Tennessee sees this as an 'affirmative action program' to benefit the suffering multitudes in Nashville?

22   Is the PMRC attempting to save future generations from SEX ITSELF? The type, the amount, and the timing of sexual information given to a child should be determined by the parents, not by people who are involved in a tax scheme cover-up.

23   The PMRC has concocted a Mythical Beast, and compounds the chicanery by demanding 'consumer guidelines' to keep it from inviting your children inside its sugar walls. Is the next step the adoption of a "PMRC National Legal Age For Comprehension of Vaginal Arousal". Many people in this room would gladly support such legislation, but, before they start drafting their bill, I urge them to consider these facts:

1. There is no conclusive scientific evidence to support the claim that exposure to any form of music will cause the listener to commit a crime or damn his soul to hell.

2. Masturbation is not illegal. If it is not illegal to do it, why should it be illegal to sing about it?

3. No medical evidence of hairy palms, warts, or blindness has been linked to masturbation or vaginal arousal, nor has it been proven that hearing references to either topic automatically turns the listener into a social liability.

4. Enforcement of anti-masturbatory legislation could prove costly and time consuming.

5. There is not enough prison space to hold all the children who do it.

24   The PMRC's proposal is most offensive in its "moral tone". It seeks to enforce a set of implied religious values on its victims. Iran has a religious government. Good for them. I like having the capitol of the United States in Washington, DC, in spite of recent efforts to move it to Lynchburg, VA.

25   Fundamentalism is not a state religion. The PMRC's request for labels regarding sexually explicit lyrics, violence, drugs, alcohol, and especially occult content reads like a catalog of phenomena abhorrent to practitioners of that faith. How a person worships is a private matter, and should not be inflicted upon or exploited by others. Understanding the Fundamentalist leanings of this organization, I think it is fair to wonder if their rating system will eventually be extended to inform parents as to whether a musical group has homosexuals in it. Will the PMRC permit musical groups to exist, but only if gay members don't sing, and are not depicted on the album cover?

26   The PMRC has demanded that record companies "re-evaluate" the contracts of those groups who do things on stage that THEY find offensive. I remind the PMRC that groups are comprised of individuals. If one guy wiggles too much, does the whole band get an "X"? If the group gets dropped from the label as a result of this 're-evaluation' process, do the other guys in the group who weren't wiggling get to sue the guy who wiggled because he ruined their careers? Do the founders of this tax-exempt organization with no members plan to indemnify record companies for any losses incurred from unfavorably decided breach of contract suits, or is there a PMRC secret agent in the Justice Department?

27   Should individual musicians be rated? If so, who is qualified to determine if the guitar player is an "X", the vocalist is a "D/A" or the drummer is a "V". If the bass player (or his Senator) belongs to a religious group that dances around with poisonous snakes, does he get an "O"? What if he has an earring in one ear, wears an Italian horn around his neck, sings about his astrological sign, practices yoga, reads the Quaballah, or owns a rosary? Will his "occult content" rating go into an old CoIntelPro computer, emerging later as a "fact", to determine if he qualifies for a home-owner loan? Will they tell you this is necessary to protect the folks next door from the possibility of 'devil-worship' lyrics creeping through the wall?

28   What hazards await the unfortunate retailer who accidently sells an "O" rated record to somebody's little Johnny? Nobody in Washinton seemed to care when Christian Terrorists bombed abortion clinics in the name of Jesus. Will you care when the "friends of the wives of big brother" blow up the shopping mall?

29   The PMRC wants ratings to start as of the date of their enactment. That leaves the current crop of 'objectionable material' untouched. What will be the status of recordings from that Golden Era to censorship? Do they become collectors' items . . . or will another "fair and unbiased committee" order them destroyed in a public ceremony?

30   Bad facts make bad law, and people who write bad laws are, in my opinion, more dangerous than songwriters who celebrate sexuality. Freedom of Speech, Freedom of Religious Thought, and the Right to Due Process for composers, performers and retailers are imperiled if the PMRC and the major labels consummate this nasty bargain. Are we expected to give up Article One so the big guys can collect an extra dollar on every blank tape and 10 to 25% on tape recorders? What's going on here? Do WE get to vote on this tax? There's an awful lot of smoke pouring out of the legislative machinery used by the PMRC to inflate this issue. Try not to inhale it. Those responsible for the vandalism should pay for the damage by voluntarily rating themselves. If they refuse, perhaps the voters could assist in awarding the Congressional "X", the Congressional "D/A", the Congressional "V", and the Congressional "O". Just like the ladies say: these ratings are necessary to protect our children. I hope it's not too late to put them where they really belong.

Analyzing the Writer's Argument

1. What, according to Zappa, are the main shortcomings of the PMRC's proposal? Does he convincingly document each of his objections? Explain.
2. In paragraph 3, Zappa uses an analogy to describe what he believes is the outlandishness of the PMRC's proposal. What is the analogy and what does it contribute to his argument?
3. At several points in his statement Zappa refers to Tipper Gore and her colleagues as "ladies" and "The Wives of Big Brother." What, if anything, does he gain with this name-calling?

4. What, according to Zappa, is the "Blank Tape Tax" bill? How is this piece of legislation related to the PMRC's labeling proposal? What conflicts of interest does Zappa believe exist? Explain. What does Zappa mean when he refers to a "tax scheme cover-up"?

5. Is Zappa justified in his charges that the PMRC "practices a curious double standard" by discussing violence and oral sex on the network news? Why or why not?

6. When Zappa introduces the subject of "Music Appreciation programs," is this a "red herring" or does it have a logical connection to his argument?

7. What does Zappa fear will happen if a rating system like the one proposed by the PMRC is established? Are his fears justified, or is he simply invoking a "slippery slope" argument?

8. Why does Zappa find the "moral tone" of the PMRC's proposal offensive? What is Zappa's own tone in this statement? How do you think members of the Senate Commerce Committee would react to this tone? Explain.

Exploring the Issues in This Essay

1. Tipper Gore, in her essay "The Smut and Sadism of Rock," claims that "most purveyors of porno rock think they can get by with anything by simply accusing their critics of advocating censorship." To what extent can this criticism be applied to Frank Zappa in his statement before the Senate Commerce Committee? Is he accusing the PMRC of advocating censorship? If not, what is he saying about the PMRC and their proposal?

2. What are your own thoughts on the subject of porno rock and music videos? Are some of the lyrics too explicit? Is it all right for some videos to celebrate the torture of women, incest, satanism, suicide, sadistic behavior, and murder? If not, what should be the limits? At what point, if any, does music stop being artistic expression and cross over into the realm of sleaze or pornography? Discuss specific examples of recordings and videos that you approve of and those, if any, you find objectionable.

Garry Wills

In Praise of Censure

> *Journalist and author Garry Wills was born in Atlanta, Georgia, in 1934. As an articulate college student, he attracted the attention of William F. Buckley, Jr., the editor of the conservative* National Review, *who published his writings even as Wills earned his M.A. and Ph.D. degrees from Yale University. His books, among them* Nixon Agonistes *(1970),* Bare Ruined Choirs *(1972), and* Inventing America *(1978), have earned him a reputation as a writer with a fresh and witty style. Wills' break with the* National Review *in the late 1960s marked what some have called his "conversion to liberalism." Wills is the Henry R. Luce Professor of American Culture and Public Policy at Northwestern University, and is a syndicated newspaper and magazine columnist.*
>
> *In the following essay, Wills argues for us to make a crucial distinction between the terms* censorship *and* censure *as a way of better understanding the positions of the forces arguing over censorship. The essay first appeared in* Time, *July 31, 1989.*

1   Rarely have the denouncers of censorship been so eager to start practicing it. When a sense of moral disorientation overcomes a society, people from the least expected quarters begin to ask, "Is nothing sacred?" Feminists join reactionaries to denounce pornography as demeaning to women. Rock musician Frank Zappa declares that when Tipper Gore, the wife of Senator Albert Gore from Tennessee, asked music companies to label sexually explicit material, she launched an illegal "conspiracy to extort." A *Penthouse* editorialist says that housewife Terry Rakolta, who asked sponsors to withdraw support from a sitcom called *Married . . . With Children*, is "yelling fire in a crowded theater," a formula that says her speech is not protected by the First Amendment.

2   But the most interesting movement to limit speech is directed at defamatory utterances against blacks, homosexuals, Jews, women

or other stigmatizable groups. It took no Terry Rakolta of the left to bring about the instant firing of Jimmy the Greek and Al Campanis from sports jobs when they made racially denigrating comments. Social pressure worked far more quickly on them than on *Married . . . With Children*, which is still on the air.

3 The rules being considered on college campuses to punish students for making racist and other defamatory remarks go beyond social and commercial pressure to actual legal muzzling. The right-wing *Dartmouth Review* and its imitators have understandably infuriated liberals who are beginning to take action against them and the racist expressions they have encouraged. The American Civil Liberties Union considered this movement important enough to make it the principal topic at its biennial meeting last month in Madison, Wis. Ironically, the regents of the University of Wisconsin had passed their own rules against defamation just before the ACLU members convened on the university's campus. Nadine Strossen, of New York University School of Law, who was defending the ACLU's traditional position on free speech, said of Wisconsin's new rules, "You can tell how bad they are by the fact that the regents had to make an amendment at the last minute exempting classroom discussion! What is surprising is that Donna Shalala [chancellor of the university] went along with it." So did constitutional lawyers on the faculty.

4 If a similar code were drawn up with right-wing imperatives in mind—one banning unpatriotic, irreligious or sexually explicit expressions on campus—the people framing Wisconsin-type rules would revert to their libertarian pasts. In this competition to suppress, is regard for freedom of expression just a matter of whose ox is getting gored at the moment? Does the left just get nervous about the Christian cross when Klansmen burn it, while the right will react only when Madonna flirts crucifixes between her thighs?

5 The cries of "un-American" are as genuine and as frequent on either side. Everyone is protecting the country. Zappa accuses Gore of undermining the moral fiber of America with the "sexual neuroses of these vigilant ladies." He argues that she threatens our freedoms with "connubial insider trading" because her husband is a Senator. Apparently her marital status should deprive her of speaking privileges in public—an argument Westbrook Pegler used to make against Eleanor Roosevelt. *Penthouse* says Rakolta is taking

us down the path toward fascism. It attacks her for living in a rich suburb—the old "radical chic" argument that rich people cannot support moral causes.

6   There is a basic distinction that cuts through this free-for-all over freedom. It is the distinction, too often neglected, between censorship and censure (the free expression of moral disapproval). What the campuses are trying to do (at least those with state money) is to use the force of government to contain freedom of speech. What Donald Wildmon, the free-lance moralist from Tupelo, Miss., does when he gets Pepsi to cancel its Madonna ad is censure the ad by calling for a boycott. Advocating boycotts is a form of speech protected by the First Amendment. As Nat Hentoff, journalistic-custodian of the First Amendment, says, "I would hate to see boycotts outlawed. Think what that would do to Cesar Chavez." Or, for that matter, to Ralph Nader. If one disapproves of a social practice, whether it is racist speech or unjust hiring in lettuce fields, one is free to denounce that and to call on others to express their disapproval. Otherwise, there would be no form of persuasive speech except passing a law. This would make the law coterminous with morality.

7   Equating morality with legality is in effect what people do when they claim that anything tolerated by law must, in the name of freedom, be approved by citizens in all their dealings with one another. As Zappa says, "Masturbation is not illegal. If it is not illegal to do it, why should it be illegal to sing about it?" He thinks this proves that Gore, who is not trying to make raunch in rock illegal, cannot even ask distributors to label it. Anything goes, as long as it's legal. The odd consequence of this argument would be a drastic narrowing of the freedom of speech. One could not call into question anything that was not against the law—including, for instance, racist speech.

8   A false ideal of tolerance has not only outlawed censorship but discouraged censoriousness (another word for censure). Most civilizations have expressed their moral values by mobilization of social opprobrium. That, rather than specific legislation, is what changed the treatment of minorities in films and TV over recent years. One can now draw opprobrious attention by gay bashing, as the Beastie Boys rock group found when their distributor told them to cut out remarks about "fags" for business reasons. Or by

anti-Semitism, as the just disbanded rap group Public Enemy has discovered.

9   It is said that only the narrow-minded are intolerant or opprobrious. Most of those who limited the distribution of Martin Scorsese's movie *The Last Temptation of Christ* had not even seen the movie. So do we guarantee freedom of speech only for the broad-minded or the better educated? Can one speak only after studying whatever one has reason, from one's beliefs, to denounce? Then most of us would be doing a great deal less speaking than we do. If one has never seen any snuff movies, is that a bar to criticizing them?

10   Others argue that asking people not to buy lettuce is different from asking them not to buy a rocker's artistic expression. Ideas (carefully disguised) lurk somewhere in the lyrics. All the more reason to keep criticism of them free. If ideas are too important to suppress, they are also too important to ignore. The whole point of free speech is not to make ideas exempt from criticism but to expose them to it.

11   One of the great mistakes of liberals in recent decades has been the ceding of moral concern to right-wingers. Just because one opposes censorship, one need not be seen as agreeing with pornographers. Why should liberals, of all people, oppose Gore when she asks that labels be put on products meant for the young, to inform those entrusted by law with the care of the young? Liberals were the first to promote "healthy" television shows like *Sesame Street* and *The Electric Company*. In the 1950s and 1960s they were the leading critics of television, of it its mindless violence, of the way it ravaged the attention span needed for reading. Who was keeping kids away from TV sets then? How did promoters of Big Bird let themselves be cast as champions of the Beastie Boys—not just of their *right* to perform but of their performance itself? Why should it be left to Gore to express moral disapproval of a group calling itself Dead Kennedys (sample lyric: "I kill children, I love to see them die")?

12   For that matter, who has been more insistent that parents should "interfere" in what their children are doing, Tipper Gore or Jesse Jackson? All through the 1970s, Jackson was traveling the high schools, telling parents to turn off TVs, make the kids finish their homework, check with teachers on their performance, get to know

what the children are doing. This kind of "interference" used to be called education.

13   Belief in the First Amendment does not pre-empt other beliefs, making one a eunuch to the interplay of opinions. It is a distortion to turn "You can express any views" into the proposition "I don't care what views you express." If liberals keep equating equality with approval, they will be repeatedly forced into weak positions.

14   A case in point is the Corcoran Gallery's sudden cancellation of an exhibit of Robert Mapplethorpe's photographs. The whole matter was needlessly confused when the director, Christina Owr-Chall, claimed she was canceling the show to *protect* it from censorship. She meant that there might be pressure to remove certain pictures—the sadomasochistic ones or those verging on kiddie porn—if the show had gone on. But she had in mind, as well, the hope of future grants from the National Endowment for the Arts, which is under criticism for the Mapplethorpe show and for another show that contained Andres Serrano's *Piss Christ*, the photograph of a crucifix in what the title says is urine. Owr-Chall is said to be yielding to censorship, when she is clearly yielding to political and financial pressure, as Pepsi yielded to commercial pressure over the Madonna ad.

15   What is at issue here is not government suppression but government subsidy. Mapplethorpe's work is not banned, but showing it might have endangered federal grants to needy artists. The idea that what the government does not support it represses is nonsensical, as one can see by reversing the statement to read: "No one is allowed to create anything without the government's subvention." What pussycats our supposedly radical artists are. They not only want the government's permission to create their artifacts, they want federal authorities to supply the materials as well. Otherwise they feel "gagged." If they are not given governmental approval (and money), they want to remain an avant-garde while being bankrolled by the Old Guard.

16   What is easily forgotten in this argument is the right of citizen taxpayers. They send representatives to Washington who are answerable for the expenditure of funds exacted from them. In general these voters want to favor their own values if government is going to get into the culture-subsidizing area at all (a proposition many find objectionable in itself). Politicians, insofar as they support the arts, will tend to favor conventional art (certainly not

masochistic art). Anybody who doubts that has no understanding of a politician's legitimate concern for his or her constituents' approval. Besides, it is quaint for those familiar with the politics of the art world to discover, with a shock, that there is politics in politics.

17 Luckily, cancellation of the Mapplethorpe show forced some artists back to the flair and cheekiness of unsubsidized art. Other results of pressure do not turn out as well. Unfortunately, people in certain regions were deprived of the chance to see *The Last Temptation of Christ* in the theater. Some, no doubt, considered it a loss that they could not buy lettuce or grapes during a Chavez boycott. Perhaps there was even a buyer perverse enough to miss driving the unsafe cars Nader helped pressure off the market. On the other hand, we do not get sports analysis made by racists. These mobilizations of social opprobrium are not examples of repression but of freedom of expression by committed people who censured without censoring, who expressed the kinds of belief the First Amendment guarantees. I do not, as a result, get whatever I approve of subsidized, either by Pepsi or the government. But neither does the law come in to silence Tipper Gore or Frank Zappa or even that filthy rag, the *Dartmouth Review*.

Analyzing the Writer's Argument

1. Why are the examples of recent attempts to limit freedom of speech interesting to Wills?

2. Why do you suppose the regents at the University of Wisconsin made a last-minute change in their rules regarding defamatory expressions and allowed such expressions in classroom discussions?

3. How does Wills define "censure"? How does it differ from censorship? Where does he define censorship? Is censorship legal? Is censure legal?

4. What does Wills mean when he writes at the end of paragraph 6, "This would make the law coterminous with morality"? What is the relationship between the law and morality?

5. Why does Wills feel that liberals have gone astray in recent decades? What have they done? What have they failed to do?

6. What, if anything, do you know from reading his essay of Wills' attitude toward subsidized art? The *Dartmouth Review*? The exhibit of Robert Mapplethorpe's photographs? Christina Owr-Chall's canceling of the Mapplethorpe show?

7. Is Wills biased in this essay? For example, does he reveal any of the conservatism that characterized his early years or does he attempt to present a balanced view of the censorship issue?
8. Is Wills arguing for anything in addition to the necessity of making the distinction between *censor* and *censure*? Explain.

Exploring the Issues in This Essay

1. Discuss the difference between censor and censure. If a community is successful in censuring an art show, has it not succeeded in censoring it? If we do not censure an art show does that mean that we support it? Is the distinction Wills makes a useful one? Explain.
2. Discuss the effect of censorship on you personally. Have you ever felt its constraints? How so? Where? With what consequences? Is it a problem that concerns you? Do you feel that there should be no censorship of any kind? Is there some degree of censorship that is acceptable to you? If so, how much? Under what circumstances?

Writing Suggestions for *Censorship*

1. Because television network news cannot possibly report on everything that happens in the world, just as no single individual can experience everything, what, then, constitutes censorship? How does it differ from selectivity? Why is it undesirable? Write an essay in which you define censorship.

2. Literally thousands of books have been banned by various individuals and groups in America. Perhaps the most famous of these books are three classics of American literature: *The Adventures of Huckleberry Finn, The Grapes of Wrath*, and *The Catcher in the Rye*. Spend enough time in the library to learn the reasons why any one of these books was found to be offensive and therefore unacceptable. Write an essay in which you argue the pros and cons of the book's banning.

3. Phyllis Schlafly argues that the public in any given community should have a right to democratically decide what their schools and libraries will provide for reading materials. Write an essay in which you argue instead that decisions about what to make available in the library and what to require students to read in the classroom should be made by professionals trained in these areas, professionals who are not subject to public influences.

4. What role should parents play in determining what their children hear and watch on radio and television? What responsibility, if any, do the media owe to parents? After reviewing the articles by Gore, Zappa, and Schlafly, write an essay arguing your position on the issue of parental rights.

5. You have been asked by executives of the music industry to develop a rating system for their products. Devise such a system and argue for its implementation. Be sure to define what you think is explicit and violent material.

6. Argue for or against the banning of beer and wine advertisements from your campus newspaper.

7. Using examples from your own experience, observations, and reading, write an essay in which you clearly differentiate censor and censure.

8. How are movies rated? Who does the rating, and how does the system work? For whom was the rating system devised? What does it accomplish? Did you and your parents make use of the rating system when you were younger? Write an essay either supporting the current rating system or arguing for its revision or elimination.

9. In 1988, in a case involving the principal of Hazelwood East High School near St. Louis, Missouri, the United States Supreme Court

ruled 5–3 that school officials had acted within their rights when they deleted stories from the school newspaper. Research the Hazelwood case in your library and write an essay in which you support or attack the Supreme Court's decision.

10. You are head of the Student Government Speakers Bureau and have just invited a speaker to address the student body. Critics have come forth threatening to disrupt and prevent the speaker from appearing. Write an editorial for your school newspaper in which you defend any speaker's First Amendment right to express his or her views on your campus.

11. Tipper Gore suggests that sometimes people who are criticized for their views attempt to protect themselves by claiming that their First Amendment right of freedom of speech has been violated. Argue against the cry of censorship as a way of promoting "anything goes" and for an individual's right to censure.

13

The Right to Die

We live in an age of medical miracles. Doctors are now equipped with machines and surgical procedures that enable them to save lives that just 10 years ago would have been lost. Surgeons routinely piece together the broken bodies of accident victims so that they can resume their daily activities. Organ transplantation has been commonplace, giving people with diseased or defective hearts, lungs, or kidneys a new lease on life. And the growing ability to treat fetuses *in utero* together with advances in obstetric care have given "high risk" babies a better chance at a normal life. But as syndicated columnist Ellen Goodman reminds us, "The miracles of survival are balanced with its horrors." All too willingly we forget about the more than 10,000 patients in America who live in a permanently vegetative state. And this number is likely to increase as new advances in biomedical technology make it possible to sustain respiration and heartbeat indefinitely in both newborns and the elderly, even when they are seriously impaired or terminally ill.

In 1976, in the now celebrated Karen Anne Quinlan case, the New Jersey Supreme Court ruled that doctors may disconnect a mechanical respirator that is keeping a comatose patient alive. The suit had been brought by Joseph and Julia Quinlan, parents who maintained that the machine was preventing their daughter from "dying with decency and dignity." Once disconnected from the respirator, Karen Anne lived for almost nine years, dying in 1985 without ever regaining consciousness. In another case, the Indiana courts upheld the parents' right to withhold treatment for a severely handicapped newborn. Born on April 9, 1982, with Down's syndrome and a blocked intestine, Baby Doe died six days later, when food and water were withdrawn and the required surgery was not performed. In response to this case, the U.S. Department of Health and Human Services created the so-called "Baby Doe Rules," a set of regulations calling for the aggressive treatment of handicapped newborns. In the wake of such cases, hospitals have developed ethics committees—composed of physicians, nurses, social workers, clergy, and psychologists—to assist doctors and the families of patients in reaching the appropriate treatment decision.

Our ability to sustain and prolong the lives of otherwise irreversibly comatose or terminally ill patients has in effect lengthened the process of dying. In doing so, it has renewed our interest in death and dying and the decisions of what action to take as each of us or one close to us approaches death. In the words of Dr. Joseph Fletcher, the noted bioethicist and former president of the Society for the Right to Die, "Good dying must at last find its place in our scheme of things, along with good birthing, good living and good loving. After all, it makes perfectly sound sense to strive for quality straight across the board, as much in our dying as in our living." While it is easy for most people to accept the sentiments of Dr. Fletcher's statement, it is not so easy to reach a consensus as to what constitutes "good dying."

The American Medical Association, for example, considers passive euthanasia—the discontinuing of life-sustaining treatment of the ill or stopping so-called heroic or extraordinary treatment—good medical practice. Why prolong the life of a suffering person whose disease is inevitably fatal, doctors ask. What is the "quality" or "meaning" of a life that is artificially prolonged with respirators, feeding tubes, and surgeries? "Death is not the greatest loss in life," writes Norman Cousins. "The greatest loss is what dies inside us while we live. The unbearable tragedy is to live without dignity or sensitivity." Members of the Society for the Right to Die believe that the individual should have control over his or her death and advocate the use of the "living will," an instrument that permits people to voice their desire not to be kept alive by artificial means when the time comes that there is no chance of recovery or of the possibility to have a meaningful life. In 1976 a right-to-die bill was passed in California. Since then more than 30 other states have passed laws recognizing living wills. Still others believe that it is not enough simply to have life-support systems disconnected; they want active euthanasia legalized. Groups like the Hemlock Society, for example, believe that a person has the right to choose death—either self-induced or doctor- or relative-assisted—to prevent unavoidable pain or a loss of dignity. "One can simply get to a point," as psychiatrist and ethicist Willard Gaylin observes, "where the pain and grief of life is in excess of the joy and pride." Although attitudes about suicide seem to be changing in response to advances in medical technology, active euthanasia is still illegal in the United States.

Euthanasia is problematic for some doctors because it involves a contradiction within the Hippocratic oath, the physicians' standard of professional ethics. The oath includes a promise to relieve suffering and pain as well as a promise to prolong and protect life. The paradox can be resolved under the principle of "double effect" developed by Catholic theologians. Under this principle the administration of a strong pain-killing drug which has as its primary effect the relieving of suffering may be ethically justified, even though the same action has a secondary effect of possibly causing death. Those actively opposed to the legalization of euthanasia consider it suicide or murder and therefore immoral. Pro-life advocates believe that all life is sacred and must be protected. They view "mercy killing" not only as a crime against God, but also as a practice that goes against some of the fundamental tenets of American society. In the words of Rita Marker, a spokesperson for the International Anti-Euthanasia Task Force, "Killing, whether called 'aid-in-dying' or any other deceptive name, is still killing, and no law can make it right." These people fear that legalized euthanasia could lead to abuses such as those that occurred during Adolf Hitler's Third Reich in Nazi Germany. Compulsory euthanasia clinics were established and boards of physicians and government officials prescribed death for those people who were suffering from incurable diseases, or for one reason or another were considered incapable of leading a productive life. As history has told us, many were selected for death for far different reasons.

In recent years a growing number of Americans have been seeking alternatives to euthanasia, ways of coping with death and dying. Various groups have established hospice programs, modeled after London's St. Christopher's Hospice, founded in 1967. The hospice concept is life affirming. It emphasizes home care and encourages family members to participate in caring for the patient. Hospice aims at easing the physical and psychological pain of the patient's illness and providing counseling to the dying person's family so that all involved can appreciate the patient's remaining life.

Barbara Huttmann

A Crime of Compassion

A patients' rights advocate, Barbara Huttmann is a nurse, teacher, and writer. Her two books, The Patient's Advocate *and* Code Blue: A Nurse's True-Life Story, *address the issue of the right of terminally ill patients to die with dignity. Born in Oakland, California, in 1935, Huttmann graduated from Cypress Community College in 1976 and received her B.S. in Nursing Administration two years later from California State University at Fullerton. As a nurse, Huttmann had seen firsthand the suffering and indignity heaped on patients who begged only for the right to die. As a result, she began to question the medical profession's right to force life on dying people through the use of so-called "heroic measures." At present Huttmann works at Children's Hospital of San Francisco where she is the Associate Director of Nursing Services.*

In the following essay, which first appeared in the "My Turn" column in Newsweek *in 1983, Huttmann tells of the bizarre efforts to prolong the life of Mac, one of her cancer patients. Her story of Mac is an emotional plea for new legislation, legislation that would protect the terminally ill patient's request for the right to die.*

1   "Murderer," a man shouted. "God help patients who get *you* for a nurse."

2   "What gives you the right to play God?" another one asked.

3   It was the Phil Donahue show where the guest is a fatted calf and the audience a 200-strong flock of vultures hungering to pick at the bones. I had told them about Mac, one of my favorite cancer patients. "We resuscitated him 52 times in just one month. I refused to resuscitate him again. I simply sat there and held his hand while he died."

4   There wasn't time to explain that Mac was a young, witty, macho cop who walked into the hospital with 32 pounds of attack equipment, looking as if he could single-handedly protect the whole

534

city, if not the entire state. "Can't get rid of this cough," he said. Otherwise, he felt great.

5 Before the day was over, tests confirmed that he had lung cancer. And before the year was over, I loved him, his wife, Maura, and their three kids as if they were my own. All the nurses loved him. And we all battled his disease for six months without ever giving death a thought. Six months isn't such a long time in the whole scheme of things, but it was long enough to see him lose his youth, his wit, his macho, his hair, his bowel and bladder control, his sense of taste and smell, and his ability to do the slightest thing for himself. It was also long enough to watch Maura's transformation from a young woman into a haggard, beaten old lady.

6 When Mac had wasted away to a 60-pound skeleton kept alive by liquid food we poured down a tube, i.v. solutions we dripped into his veins, and oxygen we piped to a mask on his face, he begged us: "Mercy . . . for God's sake, please just let me go."

7 The first time he stopped breathing, the nurse pushed the button that calls a "code blue" throughout the hospital and sends a team rushing to resuscitate the patient. Each time he stopped breathing, sometimes two or three times in one day, the code team came again. The doctors and technicians worked their miracles and walked away. The nurses stayed to wipe the saliva that drooled from his mouth, irrigate the big craters of bedsores that covered his hips, suction the lung fluids that threatened to drown him, clean the feces that burned his skin like lye, pour the liquid food down the tube attached to his stomach, put pillows between his knees to ease the bone-on-bone pain, turn him every hour to keep the bedsores from getting worse, and change his gown and linen every two hours to keep him from being soaked in perspiration.

8 At night I went home and tried to scrub away the smell of decaying flesh that seemed woven into the fabric of my uniform. It was in my hair, the upholstery of my car—there was no washing it away. And every night I prayed that Mac would die, that his agonized eyes would never again plead with me to let him die.

9 Every morning I asked his doctor for a "no-code" order. Without that order, we had to resuscitate every patient who stopped breathing. His doctor was one of several who believe we must extend life as long as we have the means and knowledge to do it. To not do it is to be liable for negligence, at least in the eyes of many people, including some nurses. I thought about what it would be

like to stand before a judge, accused of murder, if Mac stopped breathing and I didn't call a code.

10　And after the fifty-second code, when Mac was still lucid enough to beg for death again, and Maura was crumbled in my arms again, and when no amount of pain medication stilled his moaning and agony, I wondered about a spiritual judge. Was all this misery and suffering supposed to be building character or infusing us all with the sense of humility that comes from impotence?

11　Had we, the whole medical community, become so arrogant that we believed in the illusion of salvation through science? Had we become so self-righteous that we thought meddling in God's work was our duty, our moral imperative and our legal obligation? Did we really believe that we had the right to force "life" on a suffering man who had begged for the right to die?

12　Such questions haunted me more than ever early one morning when Maura went home to change her clothes and I was bathing Mac. He had been still for so long, I thought he at last had the blessed relief of coma. Then he opened his eyes and moaned, "Pain . . . no more . . . Barbara . . . do something . . . God, let me go."

13　The desperation in his eyes and voice riddled me with guilt. "I'll stop," I told him as I injected the pain medication.

14　I sat on the bed and held Mac's hands in mine. He pressed his bony fingers against my hand and muttered, "Thanks." Then there was one soft sigh and I felt his hands go cold in mine. "Mac?" I whispered, as I waited for his chest to rise and fall again.

15　A clutch of panic banded my chest, drew my finger to the code button, urged me to do something, anything . . . but sit there alone with death. I kept one finger on the button, without pressing it, as a waxen pallor slowly transformed his face from person to empty shell. Nothing I've ever done in my 47 years has taken so much effort as it took *not* to press that code button.

16　Eventually, when I was as sure as I could be that the code team would fail to bring him back, I entered the legal twilight zone and pushed the button. The team tried. And while they were trying, Maura walked into the room and shrieked, "No . . . don't let them do this to him . . . for God's sake . . . please, no more."

17　Cradling her in my arms was like cradling myself, Mac, and all those patients and nurses who had been in this place before, who do the best they can in a death-denying society.

18   So a TV audience accused me of murder. Perhaps I am guilty. If a doctor had written a no-code order, which is the only *legal* alternative, would he have felt any less guilty? Until there is legislation making it a criminal act to code a patient who has requested the right to die, we will all of us risk the same fate as Mac. For whatever reason, we developed the means to prolong life, and now we are forced to use it. We do not have the right to die.

Analyzing the Writer's Argument

1. What exactly is Huttmann arguing for in this essay? How does she attempt to persuade readers to her position? How effective did you find her strategy? Explain.
2. Do you think the people in the audience at the Donahue show were justified in calling Huttmann a "murderer" and in accusing her of playing "God"? Why or why not?
3. What made Huttmann finally decide not to press the code button? Why hadn't she done it earlier?
4. Do you agree with Huttmann's claim that America is "a death-denying society"? Explain.
5. Good narratives often have an attention-grabbing introduction and a thought-provoking conclusion. Did you find Huttmann's opening paragraphs to be effective? What does her last statement mean? Is she exaggerating the situation or simply stating the truth?
6. Huttmann asks a rhetorical question in paragraph 10 and three more in paragraph 11. Explain how these questions work in the context of her essay.
7. Explain how Huttmann's diction, especially her verbs, enhances the emotional impact of her story about Mac's last six months. Point to specific words that worked for you.

Exploring the Issues in This Essay

1. Many people believe that the right-to-die issue is a difficult one to resolve because the law and morality seem to be at odds with one another. What are the options available to people in situations where such conflicts exist (school prayer, welfare, military draft, and affirmative action are other possibilities)?

2. When Huttmann appeared on the Phil Donahue show, she was greeted by an audience that wanted to judge her actions. One man called her a "murderer," while another accused her of "play(ing) God." Can you understand why these people reacted this way? What do you think they expected Huttmann to do when Mac begged to die? What do you think you would have done had you been in Huttmann's position?

Evan R. Collins, Jr.

*The Right to Choose Life or Death**

Evan R. Collins, vice-president and resident officer of the brokerage firm Kidder, Peabody & Company, was born in Boston, Massachusetts, on November 6, 1937. After receiving his B.A. from Dartmouth College in 1959 and doing two years of postgraduate work at Dartmouth's Amos Tuck School of Business Administration, Collins launched a very successful career in investment banking with Kidder, Peabody & Company. He has also been actively involved with the Up With People program and the United Way campaigns. Currently he serves as the president of the Society for the Right to Die, an organization that believes a person should have control over his or her death and that advocates the use of a "living will."

In the following essay, first published in USA Today *in November 1984, Collins sets forth the basic philosophy of the Society for the Right to Die and softly promotes its programs and goals, especially the concept of the "living will."*

1 The public indignation that followed Gov. Richard D. Lamm's speech in March, 1984, to the Colorado Health Lawyers Association was, the governor has said, largely caused by reporters misinterpreting his statements and quoting them out of context. Certainly, many people, especially the elderly, reacted with outrage when they read in their newspapers, "We've got a duty to die, to get out of the way with our machines and our artificial hearts and everything else like that, and let the other society, our kids, build a reasonable life." His paraphrase of a statement later attributed to Leon Kass, writing in *American Scholar* magazine—"It's like if leaves fall off a tree forming the humus for the other plants to grow"— did not help. Unthinkable historical analogies were conjured up, including genocide under the Nazi regime (an angry responding

* Reprinted from USA TODAY MAGAZINE, November 1984. Copyright © 1984 by the Society for the Advancement of Education.

article by Nat Hentoff in New York's *Village Voice* was illustrated by a photograph of Hitler), or, on another scale, the "final solution" once practiced by hard-pressed Eskimo families scrabbling for survival in the farthest reaches of the Arctic: when grandmother lost her usefulness, she was left on the ice floe, possibly to become food for the polar bear that might later be hunted to feed her own family. Grandmother, it was said, stoically accepted her fate. We are not about to do the same. The idea of any of us having a "duty to die" is abhorrent.

2   Whatever legitimate outrage Gov. Lamm's reckless remarks caused, he struck a responsive chord when warned that "we should be very careful in terms of our technological miracles that we don't impose life on people who, in fact, are suffering beyond our ability to help." He might also have included people who are beyond suffering, in irreversible coma, their brain function permanently destroyed. Patients of both kinds are a common occurrence in hospitals everywhere. Typical is the inert body of an 82-year-old woman, victim of a massive coronary, lying day after day hooked up to tubes and wires with no prospect of returning to consciousness, much less to last week's exceptional vitality which her daughter remembers as she says, "That's not my mother lying there." Less typical only because it was taken to court is the case of Abe Perlmutter, presenting the distressing picture of man mortally ill with ALS ("Lou Gehrig's disease"); fully aware and desperate, wrenching out with his own hands the mechanical respirator attached to his trachea in a failed attempt to die (the hospital alarm sounded). What are we to think of Karen Ann Quinlan, who, more than eight years after the court permitted termination of life-support apparatus, still occupies a bed in a New Jersey nursing home—weighing 60-odd pounds, usually in fetal position, and kept "alive" by the artificially given food and water that her parents can't bring themselves to stop?

3   It has been estimated that the medical advances of the last 10 years exceed all the medical progress achieved in the preceding 100 years. The miracles continue to multiply, most of them beneficial in preserving life and the ability to enjoy it. However, new technology has also confronted us with dilemmas we've never had to consider before. As the distinguished bioethicist, Joseph Fletcher, expressed it, "Ethical questions jump out at us from every laboratory and clinic." The answers to those questions are not easy to

find—not for ethicists, clergymen, doctors, nurses, hospital case-workers, lawyers, judges, government agency officials, legislators, or you and me.

4   How do we determine the line between prolonging life and prolonging dying? How far should we go to sustain a life whose quality is at best only marginal? Can anyone define unacceptable "quality of life" for anyone else? If a hospital's life-sustaining equipment is limited, who is to decide its allocation, and how? Is the life of a 65-year-old upright citizen less "worth saving" than the life of a 25-year-old confirmed criminal? Should the wishes of an intermittently "confused" 90-year-old woman be heeded if she refuses recommended surgery? The list of questions could go on and on, repeatedly echoing "Who's to decide?" No wonder the elderly were alarmed by the implications of Gov. Lamm's quoted statements, envisioning a lifetime of control over their own lives eroded at the end by a battery of medical decision-makers.

5   Dr. Fletcher, professor emeritus of Christian ethics and Pastoral Theology at the Episcopal Divinity School in Cambridge, Mass., is also president emeritus of the Society for the Right to Die, an organization that was founded nearly a half-century ago. His philosophy emphasizes the human need to be in control. The Society stresses the fundamental right of self-determination—the right to determine what shall and shall not be done to one's own body. This right, established by common law and the constitutional right of privacy, includes the right to refuse treatment—the corollary of informed consent. A surprising number of patients are unaware that they can say no in a hospital, just as they are unsure of their right to leave a hospital at will.

6   Knowing these rights can be important to patients who have the capacity to listen, understand, make decisions, and communicate or act on them. However, critically ill or injured patients are often helpless—debilitated by disease, incapacitated by pain or other medication, mentally impaired or unconscious. Many of them have no prospect of recovery and would, if they could, choose not to prolong a hopeless situation.

7   It is to protect the rights of these patients that the Society for the Right to Die offers "living will" forms—documents which, with or without personalized modifications and specific additions, may be executed in advance by competent adults to serve as written evidence of their preferences regarding terminal treatment. It can be

a help to their doctors when communication is impossible, and a relief to their families who may otherwise have to bear the entire burden of making painful decisions for them. A living will can be revoked at any time. The wishes expressed by the terminally ill patient, which may contradict the preferences stated in the document, always supersede it.

8   In addition to supplying living will forms, the Society supports enactment of state laws that give legal recognition to these advance directives, make them binding on doctors and other health care professionals, and provide immunity from liability for complying with them. So far, 21 states (Alabama, Arkansas, California, Delaware, Florida, Georgia, Idaho, Illinois, Kansas, Mississippi, Nevada, New Mexico, North Carolina, Oregon, Texas, Vermont, Virginia, Washington, West Virginia, Washington, West Virginia, Wisconsin, and Wyoming) and the District of Columbia have enacted such laws. While many other legislatures have failed year after year to pass them, living will bills proliferate and support for them grows. Twenty-five states considered them during the 1984 legislative session, and six were enacted in the spring.

9   Although only two living will laws are exactly alike, most of them contain specific wording of the living will "declaration"—to be followed precisely or "substantially"—that expresses the desire not to have one's dying artificially prolonged by life-sustaining procedures if one's condition has been medically certified as terminal. The Society distributes on request the forms contained specifically in the statutes, as well as its own "Living Will Declaration," made available to people who live in states that have not yet passed living will laws. It is impossible to estimate just how many people have signed living wills in states both that have and have not passed laws recognizing them, but millions of forms have been distributed.

10   An added protection is the naming of another person to make treatment decisions on behalf of the patient, in keeping with the patient's known wishes. This is provided in some of the more recent living will laws, and is contained in the Society's Living Will Declaration form. The proxy is an optional election; not everyone has someone to appoint—especially the childless elderly, who may have no surviving family or close friends. If there is an appropriate person available, however, the proxy appointment may be helpful, providing someone on the spot to press for decisions that honor

the patient's wishes with specific reference to the patient's condition and treatment options, which can never be fully foreseen.

11   Another way of extending the rights and protecting the interests of patients who have lost the ability to make or communicate decisions is through a durable power of attorney appointment. All 50 states have durable power of attorney statutes which would theorectically permit decisions about medical treatment, as well as about property matters. Two states—California and Pennsylvania—have amended those laws expressly to cover health care decisions. California, characteristically avant garde, was the first state to pass a living will law of any kind—but its 1976 Natural Death Act is relatively restrictive and the 1983 amended durable power statute can compensate for its limitations. Pennsylvania has yet to enact a living will law.

12   The application to medical treatment decisions of durable powers of attorney in states that don't specify this use is uncertain. As a presidential commission pointed out in its March, 1983, report, *Deciding to Forego Life-Sustaining Treatment*, these laws need to be studied further with a view to safeguarding them from possible abuse in connection with health care matters. Their use, even coupled with living will directives, has not been tested to any extent.

13   Nor have living wills been widely tested in the courts. They have figured in only two known cases—peripherally in one, significantly in the other. In Texas, the issue was muddied by the fact that the patient had executed a living will quite different from the document form prescribed by the Texas Natural Death Act. The case was ultimately resolved by declaring the patient brain-dead—an anomaly, since, if he was found to meet the generally accepted medical criteria for brain death, what was his case doing in court?

14   In Florida, a living will case was carried to the state's highest court following an appellate court decision. The lower court had ruled that, although a comatose patient's living will could be admitted as evidence, it was not sufficient in itself to guarantee immunity to physicians acting in accordance with it, and that life support could be withdrawn only if a court-appointed guardian had obtained court approval to do so. Although the patient had already died, the hospital appealed the case to the Florida Supreme Court, hoping for guidance in the treatment of some 40 other comatose patients. During the last week of May, 1984—the same

week that saw enactment, finally, of a Florida living will law—the high court overturned the appellate court's ruling. It affirmed the validity of the living will, gave the right of decision to a comatose patient's family, and removed the necessity for court intervention before life support could be terminated.

15   Patients' deaths have preceded judicial resolutions in the majority of right-to-die cases that have made their way up to state supreme courts. While living wills have not played a part in them— none of the other dying patients had executed these—one notable case has been decided on the basis of "clear and convincing evidence" of the patient's prior wishes, which a living will can without doubt provide. The case concerned Brother Fox, a member of the Catholic Marianist order in a religious community in New York. At the time when the newspapers were full of the Karen Ann Quinlan case, he had expressed his own feelings about being kept alive "as a vegetable." Ironically, three and a half years later, he lapsed into a permanent coma following surgery. His superior, Father Eichner, petitioned the court for permission to withdraw Brother Fox's respirator. Though permission was granted two months later, it was not acted on. Because of the importance of the issue, the case was appealed to the Appellate Division (at which point, Brother Fox, despite continuing respiratory support, had died), and finally to the Court of Appeals, New York's highest court. The court's opinion was handed down a full year and a half after Father Eichner had initiated legal action and 14 months after Brother Fox's death. In addition to the "clear and convincing evidence" of his earlier statements, the court based its findings on Brother Fox's common law right to refuse treatment.

16   In one way or another—which is to say, on one ground or another—the highest state courts have upheld the terminal patient's right to be allowed to die in all but one major decision (*In re Storar*, New York Court of Appeals, 1981, which involved a retarded adult who had never been competent. He had terminal cancer of the liver, but the treatment in question was blood transfusion, and the court considered bleeding treatable and in a different category from untreatable cancer. The court also relied on the role of the state as surrogate parent with an interest in protecting the health of a child, which, for legal purposes, Storar was considered to be). All but one of the rulings have concerned

patients whose decision-making capacity was lost; only Abe Perlmutter, mentioned above, was judged competent.

17 Aside from the support it implies of living will declarations, Brother Fox's case is significant because the petitioner on his behalf was a Catholic priest and Brother Fox a member of the same order. A lot of the opposition to living will legislation has come from sectors of the Catholic community, despite the 1980 Vatican Declaration reiterating the church's position that, when death is inevitable and imminent, treatment which would secure only a "precarious and burdensome prolongation of life" may be, in conscience, refused.

18 Devout Catholic Peter Cinque might be viewed as an indirect victim of that opposition in New York State, which has yet to enact a living will statute. Diabetic, blind, and a multiple amputee, having endured enough, Cinque consulted with his priest and his family before asking his hospital to take him off the dialysis machine that was keeping him alive. Hospital agreement was slow in coming, and Cinque spend many days in an anguish of uncertainty. He suffered severe pain as well, since hospital authorities took him off all medication in order to assure themselves of his complete competency to make a rational decision to die. Then, abruptly, despite statements he had signed relieving them of all responsibility for the outcome (hospital personnel had supplied him with the forms refusing treatment), the hospital sent its lawyers to obtain a court order to continue the dialysis. Cinque's shock and despair may have accelerated his deterioration. At any rate, the next day, he lapsed into coma. There was a hearing in his hospital room a few days later in which, as the judge discovered, Cinque was unable to participate. A lawyer was appointed his guardian and, after more testimony, his request was finally granted. He died an hour after dialysis was discontinued.

Needed: Guidelines

19 The yes-no shift in this hospital's position is perhaps an extreme example of the uncertainties and fears that not only propel right-to-die cases into the courts, but also cause foot-dragging, half measures, fruitless treatment, and general stonewalling when it comes

to deciding whether or not what doctors call "aggressive treatment" can be stopped. Not that there aren't plenty of instances where a determination to stop it is reached between doctors and dying patients' families and quietly carried out. However, as technology advances and malpractice actions proliferate, some clarifying guidelines are sorely needed in the medical community. What is appropriate care for the dying patient?

20 One response has been the issuance of suggested "Do Not Resuscitate" policies and procedures by a handful of medical societies and many hospitals. These, in effect, are intended to eliminate the absurdity of rushing to restore respiration and heartbeat to patients for whom the failure of these functions is associated with their terminal condition; to revive them is only to prolong their dying, and serves no purpose. Sensible systems for regulating DNR orders and their implementation include appropriate communication and documentation. This point was driven home in early 1984, when a special grand jury investigating a death in a Queens, New York, hospital reported its findings. The hospital had been using an informal "purple dot" system to denote which of the patients were not to be resuscitated if they went into cardiac or pulmonary arrest. Their nursing cards, purple decal and all, were destroyed after the patients died. The system meant secrecy (there was no assurance that patients or their families were aware of the DNR decision), possible error (one nursing card was found to have *two* purple decals fixed to it—if this could happen, what else could?), and unaccountability.

21 Another response to the need came out of a conference of distinguished doctors, sponsored by the Society for the Right to Die, who met to develop guidelines on "The Physician's Responsibility Toward Hopelessly Ill Patients"—the title of the resulting article that was published in *The New England Journal of Medicine* in April, 1984. The 10 physician co-authors represent various medical disciplines and institutions in a number of states. The conclusions they reached were based on two premises: the patient has a primary role in making treatment decisions, and there should be a decrease in aggressive treatment when it would only prolong the dying process. The article spells out in detail the care its authors consider ethically correct and desirable at various stages of illness, for both competent and incompetent patients. These range from emergency

resuscitation and intensive care, if wanted, to giving comfort care only. They suggest procedures that may be withdrawn or withheld under certain conditions and if patient or family have agreed. In including artificially given food and water among these procedures, the authors confront an emotionally charged subject, one that was at issue in court cases still unresolved at the time of the article's publication. Depriving patients of nourishment is a step more freighted with feeling—and controversy—than disconnecting mechanisms such as respirators. In considering it, as in all matters affecting terminal patients, the authors urge clear communication, including telling the patient the truth about his or her condition. "The anxiety of dealing with the unknown can be far more upsetting than the grief of dealing with a known, albeit tragic, truth."

22 The article also confronts squarely the influences on doctors that may keep them from accepting the idea that "less" often can be "more" in treating terminal patients: training and tradition that emphasizes keeping the patient alive no matter what; the great temptation to use all the sophisticated medical technology that is there for the using; personal values and unconscious motivations; equating a patient's death with professional failure; and insistence on impossibly absolute prognostic certainty. In addition, of course, there is fear of liability, often more exaggerated than it need be, and often a deterrent to sensible, humane treatment.

23 The authors touch briefly on the astronomical cost of high-tech medicine, which strains public funds, escalates health insurance premiums, and can wipe out family finances. They note the increasing pressure on doctors for cost constraint. Gov. Lamm's statements highlighted this admittedly difficult and delicate point. No one would measure the value of a human life against the dollars it costs to sustain it—the thought is repugnant. Still, when it comes to perpetuating meaningless existences of thousands of comatose dying patients, it seems anything but heartless to talk about costs in money as well as in family anguish.

24 Pointing out that terminally ill patients are often cared for by specialists or members of hospital staffs who can not possibly know what the patient's wishes would be (unless the patient is competent to tell them), the authors recommend advance statements of those wishes—a living will—or, alternatively, the advance designa-

tion of a proxy. These devices, even though they do not necessarily solve every dilemma faced by a physician, can be of real help in deciding the best treatment course to recommend.

Hospitals' Viewpoints

25 It is reassuring that these 10 prestigious physicians have so strongly supported the patient's right to exercise control over terminal treatment and have recognized the usefulness of the living will. While you and I can hardly anticipate with pleasure a future time and circumstance when our own living will may be a significant piece of paper, can we at least anticipate with confidence that its instructions will be respected whenever we need them to be? Will hospitals honor them?

26 During the past year, at the suggestion of the Society for the Right to Die, hundreds of people have written to their local hospitals asking how their living will documents would be regarded if they became critically ill patients with no hope of recovery. Would the hospital honor the instructions? Did the hospital have a policy and a procedure on this?

27 Hospitals' responses were for the most part attentive and thoughtful, often formulated with legal counsel. Some of them said that the questions had spurred the creation of committees to develop living will policies. Others mentioned the risk of liability in the absence of a state law setting guidelines and offering protection. A few hospitals in states where living will laws do exist seemed not to know of them, but most in that category knew and referred to the statute. It is difficult to analyze the results of this "survey" in terms of categorical yes or no responses to the question of complying with the living will; some hospitals were clear, some waffled in their answers. However, one response appeared over and over again: hospitals do not initiate services or procedures, but produce them on doctors' orders. The obvious conclusion we *can* make is that we had better be sure to talk to our doctors about how we feel about terminal treatment.

28 If tubes and machines are abhorrent to us, what do we want as our lives are ending? What are we entitled to? Ease of pain, certainly, and, insofar as possible, relief from emotional discomfort;

but beyond these considerations, it is the assurance that we will be permitted to die with, to quote Dr. Fletcher again, "that quality of humanness, the preservation of which is what the concepts of loving concern and social justice are built upon."

29   As he wrote, "Good dying must at last find its place in our scheme of things, along with good birthing, good living and good loving. After all, it makes perfectly sound sense to strive for quality straight across the board, as much in our dying as in our living."

LIVING WILL DECLARATION
To My Family, Physician, and Medical Facility

I, _____, being of sound mind voluntarily make known my desire that my dying shall not be artificially prolonged under the following circumstances:

If I should have an injury, disease, or illness regarded by my physician as incurable and terminal, and if my physician determines that the application of life-sustaining procedures would serve only to prolong artificially the dying process, I direct that such procedures be withheld or withdrawn and that I be permitted to die. I want treatment limited to those measures that will provide me with maximum comfort and freedom from pain. Should I become unable to participate in decisions with respect to my medical treatment, it is my intention that these directions be honored by my family and physician(s) as a final expression of my legal right to refuse treatment, and I accept the consequences of this refusal.

Signed _____ Date _____

Witness _____ Witness _____

DESIGNATION CLAUSE (optional*)

Should I become comatose, incompetent, or otherwise mentally or physically incapable of communication, I authorize

_____ presently residing at _____ to make treatment decisions on my behalf in accordance with my Living Will Declaration. I have discussed my wishes concerning terminal care with this person, and I trust his/her judgment on my behalf.

Signed _____ Date _____

Witness _____ Witness _____

*If I have not designated a proxy as provided above, I understand that my Living Will Declaration shall nevertheless be given effect should the appropriate circumstances arise.

550

Analyzing the Writer's Argument

1. What is Collins' purpose in paragraphs 1 and 2? Why do you thing Governor Lamm's remarks cause people to conjure up "unthinkable historical analogies"? How effective are these two paragraphs as an introduction to the essay? Explain.

2. According to Collins, what are the dilemmas that our new technologies confront us with every day?

3. What is the basic philosophy and purpose of the Society for the Right to Die? Why does the Society offer people "living will" forms? What exactly is a "living will" and how, according to Collins, does one work?

4. What is the point of the optional designation clause in the Society's *Living Will Declaration*?

5. To what end does Collins use the examples of Brother Fox and Peter Cinque? What is the Catholic Church's position on medical treatment when death is inevitable and imminent?

6. Why does Collins believe that guidelines must be established to cover the appropriate care of dying patients and the use of living wills? What evidence does he present to document this need?

7. What is Collins' point in summarizing the article "The Physician's Responsibility Toward Hopelessly Ill Patients" in paragraphs 21 through 24? What recommendations do the ten doctors who co-authored this article make?

8. How have hospitals responded to the question of living wills? Do they appear ready to recognize and enforce them? Why does Collins believe that it is important for people to talk to their physicians about their feelings concerning terminal treatment?

9. How would you describe Collins' tone in this essay? Did you find it appropriate for both his subject and his audience? Explain why or why not.

10. Why do you suppose Collins wrote this essay? After reading the essay, did you think he was more interested in informing you about the issue or in persuading you to some action? Explain.

Exploring the Issues in This Essay

1. In paragraph 4 Collins presents us with a long list of ethical questions that our new technology has created. Why are answers to these questions so difficult to find? Do you have answers to any of these important questions? Discuss who you think should make some of these crucial decisions.

2. In 1938 the Euthanasia Society was founded in the United States. Later, this organization changed its name to the Society for the Right to Die. What in your opinion was accomplished by the name change?
3. Review the sample *Living Will Declaration* that Collins includes at the end of his essay. How do you react to it? Did anything about it surprise you? Is there anything that you would like to see added to this document? Would you consider making a living will? Explain why or why not.

James Rachels

Active and Passive Euthanasia

James Rachels, a professor of moral philosophy, is particularly concerned with exploring the ethical dimensions of contemporary social issues. He delights in enabling his students and colleagues to see meaningful connections between the principles of moral philosophy and real moral problems. Born in Columbus, Georgia, in 1941, James Rachels graduated from Mercer University and later earned his doctorate from the University of North Carolina. He has taught at New York University and the University of Miami before accepting a position at the University of Alabama in Birmingham, where he is currently the Dean of Humanities. Rachels is the editor of Moral Problems, *a reader on the ethical and moral aspects of current social questions.*

Some years ago the question of euthanasia first attracted James Rachels' attention because of what he perceived a philosophical inconsistency at the heart of the issue. Legally, active euthanasia, or "mercy killing," is considered murder, while passive euthanasia, or withholding treatment from a patient, is not. This, in fact, is the position supported by the American Medical Association, but Rachels did not quite see the issue that way. In "Active and Passive Euthanasia," first published in The New England Journal of Medicine *in 1975, he asks us to reconsider some of our basic assumptions about euthanasia. Rachels argues that allowing a patient to die is morally no better than mercy killing.*

1   The distinction between active and passive euthanasia is thought to be crucial for medical ethics. The idea is that it is permissible, at least in some cases, to withhold treatment and allow a patient to die, but it is never permissible to take any direct action designed to kill the patient. This doctrine seems to be accepted by most doctors, and it is endorsed in a statement adopted by the House of Delegates of the American Medical Association on December 4, 1973.

> The intentional termination of the life of one human being by another—mercy killing—is contrary to that for which the medical profession stands and is contrary to the policy of the American Medical Association.
>
> The cessation of the employment of extraordinary means to prolong the life of the body when there is irrefutable evidence that biological death is imminent is the decision of the patient and/or his immediate family. The advice and judgment of the physician should be freely available to the patient and/or his immediate family.

However, a strong case can be made against this doctrine. In what follows I will set out some of the relevant arguments and urge doctors to reconsider their views on this matter.

2   To begin with a familiar type of situation, a patient who is dying of incurable cancer of the throat is in terrible pain, which can no longer be satisfactorily alleviated. He is certain to die within a few days, even if present treatment is continued, but he does not want to go on living for those days since the pain is unbearable. So he asks the doctor for an end to it, and his family joins in the request.

3   Suppose the doctor agrees to withhold treatment, as the conventional doctrine says he may. The justification for his doing so is that the patient is in terrible agony, and since he is going to die anyway, it would be wrong to prolong his suffering needlessly. But now notice this. If one simply withholds treatment, it may take the patient longer to die, and so he may suffer more than he would if more direct action were taken and lethal injection given. This fact provides strong reason for thinking that, once the initial decision not to prolong his agony has been made, active euthanasia is actually preferable to passive euthanasia, rather than the reverse. To say otherwise is to endorse the option that leads to more suffering rather than less, and is contrary to the humanitarian impulse that prompts the decision not to prolong his life in the first place.

4   Part of my point is that the process of being "allowed to die" can be relatively slow and painful, whereas being given a lethal injection is relatively quick and painless. Let me give a different sort of example. In the United States about one in 600 babies is born with Down's syndrome. Most of these babies are otherwise healthy—that is, with only the usual pediatric care, they will proceed to an otherwise normal infancy. Some, however, are born with congeni-

tal defects such as intestinal obstructions that require operations if they are to live. Sometimes, the parents and the doctor will decide not to operate, and let the infant die. Anthony Shaw describes what happens then:

> ... When surgery is denied [the doctor] must try to keep the infant from suffering while natural forces sap the baby's life away. As a surgeon whose natural inclination is to use the scalpel to fight off death, standing by and watching a salvageable baby die is the most emotionally exhausting experience I know. It is easy at a conference, in a theoretical discussion, to decide that such infants should be allowed to die. It is altogether different to stand by in the nursery and watch as dehydration and infection wither a tiny being over hours and days. This is a terrible ordeal for me and the hospital staff—much more so than for the parents who never set foot in the nursery.[1]

I can understand why some people are opposed to all euthanasia, and insist that such infants must be allowed to live. I think I can also understand why other people favor destroying these babies quickly and painlessly. But why should anyone favor letting "dehydration and infection wither a tiny being over hours and days?" The doctrine that says that a baby may be allowed to dehydrate and wither but may not be given an injection that would end its life without suffering, seems so patently cruel as to require no further refutation. The strong language is not intended to offend but only to put the point in the clearest possible way.

5   My second argument is that the conventional doctrine leads to decisions concerning life and death made on irrelevant grounds.

6   Consider again the case of the infants with Down's syndrome who need operations for congenital defects unrelated to the syndrome to live. Sometimes, there is no operation, and the baby dies, but when there is no such defect, the baby lives on. Now, an operation such as that to remove an intestinal obstruction is not prohibitively difficult. The reason why such operations are not performed in these cases is, clearly, that the child has Down's syndrome and the parents and doctor judge that because of that fact it is better for the child to die.

[1] A. Shaw, "Doctor, Do We Have a Choice?" *New York Times Magazine*, January 30, 1972, p. 54. (Author's note.)

7   But notice that this situation is absurd, no matter what view one takes of the lives and potentials of such babies. If the life of such an infant is worth preserving, what does it matter if it needs a simple operation? Or, if one thinks it better that such a baby should not live on, what difference does it make that it happens to have an unobstructed intestinal tract? In either case, the matter of life and death is being decided on irrelevant grounds. It is the Down's syndrome, and not the intestines, that is the issue. That matter should be decided, if at all, on that basis, and not be allowed to depend on the essentially irrelevant question of whether the intestinal tract is blocked.

8   What makes this situation possible, of course, is the idea that when there is an intestinal blockage, one can "let the baby die," but when there is no such defect there is nothing that can be done, for one must not "kill" it. The fact that this idea leads to such results as deciding life or death on irrelevant grounds is another good reason why the doctrine should be rejected.

9   One reason why so many people think that there is an important moral difference between active and passive euthanasia is that they think killing someone is morally worse than letting someone die. But is it? Is killing, in itself, worse than letting die? To investigate this issue, two cases may be considered that are exactly alike except that one involves killing whereas the other involves letting someone die. Then, it can be asked whether this difference makes any difference to the moral assessments. It is important that the cases be exactly alike, except for this one difference, since otherwise one cannot be confident that it is this difference and not some other that accounts for any variation in the assessments of the two cases. So, let us consider this pair of cases:

10   In the first, Smith stands to gain a large inheritance if anything should happen to his six-year-old cousin. One evening while the child is taking his bath, Smith sneaks into the bathroom and drowns the child, and then arranges things so that it will look like an accident.

11   In the second, Jones also stands to gain if anything should happen to his six-year-old cousin. Like Smith, Jones sneaks in planning to drown the child in his bath. However, just as he enters the bathroom Jones sees the child slip and hit his head, and fall face down in the water. Jones is delighted; he stands by, ready to push the child's head back under if it is necessary, but it is not

necessary. With only a little thrashing about, the child drowns all by himself, "accidentally," as Jones watches and does nothing.

12 Now Smith killed the child, whereas Jones "merely" let the child die. That is the only difference between them. Did either man behave better, from a moral point of view? If the difference between killing and letting die were in itself a morally important matter, one should say that Jones's behavior was less reprehensible than Smith's. But does one really want to say that? I think not. In the first place, both men acted from the same motive, personal gain, and both had exactly the same end in view when they acted. It may be inferred from Smith's conduct that he is a bad man, although that judgment may be withdrawn or modified if certain further facts are learned about him—for example, that he is mentally deranged. But would not the very same thing be inferred about Jones from his conduct? And would not the same further considerations also be relevant to any modification of this judgment? Moreover, suppose Jones pleaded, in his own defense, "After all, I didn't do anything except just stand there and watch the child drown. I didn't kill him; I only let him die." Again, if letting die were in itself less bad than killing, this defense should have at least some weight. But it does not. Such a "defense" can only be regarded as a grotesque perversion of moral reasoning. Morally speaking, it is no defense at all.

13 Now, it may be pointed out, quite properly, that the cases of euthanasia with which doctors are concerned are not like this at all. They do not involve personal gain or the destruction of normal healthy children. Doctors are concerned only with cases in which the patient's life is of no further use to him, or in which the patient's life has become or will soon become a terrible burden. However, the point is the same in these cases: the bare difference between killing and letting die does not, in itself, make a moral difference. If a doctor lets a patient die, for humane reasons, he is in the same moral position as if he had given the patient a lethal injection for humane reasons. If his decision was wrong—if, for example, the patient's illness was in fact curable—the decision would be equally regrettable no matter which method was used to carry it out. And if the doctor's decision was the right one, the method used is not in itself important.

14 The AMA policy statement isolates the crucial issue very well; the crucial issue is "the intentional termination of the life of one

human being by another." But after identifying this issue, and forbidding "mercy killing," the statement goes on to deny that the cessation of treatment is the intentional termination of a life. This is where the mistake comes in, for what is the cessation of treatment, in these circumstances, if it is not "the intentional termination of the life of one human being by another"? Of course it is exactly that, and if it were not, there would be no point to it.

Many people will find this judgment hard to accept. One reason, I think, is that it is very easy to conflate the question of whether killing is, in itself, worse than letting die, with the very different question of whether most actual cases of killing are more reprehensible than most actual cases of letting die. Most actual cases of killing are clearly terrible (think, for example, of all the murders reported in the newspapers), and one hears of such cases every day. On the other hand, one hardly ever hears of a case of letting die, except for the actions of doctors who are motivated by humanitarian reasons. So one learns to think of killing in a much worse light than of letting die. But this does not mean that there is something about killing that makes it in itself worse than letting die, for it is not the bare difference between killing and letting die that makes the difference in these cases. Rather, the other factors—the murderer's motive of personal gain, for example, contrasted with the doctor's humanitarian motivation—account for different reactions to the different cases.

15   I have argued that killing is not in itself any worse than letting die; if my contention is right, it follows that active euthanasia is not any worse than passive euthanasia. What arguments can be given on the other side? The most common, I believe, is the following:

16   "The important difference between active and passive euthanasia is that, in passive euthanasia, the doctor does not do anything to bring about the patient's death. The doctor does nothing, and the patient dies of whatever ills already afflict him. In active euthanasia, however, the doctor does something to bring about the patient's death: he kills him. The doctor who gives the patient with cancer a lethal injection has himself caused his patient's death; whereas if he merely ceases treatment, the cancer is the cause of the death."

17   A number of points need to be made here. The first is that it is not exactly correct to say that in passive euthanasia the doctor

does nothing, for he does do one thing that is very important: he lets the patient die. "Letting someone die" is certainly different, in some respects, from other types of action—mainly in that it is a kind of action that one may perform by way of not performing certain other actions. For example, one may let a patient die by way of not giving medication, just as one may insult someone by way of not shaking his hand. But for any purpose of moral assessment, it is a type of action nonetheless. The decision to let a patient die is subject to moral appraisal in the same way that a decision to kill him would be subject to moral appraisal: it may be assessed as wise or unwise, compassionate or sadistic, right or wrong. If a doctor deliberately let a patient die who was suffering from a routinely curable illness, the doctor would certainly be to blame for what he had done, just as he would be to blame if he had needlessly killed the patient. Charges against him would then be appropriate. If so, it would be no defense at all for him to insist that he didn't "do anything." He would have done something very serious indeed, for he let his patient die.

18   Fixing the cause of death may be very important from a legal point of view, for it may determine whether criminal charges are brought against the doctor. But I do not think that this notion can be used to show a moral difference between active and passive euthanasia. The reason why it is considered bad to be the cause of someone's death is that death is regarded as a great evil—and so it is. However, if it has been decided that euthanasia—even passive euthanasia—is desirable in a given case, it has also been decided that in this instance death is no greater an evil than the patient's continued existence. And if this is true, the usual reason for not wanting to be the cause of someone's death simply does not apply.

19   Finally, doctors may think that all of this is only of academic interest—the sort of thing that philosophers may worry about but that has no practical bearing on their own work. After all, doctors must be concerned about the legal consequences of what they do, and active euthanasia is clearly forbidden by the law. But even so, doctors should also be concerned with the fact that the law is forcing upon them a moral doctrine that may well be indefensible, and has a considerable effect on their practices. Of course, most doctors are not now in the position of being coerced in this matter, for they do not regard themselves as merely going along with what

the law requires. Rather, in statements such as the AMA policy statement that I have quoted, they are endorsing this doctrine as a central point of medical ethics. In that statement, active euthanasia is condemned not merely as illegal but as "contrary to that for which the medical profession stands," whereas passive euthanasia is approved. However, the preceding considerations suggest that there is really no moral difference between the two, considered in themselves (there may be important moral differences in some cases in their *consequences*, but, as I pointed out, these differences may make active euthanasia, and not passive euthanasia, the morally preferable option). So, whereas doctors may have to discriminate between active and passive euthanasia to satisfy the law, they should not do any more than that. In particular, they should not give the distinction any added authority and weight by writing it into official statements of medical ethics.

Analyzing the Writer's Argument

1. What doctrine of medical ethics is endorsed by the American Medical Association and accepted by most doctors? What arguments does Rachels put forth to make his case against this doctrine?
2. What does Rachels see as the difference between active and passive euthanasia? Which of the two is generally considered more ethical? What example does Rachels use to show that "active euthanasia is actually preferable to passive euthanasia, rather than the reverse"?
3. To what end does Rachels use the quote from Anthony Shaw's article in paragraph 4? How is this point related to his thesis? How else does he use the example of infants with Down's syndrome?
4. How does Rachels demonstrate his belief that there is no moral difference between killing and letting die? Why does he believe that many people would find this conclusion difficult to accept? Did you find his presentation persuasive? Why or why not?
5. Who was Rachels' intended audience for this article? What did he want these readers to do after reading the essay? Is the essay relevant to others? Explain.
6. How does Rachels respond to those people who believe that there is a difference between active and passive euthanasia? Did you find his refutation convincing? Explain.

7. Is Rachels in favor of euthanasia? How do you know? Does this information make any difference in how you respond to the essay? Explain.

Exploring the Issues in This Essay

1. In paragraphs 10 and 11 Rachels gives the hypothetical cases of Smith and Jones. In terms of his argument, why do you suppose he chose to use hypothetical cases? Also, why do you think that neither case involved euthanasia? Was this a calculated argumentative strategy on Rachels' part or simply an oversight? Discuss the advantages and limitations of using hypothetical cases or situations as an argument strategy.

2. When the American Medical Association adopted its doctrine of active and passive euthanasia, was it in your opinion trying to legislate morality? Is it ever really possible to legislate such issues? How would you respond to a law that asks you to act against your own sense of what is morally right?

Frank Morriss

Euthanasia—No!

Writer, newspaper editor, and teacher, Frank Morriss was born in Pasadena, California, on March 28, 1923. He graduated from Regis College in Denver, Colorado, in 1943; and after two years in the U.S. Army, during which he served in the Pacific theater, he pursued graduate studies, eventually receiving his J.D. from Georgetown University in 1948. He has taught English and Philosophy at Regis College, and St. Michael's College in Winooski Park, Vermont, where he was also the debate coach. In addition, he has worked on the editorial staff of several Catholic newspapers and has written a number of books including The Conservative Imperative *(1965),* Catholic Perspectives: Abortion *(1979), and* The Catholic as Citizen *(1979).*

His articles frequently appear in The Wanderer, *a conservative Catholic newspaper published in St. Paul, Minnesota. Morriss strongly believes that sovereignty over life belongs to God, the Creator of life. In the following article he argues that the legalization of euthanasia would in effect open up the possibility that the state could declare certain classes of people "disposable."*

1   What I am insisting must not be done is to legalize murder or suicide for the motive of mercy. Consider what that would amount to. It would for the first time in the history of Western civilization and jurisprudence deliver to individuals sovereignty over innocent life—either someone else's life or one's own. This would be an historic reversal of the concept that no one, not individual or state or any person, is the absolute master of life, life being the highest and most fundamental good and the basic right. Not even in legalized abortion has such a claim been made; even here there has been recognized the need of holding to the idea (whether as fiction or fact) that what is killed in the womb is not a person, not an individual human life.

2   Legalized euthanasia, however, would discard such pretense and create a whole class of admittedly human persons who are subject to death, though innocent of any crime and certainly in no way aggressors or enemies of society. Conceding for the moment and only for the point of discussion that under such a law some acts of ending great pain might occur. Still, the precedent and idea that innocent life is dispensable, though for supposed "good" motive, would have put the whole common good in danger. Once the state, through law, has conceded sovereignty over life for one motive, there is no reason that any motive the state judges desirable should not be the excuse for legally disposing of innocent life. With legalized euthanasia we have entered the Hitlerian nightmare, or the Orwellian prophecy of the subjection of the individual to the omnipotent state.

3   Surely sovereignty over life is the mark of omnipotence. To claim it is to set up a type of idolatry. Since Greek recognition of the natural law, Western civilization has seen the necessity of leaving sovereignty over life to true Omnipotence, to the Creator of life. The alternative is to make the state a kind of life-devouring Moloch. It does not change that reality by insisting that euthanasia is a kind act of a benign society or government. The nature of what would be done by legalizing euthanasia is not changed even were that argument to be granted. A state holding sovereignty over innocent life is a monstrous usurper, whether benign or not.

"Mercy" as a Motive

4   Let us turn to more practical aspects of this question. Under legalized euthanasia the presumption of innocence on the part of the one taking the life surely would be established. One need only plead "mercy" as motive to invoke the protection of the law. This puts those who consider themselves burdened by guardianship of the elderly or the suffering at a distinct advantage. How difficult it would be to question the plea of mercy on the part of anyone who could summon up a tear or two, when the real motive might have been to get out from under a burden, or more crass, perhaps to come into an inheritance. If the quality of mercy is not strained, it is also very difficult to genuinely establish—or to deny. It is hidden in the depths of the human heart and conscience, and

there it should remain, not enthroned and made ruler over life by legal fiat.

5 The inalienability of life is in fact the concern of the state, for that inalienability is the basis for a safe society in which the natural law—the law dictated by man's true nature and true purpose—prevails. This applies even when it is a question of suicide, so that such an act has for all of Western civilization been outlawed, and still is in most jurisdictions.

Suicide and Euthanasia

6 But, you say, surely individuals should be able to end or have ended their own lives when suffering and pain become unendurable. But if that is to be so you have made each individual the evaluator of the worth of life. Under the evil influence of some philosophers, life has at times been held undesirable under any circumstances. The medieval Cathars and pure ones of the Albigensian heresy taught the worthlessness—even evil—of life. Suicide was considered the highest act of virtue. Can the state surrender to such a despairing philosophy?

7 Suicide is a major problem with young persons today. Legalized euthanasia would simply tell them it is not a problem—but their right. Who can set limits to the claim to "mercy" as a motive for suicide, once the idea is accepted and legalized? Despair and pessimism will in effect have been canonized by law.

Disposable People

8 Euthanasia concerns the type of society we wish to live in and bequeath to our children. Established as right, proper, and legal, euthanasia would be part of a society where all life is subject to state determination. Equal protection of the laws for any class of people the state considered disposable would be meaningless. Mercy for the suffering or elderly could next be "mercy" for the deformed, the defective, the burdensome. Those of differing values and philosophies could then be the subjects of state recognized "mercy."

9   No horror against life is impossible once we have allowed anyone but the Creator to usurp sovereignty over life. Whom the gods would destroy they first make mad. Legalized euthanasia is such madness.

Analyzing the Writer's Argument

1. What is Morriss's thesis and where does he present it?
2. What, for Morriss, is the consequence of legalizing murder or suicide for the motive of mercy? How is legalized abortion different?
3. Morriss invokes images of an "Hitlerian nightmare" and the "Orwellian prophecy of the subjection of the individual to the omnipotent state" in talking about logical consequences of legalized euthanasia. Is he overstating the case when he makes these associations? Explain.
4. Who, according to Morriss, should have sovereignty over life? What does he mean when he says, "To claim [sovereignty] is to set up a type of idolatry"?
5. How real is Morriss's fear that legalized euthanasia would put "those who consider themselves burdened by guardianship of the elderly or the suffering at a distinct advantage"? Why would it be difficult to question motive in a so-called "mercy" killing or even in suicide?
6. Is legalized euthanasia the first step, as Morriss would have us believe, in the creation of a society of "disposable people"? Explain why or why not.

Exploring the Issues in This Essay

1. To what extent does euthanasia concern "the type of society we wish to live in and bequeath to our children"? What would be the full implications of a law that legalized euthanasia? What messages would such a law send to the citizens of the country? Will "despair and pessimism," as Morriss claims, "have been canonized by law"? Explain.
2. What is the role of the state or government concerning euthanasia? Historically, why have people left the "sovereignty over life to true Omnipotence, to the Creator of life"? What happens when the state holds sovereignty over life? The state holds the power to

impose capital punishment. In what important ways is euthanasia different from the death penalty? Do you agree with Moriss when he concludes that "no horror against life is impossible once we have allowed anyone but the Creator to usurp sovereignty over life"? Explain why or why not. Should individuals have the right to end their own lives or have them ended when pain becomes unbearable?

Matthew E. Conolly

Euthanasia Is Not the Answer

*Physician, pharmacologist, and medical researcher, Matthew
E. Conolly was born in London, England, on June 12, 1940.
After graduating from London University in 1963, he pursued
a degree in medicine at the London University Medical School.
Conolly was a postdoctoral fellow at Vanderbilt University in
Nashville, Tennessee, and a consulting physician at the Royal
Postgraduate Medical School in London before becoming professor of medicine and pharmacology at UCLA, a position he
has held since 1977. The following selection has been excerpted
from a speech Conolly delivered at the Hemlock Society's Second National Voluntary Euthanasia Conference on February
9, 1985. The Hemlock Society supports active voluntary euthanasia for the terminally ill and believes that the final decision to terminate one's life is one's own. Drawing upon his
experience with the hospice movement in England, Conolly
argues that hospice care is a more meaningful, and ultimately
more satisfying or rewarding alternative to euthanasia.*

1   From the moment of our conception, each of us is engaged in
a personal battle that we must fight alone, a battle whose final
outcome is never in any doubt, for, naked, and all too often alone,
sooner or later we *all* must die.

2   We do not all make life's pilgrimage on equal terms. For some
the path is strewn with roses, and after a long and healthy life,
death comes swiftly and easily, for others it is not so. The bed
of roses is supplanted by a bed of nails, with poverty, rejection,
deformity, and humiliation the only lasting companions they ever
know.

3   I know that many people here today carry this problem of pain
in a personal way, or else it has been the lot of someone close to
you. Otherwise you would not be here. So let me say right at the
outset, that those of us who have not had to carry such a burden
dare not criticize those who have, if they should plead with us for
an early end to their dismal sojourn in this world.

Hard Cases Make Bad Laws

4   Society in general, and the medical profession in particular, cannot just turn away. We must do *something*, the question is—what?

5   The "what" we are being asked to consider today, of course, is voluntary euthanasia. So that there be no confusion, let me make it quite clear that to be opposed to the active taking of life, one does not have to be determined to keep the heart beating at all costs.

6   I believe I speak for all responsible physicians when I say that there clearly comes a time when death can no longer be held at bay, and when we must sue for peace on the enemy's terms. At such a time, attending to the patient's comfort in body, mind, and soul becomes paramount. There is no obligation, indeed no justification, for pressing on at such a time with so called life sustaining measures, be they respirators, intravenous fluids, CPR or whatever. I believe that there is no obligation to continue a treatment once it has been started, if it becomes apparent that it is doing no good. Also, withholding useless treatment and letting nature take its course is *not* equivalent to active euthanasia. Some people have attempted to blur this distinction by creating the term "passive euthanasia." The least unkind thing that can be said about this term is that it is very confusing. We do not "permit" such people to die, for, with or without our permission, they will soon be gone.

7   Today's discussion really boils down to the question—do hard and tragic cases warrant legalization of euthanasia? There can be no doubt that hard and tragic cases do occur. However, the very natural tendency to want to alleviate human tragedy by legislative change is frought with hazard, and I firmly believe that every would-be lawmaker should have tattooed on his or her face, where it can be seen in the mirror each morning, the adage that HARD CASES MAKE BAD LAWS.

8   If we take the superficially humane step of tailoring the law to the supposed wishes of an Elizabeth Bouvia (who, incidentally, later changed her mind), we will not only bring a hornet's nest of woes about our own ears, but, at a stroke, we will deny many relatives much good that we could have salvaged from a sad situation, while at the same time giving many *more* grief and guilt to contend with. Even worse, we will have denied our patients the best that could have been offered. Worst of all, that soaring of the

human spirit to heights of inspiration and courage which only adversity makes possible will be denied, and we will all, from that, grow weaker, and less able to deal with the crisis of tomorrow.

Unleashing Euthanasia

9   Let's look at these problems one by one. The first problem is that once we unleash euthanasia, once we take to ourselves the right actively to terminate a human life, we will have no means of controlling it. Adolph Hitler showed with startling clarity that once the dam is breached, the principle somewhere compromised, death in the end comes to be administered equally to all—to the unwanted fetus, to the deformed, the mentally defective, the old and the unproductive, and thence to the politically inconvenient, and finally to the ethnically unacceptable. There is no logical place to stop.

10   The founders of Hemlock no doubt mean euthanasia only for those who feel they can take no more, but if it is available for one it must be available for all. Then what about those precious people who even to the end put others before themselves? They will now have laid upon them the new and horrible thought that perhaps they ought to do away with themselves to spare their relatives more trouble or expense. What will they feel as they see their 210 days of Medicare hospice payments run out, and still they are alive. Not long ago, Governor Lamm of Colorado suggested that the old and incurable have a *duty* to get out of the way of the next generation. And can you not see where these pressures will be the greatest? It will be amongst the poor and dispossessed. Watts will have sunk in a sea of euthanasia long before the first ripple laps the shore of Brentwood. Is that what we mean to happen? Is that what we want? Is there nobility of purpose there?

11   It matters to me that my patients trust me. If they do so, it is because they believe that I will always act in their best interests. How could such trust survive if they could never be sure each time I approached the bed that I had not come to administer some coup de grace when they were not in a state to define their own wishes?

12   Those whose relatives have committed more conventional forms of suicide are often afterwards assailed by feelings of guilt and

remorse. It would be unwise to think that euthanasia would bring any less in its wake.

A Better Way

13 Speaking as a physician, I assert that unrelieved suffering need never occur, and I want to turn to this important area. Proponents of euthanasia make much of the pain and anguish so often linked in people's minds with cancer. I would not dare to pretend that the care we offer is not sometimes abysmal, whether because of the inappropriate use of aggressive technological medicine, the niggardly use of analgesics, some irrational fear of addiction in a dying patient, or a lack of compassion.

14 However, for many, the process of dying is more a case of gradually loosing life's moorings and slipping away. Oftentimes the anguish of dying is felt not by the patient but by the relatives: just as real, just as much in need of compassionate support, but hardly a reason for killing the patient!

15 But let us consider the patients who do have severe pain, turmoil, and distress, who find their helplessness or incontinence humiliating, for it is these who most engage our sympathies. It is wrong to assert that they must make a stark choice between suicide or suffering.

16 There is another way.

17 Experience with hospice care in England and the U.S. has shown repeatedly that in *every* case, pain and suffering can be overwhelmingly reduced. In many cases it can be abolished altogether. This care, which may (and for financial reasons perhaps must) include home care, is not easy. It demands infinite love and compassion. It must include the latest scientific knowledge of analgesic drugs, nerve blocks, anti-nausea medication and so on. But it can be done, it can be done, it can be done!

Life is Special

18 Time and again our patients have shown us that life, even a deformed, curtailed, and, to us, who are whole, an unimaginable

life, can be made noble and worth living. Look at Joni Earickson—paraplegic from the age of 17—now a most positive, vibrant and inspirational person who has become world famous for her triumph over adversity. Time and time again, once symptoms are relieved, patients and relatives share quality time together, when forgiveness can be sought and given—for many a time of great healing.

19   Man, made in the image of his Creator, is *different* from all other animals. For this reason, his life is special and may not be taken at will.

20   We do not know why suffering is allowed, but Old and New Testament alike are full of reassurances that we have not been, and will not ever be, abandoned by our God. "Yea, though I walk through the valley of the shadow of death, I will fear no evil *for thou art with me.*"

Call to Change Direction

21   Our modern tragedy is that man has turned his back on God, who alone can help, and has set himself up as the measure of all things. Gone then is the absolute importance of man, gone the sanctity of his life, and the meaning of it. Gone too the motivation for loving care which is our reasonable duty to the sick and dying. Goodbye love. Hello indifference.

22   With our finite minds, we cannot know fully the meaning of life, but though at times the storms of doubt may rage, I stake my life on the belief that to God we are special, that with Him, murder is unacceptable, and suicide (whatever you call it) becomes unnecessary.

23   Abandon God, and yes, you can have euthanasia. But a *good* death it can never be, and no subterfuge of law like that before us today can ever make it so.

24   My plea to the Hemlock Society is: Give up your goal of self-destruction. Instead, lend your energy, your anger, your indignation, your influence and creativity to work with us in the building of such a system of hospice care that death, however it come, need no longer be feared. Is not this a nobler cause? Is not this a better way?

Analyzing the Writer's Argument

1. What is Conolly's stance on the question of the legalization of euthanasia? What is the meaning of the old adage "hard cases make bad laws"?
2. What is Conolly's purpose in the first three paragraphs? How do they function in the context of his argument?
3. What are the specific problems that Conolly foresees if euthanasia were to be legalized? What examples does he use to illustrate each of his points? Did you find his reasoning persuasive? Explain why or why not.
4. In paragraph 13, Conolly admits that the care offered to suffering patients is sometimes "abysmal." Why do you suppose he makes such an admission? How did it affect you when you read it?
5. What does Conolly see as the alternative to the "stark choice between suicide and suffering"? Conolly admits that his alternative will not be easy. What exactly does the care he's calling for entail?
6. At the end of paragraph 17 Conolly, after discussing the tremendous amount of work and love and compassion involved in hospice care, emphatically states, "But it can be done, it can be done, it can be done!" Why does Conolly believe so strongly in this pro-life alternative? Did you find his example of Joni Earickson convincing or would you have liked him to provide additional examples? Explain.
7. In his concluding paragraphs Conolly show himself to be a man of God, a man of faith. Is it necessary to share Conolly's faith in God in order to share his belief that "life is special"? Explain. What do you think Conolly means when he says, "Abandon God, and yes, you can have euthanasia. But a *good* death it can never be"?
8. Conolly's audience for this address is the Hemlock Society, an organization favoring the legalization of euthanasia. Does Conolly display an awareness of and a sensitivity to the needs of his audience? Explain by referring to specific passages in the text of his speech. What would Conolly like the Hemlock Society to do? Why do you think he ends with two questions?

Exploring the Issues in This Essay

1. Conolly notes that often the anguish of dying is felt more by surviving relatives than by the patient. He believes that these feelings are "just as real, just as much in need of compassionate support,

but hardly a reason for killing the patient!" Do you agree with Conolly? Why do some survivors have so much difficulty dealing with the impending death of a loved one? What can be done to help these people deal with what has to be one of life's most difficult times? Is hospice care a possible solution? What does such care offer the patient? The surviving friends and relatives?

2. Conolly believes that when treating terminally ill patients there "comes a time when death can no longer be held at bay, and when we must sue for peace on the enemy's terms." Who is the enemy, and what do you suppose Conolly means by "sue for peace"? Is, then, the active taking of life a total surrender to the enemy? If so, how else can "peace" be achieved?

Writing Suggestions for
The Right to Die

1. Unlike James Rachels, Matthew Conolly believes that "withholding useless treatment and letting nature take its course is *not* equivalent to active euthanasia." Do you agree with Rachels or Conolly on this issue? Write an essay in which you present your position in a persuasive manner.

2. Write an essay in which you argue for the legalization of euthanasia or "mercy killing." Be sure to review the arguments against such legislation by Morriss and Conolly before you start to write.

3. Spend enough time in the library to learn about the Hemlock Society and the Society for the Right to Die. Write an essay in which you compare and contrast the philosophies, purposes, and programs of these two organizations.

4. Write an essay in which you summarize the arguments against the legalization of euthanasia. Which of the arguments do you find most compelling? Least compelling?

5. Matthew Conolly believes that it is wrong to have patients think that "they must make a choice between suicide or suffering." As an alternative, he advocates hospice, a concept of caring for the terminally ill which enables the patient to *live* as fully as possible. Before writing an essay on hospice as a viable alternative to euthanasia, research the Hospice Movement in your library. Where did the movement begin and why? What exactly is hospice care? When was it first introduced into the United States? How successful has the movement been in meeting the needs of the terminally ill and their families?

6. Research the controversy surrounding the case of Karen Ann Quinlan, Elizabeth Bouvia, Abe Perlmutter, or someone else whose "right-to-die" decision has been debated in the news recently. Write an essay in which you argue for or against that person's right to commit suicide or to have life support systems removed.

7. What is the status of "living wills" in your state? Are they protected by state law? If so, how far does the protection extend? If not, is a living will bill pending before your state legislature? Write a letter to one of your state legislators in which you argue for or against the legal recognition of living wills.

8. The "Right to Die" issue is a much more complex one than it might at first appear. Simple"yes/no" or "right/wrong" answers are not intellectually satisfying; they seem somehow to miss the emotional/philosophical and very personal heart of the issue. In

an essay explore the whole spectrum of responses that have been given to this controversial issue. Be sure to come to some resolve about where you stand on the question of the right to die.

9. Dr. Joseph Fletcher, a noted bioethicist and former president of the Society for the Right to Die, once wrote, "Good dying must at last find its place in our scheme of things, along with good birthing, good living and good loving. After all, it makes perfectly sound sense to strive for quality straight across the board, as much in our dying as in our living." Using materials from the essays by Collins and Conolly, argue for what you believe constitutes a "good death."

10. One of the central issues in the debate over the right to die is the question of who has or should have sovereignty over life. Drawing upon the arguments presented in the essays in this section, write an essay in which you first answer the question, "Who should have sovereignty over a person's life?" and then argue for your position.

11. In the debate over the legalization of euthanasia the concept of "quality of life" inevitably is introduced. What does this concept mean to you? At what point does a person's quality of life become so poor that that person should be permitted to end his or her own life? Write an essay in which you define "quality of life" and discuss its role in the debate over euthanasia.

14

Protecting the Environment: Preparations for the 21st Century

Those unaccustomed to thinking about our environment perhaps see it as static, concrete, immutable, self-sustaining, ever generous, vast and powerful, impervious to the forces of change, and ultimately indestructible. Such a view comes, in part, from the very short period of time that any human spends on this earth. In geologic or environmental time, a human life is fleeting. Those who think about our environment consider its history (estimated to be 4.5 billion years), study its systems, understand its processes, and reflect on their relationship to it, so their view is quite different. For such people the environment is a good deal more delicate and fragile, and, because it more closely resembles in its complexity a living organism than an insensitive piece of machinery, it is capable of becoming unbalanced or even destroyed. Its many systems are themselves made up of systems of systems, each uniquely situated, functionally interdependent, and susceptible to varying degrees of change. Should the forces at work on the environment, however, turn out to be overwhelming, the environment can sometimes be altered in irretrievable ways, and to that extent be destroyed.

As far as our personal attitudes toward the environment are concerned, all of us place ourselves along a spectrum that runs from seeing the environment as being at our disposal and fulfilling our needs to appreciating its intricacies and preserving its precarious balance. However one regards the environment, one undeniable fact deserves our attention: the ever-increasing presence of humans on spaceship earth has resulted in a major assault on our environment. Present world population is estimated to be 5.3 billion and growing at the rate of 80 million a year. If there is a single force threatening nature's balance more than any other, it is the human population and its needs. We need food, we need shelter, we need clean air and water, we need energy for transportation and temperature control, we need chemicals, and we need to dispose of the by-products of our civilization. It is not, then, the needs of any one of us but rather the magnitude and speed of our collective impact on the biosphere that is causing problems.

Our assault on nature seems almost limitless. Problems, and controversies over how to solve them, exist in the following areas: acid rain, global warming, solid waste disposal, deforestation, soil erosion, toxic waste, nuclear radiation, ozone pollution, pesticides, ocean pollution, and wildlife destruction. More specifically, waterfowl, salmon, and other wildlife are losing their habitats; in the past few years a disgusting array of garbage, untreated human waste, and medical syringes has been tossed back upon our beaches by an ocean unwilling to absorb any more; the Environmental Protection Agency estimates that half the streams in the mid-Atlantic and southeastern states—areas not previously thought to be affected—are either acidic or on the verge of becoming so as a result of acid rain; the hot summer of 1988 saw the worst air pollution in the nation's history in areas outside of our major cities.

The most compelling evidence to date, however, of the impact we as humans have on our environment is the recent Alaskan oil spill, the worst environmental disaster in our history. On March 24, 1989, the Exxon supertanker *Valdez*, carrying 10,800,000 gallons of crude oil, struck a reef and ran aground in Prince William Sound, spilling its cargo. The resulting destruction of wildlife and devastation of the ecological systems of the area are incalculable. The growing population's need for more fuel and for bigger tankers only increases the environmental risks we take to satisfy our consumerism. And none can ignore the increasing likelihood of human error in such endeavors. How we will meet our needs while at the same time safeguard the environment is one of the greatest challenges we face.

Paul and Anne Ehrlich

The Rivet Poppers

The Ehrlichs, a husband and wife team, have researched and written about world population and the ecosystems of America, Southeast Asia, Antarctica, Australia, Africa, and Latin America. Anne was born in 1933 in Des Moines, Iowa, and Paul was born in 1932 in Philadelphia, Pennsylvania. Anne attended the University of Kansas, and Paul earned his B.A. at the University of Pennsylvania and his M.A. and Ph.D. at the University of Kansas. Both are members of the Department of Biological Sciences at Stanford University. In 1968, Paul Ehrlich published The Population Bomb, *a book that pushed him to the forefront of the population control movement worldwide. Together the Ehrlichs have also written* Population, Resources, and Environment: Issues in Human Ecology *(1970),* Human Ecology: Problems and Solutions *(1973),* The End of Affluence: A Blueprint for Your Future *(1974), and* Earth *(1987) as well as numerous other publications.*

"The Rivet Poppers," taken from Extinction: The Causes and Consequences of the Disappearances of Species *(1981), offers an imaginative way of viewing how the decisions world leaders make can affect the well-being of spaceship Earth.*

1   As you walk from the terminal toward your airliner, you notice a man on a ladder busily prying rivets out of its wing. Somewhat concerned, you saunter over to the rivet popper and ask him just what the hell he's doing.

2   "I work for the airline—Growthmania Intercontinental," the man informs you, "and the airline has discovered that it can sell these rivets for two dollars apiece."

3   "But how do you know you won't fatally weaken the wing doing that?" you inquire.

4 "Don't worry," he assures you. "I'm certain the manufacturer made this plane much stronger than it needs to be, so no harm's done. Besides, I've taken lots of rivets from this wing and it hasn't fallen off yet. Growthmania Airlines needs the money; if we didn't pop the rivets, Growthmania wouldn't be able to continue expanding. And I need the commission they pay me—fifty cents a rivet!"

5 "You must be out of your mind!"

6 "I told you not to worry; I know what I'm doing. As a matter of fact, I'm going to fly on this flight also, so you can see there's absolutely nothing to be concerned about."

7 Any sane person would, of course, go back into the terminal, report the gibbering idiot and Growthmania Airlines to the FAA, and make reservations on another carrier. You never *have* to fly on an airliner. But unfortunately all of us are passengers on a very large spacecraft—one on which we have no option but to fly. And, frighteningly, it is swarming with rivet poppers behaving in ways analogous to that just described.

8 The rivet poppers on Spaceship Earth include such people as the President of the United States, the Chairman of the Soviet Communist Party, and most other politicians and decision makers; many big businessmen and small businessmen; and, inadvertently, most other people on the planet, including you and us. Philip Handler, the president of the United States National Academy of Sciences, is an important rivet popper, and so are industrialist Daniel Ludwig (who is energetically chopping down the Amazon rainforest), Senator Howard Baker, enemy of the Snail Darter, and Vice President George Bush, friend of nuclear war. Others prominent on the rivet-popper roster include Japanese whalers and woodchippers, many utility executives, the auto moguls of Detroit, the folks who run the AMAX corporation, almost all economists, the Brazilian government, Secretary of the Interior James Watt, the editors of *Science, Scientific American,* and the *Wall Street Journal,* the bosses of the pesticide industry, some of the top bureaucrats of the U.S. Department of Agriculture and some of those in the Department of the Interior, the officers of the Entomological Society of America, the faculties of every engineering school in the world, the Army Corps of Engineers, and the hierarchy of the Roman Catholic Church.

9   Now all of these people (and especially you and we) are certainly not crazy or malign. Most of them are in fact simply uninformed — which is one reason for writing a book on the processes and consequences of rivet-popping.

10   Rivet-popping on Spaceship Earth consists of aiding and abetting the extermination of species and populations of nonhuman organisms. The European Lion, the Passenger Pigeon, the Carolina Parakeet, and the Sthenele Brown Butterfly are some of the numerous rivets that are now irretrievably gone; the Chimpanzee, Mountain Gorilla, Siberian Tiger, Right Whale, and California Condor are prominent among the many rivets that are already loosened. The rest of the perhaps ten million species and billions of distinct populations still more or less hold firm. Some of these species supply or could supply important direct benefits to humanity, and all of them are involved in providing free public services without which society could not persist.

11   The natural ecological systems of Earth, which supply these vital services, are analogous to the parts of an airplane that make it a suitable vehicle for human beings. But ecosystems are much more complex than wings or engines. Ecosystems, like well-made airplanes, tend to have redundant subsystems and other "design" features that permit them to continue functioning after absorbing a certain amount of abuse. A dozen rivets, or a dozen species, might never be missed. On the other hand, a thirteenth rivet popped from a wing flap, or the extinction of a key species involved in the cycling of nitrogen, could lead to a serious accident.

12   In most cases an ecologist can no more predict the consequences of the extinction of a given species than an airline passenger can assess the loss of a single rivet. But both can easily foresee the long-term results of continually forcing species to extinction or of removing rivet after rivet. No sensible airline passenger today would accept a continuous loss of rivets from jet transports. Before much more time has passed, attitudes must be changed so that no sane passenger on Spaceship Earth will accept a continuous loss of populations or species of nonhuman organisms.

13   Over most of the several billion years during which life has flourished on this planet, its ecological systems have been under what would be described by the airline industry as "progressive mainte-

nance." Rivets have dropped out or gradually worn out, but they were continuously being replaced, in fact, over much of the time our spacecraft was being strengthened by the insertion of more rivets than were being lost. Only since about ten thousand years ago has there been any sign that that process might be more or less permanently reversed. That was when a single species, *Homo sapiens*, began its meteoric rise to planetary dominance. And only in about the last half-century has it become clear that humanity has been forcing species and populations to extinction at a rate greatly exceeding that of natural attrition and far beyond the rate at which natural processes can replace them. In the last twenty-five years or so, the disparity between the rate of loss and the rate of replacement has become alarming; in the next twenty-five years, unless something is done, it promises to become catastrophic for humanity.

14   The form of the catastrophe is, unfortunately, difficult to predict. Perhaps the most likely event will be an end of civilization in T. S. Eliot's whimper. As nature is progressively impoverished, its ability to provide a moderate climate, cleanse air and water, recycle wastes, protect crops from pests, replenish soils, and so on will be increasingly degraded. The human population will be growing as the capacity of Earth to support people is shrinking. Rising death rates and a falling quality of life will lead to a crumbling of post-industrial civilization. The end may come so gradually that the hour of its arrival may not be recognizable, but the familiar world of today will disappear within the life span of many people now alive.

15   Of course, the "bang" is always possible. For example, it is likely that destruction of the rich complex of species in the Amazon basin would trigger rapid changes in global climatic patterns. Agriculture remains heavily dependent on stable climate, and human beings remain heavily dependent on food. By the end of the century the extinction of perhaps a million species in the Amazon basin could have entrained famines in which a billion human beings perished. And if our species is very unlucky, the famines could lead to a thermonuclear war, which could extinguish civilization.

16   Fortunately, the accelerating rate of extinctions can be arrested. It will not be easy; it will require both the education of, and concerted action by, hundreds of millions of people. But no tasks are more

important, because extinctions of other organisms must be stopped before the living structure of our spacecraft is so weakened that at a moment of stress it fails and civilization is destroyed.

Analyzing the Writer's Argument

1. How does the major metaphor that the Ehrlichs use in their essay work? Why do you suppose they named the airline "Growthmania Intercontinental"? Do you think the metaphor of the spacecraft is an effective one? Why or why not?
2. How is the spaceship earth different from an airplane? What is the thirteenth rivet that the Ehrlichs refer to in paragraph 11?
3. Aside from the pervading metaphor, what facts do the Ehrlichs offer the reader? How persuasive is this combination?
4. Review the list of people the Ehrlichs call rivet poppers. What is your reaction to the list? Do you consider all the people mentioned rivet poppers? Why or why not?
5. What are the Ehrlichs arguing for? What are they arguing against?
6. What is the "bang" referred to in paragraph 15? How would this event come about according to the Ehrlichs? Do you believe that such a scenario is possible? Probable? Explain.
7. Are the Ehrlichs pessimists ultimately? What do they think must be done in order to save the world from catastrophe?

Exploring the Issues in This Essay

1. Is the extinction of various species a real problem as far as you are concerned? Are you a rivet popper? If you are, what can you do about the extinction of life forms in your time? Is the problem of extinction beyond any single person's capacity to rectify?
2. Discuss the problem of audience with "The Rivet Poppers" and *Extinction*, the book from which it was drawn. For whom do you think the Ehrlichs are writing? Is it those that are already concerned about the problems they address? Assume, for the moment, that they are writing for only those concerned about the problem of extinction and altered ecosystems. Is there value in reaching that audience? Why or why not? Does a writer ever really know who his or her audience will be? How does a writer get to the audience that most needs to hear his or her message?

TODAY, IN AMERICA, SOMEONE WILL SLAUGHTER AN ELEPHANT

PHOTO CREDITS: JOYCE POOLE / FRANK TARTARO COLOR / TURIEL & PARTNERS

FOR A BRACELET.

It is a simple and terrible fact that to get the ivory tusks of an elephant, the elephant must die. And it is another simple and terrible fact that every year Americans buy one-third of the world's ivory jewelry. And it is a final simple and terrible fact that unless the slaughter is stopped, the African elephant will be virtually extinct in ten years.

Some 70,000 elephants are killed each year to meet the worldwide demand for ivory. If this continues for each of the next ten years, there will be no elephants left in Africa by 1999.

It's a sickening thought. In ten short years we could have to explain to children why there are no more elephants. What could we tell them? That for a few bracelets, a few bangles, one of the world's most beloved and majestic creatures was exterminated?

Every single American can help stop the slaughter. The single most important way is not to buy ivory. There are many other ways to help. Call us or use this coupon to make a contribution. But please do something, and do it today. There isn't a minute to waste.

☐ **YES!** I want to help the AFRICAN WILDLIFE FOUNDATION stop the slaughter.
Enclosed is my tax-deductible contribution for:
☐ $25   ☐ $50   ☐ $100   ☐ $_____
Please print:
Name _____
Address _____
City_____ State_____ Zip _____
Please make your check payable to AWF. Thank you.
1717 Massachusetts Avenue N.W., Washington, D.C. 20036

OR CALL 1-800-344-TUSK
In the Washington, D.C. area call 1-202-265-8393

ONLY ELEPHANTS SHOULD WEAR IVORY

© African Wildlife Foundation, 1989

Courtesy of African Wildlife Foundation and Saatchi & Saatchi Advertising.

Wallace Stegner

The Gift of Wilderness

Wallace Stegner, the prolific and highly respected novelist, short story writer, and nonfiction author, was born in Lake Mills, Iowa, in 1909. He received his A.B. from the University of Utah, and his A.M. and Ph.D. from the University of Iowa. Among his novels are The Big Rock Candy Mountain *(1943),* The Preacher and the Slave *(1950),* Angle of Repose *(1971), and* The Spectator Bird *(1978). Stegner has won both the Pulitzer Prize and the National Book Award for his fiction. Among his nonfiction books are those concerned with history:* Mormon Country *(1941),* Beyond the Hundredth Meridian *(1954), and* The Gathering of Zion: The Story of the Mormon Trail *(1964).*

As in the essay that follows, Stegner's work is stirred by events of the American past and a profound consideration of our relationship to the land.

1   Once, writing in the interests of wilderness to a government commission, I quoted a letter from Sherwood Anderson to Waldo Frank, written in the 1920s. I think it is worth quoting again. "Is it not likely," Anderson wrote, "that when the country was new and men were often alone in the fields and forest they got a sense of bigness outside themselves that has now in some way been lost? . . . I am old enough to remember tales that strengthen my belief in a deep semireligious influence that was formerly at work among our people. . . . I can remember old fellows in my home town speaking feelingly of an evening spent on the big empty plains. It had taken the shrillness out of them. They had learned the trick of quiet."

2   I have a teenaged granddaughter who recently returned from a month's Outward Bound exposure to something like wilderness in Death Valley, including three days alone, with water but no food, up on a slope of the Panamints. It is a not-unheard-of kind of initiation—Christ underwent it; Indian youths on the verge of manhood traditionally went off alone to receive their visions and

acquire their adult names. I don't know if my granddaughter had any visions or heard the owl cry her name. I do know *she* cried some; and I know also that before it was over it was the greatest experience of her young life. She may have greater ones later on, but she will never quite get over this one.

3   It will probably take more than one exposure to teach her the full trick of quiet, but she knows now where to go to learn it, and she knows the mood to go in. She has felt that bigness outside herself; she has experienced the birth of awe. And if millions of Americans have not been so lucky as she, why, all the more reason to save intact some of the places to which those who are moved to do so may go, and grow by it. It might not be a bad idea to require that wilderness initiation of all American youth, as a substitute for military service.

4   I, too, have been one of the lucky ones. I spent my childhood and youth in wild, unsupervised places, and was awed very early, and never recovered. I think it must have happened first when I was five years old, in 1914, the year my family moved to the remote valley of the Frenchman River, in Saskatchewan. The town was not yet born—we were among the first fifty or so people assembled to create it. Beaver and muskrat swam in the river, and ermine, mink, coyotes, lynx, bobcats, rabbits, and birds inhabited the willow breaks. During my half dozen years there, I shot the rabbits and trapped the fur-bearers, as other frontier boys have done, and I can remember buying Canadian Victory Bonds, World War I vintage, with the proceeds from my trapline. I packed a gun before I was nine years old. But it is not my predatory experiences that I cherish. I regret them. What I most remember is certain moments, revelations, epiphanies, in which the sensuous little savage that I then was came face to face with the universe. And blinked.

5   I remember the night when I was very new there, when some cowboys from the Z-X hitched a team to a bobsled and hauled a string of us on our coasting sleds out to the Swift Current hill. They built a fire on the river ice above the ford, and we dragged our sleds to the top of the hill and shot down, blind with speed and snow, and warmed ourselves a minute at the fire, and plowed up the hill for another run.

6   It was a night of still cold, zero or so, with a full moon—a night of pure magic. I remember finding myself alone at the top of the hill, looking down at the dark moving spots of coasters, and the

red fire with black figures around it down at the bottom. It isn't a memory so much as a vision—I don't remember it, I *see* it. I see the valley, and the curving course of the river with its scratches of leafless willows and its smothered bars. I see the moon reflecting upward from a reach of wind-blown clear ice, and the white hump of the hills, and the sky like polished metal, and the moon; and behind or in front of or mixed with the moonlight, pulsing with a kind of life, the paled, washed-out green and red of the northern lights.

7   I stood there by myself, my hands numb, my face stiff with cold, my nose running, and I felt very small and insignificant and quelled, but at the same time exalted. Greenland's icy mountains, and myself at their center, one little spark of suffering warmth in the midst of all that inhuman clarity.

8   And I remember that evening spent on the big empty plains that Sherwood Anderson wrote about. In June of 1915 my father took my brother and me with him in the wagon across fifty miles of unpeopled prairie to build a house on our homestead. We were heavily loaded, the wagon was heavy and the team light, and our mare Daisy had a young foal that had a hard time keeping up. All day we plodded across nearly trackless buffalo grass in dust and heat, under siege from mosquitoes and horseflies. We lunched beside a slough where in the shallow water we ignorantly chased and captured a couple of baby mallards. Before I let mine go, I felt the thumping of that wild little heart in my hands, and that taught me something too. Night overtook us, and we camped on the trail. Five gaunt coyotes watched us eat supper, and later serenaded us. I went to sleep to their music.

9   Then in the night I awoke, not knowing where I was. Strangeness flowed around me; there was a current of cool air, a whispering, a loom of darkness overhead. In panic I reared up on my elbow and found that I was sleeping beside my brother under the wagon, and that night wind was breathing across me through the spokes of the wheel. It came from unimaginably far places, across a vast emptiness, below millions of polished stars. And yet its touch was soft, intimate, and reassuring, and my panic went away at once. That wind knew me. I knew it. Every once in a while, sixty-six years after that baptism in space and night and silence, wind across grassland can smell like that to me, as secret, perfumed, and soft, and tell me who I am.

10   It is an opportunity I wish every American could have. Having been born lucky, I wish we could expand the opportunities I benefited from, instead of extinguishing them. I wish we could establish a maximum system of wilderness preserves and then, by a mixture of protection and education, let all Americans learn to know their incomparable heritage and their unique identity.

11   We are the most various people anywhere, and every segment of us has to learn all anew the lessons both of democracy and conservation. The Laotian and Vietnamese refugees who in August 1980 were discovered poaching squirrels and pigeons in San Francisco's Golden Gate Park were Americans still suffering from the shock and deprivation of a war-blasted homeland, Americans on the road of learning how to be lucky and to conserve their luck. All of us are somewhere on a long arc between ecological ignorance and environmental responsibility. What freedom means is freedom to choose. What civilization means is some sense of *how* to choose, and among what options. If we choose badly or selfishly, we have, not always intentionally, violated the contract. On the strength of the most radical political document in human history, democracy assumes that all men are created equal and that given freedom they can learn to be better masters for themselves than any king or despot could be. But until we arrive at a land ethic that unites science, religion, and human feeling, the needs of the present and the claims of the future, Americans are constantly in danger of being what Aldo Leopold in an irritable moment called them: people remodeling the Alhambra with a bulldozer, and proud of their yardage.

12   If we conceive development to mean something beyond earthmoving, extraction, and denudation, America is one of the world's most undeveloped nations. But by its very premises, learned in wilderness, its citizens are the only proper source of controls, and the battle between short-range and long-range goals will be fought in the minds of individual citizens. Though it is entirely proper to have government agencies—and they have to be federal—to manage the residual wild places that we set aside for recreational, scientific, and spiritual reasons, they themselves have to be under citizen surveillance, for government agencies have been known to endanger the very things they ought to protect. It was San Francisco, after all, that dammed Hetch Hetchy, it was the Forest Service that granted permits to Disney Enterprises for the resor-

tification of Mineral King, it is Los Angeles that is bleeding the Owens Valley dry and destroying Mono Lake, it is the Air Force that wants to install the MX Missile tracks under the Utah-Nevada desert and in an ecosystem barely hospitable to man create an environment as artificial, sterile, and impermanent as a space shuttle.

13   We need to learn to listen to the land, hear what it says, understand what it can and can't do over the long haul; what, especially in the West, it should not be asked to do. To learn such things, we have to have access to natural wild land. As our bulldozers prepare for the sixth century of our remodeling of this Alhambra, we could look forward to a better and more rewarding national life if we learned to renounce short-term profit, and practice working for the renewable health of our earth. Instead of easing air-pollution controls in order to postpone the education of the automobile industry; instead of opening our forests to greatly increased timber cutting; instead of running our national parks to please and profit the concessionaires; instead of violating our wilderness areas by allowing oil and mineral exploration with rigs and roads and seismic detonations, we might bear in mind what those precious places are: playgrounds, schoolrooms, laboratories, yes, but above all shrines, in which we can learn to know both the natural world and ourselves, and be at least half reconciled to what we see.

Analyzing the Writer's Argument

1. What does Stegner mean when he writes in his final paragraph that "We need to listen to the land, hear what it says, understand what it can and can't do over the long haul"?
2. In paragraph 11, Stegner refers to a comment made by the naturalist Aldo Leopold. Explain Leopold's comment. Do you agree with his assessment of most Americans? Where, in the essay, does Stegner make Leopold's analogy his own?
3. Does Stegner argue inductively or deductively in this essay? Explain. What does he argue for and against in this essay? Where does he give us the clearest expression of his argument?
4. Why do you suppose Stegner shares with us his experiences in "wild, unsupervised places"?
5. What kind of audience do you think Stegner had in mind for this essay? What does he want his audience to believe? To do?

6. Where does Stegner place the blame for the ruination of our natural wild lands? Why?

7. Explain Stegner's title. Do you think it a fitting title for this essay? Why or why not?

Exploring the Issues in This Essay

1. In his final paragraph, Stegner comments on measures that we can take to work for the "renewable health of our earth." What, in addition to the suggestions he makes, can we as responsible citizens do to work toward that goal?

2. Have you ever thought about your personal relationship to the land? What are your thoughts and feelings about the area in which you live? To what part of the country or particular area do you seem attached? What accounts for the special feelings you have for that place? Do you think that one simply does or does not have special feelings about the land, or do you believe that one's attitudes can be nurtured and developed, that one can use nature's special places as "playgrounds, schoolrooms, laboratories, yes, above all shrines, in which we can learn to know both the natural world and ourselves, and be at least half reconciled to what we see"?

"*Hard to believe this was all rain forest just fifteen years ago.*"

Drawing by Dedini; ©1990 *The New Yorker* Magazine, Inc.

Rachel Carson

Our Assault on Nature

> *Rachel Carson (1907–1964) was born in Springfield, Penn-
> sylvania. She earned her A.B. degree from Pennsylvania Col-
> lege for Women in 1929 and her M.A. degree from Johns
> Hopkins University in 1932. Carson combined her intense in-
> terest in nature and her love of writing in such books as* Un-
> der the Sea-Wind: A Naturalist's Picture of Ocean Life
> *(1941),* The Sea Around Us *(1951), and* The Edge of the
> Sea *(1955). It was, however, her* Silent Spring *(1962), a
> study of the harmful effects of the herbicides and insecticides
> used by farmers, that made her an influential and controver-
> sial figure. Once denounced as an alarmist, she is now almost
> universally recognized as having been a powerful force in the
> ecology movement.*
>
> *In "Our Assault on Nature" taken from the second chapter
> of* Silent Spring, *Carson argues that "if the Bill of Rights
> contains no guarantee that a citizen shall be secure against
> lethal poisons distributed either by private individuals or by
> public officials, it is surely only because our forefathers, despite
> their considerable wisdom and foresight, could conceive of no
> such problem."*

1   It took hundreds of millions of years to produce the life that
now inhabits the earth—eons of time in which that developing and
evolving and diversifying life reached a state of adjustment and
balance with its surroundings. The environment, rigorously shaping and directing the life it supported, contained elements that
were hostile as well as supporting. Certain rocks gave out dangerous radiation; even within the light of the sun, from which all
life draws its energy, there were short-wave radiations with power
to injure. Given time—time not in years but in millennia—life ad-
justs, and a balance has been reached. For time is the essential
ingredient; but in the modern world there is no time.

2   The rapidity of change and the speed with which new situations
are created follow the impetuous and heedless pace of man rather

than the deliberate pace of nature. Radiation is no longer merely the background radiation of rocks, the bombardment of cosmic rays, the ultra-violet of the sun that have existed before there was any life on earth; radiation is now the unnatural creation of man's tampering with the atom. The chemicals to which life is asked to make its adjustment are no longer merely the calcium and silica and copper and all the rest of the minerals washed out of the rocks and carried in rivers to the sea; they are the synthetic creations of man's inventive mind, brewed in laboratories, and having no counterparts in nature.

3 To adjust to these chemicals would require time on the scale that is nature's; it would require not merely the years of a man's life but the life of generations. And even this, were it by some miracle possible, would be futile, for the new chemicals come from our laboratories in an endless stream; almost five hundred annually find their way into actual use in the United States alone. The figure is staggering and its implications are not easily grasped—500 new chemicals to which the bodies of men and animals are required somehow to adapt each year, chemicals totally outside the limits of biologic experience.

4 Among them are many that are used in our war against nature. Since the mid-1940's over 200 basic chemicals have been created for use in killing insects, weeds, rodents, and other organisms described in the modern vernacular as "pests"; and they are sold under several thousand different brand names.

5 These sprays, dusts, and aerosols are now applied almost universally to farms, gardens, forests, and homes—nonselective chemicals that have the power to kill every insect, the "good" and the "bad," to still the song of birds and the leaping of fish in the streams, to coat the leaves with a deadly film, and to linger on in soil—all this though the intended target may be only a few weeds or insects. Can anyone believe it is possible to lay down such a barrage of poisons on the surface of the earth without making it unfit for all life? They should not be called "insecticides," but "biocides."

6 The whole process of spraying seems caught up in an endless spiral. Since DDT was released for civilian use, a process of escalation has been going on in which ever more toxic materials must be found. This has happened because insects, in a triumphant vindication of Darwin's principle of the survival of the fittest, have evolved super races immune to the particular insecticide used,

hence a deadlier one has always to be developed—and then a deadlier one than that. It has happened also because destructive insects often undergo a "flareback," or resurgence, after spraying, in numbers greater than before. Thus the chemical war is never won, and all life is caught in its violent crossfire.

7   Along with the possibility of extinction by nuclear war, the central problem of our age has therefore become the contamination of our total environment with such substances of incredible potential for harm—substances that accumulate in the tissues of plants and animals and even penetrate the germ cells to shatter or alter the very material of heredity upon which the shape of the future depends.

8   Some would-be architects of our future look toward a time when it will be possible to alter the human germ plasm by design. But we may easily be doing so now by inadvertence, for many chemicals, like radiation, bring about gene mutations. It is ironic to think that man might determine his own future by something so seemingly trivial as the choice of an insect spray.

9   All this has been risked—for what? Future historians may well be amazed by our distorted sense of proportion. How could intelligent beings seek to control a few unwanted species by a method that contaminated the entire environment and brought the threat of disease and death even to their own kind? Yet this is precisely what we have done. We have done it, moreover, for reasons that collapse the moment we examine them. We are told that the enormous and expanding use of pesticides is necessary to maintain farm production. Yet is our real problem not one of *overproduction*? Our farms, despite measures to remove acreages from production and to pay farmers *not* to produce, have yielded such a staggering excess of crops that the American taxpayer by 1962 is paying out more than one billion dollars a year as the total carrying cost of the surplus-food storage program. And is the situation helped when one branch of the Agriculture Department tries to reduce production while another states, as it did in 1958, "It is believed generally that reduction of crop acreages under provisions of the Soil Bank will stimulate interest in use of chemicals to obtain maximum production on the land retained in crops."

10   All this is not to say there is no insect problem and no need of control. I am saying, rather, that control must be geared to realities,

not to mythical situations, and that methods employed must be such that they do not destroy us along with the insects.

11   The problem whose attempted solution has brought such a train of disaster in its wake is an accompaniment of our modern way of life. Long before the age of man, insects inhabited the earth— a group of extraordinarily varied and adaptable beings. Over the course of time a small percentage of the more than half a million species of insects have come into conflict with human welfare in two principal ways: as competitors for the food supply and as carriers of human disease.

12   Disease-carrying insects become important where human beings are crowded together, especially under conditions where sanitation is poor, as in time of natural disaster or war or in situations of extreme poverty and deprivation. Then control of some sort becomes necessary. It is a sobering fact, however, that the method of massive chemical control has had only limited success, and also threatens to worsen the very conditions it is intended to curb.

13   Under primitive agricultural conditions the farmer had few insect problems. These arose with the intensification of agriculture— the devotion of immense acreages to a single crop. Such a system set the stage for explosive increases in specific insect populations. Single-corp farming does not take advantage of the principles by which nature works; it is agriculture as an engineer might conceive it to be. Nature has introduced great variety into the landscape, but man has displayed a passion for simplifying it. Thus we undo the built-in checks and balances by which nature holds the species within bounds. One important natural check is a limit on the amount of suitable habitat for each species. Obviously then, an insect that lives on wheat can build up its population to much higher levels on a farm devoted to wheat than on one in which wheat is intermingled with other crops to which the insect is not adapted.

14   The same thing happens in other situations. A generation or more ago, the towns of large areas of the United States lined their streets with the noble elm tree. Now the beauty they hopefully created is threatened with complete destruction as disease sweeps through the elms, carried by a beetle that would have only limited chance to build up large populations and to spread from tree

to tree if the elms where only occasional trees in a richly diversified planting.

15   Another factor in the modern insect problem is one that must be viewed against a background of geologic and human history: the spreading of thousands of different kinds of organisms from their native homes to invade new territories. This worldwide migration has been studied and graphically described by the British ecologist Charles Elton in his book *The Ecology of Invasions*. During the Cretaceous Period, some hundred million years ago, flooding seas cut many land bridges between continents and living things found themselves confined in what Elton calls "colossal separate nature reserves." There, isolated from others of their kind, they developed many new species. When some of the land masses were joined again, about 15 million years ago, these species began to move out into new territories—a movement that is not only still in progress but is now receiving considerable assistance from man.

16   The importation of plants is the primary agent in the modern spread of species, for animals have almost invariably gone along with the plants, quarantine being a comparatively recent and not completely effective innovation. The United States Office of Plant Introduction alone has introduced almost 200,000 species and varieties of plants from all over the world. Nearly half of the 180 or so major insect enemies of plants in the United States are accidental imports from abroad, and most of them have come as hitchhikers on plants.

17   In new territory, out of reach of the restraining hand of the natural enemies that kept down its numbers in its native land, an invading plant or animal is able to become enormously abundant. Thus it is no accident that our most troublesome insects are introduced species.

18   These invasions, both the naturally occurring and those dependent on human assistance, are likely to continue indefinitely. Quarantine and massive chemical campaigns are only extremely expensive ways of buying time. We are faced, according to Dr. Elton, "with a life-and-death need not just to find new technological means of suppressing this plant or that animal"; instead we need the basic knowledge of animal populations and their relations to their surroundings that will "promote an even balance and damp down the explosive power of outbreaks and new invasions."

19   Much of the necessary knowledge is now available but we do not use it. We train ecologists in our universities and even employ them in our governmental agencies but we seldom take their advice. We allow the chemical death rain to fall as though there were no alternative, whereas in fact there are many, and our ingenuity could soon discover many more if given opportunity.

20   It is not my contention that chemical insecticides must never be used. I do contend that we have put poisonous and biologically potent chemicals indiscriminately into the hands of persons largely or wholly ignorant of their potentials for harm. We have subjected enormous numbers of people to contact with these poisons, without their consent and often without their knowledge. If the Bill of Rights contains no guarantee that a citizen shall be secure against lethal poisons distributed either by private individuals or by public officials, it is surely only because our forefathers, despite their considerable wisdom and foresight, could conceive of no such problem.

21   I contend, furthermore, that we have allowed these chemicals to be used with little or no advance investigation of their effect on soil, water, wildlife, and man himself. Future generations are unlikely to condone our lack of prudent concern for the integrity of the natural world that supports all life.

Analyzing the Writer's Argument

1. What is Carson arguing for? What is she arguing against? What kinds of evidence does Carson present for her views?
2. Does she deny that there is an insect problem and a need for control? Explain.
3. What essential ingredient, according to Carson, was necessary for life to achieve "a state of adjustment and balance"? Why is that necessary ingredient not possible in the modern world?
4. Why does Carson think that insecticides should be called "biocides"?
5. What is the "endless spiral" of the spraying process that Carson refers to? Why is it so important to initiate the process thoughtfully, if at all?
6. In what two principal ways have insects come into conflict with human welfare, according to Carson? What has been the result in each case?

7. Why is Carson so concerned about plant importations? What do plants have to do with spraying and insecticides?

8. What does Carson see as wrong with our heavy reliance on chemicals?

Exploring the Issues in This Essay

1. Rachel Carson published *Silent Spring* in 1962. What has happened since that time to confirm her observations and fears, to invalidate them? Have we tended to use fewer or even greater numbers of chemicals, in smaller or larger quantities, during the past 30 years? What still needs to be done as far as our use of chemicals is concerned?

2. Discuss your own use of insecticides. How do you feel about using such chemicals after reading Carson's essay? Have you ever used insecticides in an agricultural setting, on the family farm for example? Why and with what results? Are you in favor of continuing their use? Is Carson an alarmist about the use of insecticides? Why or why not?

Robert James Bidinotto

*What Is the Truth About Global Warming?**

Robert James Bidinotto is a staff writer for Reader's Digest
*and an award-winning journalist and lecturer who specializes
in cultural and political issues. Bidinotto was born in New
Castle, Pennsylvania, in 1949 and attended Grove City College in Pennsylvania. For several years, Bidinotto was contributing editor for* Oasis *magazine and* On Principle, *a
political newsletter. His many articles, essays, and book and
film reviews have appeared in* Reader's Digest, Success, The
Boston Herald, The American Spectator, The Freeman,
The Intellectual Activist, Reason, *and other publications.
He is as well a frequent speaker and talk show guest.*

*In the following essay, which first appeared in the February
1990 issue of* Reader's Digest, *Bidinotto presents the results
of his extensive and in-depth study of the latest information
on the global warming issue.*

1   In the summer of 1988, one of the century's worst heat waves
gripped the East Coast and had Midwest farmers wondering if
the Dust Bowl had returned. On June 23, at a Senate hearing on
global climate change, James Hansen, a respected atmospheric scientist and director of NASA's Goddard Institute for Space Studies,
gave alarming testimony. "The earth is warmer in 1988 than at any
time in the history of instrumental measurements," he said. "The
greenhouse effect is changing our climate now."

2   Hansen's remarks touched off a firestorm of publicity. A major
news magazine speculated that the Great Plains would be depop-
ulated. On NBC's "Today" show, biologist Paul Ehrlich warned
that melting polar ice could raise sea levels and inundate coastal
cities, swamping much of Florida, Washington, D.C., and the Los

Angeles basin. And in his recent book, *Global Warming*, Stephen Schneider of the National Center for Atmospheric Research imagined New York overcome by a killer heat wave, a baseball double-header in Chicago called because of a thick black haze created by huge forest fires in Canada, and Long Island devastated by a hurricane—all spawned by the "greenhouse effect."

3   In Paris last July, the leaders of seven industrial democracies, including President Bush and British Prime Minister Margaret Thatcher, called for common efforts to limit emissions of carbon dioxide and other "greenhouse gases." To accomplish this, many environmentalists have proposed draconian regulations—and huge new taxes—that could significantly affect the way we live. Warns Evironmental Protection Agency head William Reilly: "To slow down the global heating process, the scale of economic and societal intervention will be enormous."

4   The stakes are high: the public could be asked to decide between environmental catastrophe and enormous costs. But do we really have to make this choice? Many scientists believe the danger is real, but others are much less certain. What is the evidence? Here is what we know:

5   What is the greenhouse effect? When sunlight warms the earth, certain gases in the lower atmosphere, acting like the glass in a greenhouse, trap some of the heat as it radiates back into space. These greenhouse gases, primarily water vapor and including carbon dioxide, methane and man-made chlorofluorocarbons, warm our planet, making life possible.

6   If they were more abundant, greenhouse gases might trap too much heat. Venus, for example, has 60,000 times more carbon dioxide in its atmosphere than Earth, and its temperature averages above 800 degrees Fahrenheit. But if greenhouse gases were less plentiful or entirely absent, temperatures on Earth would average below freezing.

7   Because concentrations of greenhouse gases have been steadily rising, many scientists are concerned about global warming. Researchers at the Goddard Institute and at the University of East Anglia in England foresee a doubling of greenhouse gas concentrations during the next century, which might raise average global temperatures as much as nine degrees Fahrenheit.

8   What is causing the buildup? Nature accounts for most of the greenhouse gases in the atmosphere. For example, carbon diox-

ide (CO_2), the most plentiful trace gas, is released by volcanoes, oceans, decaying plants and even by our breathing. But much of the *buildup* is man-made.

9   CO_2 is given off when we burn wood or such fossil fuels as coal and oil. In fact, the amount in the atmosphere has grown more than 25 percent since the Industrial Revolution began around 200 years ago—over 11 percent since 1958 alone.

10   Methane, the next most abundant greenhouse gas, is released when organic matter decomposes in swamps, rice paddies, livestock yards—even in the guts of termites and cud-chewing animals. The amount is growing about one percent per year, partly because of increased cattle raising and use of natural gas.

11   Chlorofluorocarbons (CFCs), a third culprit, escape from refrigerators, air conditioners, plastic foam, solvents and spray cans. The amount in the atmosphere is tiny compared with CO_2, but CFCs are thousands of times more potent in absorbing heat and have also been implicated in the "ozone hole."

12   What does the ozone hole have to do with the greenhouse effect? For all practical purposes, nothing. Ozone, a naturally occurring form of oxygen, is of concern for another reason. In the upper atmosphere it helps shield us from ultraviolet sunlight, which can cause skin cancer. In 1985, scientists confirmed a temporary thinning in the ozone layer over Antarctica, leading to a new concern: if ozone thinning spreads to populated areas, it could cause an increase in the disease.

13   The ozone hole appears only from September to November, and only over the Antarctic region, and then it repairs itself when atmospheric conditions change a few weeks later. It also fluctuates: in 1988, there was little ozone thinning.

14   Ozone is constantly created and destroyed by nature. Volcanoes, for example, can release immense quantities of chlorine, some of which may get into the stratosphere and destroy ozone molecules.

15   But the most popular theory to explain the appearance of the ozone hole is that man-made chlorofluorocarbons release chlorine atoms in the upper atmosphere.

16   Despite thinning of upper atmospheric ozone over Antarctica, no increase in surface ultraviolet radiation outside of that area is expected. John E. Frederick, an atmospheric scientist who chaired a United Nations Environment Program panel on trends in atmospheric ozone, has dismissed fears of a skin-cancer epidemic as

science fiction. "You would experience a much greater increase in biologically damaging ultraviolet radiation if you moved from New York City to Atlanta than you would with the ozone depletion that we estimate will occur over the next 30 years," he says.

17 Will destruction of forests worsen the greenhouse effect? When trees and plants grow, they remove CO_2 from the air. When they are burned or decay, they release stored CO_2 back into the atmosphere. In nations such as Brazil, thousands of square miles of tropical rain forests are being cleared and burned, leading many to be concerned about further CO_2 buildup.

18 Worldwide, millions of acres are planted with seedling trees each year, however; and new studies reveal that there has been no reliable data about the impact of forest destruction on global warming. Research by Daniel Botkin and Lloyd Simpson at the University of California at Santa Barbara and by Sandra Brown at the University of Illinois at Urbana shows that the carbon content of forests had been vastly overestimated, suggesting that deforestation is not as great a source of CO_2 as was once thought.

19 Can we be certain that global warming will occur? Virtually all scientists agree that if greenhouse gases increase and all other factors remain the same, the earth will warm up. But "the crucial issue," explains Prof. S. Fred Singer, as atmospheric scientist at the Washington Institute for Values in Public Policy, "is to what extent other factors remain the same." Climatic forces interact in poorly understood ways, and some may counteract warming.

20 At any given time, for example, clouds cover 60 percent of the planet, trapping heat radiating from its surface, but also reflecting sunlight back into space. So, if the oceans heat up and produce more clouds through evaporation, the increased cover might act as a natural thermostat and keep the planet from heating up. After factoring more detailed cloud simulations into its computer models, the British Meteorological Office recently showed that current global-warming projections could be cut in half.

21 Oceans have a major effect upon climate, but scientists have only begun to understand how. Investigators at the National Center for Atmospheric Research attributed the North American drought in the summer of 1988 primarily to temperature changes in the tropical Pacific involving a current called El Niño—not to the greenhouse effect. And when ocean currents were included in recent computerized climate simulations, the Antarctic Ocean didn't

warm—diminishing the likelihood that part of its ice sheet will break up and add to coastal flooding.

22 How heat travels through the atmosphere and back into space is another big question mark for the global-warming theory. So is the sunspot cycle, as well as the effect of atmospheric pollution and volcanic particles that can reflect sunlight back into space. Such factors throw predictions about global warming into doubt.

23 So what is the bottom line? Has the earth begun to heat up? Two widely reported statistics *seem* to present a powerful case for global warming. Some temperature records show about one degree Fahrenheit of warming over the past century, a period that has also seen a noticeable increase in greenhouse gases. And the six warmest years globally since record keeping began 100 years ago have all been in the 1980s.

24 As for the past decade, the increased warmth in three of its hottest years—1983, 1987 and 1988—is almost certainly associated with El Niño events in the Pacific.

25 Paradoxically, the historical records of temperature change do not jibe with the greenhouse theory. Between 1880 and 1940, temperatures appeared to rise. Yet between 1940 and 1965, a period of much heavier fossil-fuel use and deforestation, temperatures dropped, which seems inconsistent with the greenhouse effect. And a comprehensive study of past global ocean records by researchers from Britain and M.I.T. revealed no significant rising temperature trends between 1856 and 1986. Concludes Richard Lindzen of M.I.T.'s department of Earth, Atmospheric and Planetary Sciences, "The data as we have it does not support a warming."

26 Taking everything into account, few climatologists are willing to attribute any seeming warming to the greenhouse effect. Last May, 61 scientists participating in a greenhouse workshop in Amherst, Mass., declared that "such an attribution cannot now be made with any degree of confidence."

27 Is there any other evidence of global warming? Atmospheric researchers use complex computer programs called General Circulation Models (GCMs) to plot climate change. But a computer is no more reliable than its input, and poorly understood oceanic, atmospheric and continental processes are only crudely represented even in the best GCMs.

28 Computer calculations do not even accurately predict the past: they fail to match historical greenhouse-gas concentrations to

expected temperatures. Because of these uncertainties, Stephen Schneider says in *Global Warming*, it is "an even bet that the GCMs have overestimated future warming by a factor of two."

29 In time, the computer models will undoubtedly improve. For now, the lack of evidence and reliable tools leaves proponents of global warming with little but theory.

30 Should we do anything to offset the possible warming up of the globe? Fossil fuels now provide 90 percent of the world's energy. Some environmentalists have advocated huge tax increases to discourage use of coal and other fossil fuels. Some have suggested a gasoline tax. There are also proposals that the government subsidize solar, windmill and geothermal power; that some foreign debts be swapped for protecting forests; and that worldwide population growth be slowed.

31 The buildup of greenhouse gases is cause for scientific study, but not for panic. Yet the facts sometimes get lost in the hysteria. Stephen Schneider confesses to an ethical dilemma. He admits the many uncertainties about global warming. Nevertheless, to gain public support through media coverage, he explains that sometimes scientists "have to offer up scary scenarios, make simplified, dramatic statements, and make little mention of any doubts we might have." Each scientist, he says, must decide the "right balance" between "being effective and being honest. I hope that means being both."

32 The temptation to bend fears for political ends is also ever present. "We've got to ride the global-warming issue," Sen. Timothy Wirth (D., Colo.) explained to a reporter. "Even if the theory is wrong, we will be doing the right thing in terms of economic and environmental policy."

33 But many scientists are troubled when inconclusive evidence is used for political advocacy. "The greenhouse warming has become a 'happening,'" says Richard Lindzen. To call for action, he adds, "has become a litmus test of morality."

34 We still know far too little to be stampeded into rash, expensive proposals. Before we take such steps, says Patrick J. Michaels, an associate professor of environmental sciences at the University of Virginia, "the science should be much less murky than it is now."

35 Further research and climatic monitoring are certainly warranted. If the "greenhouse signal" then emerges from the data, we can decide on the most prudent course of action.

Analyzing the Writer's Argument

1. What is the "greenhouse effect"? By what process is it brought about? Why are scientists worried about it?
2. What part do humans play in the buildup of the greenhouse effect, according to scientists?
3. Has Bidinotto explained to your satisfaction why John Frederick believes there will be no increase in ultraviolet radiation as a result of the depletion of the ozone layer? Why or why not?
4. Why is the eventuality of a dangerous buildup of the greenhouse effect still an uncertainty? Why are some scientists skeptical about it?
5. What is El Niño? What role do scientists believe it plays in the earth's temperature?
6. Why are computer models of future global warming problematic, according to Bidinotto? How may the issue of cloud cover, especially if the oceans warm, affect the computer models?
7. How does politics enter into the global warming controversy? How has the issue of global warming affected other political and governmental concerns?
8. Does Bidinotto answer the question posed in his title? Why or why not?

Exploring the Issues in This Essay

1. If instrument readings in the years ahead offer further support for the belief that the earth is warming, what should we, or what can we do about the situation? Discuss the measures mentioned by Bidinotto in paragraph 30 that might be taken to relieve the problem. Are they realistic as far as you know? Is nuclear energy a possible solution for our power needs? What can ordinary citizens do about the ozone layer depletion? Should products that contain chlorofluorocarbons be banned from manufacture and sale?
2. Discuss the importance of obtaining reliable information with an issue such as the possibility of global warming? How do responsible citizens know what a healthy degree of concern, a healthy degree of skepticism, should be, especially when the subject is scientific or technical? What roles do education, the media, politics, and governmental policies and expenditures, to name just a few of our institutions, play in our response to an issue such as global warming?

William L. Rathje

Rubbish!

William L. Rathje is an archaeologist, but not exactly an Indiana Jones. He is a garbologist, a student of solid waste in particular, who spends a good deal of his time pawing through the piles of rubbish that we have sent to landfills over the years. As the national interest increasingly focuses on the problems of solid waste disposal, on how the greatest consumer society in history will have to deal with its by-products, Rathje has found himself in great demand as a researcher, consultant, lecturer, and writer. He was born in South Bend, Indiana, in 1945, and received his B.A. from the University of Arizona in Tucson in 1967 and his Ph.D. in Archaeology from Harvard University in 1971. Since receiving his doctorate, Rathje has served on the faculty of the University of Arizona, where he is now Professor of Anthropology. With Michael B. Schiffer, he has authored Archaeology *(1982), a college textbook.*

In "Rubbish!" Rathje reveals the results of what he has already discovered on his many landfill digs and argues for yet more research so that we can make informed rather than emotional decisions about the future course of waste disposal. His article first appeared in The Atlantic *in November 1989 and was one of five articles nominated for "Best Feature Article" by the 1989 National Magazine Awards.*

1   Newspapers. Telephone books. Soiled diapers. Medicine vials encasing brightly colored pills. Brittle ossuaries of chicken bones and T-bones. Sticky green mountains of yard waste. Half-empty cans of paint and turpentine and motor oil and herbicide. Broken furniture and forsaken toys. Americans produce a lot of garbage, some of it very toxic, and our garbage is not always disposed of in a sensible way. The press in recent years has paid much attention to the filling up (and therefore the closing down) of landfills, to the potential dangers of incinerators, and to the apparent inadequacy of our recycling efforts. The use of the word "crisis"

606

in these contexts has become routine. For all the publicity, however, the precise state of affairs is not known. It may be that the lack of reliable information and the persistence of misinformation constitute the real garbage crisis.

2   But we have learned some things over the years. My program at the University of Arizona, The Garbage Project, has been looking at landfills and at garbage fresh out of the can since the early 1970s, and it has generated important insights. During the past two years I have visited all parts of the country and spoken with people who think about garbage every day—town planners, politicians, junkyard owners, landfill operators, civil engineers, microbiologists, and captains of industry—as well as many ordinary men and women who help make garbage possible. When seen in perspective, our garbage woes turn out to be serious—indeed, they have been serious for more than a century—but they are not exceptional, and they can be dealt with by disposal methods that are safe and already available. The biggest challenge we will face is to recognize that the conventional wisdom about garbage is often wrong.

3   To get some perspective on garbage let's review a few fundamentals. For most of the past two and a half million years human beings left their garbage where it fell. Oh, they sometimes tidied up their sleeping and activity areas, but that was about all. This disposal scheme functioned adequately, because hunters and gatherers frequently abandoned their campgrounds to follow game or find new stands of plants. Man faced his first garbage crisis when he became a sedentary animal—when, rather than move himself, he chose to move his garbage. The archaeologist Gordon R. Willey has argued, only partly in fun, that *Homo sapiens* may have been propelled along the path toward civilization by his need for a class at the bottom of the social hierarchy that could be assigned the task of dealing with mounting piles of garbage.

4   This brings us to an important truth about garbage: There are no ways of dealing with it that haven't been known for many thousands of years. These ways are essentially four: dumping it, burning it, converting it into something that can be used again, and minimizing the volume of material goods—future garbage—that is produced in the first place ("source reduction," as it is called). Every civilization of any complexity has used all four methods to varying degrees. . . .

An Unknown Quantity

5 What most people call garbage, professionals call solid waste.
The waste that we're most familiar with, from the households and
institutions and small businesses of towns and cities, is "municipal solid waste," or MSW. Professionals talk about what we all
throw away as entering the "solid-waste stream," and the figure
of speech is apt. Waste flows unceasingly, fed by hundreds of millions of tributaries. While many normal activities come to a halt
on weekends and holidays, the production of garbage flows on.
Indeed, days of rest tend to create the largest waves of garbage.
Christmas is a solid-waste tsunami.

6 One might think that something for which professionals have a
technical term of long standing should also be precisely calibrated
in terms of volume. As we shall see, this is not the case with
MSW. Nonetheless, there has been a good deal of vivid imagery
relating to volume. Katie Kelly, in her book *Garbage* (1973), asserted
that the amount of MSW produced in the United States annually
would fill five million trucks; these, "placed end to end, would
stretch around the world twice." In December of 1987 *Newsday*
estimated that a year's worth of America's solid waste would fill
the twin towers of 187 World Trade Centers. In 1985 *The Baltimore
Sun* claimed that Baltimore generates enough garbage every day
to fill Memorial Stadium to a depth of nine feet—a ballpark figure
if ever there was one.

7 Calculating the total annual volume or weight of garbage in the
United States is difficult because there is, of course, no way one can
actually measure or weigh more than a fraction of what is thrown
out. All studies have had to take shortcuts. Not surprisingly, estimates of the size of the U.S. solid-waste stream are quite diverse.
Figures are most commonly expressed in pounds discarded per
person per day, and the studies that I have seen from the past
decade and a half give the following rates: 2.9 pounds per person
per day, 3.02 pounds, 4.24, 4.28, 5.0, and 8.0. My own view is that
the higher estimates significantly overstate the problem. Garbage
Project studies of actual refuse reveal that even three pounds of
garbage per person per day may be too high an estimate for many
parts of the country, a conclusion that has been corroborated by
weight-sorts in many communities. Americans are wasteful, but
to some degree we have been conditioned to think of ourselves as

more wasteful than we truly are—and certainly as more wasteful than we used to be.

8   Evidence all around us reinforces such perceptions. Fast-food packaging is ubiquitous and conspicuous. Planned obsolescence is a cliché. Our society is filled with symbolic reminders of waste. What we forget is everything that is no longer there to see. We do not see the 1,200 pounds per year of coal ash that every American generated at home at the turn of the century and that was usually dumped on the poor side of town. We do not see the hundreds of thousands of dead horses that once had to be disposed of by American cities every year. We do not look behind modern packaging and see the food waste that it has prevented, or the garbage that it has saved us from making. (Considering the difference in terms of garbage generation between making orange juice from concentrate and orange juice from scratch; and consider the fact that producers of orange-juice concentrate sell the leftover orange rinds as feed, while households don't.) The average household in Mexico City produces one third more garbage a day than does the average American household. The reason for the relatively favorable U.S. showing is packaging—which is to say, modernity. No, Americans are not suddenly producing more garbage. Per capita our record is, at *worst*, one of relative stability.

What's in a Landfill?

9   A sanitary landfill is typically a depression lined with clays, in which each day's deposit of fresh garbage is covered with a layer of dirt or plastic or both. A great deal of mythology has built up around the modern landfill. We have stuffed it with the contents of our imaginations. It is a fact, however, that there is an acute shortage of sanitary landfills for the time being, especially in the northeastern United States. From 1982 to 1987 some 3,000 landfills have been filled up and shut down nationwide. The customary formulation of the problem we face (you will find it in virtually every newspaper or magazine article on the subject) is that 50 percent of the landfills now in use will close down within five years. As it happens, that has always been true—it was true in 1970 and in 1960—because most landfills are designed to be in use for only about ten years. As noted, we are not producing more house-

hold garbage per capita (though we are probably producing more garbage overall, there being more and more of us). The problem is that old landfills are not being replaced. Texas, for example, awarded some 250 permits a year for landfills in the mid-seventies but awarded fewer than fifty last year.

10   The idea persists nevertheless that we are filling up landfills at an exponential rate, and that certain products with a high public profile are disproportionately responsible. I recently ran across articles in two different newspapers from Oregon in which the finger of blame was pointed at disposable diapers; one of them claimed that disposable diapers accounted for a quarter of the contents of local landfills and the other put the figure at "five percent to thirty-two percent." A recent editorial in *The New York Times* singled out fast-food packaging for straining the capacity of the nation's landfills. Fast-food packaging is, perhaps not surprisingly, almost everyone's villain of choice. I have over the years asked many people who have never seen the inside of a landfill to estimate what percentage of the contents consists of fast-food packaging, and the answers I have gotten have ranged from five to 35 percent, with most estimates either 20 or 30 percent.

11   The physical reality inside a landfill is considerably different from what you might suppose. I spent some time with The Garbage Project's team over the past two years digging into seven landfills: two outside Chicago, two in the San Francisco Bay area, two in Tucson, and one in Phoenix. We exhumed 16,000 pounds of garbage, weighing every item we found and sorting them all into twenty-seven basic categories and then into 162 sub-groupings. In those eight tons of garbage and dirt cover there were fewer than sixteen pounds of fast-food packaging; in other words, only about a tenth of one percent of the landfills' contents by weight consisted of fast-food packaging. Less than one percent of the contents by weight was disposable diapers. The entire category of things made from plastic accounted for less than five percent of the landfills' contents by weight, and for only 12 percent by volume. The real culprit in every landfill is plain old paper—non-fast-food paper, and mostly paper that isn't for packaging. Paper accounts for 40 to 50 percent of everything we throw away, both by weight and by volume.

12   If fast-food packaging is the Emperor's New Clothes of garbage, then a number of categories of paper goods collectively deserve the

role of Invisible Man. In all the hand-wringing over the garbage crisis, has a single voice been raised against the proliferation of telephone books? Each two-volume set of Yellow Pages distributed in Phoenix last year—to be thrown out this year—weighed 8.63 pounds, for a total of 6,000 tons of wastepaper. And competitors of the Yellow Pages have appeared virtually everywhere. Dig a trench through a landfill and you will see layers of phone books, like geological strata, or layers of cake. Just as conspicuous as telephone books are newspapers, which make up 10 to 18 percent of the contents of a typical municipal landfill by volume. Even after several years of burial they are usually well preserved. During a recent landfill dig in Phoenix, I found newspapers dating back to 1952 that looked so fresh you might read one over breakfast. Deep within landfills, copies of that *New York Times* editorial about fast-food containers will remain legible until well into the next century.

13   As the foregoing suggests, the notion that much biodegradation occurs inside lined landfills is largely a popular myth. Making discards out of theoretically biodegradable materials, such as paper, or plastic made with cornstarch, is often proposed as a solution to our garbage woes (as things biodegrade, the theory goes, there will be more room for additional refuse). Laboratories can indeed biodegrade newspapers into gray slime in a few weeks or months, if the newspapers are finely ground and placed in ideal conditions. The difficulty, of course, is that newspapers in landfills are not ground up, conditions are far from ideal, and biodegradation does not follow laboratory schedules. Some food and yard debris does degrade, but at a very, very slow rate (by 25 to 50 percent over ten to fifteen years). The remainder of the refuse in landfills seems to retain its original weight, volume, and form. It is, in effect, mummified. This may be a blessing, because if paper did degrade rapidly, the result would be an enormous amount of inks and paint that could leach into groundwater.

14   The fact that plastic does not biodegrade, which is often cited as one of its great defects, may actually be one of its great virtues. Much of plastic's bad reputation is undeserved. Because plastic bottles take up so much room in our kitchen trash cans, we infer that they take up a lot of room in landfills. In fact by the time garbage has been compressed in garbage trucks (which exert a pressure of up to fifty pounds per square inch on their loads) and buried for a year or two under tons of refuse, anything plastic has

been squashed flat. In terms of landfill volume, plastic's share has remained unchanged since 1970. And plastic, being inert, doesn't introduce toxic chemicals into the environment.

15 A new kind of plastic that is biodegradable may in fact represent a step backward. The definition of "biodegradable" plastic used by most manufacturers focuses on tensile strength. Plastics "totally" degrade when their tensile strength is reduced by 50 percent. At that point—after as long as twenty years—a biodegradable plastic item will have degenerated into many little plastic pieces, but the total volume of plastic will not have changed at all. The degeneration agent used in biodegradable plastic, usually mostly cornstarch, makes up no more than 6 percent of a biodegradable plastic item's total volume; the 94 percent that's left represents more plastic than would be contained in the same item made with nonbiodegradable plastic, because items made with biodegradable plastic have to be thicker to compensate for the weakening effect of the degenerating agent. . . .

16 A rough consensus has emerged among specialists as to how America can at least manage its garbage, if not make it pretty or go away. Safely sited and designed landfills should be employed in the three quarters of the country where there is still room for them. Incinerators with appropriate safety devices and trained workers can be usefully sited anywhere but make the most sense in the Northeast. And states and municipalities need to cut deals with wastepaper and scrap dealers on splitting the money to be made from recycling. This is a minimum. Several additional steps could be taken to reduce the biggest component of garbage: paper. Freight rates could be revised to make the transport of paper for recycling cheaper than the transport of wood for pulp. Also, many things could be done to increase the demand for recycled paper. For example, the federal government, which uses more paper by far than any other institution in America, could insist that most federal paperwork be done on recycled paper. Beyond confronting the biggest-ticket item head-on, most garbage specialists would recommend a highly selective attack on a few kinds of plastic: not because plastic doesn't degrade or is ugly or bulky but because recycling certain plastics in household garbage would yield high-grade costly resins for new plastics and make incineration easier on the furnace grates, and perhaps safer. Finally, we need to expand our knowledge base. At present we have more

reliable information about Neptune than we do about this country's solid-waste stream.

Analyzing the Writer's Argument

1. What is Rathje arguing for in this essay? Is it strictly speaking what you would call an argument? Why or why not?
2. What are the four known ways of dealing with garbage? Does it in any way help to know that there are only four ways of dealing with it?
3. When he actually studied garbage did Rathje find that the amount of garbage disposed of per person per day was greater or lesser than studies had led him to believe? Of what use is this information to those who are concerned about the impact of garbage on the environment?
4. Why does Rathje call fast-food packaging "the Emperor's New Clothes of garbage"? What single item is the real culprit?
5. Does the fact that Rathje has actually sorted through landfills and studied garbage make him an authority on garbage? Do you accept, for example, his argument about plastics? Why or why not?
6. Do the proposals that Rathje makes in his final paragraph seem realistic to you? Is there anything new in his proposals?

Exploring the Issues in This Essay

1. Much has been said lately concerning the problem of landfills becoming clogged with disposable diapers. In fact, many consumers are turning away from disposable diapers and returning to cloth diapers. Does Rathje's experience with landfills confirm that disposable diapers are a big problem? If no, how then does one reconcile these opposing views?
2. Discuss solid waste disposal in your area with your classmates. What factual information does the class have? For example, have more landfills in your area been closed than have been allowed to open? What happens to the garbage that is taken away from the dormitory? Do officials at your college or university regard solid waste as a growing problem or a stabilized situation? What views do people hold for which they have no factual information? Is there a garbage "crisis" as far as you and your classmates can tell?

Isaac Asimov

The Case Against Man

A very popular and prolific science and science fiction writer, Isaac Asimov was born in the Soviet Union and came to the United States in 1923. After earning all three of his degrees from Columbia University, he began a teaching career at Boston University as a biochemist. As of 1984 Asimov had published 300 books over an impressive range of topics from the Bible to Shakespeare to detective fiction and history, all of them marked by a lucid and engaging prose style.

In "The Case Against Man," from his Science Past— Science Future, *Asimov examines the interrelatedness of all life, offers statistical data regarding the growth of the human population, and argues for population control. Although written in 1970, the population estimate provided by Asimov in "The Case Against Man" is nearly on schedule, a fact that would seem to lend further credibility to his argument about the need for population control.*

1   The first mistake is to think of mankind as a thing in itself. It isn't. It is part of an intricate web of life. And we can't think even of life as a thing in itself. It isn't. It is part of the intricate structure of a planet bathed by energy from the Sun.

2   The Earth, in the nearly 5 billion years since it assumed approximately its present form, has undergone a vast evolution. When it first came into being, it very likely lacked what we would today call an ocean and an atmosphere. These were formed by the gradual outward movement of material as the solid interior settled together.

3   Nor were ocean, atmosphere, and solid crust independent of each other after formation. There is interaction always: evaporation, condensation, solution, weathering. Far within the solid crust there are slow, continuing changes, too, of which hot springs, volcanoes, and earthquakes are the more noticeable manifestations here on the surface.

4   Between 2 billion and 3 billion years ago, portions of the surface water, bathed by the energetic radiation from the Sun, developed complicated compounds in organization sufficiently versatile to qualify as what we call "life." Life forms have become more complex and more various ever since.

5   But the life forms are as much part of the structure of the Earth as any inanimate portion is. It is all an inseparable part of a whole. If any animal is isolated totally from other forms of life, then death by starvation will surely follow. If isolated from water, death by dehydration will follow even faster. If isolated from air, whether free or dissolved in water, death by asphyxiation will follow still faster. If isolated from the Sun, animals will survive for a time, but plants would die, and if all plants died, all animals would starve.

6   It works in reverse, too, for the inanimate portion of Earth is shaped and molded by life. The nature of the atmosphere has been changed by plant activity (which adds to the air the free oxygen it could not otherwise retain). The soil is turned by earthworms, while enormous ocean reefs are formed by coral.

7   The entire planet, plus solar energy, is one enormous intricately interrelated system. The entire planet is a life form made up of nonliving portions and a large variety of living portions (as our own body is made up of nonliving crystals in bones and nonliving water in blood, as well as of a large variety of living portions).

8   In fact, we can pursue the analogy. A man is composed of 50 trillion cells of a variety of types, all interrelated and interdependent. Loss of some of those cells, such as those making up an entire leg, will seriously handicap all the rest of the organism: serious damage to a relatively few cells in an organ, such as the heart or kidneys, may end by killing all 50 trillion.

9   In the same way, on a planetary scale, the chopping down of an entire forest may not threaten Earth's life in general, but it will produce serious changes in the life forms of the region and even in the nature of the water runoff and, therefore, in the details of geological structure. A serious decline in the bee population will affect the numbers of those plants that depend on bees for fertilization, then the numbers of those animals that depend on those particular bee-fertilized plants, and so on.

10   Or consider cell growth. Cells in those organs that suffer constant wear and tear—as in the skin or in the intestinal lining—grow and multiply all life long. Other cells, not so exposed, as in nerve

and muscle, do not multiply at all in the adult, under any circumstances. Still other organs, ordinarily quiescent, as liver and bone, stand ready to grow if that is necessary to replace damage. When the proper repairs are made, growth stops.

11 In a much looser and more flexible way, the same is true of the "planet organism" (which we study in the science called ecology). If cougars grow too numerous, the deer they live on are decimated, and some of the cougars die of starvation, so that their "proper number" is restored. If too many cougars die, then the deer multiply with particular rapidity, and cougars multiply quickly in turn, till the additional predators bring down the number of deer again. Barring interference from outside, the eaters and the eaten retain their proper numbers, and both are the better for it. (If the cougars are all killed off, deer would multiply to the point where they destroy the plants they live off, and more would then die of starvation than would have died of cougars.)

12 The neat economy of growth within an organism such as a human being is sometimes—for what reason, we know not—disrupted, and a group of cells begins growing without limit. This is the dread disease of cancer, and unless that growing group of cells is somehow stopped, the wild growth will throw all the body structure out of true and end by killing the organism itself.

13 In ecology, the same would happen if, for some reason, one particular type of organism began to multiply without limit, killing its competitors and increasing its own food supply at the expense of that of others. That, too, could end only in the destruction of the larger system—most or all of life and even of certain aspects of the inanimate environment.

14 And this is exactly what is happening at this moment. For thousands of years, the single species Homo sapiens, to which you and I have the dubious honor of belonging, has been increasing in numbers. In the past couple of centuries, the rate of increase has itself increased explosively.

15 At the time of Julius Caesar, when Earth's human population is estimated to have been 150 million, that population was increasing at a rate such that it would double in 1,000 years if that rate remained steady. Today, with Earth's population estimated at about 4,000 million (26 times what it was in Caesar's time), it is increasing at a rate which, if steady, will cause it to double in 35 years.

16   The present rate of increase of Earth's swarming human population qualifies Homo sapiens as an ecological cancer, which will destroy the ecology just as surely as any ordinary cancer would destroy an organism.

17   The cure? Just what it is for any cancer. The cancerous growth must somehow be stopped.

18   Of course, it will be. If we do nothing at all, the growth will stop, as a cancerous growth in a man will stop if nothing is done. The man dies and the cancer dies with him. And, analogously, the ecology will die and man will die with it.

19   How can the human population explosion be stopped? By raising the deathrate, or by lowering the birthrate. There are no other alternatives. The deathrate will rise spontaneously and finally catastrophically, if we do nothing—and that within a few decades. To make the birthrate fall, somehow (almost *any* how, in fact), is surely preferable, and that is therefore the first order of mankind's business today.

20   Failing this, mankind would stand at the bar of abstract justice (for there may be no posterity to judge) as the mass murderer of life generally, his own included, and mass disrupter of the intricate planetary development that made life in its present glory possible in the first place.

21   Am I too pessimistic? Can we allow the present rate of population increase to continue indefinitely, or at least for a good long time? Can we count on science to develop methods for cleaning up as we pollute, for replacing wasted resources with substitutes, for finding new food, new materials, more and better life for our waxing numbers?

22   Impossible! If the numbers continue to wax at the present rate.

23   Let us begin with a few estimates (admittedly not precise, but in the rough neighborhood of the truth).

24   The total mass of living objects on Earth is perhaps 20 trillion tons. There is usually a balance between eaters and eaten that is about 1 to 10 in favor of the eaten. There would therefore be about 10 times as much plant life (the eaten) as animal life (the eaters) on Earth. There is, in other words, just a little under 2 trillion tons of animal life on Earth.

25   But this is all the animal life that can exist, given the present quantity of plant life. If more animal life is somehow produced,

it will strip down the plant life, reduce the food supply, and then enough animals will starve to restore the balance. If one species of animal life increases in mass, it can only be because other species correspondingly decrease. For every additional pound of human flesh on Earth, a pound of some other form of flesh must disappear.

26 The total mass of humanity now on Earth may be estimated at about 200 million tons, or one ten-thousandth the mass of all animal life. If mankind increases in numbers ten thousandfold, then Homo sapiens will be, perforce, the *only* animal species alive on Earth. It will be a world without elephants or lions, without cats or dogs, without fish or lobsters, without worms or bugs. What's more, to support the mass of human life, all the plant world must be put to service. Only plants edible to man must remain, and only those plants most concentratedly edible and with minimum waste.

27 At the present moment, the average density of population of the Earth's land surface is about 73 people per square mile. Increase that ten thousandfold and the average density will become 730,000 people per square mile, or more than seven times the density of the workday population of Manhattan. Even if we assume that mankind will somehow spread itself into vast cities floating on the ocean surface (or resting on the ocean floor), the average density of human life at the time when the last nonhuman animal must be killed would be 310,000 people per square mile over all the world, land and sea alike, or a little better than three times the density of modern Manhattan at noon.

28 We have the vision, then, of high-rise apartments, higher and more thickly spaced than in Manhattan at present, spreading all over the world, across all the mountains, across the Sahara Desert, across Antarctica, across all the oceans; all with their load of humanity and with no other form of animal life beside. And on the roof of all those buildings are the algae farms, with little plant cells exposed to the Sun so that they might grow rapidly and, without waste, form protein for all the mighty population of 35 trillion human beings.

29 Is that tolerable? Even if science produced all the energy and materials mankind could want, kept them all fed with algae, all educated, all amused—is the planetary high-rise tolerable?

30   And if it were, can we double the population further in 35 more years? And then double it again in another 35 years? Where will the food come from? What will persuade the algae to multiply faster than the light energy they absorb makes possible? What will speed up the Sun to add the energy to make it possible? And if vast supplies of fusion energy are added to supplement the Sun, how will we get rid of the equally vast supplies of heat that will be produced? And after the icecaps are melted and the oceans boiled into steam, what?

31   Can we bleed off the mass of humanity to other worlds? Right now, the number of human beings on Earth is increasing by 80 million per year, and each year that number goes up by 1 and a fraction percent. Can we really suppose that we can send 80 million people per year to the Moon, Mars, and elsewhere, and engineer those worlds to support those people? And even so, merely remain in the same place ourselves?

32   No! Not the most optimistic visionary in the world could honestly convince himself that space travel is the solution to our population problem, if the present rate of increase is sustained.

33   But when will this planetary high-rise culture come about? How long will it take to increase Earth's population to that impossible point at the present doubling rate of once every 35 years? If it will take 1 million years or even 100,000, then, for goodness sake, let's not worry just yet.

34   Well, we don't have that kind of time. We will reach that dead end in no more than 460 years.

35   At the rate we are going, without birth control, then even if science serves us in an absolutely ideal way, we will reach the planetary high-rise with no animals but man, with no plants but algae, with no room for even one more person, by A.D. 2430.

36   And if science serves us in less than an ideal way (as it certainly will), the end will come sooner, much sooner, and mankind will start fading long, long before he is forced to construct that building that will cover all the Earth's surface.

37   So if birth control *must* come by A.D. 2430 at the very latest, even in an ideal world of advancing science, let it come *now*, in heaven's name, while there are still oak trees in the world and daisies and tigers and butterflies, and while there is still open land and space, and before the cancer called man proves fatal to life and the planet.

Analyzing the Writer's Argument

1. Does Asimov argue inductively or deductively in this essay? Explain.
2. What is the analogy that Asimov begins to use in paragraph 7? Explain how it works. Do you find it useful in thinking about population? Why or why not?
3. At what points in his essay does Asimov take into account arguments that are opposed to his own? What effect do such considerations have upon you as a reader?
4. In paragraph 14, why does Asimov refer to Homo sapiens as a group "to which you and I have the dubious honor of belonging"?
5. Is it fair to refer to the growth of the human population as a cancerous growth as Asimov does in paragraphs 16–18, or to humankind as a cancer as he does in paragraph 37? Why or why not?
6. How, according to Asimov, can the human population explosion be stopped?
7. In paragraph 15, Asimov estimates the world population at 4,000 million (1970). In paragraph 31, he estimates that the world population is growing by 80 million per year. By his estimate, the 1990 population would be 5,600 million. According to the *1990 World Almanac*, the 1990 population was estimated to be 5,300 million. How do you think Asimov would respond to the discrepancy between his prediction and the actual estimate?

Exploring the Issues in This Essay

1. Why include Asimov's essay in a section of *Controversies* concerning the environment? Is world population an environmental issue? Why or why not? Why do you suppose population control isn't receiving greater attention in the popular press? Are people bored by it? Do they feel that it is beyond their control?
2. Is Asimov, as he himself asks, a pessimist? What is he overlooking, if anything, in his discussion of population growth? Discuss possible solutions for the problem that Asimov raises. Are there, for example, ways of providing food, fuel, and shelter for the growing world population that Asimov has not considered?

Writing Suggestions for
Protecting the Environment: Preparations for the 21st Century

1. Spend some time researching the problem of acid rain in preparation for writing an essay on it. What is it? How do experts think it is caused? What are its effects? What has been the federal government's position with regard to it? Is the problem of acid rain something that Carson would have included in her essay if she knew about it? Or, is it really a different problem?

2. You have just returned from a camping trip in the Rockies that lasted two weeks. You have not spent, like Stegner's granddaughter, time alone and with water but no food. You understand perfectly, however, what Sherwood Anderson meant by the "trick of quiet." Based on what you have experienced and what you have learned by reading Stegner's essay, write an essay in which you attempt to define the concept for those who may not know what it means.

3. Much publicity has been devoted recently to the destruction of vast areas of the Amazonian rain forest by commercial interests. Trees remove CO_2 from the air, but they return it to the atmosphere as they decay or are burned. In his essay, Bidinotto cites research by Daniel Botkin and Lloyd Simpson at the University of California at Santa Barbara and by Sandra Brown at the University of Illinois at Urbana that "shows that the carbon content of forests had been vastly overestimated, suggesting that deforestation is not as great a source of CO_2 as was once thought." Research the problem in your library and write an essay in which you argue for or against continued deforestation in nations such as Brazil.

4. If you agree with Rathje's claim that paper represents one of the biggest solid waste problems, write a guest editorial for either your school or local newspaper arguing for the campus or local community to begin recycling immediately. Use material from Rathje's essay and be sure to offer a proposal for how the recycling effort should be carried out.

5. Some believe the "greenhouse effect" to be caused, in part, by the use of fossilized fuels, chiefly coal and oil. Consequently, there has been a renewed call for the construction of more nuclear power plants. Using information provided by the writers in this section, write an essay in which you argue for the construction of more nuclear power plants.

6. Write an essay in which you argue against Rathje's view of disposable diapers as a landfill problem. Are disposable diapers simply a landfill problem or do they represent a health problem as well? You may want to interview local public interest officials and perhaps call local diaper services to hear what legitimate arguments (e.g., those not having to do with business competition) they have? You may also want to check the *Reader's Guide to Periodical Literature* for magazine articles representing both pro and con sides of the question. Finally, you should read or reread Lisa Denis's essay "What Are Disposable Diapers?" that begins on p. 20.

7. Many of our environmental problems seem to be the by-product of our technological age. It is not surprising, therefore, that many people, especially those that are trained in technology and who work in technological fields, think that our problems can also be solved by technology. Perhaps you yourself think this way. Write an essay in which you argue a "techno-fix" solution to our environmental problems.

8. A relatively new field has emerged in the study of the environment called "ecofeminism." Write an essay in which you attempt to define the field, identify its major figures, and explain what the field is all about.

9. As in any field of study there are a number of terms that people unfamiliar with the field do not know or that people in the field use in different and sometimes confusing ways, so definition becomes an important exercise. Choose one of the following, or a similar subject of your own choosing, and write an essay in which you attempt to "come to terms" with the subject: ecosystem, ecofeminism, Spaceship Earth, solid waste, greenhouse effect, ozone layer, environment, wilderness, nature, biodegradable, deep ecology, and social ecology.

10. In his essay, Bidinotto quotes scientist Stephen Schneider as saying that sometimes scientists "have to offer up scary scenarios, make simplified, dramatic statements, and make little mention of any doubts they have." Write an essay in which you argue against such a philosophy and practice on the grounds that such an attitude could have many potentially dangerous consequences. For example, dramatizing the significance of scientific findings could lead to the public and government officials becoming insensitive and failing to act when there is a real need to do so.

11. Does the plastic styrofoam used in fast-food packaging represent an environmental threat? Write an essay in which you argue the pros and cons of the question.

12. If there is no bottle and can law in your state, write a letter to either your state representative or senator proposing such a law. You will, of course, want to see how the law is written and how it actually works in states where it is in effect.

13. What is a corporation's responsibility for environmental protection? Should corporations be held liable for actions they take that have an adverse impact on the environment? Spend enough time in your library to investigate the question, take a stand on the issue, and write an essay in which you argue your position. The results of the court case against Exxon's *Valdez* supertanker disaster in Alaska would be a good case in point to use as an example in your argument.

Glossary of
Rhetorical Terms

Analogy: a process of reasoning that employs comparison to explain something unfamiliar by comparing it to something familiar.

Anticipating the opposition: the process of imagining what objections an opponent will make in an argument.

Argumentation: a process of reasoning and providing evidence about controversial issues in order to encourage the reader to adopt a specific position, make a given decision, or pursue a particular course of action.

Assertion: a declaration or statement of belief.

Assumption: a fact or statement taken for granted.

Attitude: the writer's opinion of a subject.

Audience: the intended readership for a writer's work.

Authority: an expert in a field used as a source of information for an argument.

Case study: an intensive analysis of a person or community.

Cause and effect: an explanation of the reasons for an occurrence or the consequences of an action.

Claim: the point that a writer of an argument is trying to prove.

Classification: see **Division and classification**.

Coherence: a quality in writing achieved through the logical sequence of ideas, the purposeful repetition of key words, and transitional words and expressions.

625

Comparison and contrast: the process of reasoning that points out the similarities or differences between two or more subjects in the same class or category.

Concession: acknowledging the merits of the opposition's counterargument.

Connotation: the implied or suggested meaning of a word. See **Denotation**.

Con position: the side of an argument that takes opposition to an assertion, sometimes called the negative position.

Controlling idea: see **Thesis**.

Counterargument: a reasoned response to an opponent's objection.

Data: factual information used as a basis for reasoning, discussion, or calculation.

Deduction: the process of reasoning from stated premises to a conclusion. See also **Syllogism**.

Definition: the clarification of the meaning of a word or phrase.

Denotation: the dictionary meaning of a word, the literal meaning. See **Connotation**.

Description: type of writing that emphasizes how a person, place, or thing is perceived by the five senses.

Diction: choice and use of words that mean exactly what the writer intends and that are well-suited to the writer's purpose in writing and audience.

Division and classification: a process of reasoning that first establishes categories and then arranges or sorts items into these categories according to their characteristics.

Documentation: see **Evidence**.

Enthymeme: a syllogistic statement in which either the major or minor premise is implicit.

Evidence: all information—expert testimony, facts, statistics, case studies, personal experiences, and so on—used to support a claim or thesis.

Example: an illustration used to develop or clarify a larger idea.

Exposition: a type of writing that seeks to clarify, explain, and inform.

Fact: a piece of information that is presented as having objective reality or regarded as verifiable.

Fallacy: see **Logical fallacies**.

Illustration: the use of examples to explain or to make ideas both clear and concrete.

Induction: the process of reasoning to a conclusion about all members of a class through an examination of only a few members of that class.

Logical fallacies: an error in reasoning that renders an argument invalid. For a complete discussion of the more common logical fallacies, see pp. 19–20.

Narration: telling a story, relating a sequence of events.

Opinion: a belief stronger than impression and less strong than positive knowledge.

Organization: the pattern of order that a writer imposes on his or her material.

Paragraph: a series of closely related sentences that develop a central idea.

Persuasion: an appeal to emotion used to compel an action.

Point of view: the grammatical person in a piece of writing; or, the attitude a writer takes towards a subject.

Premise: a generalization or assumption on which an argument is based.

Process analysis: an explanation of how something works or step-by-step directions for doing something.

Proposition: the point to be discussed or maintained in argument.

Pro position: the side of an argument that supports an assertion, sometimes called the affirmative position.

Purpose: what the writer wants to accomplish in a piece of writing.

Reason: a statement offered in explanation or justification of a claim.

Refutation: lessening the credibility of a position by showing it to be false or erroneous.

Rhetorical question: a question that requires no answer from the reader.

Statistics: a collection of quantitative data.

Strategy: the rhetorical choices a writer makes to achieve his or her purpose.

Supporting evidence: see **Evidence**.

Syllogism: see **Deduction**.

Testimony: first-hand authentication of a fact.

Thesis: the main idea or claim of an essay.

Tone: the manner (serious, angry, cheerful, cynical, etc.) in which a writer relates to an audience.

Transitions: words or phrases that link sentences, paragraphs, and larger units of a composition to enhance coherence.

Warrant: an explicit or implicit generalization that underlies an argument and establishes a connection between the evidence and the claim.

ACKNOWLEDGMENTS

African Wildlife Foundation and Saatchi & Saatchi Advertising. "Only elephants should wear ivory." Copyright © 1989. *People Magazine*, November 13, 1989. Reprinted by permission of the African Wildlife Foundation and Saatchi & Saatchi Advertising.

American Library Association. "Puzzled by Banned Books?" Reprinted with permission of the American Library Association, from *Banned Books Week 1987: Celebrating the Freedom to Read*, produced by the Office for Intellectual Freedom, pp. 49–50; copyright © ALA 1987.

American Medical Association White Paper (Loeb, Hendee, Smith, Schwarz). "Use of Animals in Biomedical Research: An AMA White Paper." Copyright © 1989. AMA White Paper, 1989, pp. 4–5, 10–16, 18–19, 23–24.

Anderson, Bernard E. "An Economic Defense of Affirmative Action." Copyright © 1982. *Black Enterprise*, May 1982.

Asimov, Isaac. "The Case Against Man", copyright © 1970 by Field Enterprises, Inc. From SCIENCE PAST-SCIENCE FUTURE by Isaac Asimov. Used by permission of Doubleday, a division of Bantam, Doubleday, Dell Publishing Group, Inc.

Auth. "The War on Drugs." AUTH COPYRIGHT 1990 Philadelphia Inquirer. Reprinted with permission of Universal Press Syndicate. All rights reserved.

Bennett, William. "Should Drugs Be Legalized?" Reprinted with permission from the March 1990 Reader's Digest. Copyright © 1990 by The Reader's Digest Assn., Inc.

Bidinotto, Robert Jones. "What Is the Truth About Global Warming?" Reprinted with permission from the February 1990 Reader's Digest. Copyright © 1990 by The Reader's Digest Assn., Inc.

Brady, Judy. "Why I Want a Wife." Copyright © 1971. *Ms.* Magazine, 1971. Reprinted by permission of the author.

Buckley, William F., Jr. "Identify All the Carriers." *The New York Times*, March 18, 1986. Copyright © 1986 by The New York Times Company. Reprinted by permission.

Califano, Joseph, and Screvane, Paul "Pro/Con:Restrict Smoking in Public Places?" Copyright, July 21, 1986, U.S. News & World Report.

Carson, Rachel. "Our Assault on Nature." Excerpts from SILENT SPRING by Rachel L. Carson. Copyright © 1962 by Rachel L. Carson. Reprinted by permission of Houghton Mifflin Co.

Cheney, Lynne V. "Students of Success." *Newsweek*, "My Turn" column, September 1, 1986. Reprinted by permission of the author.

Coan, Marvin L. "Let the Convicted Person Decide." *Louisville Courier-Journal*, August 1, 1980, p. A9. Reprinted by permission of the author.

629

Collins, Evan R., Jr. "The Right to Choose Life or Death." Reprinted from USA TODAY MAGAZINE, November copyright 1984 by the Society for the Advancement of Education.

Conolly, Matthew E. "Euthanasia Is Not the Answer." Excerpt from speech delivered at the Hemlock Society's Second National Voluntary Euthanasia Conference, February 9, 1985. Reprinted by permission of the author.

Cousins, Norman. "Pain Is Not the Ultimate Enemy." Reprinted from ANATOMY OF AN ILLNESS, As Perceived by the Patient, by Norman Cousins, by permission of W. W. Norton & Company, Inc. Copyright © 1979 by W. W. Norton & Company, Inc.

Curtis, Patricia. "The Argument Against Animal Experimentation." *New York Times Magazine*, December 31, 1978. Copyright © 1978 by The New York Times Company. Reprinted by permission.

Darrow, Clarence: "The Futility of the Death Penalty," by Clarence Darrow. From Arthur and Lila Weinberg, *Verdicts Out of Court* (Chicago: Ivan R. Dee, Inc., 1989). Arthur and Lila Weinberg, 1963, 1969. Reprinted with permission.

DeBakey, Michael E., M.D. "Holding Human Health Hostage." Reprinted by permission of the author.

Dedini, Eldon. Drawing by Dedini; © 1990 The New Yorker Magazine, Inc.

Denis, Lisa. "What Are Disposable Diapers?" In Alfred Rosa and Paul Eschholz, *Controversies: Contemporary Arguments for College Writers.* Copyright © 1991. Macmillan Publishing Company, New York, 1991.

Ehrenreich, Barbara. 'The "Playboy" Man and the American Family.' Copyright © 1983. *Ms.* Magazine, June 1983. Reprinted by permission of the author.

Ehrlich, Paul and Anne. "The Rivet Poppers." From EXTINCTION: THE CAUSES AND CONSEQUENCES OF THE DISAPPEARANCE OF SPECIES by Paul R. Ehrlich and Anne H. Ehrlich. Copyright © 1981 by Paul R. and Anne H. Ehrlich. Reprinted by permission of Random House, Inc.

Francke, Linda Bird. "The Ambivalence of Abortion." From THE AMBIVALENCE OF ABORTION by Linda Bird Francke. Copyright © 1978 by Linda Bird Francke. Reprinted by permission of Random House, Inc.

Gallup, George, Jr.: "The Faltering Family" from FORECAST 2000 by George Gallup, Jr. with William Proctor. Copyright © 1984 by George Gallup, Jr. Reprinted by permission of William Morrow & Co.

Gansberg, Martin. "38 Who Saw Murder Didn't Call the Police." *New York Times Magazine*, March 17, 1964. Copyright © 1964 by The New York Times Company. Reprinted by permission.

Goldberg, Bernard R. "TV Insults Men, Too." *The New York Times*, March 14, 1989. Copyright © 1989 by The New York Times Company. Reprinted by permission.

Goldstein, Richard. "AIDS and the Social Contract." Copyright © 1987. *The Village Voice*, December 29, 1987. Reprinted by permission of the author and the Village Voice.

Goldwater, Barry. "Why Gun Control Laws Don't Work." Reprinted with permission from the December 1975 Reader's Digest. Copyright © 1975 by The Reader's Digest Assn., Inc.

Gore, Tipper. "The Smut and Sadism of Rock." Reprinted by permission of the author.

Gould, Stephen J. "The Terrifying Normalcy of AIDS." *New York Times Magazine*, April 19, 1987. Copyright © 1987 by The New York Times Company. Reprinted by permission.

Handgun Control, Inc. "A $29 handgun shattered my family's life." From Handgun Control, Inc. information packet. Reprinted by permission.

Hardin, Garrett. "Lifeboat Ethics: The Case Against Helping the Poor." *Psychology Today*, September 1974. Reprinted with permission from PSYCHOLOGY TODAY MAGAZINE. Copyright © 1974 (PT Partners, L.P.).

Harris, Jean. "Inside Story." *New York Magazine*, June 13, 1983. Copyright © 1990 by News Group Publications, Inc. All rights reserved.

Hentoff, Nat. "When Nice People Burn Books." *The Progressive*, February 1983. Reprinted by permission from *The Progressive*, 409 East Main Street, Madison, WI 53703.

Hughes, Robert. "The NRA in a Hunter's Sights." *Time*, April 3, 1989, p. 86. Copyright 1989 The Time Inc. Magazine Company. Reprinted by permission.

Hull, John D. "Slow Descent into Hell." *Time*, February 2, 1987. Copyright 1987 Time Inc. Reprinted by permission.

Huttmann, Barbara. "A Crime of Compassion." *Newsweek*, "My Turn" column, 1983. Reprinted by permission of the author.

Keillor, Garrison. "My Stepmother, Myself." From HAPPY TO BE HERE by Garrison Keillor. Copyright © 1982 by Garrison Keillor. Reprinted by permission of the publisher, Viking Penguin, a division of Penguin Books USA Inc.

Kennedy, Edward M. "The Need for Gun Control Legislation." *The Los Angeles Times*, April 15, 1981. Reprinted by permission of the author.

King, Martin Luther, Jr. "I Have a Dream." Speech delivered in Washington D.C., August 28, 1963. Copyright © 1963 by Martin Luther King, Jr. Reprinted by permission of Joan Daves.

Koch, Edward I. "Death and Justice: How Capital Punishment Affirms Life." Copyright © 1985. *New Republic*, April 15, 1985.

Lambert, Bruce. "Unlikely AIDS Sufferer's Message: Even You Can Get It." *The New York Times*, March 11, 1989, p. 29. Copyright © 1989 by The New York Times Company. Reprinted by permission.

Lear, Norman. "Cashing in the Commonweal for the Commonwheel of Fortune." First printed as "Our Babylon" in National Weekly Edition of the *Washington Post*, April 20, 1987. Copyright © 1987 Norman Lear.

List, Shelley. "Each Starving Child Is Your Child." *The Los Angeles Times*, 1985. Reprinted by permission of the author.

Marin, Peter. "Helping and Hating the Homeless." Copyright © 1987 by *Harper's Magazine*. All rights reserved. Reprinted from the January issue by special permission.

Mead, Margaret: "Can the American Family Survive?" from ASPECTS OF THE PRESENT by Margaret Mead and Rhoda Metraux. Copyright © 1980 by Mary Catherine Bateson Kassarjian and Rhoda Metraux. Reprinted by permission of William Morrow & Co., Inc.

Mead, Margaret. "One Vote for This Age of Anxiety." *The New York Times*, March 20, 1956. Copyright © 1956 by The New York Times Company. Reprinted by permission.

Mencken, H. L. "The Penalty of Death." Copyright 1926 by Alfred A. Knopf, Inc. and renewed 1954 by H. L. Mencken. Reprinted from A MENCKEN CHRESTOMATHY by H. L. Menchen, by permission of the publisher.

Mirachi, Joseph. Drawing by Joe Mirachi; © 1989 The New Yorker Magazine, Inc.

Moreu. "Nice work, Joan of Arc!" (cartoon). Copyright © 1990. College Press Service.

Morriss, Frank. "Euthanasia—No!" Reprinted by permission of the author.

Nachman, Gerald. "Biting the Bullets." From *Out on a Whim: Some Very Close Brushes With Life* by Gerald Nachman (New York: Doubleday, 1983). Reprinted by permission of the author and the author's agents, Scott Meredith Literary Agency, Inc., 845 Third Avenue, New York, New York 10022.

Nadelmann, Ethan A. "Shooting Up." Copyright © 1988. *The New Republic*, June 13, 1988.

National Rifle Association of America. "I'm the NRA." Copyright © 1989. *Newsweek*, April 10, 1989. Reprinted by permission of the National Rifle Association of America.

New York Magazine. "Today Fur . . . " (art work). From *New York Magazine*, January 15, 1990. Reprinted by permission.

Orwell, George: "A Hanging" from *Shooting an Elephant and Other Essays* by George Orwell, copyright 1950 by Sonia Brownell Orwell and renewed 1978 by Sonia Pitt-Rivers, reprinted by permission of Harcourt Brace Jovanovich, Inc.

Partnership for a Drug-Free America. "Cocaine Lies." Copyright © 1987, DDB Needham Worldwide, Inc. Reprinted by permission of Partnership for a Drug-Free America.

PLAN International USA. "Here's your chance to achieve a small moral victory." Reprinted by permission of PLAN International USA.

Planned Parenthood Federation of America. "What every man should know about abortion." Copyright © 1989. Reprinted by permission. Planned Parenthood® Federation of America, Inc.

Rachels, James. "Active and Passive Euthanasia." *The New England Journal of Medicine*, vol. 292, 1975, pp. 78–80. Copyright 1975 Massachusetts Medical Society. Reprinted by permission of The New England Journal of Medicine.

Rathje, William L. "Rubbish!" *The Atlantic Monthly*, December 1989, pp. 99–109. Reprinted by permission of the author.

Reilly, Donald. Drawing by Donald Reilly; © 1974 The New Yorker Magazine, Inc.

Rivers, Caryl. "What Should Be Done About Rock Lyrics?" *The Boston Globe*, September 15, 1985. Reprinted by permission of the author.

Rodriguez, Richard. "Does America Still Exist?" *Harper's Magazine*, March 1984. Reprinted by permission of Georges Borchardt, Inc. for the author. Copyright © 1984 by Richard Rodriguez.

Rosenberger, Jack. "Whose Life Is It, Anyway?" *New York Magazine*, January 15, 1990, pp. 30–31. Copyright © 1990 News America Publishing, Inc. All rights reserved. Reprinted with the permission of *New York* Magazine.

Rye, Teresa K. "How I Benefited from Animal Research." Speech delivered at a symposium on animal experimentation at the National Academy of Science, 1984. Reprinted by permission of the author.

Schlafly, Phyllis. "Citizen's Bill of Rights About Schools and Libraries." *The Phyllis Schlafly Report*, vol. 16, no. 7, February 1983, p. 4. Reprinted by permission of the author.

Seligmann, Jean. "The Medical Quandary." From NEWSWEEK, January 14, 1985. Copyright © 1985, Newsweek, Inc. All rights reserved. Reprinted by permission.

Smith, Adam. "Fifty Million Handguns." Copyright © 1981. *Esquire*, April 1981.

Staples, Brent. "A Brother's Murder." *The New York Times Magazine*, March 30, 1986. Copyright © 1986 by The New York Times Company. Reprinted by permission.

Stegner, Wallace. "The Gift of Wilderness." Excerpt(s) from ONE WAY TO SPELL MAN by Wallace Stegner, copyright © 1982 by Wallace Stegner. Used by permission of Doubleday, a division of Bantam, Doubleday, Dell Publishing Group, Inc.

Steinem, Gloria. "The Importance of Work." From OUTRAGEOUS ACTS AND EVERYDAY REBELLIONS by Gloria Steinem. Copyright © 1983 by Gloria Steinem, © 1984 by East Toledo Productions, Inc. Reprinted by permission of Henry Holt and Company, Inc.

Sweet, Ellen. "Date Rape: The Story of an Epidemic and Those Who Deny It." *Ms.* Magazine, October 1985. Reprinted by permission of the author.

Tisdale, Sallie. "We Do Abortions Here." *Harper's Magazine*, October 1987. Copyright © 1988 by Sallie Tisdale. Reprinted by permission of the author c/o John Brockman Associates, Inc.

Weltner, Linda. "Every 23 Minutes. . . ." *Boston Globe*, June 6, 1986. Reprinted by permission of the author.

White, Joseph L. "Black Family Life." From Joseph L. White, THE PSYCHOLOGY OF BLACKS: An Afro-American Perspective, © 1984, pp. 60–70, 80–82. Reprinted by permission of Prentice Hall, Inc., Englewood Cliffs, New Jersey.

Index